Financial Structure and Economic Organization

To my wife, Pramerudee, for her love and constant encouragement
and to my father, Roswell, the economist I strive to imitate

Financial Structure and Economic Organization

Key Elements and Patterns in Theory and History

Robert M. Townsend

Basil Blackwell

First published 1990

Basil Blackwell, Inc.
3 Cambridge Center
Cambridge, MA 02142, USA

Basil Blackwell Ltd
108 Cowley Road, Oxford, OX4 1JF, UK

Library of Congress Cataloging in Publication Data

ISBN 155786 0394

British Library Cataloguing in Publication Data

A CIP catalogue record for this book is available from the British Library.

FSC www.fsc.org MIX Paper from responsible sources FSC® C013604

Typeset in 10 on 12pt Times by P&R Typesetters Ltd, Salisbury, Wiltshire

Contents

Acknowledgments

The author would like to thank the publishers and co-authors of the following articles for permission to reproduce them in this volume:

"Models of Money with Spatially Separated Agents." In *Models of Monetary Economies*, eds J. Kareken and N. Wallace (Minneapolis, MN: The Federal Reserve Bank of Minneapolis, 1980). The author would like to state that the views expressed in this article are his and not necessarily those of the Federal Reserve Bank of Minneapolis or the Federal Reserve System.

"A Model of Circulating Private Debt: An Example with a Coordination Problem," with Neil Wallace. In *Contractual Arrangements for Intertemporal Trade*, eds Edward C. Prescott and Neil Wallace, University of Minnesota Press, 1987.

"Financial Structure and Economic Activity," *American Economic Review* 73(5), December 1983, pp. 895–911.

"Optimal Contracts and Competitive Markets with Costly State Verification," *Journal of Economic Theory*, 21(2), October 1979, pp. 265–93. Copyright © 1979 by Academic Press, Inc. All rights of reproduction in any form reserved.

"Resource Allocation under Asymmetric Information," with Milton Harris, *Econometrica* 49(1), January 1981, pp. 33–69.

"Optimal Multiperiod Contracts and the Gain from Enduring Relationships under Private Information," *Journal of Political Economy*, 90(6), 1982, pp. 116–86. © 1982 by The University of Chicago. All rights reserved.

"Economic Organization with Limited Communication," *American Economic Review* 77(5), December 1987, pp. 954–70.

"Intermediation with Costly Bilateral Exchange," *Review of Economic Studies* 55, 1978, pp. 417–25.

"Theories of Intermediated Structures," originally published in the Carnegie-Rochester Conference Series on Public Policy 18, 1983, *Money, Monetary Policy and Financial Institutions*, a supplemental series to the *Journal of Monetary Economics*.

"Asset Return Anomalies in a Monetary Economy," *Journal of Economic Theory*, 41(5), April 1987, pp. 219–47. Copyright © 1987 by Academic Press, Inc. All rights of reproduction in any form reserved.

"Market Anticipations, Rational Expectations, and Bayesian Analysis," *International Economic Review*, 19(2), June 1978, pp. 481–94.

"Forecasting the Forecasts of Others," *Journal of Political Economy*, 91(4), 1983, pp. 546–87. © 1983 by The University of Chicago. All rights reserved.

"Equilibrium Theory with Disparate Expectations and Learning: Some Issues and Methods," *Individual Forecasting and Aggregate Outcomes: "Rational Expectations" Examined*, eds Edmund S. Phelps and Roman Frydman, Cambridge University Press, 1983.

"Pareto Optima and Competitive Equilibria with Adverse Selection and Moral Hazard," with Edward C. Prescott, *Econometrica*, 52(1), January 1984.

"General Competitive Analysis in an Economy with Private Information," with Edward Prescott, in *International Economic Review*, 25(1), February 1984, pp. 1–20.

Part I
Introduction

1

Key Elements and Patterns in Theory and Early European History

Annotated table of contents

1 Introductory remarks

The relationship of theories of economic organization and financial structure to European medieval history is examined. That is, key features in environments of theories are matched with key features in actual historical environments, diverse organizational and financial arrangements in theories and in historical regimes are emphasized, and the mapping of environments to arrangements in theory and in practice is pursued.

2 Spatial separation as a key element

2.1 The varying spatial configurations of Roman, Byzantine, and Islamic Empires and the broad movement of various peoples over space is emphasized. The economic disintegration of northwest Europe is featured.
2.2 The economics of feudalism in the depth of the decline of northwest Europe is the economics of spatial separation for the most part, economies of virtually self-contained medieval villages or of self-contained clusters of villages constituting larger estates.
2.3 Improved military and agricultural technologies are associated with the resurgence of northwest Europe and renewed far-reaching spatial exchange.
2.4 Regional centers of commercial growth in Flanders and in Italy are

---

I want to thank Jeffrey Lacker, Julio Rotemberg, Thomas Sargent, and Bruce Smith for providing detailed comments on earlier drafts and the National Science Foundation grant SES-8708242 for research support. I assume full responsibility for any errors and for the views expressed herein.

eventually linked by well-established land trade routes featuring centrally located massive international fairs. Towns in these regions and along these routes are established, outside older medieval villages, frequently as working bases for itinerant merchants and the requisite service sector. Fairs and markets are highly structured in time and space, allowing for regular periodic exchange and the movement of goods within and across regions.

2.5 The invention of larger ships featuring the rudder and the invention of the crossbow are associated with a radical restructuring of exchange arrangements featuring larger Atlantic seaports and permanent colonial merchant settlements.

3 Models of financial arrangements relying on spatial separation

3.1 Separation of agents in space with once and for all exchange in markets at selected points in space can deliver a theory of valued currency. In contrast, implementation of efficient arrangements in spatially isolated villages would require no currency, in theory. The prediction, then, is increasing use of currency with increasing spatial exchange. This prediction is taken to medieval observations on the initial dearth of circulating coinage, the then apparent proliferation of mints, the increasing use of larger denomination units, and the commutation of rents and services in medieval villages near commercial centers.

3.2 If agents meet periodically or, more weakly, if there exist chains of pairings of agents so that one can trace paths from agents back to themselves through various intermediate parties, then theory predicts the emergence of simple private debt and even circulating IOUs. The salient spatial character of early medieval debt instruments is then emphasized, along with the eventual emergence of negotiable bills of exchange.

3.3 If agents meet, in theory, at a point in space, Walrasian-like credit arrangements allow multilateral exchange without specie. In practice, medieval oral assignment banking, allowing account book transfers of credits and mitigating portage of valuable coin, may have been an attempt at something similar, especially at the massive international fairs. Oral assignment systems seem also to have been used to transfer various financial instruments without hand to hand exchange.

3.4 As agents become more interconnected over space, so that asset holding time is lessened, deferred exchange is lessened and production for the market is furthered. This delivers a theory which explains the association of increasing commerce and spatial exchange with a rise in per capita income and the increasing use of debt instruments relative to currency. Medieval observations seem not inconsistent, though not well measured.

4 Uncertainty as a key element

The extent of variability in grain yields and the relatively low cross-space correlations in yields in a typical medieval English village are examples of the importance of uncertainty in economic life.

5 Private information as a key element

5.1 The determination of Pareto optimal arrangements as solutions to concave programming problems is possible despite the presence of private information held by some parties. Incentive compatibility conditions can be derived as necessary and sufficient constraints, capturing all the restrictions implied by private information on potential arrangements. Environments with (stochastic) audit possibilities and multiperiod environments can be analyzed.
5.2 Private information on labor effort or on output may be a key feature in helping to understand, or at least analyze formally, the fragmentation of medieval village land, the existence of land held in demesne by the lord and the use of reeves on the lord's land, and the apparently limited direct transfers from villagers to the lord and across the villages constituting a medieval estate.
5.3 Private information may also help us to understand, in part, the nature of early Italian firms. Multiperiod tie-ins are emphasized.

6 Limited communication as a key element

6.1 Efficient arrangements under private information require that messages be sent from and to parties with that information. But messages over space are naturally limited by available communication technologies, allowing a formalization of oral assignment, portable token, written message, and telecommunication systems.
6.2 Financial instruments can then be reinterpreted as communication devices, and the medieval material on oral command banking, written bills of exchange, and checks can be re-examined.
6.3 Currency can be interpreted in this way as a portable record-keeping device, and decentralized taxation possibilities by state authorities can be examined. Devaluations of coins as explicit or implicit taxation may be a related phenomenon, though an enigma is uncovered.

7 Limited commitment and costly enforcement

Theories with limited commitment and costly enforcement are needed to explain the conflicts among empires and nomadic peoples, the apparent absence of many contingencies in early medieval contracts, and the enduring relationships in early Italian firms.

8 The anomalies and enigmas of failing institutions and volatile markets

8.1 Despite their aforementioned beneficial role in exchange, medieval banks engaged in risky intermediation and often failed dramatically. Arrangements seem surprisingly naive.
8.2 Medieval financial markets have also suffered from what seems to be excess volatility.

9 On modeling limited market participation – some alternative attacks

Models in which not all agents are systematically linked up to one another are needed.

9.1 One approach is to posit a fixed cost of bilateral exchange. Balanced against a gain from portfolio diversification, this gives rise to subclusters of agent coalitions as an unblockable core structure. Thus an efficient solution to the resource-allocation problem is not achievable by the coalition of the whole. A second related but more decentralized approach is to imagine subgroups that must be formed by intermediaries who compete by proposing terms of exchange.
9.2 Asset structures can be made more limited by suitably altered spatial itineraries. In such theories credit and other assets can be used within groups and currency alone is used for transactions across groups.
9.3 If market structure is imposed exogenously, nontrivial signal extraction problems emerge as agents use prices to learn about underlying state variables and to learn about the beliefs of others. A competitive equilibrium with rational learning can display much volatility relative to common information competitive systems.
9.4 On the other hand, if there is private information but market structure is otherwise complete, then theorems of standard competitive analysis may apply, that is, apply in the space of *ex ante* information-constrained contracts. Still some adverse selection environments seem to defy standard decentralization.
9.5 Some concluding remarks.

1 Introductory remarks

The essays in this book are an attempt to understand a little better how groups of agents organize themselves for economic purposes, with a special interest in the financial arrangements they adopt. Many of the essays begin by describing some economic environment in which the agents are imagined to be situated, and then delivering economic organization and financial structure as efficient or competitively determined arrangements for that environment. This way of proceeding is not unusual in other contexts, at least for "regular," "smooth," or "convex" environments. Indeed one might say that the essays in this book are neoclassical models of economic organization and financial structure. However, the models incorporate the transactions costs and impediments to trade often thought to make neoclassical analysis difficult or inapplicable.

A few years ago I began reading early European history in earnest.[1] What struck me, though it was far from precise in my mind at the time, was a certain parallel of the descriptive historical material with stylized models like those described in this collection. In the historical material one obtains a sense of the elements in environments, across economies at a point in time, and in a given economy over time, which are crucial. Economic agents are separated in time and space; economic life is full of uncertainty; there is often private information among agents; there are sometimes difficulties of communication among agents; there can be difficulties in persuading agents to commit to arrangements – the difficulties of costly and limited enforcement. What struck me was that these key elements are the key features of the environments of my theories. Also, one can read in this history about strikingly diverse forms of economic organization and financial structure, again with dramatic changes in these forms both cross-sectionally and over time. These observations fueled my interest in trying to understand the arrangements. What causes arrangements to differ so much? Is there some connection with the underlying economic environments? My theories seemed to be helping me to think about these questions.

In what follows in this introduction, then, I would like to share with the reader some of this history,[2] emphasizing the key elements and the variety in outcomes. I would also like to share, though this is more difficult, the connection I see between the observations and the theories. I will try to point out when a theory or class of theories seems useful in interpreting observations, when it helps in understanding what was occurring. I will also try to point out when a theory is inadequate and when observations seem anomalous, to dictate trial model extensions.

In outline, I will proceed through the various key elements, illustrating the importance of each by at least one environment observed in history. The importance of spatial separation is covered first, for a natural by-product is the historical background necessary for further analysis. Indeed, the reader is forewarned to be patient as there is much background material to cover. One becomes impatient for theories with spatial separation which might help in understanding some of the observations. But the observations are too bold or sweeping for this. I do not offer here a theory of the decline of the Roman Empire or, for that matter, a theory of regional economic growth and the emergence of cities. Again, however, the observations do convey the importance of geographical proximity and of separation of agents in space, and provide background material for the observations and theories which follow. What follows in the essay is a discussion of the importance of other key elements – uncertainty, private information, limited communication, and limited commitment. But throughout the chapter, that is, for each historical environment featuring a key element, I will try to interpret at least one observed historical outcome by using a parallel theory. For example, spatial separation is used as a key element in theories of currency, limited communication is used as a key element in interpreting various financial instruments, and so on. Finally, at the end of this chapter, I will interpret a class of theories as an attempt to come to grips with some observations which are otherwise anomalous to neoclassical models. The reader is urged at this point to scan the annotated table of contents to this introductory chapter to fix the outline, so that he does not become lost in the details which follow.

Finally, I want to conclude these introductory remarks with a few comments on the open-ended nature of the observational–historical material and the theoretical material. On the historical side, a natural question to ask, given the "grand" scope of this essay, is why it focuses, nevertheless, on early European experience. The practical answer is that I needed to impose *some* boundaries! However, early European experience does serve well, as many of the financial arrangements of contemporary developed economies emerged in this period. It is hoped that a study of the origins of these arrangements might contribute to an understanding of their role in contemporary economies. Also, a given arrangement may be easier to understand when surrounding institutions such as banking, securities markets, or enforcement systems are simpler and less developed. By going back in time I hope to "isolate" some current arrangement from the entangling web of contemporary institutions.

Having said this, we can easily imagine extending the historical inquiry to other technologically simpler economies such as those in Asia or, closer to home, the British colonies in America. I believe that there is evidence that many aspects of the early European experience described in this chapter are not unique. More generally, however, in extending the inquiry to a larger sample we can obtain more evidence for which theories are useful, and guidance for which theories might be developed further.

The extent to which a case is made for or against a given theory by "fitting" it to observations is also open ended. As noted, I did not set out with particular theories in mind when I began reading the historical material, and though several may have emerged as useful in interpreting observations, further efforts to "fit" or "refute" could be made. Neither have I attempted to run a race between my own theories and plausible alternatives, except implicitly in emphasizing the importance of key elements in practice and the apparent fact that economic organization and financial structure are endogenous.

2 Spatial separation as a key element

2.1 The decline into feudalism – spatial marauders and hostile neighbors

At its height, the Roman Empire was an integrated economy, essentially along the shores of the Mediterranean Sea. Except for the north of France, Britain, and the Rhineland, no part of the Empire was more than 200 miles from its coast. It was, in fact, easier to ship grain across the entire sea than to transport it over land, by donkeys, mules, or oxen, for a distance of 70 miles or greater. A sea voyage from Marseilles to Alexandria, for example, was on average 30 days, and most trips were far shorter. Inland, river transport was preferred, on the Rhine, Rhone, Danube, and their tributaries, though Rome had also constructed a network of roads. Much of the transport of goods was associated with the supply of Rome, with a population of over a million, and also the supply of military outposts. There were also cities in Asia, Syria, Egypt, Tunisia, southern Spain, Greece, Italy, and Provence. That is, the Roman Empire in its entirety was largely self-sufficient, but many of its regions were not. Of course the Mediterranean could also be used for the efficient dispatch of armies. The reader is urged to consult the map "The Economy of the Roman World," *Times Atlas of World History*, pp. 90–1, for a visual image of the situation.

The Empire was surrounded by peoples known as barbarians – Celts in Wales and Scotland, Germans in the heart of Europe, Persians in the east, and Arabs in the south. Many of these people were townless, more or less nomadic, and frequently bellicose, but the Empire was successful in drawing a line over which they were not allowed to pass. Lines of forts in Germany and Palestine literally mark the boundaries of control. The maps "The Frontiers in Germany" and "The Syrian Lines," *Times Atlas*, p. 88, tell the story. Military and political accommodations favored Rome. Barbarians were integrated into Roman legions and fought for Rome.

Eventually, though, the Empire weakened. McNeill (1974) believes that Rome suffered dramatic losses in population, owing to the appearance of malaria and other infectious diseases spread, ironically, by its commerce and made lethal in large cities. The commercial class was especially vulnerable, forcing regions of the Empire to become more self-sufficient. Distant armies were increasingly more responsible for their own supplies – the beginnings of a feudalization of sorts. At the same time German peoples seem to have developed the moldboard plow, allowing grain cultivation in clay soils and previously unproductive forested lands. German populations were increasing. Finally, pastoral nomads in the steppes of Asia developed the stirrup, making mounted lancers and archers an overwhelming force. Large confederacies of mobile cavalry moved west, starting with the Huns in 370 who reached across the entirety of Europe into France by 451. They were followed out of Asia by the Avars, 568–803. This turmoil set in motion broad incredible movements of Germanic and Slavic peoples. The Angles overran Britain in 429, and were victorious by 500. The Ostrogoths moved through central Europe into northern Italy. The Visigoths moved through Asia Minor. The Vandals moved from central Europe into northern France, then down into Spain, across the northern African coast, and up into the Mediterranean islands and Italy. Details of these movements are shown in the map "Germanic and Slavic Invasions of Europe," *Times Atlas*, p. 98.

Sometimes these tribes moved peacefully, a few thousand at a time. But more frequently one has a picture of plundering, killing, and the burning of existing towns. For example, Romano-British villages in Sussex and Wessex were converted to a maze of grass-covered mounds, and it appears that in some areas the British were exterminated. Occasionally more organized battles were waged against Roman soldiers. Rome itself was eventually sacked, and the Empire moved east with its capital at Constantinople, formalizing an earlier move in 330.

For the most part these invasions were not unique events. Rather, they consisted of a series of waves. One tribe might settle, adopt Christianity and an agrarian life, with various political and military alliances and accommodations, only to be driven from its settlement by another onslaught. The overall picture is of an Empire in significant and repeated turmoil, crumbling in the west.

The effect of all this turmoil was mixed. On the one hand, the weakening power of any centralized state and associated internal disorders made the transport of goods precarious, especially in the interior of Britain, Gaul, and Spain. In these regions cities apparently declined into nothing. At least this is the thesis of Pirenne (1948), disputed now as too bold but accurate in its broad outline if not in its details. On the other hand, the Empire apparently retained control of the East and the shores of the Mediterranean. Pirenne believes there was still active commerce – textiles from Constantinople and Alexandria; wines, oils, and spices from Syria; papyrus from Egypt; wheat from parts of Spain; and wines from Gaul and Italy. Marseilles remained active, involved in the shipping of all these products and harboring a professional merchant class including Jews and Syrians. To some extent this activity permeated inland France. At least there were fairly large towns south of the Loire. Pirenne also notes that much revenue was obtained from bridges and fords, and that tax collectors were regarded as important functionaries.

This situation did not endure. There followed the great Islamic invasions of the seventh and eighth centuries. Syria fell to Islam and the united tribes of Mohammed between 634 and 638, followed by the Persian Empire in 637–51 and, pushing east, parts of India by 712. Pushing west, Egypt fell during 640–3, Roman Africa by about 700, and the Iberian peninsula by

712. These incursions were essentially stopped by Constantinople in the east in 711 and by Charles Mantel in France in 732. However, the Islamic Empire remained in force for some time. Details are given in the map "The Spread of Islam," *Times Atlas*, p. 104.

In effect, the Roman Empire had fallen into a tripartite division. First there was the Byzantine Empire, centered at Constantinople, a city with a population still close to a million in the eighth century, which controlled Asia Minor and the Balkan peninsula. In effect, Rome had adopted a more defensible position militarily and had developed a portfolio of spatially separated suppliers. Water facilitated the transport of goods. When supplies from the Aegean were interrupted, supplies from the Black Sea continued.

Second, of course, was the Islamic Empire itself, a flourishing civilization with shipping, traveling merchants, trade and communication networks, and great achievements in science. The Islamic Empire assumed the prior cultural dominance of Greece and Rome. Political accommodations allowed intermittent trade between the Byzantine and Islamic realms.

Finally, there was western Europe, that is, contemporary France, Britain, Germany, Belgium, and the Low Countries, essentially coalitions of Germanic tribes with varying degrees of centralized authority over time and space. But western Europe never reached a political accommodation with Islam, and with the loss of the Mediterranean it was blocked off from the Byzantine Empire as well.

One particularly centralized period in western Europe was the reign of Charlemagne. Ironically, Pirenne uses that period to argue how poor and factionalized western Europe had become, in effect a closed state with few foreign markets and little communication with the exterior. Provence, containing Marseilles, had now become the poorest province. There was some trade in indispensable commodities such as wine and salt, and in the north, in Flanders, slate, glassware, pottery, and a few slaves. However, according to Pirenne, there was really no regular commercial activity – no merchant class and no revenue from commerce. Charlemagne maintained an itinerant court, traveling around the kingdom on a regular periodic basis. Apparently, shipment of goods was too costly and too precarious. Charlemagne's military dominance arose from numbers – numerous foot soldiers together with a few heavy cavalrymen equipped with armor and lances.

Even this rather dismal state of affairs was not to endure, as western Europe fell prey to another series of so-called barbarian invasions. In the eighth and ninth centuries Vikings from Denmark and Norway conducted raids on the European continent, not only from the North Sea but also from the Atlantic coast and even from the Mediterranean. As Pirenne puts it, every river which emptied into one of these seas was at one time or another ascended by skillfully constructed barks. River valleys of the Rhine, Meuse, Scheldt, Seine, Loire, Garonne, and Rhone were the scene of systematic and persistent pillaging, with devastation so complete that at times the entire population disappeared. The leading Carolingian ports of Durstedt and Quentovic on the North Sea were destroyed and never rebuilt. Charlemagne-type defenses were no match for rapidly moving unpredictable enemies. Off the continent, Britain and Ireland were pillaged by 787 in a series of conflicts mixed with military settlements. London fell to the Danes as late as 1013.

In addition, back on the continent, Magyars executed terrifying cavalry raids, continuing the devastation that nomadic Huns from the east had wrought earlier. Meanwhile, Saracen Arabs occupied Sicily and then conducted raids, harassing local populations such as those living in the Rhone delta with slaughter, robbery, or slavery, and preying on pilgrims taking the land route between France and Italy. Marseilles, Arles, Frejus, Aix, and Genoa were abandoned. The map "The 9th and 10th Century Invasions of Europe: Vikings, Magyars, Saracens," *Times Atlas*, p. 111, summarizes these incursions.

With the demise of any semblance of a centralized state there was much internal disorder. Peasant communities were at the mercy of wandering bands of habitual fighters. These would capture whole villages, take them under protection, and guard them from further marauders. Indeed, great fighting men came to possess many such villages, with a retinue of horsemen moving from one village to another throughout the year. With the continual turmoil, life became even more self-sufficient – trade disappeared to a large extent and cities became depopulated, except for monastic centers. Roads fell into neglect. In fact, villagers used some roads as local quarries. Essentially, between 814 and 987 feudalism spread all over western Europe.

2.2 *Feudalism and the spatially separated clusters of autarkic medieval villages*

It seems from a reading of Pirenne (1948), Duby (1974), and others that at the depth of the decline, varying by dates and regions, economic life reverted to something close to autarky. Villagers gathered together into a nucleated village under the protection of a local strongman, farmed the land adjacent to the village with their own labor and oxen, and ate the produce – a closed system in many respects. Further, with their own court system and lack of safe alternatives elsewhere, one can imagine that each village was an entire economy. An exception would be the groups of villages which together formed the estates of a great lord such as the Bishop of Winchester. Then cross-villa transfers were possible, if not large in magnitude. Yet significant cross-regional movements of goods were apparently rare. Exchanges were primarily within the village, of goods for military services, for example.

A problem in studying these autarkic village economies is that much evidence on their nature comes too late, when, as is noted below, markets and interregional, international exchange played larger roles. For example, it is only in the twelfth, thirteenth, and fourteenth centuries that the court rolls, surveys, customs, and estate accounts come to us from England, allowing Bennett (1937), Homans (1941), Postan (1972), and others to portray medieval life. However, there seems to be little doubt that the extreme prototype of a closed village economy represents a useful abstraction for life earlier in many regions.

2.3 *Military dominance and the re-emergence of commerce over space*

The elements of revival in northwest Europe – the moldboard plow and armed cavalry – had been developing for centuries. However, as McNeill (1974) suggests, the barbarian incursions of the tenth century may have forced a dramatic change. It became worthwhile to reorganize in such a way that a surplus of food could be used to support knights, the local cavalry. The surplus required was nontrivial; knights specialized in military skills, did not farm, and used large horses requiring much grain. However, losses from barbarian pillage and internal disorder were great, and, once in place, bands of lanced, armored, and mounted knights could rapidly mobilize against horseless and relatively immobile Viking raiders.

Thus armed Norman knights eventually took the offensive against Moslems and others in their way. The strategic Saracen outputs of Montpellier and Frainet on the Mediterranean fell by 972. Britain fell to William the Conqueror in 1066. Robert Guiscard conquered southern Italy in 1091. Normans and Flemings played a key role in the First Crusade, 1096–9, establishing a dramatic if temporary Latin kingdom in Palestine, and Christian knights in Spain eventually dealt mortal blows to Moslems there.

In northwest Europe, German knights and the associated agro-military systems were less successful. Yield-to-seed ratios were lower, generating less of a surplus, and lands further east had to cope with nomadic raiders such as the Magyars mounted on fast-moving quickly turning ponies. Knights were at a disadvantage, as McNeill puts it. Otto I, using mountainous terrain, checked and held the Hungarians along the Danube in 955, establishing a West German Empire.

The Vikings themselves turned to trade and eventual settlement during this resurgence, beginning in western France with the surrender of Normandy to Rollo in 912. Indeed, though the region was depopulated at the time, the French descendants of these Viking settlers became the Normans just mentioned. In England five boroughs in the Midlands were settled by Vikings. Indeed, the Swedes established a far-flung trading empire, reaching Kiev in Russia, relying on the north–south flow of the Dnieper, the Volga, and other Russian rivers. This put them in contact with the Black Sea and Byzantium, on the one hand, and with the Caspian and Baghdad, on the other.

In the south, Italian cities developed militarily and became aggressive. The southern Italian city of Amalfi, part of the Byzantine Empire, had traded indiscriminately with the Moslems as well as with Constantinople, though eventually it was raided by Saracens. Then Venice cleared the Adriatic of Dalmatian pirates and freed Bari on the straits of Otranto from Moslem rule. Much later, in 1123, Venice achieved a key naval victory at Ascalon. Meanwhile, Pisa took Corsica in 1016, Sardinia in 1050, Bone on the African coast in 1034, parts of Sicily in 1063, Mahdia on the African coast in 1087, and the Balearic Islands in 1115–43. Genoa aided somewhat later, and reached Bougie on the African coast in 1136.

Here and elsewhere a word of caution is in order. Genoa entered into treaties with Moslems on the North African coast, rather than defeating them militarily. Genoa and Pisa themselves were often in military conflict with one another, a tradition continued by later Italian city-states competing for trade areas. Finally, the Normans were also adversaries at times, taking southern Italy, as mentioned earlier.

Part of the Italian expansion came at the expense of Byzantium. Venetian trading rights lessened the flow of taxes from commerce, and crusaders eventually attacked the city though the occupation was temporary. Byzantium was also weakened by the loss of products from Asia Minor, as a result of nomadic incursions; Turkish bands there converted farm land to grassland. Eventually the city fell under Turkish control and its trade was absorbed by the Italians. In addition, the Mongols from Asia extended their dominion westward, crushing the Scandinavian empire in Russia, for example. However, the highly organized Mongols were receptive to the Italians. An economic alliance extended Italian reaches far east into Asia.

2.4 *Towns, markets, and fairs: search and exchange organized in time and space*

Realization of potential gains from trade had been increasing from the tenth century onward, with numerous setbacks. In the north, Flanders had the technology for making fine wool cloth, something it never lost despite the previous decline with Viking raids. The Scandinavian countries had honey, furs, skins, hunting hawks, and other forest products. France was capable of producing a surplus of wine from the Burgundy, Loire, and Bordeaux regions, and England, especially after the conquest, was a ready market. England itself had tin, lead, and also, led at first by Cistercian monks, wool from grazing sheep.

It seems that the development of towns and cities is related to this commerce and to the terrain. Large numbers of rivers in Belgium and Flanders provided natural trading ports, and cities began to flourish. Bruges on the Zwin took the lead, together with Cambrai, Valenciennes, Ghent, Antwerp, and Tournai on the Scheldt; Liège, Huy, Danant, and Verdun on the Meuse; and Cologne and Mainz on the rhine (see Pounds, 1974, figure 7.1).

In the south we have already noted the trade roles played by Venice and by Genoa and Pisa. Spices, silk, ornaments, and luxury goods were imported through these cities in exchange, at first, for slaves and bullion. Local regional growth was not far behind. In the fertile plains of Tuscany old towns – Lucca, Florence, Siena – took on new life. Somewhat later, further north in the Lombard plain on the tributaries of the Po, Pavia, Brescia, Verona, Piacenza, Padua, Asti, and Milan emerged (see Pounds, 1974, figure 6.2).

The development of Venice and the Lombard cities was not unrelated to the eventual link between these northern and southern regional centers. Trade routes developed over western Alpine passes, feeding into the Rhone–Saône river valleys in France, and extending north to Flanders. These land routes could also be accessed by sea from Genoa by various shifting ports on the Mediterranean and the more permanent and growing Marseilles. By 1150 northern and southern commerce joined in dramatic international fairs a little southwest of Paris, at Lagne, Provins, Bar-sur-Aube, and Troyes. The map "The Medieval Economy at its Height," *Rand McNally Atlas of World History*, p. 28, depicts this state of affairs.

It is more difficult to document what was happening beneath the appearance of regional centers and interregional fairs. Records are scant. Yet the scenario sketched by Pirenne (1948) seems largely consistent with the evidence. The links among trade, towns, and markets become more apparent.

It seems that economic exchange re-emerged relatively early throughout western Europe with the activity of itinerant merchants. (Indeed, it bears repeating that trade never dwindled to zero.) At first barefoot and poor, these "young sons," reflecting population growth, may have wandered about looking for opportunities, symptomatic of Europe's backward condition, as Braudel (1979) has argued. However, we should not draw the conclusion that these early itinerants were unorganized. They would form groups for security, with horses and wagons encircled by men carrying bows and swords. Throughout this period, even with the growth in commerce, one cannot divorce commerce from military concerns.

Itinerant merchants needed places to stay for brief if not more sustained periods: at night, on intervals between trips, during bad weather, and during the winter when roads became impassable. Naturally enough, they would end up together at obvious places along the obvious trade routes – for example, at ports or landing places along coasts and rivers. The obvious places were often near fortified feudal villages, for these trading routes had also been the paths of previous invaders. Indeed, traveling merchants began to set up their own towns with wooden palisades or forts to withstand bandits, if not a sustained attack. By the twelfth century these outside-towns or faubourgs frequently had walls and towers. Military concerns were still at the forefront, but the number of merchants was increasing. In time permanent headquarters were established.

These groups of merchants or porters in their faubourgs were viewed as foreigners, outside the jurisdiction of the feudal system. The church, it seems, took an especially negative attitude. But the merchants wanted to come and go and to conduct their own business. The natural outcome of this tension was a formal agreement between the merchants as a group and the local lord – an explicit town charter. Under these, merchants had the right to administer their own merchant law, with its tribunals, penal code, and police, used for contract enforcement, debt and bankruptcy, and apprehending thieves. Anyone who had lived in a town for more than a year and a day was to be given free status, outside the domain of the lord; local serfs were exempted from this provision, but others were welcomed. This brings us to an obvious point: the lord himself partly benefited from the arrangement. Merchant towns provided some income, mostly from the grant of land, and town infantry for additional defense of the fortress.

Events did not proceed smoothly everywhere. Though many towns in Germany obtained free status as organized communes, there was occasional resort to violence, especially against an ecclesiastical lord. Indeed, feudal lords receded into the background in various places and became indistinguishable from the middle commercial class. Parts of Germany were an exception, however, as noted below.

Again, in time, towns and cities became centers of more permanent population, including nonmerchants. Men were needed for loading and unloading merchandise, for rigging and equipping boats, for manufacturing casts, chests, and carts, and so on. Certain artisan groups from regional villages were attracted: bakers, brewers, butchers, and smiths. For example, Pounds (1974) notes from tax rolls the relatively large numbers of butchers and bakers in towns like Toulouse and Milan. Eventually, towns started to draw in craftsmen generally, such as cloth weavers in Flanders, silk weavers in Lucca, and, later, iron and copper workers, despite the need to transport raw materials. Symptomatic also of the commercial nature of towns was the relatively high number of notaries.

Merchant residents of the towns benefited from this growth in population. In fact, they occasionally forbade craftsmen from trading in the country. At the same time, town residents were dependent on rural peasants to supply goods to the town, and rules and regulations to protect food supplies proliferated. The line between trade and tribute is difficult to draw.

Indeed, it seems that the larger the town or city, the larger was the number of trade, service, and craft activities relative to agricultural activities. Yet these nonagrarian people needed to be fed – hence the intense concern with control over adjacent agricultural areas. This suggests in fact a limit on town size, or on the configuration of towns in a region, if the region is closed in food supplies. Conversely, expanded agricultural areas and increased interregional trade in food allow greater specialization of the population in commercial activities. For example, towns and cities in northwest Europe and Italy were relatively small, with only a handful over 50,000 in population, a few more between 25,000 and 50,000, a number of large "cities" over 10,000, and the bulk of the rest between 1,000 and 2,000. In contrast, Byzantium with its trading empire had between 500,000 and a million inhabitants.

As commercial activities grew in Italy and northwest Europe, so did the number of towns and cities. Maps of Germany such as "The Colonization of the Black Forest" and those of France such as "The Clearance and Settlement of Northeastern France," *Times Atlas*, p. 121, tell the dramatic story. Some caution is in order, however. There was active settlement of underpopulated regions in France and Germany, for example, so that an increase in the number of towns need not have reflected increased commercialization. Some regions were settled by towns with fortifications for military–political reasons, as with the settlement of Wales by the English. Active exchange need not have followed.

Patterns of trade among towns and regions are difficult to document. Pounds (1974) contrasts two towns in Germany in the fifteenth century. Espalion had a market in which pastoral products of the mountains were exchanged for grain from the lowlands. In contrast, Rheinfelden seems to have operated for an area of 300 km^2, overlapping the service area of neighboring towns. Only Rheinfelden had manufactured articles for sale, including some of distant origin: salt from Salzburon and Lorraine, timber and fish brought from the lower Rhine, and spices, sugar, cotton, and luxury fabrics. With no other source of exchange it seems that Rheinfelden must have exported local crafts and a surplus of agricultural products from its region.

It is also clear from this example that the distinction between local and "international" trade should not be overdrawn. Interregional trade was probably important as well. Pounds (1974) notes patterns of specialization, with certain cities specializing in particular cloth, leather, or metal items and having a reputation for quality of merchandise. These were in "local" demand.

In contrast with the search models of Diamond (1982) and Mortensen (1974), in which traders run into one another at random, trade in medieval Europe was highly organized in time and space. Some villages had markets and some did not; this was known. Towns with markets held these only on specified days, usually once or twice a week. Apparently, not all towns had markets on the same day, allowing, we might speculate, cross-market coordination. Larger regional fairs met at specified times, maybe once or twice a year.

This highly structured nature of markets culminated with the fairs in Champagne mentioned earlier. The fairs were organized directly by the Count of Champagne, a powerful feudal lord. He supplied virtually everything needed for the duration of each fair: booths to be rented by merchants, money changers to handle diverse coins, police to keep order, and judges to give a quick decision in case of disputes. The fairs were profitable to the Count: he obtained revenue from the rents of booths, from the money changers' fees, from the fines for offenses committed, and from a sales tax on all goods brought to the fair. Further, fairs were organized in such a way as to encourage broad participation: merchants were exempted from reprisals for crimes committed or for debts contracted outside the fairs; lawsuits against merchants were temporarily dropped; the canonical prohibition against usury was set aside; death and inheritance taxes were outlawed. Finally, the Count was able to provide protection for merchants along their entire Rhone–Saône trade route. This was done by entering into alliances with lesser lords who become vassals of the Count. In return he allocated them revenue from the fairs.

The internal organization of the fairs of Champagne was also structured. Each of the fairs lasted approximately six weeks, within which various trading periods were clearly established. The first week was for entry of goods, followed by ten days for cloth sales, 11 days for leather, two weeks for drugs and spices, and finally a period for settling of accounts and making payments (this is discussed further below).

The six fairs of Champagne met in four cities and covered the entire year; that is, one fair was under way at any time in at least one place, virtually. Further, there is an interesting pattern in the annual calendar, with fairs at Lagne, then at Bar-sur-Aube, then at Provins, then at Troyes, then at Provins again, then at Troyes again, and so on, with a repetition of the cycle the following year. A map thus reveals a pendulum swinging from east to west and back again. Presumably this had something to do with the distribution system and convenience to regional participants.

The fairs of Champagne began to decline in the late thirteenth century with the development of alternative routes over the Alps and the growth of trade in Germany. However, international fairs *per se* continued to flourish, at Geneva and Lyons on the Rhone–Saône routes, on into the fifteenth and sixteenth centuries.

2.5 Transportation innovation, the Atlantic coast trade, and a massive locational shift

What emerges then is a picture of Europe in which towns and regions are interwoven by markets and fairs, with transportation and military technology as key determinants. If this picture is correct, then it would seem that a significant change in these key determinants could have altered the picture dramatically. This occurred at the turn of the thirteenth century.

The first innovation was the use of the rudder which was located directly astern. Galleys no longer needed to rely on steering oars and the requisite oarsmen, and no longer needed to allow space for carrying supplies for the latter. Further, the rudder made possible much better control of vessels in heavy seas; vessels could steer more directly into the wind. Thus, equipped with multiple sails and masts, and decked over against bad weather, it became possible to sail year round, even in the Atlantic. Larger cargoes or, better put, larger containers were accommodated with increasing use of block and tackle. Finally came the development of the crossbow. As McNeill (1974) puts it succinctly, a well-aimed bolt could pierce armor and the supremacy of the knight ended. In 1282 Normans were defeated at sea by Catalan bowmen.

Evidence for improved shipping is apparent from dates of the great expeditions. In 1278 the Genoese sent galleys through the Strait of Gibraltar to Flanders and England, voyages which became more or less regular by 1298. In 1291 two brothers of the Genoese Vivaldi family sailed through the Strait of Gibraltar with the aim of reaching India. A series of Italian expeditions followed, probing further south along the African coast. In 1312 Mallocello discovered the Canary Islands, and in 1330 an anonymous explorer discovered the Madeira Islands. Then in 1351, under Prince Henry the Navigator, Portugal joined in these efforts.

Larger ocean-going vessels could not be beached for repairs; they required deep and protected harbors. Thus shipping inevitably became more concentrated on and oriented to the Atlantic. Sluys, the seaport of Bruges, became a permanent terminal point of commercial trade. Later, with larger vessels, this trade moved to Antwerp. There the Scheldt was deep and provided good wharf facilities, far enough from the sea to be safe from casual marauders. Antwerp was also well linked to its hinterland by many tributaries and canals. Activities in Antwerp peaked in the sixteenth century and then declined sharply as religious wars between the Dutch and Spanish cut its access to the sea. But Amsterdam, and also London, followed, with substantial inland ports. Associated with the rise of Antwerp, Amsterdam, and London was a decline in trade on the Mediterranean.

Trade patterns shifted dramatically during this period. The great land trade fairs of Champagne, with their periodic meetings and itinerant merchants, declined in importance. In their place arose a more systematic wholesale trade at the great shipping ports. Again, first at Bruges, there were docks, cranes, large warehouses, and goods shipped on consignment to Italian merchant partners established abroad in permanent colonial settlements. These advances came hand in hand with a change in the composition of trade. It now became economical to ship cheaper bulk commodities: raw wool, salt, grain, timber, alum, and iron as well as the spices, cloth, and luxury manufactures of earlier trade. This is evident in the emergence of a Baltic trade, supplying east German settlements with salt. Salt-preserved herring and rye bread yielded a sufficiently balanced diet to enable settlers to survive the winter reasonably well nourished. In return, grain and timber were exported. A landed aristocracy took charge of this trade in the interior of Germany, in league with an alliance of towns known as the Hanse.

3 Models of financial arrangements relying on spatial separation

3.1 Spatial exchange and the role of currency

Thus far I have argued that spatial separation must have been a key element in the environment of the early medieval economy. But can more be said? Are models or theories which make spatial separation a key element useful in thinking about observations from the medieval economy?

One class of models which makes use of spatial separation is the class of models of currency with spatially separated agents. In "Models of money with spatially separated agents" (Townsend, 1980, this volume, ch. 2) agents are assumed to travel over space following an exogenously given itinerary. When some subset of these meet at a point in time at a given location, some have previously acquired pieces of paper, an intrinsically useless object, and some have on hand an endowed or produced good. An absence of double coincidence of wants makes either intertemporal or atemporal trade in goods alone impossible. Yet there can be beneficial exchange under competitive equilibria with valued paper or currency. Currency is valued at any date and location because agents know that it will be valued in the future. It serves as a store of value in decentralized exchange or exchange–production economies – economies in which agents meet at most once and share no common trading partners or meet repeatedly but with similar endowment positions. In these economies more elaborate arrangements among agents over time are not possible. They cannot make longer commitments because they are not around to honor them or will not have the resources to do so. Thus without currency life would be Pareto inferior.

This class of models stands in sharp contrast with the class of models which forms the literature on contract theory and mechanism design, of which several chapters in this book are examples. In their simplest form these contract models neglect information and commitment problems by assuming full information and perfect costless enforcement. Then the determination of an optimal arrangement reduces simply to finding the solution to a Pareto problem, a programming problem. Essentially, for a given environment, the utilities' possibilities set is filled in by consideration of all resource-feasible plans. Optimal plans lie on the frontier of this set. Then, to achieve a given optimum, agents just carry out the associated plan. In particular, there is no need for currency, even though endowments can differ significantly from consumptions.

The crude prediction of these theories, therefore, is that when there is little or no spatial exchange, that is, when agents are clustered together into more or less self-contained communities with transfers within but not across communities, there will be little or no use of currency. Conversely, with an increase in spatial exchange there should be an increase in the use of currency. Observations from the medieval economy are suggestive of these predictions. Unfortunately, the evidence is indirect as hand-to-hand payments are infrequently observed. Therefore some caution is in order, to say the least.

Perhaps the most direct evidence for the absence or use of currency concerns accounts of the use of coins and the operation of mints. This is hazardous because nothing in the theory described argues for metallic money. Other commodities would do as well. Indeed, the model described is not a model of commodity money at all! Nevertheless, if currency is associated with minted metallic coins, then we seem to see a strong association of the type predicted by the theory.

Rome minted its own coins, and these were used widely in commercial exchange, at least before the decline. Similarly, Byzantine and Islamic coins were minted continually throughout the medieval period. However, in northwest Europe there seems to have been a decline, albeit not uniform, in the circulation of coins.

The first evidence of this concerns the use of gold. By the seventh century newly minted Byzantine and Islamic gold coins did not make their way to northwest Europe. Nor were local mints issuing gold coins. Indeed, the conclusion of historians like Painter (1951), Cipolla (1964), and Duby (1974) is that gold coins had disappeared from circulation.

Silver coins were minted in northwest Europe in the seventh century. In fact the number of mints *per se* proliferated. Duby (1974) notes that mints were especially active in regions of commercial transactions, near Marseilles, for example, and what was left of the Mediterranean trade; near Quentovic and also near Huy and Maastricht on the Meuse; and in Burgundy on the road from the Saône to Neustria. Later, Charlemagne seemed to have centralized operations and implemented the silver pound–shilling–pence system. However, numerous authors indicate that only the smallest coin in value, the pence or penny, was actually minted. The shilling and pound were units of account. Indeed, both gold and silver were regarded more as precious metals than as the monies predicted by the theory. Silver coins were not in common circulation in England and Germany until the tenth century. Cloth, jewelry, and animals may have appeared frequently in exchange, thought it is not apparent whether or not these were commodity monies.

By the first stages of the commercial revolution, however, coins again began to dominate in recorded exchange transactions. More and more, payments in kind became exceptions, such as in loans. For a while pepper and spices were used, especially in great commercial centers, presumably because of an absence of precious metals, but eventually this practice also died out. The impression is also given that local mints became more and more active, though this is hard to document. In any event, heavier silver coins called groats (in effect, shillings) were minted in Genoa in 1172, in Florence in 1182, and in Venice in 1192. In 1266 Louis XI issued the heavier groat of Tours, and this was imitated in Flanders, in the northern Netherlands, and in Germany. Finally, Europe resumed the minting of gold coins, first in Sicily in 1231 by the Holy Roman Emperor Frederick II, though these did not circulate widely, and then in Genoa in 1250, in Florence in 1252, and in Venice in 1284. Apparently, the gold coins of Florence circulated widely from 1252 to 1400, and those of Venice in the fifteenth century. France also issued gold coins in the thirteenth century, as did Flanders and England in the fourteenth.

Complementary evidence for the proliferation of coins and for monetary exchange is the increasing use of coins as units of account for goods and services, this being obvious by the eleventh century. Associated with this is the commutation of rents and services in the agrarian sector, beginning near the great towns by 1100 and somewhat later for towns further from trade routes. Apparently, local lords accepted monetary payments for the use of the oven and the mill and in place of commodity taxes on chickens, pigs, and so on, in effect monetizing the previous transfer. Eventually, lords in some localities accepted rents from previous serfs for the latter's use of the land, with the former leaving entirely. Alternatively, lords took over entire estates, evicting serfs in some way, and producing wool or grain for export, presumably for money. There is some explicit evidence of the existence of active wage labor markets, in Portugal from 1253 to 1379, in Burgundy in 1393 where there were daily meetings in a town square between employers and laborers, and in Hamburg in 1480 where laborers and servant girls were hired. Braudel (1979) estimates that in England by 1500 half or even two-thirds of the households received money wages, though there remained a large number of isolated units.

3.2 Spatial exchange and the role of debt

Some of the theories of currency with spatially separated agents suffer from what may appear to be an unrealistic element: the itineraries of agents are such that any two agents meet at most once and share no common trading partners. For example, agents are imagined to be traveling on a highway which extends without limit in either direction, so that two agents pass each other at most once. In short, the itinerary appears contrived, and not a realistic description of medieval life. With less contrived itineraries, the prediction might be different; something else might emerge.

Precisely this question is explored in "Circulating private debt: an example with a coordination problem" (Townsend and Wallace, 1982, this volume, ch. 3). In this description the highway is bent around on itself to form a circle. Then agents meet one another repeatedly, at least once every revolution as it were. In addition, agents share common trading partners, so that paths or chains of agent pairings – a path from one agent back to himself through some, perhaps many, intermediate parties – can be traced out.

The altered model creates the possibility of valued private debt. Agents who are paired periodically can issue simple IOUs promising repayment at the dates and locations of future pairings. Indeed, if whole groups of agents follow more or less similar itineraries, these IOUs can be priced competitively. Moreover, the existence of chains of agents through intermediate parties creates the possibility, often helpful, of circulating private debt – IOUs which are passed to third parties before they are redeemed by the issuer. Again, these can be priced competitively.

One can imagine that a careful mixture of the currency and debt models would yield coexistence of the two types of objects. One might also speculate that systems with private debt and currency might dominate systems with currency alone, or at least that profitable or utility-improving possibilities might be present for some agents if the system had been restricted exogenously to currency alone. Finally, and bolder, one might imagine agents deliberately altering their itineraries so as to allow some private debt. It is not inconceivable that the underlying structure of trade and markets itself would be tempered by this pressure.

Again, observations from the early medieval economy serve to document the presence of private spatially motivated debt. Further, observations given here and below are at least suggestive of pressure on market structure.

Fortunately, we are blessed with actual copies of the early contracts of medieval towns, for these were notarized and thus preserved as public documents in archives. An excellent sample collection is given by Lopez and Raymond (1955). The most common contracts in this collection are standard loan contracts – promises to pay stated amounts of specified currencies at a specified future date. Prominent among these are exchange contracts in which the spatial aspect is striking. A borrower of coin at a given date and location would promise to make payment to the lender or his accredited messenger at some future date and distinct location. Examples are the contracts executed in Italian cities with promises to pay at the great international trade fairs of Lagne and Provins (Lopez and Raymond, 1955).

The spatial aspect is also prominent with the sea loan. This was like a standard loan except that it was understood that specific goods or goods bought with currency were to be carried by ship to a specified port and sold there for a monetary return. The goods were considered as collateral for this loan. More elaborate still was the commenda. In it the lender was not promised a specified amount on return of the ship. Rather, a three-fourths share of the profits went to the investor, and the rest to the traveling party. Both would share in the loss if the return were less than the investment. The traveling party himself could act as investor in the venture, altering the divisions. There could be many investors; a contract issued in Genoa in 1198 had 15. The analog of the sea contract for land shipments, for example for shipment of goods to a fair, was the *societates terrae.*

Circulating private debt, paper IOUs which passed from hand to hand, emerged also, though this took some time. As was noted above, Italians settled in places like Bruges as representatives of home trading companies or banks. This allowed parties in distinct cities to issue bills of exchange. For example, a partner in Bruges would borrow money from a merchant in Bruges and instruct his partner in Florence to pay back the loan in Florence at a specified future date, either to the lender or to the latter's trading partner. In effect, this was an exchange contract described earlier except that the second partner, not the issuer, was obliged to pay. Active markets in bills, with many merchant–suppliers and merchant–demanders, emerged in Bruges by 1420, and their dominance continued in the fourteenth and fifteenth centuries. Later Antwerp dominated the bill market. Finally, as noted, bills began to circulate, in Bruges by 1577, in London by 1600, in France by 1604, and in Antwerp in 1610, according to Usher (1943). Earlier predecessors uncovered by Usher include two unfolded unsealed notes payable to the bearer, dated 1399 and 1400. English fair bonds, described below, may have been negotiable by the beginning of the fourteenth century, though Usher disputes this.

There are observations on private debt and its circulation with which the theory cannot yet come to grips. Why did it take so long for bills of exchange to circulate? What determines the contingencies which a simple loan contract might have? Why were regulations constantly proposed to limit markets and the circulation of bills? Some of these questions will be taken up below, if not answered, when more key elements have been introduced.

3.3 Walrasian-like credit arrangements at a point in space

A payments system with which economists are familiar is the Walrasian auction. In the pure exchange version a group of agents are gathered together, carrying various collections of goods as endowments. Then prices are called out specifying credits in units of account for goods sold and debits in units of account for goods purchased. Agents then choose their maximizing plans of exchange. As these are carried out, purchases and sales are registered on some account book for example. At the end of the auction debits must not exceed credits for each agent – the familiar budget constraint. If prices are initially chosen correctly, goods will change hands voluntarily and all accounts will balance in the end. The account system suffices. Currency is never used.

I would like to entertain here the somewhat wild thought that this Walrasian system might represent a viable, indeed beneficial, payments arrangement. Something close to it might be adopted in practice if a group of agents were to find themselves in something close to the environment described above. Indeed, as a more elaborate system allowing even greater interconnections among agents, one might assume that there would be pressures for agents to coalesce together so that Walrasian-like systems could emerge.

Do these wild thoughts receive any support from the medieval observations? To answer that question it is useful to review what is known about medieval banking.

It seems that early bankers were closely associated with the currency system and coins. That is, early bankers were essentially money changers, with coins of various kinds placed each day on a portable table or bench near the local exchange or market. Overnight, for example, such bankers had need of places of relative safekeeping, and we might well imagine that outsiders deposited their coins with these early bankers for that purpose. Apparently, some such bankers also had "surplus" coins which they were willing to lend. As we will see, bankers kept written records or accounts of these transactions, so that a more or less contemporary banking system came into being. In fact we know from Usher (1943) that this was going on in Barcelona by 1200 and presumably before that in Italy, especially Genoa. According to DeRoover (1948), banking was established in Bruges by 1265, if not earlier; DeRoover studied the account books of two bankers in Bruges, named Ruyelle and de Marke, from 1369 to 1370 and from 1366 to 1369 respectively.

A peculiar feature of medieval banking was its predominantly oral character, emphasized by Usher (1943). Accounts could not be transferred by written commands as with checks but rather required the physical presence of all parties. That is, in order for a depositor of coins to transfer his account to a seller of desired goods, both the depositor and the seller had to walk to the banker, give him oral instructions, and witness the transfer. By contemporary standards this system seems incredibly awkward. No doubt it made banking an essentially local operation. However, such local operations were apparently not that inconvenient because, as noted, bankers were mobile and were frequently located near the local commodity exchange during the day.

A typical banker did keep written records and a variety of books. In Bruges, according to DeRoover, there was at least a cashbook, a daily record of coins in and coins out; a book which kept track of transactions with the local mint; a book for direct investments in business and commerce, though there is no existing record of this; a book of ledgers of the accounts of individual customers, with debit and credit columns; and finally a journal which recorded all daily transactions. Apparently, though, this was not a sophisticated system. Without double-entry bookkeeping, it was rarely possible to find out how well the business was doing; there were no periodic statements of net worth. However, the importance of written records should not be de-emphasized. The journal in particular was a key part of the banking system. According to Usher, it was a sequence of written formal contracts with the same force as separate individual agreements executed with a public independent notary. The banker was required to state at intervals that his journal was a true record of all transactions of his business, and it was equivalent, apparently, to the registers of contracts of public notaries. Thus assignment was supposedly guaranteed by a public authority. Of course, special care was taken with the journal. It had to be kept in strict chronological order, without blanks or erasures, and with numerical entries in Roman numerals. The tearing out of leaves from the journal was viewed with great suspicion.

A key aspect of this banking system, then, is that credit transfers were possible. That is, the obligation of the debtor (purchaser) could be eliminated by written transfer of a credit in the books of a banker. In effect, the debts of the banker could be reassigned. Further, bankers could and did create credit by written entries in their books, even without the deposit of lawful currencies; a customer was simply granted an overdraft. Finally, bankers could and did keep accounts with one another, giving rise to a kind of interbank clearing system that potentially increased the scope of their operation.

Apparently, merchants came close to realizing the full set of possibilities of this banking transfer system with the great international trade fairs of Champagne. As noted above, such fairs had prespecified days, first for the introduction of goods, then for transactions in cloth, leather goods, and drugs and spices, and last, at the end, for settlements. There seems to be little doubt that bankers played a key role in this sequence. Indeed, Usher (1943) believes that traders brought relatively few coins with them to the fair. Somehow, then, potential sellers received credit from bankers for goods not yet sold, and this credit was transferred to other sellers relatively early on in the fair sequence. Similarly, book credits to these early buyers were not demand assets of the banker; payments were not due until the close of the fair. Again, Usher (1943) believes that only a small fraction of the transactions were actually discharged in specie. According to Clough and Rapp (1975) all principals did come together in the settlement period, so that in theory at least, if not in practice, relatively little specie was needed. Indeed, if market-clearing prices were somehow posted as if in a Walrasian auction (which of course they were not), then no coins whatever would be needed.

A complete separation of a book-transfer payment system from coins or specie is hard to imagine. Again, however, it appears that medieval merchants came quite close at times. Supporting evidence is provided by the use at various dates and locations of pure units of account for record-keeping purposes, as noted by Cipolla (1956). In fact we have already noted this use of pounds and shillings in Carolingian times. Later, accounts were kept in circulating coins of various denominations to facilitate record-keeping. Subsequent devaluations changed the relative value of circulating coins, potentially destroying the record-keeping system. However, merchants in Milan after 1340, for example, continued to use older coins in their record-keeping systems with the understanding that they were pure fictional units of account.

In short, then, record-keeping in units of account was not a problem. But what about actual payments? Certainly there was some uncertainty at the fair, about the valuation of goods for example. Some coins must have been needed. Again, however, medieval merchants were willing to extend their bookkeeping system to cope with this problem. Credit was extended to the next fair by having the debtor issue a personal IOU. Frequently the money changers (bankers) were used as intermediaries, extending credit for promises of future payment. Either way there arose well-documented exchange contracts or *lettres de foire*. With such letters, the requirements that accounts be balanced, essentially at a point in time, could be replaced by the requirement that accounts be balanced over time. Further, the regular periodic meetings of fairs and the use of *lettres de foire* gave rise to apparently massive international settlement periods, at the fairs of Lyon for example. Merchants could all write contracts payable at one of the fairs, with accounts settled at the outset in the centralized multilateral bank credit system. These international financial fairs persisted well beyond the trade in commodities which fathered them originally.

There is also evidence that the banking transfer systems of large commercial cities greatly facilitated payments on a continual daily basis. In his study of the account books of two of the 15 bankers of Bruges, for example, DeRoover uncovers literally thousands of within-bank relatively rapid transfers of account. New accounts were opened as an assignment from an original depositor, then transferred, perhaps within the day, to a third party, and so on. These and other book transfers apparently outnumber cash transactions by a large amount. Thus DeRoover speculates that regular customers made extensive use of the transfer system, with most local payments made by assignment on their bank accounts. Further, this practice must have been facilitated by the existence of interbank accounts, for DeRoover finds that *each* banker had an account *with every other banker.* We do not know the actual physical process involved, but it seems that an outside claimant did not have to withdraw specie to transfer his newly acquired account to his own bank. As to the global nature of the payment system of Bruges, we can only speculate. One of DeRoover's ledgers shows 11,000 accounts, while he estimates the population of Bruges at not more than 45,000. He concludes that every merchant, broker, innkeeper, and draper had bank accounts, and probably also realtors, furriers, and goldsmiths. DeRoover's point is that the banking transfer system consisted of more than just a few major accounts but rather was recruited at large from the moderately well-to-do.

Banking-like record-keeping systems would also allow transfers among agents through chains of pairings, as described earlier. Even if liabilities did not pass from hand to hand, they could be passed on the books at a centralized location visited by participating parties. It appears that this occurred early, making the enigmatic absence of circulating private debt less puzzling.

One type of debt or obligation which emerged early was the promise of a series of payments or rents backed by specific property. Issuers of these types of annuities received in turn a fixed payment at the outset, perhaps to finance the acquisition of the property itself. In any event such devices were soon used to fund long-term public debts, with the holder of an annuity giving up a fixed initial payment to the public authority for the promise of sequences of "rents," backed in this case by specified tax revenues. Usher finds that funded debts of this type appeared in Italy in the thirteenth century and in Catalonia and Germany in the fourteenth century. Further, and more to the point here, annuities or shares in the public debt were actively traded, for example in Genoa as early as 1200–1225 according to Lopez and Raymond (1955), but sales were registered in transfer books. Indeed, Usher (1943) notes that the organization of the funded debt was roughly contemporaneous with the development of oral-command deposit-transfer banking, with sales effected on the books of banks. Again, it seems that active security markets existed without the hand-to-hand transfer of paper instruments, that is, without negotiable securities. Centralized record-keeping devices sufficed.

As Usher (1943) and DeRoover (1948) emphasize, negotiable securities did not emerge until the seventeenth century. However, Braudel (1979) notes the existence of active markets in stocks or shares by the thirteenth century. Shares in a silver mine near Siena were issued and sold then, as were shares in salt mines, in metal works in Syria, and in French copper mines. In fact by the fifteenth century stock was issued in mines in central Europe and became the object of speculation. Shares were also issued in partnerships, for example in mills in Toulouse, again by the thirteenth century. Apparently these could be sold. We also know from Lopez and Raymond (1955) that shares in commendas could be bought and sold in Genoa by the thirteenth century, and Clough and Rapp (1975) note that shares in the construction of a ship could be bought there by the same date. Indeed, a state-operated trading company was issuing shares in Genoa by 1346. The point, again, is that a reconciliation of Usher (1943) and DeRoover (1948) on the absence of negotiable securities with Lopez and Raymond (1955), Clough and Rapp (1975), and Braudel (1979) on active financial markets requires that these active security markets be supported by relatively centralized bookkeeping systems.

3.4 Spatial interconnectedness and a theory of growth

It is apparent from the spatial theories described above that the degree of interconnectedness of agents in space and over time has a bearing on the financial arrangements that are adopted. As one moves from autarky, to infinitely extended highway travel, to revolving circles, and finally to concentrated group meetings, one sees no financial instruments *per se*, currency, IOUs and circulating private debt, and Walrasian-like arrangements respectively. Indeed, in "Financial structure and economic activity" (Townsend, 1983, this volume, ch. 4) this idea is exploited to deliver systematic correlations between financial instruments in use and economic activity. Essentially, as agents become more interconnected, there is less deferred consumption. For example, we can compare the model of currency with the model of Walrasian credit. In the model of currency, agents work to manufacture home-produced goods. These can then be sold for currency which is held at least one period before acquisition of market-produced goods. In the model of Walrasian credit, consumption of market-produced goods occurs within the period of production. Thus, if economic agents discount the future, market-produced goods are more expensive in the currency regime than in the Walrasian regime. Mild substitution assumptions thus deliver less labor effort and fewer market purchases in the currency regime relative to the Walrasian regime. Finally, if the degree of interconnectedness is varied exogenously, for example is increasing over time, then we would see an increase in both measured economic activity and the ratio of debt to currency.

We obtain a rough impression that these correlations hold up in the medieval period under consideration. Again, in northwest Europe we see increasing spatial connectedness, increasing production for the market, increasing use of currency overall, and an eventually increasing ratio of private debt to currency. Not too much should be claimed for the accuracy of the observations, but the suggestion is clear nonetheless.

4 Uncertainty as a key element

Uncertainty appears to have been a salient feature of economic life in the medieval period. Many examples might serve to make this point, but one should suffice here – the example of medieval agriculture.

Two aspects of uncertainty about crop yields stand out. First, there was enormous variability. Using data on yields of various grains from Winchester and other English estates, for example, McCloskey (1976) has computed an average coefficient of variation of output net of seed at 0.347. If half the average output is taken as the minimal subsistence level, as it often is in the literature, then a calculation reveals that output fell below subsistence roughly once every 13 years. On the assumption that output was eaten, or sold to acquire consumption indirectly, the prediction is famine and starvation for a large number of people. Indeed, famines did occur in England in the thirteenth and fourteenth centuries at roughly that frequency.

The second aspect of uncertainty that stands out is that yields were *not* highly correlated over space at a point in time. Yields in the two or three square mile area comprising the land of a village could vary enormously. There is not enough space here to summarize McCloskey's (1976) evidence on this. Suffice it to note that the correlation of yields seems to fall roughly 14 points per mile within some range. On the assumption that households were virtually autarkic in consumption, something which is explored further below, we would predict with McCloskey that households would be concerned about their portfolios of land plots, that they would diversify spatially. In fact a typical villager with 30 acres held from 30 to 60 strips, as illustrated dramatically in the map of landholdings of Elford, Stratfordshire (Homans, 1941). The same argument might be used to understand why various estates and monasteries held spatially separated villas, as is evident in the map of villas recorded in the surviving ninth century French polyptyques (Pounds, 1974) or the map of the estates of Ramsey Abbey (Raftis, 1957).

The model used by McCloskey (1976) and the observations he has garnered are intriguing. In particular, McCloskey-like environments can be studied with the use of programming problems for the determination of Pareto optimal allocations – the contract-theoretic mechanism design approach mentioned above. Essentially, the problem of maximizing a weighted sum of the utilities of the households of the model by choice of consumption assignments is solved subject to the constraints implied by finite resources. The natural space for this problem is the state contingent commodity space of Arrow (1953) and Debreu (1959). With a solution in hand, the implications of full risk bearing for the autarky hypothesis and for the land portfolio problem generally can be examined systematically. I am pursuing this in ongoing research.

Many of the essays in this book, representing previous research, also incorporate uncertainty as a key element. Virtually all the essays with private information do this – the next key element to be considered.

5 Private information as a key element

5.1 How to handle private information in theory

In many applications the existence of some key privately observed components can be postulated. For example, households in a medieval village might have had private information on their labor effort; others might have made guesses about efforts from observed outputs, or they might have monitored occasionally, using up resources to do so. Or, agents in the spatially dispersed outposts of early Italian trading companies might have had private information on aspects of the environment under which they operated; managers back home might have made guesses about underlying circumstances from observed or reported profits, or they might have engaged in costly audits. But how is a modeler to handle private information theoretically? For example, how can consumption–labor assignments and institutions be delivered as endogenous in such settings, so that the effect of private information on arrangements can be investigated systematically?

This problem is attacked in "Allocation mechanisms for asymmetrically informed agents" (Harris and Townsend, 1978, this volume, ch. 6) and "Resource allocation under asymmetric information" (Harris and Townsend, 1981, this volume, ch. 7). The idea is to search over *all* possible feasible arrangements. Yet because it is cumbersome if not impossible to do this directly, we seek to discover the universal characteristics of the equilibrium allocations of arrangements, characteristics intimately associated with private information. Then, inequalities capturing these characteristics are appended as constraints onto the full information programming problems described above. The solutions are naturally termed "private information constrained optima." Further, to implement any constrained optimum, agents need merely report on privately observed parameters; owing to the imposition of the constraints they can be assumed to report truthfully, to reveal these parameters as it were. Hence these methods are termed "revelation principle" methods. Harris and Townsend (1978, this volume, ch. 6) develop and illustrate the methods in a pure exchange context. The arguments are generalized and refined so that they can be applied widely in Harris and Townsend (1981, this volume, ch. 7).

In the paper "Optimal contracts and competitive markets with costly state verification" (Townsend, 1979, this volume, ch. 5) revelation principle methods, or a predecessor to them, are used to determine optimal auditing policy and optimal contracts when there is private information on output (or profits). Deterministic audits over some, but not all, reported outputs yield simple debt contracts as the efficient arrangement. Random audits are shown to help further, though a tight characterization of the arrangement is lost.

In the paper "Optimal multiperiod contracts and the gain from enduring relationships under private information" (Townsend, 1982, this volume, ch. 8) revelation principle methods are used to examine the features of multiperiod arrangements. It turns out that intertemporal tie-ins – dependence of the current arrangement on the history of past observables or past claims – are the hallmark of multiperiod private information environments. In that sense there are gains to enduring relationships, a gain over a sequence of single-period information-constrained optima.

5.2 *Private information in the medieval village – some questions*

I am reminded of these private information papers in reading about the medieval village economy. For the clusters of monastic villages constituting an estate, for example, one wonders whether there was variability in the commodity bundles transferred to the central monastery, whether there was any effort to audit villa yields, and whether there was any dependence in the transfers over time, say forgiveness of requirements in return for promises of greater produce later on. Within a village with lands held in demesne, farmed for a lord by the villagers, one wonders whether labor efforts were observed continually, as might be suggested by the presence of reeves, haywards, and bailiffs, whether this could have been efficient for the parameters of the environment, and whether a more variable monitoring policy might have been in place. For villages as a whole one wonders whether private information might partially rationalize limited *ex post* transfers of grain, something close to the autarky hypothesis. With nontrivial information-constrained *ex post* transfers, one wonders whether one could rationalize observed dispersed landholdings, the existence of land held in demesne, and the apparent absence of borrowing–lending arrangements between the lord and the villagers.

5.3 *Private information and early firms – the gain from enduring relationships*

Though the association is far from close, I am reminded of these private information papers in reading about the nature and operation of early Italian firms – firms which operated with spatially dispersed divisions in Bruges, for example. Here are some of these observations for the reader. They emphasize intertemporal tie-ins but suggest that a closer examination of the observations and that extensions of the theory might be fruitful projects.

DeRoover (1948) identifies two types of Italian organizations in Bruges. One, the "centralized" firm, was common in the fourteenth century. Under it, capital invested in an enterprise was divided into shares held primarily by family members and also, to some extent, by outsiders. For example, the

Peruzzi Company in 1297 consisted of ten partners, including three Peruzzi brothers. The Bardi Company in 1331 had six family members holding $36\frac{3}{4}$ shares and five outsiders holding $21\frac{1}{4}$ shares. Like the earlier commenda agreements, profits of the firm were divided according to these shares, that is, according to initial investments. Indeed, these companies really represented a series of successive partnerships; at the terminal date of each partnership, as with the end of a commenda, books were closed, financial statements were prepared, and the old firm was liquidated (while the new one continued in existence). For example, the Peruzzi Company was "reorganized" in this way in 1308, 1310, 1312, 1324, 1331, and 1335. We might also note that the Peruzzi Company, like others of its kind, had branches not only in Bruges but also in other trading centers, 15 branches in total.

The other type of organization identified by DeRoover (1948) is the "decentralized" firm, which became increasingly popular after a series of failures of centralized firms in 1345. Indeed, under the "decentralized" firm, such as that of the Medici, each of the many branches was essentially an independent legal entity; overall there was a kind of loose combination of quasi-independent partnerships. But, in fact, senior partners based in Italy, such as Lorenzo and Cosimo de Medici, decided all important matters of policy. Also, profits were not divided according to initial capital investments, but were allocated more toward senior partners. The branches were sometimes run by salaried factors.

Neither form of organization was original to the fourteenth century in Europe. Indeed, Lopez and Raymond (1955) emphasize in their study of contracts that any line between the *societates terrae*, the land-trade analog of the commenda, and these firms or compagnia is hard to draw. They display company charters dated Venice 1179, Marseilles 1248, Lucca 1259, and Genoa 1308. However, some distinguishing features can be identified. First of all, in the company charters there is unlimited liability for each of the partners; they were all responsible for all debts and were liable up to all their worldly goods, not just initial investments. Second, company charters, unlike *societates terrae*, are really *informal* agreements among merchants, not notarized public documents; company charters are holograph documents written and certified by merchants themselves. Indeed, early firms were just associations of family members brought together for some kind of business purpose, the word *com* meaning with and *pan* meaning bread, invoking an image of all things shared. Lopez and Raymond (1955) also display relatively early factor or agency contracts in which one party swears to serve another in good faith.

It is difficult to find a common motive for the formation of these early firms or agency relationships, but it might be guessed that, like the later Italian companies with branches in Bruges, they were established to extend the scope of operations in land trade, to solve the decentralization problem of spatial separation which such extended operations entailed. Indeed, early firms were especially associated with inland Italian cities, unlike the association of the commenda with seaports. Braudel (1979) seems to draw the same conclusion, noting for example the powerful role played "deep in Germany" by three family firms from 1380 to 1530.

The key idea, then, is that the decentralization of activity within a firm results in information which is private to individual partners or factors. However, with private information there can be damning consequences if agents are ruthless in the pursuit of their own self-interest. A way out of this dilemma is to provide intertemporal links, tying future transfers or potential transfers to present outcomes, or even to present claims about unobserved events. Thus private information should give rise to multiperiod agreements and, as regards incentives, the longer are the agreements the better (potentially) for all parties concerned. Of course relatively long agreements are in fact what we observe with these early companies. There is also ample evidence of explicit intertemporal tie-ins. Partners shared in future profits. Salaried factors could be reprimanded and denied promotion or increase of salary if they neglected their duty or if the performance of the branch fell short of the expectations of the senior partner. In extreme cases salaries of factors could be cut and incompetent factors recalled.

The absence of any outside enforcement device is a hallmark of these partnerships and factor relationships; all concerned entered into an enduring relationship with one another. Thus, as regards enforcement, there seemed to be no real need to write much down. Thus it is not surprising that the holograph records we have are sometimes vague, often just acknowledging the existence of a relationship. In the documents of Lopez and Raymond (1955) we find that one partner is to do business with an initial investment as best he can and to promise to tell the other the truth and to be honest in everything, that two partners are to trade and do business whenever they may be of the opinion that it is good and advantageous for the company, according as they will in the future come to mutual agreement, and that a factor is to carry out the business of the principal and to gain a profit, acting in good faith and without fraud.

Occasional agreements are, however, somewhat more detailed in nature. The agreement of one Angolo Tani in Bruges with Lorenzo de Medici in Florence is replete with guidelines. Tani is not allowed to leave Bruges except for business trips to cities like Antwerp, is not allowed to play cards or dice or to have relations with any married woman, virgin, or religious, is not to hire factors without approval, is not to invest in any other company whatever, is permitted to lend money only to merchants by giving credit on his books or by purchasing their exchange contracts, is not to purchase wool or cloth exceeding 600 pounds in value per year, is not to underwrite insurance with specified exceptions, and is not to sell foreign exchange to lords, except with written permission. Yet despite all this detail it seems that Tani was left with considerable discretion, as contrasted for example with the detailed and exacting landlord–serf agreements on the medieval manor. That of course is what we would expect from principal–agent theory when labor effort is unobserved; it is understood that the agent will optimize, given his particular situation and the overall nature of the agreement.

6 Limited communication as a key element

6.1 *A model of communication-accounting systems*

In the previous section it was argued that agents with private information could usefully send messages to one another about privately observed shocks or recommended actions. If, in addition, these agents are spatially separated then the available communication technology comes into play. This idea is analyzed in "Economic organization with limited communication" (Townsend, 1987a, this volume, ch. 9); oral assignment, portable token, written message, and telecommunication systems are presented formally as the communication technology is varied exogenously.

In an oral assignment system agents must literally make physical contact with one another in order to send a message or find out what someone else said. Thus an intermediary can emerge as agents report to a common location or a common agent. In a portable token system agents receive, under the rules of a contract or mechanism, a prespecified number of tokens as evidence of having taken certain actions or made certain announcements. Later, possibly at a distinct location, these tokens serve as evidence of the past history. They can still serve this role, at least partially, even if they can be concealed and only displayed at the discretion of the holder. Multiple portable token systems allow more history to be conveyed, overcoming some concealment difficulties. Written message systems represent in this framework the limit of multiple portable token systems. Finally, perfect costless telecommunications allow agents to be linked instantaneously and without cost to a central record-keeping system.

6.2 *Financial instruments as communication devices*

The importance of less than perfect communication systems in medieval history is apparent from the discussion in earlier sections, that is, from the discussion of other key elements. As was noted earlier, for example, banking was predominantly oral in character for several hundred years. That is, it was an oral assignment system, backed by written ledgers at the bank. Another example would be the bills of exchange discussed earlier. Again, these were written messages sent among trading partners in distinct cities. The bill was not a notarized agreement; it was a mere letter, or series of letters, written by the maker, folded and sealed, and sent at intervals.

Related to the bill of exchange was the order of payment in which a depositor asks his banker, or someone who owes him money, to pay a specified third party. Indeed, to the extent that the banker is a trading partner, an order of payment is exactly like a bill. Apparently, however, orders were drawn on less closely related agents. They appear to have been used in Florence by the end of the fourteenth century and in Genoa by the early fifteenth century. What is not so obvious is how these orders were transmitted to the banker. Indeed, orders to pay carried by a third party to the bank are essentially checks. Yet Usher (1943) emphasizes that checks were slow to emerge. At first, at least, only factors, servants, or family members of the initial depositor could present with any force written instruments from their principals. Thus fraud, the distortion of messages, seems to have been a real possibility, something which is not in the theoretical model. The introduction of fraud coupled with aspects of enduring relationships might make for an interesting and realistic extension of the theory, motivated by the observations here.

6.3 *Currency as a creation of the state*

The theory discussed above also suggests that portable tokens can serve as communication devices – evidence of past histories. This suggests the idea that currency can at times be interpreted as playing that role. Suppose, for example, that the king or local strongman were to issue tokens as "payment" for produce received, or confiscated, or for services rendered to him. If this tax fell on one person, it might be disproportionate. However, if the king were to require that tokens be surrendered as taxes by everyone, periodically, then the initial holder could pass some of the tokens to a third party in return for goods and services. These tokens would be evidence, though not thought of that way, of having supplied goods or services to the monarch. Further, anyone showing up with tokens at the time of periodic assessments would be providing evidence that they had supplied goods to the monarch either directly or indirectly as third-party suppliers.

However wild this idea, there is some evidence that currencies as tokens were creations of the "state," part of explicit or implicit social agreements. The evidence is complicated by the fact that tokens were actually metallic objects, partial if not full-bodied coins. The theory above does not require this. However, metallic coins with variable proportions over time seem to present their own taxation possibilities, as noted below.

Indirect evidence for the explicit social character of currency is provided by the wide variety of currency areas, locations which issued and circulated their own silver or vellon coins (vellon is an alloy of copper and silver). There were at least five separate currency areas in north and central Italy; apparently, many German and Flemish towns were also minting their own coins; Majorca, Sardinia, Valencia, and Barcelona controlled their own silver and vellon currencies; and in France there were innumerable local coinages with two dominant currency areas centered around Paris and Tours respectively. According to Cipolla (1964), small (fractional) coins served the needs of local transactions; beyond some well-defined area, such coins were not always accepted.

There is also direct evidence that local currencies were associated with explicit social agreements, namely town charters with the prince. Apparently, in some localities the prince retained his feudal privilege of minting coins but was not allowed to alter the metallic content of coins at will. This idea was embodied in the agreement of Louis VII in 1137 with the citizens of Orleans and Etamps not to make alterations in the currencies of their towns; apparently, there were similar agreements with princes or monarchs in Spain and Germany. More generally, it seems that mint masters were subject to some kind of public control. In Bruges, at least, explicit regulations prohibited the melting down of coins in circulation or even the assaying of coins other than through money changers. These money changers were required to take all bullion to the local mint, and export of bullion or coins was prohibited. Further, foreign (nonlocal) coins were not supposed to circulate. Similarly, in Spain, local agents were obliged to deal with the mints through money changers who set fees and did not allow perfect convertibility. Usher (1943) finds that in many states mints (or money changers) did not buy or sell on demand.

We might wonder whether some of these regulations had any force; at least enforcement must have been difficult. However, strong evidence for the monopoly or social character of local mints and coins is provided by the pervasive and persistent debasement of local coins. This debasement, however accomplished (see below), is hard to understand in the absence of a grant of local monopoly or some *de facto* social agreement. In fact such debasement generally did not take place with gold coins which circulated across "national" boundaries.

It is evident from table 1.1 (from Cipolla, 1964) that the silver content of a penny was successively lowered in the various currency areas of Italy, which Cipolla terms the van of the debasement movement. England, however,

Table 1.1 Grams of pure silver corresponding to a pound-tale (240 pennies)

Year	*England*	*France*	*Genoa*	*Milan*	*Venice*	*Florence*
800	330	390		390	390	
1250	324	80	70	70	20	35
1500	172	22	13	9	6	6

managed to have a relatively stable currency relatively early, and France lies somewhere between these two extremes. Apparently, the debasement of vellon coins was at least equal to that of silver coins, if not more extreme (Lopez and Raymond, 1955). In contrast Cipolla (1956) notes that the gold coins which circulated as international currencies, the coins of Constantinople and Baghdad, and also of Venice and Florence, had remarkably stable metallic contents in weight and fineness. For example, the gold coins of the Byzantine and Islamic Empires remained stable up to the eleventh century, and the coins of Florence, after their issue in 1252, up to 1400.

It seems hard to reconcile these facts with some kind of free-market theory of both gold and silver coins. It is sometimes claimed, as by Cipolla (1964), that in the face of a rather dramatic monetization of the economy and relatively inelastic supplies of precious metals the relative value of gold and silver increased throughout the Commercial Revolution. This chronic shortage of money could be alleviated to some extent by the creation of coins with less metallic content. But why then the asymmetry as between gold and silver coins? Similarly, it is sometimes claimed, as in DeRoover (1948), that debasements of silver coins were associated with balance-of-payments difficulties and a regional shortage of specie. But then why was this phenomenon so pervasive across regions and time spans? Again, why the asymmetric experience as between gold and silver?

The answer might be that in one way or another gold coins and perhaps large silver coins were in effect provided on a somewhat competitive or decentralized basis, but that small silver coins and vellon coins were not. Gold coins of stable metallic content were issued by large trading centers which found it to their advantage to be able to have their currency adopted as an international standard. In a sense, they provided a service (for payment of course), portable units of relatively high and known value, obviating the need for costly state verification at every transaction among relatively anonymous international merchants. It may well be that others were waiting in the wings, so to speak, ready to supply a similar service. In contrast, it seems evident that minters of local silver and vellon coins were given an explicit monopoly. Perhaps only local residents could keep track of monetary ordinances establishing the metallic content of coins. Indeed, perhaps these coins had become virtual tokens, and only local residents would accept them in exchange, as if local coins and devaluations had become part of a well-known and well-understood system of taxation. We might note that England, with a relatively stable penny, had alternative sources of revenue. We might also note in the decretals of Innocent IV, from 1243 to 1245, as guidelines to princes, that the value of coins was to be equal to the value of metal less minting costs, but that the prince was allowed to draw *profit* from the coinage *in case of need.*

Unfortunately, it is not clear how the prince was to profit or, equivalently, how the taxes were to be administered. Some possibilities suggested by a reading of history are given below.

1 There are references in the literature to "calling in the coins" – apparently a prince could collect coins of one metallic content and hand out coins of another lower content. One German prince is said to have done this on average three times a year for 38 years (Clough and Rapp, 1975). This is a clear if not extraordinary tax. More frequently, older coins of the same denomination but with higher weight would not disappear from circulation; efforts to collect the older coins were only partially successful in France, for example.

2 Minters might try to put less metal in coins surreptitiously. However, it seems clear from the literature that there were more or less reliable commercial ratings of coins. Merchants, for example, would gather valuable coins in bags sealed with colored wax to indicate the standard (Lopez and Raymond, 1955). Contracts often made a distinction as between various types of gold Byzantine hypers, distinguished by the image on the coin (Lopez and Raymond, 1955). Usher (1943) gives the impression that many issues of new coins with relatively less silver were *fully announced*.

3 Official ratings of coins might just define the values at which designated coins were to be accepted in payment for services or goods provided to the public authority, either on current account or for past public borrowings. The latter would be a clear default, in effect a tax levied on creditors.

4 Coins may have had a value in exchange beyond their value as metal, say because they were accepted as tokens, as Cipolla (1956) suggests. In that event, those who brought their bullion to the mint received something of value even if they received relatively little metal. The bullion in turn represented pure profit to the mint. Did mints recognize this possibility early on? In any event, it seems that seigniorage or mint charges were considerable – $\frac{1}{2}$–1 percent on vellon coins. Indeed, DeRoover (1948) argues that mint charges varied up to 50 percent on small silver and vellon coins.

5 Finally and related to point 3 above, coins could have a value in exchange different from their value as actual metal if someone were able to fix a price. It is suggested by Cipolla (1956) that wage earners were subject to this plight, paid in nominal units of coins and taxed by merchants under debasement, and suggested by DeRoover (1948) that bankers could fix accounts in terms of nominal coins, not real metal, and would push for debasement to prevent failures.

7 Limited commitment and costly enforcement

Much emphasis has been given in preceding sections to the programming approach for the determination of social arrangements. Uncertainty, private information, and limited communication were all discussed in that context. Yet agents are often unable to make plans in advance of meeting one another, as in the spatial models of currency and valued private debt discussed at the outset. Though the essays in this book do not appear to have much bearing on the enormous movements of people associated with the fall of the Roman Empire and subsequent rise of northwest Europe, aspects of limited commitment are overwhelming, to say the least! Force, or threat of force, was used period by period in containment, in pillage, or in extraction of tribute.

Implicit also in some of the discussions of earlier sections are aspects of limited commitment and costly enforcement. For example, the contracts of early medieval towns were notarized documents, suggesting third-party enforcement. Suppose in fact that a third party would have to be called in to enforce the agreement if either party attempted to default. The contract would serve as evidence of the initial agreement, as in the model of limited communication. If enforcement were costly, then the number of contingencies might be limited, as in the simpler "Optimal contracts and competitive markets with costly state verification" (Townsend, 1979, this volume, ch. 5).

Indeed, these early documents are striking in the paucity of explicit contingencies. Standard loan contracts in the Lopez and Raymond (1955) collection are typically for one year or less. In one there is an explicit monetary penalty for payment beyond maturity. In another, it is stated that the borrower can pay the debt off early and that such payment must be accepted. So much for multiperiod contingencies. Exchange contracts had some contingencies. In one, if the borrower was unable to pay because a specified caravan did not arrive at a specified place, then he could repay at a distinct date and location. In the sea loan, repayment was conditioned on the ship arriving safely, at risk of fortunes of God, the sea, and hostile peoples. In short, there are some important contingencies, but these are not the detailed social arrangements that theory might suggest.

Aspects of limited commitment and less than perfect enforcement are implicit also in the discussion of Italian firms. Presumably, factors participated voluntarily in the sense that they could default and flee if they pleased. Indeed, as noted, factor contracts were not notarized; at best they were informal documents. Thus the promise of future profits and the loss from banishment must have kept agents in the arrangement. Braudel (1979) recounts the story of a factor in a foreign port who successfully evades pursuing police only to show up and fling himself at his "master's" feet.

8 The anomalies and enigmas of failing institutions and volatile markets

Of course not all the observations from the medieval period are readily interpreted by existing theory. A few of the anomalies are emphasized in this section. Possible alternative approaches are reserved for the next.

8.1 The enigma of bank failures

It seems from theory and from the operation of the Champagne fairs that a banking book-transfer system can facilitate routine and more or less systematic payments. No doubt the banking transfer systems of Barcelona and Bruges played such a role. However, there is also little doubt that the banks of Barcelona and Bruges engaged extensively in intermediary-investment activities, financing relatively long term and occasionally risky commercial undertakings. The account books studied by DeRoover (1948) reveal many small overdraft loans, and, more to the point, a few relatively large overdrafts which seem to have absorbed most of the bank's resources. Apparently, the latter were not temporary accounts but rather were investment loans in which the banker entered into a partnership with the borrower, furnishing him with working capital. An example of this in the account books is the overdraft account of one Mademoiselle Rudevorde who ran an inn patronized by foreign merchants. The risk of loans in Bruges and elsewhere is explicitly acknowledged by the requirement of collateral of jewels or plate, an assignment of revenue from the borrower's property, or the assignment of tax collection proceeds in the case of loans to municipal authorities. Further, the municipal authorities themselves attempted to control the portfolios of banks, as in Venice in 1274 where banks were prohibited from trading in speculative commodities such as iron, copper, and tin, and from having more than two-fifths of their investments in the public debt. In Barcelona public money changers who could accept deposits were required to post a bond to the equivalent of 180,000 dollars in nineteenth century US prices, according to Usher! Having done so, such bankers could place cloths of certification on their banking tables at the exchange.

Despite all these precautions, banks frequently failed, as did Ruyelle in Bruges in 1370. Earlier, in Bruges in 1309, the number of money changers had fallen from 19 to 14. According to one Venetian senator, of the 103 bankers that existed at one time or another in Venice, 96 came to a bad end. Further, securities were often inadequate to cover losses. One Señor Costello was beheaded in front of his bank in Barcelona in 1360.

In the face of all this risk it might be guessed that the liabilities of the bank might make a sharp distinction between depositors using the bank as a convenient means of payment and depositors using the bank as an investment-intermediary device. Unfortunately the evidence for this is far from clear. Perhaps an extreme view is adopted by DeRoover (1948) who believes that most deposit liabilities were payable on demand, as if the funds were merely deposited for safekeeping, whereas the funds were actually used to finance investment projects and thus were not in the bank. DeRoover estimates the reserve-to-deposit ratio of the banker Ruyelle in 1370 at 29.3 percent. DeRoover also states that banks were subject to runs on false rumors, imminence of war, news that a commercial venture had gone wrong, or failure of a merchant in debt to a bank. He also adopts the position that demand deposits did not bear interest. Of course DeRoover is not alone in emphasizing the importance of demand deposits; Usher (1943) also finds abundant evidence that deposits on current account were consciously recognized as the primary activity of a bank. There is also the evidence of municipal legislation, for example in Barcelona in 1444, which was meant to ensure payment upon demand to persons having credit entries in a bank, and also in Liège in 1350.

The problem of inference is that many deposit liabilities of a bank appear as mere entries in the bank's ledgers, apparently leaving unspecified the nature of the obligations in favor of depositors. However, depositors may have known. Usher draws a sharp distinction between various types of deposits and notes that rather subtle questions of timing and obligation were sometimes made. In one class of deposits, monies and valuables placed in safekeeping were carefully described, sealed in bags, and stored in strongboxes. In a second class of deposits involving the transfer of real estate, funds were deposited by an individual to the credit of a notary, to be transferred by the notary to a designated party when stated conditions were satisfied. In 1433, 28 percent of the deposits of the Bank of Deposit of Barcelona were of the latter kind, though it is not known if this was typical. Finally, we do have some explicit bank deposit contracts available in the collection of Lopez and Raymond (1955). Unfortunately, though, these do not settle the issue. In one, the banker accepts 50 pounds from a depositor with the explicit intent of employing them in trade in Genoa, promising to give the depositor some profit at the banker's discretion. However, the banker also promises to return the 50 pounds with profit to the depositor within eight days of request. From the point of view of theory this contract seems enigmatic.

To summarize the discussion, then, medieval banking systems appear to have been made vulnerable by investment-intermediary activities. Such activities in themselves are beneficial, but so apparently are the activities of a more mundane bank transfer system. Why put the latter in jeopardy? How do we explain the lack of separation? Were more efficient arrangements available? If so, why were they not adopted?

8.2 The enigma of volatile markets

As was emphasized before, notes, bills, and IOUs were traded in a sense in a security market, with the term interpreted generously to mean the coming together of merchants, bankers, and brokers. Indeed, the impression is gained that participation in markets increased generally throughout the period of study so that by the sixteenth century, in Antwerp for example, one witnesses the development of the Bourse, housing in effect a commodity exchange for sales on the basis of samples and for contracts of future delivery, a short-term money market for the borrowing and lending of funds, security exchanges for transactions in bonds and stocks, and underwriting offices for the trade of insurers. The conglomeration of all these people at one place at various points in time in conjunction with still prevalent difficulties of transportation and communication across space and time seems to have played a part in the speculation, second guessing, and erratic movements of prices prominent in the Netherlands in the tulip mania in 1630, then in France in stock on Law's Mississippi Company in the early eighteenth century, and in England in stock in the South Sea Company shortly thereafter.

Again we have the obvious questions. Are erratic price movements and speculation inevitable? How do we explain them? Could alternative superior systems have been implemented? If so, why were they not adopted?

9 On modeling limited market participation – some alternative attacks

An obvious starting point for addressing the apparent enigmas of banking is to try to model banks and intermediaries as institutions – to construct models in which agents emerge endogenously as go-betweens for other agents. Perhaps out of this would come an understanding of the limits on banks, especially in environments which dictate that not all agents be linked up to one another. Similarly, a natural starting point for addressing the apparent enigmas of volatile asset markets is to try to model asset markets in environments in which it is not efficient for all agents to be linked up to one another, in which market participation is limited endogenously. My own efforts to model banks and limited assets markets are now briefly described.

9.1 *Intermediation with costly exchange and endogenous marketeers*

In "Intermediation with costly bilateral exchange" (Townsend, 1978a, this volume, ch. 10) I explore the simple idea that it might be costly for agents to be linked up to one another, that is, more specifically, that there be a fixed cost for each bilateral link. The motive to form links is risk aversion: endowments are independent and identically distributed across risk-averse agents, and so diversified portfolios are possible and beneficial. However, the fixed costs of larger group size can limit this diversification optimally. In fact, for particular parameter configurations, clusters of agents emerge endogenously. The equilibrium concept employed is the core, that a configuration of clusters and allocations within clusters be such that no new group can form and block, that is, do better on its own. Of course feasible allocations for coalitions take into account the costs of exchange within groups. What I like about this simple model is that not all agents deal with one another in equilibrium. In effect the solution to a programming problem is not implemented by a coalition of the whole, even though it is in the core.

In this and subsequent efforts I have tried to impose even less structure a priori, supposing that agents can compete with one another in proposing arrangements and in responding to proposals. This was done in "Theories of intermediated structures" (Townsend, 1983d, this volume, ch. 11), for example, by supposing that any agent can propose to act as an intermediary, calling out terms of trade for coalitions of agents, and that agents can respond to these proposals by choices of intermediaries and the amounts to trade. The key is that no central plan limits this behavior. However, the result in the model with costly bilateral exchange is the same core allocations as before. The result in the pure exchange marketeers model is the standard competitive core allocation, at least as the number of agents gets large. These papers, then, seem to help to explain the emergence of "competitive" outcomes and prices when agents meet without precommitment. They do not, however, explain many of the anomalies of limited market participation. At best small numbers can make the competitive outcome a poor approximation to reality, but this happens in the theory less frequently than one might have supposed.

These modeling efforts are also vulnerable to the charge that the structure, the "decentralized" games in this instance, still comes from the modeler. Perhaps there is even less structure in reality, and this is the cause of failure and erratic markets. Therefore further avenues need to be explored.

9.2 *Endogenous asset structures with spatially separated agents*

An alternative systematic way to limit links among agents, to limit asset market participation, is to let separation of agents in space dictate all arrangements. In "Asset return anomalies in a monetary economy" (Townsend, 1987, this volume, ch. 12) arrangements are naturally competitive when large numbers of strangers meet with one another; again, they are meeting once and never more. This is what gives rise to valued currency, to effect some exchange. In contrast, if large numbers of cohort agents travel with one another, then asset markets can be complete *within* these groups. As with standard representative consumer models, any asset whatever, including assets with payments in monetary terms, can be priced for the group since there is a role for currency in the "outside" economy. In this model asset returns are anomalous relative to the model with no separation in space and no currency. One would see rate-of-return dominance, for example. Therefore there is some success in this approach.

A complaint, perhaps, is that the environments are too stylized and the asset trades in these environments are not sufficiently limited. This would argue for the further work along the same but generalized lines. In fact there are hints that this might lead to phenomena more closely associated with some of the enigmas. In Townsend and Wallace (1987, this volume, ch. 3) the determination of an equilibrium seems to require coordination across spatially dispersed agents, a coordination which is supposed to be impossible given the implicitly assumed limits on communication. It is not obvious how coordination is to be achieved, if at all. Indeed, one is reminded in the model of actual medieval efforts to limit circulating private debt and to establish central clearing houses, the beginnings of central banks!

Still, the Townsend–Wallace model itself fails to make a determinate prediction. Nor is it clear that it could easily be extended to capture volatile prices – movements in prices induced by the revelation of information in environments with asymmetrically informed traders.

9.3 *The volatility of prices in equilibrium systems with optimal signal extraction*

Equilibrium pricing in models with asymmetrically informed agents is investigated in "Market anticipations, rational expectations and Bayesian analysis" (Townsend, 1978b, this volume, ch. 13), "Forecasting the forecasts of others" (Townsend, 1983b, this volume, ch. 14), and "Equilibrium theory with learning and disparate expectations: some issues and methods" (Townsend, 1983c, this volume, ch. 15). In this class of models, market structure is limited exogenously, not endogenously as desired, but there is scope for optimal learning from prices. That is, prices of the objects which are allowed to be traded clear markets period by period, with each agent solving his own dynamic optimization problem, taking into account the information gleaned from prices. If the exogenous parts of information sets differ across sets of agents, then innovations to underlying random variables can set off erratic and fluctuating price movements, as agents second guess one another as well as the underlying state of the system. For example, in "Equilibrium theory with learning and disparate expectations" (Townsend, 1983c, this volume, ch. 15) a positive temporary shock to demand can be viewed by each of a set of firms as a possible permanent shock, and outputs of all firms increase. Informed firms catch on exponentially as they see or infer industry output, but uninformed firms which do not infer industry output respond to their own shadow, unknowingly, as the price drop from increased output signals a possible decline in the permanent component. This delivers prolonged oscillating movements in prices and seems to capture an important aspect of the volatile asset market scenario.

Though apparently successful on their own terms, these models beg the question of why markets were limited in the first place. Private information is a key aspect of the story, but private information was not used to limit market structure.

9.4 *Competitive equilibrium in information-constrained commodity spaces*

The effect of private information alone on market structure is examined systematically in "General competitive analysis in an economy with private information" (Prescott and Townsend, 1984a, this volume, ch. 17) and "Pareto optima and competitive equilibria with adverse selection and moral hazard" (Prescott and Townsend, 1984b, this volume, ch. 16). In brief, we follow the programming approach to the determination of Pareto optimal allocations, with endogenously derived information constraints explicitly imposed. But then we attempt to decentralize the optima in the standard way, finding prices for commodity allocations in a planning period market which satisfy individual maximization and market-clearing postulates. Perhaps the surprising part of this endeavor is that in some circumstances the theorems of classical competitive analysis apply. Decentralized competitive equilibria in the enriched commodity spaces do exist and support the Pareto optima.

There is one class of private information environments for which these theorems fail, examples of which are the Spence (1974) signalling environment and the Rothschild–Stiglitz (1976) insurance environment. Prescott and Townsend did not discover a way to decentralize the optima for these environments. We showed that the problem is not due to imposed market structure or to the presumed structure of competition. The problem is one of private information.

More generally what is missing in the work of Prescott and Townsend, even in environments for which the classical theorems hold, is some further aspect of decentralization – implementation of constrained optima in period-by-period markets.

9.5 *Concluding remarks*

It does seem that aspects of costly exchange, spatial separation, private information, limited communication, and limited commitment will ultimately give us some of the models we need to interpret historical observations on financial structure and economic organization. But it would be wrong to claim too much. I know all too well how difficult it is to combine subsets of these elements within a single model, and no doubt there will be further problems and more than a few surprises along the way. Still, in making the point that observed arrangements might be better understood as the product of key elements, I hope that this introduction will prove useful.

Notes

1 The specific sources are listed in the bibliography at the end of this chapter.
2 As I synthesize and summarize I do not cite specific authors or sources by page. The reader is urged to consult the bibliography as interests dictate. More detailed citations are contained in the working paper (University of Chicago).

Bibliography

Arrow, K.J. (1953) Le rôle des valeurs boursières pour la répartition la meilleure des risques. In *Econometrie*, pp. 41–8. Paris: Centre Nationale de la Recherche Scientifique.

Barraclough, G. (ed.) (1985) *The Times Atlas of World History*. Maplewood, NJ: Hammon.

Bennett, A.S. (1937) *Life on the English Manor: A Study of Peasant Conditions*. Cambridge: Cambridge University Press.

Braudel, F. (1979) *The Wheels of Commerce: Civilization and Capitalism 15th–18th Centuries*, vol. 2. New York: Harper and Row.

Cipolla, C.M. (1956) *Money, Prices, and Civilization in the Mediterranean World*. Princeton, NJ: Princeton University Press.

—— (1964) Currency depreciation in medieval Europe. In *Change in Medieval Society*, ed. S.L. Thrupp. New York: Appleton-Century-Crofts.

Clough, S.B. and Rapp, R.T. (1975) *European Economic History*. New York: McGraw-Hill.

Darby, H.C. (1973) *A New Historical Geography of England before 1600*. Cambridge: Cambridge University Press.

Debreu, G. (1959) *Theory of Value: An Axiomatic Analysis of Economic Equilibrium*. New York: Wiley for Cowles Foundation.

DeRoover, R. (1948) *Money, Banking and Credit in Mediaeval Bruges*. Cambridge, MA: Mediaeval Academy of America.

Diamond, P. (1982) Aggregate demand management in search equilibrium. *Journal of Political Economy* 90(5), 881–94.

Duby, G. (1974) *The Early Growth of the European Economy: Warriors and Peasants from the Seventh to the Twelfth Century*. Ithaca, NY: Cornell University Press.

Harris, M. and Townsend, R.M. (1978) Allocation mechanisms for asymmetrically informed agents. GSIA Working Paper 35-76-77, Carnegie–Mellon University, Pittsburgh, PA. Reprinted in this volume as chapter 6.

—— and —— (1981) Resource allocation under asymmetric information. *Econometrica* 49(1), 33–64. Reprinted in this volume as chapter 7.

Homans, G.C. (1941) *English Villagers of the Thirteenth Century*. Cambridge, MA: Harvard University Press.

Koebner, R. (1941) The settlement and colonisation of Europe. In *The Cambridge Economic History of Europe: The Agrarian Life of the Middle Ages*, vol. 1, ch. 1, pp. 1–88. Cambridge: Cambridge University Press.

Lopez, R.S. and Raymond, I.W. (1955) *Medieval Trade in the Mediterranean World.* New York: Columbia University Press.

McCloskey, D. (1976) English open fields as behavior towards risk. In *Research in Economic History*, vol. 1, ed. P. Uselding, pp. 124–70. Greenwich, CT: JAI Press.

—— and Nash, J. (1984) Corn at interest: the extent and cost of grain storage in medieval England. *American Economic Review* 74, 174–87.

McNeill, W.H. (1974) *The Shape of European History.* Oxford: Oxford University Press.

Mortensen, D. (1974) Search equilibrium and the core in a decentralized pure exchange economy. Manuscript, Northwestern University, Evanston, IL.

Nabholz, H. (1941) Medieval agrarian society in transition. In *The Cambridge Economic History of Europe: The Agrarian Life of the Middle Ages*, vol. 1, ch. 8, pp. 493–554. Cambridge: Cambridge University Press.

Orwin, C.S. and Orwin, C.S. (1954) *The Open Fields*, 2nd edn. Oxford: Oxford University Press.

Painter, S. (1951) *Medieval Society.* Ithaca, NY: Cornell University Press.

Palmer, R.R. and Colton, J. (1965) *A History of the Modern World*, 3rd edn. New York: Knopf.

Pirenne, H. (1948) *Medieval Cities: Their Origins and the Revival of Trade.* Princeton, NJ: Princeton University Press.

Postan, M.M. (1972) *The Medieval Economy and Society.* Harmondsworth: Penguin.

Pounds, N.J.G. (1974) *An Economic History of Medieval Europe.* New York: Longman.

Prescott, E.C. and Townsend, R.M. (1984a) General competitive analysis in an economy with private information. *International Economic Review* 25(1), 1–20. Reprinted in this volume as chapter 17.

—— and —— (1984b) Pareto optima and competitive equilibria with adverse selection and moral hazard. *Econometrica* 52(1), 21–45. Reprinted in this volume as chapter 16.

Raftis, J.A. (1957) *The Estates of Ramsey Abbey.* Toronto: Pontifical Institute of Mediaeval Studies.

Rand McNally Atlas of the World History (1984) Chicago, IL: Rand McNally.

Rothschild, M. and Stiglitz, J. (1976) Equilibrium in competitive insurance markets: an essay on the economics of imperfect information. *Quarterly Journal of Economics* 90, 629–49.

Spence, A.M. (1974) *Market Signaling: Information Transfer in Hiring and Related Screening Process.* Cambridge, MA: Harvard University Press.

Townsend, R.M. (1978a) Intermediation with costly bilateral exchange. *Review of Economic Studies* 45(3), 417–25. Reprinted in this volume as chapter 10.

—— (1978b) Market anticipations, rational expectations, and Bayesian analysis. *International Economic Review* 19(2), 481–94. Reprinted in this volume as chapter 13.

—— (1979) Optimal contracts and competitive markets with costly state verification. *Journal of Economic Theory* 21(2), 265–93. Reprinted in this volume as chapter 5.

—— (1980) Models of money with spatially separated agents. In *Models of Monetary Economies*, eds J. Kareken and N. Wallace. Minneapolis, MN: Federal Reserve Bank of Minneapolis. Reprinted in this volume as chapter 2.

——(1982) Optimal multiperiod contracts and the gain from enduring relationships under private information. *Journal of Political Economy* 90(6), 1166–86. Reprinted in this volume as chapter 8.

——(1983a) Financial structure and economic activity. *American Economic Review* 73(5), 895–911. Reprinted in this volume as chapter 4.

——(1983b) Forecasting the forecasts of others. *Journal of Political Economy* 91(4), 546–87. Reprinted in this volume as chapter 14.

——(1983c) Equilibrium theory with disparate expectations and learning: some issues and methods. In *Individual Forecasting and Aggregate Outcomes: "Rational Expectations," Examined*, eds B.S. Phelps and R. Frydman. Cambridge: Cambridge University Press. Reprinted in this volume as chapter 15.

——(1983d) Theories of intermediated structures. *Carnegie–Rochester Conference Series on Public Policy*, vol. 18, *Money, Monetary Policy and Financial Institutions*. Reprinted in this volume as chapter 11.

——(1987) Asset return anomalies in a monetary economy. *Journal of Economic Theory* 41(5), 219–47. Reprinted in this volume as chapter 12.

——and Wallace, N. (1987) Circulating private debt: an example with a coordination problem. In *Contractual Arrangements for Intertemporal Trade*, eds E.C. Prescott and N. Wallace. Minneapolis, MN: University of Minnesota Press. Reprinted in this volume as chapter 3.

Usher, A.P. (1943) *The Early History of Deposit Banking in Mediterranean Europe*. Cambridge, MA: Harvard University Press.

Part II
Spatial Separation as a Key Element in Theories of Financial Arrangements

2

Models of Money with Spatially Separated Agents

1 Introduction

Three models which explain the observation that money is used in payment for commodities and barter is not prevalent are presented in this chapter. In each of these models money is intrinsically useless, inasmuch as it does not enter directly into either utility functions or production functions, and is inconvertible, inasmuch as no one stands ready to convert money into anything else.[1] Moreover, money does not enter any of the models by way of legal restrictions[2] or by way of a requirement that commodities cannot be acquired without it, *à la* Clower (1967).[3] Rather, money is explained in the sense that the following procedure is adopted. First, the environment is specified carefully and completely – the agents of the model, their preferences and endowments, and, most important, who can communicate with whom. It is then established that there exists a monetary equilibrium, that is, a competitive equilibrium in which a fixed-supply money has value.

It is widely accepted that money cannot be explained in this sense in a standard general equilibrium model (see, for example, Hahn, 1965). In a Walrasian model, at least, money cannot facilitate exchange; the nonmonetary competitive equilibria are Pareto optimal. (Note again that a distinction is

---

Reprinted from *Models of Monetary Economies*, eds J. Kareken and N. Wallace (Minneapolis, MN: Federal Reserve Bank of Minneapolis, 1980). This chapter would not have been written without the benefit of many stimulating conversations on money and debt with Neil Wallace, whom I would also like to thank for innumerable contributions to the present draft. I am also much indebted to John Bryant for several very useful conversations and for an example which played a crucial role in the development of this chapter, to Robert E. Lucas Jr for several conversations on the Cass–Yaari model, and to Thomas J. Sargent for helpful comments. I assume full responsibility for any errors. Support for this research from the Federal Reserve Bank of Minneapolis is gratefully acknowledged.

maintained here between money – fiat money, that is – and private credit.) Thus, to incorporate money into a model something must inhibit the operation of markets.[4] Moreover, if terminal conditions are to be avoided, time must be infinite.

In the model of Samuelson (1958) some markets are precluded in an obvious way: there can be no transactions between the current young and the young of the next generation; unborn individuals cannot trade. In versions of this overlapping generations model, a monetary equilibrium exists which improves upon the nonmonetary equilibrium. In fact, in some versions, the monetary equilibrium is itself optimal and is associated with nonbinding nonnegativity constraints on the holding of money balances. Yet we wonder whether the properties of the overlapping generations model carry over to alternative models which explain money in the above sense.

In the models in this chapter, markets are precluded in another way, by spatially separating agents. Infinitely lived agents who discount future over present consumption are allocated over time into distinct markets or islands. The crucial idea here is that markets must clear on each island in every time period. There can be no communication across islands; that is, there is no central market or exchange system. Certainly this way of decentralizing an economy is not new. Lucas (1972) uses such islands to explain the movement of economic aggregates.[5] More to the point, the explicit pairing of agents is a scheme used in various recent microeconomic approaches to money, including Feldman (1973), Ostroy (1973), Ostroy and Starr (1974), and Harris (1979). Yet, for the most part, these approaches are not really dynamic equilibrium theories. An important exception is Harris, but he is concerned with commodity money, not with outside indebtedness.

In two of the models in this chapter, the turnpike model of exchange (section 2) and Lucas's version of the Cass–Yaari (1966) model (section 4), there exists a monetary equilibrium, that is, a competitive equilibrium with valued money. Therefore, as claimed, these models explain money. As in the overlapping generations construct, this monetary equilibrium improves upon the nonmonetary equilibrium (autarky). Unlike the overlapping generations model, however, the monetary equilibria in these models with spatially separated agents are nonoptimal and are associated with binding nonnegativity constraints on the holding of money balances. Thus the decentralization of spatial separation is not completely overcome with money.[6]

The argument as to why no optimal allocation can be supported as a monetary equilibrium in these models is fairly intuitive. Suppose that all agents are of the same age and all discount the future at the same rate, as in the turnpike model and Lucas's version of the Cass–Yaari model. Then, if an optimal allocation is to be supported, there must be a rate of deflation equal to the common discount rate. But in the absence of taxes, such a deflation is inconsistent with individual maximization, as real wealth (real money balances) would be unbounded. That no stationary monetary equilibrium can be optimal is an immediate corollary.

As Grandmont and Younes (1972, 1973) point out, the latter conclusion appears frequently in the literature (see, for example, Samuelson, 1968, 1969; Friedman, 1969; Clower, 1970; Johnson, 1970), where the argument turns on a divergence between the positive marginal utility of real money balances and the zero marginal cost of creating them. Grandmont and Younes are critical of this literature, and they are not alone; Clower (1970), for example, argues quite forcefully that these welfare questions must be addressed in a model which makes explicit the monetary exchange process. Grandmont and Younes do establish the aforementioned conclusion rigorously in a general equilibrium monetary economy. Yet, as they note (Grandmont and Younes, 1972, p. 357), even in their model money is introduced "in a very crude way by imposing constraints on transactions." That is, in contrast with the models of this chapter, their model does not explain money. In this respect, at least, this chapter can be viewed as an important extension of Grandmont and Younes and of this literature.

If lump-sum taxes on money balances are permitted, then the models with spatially separated agents in this chapter can also produce Friedman's (1969) conclusions on the optimal quantity of money. That is, with lump-sum taxes, optimal allocations can be supported in an interventionist monetary equilibrium in which the rate of interest on money equals the common discount rate and in which agents are satiated with money balances, that is, the nonnegativity constraints on money balances are nonbinding (see also Grandmont and Younes, 1972; Bewley, 1980).

Speaking rather loosely, the overlapping generations model overturns these welfare results by pairing agents of different ages and therefore different rates of discount.[7] This is argued more fully in section 3, where the turnpike model is modified to incorporate finitely lived agents and hence becomes an overlapping generations model. It is hoped that an essential feature of the overlapping generations model is revealed.

As noted above, monetary economics necessarily involves the economics of infinity. In the overlapping generations model there is an infinite number of generations, though a finite number of agents are alive at any one date. In the turnpike model and in the Cass–Yaari model presented here, an infinite number of agents are alive at any one date. This specification ensures that no private debt is traded, so that its exclusion is endogenous, that is, not imposed by the modeler. Section 5 offers some preliminary comments on private debt (inside money) in the context of a modified turnpike model without the contemporaneous infinity.

Finally, a caveat is in order. The intent in what follows is to understand the implications of various exchange structures for monetary equilibria. Thus, again speaking rather loosely, preferences and endowments are held fixed across models as the exchange structure is varied. To this end, maximum generality is not pursued within the context of each model. Agents are assumed throughout to have preferences and endowments of a very special form. Moreover, certain strong symmetry conditions (on the class of allocations under consideration) are imposed exogenously, without elaboration. Finally, it should be noted that the models in this chapter are successful in explaining money without the introduction of uncertainty; it remains an open question whether these models can approximate economies in which moral hazard and bankruptcy play a crucial role.[8]

2 A turnpike model of exchange

In the turnpike model each of a countably infinite number of agents is allocated into one of a countably infinite number of spatially distinct markets or islands in each period of her or his life. The exogenous allocation procedure is such that any two agents are paired at most once during their lifetimes, and, moreover, they share no common third agent as a trading partner. All agents are born at time zero, so that at any time t all agents are of the same age. Each lives for ever and faces a sequence of endowments of the single consumption good of the model which alternates between zero and one unit. At any time $t \geqslant 0$ an agent who has an endowment of one unit is paired with an agent who has an endowment of zero. The consumption good cannot be stored.

An economy with these characteristics is depicted in figure 2.1. Each agent is imagined to be traveling on a turnpike, either east or west. The arrows indicate the direction of travel, and the spikes indicate the markets. The numbers 0 and 1 index the endowment of an agent located at the indicated position. Initially, at $t = 0$, there is one agent at each position. It should be emphasized here that no agents have control over their lifetime itineraries. Each agent moves forward one market in each period. Also, these markets

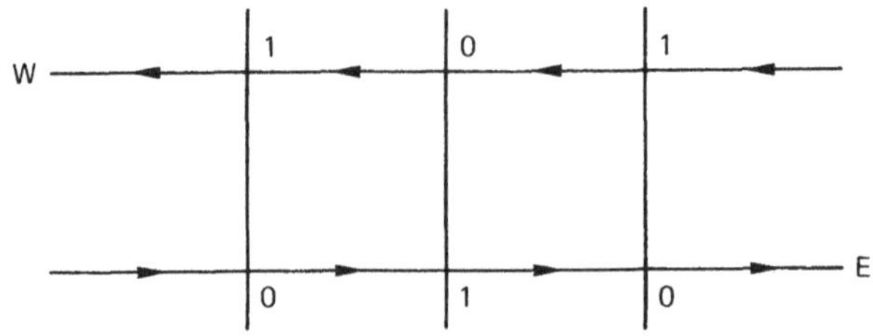

Figure 2.1. The turnpike model

are isolated from one another; there can be no transactions or communication among them at any time.

Each agent has preferences over her or his (infinite) lifetime consumption sequence $\{c_t\}_{t=0}^{\infty}$ as described by the utility function $\Sigma_{t=0}^{\infty}\beta^t U(c_t)$ where $c_t \geqslant 0$, $0<\beta<1$, and $U(\cdot)$ is strictly concave, strictly increasing, bounded, and continuously differentiable with $U'(0)=\infty$. Thus all agents have the same time-separable utility function of a rather special form and, in particular, all discount future over present consumption at the same rate β.[9]

This model displays a well-known property: the absence of double coincidence of wants. At each time t, considered in isolation, there can be no Pareto improving bilateral trade; there is only one consumption good, and more is preferred to less. We may ask, of course, whether borrowing and lending might not improve matters. Section 5 below is devoted entirely to this question in a slightly modified context, but it should be noted here that, in a sense which will be made precise, there can be no private debt in the present model. For consider an agent at time t who has zero units of the consumption good. Such an agent might wish to issue an IOU, to be honored in better times when the agent has one unit of the consumption good. Similarly, the agent's partner at time t, who has one unit, might be inclined to accept such an IOU. Yet the model is constructed in such a way that the IOU can never be redeemed by the issuer; the pair will never meet again, and the purchaser of such an IOU can only pass it along to an agent "behind" the issuer. Thus, if we take as a defining characteristic of private debt that it ultimately be redeemed by the issuer, there can be no private debt in this model.[10]

Having specified the environment for this model, our next step is to characterize Pareto optimal allocations. For this purpose a strong symmetry condition is imposed: in any allocation, agents cannot be distinguished by their initial market position. That is, any agent who begins life with zero units of the consumption good must be treated in the same way as any other agent who begins with zero units, independent of the initial location. All such agents are hereafter referred to as agents of *type A*. A similar restriction is placed on those who begin with one unit, agents of *type B*. It bears repeating here that when an allocation is termed optimal below, it is only established to be optimal in the class of symmetric allocations; there remains the possibility of a nonsymmetric allocation which is Pareto superior.

Now let c_t^i denote the number of units of consumption of an agent of type i at time t. Then an *allocation* $\{c_t^A\}_{t=0}^{\infty}$, $\{c_t^B\}_{t=0}^{\infty}$ is said to be *feasible* if

$$c_t^A + c_t^B \leqslant 1,\ c_t^A \geqslant 0,\ c_t^B \geqslant 0 \qquad \text{all } t \geqslant 0 \tag{2.1}$$

(An allocation is said to be *interior* if consumption is strictly positive for each agent type in each time period.) It can be assumed without loss of generality in what follows that resources are fully utilized. Then, to determine an interior Pareto optimal allocation it is enough to maximize a weighted average of the utilities of the two agent types, subject to the resource constraints, as is established below. This yields the following problem.

Problem 2.1

$$\max_{\{c_t^A\}_{t=0}^{\infty}, \{c_t^B\}_{t=0}^{\infty}} \quad w^A\left\{\sum_{t=0}^{\infty} \beta^t U(c_t^A)\right\} + w^B\left\{\sum_{t=0}^{\infty} \beta^t U(c_t^B)\right\}$$

subject to (2.1) where $w^A > 0$, $w^B > 0$, $w^A + w^B = 1$. Necessary and sufficient first-order conditions for problem 2.1 are

$$w^i \beta^t U'(c_t^i) - \theta_t = 0 \quad i = \text{A, B} \qquad t \geq 0 \tag{2.2}$$

where the θ_t are positive Lagrange multipliers. Trivial manipulation of (2.2) yields

$$\frac{U'(c_t^A)}{U'(c_\tau^A)} = \frac{U'(c_t^B)}{U'(c_\tau^B)} \qquad \text{all } t, \tau \geq 0 \tag{2.3}$$

Conditions (2.1) and (2.3) are fully equivalent to (see figure 2.2)

$$c_t^A = \lambda,\ c_t^B = 1 - \lambda,\ 0 < \lambda < 1 \qquad \text{all } t \geq 0 \tag{2.4}$$

Thus a necessary and sufficient condition for a feasible interior allocation $\{c_t^A\}_{t=0}^{\infty}$, $\{c_t^B\}_{t=0}^{\infty}$ to be optimal is that each agent of type A receives λ units of the consumption good in each period t. That this condition is necessary for optimality follows from the obvious fact that, if condition (2.3) is not satisfied for some periods t and τ, then there is a Pareto superior feasible allocation. That this condition is sufficient is also obvious. Suppose that there exists a feasible allocation which is Pareto superior. Then it would satisfy constraint (2.1) and increase the value of the objective function in problem 2.1, which is a contradiction. Hereafter, then, reference will be made to an *interior optimum* λ in which both agents receive constant consumption.

The question can now be raised as to whether optimal allocations can be supported in competitive equilibria with valued fiat money. To do so we must discuss carefully what we mean by *fiat money* and *competitive markets* in the context of this model. A unit of fiat money is imagined to be a physical commodity, say a piece of paper, which can be carried costlessly and used in exchange by the agents as they travel among islands. As a commodity, the stock of fiat money in the possession of any trader at any time cannot be negative. On each island and at each time period there is assumed to be

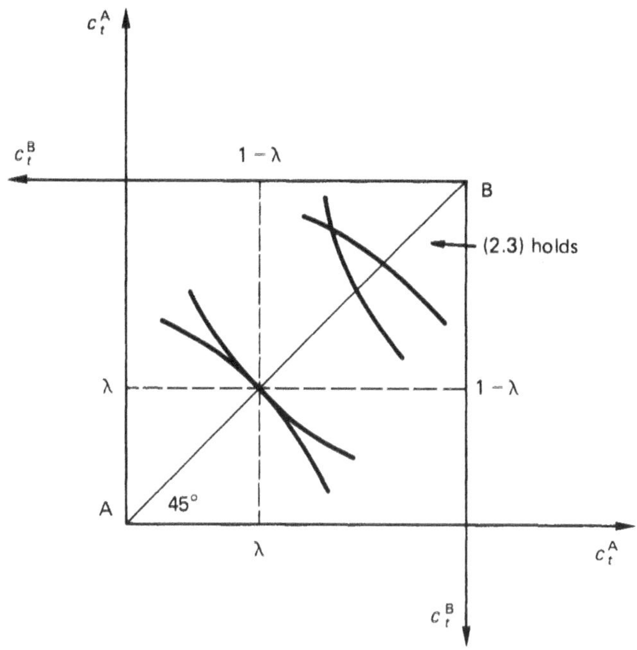

Figure 2.2. Optimal allocations in the turnpike model

a competitive market in which fiat money can be exchanged for the consumption good at a specified rate. That is, agents take the price of the consumption good as given and maximize utility by choice of the amount to consume and the amount of money balances to carry over into the next period. No attempt is made here to justify the price-taking assumption or to defend the competitive equilibrium concept; to the extent that the mechanism which underlies the equilibrium concept requires a large (perhaps infinite) number of agents, each agent discussed above can be taken as representative of agents in identical situations.

Consistent with the symmetry assumption, attention will be restricted to monetary equilibria in which the price of the consumption good in terms of money at any time t is the same in each market. This price is denoted p_t and is assumed to be finite and strictly positive. Also, let M_t^i denote the number of units of fiat money chosen at time $t-1$ by agent type i and carried over into period t, z_t^i denote the number of units of a lump-sum tax on money balances (or subsidy, if negative) on agent type i at the beginning of period t, and y_t^i denote the endowment of agent type i at time t. Then, taking as given the sequences $\{p_t\}_{t=0}^{\infty}$, $\{z_t^i\}_{t=0}^{\infty}$, and the initial money balances M_0^i, each agent of type i is confronted with the following problem.

Problem 2.2

$$\max_{\{c_t^i\}_{t=0}^\infty, \{M_t^i\}_{t=1}^\infty} \sum_{t=0}^{\infty} \beta^t U(c_t^i)$$

subject to

$$\begin{aligned} &c_t^i \geqslant 0 && \text{all } t \geqslant 0 \\ &M_t^i \geqslant 0 && \text{all } t \geqslant 0 \qquad (2.5) \\ &p_t c_t^i + M_{t+1}^i \leqslant p_t y_t^i + M_t^i - z_t^i && \text{all } t \geqslant 0 \end{aligned}$$

given $M_0^i \geqslant 0$, $z_0^i = 0$. Here (2.5) is the budget constraint which prevails in period t. With $U'(0) = \infty$, the nonnegativity constraint on consumption need not be made explicit; in contrast, the nonnegativity constraint on money balances may be binding. Assuming without loss of generality that the budget constraint (2.5) holds as an equality, so that in effect only $\{M_t^i\}_{t=1}^\infty$ need be chosen, and making the obvious substitution for the c_t^i, we obtain necessary Euler conditions for a maximum:

$$-\frac{\beta^{t-1} U'(c_{t-1}^i)}{p_{t-1}} + \frac{\beta^t U'(c_t^i)}{p_t} + \theta_t^i = 0 \qquad \text{all } t \geqslant 1 \tag{2.6}$$

where θ_t^i is the Lagrange multiplier associated with the nonnegativity constraint on money balances, that is,

$$\theta_t^i \geqslant 0 \qquad M_t^i \geqslant 0 \qquad \theta_t^i M_t^i = 0$$

Thus

$$\frac{U'(c_{t-1}^i)}{\beta U'(c_t^i)} \geqslant \frac{p_{t-1}}{p_t} \qquad \text{all } t \geqslant 1 \tag{2.7}$$

which must hold as an equality if $M_t^i > 0$ and as an inequality if and only if $\theta_t^i > 0$, that is, when the marginal utility of a unit of fiat money spent on period $t-1$ consumption exceeds the marginal utility of a unit of fiat money spent on period t consumption and there is no more fiat money to spend in period $t-1$.

A competitive equilibrium with valued fiat money can now be defined.

Definition

A monetary equilibrium is a sequence of finite positive prices $\{p_t^*\}_{t=0}^\infty$ and sequences of consumptions $\{c_t^{i*}\}_{t=0}^{\infty}$, money balances $\{M_t^{i*}\}_{t=0}^{\infty}$, and lump-sum taxes $\{z_t^{i*}\}_{t=0}^{\infty}$ for each agent type $i = \mathrm{A, B}$ such that

- maximization: the sequences $\{c_t^{i*}\}_{t=0}^{\infty}$, $\{M_t^{i*}\}_{t=1}^{\infty}$ solve problem 2.2 relative to $\{p_t^*\}_{t=0}^{\infty}$, $\{z_t^{i*}\}_{t=0}^{\infty}$, and M_0^{i*}
- market clearing: $c_t^{A*} + c_t^{B*} = 1$, all $t \geq 0$

We can now ask whether optimal allocations can be supported in a monetary equilibrium without intervention. The answer is summarized in the following proposition.

Proposition 2.1
No interior optimum λ can be supported in a monetary equilibrium without intervention, that is, with $z_t^{i*} \equiv 0$ for all $i = \mathrm{A, B}$.

Proof. The proof is by contradiction. Thus, suppose that the allocation $c_t^{\mathrm{A}} = \lambda$, $c_t^{\mathrm{B}} = 1 - \lambda$, all $t \geq 0$, can be supported in a monetary equilibrium without intervention. With $z_t^{i*} \equiv 0$, with $y_t^{\mathrm{A}} = 0$ for t even and $y_t^{\mathrm{B}} = 0$ for t odd, and with $U'(0) = \infty$, it is clear that the nonnegativity constraint on money balances cannot be binding for agent type A for choices made when t is odd or for agent type B for choices made when t is even. Thus from (2.7), equilibrium prices $\{p_t^*\}_{t=0}^{\infty}$ must satisfy

$$\frac{U'(\lambda)}{\beta U'(\lambda)} = \frac{p_{t-1}^*}{p_t^*} \qquad t \geq 2, \ t \text{ even}$$

$$\frac{U'(1-\lambda)}{\beta U'(1-\lambda)} = \frac{p_{t-1}^*}{p_t^*} \qquad t \geq 1, \ t \text{ odd}$$

It follows that

$$p_t^* = \beta p_{t-1}^* \qquad \text{all } t \geq 1 \tag{2.8}$$

that is the rate of deflation must be $1 - \beta$. Now consider the evolution of money balances of agent type B given the price sequence $\{p_t^*\}_{t=0}^{\infty}$ and the specified consumption sequence $c_t^{\mathrm{B}} = 1 - \lambda$, all $t \geq 0$. Agent type B begins life with $M_0^{\mathrm{B}*} \geq 0$ units of fiat money, acquires $p_0^* \lambda$ units in period 0, and spends $p_1^*(1 - \lambda)$ units in period 1. Thus

$$M_2^{\mathrm{B}*} - M_0^{\mathrm{B}*} = p_0^* \lambda - p_1^*(1 - \lambda) \tag{2.9}$$

Clearly the increment to money balances from $t = 0$ to $t = 2$, the left-hand side of (2.9), is nonnegative if the right-hand side is nonnegative. Substituting from (2.8), the right-hand side is nonnegative if

$$\frac{\lambda}{1-\lambda} \geqslant \beta \tag{2.10}$$

In fact, it can readily be verified that the increment to money balances is nonnegative for agent type B from t to $t+2$ for all t even, if (2.10) holds. Similar calculations establish that the increment to money balances is nonnegative for agent type A from t to $t+2$ for all t odd, if

$$\frac{1-\lambda}{\lambda} \geqslant \beta \tag{2.11}$$

The left-hand sides of inequalities (2.10) and (2.11) are plotted in figure 2.3 as functions of the parameter λ. As figure 2.3 makes clear, with the discount rate β fixed, $0 < \beta < 1$, at least one of the relationships (2.10) and (2.11) must hold as a strict inequality for any value of λ between zero and unity. That is, at least one agent type will be accumulating money balances over time in the above sense. But then this cannot be an equilibrium. For, if (2.10) holds

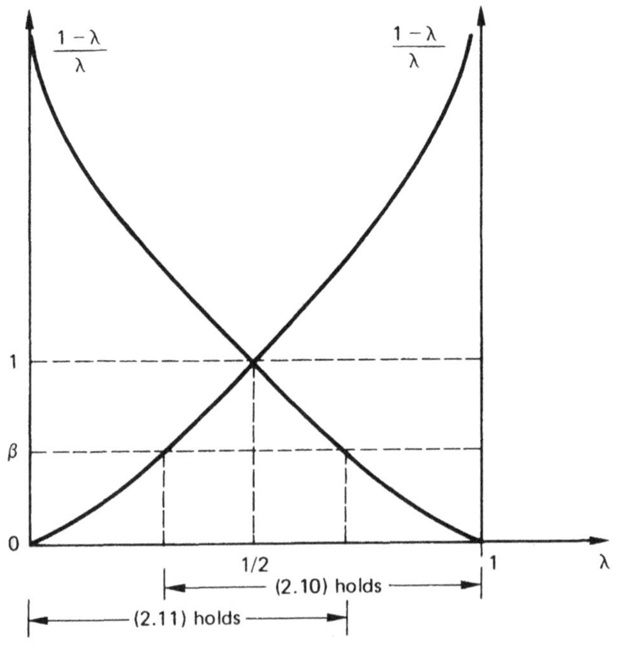

Figure 2.3. The relationship between λ and β

as a strict inequality, for example, agent type B could spend these excess balances at $t \geq 1$, t odd, and improve upon the consumption sequence $c_t^{B*} \equiv 1 - \lambda$. This completes the proof.

Thus, if an optimal allocation is to be attained in a monetary equilibrium, the rate of deflation must be $1 - \beta$, and consequently there must be some intervention by way of taxes and/or subsidies. That at least some optimal allocations can be supported in this way is established in the following proposition.

Proposition 2.2
Any interior optimum λ with $\beta \leqslant \lambda/(1-\lambda)$ and $\beta \leqslant (1-\lambda)/\lambda$ can be supported in a monetary equilibrium with rate of deflation $1-\beta$, with $z_t^{B*} = p_{t-1}^*\{\lambda - \beta(1-\lambda)\} \geqslant 0$ for $t \geqslant 1$, t odd, and $z_t^{B*} = 0$ otherwise, and with $z_t^{A*} = p_{t-1}^*\{(1-\lambda) - \lambda\beta\} \geqslant 0$ for $t \geqslant 2$, t even, and $z_t^{A*} = 0$ otherwise.

The proof is given in the appendix.

Given propositions (2.1) and (2.2), we may well ask whether there exist any monetary equilibria which do not require intervention. The search for such equilibria is facilitated by the following proposition which suggests that the search can be limited to equilibria in which the nonnegativity constraints on money balances play an important role.

Proposition 2.3
Any monetary equilibrium with nonbinding nonnegativity constraints on money balances on each agent in each period supports an optimal allocation and hence requires some intervention.

Proof. By hypothesis, $\theta_t^{i*} \equiv 0$. Thus from (2.6) it follows that

$$\frac{\beta^{t-1}U'(c_{t-1}^{i*})}{\beta^t U'(c_t^{i*})} = \frac{p_{t-1}^*}{p_t^*} \qquad i = \text{A, B} \qquad \text{all } t \geqslant 1 \tag{2.12}$$

Manipulation of (2.12) yields

$$\frac{\beta^t U'(c_t^{i*})}{\beta^\tau U'(c_\tau^{i*})} = \frac{p_t^*}{p_\tau^*} \qquad i = \text{A, B} \qquad \text{all } t, \tau \geqslant 0 \tag{2.13}$$

As (2.13) holds for both i,

$$\frac{U'(c_t^{A*})}{U'(c_\tau^{A*})} = \frac{U'(c_t^{B*})}{U'(c_\tau^{B*})} \qquad \text{all } t, \tau \geqslant 0 \tag{2.14}$$

Condition (2.14) and the market-clearing condition of an equilibrium are sufficient for an optimum as discussed above. The conclusion of this proposition follows from proposition 2.1. This completes the proof.

The search for a noninterventional monetary equilibrium is also facilitated by the observation that, roughly speaking, a time trend to prices, say a constant rate of deflation $1 - \beta$ as in proposition 2.2, would seem to necessitate intervention in order to keep purchasing power constant. That is, we might search for an equilibrium in which prices remain constant over time at some value $p^* > 0$. Thus it may be guessed that, in a noninterventionist monetary equilibrium, each agent of type B will have one unit of purchasing power to be allocated over consumption in each pair of periods $(t, t+1)$, $t \geqslant 0$, t even, selling the consumption good for money in period t and spending all accumulated money balances in period $t+1$, with a binding nonnegativity constraint on money balances at $t+1$. This will generate consumptions c^* and c^{**}, as shown in figure 2.4. Of course, each agent of type A will be doing the same thing in each pair of periods $(t+1,\ t+2)$, $t \geqslant 0$, t even. This discussion is summarized in the following proposition.

Proposition 2.4
There exists a noninterventionist monetary equilibrium with constant prices, with binding nonnegativity constraints on money balances in every other period, and with alternating consumption sequences. In particular, for taxes and prices

$$z_t^{i*} \equiv 0,\ p_t^* \equiv p^* > 0$$

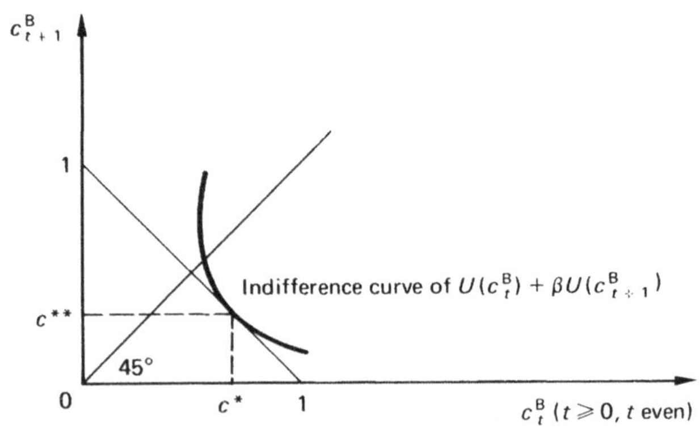

Figure 2.4. The monetary equilibrium of the turnpike

and for agent A, $M_0^{A*} = p^* c^{**}$ and

$$c_t^{A*} = c^{**},\ M_{t+1}^{A*} = 0,\ \theta_{t+1}^{A*} > 0 \qquad t \geq 0,\ t \text{ even}$$
$$c_t^{A} = c^{*},\ M_{t+1}^{A*} = p^* c^{**},\ \theta_{t+1}^{A*} = 0 \quad t \geq 1,\ t \text{ odd}$$

and for agent B, $M_0^{B*} = 0$ and

$$c_t^{B} = c^{*},\ M_{t+1}^{B*} = p^* c^{**},\ \theta_{t+1}^{B*} = 0 \quad t \geq 0,\ t \text{ even}$$
$$c_t^{B} = c^{**},\ M_{t+1}^{B} = 0,\ \theta_{t+1}^{B} > 0 \qquad t \geq 1,\ t \text{ odd}$$

and where c^* and c^{**} satisfy

$$\frac{U'(c^*)}{\beta U'(c^{**})} = 1 \qquad c^* + c^{**} = 1$$

the equilibrium allocation is nonoptimal but Pareto superior to autarky.

The proof is given in the appendix.

The proof of proposition 2.4 utilizes the fact that, for agent type A,

$$p_t c_t^A + p_{t+1} c_{t+1}^A = p_{t+1} y_{t+1}^A + M_t^A - M_{t+2}^A \qquad t \geq 0,\ t \text{ even} \tag{2.15}$$
$$p_t c_t^A \leqslant M_t^A \qquad t \geq 0,\ t \text{ even} \tag{2.16}$$

where (2.15) is the money balance accumulation equation and (2.16) follows from the restriction that $M_{t+1}^A \geq 0$. If we let $c_t^A = c^1$, $c_{t+1}^A = c^2$, $p_t = p^1$, $p_{t+1} = p^2$, $y_{t+1}^A = y^2$, $M_t^A = M$, and $M_{t+2}^A = M'$, equations (2.15) and (2.16) can be written as

$$p^1 c^1 + p^2 c^2 = p^2 y^2 + M - M' \tag{2.17}$$
$$p^1 c^1 \leqslant M \tag{2.18}$$

Thus (2.17) appears as a money balance accumulation equation in a two-commodity model and (2.18) is a semi-Clower constraint that the valuation of consumption of the first commodity does not exceed the initial money balance. This formulation leads us to inquire as to the effect of a more standard Clower constraint of the form

$$p^1 c^1 + p^2 c^2 \leqslant M \tag{2.19}$$

that the total valuation of consumption be bounded by initial money balances.

Constraint (2.19) is not derived entirely from the technology of exchange. Imposed in addition is the requirement that agents bid in competitive markets for their own production. That is, agent type A at time $t+1$ as a producer is required to place all production y_{t+1}^{A} on the market and pay cash in advance for any consumption c_{t+1}^{A}.

Motivated by the above discussion, consider the following definition.

Definition

A Clower-type monetary equilibrium is a sequence of finite positive prices $\{p_t^*\}_{t=0}^{\infty}$ and sequences of consumptions $\{c_t^{i*}\}_{t=0}^{\infty}$ and money balances $\{M_t^{i*}\}_{t=0}^{\infty}$ for each agent type $i = \mathrm{A, B}$ such that

- maximization for type A: the sequences $\{c_t^{A*}\}_{t=0}^{\infty}$, $\{M_t^{A*}\}_{t=1}^{\infty}$ solve

$$\max_{\{c_t^A\}_{t=0}^{\infty}, \{M_t^A\}_{t=1}^{\infty}} \sum_{\substack{t \geqslant 0 \\ t\,\text{even}}} \beta^t \{U(c_t^A) + \beta U(c_{t+1}^A)\}$$

subject to

$$p_t^* c_t^A + p_{t+1}^* c_{t+1}^A = p_{t+1}^* y_{t+1}^A + M_t^A - M_{t+2}^A \qquad t \geqslant 0,\ t \text{ even}$$

$$p_t^* c_t^A + p_{t+1}^* c_{t+1}^A \leqslant M_t^A \qquad t \geqslant 0,\ t \text{ even}$$

$$M_{t+1}^A = M_t^A - p_t^* c_t^A \qquad t \geqslant 0,\ t \text{ even}$$

given $M_0^{A*} \geqslant 0$;

- maximization for type B: the sequences $\{c_t^{B*}\}_{t=0}^{\infty}$, $\{M_t^{B*}\}_{t=1}^{\infty}$ solve

$$\max_{\{c_t^B\}_{t=0}^{\infty}, \{M_t^B\}_{t=1}^{\infty}} \left[U(c_0^B) + \sum_{\substack{t \geqslant 1 \\ t\,\text{odd}}} \beta^{t-1} \{\beta U(c_t^B) + \beta^2 U(c_{t+1}^B)\} \right]$$

subject to

$$p_t^* c_t^B + p_{t+1}^* c_{t+1}^B = p_{t+1}^* y_{t+1}^B + M_t^B - M_{t+2}^B \qquad t \geqslant 1,\ t \text{ odd}$$

$$p_t^* c_t^B + p_{t+1}^* c_{t+1}^B \leqslant M_t^B \qquad t \geqslant 1,\ t \text{ odd}$$

$$M_{t+1}^B = M_t^B - p_t^* c_t^B \qquad t \geqslant 1,\ t \text{ odd}$$

$$p_0^* c_0^B = p_0^* y_0^B + M_0^B - M_1^B$$

$$p_0^* c_0^B \leqslant M_0^B$$

given $M_0^{B*} \geqslant 0$;

- market clearing: $c_t^{A*} + c_t^{B*} = 1$, $t \geqslant 0$.

This leads to the following proposition.

Proposition 2.5
If there exists a Clower-type monetary equilibrium with constant prices, that is with $p_t^* \equiv p^* > 0$, and with a symmetric consumption sequence, that is, with $c_{t+1}^{B*} = c_t^{A*}$ for all $t \geqslant 0$, then $c_{t+1}^{B*} = c_t^{A*} = c^*$ and $c_{t+1}^{A*} = c_t^{B*} = c^{**}$ for $t \geqslant 0$, t even, where c^* and c^{**} are defined in proposition 2.4. This allocation is nonoptimal but is Pareto superior to autarky.

Proof. The necessary conditions for a maximum include

$$\beta^t U'(c_t^{A*}) - \theta_t^A p^* - \gamma_t^A p^* = 0 \qquad t \geqslant 0,\ t \text{ even}$$

$$\beta^t \beta U'(c_{t+1}^{A*}) - \theta_t^A p^* - \gamma_t^A p^* = 0 \qquad t \geqslant 0,\ t \text{ even}$$

where $\theta_t^A > 0$ and $\gamma_t^A \geqslant 0$ are Lagrange multipliers. Thus

$$\frac{U'(c_t^{A*})}{\beta U'(c_{t+1}^{A*})} = 1 \qquad t \geqslant 0,\ t \text{ even} \tag{2.20}$$

Similarly for agent type B

$$\frac{U'(c_t^{B*})}{\beta U'(c_{t+1}^{B*})} = 1 \qquad t \geqslant 1,\ t \text{ odd} \tag{2.21}$$

Market clearing and the symmetry hypothesis imply

$$c_{t+1}^{B*} + c_t^{B*} = 1 \qquad \text{all } t \geqslant 0 \tag{2.22}$$

The unique solution to (2.21) and (2.22) is $c_t^{B*} = c^*$ and $c_{t+1}^{B*} = c^{**}$ for $t \geqslant 1$, t odd, and by the symmetry hypothesis $c_t^{A*} = c^*$, $c_{t+1}^{A*} = c^{**}$ for $t \geqslant 0$, t even. Thus by market clearing $c_0^{B*} = c^{**}$ also. It is obvious that this allocation is nonoptimal. Note also that for agent type A, for example, the consumption pair (c^*, c^{**}) dominates the endowment pair $(0, 1)$ in periods $(t, t+1)$ for $t \geqslant 0$, t even. This completes the proof.

It should be noted here that the imposition of the full Clower constraint (2.19) reverses the consumption sequences from those of proposition 2.4. Yet in this model the intervention implicit in the Clower constraint is not enough to attain optimal allocations.

In closing this section it should be noted that as the discount rate goes to zero or, equivalently, as the frequency of transactions (pairings) increases, the turnpike model comes close to producing the welfare result of the overlapping generations construct – that there exists an optimal noninterventionist monetary equilibrium. To see this note, for example, that the amount of taxation needed to support the optimal allocation $\lambda = 1/2$ goes to zero as $\beta \to 1$ (see proposition 2.2). Alternatively, note that the noninterventionist monetary equilibrium consumption sequences approach the constant $\lambda = 1/2$ as $\beta \to 1$ (see proposition 2.4 and figure 2.4). It may well be that this welfare result holds exactly in the limit, as $\beta = 1$, if agents use the overtaking criterion to evaluate consumption paths.[11]

3 A generalized overlapping generations model

The turnpike model can be contrasted with the overlapping generations model of Samuelson (1958) which, as is well known, yields (under specified assumptions) an optimal noninterventionist monetary equilibrium. It should prove useful, then, to discover those elements which lead to the different implications of the two models. The intent of this section is to modify the turnpike model to make it more comparable with the standard overlapping generations construct. In other words, the overlapping generations model is generalized; in so doing, its essential features are revealed.

The obvious modification of the turnpike model produces the model shown in figure 2.5. In effect, the turnpike model has been truncated at both ends. Here one agent is born in each period at the beginning of the eastern and western routes, and each agent lives four periods. Note that agents aged zero and three periods are paired, as are agents aged one and two periods.

Preliminary work with this model indicated that an optimal allocation can be supported as a noninterventionist monetary equilibrium, as with the standard overlapping generations model. In such an equilibrium, prices first fall and then rise over each agent's lifetime. Moreover, the (even-aged) lifetimes of each agent can be made arbitrarily long by truncating the model further out, without altering these conclusions. However, it should be noted that the age pairings in this class of models are extreme, the youngest trading

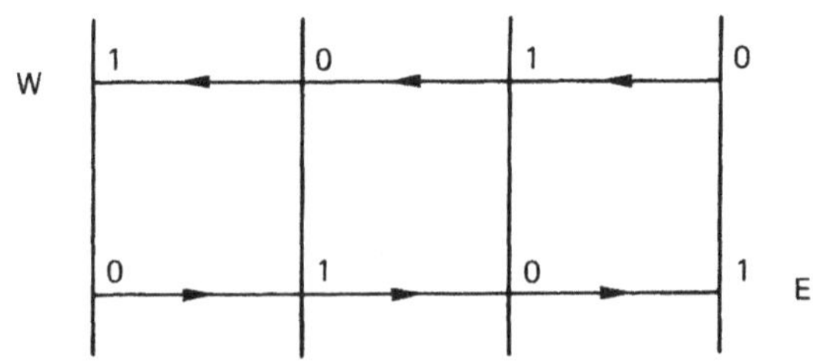

Figure 2.5. A truncated turnpike

with the oldest, the next-to-youngest trading with the next-to-oldest, and so on, whereas in the turnpike model trading partners are of the same age. Thus a more natural comparison would be to a modified model in which trading partners are more or less the same age. This produces the generalized overlapping generations model which is examined in the remainder of this section.

As in the turnpike model, each of a countably infinite number of agents faces an endowment sequence of the single nonstorable consumption good over her or his infinite lifetime which alternates between unity and zero. Yet here all agents are not of the same age; one representative trader is born in each period t, $t \geqslant 0$, and begins life with an endowment of one unit. Each agent is again allocated into one of a countably infinite number of spatially distinct markets in each period of life, but here the allocation procedure is such that each agent is paired with an agent who is either one period older or one period younger. The scheme is illustrated in figure 2.6. The arrows indicate the direction of travel, and the numbers on the right of the market spikes indicate the endowment of an agent whose age is indicated on the left.

For our purpose the economy will be envisaged as beginning at time $t = 0$ but populated with agents born at times $t = -h$, $h \geqslant 1$. Thus at time $t = 0$, island $k = j/2, j \geqslant 0, j$ even, is inhabited with two (representative) agents, one born at time $-j$ with an endowment of one unit and one born at time $-(j+1)$ with an endowment of zero units. At time $t = 1$, one new (representative) agent is born and enters market 0, while the other agents move forward as indicated, and so on. Note that if agents were to live two periods only, attention could be restricted to market 0 alone, an economy which is identical with the simplest two-period overlapping generations model. As will be shown, the present generalization retains the characteristics of that economy.

As in the turnpike model, there is a sense in which there can be no private debt in this model. Here, unlike in the turnpike model, agents meet each other infinitely often: an agent born at time t is paired with an agent born at time $t+1$ when the former is of age 0, 2, 4, ..., and an agent born at time

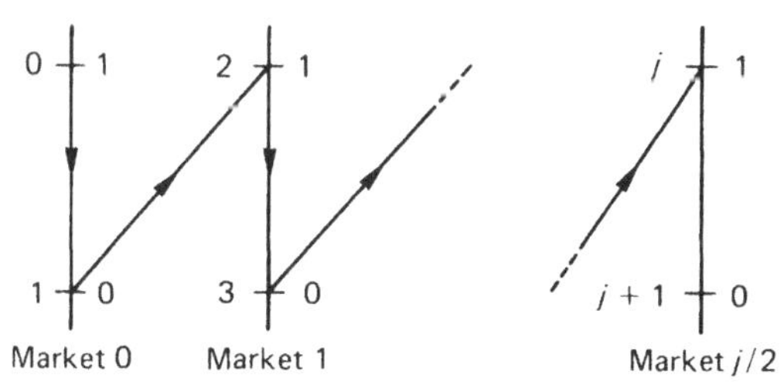

Figure 2.6. Generalized overlapping generations

t is paired with an agent born at time $t-1$ when the former is of age 1, 3, 5, ... Yet when they meet, each of the pair has the same relative endowment position. An IOU issued by an agent of an odd age who has zero units of the consumption good can never be redeemed by the issuer – she or he will have zero units when the pair meet again.

To describe preferences, feasible allocations, and Pareto optimal allocations, some additional notation is needed. Thus let $\{y_j\}_{j=0}^{\infty}$ denote the endowment sequence of a typical agent over her or his lifetime, where y_j is the endowment of an agent of age j. Then $y_j = 1$ for $j \geqslant 0$, j even, and $y_j = 0$ for $j \geqslant 1$, j odd. Let $c_j(t)$ denote the consumption of an agent born at time t who is of age j, $j \geqslant 0$, all t. Individual agents have the same preferences as they did in the turnpike model. That is, the objective function of an agent born at time $t \geqslant 0$ is $\Sigma_{j=0}^{\infty} \beta^j U\{c_j(t)\}$ where $0 < \beta < 1$ and $U(\cdot)$ is strictly concave, strictly increasing, bounded, and continuously differentiable with $U'(0) = \infty$. The objective function of an agent born at time $-h < 0$ is $\Sigma_{j=h}^{\infty} \beta^{j-h} U\{c_j(-h)\}$. An *allocation* is a consumption sequence $\{c_j(t)\}_{j=0}^{\infty}$ for each agent born at time $t \geqslant 0$ and a consumption sequence $\{c_j(-h)\}_{j=h}^{\infty}$ for each agent born at time $-h \leqslant 0$. By construction there is only one unit of the consumption good among the two traders of any market at any point in time. Thus an allocation is said to be *feasible* if

$$\begin{aligned} &c_j(t) + c_{j+1}(t-1) \leqslant 1 \qquad && t \geqslant 0, j \geqslant 0, j \text{ even} \\ &c_j(-h) + c_{j+1}(-h-1) \leqslant 1 \qquad && h \geqslant 1, j \geqslant h, j \text{ even} \end{aligned} \tag{2.23}$$

It will be assumed in what follows, without loss of generality, that these constraints must hold as equalities.

The next step is to define Pareto optimal allocations. For this purpose, a strong symmetry condition is imposed, namely that agents of identical ages be treated identically even though they can be distinguished by birthdate. That is,

$$c_j(t) = c_j(\tau) = c_j \geqslant 0, j \geqslant 0 \qquad \text{all } t, \tau \tag{2.24}$$

Then an allocation $\{c_j\}_{j=0}^{\infty}$ is said to be *optimal* if there does not exist another allocation $\{\tilde{c}_j\}_{j=0}^{\infty}$ with the property that

$$\sum_{j=h}^{\infty} \beta^{j-h} U(\tilde{c}_j) \geqslant \sum_{j=h}^{\infty} \beta^{j-h} U(c_j) \qquad h \geqslant 0 \tag{2.25}$$

with strict inequality for at least one such h. Note that for $h = 0$ the terms in (2.25) represent the utility of one agent born at time $t \geqslant 0$, and for $h > 0$ they represent the utility of an agent born at time $t = -h$. Thus the preferences of all agents are taken into account.

It is now claimed that the solution $\{c_j^*\}_{j=0}^{\infty}$ of the following problem is optimal in the above sense.

Problem 2.3

$$\max_{\{c_j\}_{j=0}^{\infty}} \sum_{j=0}^{\infty} \beta^j U(c_j)$$

subject to

$$c_j + c_{j+1} = 1 \qquad c_j \geqslant 0, j \geqslant 0, j \text{ even}$$

To establish the claim, note that, owing to the time-separable nature of the objective function and of the constraints, the unique solution to this problem is

$$c_j^* = c^*,\ c_{j+1}^* = c^{**} \qquad j \geqslant 0, j \text{ even}$$

where

$$\frac{U'(c^*)}{\beta U'(c^{**})} = 1 \qquad c^* + c^{**} = 1$$

Now suppose that there exists a feasible allocation $\{\tilde{c}_j\}_{j=0}^{\infty}$ which Pareto dominates $\{c_j^*\}_{j=0}^{\infty}$. If an agent born at time $t \geqslant 0$ is to be better off under $\{\tilde{c}_j\}_{j=0}^{\infty}$, then consumption must be increased for at least one element $\tilde{c}_i$. Suppose that $i \geqslant 0$ is even. Then feasibility requires that $\tilde{c}_{i+1}$ be decreased. But c^* and c^{**} are chosen in such a way that such changes can only make the agent born at time t worse off, that is,

$$U(\tilde{c}_i) + \beta U(\tilde{c}_{i+1}) < U(c_i^*) + \beta U(c_{i+1}^*)$$

A similar argument applies for $i \geqslant 0$ and odd. Hence if $\{\tilde{c}_j\}_{j=0}^{\infty}$ is to Pareto dominate $\{c_j^*\}_{j=0}^{\infty}$, it must make at least one agent born at time $-h < 0$ better off. By the above argument, an increase in utility is possible only for the relatively old person of some market at time $t = 0$, that is, only if there is an increase in the element $c_h(-h)$, $h \geqslant 1$, h odd. But then the representative trader born at time $t \geqslant 0$ must be made worse off, and, by the above argument, there can be no compensating changes elsewhere. This establishes the claim.

Unlike the procedure in the turnpike model, no attempt is made here to characterize all possible Pareto optimal allocations in the restricted class. In the simple two-period overlapping generations model, other optimal allocations in the above sense do exist. Moreover, under specified assumptions, each of these can be supported in a monetary equilibrium with deflation and lump-sum taxation. Further, there exist monetary equilibria with inflation and lump-sum subsidization which are nonoptimal. Analogs of these results could be sought here. Instead, attention will be limited to generalizing the well-known proposition mentioned at the onset of this section, that there exists a noninterventionist monetary equilibrium which supports the above described optimal allocation.

To define a monetary equilibrium, some additional notation is needed. Let p_t^k denote the price of the consumption good in market k at time t, $k \geqslant 0$, $t \geqslant 0$. Let $M_j(t)$ denote the money balances held by the agent born at time t at the beginning of period j of that agent's life, chosen at age $j-1$. As attention is restricted to noninterventionist equilibria, no notation for lump-sum taxes is needed. As before, each agent takes initial money balances and the sequence of future prices as given, and maximizes utility by choice of the sequences of money balances and consumptions over her or his infinite lifetime. Thus, for an agent born at time $t \geqslant 0$, consider the following problem.

Problem 2.4

$$\max_{\{c_j(t)\}_{j=0}^{\infty}, \{M_j(t)\}_{j=1}^{\infty}} \sum_{j=0}^{\infty} \beta^j U\{c_j(t)\}$$

subject to

$$c_j(t) \geqslant 0,\ M_j(t) \geqslant 0 \qquad j \geqslant 0$$

$$p_{t+j}^k y_j + M_j(t) = p_{t+j}^k c_j(t) + M_{j+1}(t) \qquad j \geqslant 0 \tag{2.26}$$

given

$$M_0(t) \geqslant 0, \qquad k = \begin{cases} j/2 & j \text{ even}, j \geqslant 0 \\ (j-1)/2 & j \text{ odd}, j \geqslant 1 \end{cases}$$

Similarly, for an agent born at time $-h < 0$, consider the following problem.

Problem 2.5

$$\max_{\{c_j(-h)\}_{j=h}^{\infty}, \{M_j(-h)\}_{j=h+1}^{\infty}} \sum_{j=h}^{\infty} \beta^{j-h} U\{c_j(-h)\}$$

subject to

$$
\begin{aligned}
&c_j(-h) \geqslant 0,\ M_j(-h) \geqslant 0 && j \geqslant h \\
&p^k_{j-h} y_j + M_j(-h) = p^k_{j-h} c_j(-h) + M_{j+1}(-h) && j \geqslant h
\end{aligned}
\tag{2.27}
$$

given

$$
M_h(-h) \geqslant 0, \qquad k = \begin{cases} j/2 & j \text{ even}, j \geqslant h \\ (j-1)/2 & j \text{ odd}, j \geqslant h \end{cases}
$$

We can now write the following definition formally.

Definition
A monetary equilibrium is a sequence of finite positive prices $\{p^{k*}_t\}^{\infty}_{t=0}$ for each market $k \geqslant 0$, sequences of consumptions $\{c^*_j(t)\}^{\infty}_{j=0}$, and money balances $\{M^*_j(t)\}^{\infty}_{j=0}$ for the agent born at each time $t \geqslant 0$, and sequences of consumptions $\{c^*_j(-h)\}^{\infty}_{j=h}$ and money balances $\{M^*_j(-h)\}^{\infty}_{j=h}$ for the agent born at each time $-h < 0$ such that

- maximization for agent t: the sequences $\{c^*_j(t)\}^{\infty}_{j=0}$ and $\{M^*_j(t)\}^{\infty}_{j=1}$ solve problem 2.4 given $M^*_0(t)$;
- maximization for agent $-h$: the sequences $\{c^*_j(-h)\}^{\infty}_{j=h}$ and $\{M^*_j(-h)\}^{\infty}_{j=h+1}$ solve problem 2.5 given $M^*_h(-h)$;
- market clearing:

$$
\begin{aligned}
c^*_j(t) + c^*_{j+1}(t-1) &= 1 && t \geqslant 0, j \geqslant 0, j \text{ even} \\
c^*_j(-h) + c^*_{j+1}(-h-1) &= 1 && h \geqslant 1, j \geqslant h, j \text{ even}
\end{aligned}
$$

To characterize one of the monetary equilibria of this model, return for a moment to problem 2.4. On differentiating with respect to $M_j(t)$, familiar necessary conditions for a maximum are obtained:

$$
-\frac{\beta^{j-1} U'\{c_{j-1}(t)\}}{p^k_{t+j-1}} + \frac{\beta^j U'\{c_j(t)\}}{p^k_{t+j}} + \theta_j(t) = 0 \qquad j \geqslant 1 \tag{2.28}
$$

where $\theta_j(t)$ is the nonnegative Lagrange multiplier associated with the constraint $M_j(t) \geqslant 0$. Expression (2.28) yields

$$
\frac{U'\{c_{j-1}(t)\}}{\beta U'\{c_j(t)\}} \geqslant \frac{p^k_{t+j-1}}{p^k_{t+j}} \qquad j \geqslant 1 \tag{2.29}
$$

where equality prevails if $M_j(t) > 0$. As before with $U'(0) = \infty$ and $y_j = 0$ for $j \geqslant 1, j$ odd, it is obvious that equality must prevail for $j \geqslant 1, j$ odd, and all $t > 0$.

Now suppose that the optimal allocation $c_j^* = c^*$, $c_{j+1}^* = c^{**}, j \geqslant 0, j$ even, were to be supported in a monetary equilibrium. Then, with $j = 1$ in (2.29) as an equality,

$$1 = \frac{U'(c^*)}{\beta U'(c^{**})} = \frac{p_t^{0*}}{p_{t+1}^{0*}} \qquad \text{all } t \geqslant 0$$

where the equality on the left follows from the construction of c^* and c^{**}. That is, the price in market 0 must remain constant over time. A similar argument yields the fact that the price of each market $k \geqslant 0$ must remain constant over time. Moreover, suppose that (2.29) were to hold as an equality in such an equilibrium for j even as well. (That is, suppose that the nonnegativity constraints on money balances were never binding.) Then, with $j = 2$ in (2.29) as an equality,

$$\frac{1}{\beta^2} = \frac{U'(c^{**})}{\beta U'(c^*)} = \frac{p_{t+1}^{0*}}{p_{t+2}^{1*}} \qquad \text{all } t \geqslant 0$$

where again the equality on the left follows from the construction of c^* and c^{**}. That is, $p_{t+1}^{0*} > p_{t+2}^{1*}$ so that the price level would decrease as the agent born at time t moves across markets, from market 0 at time $t + 1$ to market 1 at time $t + 2$. Again j even and $t \geqslant 0$ were arbitrary, and so this relationship would hold across any two adjacent markets for any time period t.

Thus we can guess that the optimal allocation c^*, c^{**} can be supported in a monetary equilibrium with constant prices over time in each market, with deflation cross-sectionally over markets, and with deflation in every other period of each agent's lifetime. Before establishing this conjecture formally, it may be instructive to answer this question: how can it be that there exists a noninterventionist monetary equilibrium in this model with deflation but without taxation? The answer, of course, is that the price level stays constant in each market. In equilibrium the relatively old person of each market passes along *all* of her or his money holdings to the relatively young person, who then does the same in the next period. That is, money itself never moves across markets, and so real balances stay constant in each market. In equilibrium, nominal money balances decline over markets with the price level; real balances stay constant over markets.

This discussion is now summarized in the following proposition.

Proposition 2.6

The optimal allocation c^*, c^{**} can be supported in a (noninterventionist) monetary equilibrium with constant prices over time in each market, with deflation rate $1-\beta^2$ across adjacent markets, and with nonbinding nonegativity constraints on money balances for each agent of any age. In particular, for prices,

$$p_t^{k*} \equiv p^{k*} > 0 \qquad k \geqslant 0$$

$$p^{k*} = \beta^2 p^{k-1*} \qquad k \geqslant 1$$

and for the agent born at each time $t \geqslant 0$

$$c_j^*(t) = c^*, \ M_{j+1}^*(t) = p^{k*}c^{**} \qquad j \geqslant 0, j \text{ even}$$

$$c_j^*(t) = c^{**}, \ M_{j+1}^*(t) = 0 \qquad j \geqslant 1, j \text{ odd}$$

where k is defined in problem 2.4, and for the agent born at each time $-h<0$

$$c_j^*(-h) = c^*, \ M_{j+1}^*(-h) = p^{k*}c^{**} \qquad j \geqslant h, j \text{ even}$$

$$c_j^*(-h) = c^{**}, \ M_{j+1}^*(-h) = 0 \qquad j \geqslant h, j \text{ odd}$$

where k is defined in problem 2.5.

The proof is given in the appendix.

Thus it has been established that there exists an optimal allocation in this model which can be supported in a noninterventionist monetary equilibrium. Yet proposition 2.1 asserts that this is not possible in the turnpike model. Wherein lies the difference?

It should be noted that the allocation $c_j = c^*$, $c_{j+1} = c^{**}$ for $j \geqslant 0$, j even, is optimal here in this generalized overlapping generations model but is not optimal in the turnpike model. (More specifically, the allocation $c_t^{\mathrm{B}} = c^*$, $c_{t+1}^{\mathrm{B}} = c^{**}$, $t \geqslant 0$, t even, is not optimal in the turnpike model, though it can be supported in a noninterventionist monetary equilibrium.) This result turns on the fact that in the overlapping generations model agents are paired at different ages. The optimal allocation takes into account that the young in each market prefer present over future consumption. Thus the age structure seems to be crucial.

4 The Lucas version of the Cass–Yaari model

Thus far, attention has been restricted to models which have the property that money allows the economy to achieve a Pareto superior allocation of goods over time, relative to autarky. For the individual, money plays a role in equating, at least partially, intertemporal marginal rates of substitution. This has led some to claim that money in such models serves as a store of value rather than as a medium of exchange. This section presents a third model with spatially separated agents in which money plays a role in achieving intratemporal efficiency (as well). In essence, the model is the well-known Cass–Yaari (1966) circle, but with trader pairs and a timing of transactions as suggested by Lucas.[12]

The model consists of a countably infinite number of households and a countably infinite number of perishable commodities. Each (representative) household consists of a pair of agents and is imagined to be located on the real line, say one household per integer (see figure 2.7). Each household i lives for ever and faces an endowment sequence of commodity i which is constant, say one unit in each period $t \geqslant 0$. In each period t, each member of household i is capable of moving half the distance to one of the two adjacent integers, $i+1$ and $i-1$. Thus, in each period t, each household i is physically capable of carrying out transactions with households $i-1$ and $i+1$ in two spatially separated markets. There is no storage.

Household i cares only about commodities i and $i+1$, and discounts future over present consumption. Thus, if $c_{it}(i)$ and $c_{i+1,t}(i)$ denote the number of units of consumption by household i at time t of commodities i and $i+1$ respectively, the preferences of household i are represented by the utility function $\Sigma_{t=0}^{\infty} \beta^t V\{c_{it}(i), c_{i+1,t}(i)\}$, $0 < \beta < 1$. Here also $V\{\cdot,\cdot\}$ is strictly concave, strictly increasing, bounded, and continuously differentiable with indifference curves which are asymptotic to the axes. (A particular functional form will be assumed for some purposes in what follows.)

As Cass and Yaari note, this model displays the absence of double coincidence of wants. At each time t each household i can trade with household $i+1$, but i has no commodity that $i+1$ wants. It should also be noted that this model reverses the construction of Cass and Yaari, breaking their circle at some point and spreading it back out over the real line with infinite extensions.[13] As in the turnpike model, this serves to eliminate the possibility of private debt. Household i may issue an IOU to household $i+1$ in exchange for commodity $i+1$, but this IOU can be returned to household i only by household $i+1$ and, as noted, i has no commodity that $i+1$ wants.

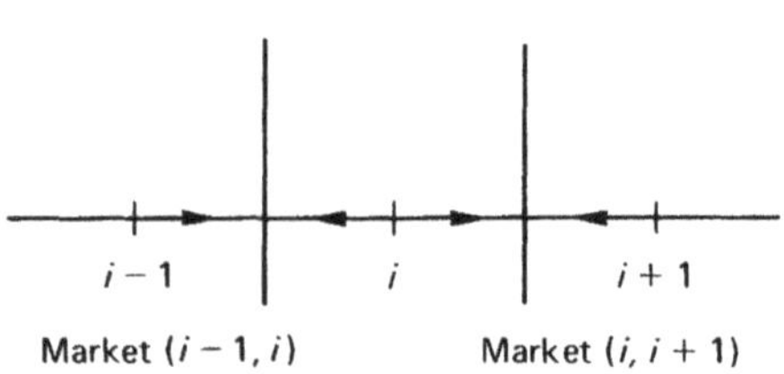

Figure 2.7. Lucas's version of the Cass–Yaari model

The next step in the analysis is to define feasible allocations and characterize those allocations which are Pareto optimal. Without loss of generality attention is restricted to those allocations in which each household receives at most those commodities which enter its utility function. Thus an *allocation* is a sequence of consumptions $\{c_{it}(i), c_{i+1,t}(i)\}_{t=0}^{\infty}$ for each household i. An allocation is said to be *feasible* if

$$\begin{aligned} &c_{it}(i) + c_{it}(i-1) \leqslant 1 && t \geqslant 0, \text{ all integers } i \\ &c_{it}(i) \geqslant 0,\ c_{it}(i-1) \geqslant 0 && t \geqslant 0, \text{ all integers } i \end{aligned} \tag{2.30}$$

Also, without loss of generality, the resource constraint in (2.30) is assumed to hold as an equality. Now in order to characterize Pareto optimal allocations, a strong symmetry condition is imposed – that in any feasible allocation each household i be treated identically with respect to its own consumption of commodity i and other households' consumption of commodity $i+1$. That is, an allocation $\{c_{it}(i), c_{i+1,t}(i)\}_{t=0}^{\infty}$ for all i is said to be *symmetric* if

$$c_{it}(i) = c_t^1,\ c_{i+1,t}(i) = c_t^2 \qquad t \geqslant 0, \text{ all integers } i \tag{2.31}$$

Within the class of such symmetric allocations, then, feasibility is equivalent to

$$c_t^1 + c_t^2 = 1,\ c_t^1 \geqslant 0,\ c_t^2 \geqslant 0 \qquad t \geqslant 0 \tag{2.32}$$

It is now claimed that, subject to this symmetry restriction, the unique Pareto optimal allocation can be found as the solution to the following problem.

Problem 2.6

$$\max_{\{c_t^1, c_t^2\}_{t=0}^{\infty}} \sum_{t=0}^{\infty} \beta^t V(c_t^1, c_t^2)$$

subject to (2.32). Since the objective function and constraint sets are time separable, it is obvious that the unique solution $\{c_t^{1*}, c_t^{2*}\}_{t=0}^{\infty}$ to this problem satisfies

$$c_t^{1*} = c^{1*},\ c_t^{2*} = c^{2*} \qquad \text{all } t \geqslant 0$$

where (see figure 2.8)

$$\frac{V_1(c^{1*}, c^{2*})}{V_2(c^{1*}, c^{2*})} = 1, \qquad c^{1*} + c^{2*} = 1 \tag{2.33}$$

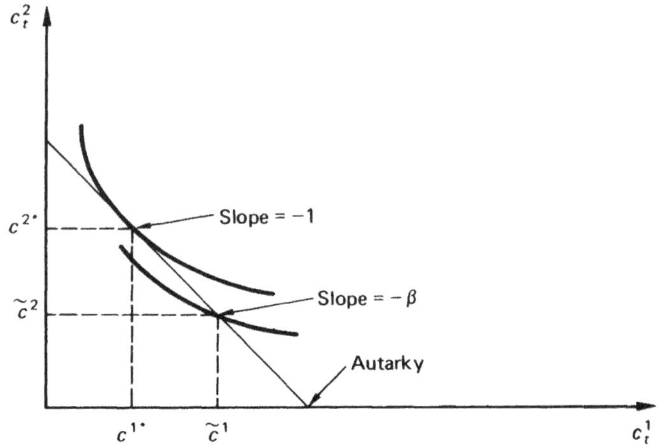

Figure 2.8. Equilibria in Lucas's version of the Cass–Yaari model

Any symmetric feasible allocation which is supposed to improve upon this solution must satisfy (2.32) and increase utility in some period t. The choice of c^{1*} and c^{2*} makes this impossible. Similarly, any symmetric feasible allocation which differs from this solution can be improved upon and hence is not an optimum. Finally, note that the unique Pareto optimum is defined completely by intratemporal considerations.

As before, we now seek to discover the relationship between optimal allocations and monetary equilibria. Thus, suppose that at each time $t \geqslant 0$ households i and $i+1$ meet in a competitive market in which commodity $i+1$ can be exchanged for fiat money. Thus, let $p_{i+1,t}$ denote the price of commodity $i+1$ in terms of fiat money at time $t \geqslant 0$. Also, let $M_t(i)$ denote the number of units of fiat money held by household i at the beginning of period t, and let $z_t(i)$ denote the lump-sum tax. Finally, let $y_{it}(i)$ denote the endowment of commodity i of household i at time t, so that $y_{it}(i) \equiv 1$. At the beginning of each period t, one member of household i travels to the market $(i, i+1)$ with some of the beginning-of-period money balances and purchases commodity $i+1$ at the price $p_{i+1,t}$. Similarly, the other member of household i travels to the market $(i-1, i)$ with some of the endowment of commodity i and sells it for fiat money at the price p_{it}. At the end of each period t, both members of household i return to their original location and consume. Thus, taking the price sequence $\{p_{it}, p_{i+1,t}\}_{t=0}^{\infty}$ and the tax sequence $\{z_t(i)\}_{t=0}^{\infty}$ as given, each household i is confronted with the following problem.

Problem 2.7

$$\max_{\{c_{it}(i),\, c_{i+1,t}(i)\}_{t=0}^{\infty},\ \{M_t(i)\}_{t=1}^{\infty}} \sum_{t=0}^{\infty} \beta^t V\{c_{it}(i), c_{i+1,t}(i)\}$$

subject to

$$c_{it}(i) \geqslant 0,\ c_{i+1,t}(i) \geqslant 0,\ M_t(i) \geqslant 0 \qquad t \geqslant 0$$

$$p_{it}y_{it}(i) + M_t(i) - z_t(i) = p_{it}c_{it}(i) + p_{i+1,t}c_{i+1,t}(i) + M_{t+1}(i) \qquad t \geqslant 0 \quad (2.34)$$

$$p_{i+1,t}c_{i+1,t}(i) \leqslant M_t(i) \qquad t \geqslant 0 \quad (2.35)$$

given $M_0(i) \geqslant 0$, $z_0(i) = 0$.

Here (2.34) is the money balance accumulation equation, and (2.35) is the constraint that the valuation of consumption of commodity $i+1$ by household i is bounded by beginning-of-period money balances. Thus (2.35) is very much in the spirit of a Clower constraint. But here this constraint is generated by the underlying exchange technology of the model.[14]

In what follows, attention will be restricted to equilibria which are symmetric across households in that $\{p_{it}\}_{t=0}^{\infty} = \{p_t\}_{t=0}^{\infty}$ for all commodities i, and $\{z_t(i)\}_{t=0}^{\infty} = \{z_t\}_{t=0}^{\infty}$, $\{M_t(i)\}_{t=0}^{\infty} = \{M_t\}_{t=0}^{\infty}$, and $\{c_{it}(i), c_{i+1,t}(i)\}_{t=0}^{\infty} = \{c_t^1, c_t^2\}_{t=0}^{\infty}$ for all households i. Under these symmetry restrictions the problem of each household i is the same, namely the problem of the representative household.

Problem 2.8

$$\max_{\{c_t^1, c_t^2\}_{t=0}^{\infty}, \{M_t\}_{t=1}^{\infty}} \sum_{t=0}^{\infty} \beta^t V(c_t^1, c_t^2)$$

subject to

$$c_t^1 \geqslant 0,\ c_t^2 \geqslant 0,\ M_t \geqslant 0 \qquad t \geqslant 0$$

$$p_t y_t + M_t - z_t = p_t c_t^1 + p_t c_t^2 + M_{t+1} \quad (2.36)$$

$$p_t c_t^2 \leqslant M_t \quad (2.37)$$

given $M_0 \geqslant 0$, $z_0 = 0$ with $y_t \equiv 1$.

The above discusstion leads to the following definition.

Definition

A symmetric monetary equilibrium is a sequence of finite positive prices $\{p_t^*\}_{t=0}^{\infty}$ and sequences of consumptions $\{c_t^{1*}, c_t^{2*}\}_{t=0}^{\infty}$, money balances $\{M_t^*\}_{t=0}^{\infty}$, and taxes $\{z_t^*\}_{t=0}^{\infty}$ such that

- maximization: the sequences $\{c_t^{1*}, c_t^{2*}\}_{t=0}^{\infty}$ and $\{M_t^*\}_{t=1}^{\infty}$ solve problem 2.8 relative to $\{p_t^*\}_{t=0}^{\infty}$, $\{z_t^{\infty}\}_{t=0}^{\infty}$, and M_0^*;

- market clearing: $c_t^{1*} + c_t^{2*} = 1$, all $t \geqslant 0$.

In order to discover the relationship between symmetric monetary equilibria and optimal allocations it is useful to consider the necessary Euler conditions for a maximum to problem 2.8. If we assume nonbinding nonnegativity constraints on money balances (and consumption) and follow Locay and Palmon (1978), these are of the form

$$-\beta^t V_1(c_t^1, c_t^2) + \beta^t V_2(c_t^1, c_t^2) - p_t^* \theta_t = 0 \qquad t \geqslant 0 \tag{2.38}$$

$$V_1(c_{t-1}^1, c_{t-1}^2) = \frac{p_{t-1}^*}{p_t^*} \beta V_2(c_t^1, c_t^2) \qquad t \geqslant 1 \tag{2.39}$$

where θ_t is the nonnegative Lagrange multiplier associated with the constraint (2.37). One implication is almost immediate.

Proposition 2.7
The optimal allocation c^{1*}, c^{2*} cannot be supported in a noninterventionist symmetric monetary equilibrium, that is, with $z_t^* \equiv 0$.

Proof. Assume the contrary. Then it follows from (2.39) and the construction of the optimum (2.33) that in such an equilibrium the rate of deflation must be $1 - \beta$, that is,

$$p_t^* = \beta p_{t-1}^* \qquad t \geqslant 1 \tag{2.40}$$

Also, from the money balance accumulation equation (2.36) and the feasibility of the optimum,

$$M_{t+1}^* - M_t^* = p_t^*(y_t - c^{1*} - c^{2*}) = 0 \qquad t \geqslant 1 \tag{2.41}$$

Now consider constraint (2.37) at $t = 0$:

$$p_0^* c^{2*} \leqslant M_0^* \tag{2.42}$$

Repeated substitution of (2.40) and (2.41) into (2.42) yields

$$p_t^* c^{2*} < M_t^* \qquad \text{all } t \geqslant 1 \tag{2.43}$$

Then, holding the consumption sequence $\{c_t^1\}_{t=0}^{\infty}$ fixed identically at c^{1*}, the representative household could increase consumption of c_t^2 over c^{2*} in every period $t \geqslant 1$ by spending the surplus money balances. This is the desired contradiction, and it completes the proof. (For an alternative argument see Locay and Palmon (1978).)

Proposition 2.7 of this model is the analog of proposition 2.1 in the turnpike model. It seems that propositions 2.2 and 2.4 of the turnpike model also have analogs here; that is, the optimal allocation can be supported in an interventionist monetary equilibrium, and there exists a noninterventionist monetary equilibrium which is nonoptimal but Pareto superior to autarky.[15] For, according to Locay and Palmon (1978), the necessary transversality condition for the maximization problem confronting the representative household is

$$\lim_{t\to\infty} \frac{\beta^t M_t V_2(c_t^1, c_t^2)}{p_t} = 0 \tag{2.44}$$

Then for the interventionist monetary equilibrium which is to support the optimal allocation c^{1*}, c^{2*}, consider the following specification. Let $M_0^* = p_0^* c^{2*}$ so that the representative household spends all initial money balances on the consumption good with which it is not endowed. Similarly, in each period t let the representative household spend all after-tax money holdings on this commodity, acquiring additional money from the sale of the endowment commodity $y_t - c^{1*}$. Also, let the rate of deflation be $1-\beta$. In summary, then, let

$$M_{t+1}^* = p_t^*(y_t - c^{1*}) \qquad t \geqslant 0 \tag{2.45}$$

$$z_t^* = (M_t^* - p_t^* c^{2*}) > 0 \quad t \geqslant 1 \tag{2.46}$$

$$p_t^* = \beta p_{t-1}^* \qquad t \geqslant 1 \tag{2.47}$$

It is apparent that this specification satisfies the necessary and sufficient conditions for a maximum, (2.38), (2.39), and (2.44), with the nonbinding constraint (2.37), that is, $\theta_t \equiv 0$.

For the noninterventionist monetary equilibrium, consider the following specification. First, let prices be constant; then, motivated by (2.39), let $c_t^1 \equiv \tilde{c}^1$, $c_t^2 \equiv \tilde{c}^2$, where $\tilde{c}^1$ and $\tilde{c}^2$ are uniquely defined by

$$\frac{V_1(\tilde{c}^1, \tilde{c}^2)}{V_2(\tilde{c}^1, \tilde{c}^2)} = \beta \qquad \tilde{c}^1 + \tilde{c}^2 = 1 \tag{2.48}$$

Again, suppose that all beginning-of-period money balances are spent on the other households' consumption good, and that these are replenished from the sale of the households' own consumption good. That is, let

$$M^*_{t+1} = p^*_t(y_t - \tilde{c}^1) \tag{2.49}$$

$$M^*_t = p^*_t \tilde{c}^2 \tag{2.50}$$

$$p^*_t \equiv p^* > 0 \tag{2.51}$$

Again, the necessary and sufficient first-order conditions for a maximum are satisfied, this time with the binding constraint (2.37), that is, $\theta_t > 0$. It is clear that this consumption sequence is nonoptimal but Pareto superior to autarky (see figure 2.8).

The reader may be struck by the similarity of the above results to those of the turnpike model. To repeat, optimal allocations cannot be supported in a noninterventionist monetary equilibrium, but there exists a monetary equilibrium with constant prices and binding constraints which is Pareto superior to autarky.[16] Yet here, unlike the turnpike model, the imposition of a stronger Clower-type constraint may be sufficient to generate a monetary equilibrium without taxation which is optimal. In fact, the imposition of such a constraint can convert the Cass–Yaari model into Lucas's model of money with certainty (Lucas, 1980). These results are now established.

The above scheme is modified in two ways. First, the utility function $V(\cdot, \cdot)$ is assumed to be of the form

$$V(c^1, c^2) = U\left\{\left(\frac{c^1}{\alpha_1}\right)^{\alpha_1}\left(\frac{c^2}{\alpha_2}\right)^{\alpha_2}\right\}$$

where $\alpha_1 > 0$, $\alpha_2 > 0$, and $\alpha_1 + \alpha_2 = 1$, and where $U(\cdot)$ satisfies all the assumptions of the previous two sections. Second, the constraint (2.37) in problem 2.8 is strengthened to

$$p_t c^1_t + p_t c^2_t \leqslant M_t \tag{2.52}$$

As in section 2, the idea here is that the member of household i who travels to the market $(i-1, i)$ with the endowment $y_{it}(i) = 1$ must pay cash in advance for any units of commodity i which she or he is to take home. Again, a *Clower-type symmetric monetary equilibrium* can be defined in the obvious way, with (2.52) replacing (2.37) in problem 2.8, and $z^*_t \equiv 0$. This leads to the following proposition.

Proposition 2.8

The optimal allocations c^{1*}, c^{2*} can be supported in a Clower-type symmetric monetary equilibrium with constant prices. In particular, $c_t^{1*} \equiv c^{1*}$, $c_t^{2*} \equiv c^{2*}$, $p_t^* \equiv p^* > 0$, and $M_t^* = p^* y_t$ for all $t > 0$.

Proof. First let c_t denote real consumption expenditures in period t, that is,

$$p^* c_t^1 + p^* c_t^2 = p^* c_t \tag{2.53}$$

Substitution of (2.53) into the budget constraint (2.36) yields

$$p^* y_t + M_t - M_{t+1} = p^* c_t \tag{2.54}$$

Now if we fix M_t and M_{t+1}, the intratemporal period t decision problem of the representative household is of the form

$$\max_{c_t^1 \geqslant 0,\, c_t^2 \geqslant 0} U\left\{\left(\frac{c^1}{\alpha_1}\right)^{\alpha_1}\left(\frac{c^2}{\alpha_2}\right)^{\alpha_2}\right\}$$

subject to

$$p^* c_t^1 + p^* c_t^2 = p^* c_t$$

The unique solution to this problem is

$$c_t^1 = \alpha_1 c_t, \; c_t^2 = \alpha_2 c_t$$

and so the indirect utility as a function of c_t is just $U(c_t)$. Hence the problem of the representative household is reduced to

$$\max_{\{M_t\}_{t=1}^{\infty}} \sum_{t=0}^{\infty} \beta^t U(c_t)$$

subject to

$$M_t \geqslant 0,\; c_t \geqslant 0 \qquad t \geqslant 0$$

$$p^* y + M_t - M_{t+1} = p^* c_t$$

$$p^* c_t \leqslant M_t$$

given $M_0^* = p^* y$ where $y = 1$. Lucas (1980) establishes that $M_t \equiv p^* y$ is the unique solution to this problem. Thus $p^* c_t = p^* y$ for all $t \geqslant 0$, and so the solution to the intratemporal problem must be $c_t^{*1} = c^{1*}$, $c_t^{*2} = c^{2*}$ for all $t \geqslant 0$, the optimum. This completes the proof.

That the imposition of a strong Clower-type constraint generates an optimal allocation in this model and not in the turnpike model is somewhat puzzling. This result seems to turn on the facts that there is only one representative agent in this model, whereas there are two representative agents in the turnpike model, and that optimal allocations are defined accordingly.

5 Circles and private debt

As noted in section 1, there are an infinite number of agents alive at any one date both in the turnpike model and in the version of the Cass–Yaari model just presented. This specification ensured that the exclusion of private debt was indeed endogenous. With the removal of this contemporaneous infinity, the role of private debt can be analyzed. This section is intended to be illustrative of the kind of analysis which can be undertaken.

The contemporaneous infinity is removed from the turnpike model by converting it into a circle. This is done in figure 2.9 for an economy with eight agents. As before, arrows indicate the direction of travel, spikes indicate islands or markets, and numbers index the endowment of the agent at the indicated position.

Focusing on the pairings of agents in this model, it becomes clear that the set of agents can be partitioned into two groups or subeconomies, where agents in a subeconomy trade only with other agents of that subeconomy. Thus the essential features of the model depicted in figure 2.9 can be captured by the simpler model depicted in figure 2.10. Here there are only two markets,

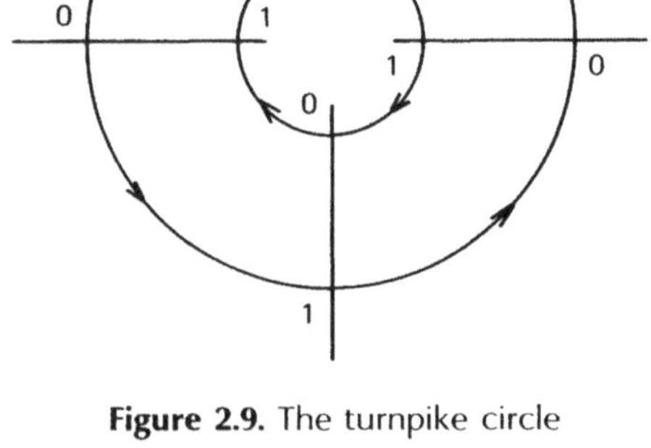

Figure 2.9. The turnpike circle

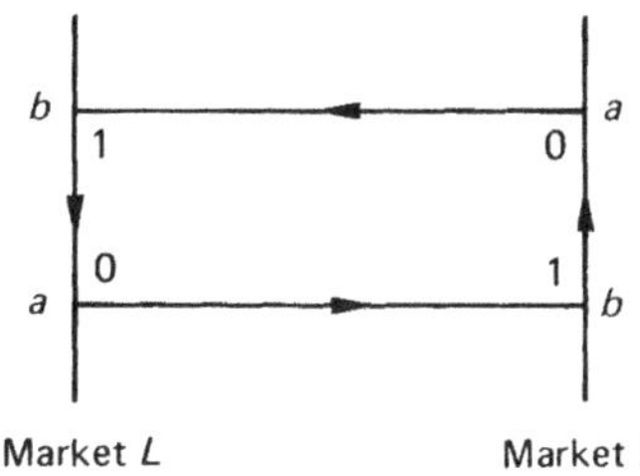

Figure 2.10. The debt model

labeled L and R, and four agents, labeled a, a', b, and b' at their initial positions. To understand the way agents are paired over time, consider the itinerary of one of the agents. Agent a, of type A, begins in period 0 with zero units of the consumption good and is paired in market L with agent b, of type B, who has one unit. In period 1, agent a is allocated to market R with one unit, and is paired with agent b'. Continuing, agent a stays in market R in period 2 and finally moves back to market L in period 3. Period 4 is the same as period 0.

The fact that agents meet repeatedly in this version of the turnpike model has no bearing on the determination of optimal allocations. Under the symmetry condition imposed in section 2, an (interior) optimum has the property that each agent of type A receives λ units of the consumption good in each period. In fact, all the propositions of section 2 apply to this economy if we accept the exogenous exclusion of debt. Yet now there may be private debt equilibria. That is, debt can be used as a means of payment.

For the purpose of discussing private debt in this economy, attention is restricted first to the obvious four-period version of this model. (Again this has no effect on the properties of optima.) A particular scheme is considered. In the initial period, $t = 0$, each agent of type A is permitted to issue IOUs, where one such IOU is a promise to pay to the holder $1 + r$ units of the consumption good in period 3. Both the interest rate r and the price $p_0 > 0$ of the consumption good, in terms of such IOUs in period 0, are taken as given by agents a and a'. Thus the problem confronting each agent of type A in period 0 is as follows.

Problem 2.9

$$\max_{B_0^A \geq 0,\, c_0^A \geq 0,\, c_3^A \geq 0} \quad U(c_0^A) + \beta^3 U(c_3^A)$$

subject to

$$p_0 c_0^A \leq B_0^A \tag{2.55}$$

$$c_3^{\mathrm{A}} \leqslant y_3^{\mathrm{A}} - (B_0^{\mathrm{A}} + z_3^{\mathrm{A}})(1+r) \tag{2.56}$$

where B_0^{A} is the number of IOUs issued by an agent of type A and $-z_3^{\mathrm{A}}$ is a lump-sum forgiveness (subsidy) of debt in period 3. The above two budget constraints can be assumed to hold as equalities. Here the nonnegativity constraints can be ignored, yielding the necessary first-order condition

$$\frac{U'(c_0^{\mathrm{A}})}{p_0} = \beta^3 U'(c_3^{\mathrm{A}})(1+r) \tag{2.57}$$

In periods 1 and 2 the debt issued by agents a and a' is traded in markets L and R respectively. In particular, agent a can purchase the debt (of a') in market R in period 1 and sell the debt in market R in period 2. Then if p_1 and p_2 denote the price of the consumption good in terms of IOUs in periods 1 and 2 respectively, the problem confronting each agent of type A in period 1 is as follows.

Problem 2.10

$$\max_{B_2^{\mathrm{A}} \geqslant 0,\, c_1^{\mathrm{A}} \geqslant 0,\, c_2^{\mathrm{A}} \geqslant 0} \quad \beta U(c_1^{\mathrm{A}}) + \beta^2 U(c_2^{\mathrm{A}})$$

subject to

$$p_1 c_1^{\mathrm{A}} \leqslant p_1 y_1^{\mathrm{A}} - B_2^{\mathrm{A}} \tag{2.58}$$

$$p_2 c_2^{\mathrm{A}} \leqslant B_2^{\mathrm{A}} - z_2^{\mathrm{A}} \tag{2.59}$$

where B_2^{A} is the number of IOUs acquired by agent type a in period 1 and z_2^{A} is a lump-sum tax (confiscation) of IOUs in period 2. With $z_2^{\mathrm{A}} \geqslant 0$ the nonnegativity constraints can be ignored, yielding the necessary first-order condition

$$\frac{\beta U'(c_1^{\mathrm{A}})}{p_1} = \frac{\beta^2 U'(c_2^{\mathrm{A}})}{p_2} \tag{2.60}$$

It is now obvious that the problem confronting each agent of type B in period 0 is as follows.

Problem 2.11

$$\max_{B_1^B \geqslant 0,\, c_0^B \geqslant 0,\, c_1^B \geqslant 0} \quad U(c_0^B) + \beta U(c_1^B)$$

$$p_0 c_0^B \leqslant p_0 y_0^B - B_1^B \tag{2.61}$$

$$p_1 c_1^B \leqslant B_1^B - z_1^B \tag{2.62}$$

where B_1^B is the member of IOUs acquired by an agent of type B in period 0 and $z_1^B \geqslant 0$ is the lump-sum confiscation in period 1. The necessary first-order condition is

$$\frac{U'(c_0^B)}{p_0} = \frac{\beta U'(c_1^B)}{p_1} \tag{2.63}$$

The following problem is obtained in a similar manner.

Problem 2.12

$$\max_{B_3^B \geqslant 0,\, c_2^B \geqslant 0,\, c_3^B \geqslant 0} \quad \beta^2 U(c_2^B) + \beta^3 U(c_3^B)$$

$$p_2 c_2^B \leqslant p_2 y_2^B - B_3^B \tag{2.64}$$

$$c_3^B \leqslant (B_3^B - z_3^B)(1 + r) \tag{2.65}$$

with the necessary first-order condition

$$\frac{\beta^2 U'(c_2^B)}{p_2} = \beta^3 U'(c_3^B)(1 + r) \tag{2.66}$$

These procedures lead to the following definition.

Definition

A private debt equilibrium is an interest rate r^*, a sequence of finite positive prices $\{p_t^*\}_{t=0}^2$, and sequences of lump-sum taxes $\{z_t^{A*}\}_{t=2,3}$, $\{z_t^{B*}\}_{t=1,3}$, consumptions $\{c_t^{A*}\}_{t=0}^3$, $\{c_t^{B*}\}_{t=0}^3$, and debt decisions $\{B_t^{A*}\}_{t=0,2}$, $\{B_t^{B*}\}_{t=1,3}$ such that

- maximization for A: c_0^{A*}, c_3^{A*}, B_0^{A*} solve problem 2.9 relative to r^*, p_0^*, z_3^{A*}, and c_1^{A*}, c_2^{A*}, B_2^{A*} solve problem 2.10 relative to p_1^*, p_2^*, z_2^{A*};

- maximization for B: c_0^{B*}, c_1^{B*}, B_1^{B*} solve problem 2.11 relative to p_0^*, p_1^*, z_1^{B*}, and c_2^{B*}, c_3^{B*}, B_2^{B*} solve problem 2.12 relative to p_2^*, r^*, z_3^{B*};
- market clearing: $c_t^{A*} + c_t^{B*} = 1$, $t = 0, 1, 2, 3$.

A major point of this section is that the decentralization of the turnpike model cannot be overcome with private debt alone. To see this, suppose for the moment that all four agents of the above model were in the same market in each of the four periods. Then there is a (centralized) Arrow–Debreu competitive equilibrium with

$$p_t^* = \beta p_{t-1}^* \qquad t = 1, 2 \qquad 1 + r^* = \frac{1}{\beta^3}$$

$$c_t^{A*} \equiv \frac{\beta}{1+\beta} \qquad c_t^{B*} \equiv \frac{1}{1+\beta} \qquad t = 0, 1, 2, 3$$

Of course this allocation is optimal. Yet it turns out that neither this allocation nor any other optimal allocation can be achieved in the decentralized economy under a private debt equilibrium without taxation. More formally, consider the following proposition.

Proposition 2.9
No interior optimum λ can be supported in a private debt equilibrium without taxation, that is, with $z_t^{i*} \equiv 0$ for $i = \text{A, B}$.

Proof. Suppose that the contrary holds. Then from problem 2.11 and equation (2.63), $p_1^* = \beta p_0^*$. Budget constraint (2.61) as an equality yields $B_1^{B*} = p_0^* \lambda$. Substitution into (2.62) yields $\beta = \lambda/(1-\lambda)$. From problem 2.10 and (2.60), $p_2^* = \beta p_1^*$. Budget constraint (2.58) as an equality yields $B_2^{A*} = p_1^*(1-\lambda)$. Substitution into (2.59) yields $\beta = (1-\lambda)/\lambda$. Figure 2.3 makes clear with $\beta < 1$ that these two specifications of β are inconsistent. This completes the proof.

Proposition 2.9 and its analog proposition 2.1 suggest that inside money in the turnpike model acts very much like outside money. In fact, the analog of proposition 2.2 can be obtained as well.

Proposition 2.10
Any interior optimum λ with $\beta \leqslant \{\lambda/(1-\lambda)\}$ and $\beta \leqslant \{(1-\lambda)/\lambda\}$ can be supported in a private debt equilibrium with lump-sum taxation and forgiveness of debt.

Proof. From problem 2.9 and (2.57) let $(1 + r^*) p_0^* \beta^3 = 1$. From (2.55) let

$p_0^* \lambda = B_0^{A*}$, and from (2.56) let $z_3^{A*} = (1-\lambda)\beta^3 p_0^* - \lambda p_0^*$. From problem 2.10 and (2.60) let $p_2^* = \beta p_1^*$. From (2.58) let $B_2^{A*} = p_1^*(1-\lambda)$, and from (2.59) let $0 \leqslant z_2^{A*} = p_1^*\{(1-\lambda) - \beta\lambda\}$. From problem 2.11 and (2.63) let $p_1^* = \beta p_0^*$. From (2.61) let $B_1^{B*} = \lambda p_0^*$, and from (2.62) let $0 \leqslant z_1^{B*} = p_0^*\{\lambda - (1-\lambda)\beta\}$. Finally, from problem 2.12 and (2.66) let $\beta p_2^*(1+r^*) = 1$. From (2.64) let $B_3^{B*} = p_2^* \lambda$, and from (2.65) let $0 \leqslant z_3^{B*} = p_2^*\{\lambda - (1-\lambda)\beta\}$. Now, by construction, all the first-order conditions for maxima are satisfied, with the budget constraints as equalities in every period. This is sufficient for the proposed solution to satisfy the maximizing conditions of an equilibrium. The market-clearing condition is also satisfied by construction. Finally, it can be noted as a check on the above procedure that the sum of the confiscations of debt equals the lump-sum forgiveness in period 3. This completes the proof.

Thus proposition 2.10 establishes that an optimal allocation can be achieved with nontrivial intervention in private credit markets. At this point we may well ask whether there exists a private debt equilibrium without such lump-sum taxation and forgiveness of debt which is Pareto nonoptimal but Pareto superior to autarky. In particular, can the allocations of the noninterventionist monetary equilibrium of proposition 2.4 be achieved? Perhaps it is now obvious from section 2 and the above analysis that this question can be answered in the affirmative if we are willing to impose an upper bound on the issue of IOUs. That is, in problem 2.9 impose the additional exogenous constraint that $B_0^A \leqslant d$ for some constant d and define a *constrained private debt equilibrium* in the obvious way. The proposition below follows.

Proposition 2.11

There exists a constrained private debt equilibrium with a binding constraint on the issue of IOUs in period 0. In particular,

$$r^* = 0;\ p_t^* = 1,\ t = 0, 1, 2;\ z_t^{i*} \equiv 0,\ i = \text{A, B}$$

$$c_t^{A*} = c^{**},\ c_{t+1}^{A*} = c^*,\ B_t^{A*} = c^{**} = d,\ t = 0, 2$$

$$c_t^{B*} = c^*,\ c_{t+1}^{B} = c^{**},\ B_{t+1}^{B*} = c^{**},\ t = 0, 2$$

Proof. The relevant first-order conditions and budget constraints are satisfied for problems 2.10, 2.11, and 2.12 and modified problem 2.9. This completes the proof.

Proposition 2.11 turns on the fact that the constraint on the issue of inside money plays the role of a nonnegativity constraint on money balances in the same economy with fiat money. This, together with proposition 2.3, may lead us to the conjecture that a private debt equilibrium without taxation and without such exogenously imposed constraints does not exist. Yet it can be established that, for the simple four-period economy described above, there does exist at least one such equilibrium.[17] Clearly we can introduce private debt into an infinite-period economy by duplication of the four-period scheme every four periods. What is not yet clear is the extent to which such equilibria rest on the rather special assumptions which have been loaded into the four-period scheme: that only agents of type A can issue debt in every fourth period, that this debt can only be redeemed four periods after it is issued, and so on. It would seem that a completely unrestricted private debt economy would be plagued by Ponzi schemes. An open and intriguing question is whether relatively unrestricted debt and fiat money can coexist; this is the subject of ongoing research.

6 Concluding remarks

The contention of this chapter is obvious: models of money with spatially separated agents should be taken seriously as models of money. Certainly these communication-cost models explain money in a rigorous way, at least subject to the implicit restrictions of the competitive paradigm. But more research is needed. Remaining to be investigated, for example, are the issues of asset dominance and capital over accumulation when storage is allowed. To be looked at also is the problem of multiple monetary equilibria, especially without all the exogenously imposed symmetry restrictions.

Ultimately, though, it is difficult to make judgments on the relative merits of models in the abstract without reference either to actual observations or to policy questions. We would like to know, for example, whether models with spatially separated agents can be modified to explain the existence of both inside and outside money. Wallace (1980) has established that the overlapping generations construct is not subject to this criticism. As for policy issues, the overlapping generations construct has been shown by Bryant and Wallace (1979, 1980) and Kareken and Wallace (1977, 1978) to have strong policy implications for open-market operations and international financial arrangements respectively. It remains to be seen whether other models can do as well on this account and, if so, whether the implications will be the same.

In closing, let us return to the claim that the three models in this chapter explain the use of money. This claim is equivalent to the statement that in each of the models there exists a (noninterventionist) monetary equilibrium in which money has value. Thus the approach of this chapter relies heavily on the competitive paradigm. Ideally, though, competitive equilibrium allocations should be viewed as the outcome of an explicit game or mechanism (for example, see Shubik, 1973; Townsend, 1978; Prescott and Townsend, 1980), but this raises an obvious question: why has the competitive mechanism been imposed as opposed to some other?

In this regard, consider the welfare theorems of this chapter. These theorems are consistent with the view that the operation of competitive markets is possible though direct redistribution of endowments is not, or at least that the first scheme is less onerous than the second. Putting this in another way, if the agents of the model could agree to direct redistribution of the endowments, then Pareto optimal allocations could be achieved without the use of money. The welfare theorems of this paper are also consistent with the view that the operation of competitive markets along with lump-sum taxation of money is more appealing than direct redistribution. Clearly this second view is even more tenuous than the first. Finally, it should be noted that, in Lucas's version of the Cass–Yaari model, optimal allocations can be achieved with either lump-sum taxation or the imposition of a Clower constraint, requiring the use of money to purchase commodities. Is there any sense in which one of these schemes is preferable to the other?

The point of this discussion is that in the context of the specified economic environments of the models of this chapter, any criterion used to select from among various schemes is *ad hoc* and thus unsatisfactory. What is needed is theory in which the choice of social arrangements or games is endogenous. That is, the environment of the model should be sufficiently rich that certain games or constraints are either technically infeasible or too costly (if not impossible) to enforce. Models with moral hazard and asymmetric information may be needed, as was suggested at the outset (compare Harris and Townsend, 1978, this volume, ch. 6; 1981, this volume, ch. 7; Townsend, 1979, this volume, ch. 5). It would seem to be particularly important in monetary economics to make the choice of joint arrangements endogenous, that is, to solve Shubik's start-up problem (Shubik, 1980). As Bryant (1979) has emphasized, the seigniorage associated with the issue of money must be allocated.

Appendix

Proof of Proposition 2.2

First, let $p_t^* = \beta p_{t-1}^*$, all $t \geqslant 1$. Next, for agent type A let $c_0^{A*} = \lambda$, $M_0^{A*}/p_0^* = \lambda$, and $M_1^{A*} = 0$ so that agent type A spends all of her or his initial money balances on consumption. Subsequently, tax as needed to maintain the consumption sequence $c_t^{A*} \equiv \lambda$ with money balances returning to zero in every other period:

$$y_t^A = 1,\ c_t^{A*} = \lambda,\ z_t^{A*} = 0,\ M_{t+1}^{A*} = p_t^*(1-\lambda) \qquad t \geqslant 1,\ t \text{ odd}$$

$$y_t^A = 0,\ c_t^{A*} = \lambda,\ z_t^{A*} = p_t^*\left(\frac{1-\lambda}{\beta} - \lambda\right) \geqslant 0,\ M_{t+1}^{A*} = 0$$

$$t \geqslant 2,\ t \text{ even}$$

Similarly, for agent type B let $M_0^{B*} = 0$ and

$$y_t^B = 1,\ c_t^{B*} = 1-\lambda,\ z_t^{B*} = 0,\ M_{t+1}^{B*} = p_t^*\lambda \qquad t \geqslant 0,\ t \text{ even}$$

$$y_t^B = 0,\ c_t^{B*} = 1-\lambda,\ z_t^{B*} = p_t^*\left\{\frac{\lambda}{\beta} - (1-\lambda)\right\} \geqslant 0,\ M_{t+1}^{B*} = 0$$

$$t \geqslant 1,\ t \text{ odd}$$

By construction, the market-clearing condition is satisfied, and so it remains to verify that the above specification constitutes a solution to the maximization problem confronting each agent type i given M_0^{i*}, $\{p_t^*\}_{t=0}^{\infty}$, $\{z_t^{*i}\}_{t=0}^{\infty}$. This will be done explicitly for agent type B; the argument for agent type A follows immediately.

Consider first any consumption sequence $\{\hat{c}_t^B\}_{t=0}^{\infty}$ and associated money balance sequence $\{\hat{M}_t^B\}_{t=1}^{\infty}$ which are assumed to solve the maximization problem of agent type B. With $p_t^* y_t^B - z_t^{B*} \leqslant 0$, all $t \geqslant 1$, t odd, it follows that $\hat{M}_t^B > 0$ for $t \geqslant 1$, t odd. Hence (2.7) must hold as an equality at such times, that is,

$$\frac{U'(\hat{c}_{t-1}^B)}{\beta U'(\hat{c}_t^B)} = \frac{p_{t-1}^*}{p_t^*} = \frac{1}{\beta} \qquad t \geqslant 1,\ t \text{ odd} \tag{2.A1}$$

It follows that

$$\hat{c}_{t-1}^B = \hat{c}_t^B \qquad t \geqslant 1,\ t \text{ odd} \tag{2.A2}$$

Next, convert the problem of agent type B into real terms. In particular, let $w_t^B = (p_t^* y_t^B - z_t^{B*})/p_t^*$ so that

$$w_t^B = 1 \qquad t \geqslant 0,\ t \text{ even}$$

$$w_t^B = -\left\{\frac{\lambda}{\beta} - (1-\lambda)\right\} \qquad t \geqslant 1,\ t \text{ odd}$$

Also let $m_t^B \equiv M_t^B / p_t^*$ denote real money balances held by agent type B at the beginning of period t. From the budget constraint (2.5) as an equality and utilizing the fact that $p_t^* = \beta p_{t-1}^*$, all $t \geqslant 1$, it follows that

$$c_t^{\mathrm{B}} + \beta m_{t+1}^{\mathrm{B}} = w_t^{\mathrm{B}} + m_t^{\mathrm{B}} \qquad \text{all } t \geqslant 0 \tag{2.A3}$$

Then, from (2.A2), setting $c_t^{\mathrm{B}} = c_{t+1}^{\mathrm{B}}$ for $t \geqslant 0$, t even, and solving for m_{t+1}^{B} we obtain

$$(1+\beta)m_{t+1}^{\mathrm{B}} = w_t^{\mathrm{B}} - w_{t+1}^{\mathrm{B}} + m_t^{\mathrm{B}} + \beta m_{t+2}^{\mathrm{B}} \qquad t \geqslant 0,\ t \text{ even} \tag{2.A4}$$

$$(1+\beta)c_t^{\mathrm{B}} = (1+\beta)c_{t+1}^{\mathrm{B}} = w_t^{\mathrm{B}} + \beta w_{t+1}^{\mathrm{B}} + m_t^{\mathrm{B}} - \beta^2 m_{t+2}^{\mathrm{B}} \qquad t \geqslant 0,\ t \text{ even} \tag{2.A5}$$

Following the methods of Lucas and Prescott (1971) it can be established that there exists a bounded continuous function $V(\cdot)$ satisfying the functional equation

$$V(m_0^{\mathrm{B}}) = \max_{m_2^{\mathrm{B}}} [\{U(c_0^{\mathrm{B}}) + \beta U(c_1^{\mathrm{B}})\} + \beta^2 V(m_2^{\mathrm{B}})]$$

subject to

$$0 \leqslant m_2^{\mathrm{B}} \leqslant \frac{w_1^{\mathrm{B}} - w_0^{\mathrm{B}} - m_0^{\mathrm{B}}}{\beta}$$

$$c_0^{\mathrm{B}} \text{ and } c_1^{\mathrm{B}} \text{ satisfy (2.A5) at } t = 0$$

given $m_0^{\mathrm{B}} \geqslant 0$. (Here the upper bound on m_2^{B} follows from (2.A4) at $t = 0$ and the constraint $m_1^{\mathrm{B}} \geqslant 0$. Note that the constraint set on m_2^{B} is compact and the objective function, in braces above, as an indirect function of m_2^{B}, is bounded and continuous.) Here, then, the solution $m_2^{\mathrm{B}} = \Psi(m_0^{\mathrm{B}})$ is the *stationary policy function* which solves

$$\max_{\{m_t^{\mathrm{B}}\}_{t=2}^{T}} \sum_{\substack{t \geqslant 0 \\ t\,\text{even}}} \beta^t \{U(c_t^{\mathrm{B}}) + \beta U(c_{t+1}^{\mathrm{B}})\}$$

subject to

$$0 \leqslant m_{t+2}^{\mathrm{B}} \leqslant \frac{w_{t+1}^{\mathrm{B}} - w_t^{\mathrm{B}} - m_t^{\mathrm{B}}}{\beta}$$

$$c_t^{\mathrm{B}} \text{ and } c_{t+1}^{\mathrm{B}} \text{ satisfy (2.A5)}$$

given $m_0^{\mathrm{B}} \geqslant 0$. Thus there does exist at least one solution to the problem confronting agent type B.

Clearly, the proposed solution

$$c_t^{\mathrm{B}} \equiv 1-\lambda,\ m_t^{\mathrm{B}*}=0 \qquad t \geqslant 2,\ t \text{ even}$$

$$m_t^{\mathrm{B}*}=\frac{\lambda}{\beta} \qquad t \geqslant 1,\ t \text{ odd}$$

satisfies (2.7) with equality in every period. By construction the budget constraint (2.5) is also satisfied as an equality in every period. Now suppose that there exist a consumption sequence $\{\hat{c}_t^{\mathrm{B}}\}_{t=0}^{\infty}$ and its associated real money balance sequence $\{\hat{m}_t^{\mathrm{B}}\}_{t=1}^{\infty}$ which do better than the proposed solution, and consider the first-period τ at which $\hat{c}_\tau^{\mathrm{B}} \neq 1-\lambda$. (Note from (2.A2) that τ must be even.) Clearly, $\hat{c}_\tau^{\mathrm{B}} > 1-\lambda$ is not feasible, for with $\hat{c}_{\tau+1}^{\mathrm{B}} > 1-\lambda$ also, we obtain $\hat{m}_{\tau+2}^{\mathrm{B}} < 0$. Nor is $\hat{c}_\tau^{\mathrm{B}} < 1-\lambda$ possible. For in this case $\hat{c}_{\tau+1}^{\mathrm{B}} < 1-\lambda$, so $\hat{m}_{\tau+2}^{\mathrm{B}} > 0$. Thus (2.7) would hold as an equality at $t=\tau+2$, so that $\hat{c}_{\tau+2}^{\mathrm{B}} < 1-\lambda$ also, and so on. That is, the consumption path would be maintained below the proposed solution for all $t \geqslant \tau$, and this cannot improve matters. Hence the proposed solution is indeed maximizing.

A virtually identical argument establishes that, given $c_0^{\mathrm{A}*}=\lambda$, $m_0^{\mathrm{A}*}=\lambda$, and $m_1^{\mathrm{A}*}=0$, the sequences $\{c_t^{\mathrm{A}*}\}_{t=1}^{\infty}$ and $\{m_t^{\mathrm{A}*}\}_{t=2}^{\infty}$ solve the problem of agent type A from $t=1$ onward. In particular, by the principle of optimality, at $t=2$ given

$$m_2^{\mathrm{A}*}=\frac{1-\lambda}{\beta},\ w_2^{\mathrm{A}}=-\left(\frac{1-\lambda}{\beta}-\lambda\right),\ m_2^{\mathrm{A}*}+w_2^{\mathrm{A}}=\lambda$$

the sequences $\{c_t^{\mathrm{A}*}\}_{t=2}^{\infty}$, $\{m_t^{\mathrm{A}*}\}_{t=3}^{\infty}$ solve the problem of agent type A. But given $m_0^{\mathrm{A}*}=\lambda$ this implies that $\{c_t^{\mathrm{A}*}\}_{t=0}^{\infty}$ and $\{m_t^{\mathrm{A}*}\}_{t=1}^{\infty}$ solve the problem of agent type A, as desired.

Proof of Proposition 2.4

By construction, the market-clearing condition of an equilibrium is satisfied, and so it remains to verify that the specification of the proposition is consistent with maximization. This will be done explicitly for agent type A.

Consider first any consumption sequence $\{c_t^{\mathrm{A}}\}_{t=0}^{\infty}$ and its associated money balance sequence $\{M_t\}_{t=1}^{\infty}$ which satisfy the budget constraint (2.5) as an equality, that is,

$$M_t^{\mathrm{A}}=p^*c_t^{\mathrm{A}}+M_{t+1}^{\mathrm{A}} \qquad t \geqslant 0,\ t \text{ even} \tag{2.A6}$$

$$p^*y_{t+1}^{\mathrm{A}}+M_{t+1}^{\mathrm{A}}=p^*c_{t+1}^{\mathrm{A}}+M_{t+2}^{\mathrm{A}} \qquad t \geqslant 0,\ t \text{ even} \tag{2.A7}$$

Solving (2.A6) for M_{t+1}^{A} and substituting into (2.A7) yields

$$p^*c_t^A + p^*c_{t+1}^A = p^*y_{t+1}^A + M_t^A - M_{t+2}^A \qquad t \geqslant 0,\ t \text{ even} \qquad (2.A8)$$

From (2.A6) also, with $M_{t+1}^{A} \geqslant 0$,

$$p^*c_t^A \leqslant M_t^A \qquad t \geqslant 0,\ t \text{ even} \qquad (2.A9)$$

Again following the methods of Lucas and Prescott (1971), it can be established that there exists a continuous bounded function $V(\cdot)$ which satisfies the functional equation

$$V(M_0^A) = \max_{M_2^A, c_0^A} \left[U(c_0^A) + \beta U \left\{ \frac{M_0^A + p^*y_1^A - M_2^A - p^*c_0^A}{p^*} \right\} + \beta^2 V(M_2^A) \right]$$

subject to

$$0 \leqslant p^*c_0^A \leqslant M_0^A$$
$$0 \leqslant M_2^A \leqslant p^*y_1^A + M_0^A - p^*c_0^A$$

given $M_0^A \geqslant 0$. Here, then, the solution $(M_2^A, c_0^A) = \phi(M_0^A)$ is the stationary policy function which solves

$$\max_{\{c_t^A\},\{M_t^A\}} \sum_{\substack{t \geqslant 0 \\ t \text{ even}}} \beta^t \left\{ U(c_t^A) + \beta U\left(\frac{M_t^A + p^*y_{t+1}^A - M_{t+2}^A - p^*c_t^A}{p^*} \right) \right\}$$

subject to

$$0 \leqslant p^*c_t^A \leqslant M_t^A$$
$$0 \leqslant M_{t+2}^A \leqslant p^*y_{t+1}^A + M_t^A - p^*c_t^A$$

given $M_0^A \geqslant 0$. Thus there does exist a solution to the problem of agent A.

Clearly, the proposed solution satisfies (2.7) as an equality for $t \geqslant 0$, t even, and as an inequality for $t \geqslant 1$, t odd, that is,

$$\frac{U'(c_{t-1}^{A*})}{\beta U'(c_t^{A*})} = \frac{U'(c^{**})}{\beta U'(c^*)} = \frac{1}{\beta^2} > 1 \qquad t \geqslant 1,\ t \text{ odd} \qquad (2.A10)$$

Also, the budget constraint is satisfied as an equality in every period. Now fix $\hat{c}_0^A = c_0^{A*}$, $\hat{M}_1^A = M_1^{A*}$, and suppose that there exist a consumption sequence $\{\hat{c}_t^A\}_{t=1}^{\infty}$ and an associated money balance sequence $\{\hat{M}_t^A\}_{t=2}^{\infty}$ which do better than the proposed solution from $t=1$ onward. Consider the first-period τ for which $\hat{c}_\tau^A \neq c_\tau^{A*}$. Since (2.7) will be satisfied as an equality for $t \geqslant 2$, t even, it follows that $\tau \geqslant 1$ and is odd. Clearly, $\hat{c}_\tau^A > c_\tau^{A*}$ is not feasible, for with $\hat{c}_{\tau+1}^A > \hat{c}_{\tau+1}^{A*}$ also, we obtain $\hat{M}_{\tau+2}^A < 0$. Nor is $\hat{c}_\tau^A < c_\tau^{A*}$ possible. For in this case $\hat{c}_{\tau+1}^A < c_{\tau+1}^{A*}$ also, and $\hat{M}_{\tau+2}^A > 0$. Thus (2.7) must hold as an equality at $t=\tau+2$, and so from (2.A10) $\hat{c}_{\tau+2}^A < c_{\tau+2}^{A*}$, and so on. This cannot be an improvement. Thus $\{c_t^{A*}\}_{t=1}^\infty, \{M_t^{A*}\}_{t=2}^\infty$ is indeed maximal for agent A from $t=1$ onward and so, by the principle of optimality, is optimal from $t=2$ onward with c_1^{A*} and M_2^{A*} given. But this implies $\{c_t^{A*}\}_{t=0}^\infty, \{M_t^{A*}\}_{t=1}^\infty$ is maximal for agent A at $t=0$, as claimed. A virtually identical argument (without the last step) establishes that the specified solution is maximal for agent type B as well.

Finally, note that for agent A, for example, from (2.A10) and (2.6), $\theta_t^{A*} > 0$ for $t \geqslant 1$, t odd. Similarly, $\theta_t^{B*} > 0$ for $t \geqslant 0$, t even.

That the equilibrium allocation is nonoptimal is obvious from the fact that the consumption sequences are not constant. That it is Pareto superior to autarky is also obvious, but it is instructive to note that for agent A, for example, c^{**} dominates 0 in period 0, and the consumption pair (c^*, c^{**}) dominates the endowment pair $(1, 0)$ in periods $(t, t+1)$, $t \geqslant 1$, t odd.

Proof of Proposition 2.6

It is first established that the above specification is maximizing for the agent born at time $t \geqslant 0$. Consider first any consumption sequence $\{c_j(t)\}_{j=0}^\infty$ and associated money balance sequence $\{M_j(t)\}_{j=1}^\infty$ which satisfy the budget constraints (2.26) as equalities, $j \geqslant 0$, j even. Substitution for $M_{j+1}(t)$ yields

$$M_j(t) + p_{t+j}^{k*} y_j - M_{j+2}(t) = p_{t+j}^{k*} c_j(t) + p_{t+j+1}^{k*} c_{j+1}(t) \qquad (2.A11)$$

If we define real money balances $m_i(t) = M_i(t)/p_{t+i}^{k*}$, $i = j, j+2$, and recall the specified relationship

$$p_{t+j}^{k*} = p_{t+j+1}^{k*} = \frac{1}{\beta^2} p_{t+j+2}^{k*}$$

(2.A11) then yields

$$m_j(t) + y_j = c_j(t) + c_{j+1}(t) + \beta^2 m_{j+2}(t) \qquad j \geqslant 0, j \text{ even}$$

Now, holding $m_j(t)$ and $m_{j+2}(t)$ fixed, define real disposable income $d_j(t)$ by

$$d_j(t) = m_j(t) + y_j - \beta^2 m_{j+2}(t) \qquad j \geqslant 0, j \text{ even} \qquad (2.A12)$$

and consider the following problem in isolation:

$$\max_{c_j(t)\geqslant 0,\, c_{j+1}(t)\geqslant 0} [U\{c_j(t)\} + \beta U\{c_{j+1}(t)\}]$$

subject to

$$c_j(t) + c_{j+1}(t) = d_j(t)$$

Solving for the maximizing $c_j(t)$ and $c_{j+1}(t)$ as continuous functions of $d_j(t)$, substitution into the objective function then yields the bounded continuous indirect utility function, denoted here by $W\{d_j(t)\}$. Thus problem (2.4) reduces to

$$\max_{\{m_j(t)\}_j} \sum_{\substack{j\geqslant 0\\ j\,\text{even}}} \beta^j W\{d_j(t)\}$$

subject to (2.A12) and

$$m_j(t) \geqslant 0 \qquad j\geqslant 2, j \text{ even, given } m_0(t)\geqslant 0$$

Again the functional equation approach yields a stationary policy which solves this problem.

It is clear from the discussion preceding the proposition that the specified solution to problem 2.4 satisfies the necessary first-order conditions (2.28) as equalities. (The budget constraints also hold as equalities.) Now suppose that there exist a consumption sequence $\{\hat{c}_j(t)\}_{j=0}^{\infty}$ and an associated money balance sequence $\{\hat{m}_j(t)\}_{j=1}^{\infty}$ which do better than the proposed solution, and consider the first age g for which $\hat{c}_g(t) \neq c_g^*(t)$. A now familiar argument leads to a contradiction.

It follows from the principle of optimality that for any $h \geqslant 1$ the sequences $\{c_j^*(t)\}_{j=h}^{\infty}$, $\{m_j^*(t)\}_{j=h+1}^{\infty}$ are maximal for agent t given $m_h^*(t)$. But then, by symmetry, the sequences $\{c_j^*(-h)\}_{j=h}^{\infty}$, $\{m_j^*(-h)\}_{j=h+1}^{\infty}$ are maximal for the agent born at each period $-h$, given $m_h^*(-h)$, as we needed to show.

Notes

1 The terminology here is that of Wallace (1980).
2 But see the concluding section for a qualification to this statement.
3 The implications of such Clower constraints over and above the constraints implied by the technology of exchange are examined, however.
4 See Wallace (1980) and the discussion in Hahn (1973) on inessential money.

5 A case can be made that models of money with spatially separated agents are of interest in their own right, quite apart from providing an alternative to overlapping generations.

6 On an a priori basis this should not be a surprise; indeed, versions of the overlapping generations model have been criticized for producing optimal monetary equilibria. See Wallace (1980).

7 Cass et al. (1980) argue that the inefficiency of monetary equilibrium emerges in the overlapping generations model under alternative assumptions.

8 See Brunner and Meltzer (1971).

9 Recall the caveat at the end of section 1.

10 If there are limitations on the issue of IOUs, there can exist equilibria in which IOUs have value and are never redeemed. Such equilibria are virtually indistinguishable from equilibria with valued fiat money, as defined below.

11 This is left as an open question. It should be noted, however, that Grandmont and Younes (1972) establish certain results in the limit, at $\beta = 1$, using the overtaking criterion.

12 For the most part this section reports some results known to Lucas and his students and suggested by Lucas in various conversations; the interested reader is urged to consult Locay and Palmon (1978), on which this section draws heavily. The model is presented here both because it does not seem to be known generally and because it offers a natural comparison with the other two models.

13 Lucas's version of the Cass–Yaari model retains the circle.

14 It is curious to note that (2.35) corresponds to the transaction constraint in Grandmont and Younes (1972, 1973) for $k = 0$, a case which is not really analyzed there.

15 Grandmont and Younes (1972, 1973) establish all these results for the case $0 < k < 1$ in their transaction constraint.

16 Again we obtain asymptotic welfare results as $\beta \to 1$ (compare with the discussion at the end of section 2).

17 The example is due to Neil Wallace.

References

Bewley, T. (1980) The optimum quantity of money. In *Models of Monetary Economies*, eds J. Kareken and N. Wallace, pp. 169–210. Minneapolis, MN: Federal Reserve Bank of Minneapolis.

Brunner, K. and Meltzer, A.H. (1971) The uses of money: money in the theory of an exchange economy. *American Economic Review* 61, 784–805.

Bryant, J. (1979) The political economy of overlapping generations. Research Department Staff Report 43, Federal Reserve Bank of Minneapolis, Minneapolis, MN.

—— and Wallace, N. (1979) The inefficiency of interest-bearing national debt. *Journal of Political Economy* 87, 365–81.

—— and —— (1980) Open market operations in a model of regulated, insured intermediaries. *Journal of Political Economy* 88, 146–73.

Cass, D. and Yaari, M. (1966) A re-examination of the pure consumption loans model. *Journal of Political Economy* 74, 353–67.

——, Okuno, M. and Zilcha, I. (1980) The role of money in supporting the Pareto optimality of competitive equilibrium in consumption loan type models. In *Models of Monetary Economies*, eds J. Kareken and N. Wallace, pp. 13–48. Minneapolis, MN: Federal Reserve Bank of Minneapolis.

Clower, R.W. (1967) A reconsideration of the microfoundations of monetary theory. *Western Economic Journal* 6, 1–8.

—— (1970) Is there an optimal money supply? *Journal of Finance* 25, 425–33.

Feldman, A.M. (1973) Bilateral trading processes, pairwise optimality, and Pareto optimality. *Review of Economic Studies* 40, 463–73.

Friedman, M. (1969) *The Optimum Quantity of Money and Other Essays*. Chicago, IL: Aldine.

Grandmont, J.M. and Younes, Y. (1972) On the role of money and the existence of a monetary equilibrium. *Review of Economic Studies* 39, 355–72.

—— and —— (1973) On the efficiency of a monetary equilibrium. *Review of Economic Studies* 40, 149–65.

Hahn, F.H. (1965) On some problems of proving the existence of an equilibrium in a monetary economy. In *The Theory of Interest Rates*, eds F.H. Hahn and F.P.R. Brechling, pp. 126–35. London: Macmillan.

—— (1973) On the foundations of monetary theory. In *Essays in Modern Economics*, eds M. Parkin and A.R. Nobay, pp. 230–42. New York: Harper & Row.

Harris, M. (1979) Expectations and money in a dynamic exchange economy. *Econometrica* 47, 1403–19.

—— and Townsend, R.M. (1978) Allocation mechanisms for asymmetrically informed agents. GSIA Working Paper 35-76-77, Carnegie–Mellon University, Pittsburgh, PA. Reprinted in this volume as chapter 6.

—— and —— (1981) Resource allocation under asymmetric information. *Econometrica* 49(1), 33–64. Reprinted in this volume as chapter 7.

Johnson, H.G. (1970) Is there an optimal money supply? *Journal of Finance* 25, 435–42.

Kareken, J.H. and Wallace, N. (1977) Portfolio autarky: a welfare analysis. *Journal of International Economics* 7, 19–43.

—— and —— (1978) Samuelson's consumption–loan model with country-specific fiat monies. Research Department Staff Report 24, Federal Reserve Bank of Minneapolis, Minneapolis, MN.

Locay, L. and Palmon, O. (1978) The optimum quantity of money in a perfect foresight monetary model. Working Paper, University of Chicago.

Lucas, R.E., Jr (1972) Expectations and the neutrality of money. *Journal of Economic Theory* 4, 103–24.

—— (1980) Equilibrium in a pure currency economy. In *Models of Monetary Economies*, eds J. Kareken and N. Wallace, pp. 131–46. Minneapolis, MN: Federal Reserve Bank of Minneapolis.

—— and Prescott, E.C. (1971) Investment under uncertainty. *Econometrica* 39, 659–81.

Ostroy, J.M. (1973) The informational efficiency of monetary exchange. *American Economic Review* 63, 597–610.

—— and Starr, R.M. (1974) Money and the decentralization of exchange. *Econometrica* 42, 1093–113.

Prescott, E.C. and Townsend, R.M. (1980) Equilibrium under uncertainty: multi-agent statistical decision theory. In *Studies in Bayesian Econometrics and Statistics in Honor of Harold Jeffreys*, ed. A. Zellner, pp. 169–94. Amsterdam: North-Holland.

Samuelson, P.A. (1958) An exact consumption–loan model of interest with or without the social contrivance of money. *Journal of Political Economy* 66, 467–82.

—— (1968) What classical and neoclassical monetary theory really was. *Canadian Journal of Economics* 1, 1–15.

—— (1969) Nonoptimality of money holding under laissez faire. *Canadian Journal of Economics* 2, 303–8.

Shubik, M. (1973) Commodity money, oligopoly, credit and bankruptcy in a general equilibrium model. *Western Economic Journal* 11, 24–38.

—— (1980) The capital stock modified competitive equilibrium. In *Models of Monetary Economies*, eds J. Kareken and N. Wallace, pp. 97–130. Minneapolis, MN: Federal Reserve Bank of Minneapolis.

Townsend, R.M. (1978) Equilibrium with endogenous marketeers. Working Paper, Carnegie–Mellon University, Pittsburgh, PA.

—— (1979) Optimal contracts and competitive markets with costly state verification. *Journal of Economic Theory* 21(2), 265–93. Reprinted in this volume as chapter 5.

3

Circulating Private Debt: an Example with a Coordination Problem

with Neil Wallace

1 Introduction

A seemingly central observation for monetary economics is that some objects – often referred to as monies – appear in exchange much more frequently than others. In this chapter we present and study a model that generates a version of this observation for private securities; in the model, some securities are traded frequently, or circulate, whereas others are not. In this and other respects, the securities in our model resemble historically observed bills of exchange.

The model that we use to explain the existence of circulating securities is one of intertemporal trade in spatially and informationally separated markets. The assumption that trade occurs in separate markets has been used by Ostroy (1973), Ostroy and Starr (1974), and Harris (1979) to model the transaction patterns of commodities, and by Townsend (1980, this volume, ch. 2) to model that of fiat money. We use it here to model the transaction patterns of private securities. Adopting this assumption is consistent with the general view that fruitful theories of the pattern of exchange and of media of exchange require settings in which it is somehow difficult to carry out exchange.

Reprinted from *Contractual Arrangements for Intertemporal Trade*, eds E.C. Prescott and N. Wallace (Minneapolis, MN: University of Minnesota Press, 1987). A version of this chapter entitled "A model of circulating private debt" was presented at the Econometric Society Summer Meeting, Cornell University, June 16–19, 1982, and at seminars at several universities. Helpful comments from the participants of these seminars and from Alvin Roth and Allan Drazen are gratefully acknowledged. We are indebted to the Federal Reserve Bank of Minneapolis for financial support. However, the views expressed are those of the authors and not those of the Bank or the Federal Reserve System.

The difficulty of carrying out exchange under our assumptions shows up in two distinct ways. One is market incompleteness: it can happen that some physically feasible and beneficial trades cannot be accomplished. This, as we will see, is an obvious implication of our assumptions and therefore does not require extended discussion. The other is much less obvious: it turns out to resemble the problem in a Schelling pure coordination game.

As described by Schelling (1960), a *pure coordination game* is one in which there is no communication and no conflict, and in which the problem facing the players is to choose strategies that are coordinated. In our model, it can happen that the quantities of securities that are required to support an equilibrium and that are issued by individuals at the same time in spatially and informationally separated markets must satisfy restrictions not implied by individual maximization and by market clearing in each separate market. In other words, the utility-maximizing choices of quantities of securities – the strategies of individuals – are not in general unique but must somehow be coordinated across informationally separated markets if they are to be consistent with the existence of an equilibrium.

This (coordination) problem arises only in some versions of our model. In fact, there is a close connection between its appearance and that of circulating securities; the problem does not appear unless there is a role for circulating securities. In this sense, the model is consistent with the widely held view that problems – perhaps in the form of chaotic conditions – sometimes arise in credit markets with unregulated issue of private securities that play an important role in exchange.[1] Although this view is widely held, there are few, if any, other models that provide an interpretation of it.[2]

Our presentation is organized as follows. We begin in section 2 with an introductory description of our model and of the example we use to display the coordination problem. In section 3 we describe a somewhat general class of environments, introduce our notation, and formally describe our equilibrium concept. In section 4 we establish for our example equivalence between our equilibrium and that implied by complete date–location contingent markets with complete participation. In section 5, we use that equivalence to display the transaction patterns of the securities issued. Finally, in section 6 we use it to display the coordination problem.

2 Preliminary description: some example economies

We study setups with a finite number of finite-lived people who meet deterministically at prescribed locations and prescribed times. The example we focus on is an economy of four people who meet according to the pattern laid out in table 3.1. Although the coordination problem arises only in the four-period version of this setup, in this section we also comment on the two- and three-period versions. In this example, at date 1, persons 1 and 2 are together at location 1, whereas persons 3 and 4 are together at location 2. Persons 1 and 4 always stay at those locations, whereas persons 2 and 3 switch locations each period.

As regards commodities or consumption goods, we assume that there is one commodity for each location–date combination. Equivalently, we assume that there is one good that is indexed by location and date. The setup is pure exchange in the usual sense: goods indexed by one location–date combination cannot be transformed into goods indexed by another location–date combination; that is, there is no transportation, production, or storage technology for goods. If J denotes the number of locations and T the number of dates, the commodity space has dimensions JT. We assume that each person obtains utility from commodities and has positive endowments of commodities in a proper subset whose elements correspond to the location–date combinations that the person visits. In figure 3.1 we indicate by crosses the subspace of the $2T$ commodity space that is relevant in the above sense for each of the persons in the four-person four-period economy.

As regards private securities, we let the spatial separation limit trades in securities in what seems to be a natural way. First, at a particular time, a person can trade securities only with someone he or she meets. Second, although securities can be transported, they can move only with a person. Finally, we do not allow people to renege on their debts or to counterfeit others' debts. Securities or debts in our model take the form of promises to pay stated amounts of goods that are date and location specific. We assume that, if the promise is presented at the relevant date and location, then it is honored.

To suggest how these rules and our spatial separation work, we briefly describe some of their implications for the example in table 3.1.

If $T = 2$, that is, if the economy lasts only two periods, then no trade is possible in the table 3.1 economy under our security trading rules. For example, person 1 cannot sell a promise to person 2 because person 2 can neither redeem it at date 2 nor pass it on to person 4, who has no use for it at date 2, the assumed last date. Note in this connection that there is a

Table 3.1 Who meets whom when

	Location	
Date	1	2
1	(1, 2)	(3, 4)
2	(1, 3)	(2, 4)
3	(1, 2)	(3, 4)
4	(1, 3)	(2, 4)

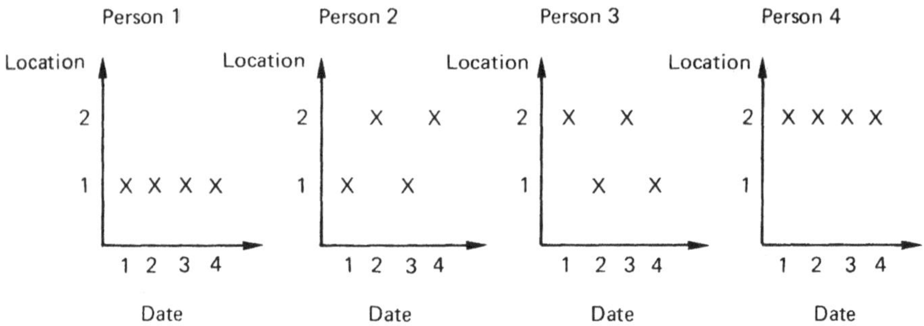

Figure 3.1. Relevant commodity subspaces in the economy shown in table 3.1

complete absence of double coincidence in the table 3.1, $T = 2$, example; as shown in figure 3.1, for $T = 2$ no pair of persons has endowments and cares about a common two-dimensional subspace of the commodity space. From what we have just seen, the kinds of private securities we allow do not at all overcome this particular absence of double coincidence. Note, by the way, that there is potentially something to overcome in the sense that there can exist redistributions of the endowments that give rise to allocations that are Pareto superior to the endowment allocation. Put differently, if all four people were together at some time zero and traded in complete (location- and date-contingent) markets, something we rule out, then the endowment would not necessarily be a competitive equilibrium.

If $T = 3$ in the table 3.1 economy, our rules are consistent with some trade in private securities. It is easy to see, however, that only the following kinds of securities are traded: persons who meet at date 1 can trade debts due at date 3 when they meet again. For example, person 1 can issue a promise to pay a good at location 1, date 3, a promise that person 2 holds until he or she again meets person 1. Thus, such securities do not circulate; they are not traded in a secondary market and are not used to make third-party payments. Corresponding to this noncirculating characteristic is the fact that such securities do no more than accomplish trades for which there is a double coincidence. For example, as is clear from figure 3.1, persons 1 and 2 have a double coincidence between goods at location 1, date 1, and goods at location 1, date 3. Note also that there remains a degree of market incompleteness in the $T = 3$ economy; in particular, the two goods at date 2 cannot be traded.

If $T = 4$ in the table 3.1 economy, then our security trading rules are consistent not only with the existence of several noncirculating securities but also with the existence of several circulating securities. At date 1, person 1 can issue to person 2 a promise to pay a good at location 1, date 4. This promise can be redeemed by being passed from person 2 to person 4 at date 2, from person 4 to person 3 at date 3, and from person 3 to person 1 – the issuer – at date 4. Similarly, each of persons 2, 3, and 4 can issue at date 1 a promise of a good at date 4 at some location. Whether such securities are in fact issued is one of the questions taken up below.

3 Debt equilibria in the general spatial separation setup

In this section we describe the general class of economies under consideration and define a competitive debt equilibrium.

We assume an economy with G persons, each of whom lives T periods. At each time t, each person g can be paired with some other person or with no one. These pairings occur at (isolated) locations. Thus we assume that person g is assigned to some location i at each time t and that in that location there either is or is not a single trading partner. We let there be $J \geqslant G/2$ locations.

If person g is in location i at time t, then he or she is endowed with some positive number w_{it}^g of units of the consumption good at location i, date t. For other location–date combinations, the endowment is zero. Let w^g denote the entire JT-dimensional endowment vector for person g. Also let c_{it}^g denote the nonnegative number of units of location i–date t consumption of person g and let c^g denote the entire JT-dimensional consumption vector for person g. The preferences of each person g are described by a utility function $U^g(c^g)$ that is continuous, concave, and strictly increasing in the T-dimensional subspace that is relevant for g.

We restrict attention to securities that can be redeemed. Thus, if d_{st}^f, which is nonnegative, denotes securities issued by person f at time s to pay d_{st}^f units of the consumption good where f will be at time t, we consider only triplets (f, s, t) with the property that there is a path or chain of pairings leading from where f is at s to where f is at t.

We let $p_{st}^f(i, u)$ be the price per unit of d_{st}^f at location i, date u, in units of good (i, u). However, we define such a price only for pairs (i, u) that potentially admit of a nontrivial trade in d_{st}^f. (This allows us to avoid having to determine a price for d_{st}^f in a market where demand and supply are identically zero and also allows us to restrict attention to positive prices.) Thus, suppose that h and g meet at (i, u). We say that h is a *potential demander* of d_{st}^f at (i, u) if there is a route from h at u to f at t. We say that h is a *potential supplier* of d_{st}^f at (i, u) if there is a route from f at s to h at u. We say that there is a *market* in d_{st}^f at (i, u) if and only if h is a potential demander and g is a potential supplier at (i, u), or vice versa.

We let $d_{st}^{fg}(i, u)$ be the excess demand by g at (i, u) for d_{st}^f. In terms of this notation, our debt trading rules are

$$\sum_{u=s}^{t} d_{st}^{ff}(\cdot, u) \geqslant 0 \qquad \text{for each } f$$

$$\sum_{u=s}^{t'} d_{st}^{fg}(\cdot, u) \geqslant 0 \qquad \text{for each } t' \geqslant s \text{ and } g \neq f \tag{3.1}$$

where, in each case, the locations range over those that the demander visits. The first inequality says that f must end up demanding as much as f issues, which expresses our no-reneging rule. The second says that $g \neq f$ cannot supply d_{st}^{f} without having previously acquired it. Finally, as a convention, if there is not a market in d_{st}^{f} at (i, u), we set $d_{st}^{fg}(i, u) \equiv 0$.

Then, as budget constraints for any person g, we can write

$$w_{iu}^{g} \geqslant c_{iu}^{g} + \sum d_{st}^{fg}(i, u) p_{st}^{f}(i, u) \tag{3.2}$$

There are T such constraints, one for each (i, u) that g visits. The summation in (3.2) is over all securities – all (f, s, t) – for which a market exists at (i, u).

Now, if d^g denotes the vector of debt demands of g over *all* securities that can be issued, a vector that has many zeros, we can give the following definition of a debt equilibrium or a competitive perfect-foresight equilibrium under our security trading rules.

Definition.
A debt equilibrium is a specification of consumption and debt demands – c^g and d^g for each $g = 1, 2, \ldots, G$ – and positive security prices $p_{st}^{f}(i, u)$ such that (a) c^g and d^g maximize $U^g(c^g)$ subject to (3.1) and (3.2), and (b) $\Sigma_g(c_{iu}^{g} - w_{iu}^{g}) = 0$ for each (i, u) and $\Sigma_g d_{st}^{fg}(i, u) = 0$ for each (i, u) and all potentially redeemable d_{st}^{f}.

Although it may seem strange to be considering competitive (price-taking) equilibrium in markets with only two traders, everything we do also holds for setups in which each of our persons is a trader type and in which there are many traders of each type.

Although we do not appeal to a general existence result in what follows, we include, in the appendix, a proof that every economy in our class of spatial separation setups has a debt equilibrium. The proof draws heavily on Debreu (1959), although with modifications connected with the fact that the objects traded – the securities – are not ultimate consumption goods and are not bounded in an obvious way.

4 Debt equilibria and complete-markets equilibria

In this section we establish equivalence for the table 3.1, $T = 4$, economy between the equilibrium allocations and prices of complete date–location contingent markets and the allocations and prices of debt equilibria. This proves useful in describing the transaction pattern implications of the theory and the coordination problem. We begin by showing that any complete-markets equilibrium (CME) consumption allocation can be supported by a debt equilibrium (DE).

To show that any CME can be supported by a DE in the table 3.1, $T = 4$, economy, we start with a given CME. We describe this by individual consumption excess demands $e^g_{it} \equiv c^g_{it} - w^g_{it}$ and by associated prices s_{it} (in terms of an abstract unit of account). These constitute a CME if they satisfy

$$\sum_i \sum_t e^g_{it} s_{it} = 0 \qquad \text{for each } g \tag{3.3}$$

$$\sum_g e^g_{it} = 0 \qquad \text{for each } (i, t) \tag{3.4}$$

and if, in addition, for each g, the e^g_{it} are utility maximizing for g subject to (3.3).

A corresponding DE consists of positive debt prices and nonnegative market-clearing debt quantities such that (a) the debt quantities and the given CME e^g_{it} satisfy each person's debt budget constraints and (b) the debt quantities and the given CME e^g_{it} are utility maximizing for each person given those debt prices.

Our first step is to produce candidate debt prices for the table 3.1, $T = 4$, economy. This candidate is produced by matching the terms of trade between consumption goods implied by unconstrained trades in debts to the corresponding terms of trade given by the CME prices. Thus, for example, for person 1, $p^1_{14}(1, 1)$ implies a trade between goods at location 1, date 1, and location 1, date 4. (Recall that, given our way of measuring debt quantities, $p^1_{14}(1, 4) = 1$.) Thus we let $p^1_{14}(1, 1) = s_{14}/s_{11}$. In general, then, each debt price is taken to be a ratio of CME prices with the numerator corresponding to the redemption location–date and the denominator to the location–date of the current trade.

For noncirculating debts, then, our candidate is

$$\begin{aligned} &\{p^1_{13}(1, 1), p^3_{13}(2, 1), p^1_{24}(1, 2), p^2_{24}(2, 2)\} \\ &= \{p^2_{13}(1, 1), p^4_{13}(2, 1), p^3_{24}(1, 2), p^4_{24}(2, 2)\} \\ &= (s_{13}/s_{11}, s_{23}/s_{21}, s_{14}/s_{12}, s_{24}/s_{22}) \end{aligned} \tag{3.5}$$

whereas, for circulating debts, it is

$$\begin{bmatrix} p_{14}^1(1,1), p_{14}^1(2,2), p_{14}^1(2,3) \\ p_{14}^2(1,1), p_{14}^2(1,2), p_{14}^2(2,3) \\ p_{14}^3(2,1), p_{14}^3(2,2), p_{14}^3(1,3) \\ p_{14}^4(2,1), p_{14}^4(1,2), p_{14}^4(1,3) \end{bmatrix} = \begin{bmatrix} s_{14}/s_{11}, s_{14}/s_{22}, s_{14}/s_{23} \\ s_{24}/s_{11}, s_{24}/s_{12}, s_{24}/s_{23} \\ s_{14}/s_{21}, s_{14}/s_{22}, s_{14}/s_{13} \\ s_{24}/s_{21}, s_{24}/s_{12}, s_{24}/s_{13} \end{bmatrix} \tag{3.6}$$

We can immediately indicate that this shows that satisfaction of (a) implies satisfaction of (b). To see this, multiply the debt constraint for e_{it}^g (equation (3.2)) by s_{it} and sum over i and t. Using (3.5) and (3.6) gives the result as (3.3) in which debt quantities do not appear. Thus, at prices given by (3.5) and (3.6), the debt constraints for any person are at least as constraining as (3.3). Therefore, if we can produce market-clearing debt quantities d_{st}^f which make the CME e_{it}^g feasible choices subject to the budget constraints (3.2), then they are certainly utility-maximizing choices. That is, (a) implies (b).

To motivate how we produce debt quantities, recall that a CME consists of arbitrary s_{it} and e_{it}^g that satisfy (3.3) and (3.4), and zero restrictions for those e_{it}^g that correspond to (i, t) that g does not visit. For the table 3.1, $T = 4$, economy, there are $3 + 8 + 16$ *independent* constraints on the 32 e_{it}^g. This leaves us free to choose five e_{it}^g arbitrarily, but not any five. For example, e_{11}^1 and e_{11}^2 cannot both be chosen arbitrarily because (3.4) and the zero restrictions imply that these sum to zero. Similarly, e_{11}^1, e_{12}^1, e_{13}^1, and e_{14}^1 cannot each be chosen arbitrarily since (3.3) must be satisfied. We arrive at candidates for equilibrium debt quantities by finding some that satisfy constraints (3.1) and (3.2) and the relevant debt market-clearing conditions for a set of e_{it}^g that can be chosen arbitrarily.

For the table 3.1, $T = 4$, economy, the following equations are the debt budget constraints, at prices satisfying (3.5) and (3.6), for five e_{it}^g that *can* be chosen arbitrarily:

$$(e_{21}^4, e_{22}^4, e_{11}^1, e_{12}^1, e_{13}^1)' = Ad \tag{3.7}$$

where

$$A = \begin{bmatrix} s_{23}/s_{21} & 0 & 0 & 0 & 0 & 0 & -s_{14}/s_{21} & s_{24}/s_{21} \\ 0 & s_{24}/s_{22} & 0 & 0 & -s_{14}/s_{22} & 0 & s_{14}/s_{22} & 0 \\ 0 & 0 & s_{13}/s_{11} & 0 & s_{14}/s_{11} & -s_{24}/s_{11} & 0 & 0 \\ 0 & 0 & 0 & s_{14}/s_{12} & 0 & s_{24}/s_{12} & 0 & -s_{24}/s_{12} \\ 0 & 0 & -1 & 0 & 0 & 0 & -s_{14}/s_{13} & s_{24}/s_{13} \end{bmatrix}$$

and $d = (d^4_{13} - d^3_{13}, d^4_{24} - d^2_{24}, d^1_{13} - d^2_{13}, d^1_{24} - d^3_{24}, d^1_{14}, d^2_{14}, d^3_{14}, d^4_{14})'$. Note that zeros in the matrix A do not denote zero debt prices, but rather that the particular debt cannot be traded at the relevant location–date combination. Note also that the relevant debt market-clearing conditions are imposed in equation (3.7). Thus, for example, the equilibrium demands for d^3_{14} at dates 1, 2, and 3 are imposed in the first, second, and fifth equations respectively of (3.7).

To see that there are *nonnegative* debt quantities that satisfy (3.7) for arbitrary s_{it} and an arbitrary left-hand side of (3.7), consider an equivalent set of equations obtained by replacing the last equation of (3.7) by itself plus a multiple s_{11}/s_{13} of the third equation, namely

$$[e^4_{21}, e^4_{22}, e^1_{11}, e^1_{12}, e^1_{13} + (s_{11}/s_{13})e^1_{11}]' = \{A_1, A_2, A_3, A_4, A_5 + (s_{11}/s_{13})A_3\}'d \tag{3.8}$$

where A_i denotes the ith row of the matrix A. Note that in each of the first four equations of (3.8), there appears (with a nonzero coefficient) a difference between noncirculating debts that does not appear in any other equation. Thus, for any quantities of the other debts, each of the first four equations can be satisfied by choosing *nonnegative* quantities of the noncirculating debts that appear in that equation only. This allows us to choose nonnegative quantities of the circulating debts in any way that satisfies the last equation of (3.8), namely

$$e^1_{13} + (s_{11}/s_{13})e^1_{11} = (s_{14}/s_{13})(d^1_{14} - d^3_{14}) - (s_{24}/s_{13})(d^2_{14} - d^4_{14}) \tag{3.9}$$

Equation (3.9) is easily satisfied; if the left-hand side is positive (negative), it can be satisfied by setting at zero all but d^1_{14} (d^3_{14}).

Given debt quantities that satisfy (3.8), all that remains is to show that they, (3.5) and (3.6), and the 11 other potentially nonzero CME e^g_{it} satisfy the associated debt budget constraints. Two facts imply that they do. First, if, for any g, three debt budget constraints are satisfied at equality (as they are for person 1), then the fourth is also; note that we have already referred to the fact that (3.5) and (3.6) imply that the debt budget constraints satisfy (3.3). Second, we know that if g and h meet at (i, t), then the debt budget constraint for e^g_{it} is minus that for e^h_{it}. Thus, if debt prices and quantities are such that the debt budget constraint for g implies the CME e^g_{it}, then the debt budget constraint for h implies minus the CME e^g_{it}. But, by (3.4), this is the CME value of e^h_{it}. This concludes our argument that any CME for the table 3.1, $T = 4$, economy can be supported by a DE.

The converse – that any DE consumption excess demands are also CME excess demands in the table 3.1, $T = 4$, economy – is established in the appendix.

5 Debt equilibrium transaction patterns

We now show that most table 3.1, $T=4$, environments imply, rather than just permit, the existence of several private securities that play different roles in exchange. We then describe two ways of summarizing these different roles.

The coexistence of circulating and noncirculating private debts can be demonstrated using the equivalence results of section 4. That is, for some setups for which DEs and CMEs coincide, we now show that some CMEs can be supported *only* by DEs with both circulating and noncirculating securities.

From (3.9), if $e_{13}^1+(s_{11}/s_{13})e_{11}^1 \neq 0$, then some circulating debt, d_{14}^h for some h, must be positive. Notice also that by multiplying the fifth equation of (3.7) by s_{13}/s_{21} and subtracting it from the first, we obtain an equation for $e_{21}^4-(s_{13}/s_{21})e_{13}^1$ that contains only noncirculating debts. Thus, if a table 3.1, $T=4$, setup is such that any CME satisfies $e_{13}^1+(s_{11}/s_{13})e_{11}^1 \neq 0$ and $e_{21}^4-(s_{13}/s_{21})e_{13}^1 \neq 0$, then every DE for that setup displays positive amounts of both circulating and noncirculating debts.[3]

We now describe two ways of summarizing the different exchange roles played by the different objects in debt equilibria in our setups. One way is in terms of a payments matrix (see Clower, 1967); the other is in terms of transaction velocities.

By a payments matrix we mean an $N \times N$ matrix, where N is the number of objects observed in a debt equilibrium, in which the (i,j)th element is unity if object i is observed to trade for object j and is zero otherwise. Thus, for a table 3.1, $T=4$, economy, N equals the number of distinct consumption goods – eight – plus the number of distinct private securities issued in an equilibrium. If the transaction pattern is such that each consumption good is traded for one circulating and one noncirculating security, then there are two nonzero elements in each row corresponding to a consumption good or to a noncirculating debt, and there are four in each row corresponding to a circulating debt. Note, by the way, that nontrivial spatial setups seem not to produce equilibria in which *one* object trades for *every* other object.

By the transaction velocity of an object, we mean the ratio of the average amount traded per date to the average stock, a pure number per unit time. For example, for a table 3.1, $T=4$, economy, the following transaction velocity pattern among objects shows up in a debt equilibrium. For a consumption good at location i, date t, the *average* stock outstanding can be taken to be the total endowment divided by 4 (at dates other than t, the stock of this good is zero), whereas the average amount traded per date is the amount traded at t divided by 4. Thus the transaction velocity is in the interval $(0,1)$. Computed in a similar way, the transaction velocity of noncirculating debt in such an economy is $2/3$ (such debt is outstanding for three dates and the entire stock is traded at two of those dates), whereas that of circulating debt is unity (the maximum possible velocity given our choice of time unit).

Thus, either in terms of a payments matrix or in terms of the pattern of transaction velocities across objects, our setups can imply different exchange roles for different objects and, in particular, a relatively prominent exchange role for what we have been calling circulating debt.

6 The coordination problem

Although a debt equilibrium exists in a table 3.1, $T=4$, economy, there is a difficulty in arriving at debt quantities that achieve it. This difficulty can be described as follows.

Individual equilibrium debt demands are correspondences, not functions; that is, when faced with equilibrium debt prices, each of many vectors of debt quantities achieves a given equilibrium vector of consumption for each individual. Of course, not surprisingly, in order to be a debt equilibrium, the vectors chosen from these individual correspondences must satisfy a restriction. In particular, the quantities of circulating debts must satisfy equation (3.9), which we rewrite here as

$$d_{14}^{1}-(s_{24}/s_{14})d_{14}^{2}=b+d_{14}^{3}-(s_{24}/s_{14})d_{14}^{4} \tag{3.10}$$

where $b=(s_{13}/s_{14})\{e_{13}^{1}+(s_{11}/s_{13})e_{11}^{1}\}$. Equation (3.10) says that a linear function of the circulating debts issued in location 1 must equal a linear function of those issued in location 2. What distinguishes this situation from others in which demands are correspondences is that, if people in one location at date 1 do not observe the quantities issued in the other location at date 1, then whether a vector of debt quantities is consistent or inconsistent with equation (3.10) is not revealed at date 1. Corresponding to any nonnegative pair of circulating debts issued in location 1 at date 1 is a net trade of noncirculating debts in location 1 at date 1, with a magnitude of $d_{13}^{1}-d_{13}^{2}$, consistent with the equilibrium date 1, location 1 consumption trade and with market clearing in the debts traded in location 1 at date 1 (see the third row of equation (3.8)). A similar situation prevails in location 2 at date 1 (see the first row of equation (3.8)). Only at date 2 and thereafter is it revealed whether the quantities chosen at date 1 are consistent with equation (3.10) and hence with equilibrium consumption trades at subsequent dates.

We call this difficulty a coordination problem because arriving at quantities that satisfy equation (3.10) calls for communication across locations, which is precluded by assumption. In that respect, our situation resembles those described by Schelling (1960) as giving rise to coordination problems. The absence of communication across locations is, by the way, consistent with one interpretation of our concept of a perfect-foresight equilibrium. That concept can be interpreted to mean that each person knows the endowments and preferences of each other person and hence knows the equilibrium consumption excess demands and debt prices. Such knowledge is consistent with people in one location not knowing the debt quantities issued in the other location.

Our coordination problems bears some resemblance to a result obtained by Ostroy (1973) and Ostroy and Starr (1974) in their study of the decentralization of exchange. In their model, knowledge of equilibrium prices of commodities is not enough to guide people to the trades that produce the equilibrium allocation in one round of bilateral trading if the trading rules are informationally decentralized. In our model, knowledge of current and future equilibrium prices of securities is not enough to guide people to the quantities of securities required to support an equilibrium if security transactions in other markets are not observed. Of course, both private debt in our model and money in their model alleviate a *quid pro quo* requirement and facilitate the attainment of equilibrium. There is a sense, though, in which the monetary exchange process is informationally centralized in their model. It requires that budget balance information be transmitted to a monetary authority or that there be implicit agreement about which commodity is to be used to cover budget deficits and surpluses. One interpretation of our coordination problem is that a debt equilibrium also requires centralization.

7 Concluding remarks

As promised, we have described a class of environments that, in general, give rise to private securities that circulate. The crucial feature in our environments is separated or segmented markets among which people move over time. We have also demonstrated that, in some of the environments in which circulating securities appear, a problem resembling a Schelling coordination problem also appears. Since there is nothing particularly strange about our physical environment or our security trading rules and equilibrium concept, we believe that the model shows promise as an explanation for why actual credit markets appear not to work well at times. However, except for breaking down barriers to communication, the model does not suggest to us any way of solving the coordination problem.

Appendix

Existence of a debt equilibrium

Here we prove that the debt equilibrium defined in section 3 exists. We first prove existence with imposed arbitrary bounds on debt demands. We then argue by taking the appropriate limit that there exists some equilibrium.

Let C be the space of JT-tuples, each element of which is in $[0, w]$, where $w > w_{iu}$ for all (i, u) and where w_{iu} is the social endowment of good (i, u). Also let D be the space of n-tuples, each element of which is in $[-d, d]$, where $d > 0$ and where n is the number of elements in d^g. Note that d is the arbitrary bound on debt demands. Let P^h_{st} be the n'-dimensional simplex for d^h_{st}, where n' is the number of location–date combinations where there is a market for d^h_{st}, and let P be the product space of the P^h_{st}, a finite product of finite-dimensional simplexes. Finally, for each $p \in P$, let $\gamma^g(p, w^g) = \{(c^g, d^g) \in C \times D$ that satisfy constraints (3.1) and (3.2)$\}$. We are now in a position to follow Debreu's (1959) proof of the existence of a standard competitive equilibrium.

Since $C \times D$ restricted by (3.1) and (3.2) is compact and convex, it follows from (1) of section 4.8 of Debreu (p. 63), modified for vector constraints, that $\gamma^g(p, w^g)$ is a continuous correspondence in p. The key to this assertion is that the right-hand side of (3.2) takes a value of zero at zero consumption and debt demands. Since zero is strictly less than w^g_{iu}, the exceptional case of minimum wealth does not occur.

Now, since the bounded competitive maximization problem of g involves maximizing a continuous function on a compact set, there exists a nonempty maximizing correspondence of security demands denoted $\phi^g(p)$. By theorem 4 of section 1.8 of Debreu (p. 19), $\phi^g(p)$ is upper semicontinuous; it is also convex. Now let $\Phi(p) = \Sigma_g \phi^g(p)$. Clearly, $\Phi(p)$ is in the space of n-tuples, each element of which is in the interval $[-Gd, Gd]$. We denote this compact convex set by Z.

Now consider the correspondence ρ from $P \times Z$ into itself defined by $\rho(p, z) = \mu(z) \times \Phi(p)$, where $\mu(z) = \{p \in P$ that maximize pz for $z \in Z\}$. Following Debreu (p. 82), $\mu(z)$ is an upper semicontinuous correspondence from Z to P with $\mu(z)$ nonempty and convex. It follows that $\rho(p, z)$ is a nonempty, upper semicontinuous, and convex correspondence on $P \times Z$, which is a nonempty, compact, and convex set. Therefore ρ has a fixed point, namely (p^*, z^*) such that $p^* \in \mu(z^*)$ and $z^* \in \Phi(p^*)$.

We now establish that $\Phi(p^*) = 0$. Consider the subvector of $\Phi(p^*)$ associated with a particular debt d^h_{st}. If this subvector is not zero, then some element must be positive because constraint (3.1) does not permit the sum of these elements to be negative. Therefore suppose that some elements of the subvector are positive. The correspondence μ sets debt prices at positive levels for at least one of these positive elements and for no nonpositive element. This, in turn, implies that more of d^h_{st} is being demanded at positive prices over all location–date combinations than is being supplied at positive prices. This contradicts individual maximization for someone and hence implies that the subvector of $\Phi(p^*)$ associated with d^h_{st} is zero. It follows that $\Phi(p^*) = 0$. Moreover, a similar argument implies that no component of p^* can be zero.

We can now show that the consumptions implied by z^* and p^* satisfy market clearing for each (i, u). For each g, individual maximization implies that (3.2) holds with equality. Therefore suppose that we sum (3.2) at a given (i, u) over g. Then market clearing in consumptions follows from $\Phi(p^*) = 0$.

We have thus established the existence of a debt equilibrium with arbitrary imposed debt bounds d. If we double these bounds, we can again establish existence. Continuing in this way, we can construct a sequence of debt equilibria for economies with larger and larger debt bounds. As the associated sequence of debt equilibrium prices and consumptions has elements in the same compact space, there exists a convergent subsequence – say with limit prices and consumptions $\bar{p}$ and $\bar{c}^g$ respectively.

Now consider the problem confronting a typical person g in the limit economy at prices $\bar{p}$ and no imposed debt bounds whatever. The space of feasible consumptions for such a person (the budget set at prices $\bar{p}$ projected onto the space of consumptions) is compact and the objective function is continuous, and so there exists a solution – some maximizing choice of consumptions $\hat{c}^g$. Also, by construction, $\bar{c}^g$ is feasible in the limit economy. Suppose that $U^g(\hat{c}^g) > U^g(\bar{c}^g)$. Then for some kth economy associated with the convergent subsequence, with debt bounds sufficiently large and prices sufficiently close to $\bar{p}$, we can find a feasible consumption vector with utility arbitrarily close to $U^g(\hat{c}^g)$. But along the convergent subsequence, utility must converge to $U^g(\bar{c}^g)$. We have thus contradicted maximization for person g in the kth economy. Thus $U^g(\hat{c}^g) = U(\bar{c}^g)$, and $\bar{c}^g$ solves the maximization problem of person g in the limit economy. Recall that person g was arbitrary.

We have thus established that consumptions $\bar{c}^g$ are all maximizing in the limit economy. Also, by construction, the $\bar{c}^g$ satisfy market clearing in the limit economy (this was a property of each economy in the convergent subsequence, by virtue of equilibrium). It only remains then to specify market-clearing debt demands for each person g in the budget set of persons g and consistent with the choice of $\bar{c}^g$. This is done as follows. First, specify person 1's debt demands in his or her budget set consistent with $\bar{c}^1$. For market clearing, let these determine the debt demands of each person with whom person 1 trades at specified dates and locations. Next, consider person 2. If there are no debt demands that remain to be determined for this person, then we are done. To suppose otherwise is to contradict the fact that $\bar{c}^1$ and $\bar{c}^2$ are market clearing and the fact that person 1's debt demands are in the budget set of person 1. If any debts remain to be determined, choose these consistent with $\bar{c}^2$. Continue in this way for person 3, and so on through person G. In the end, then, we have constructed an equilibrium in the limit economy, with no bounds on debts. Recall also that the (fixed) bounds on consumptions need not be imposed in the limit economy, by the choice of the bound w.

Debt equilibrium excess demands imply complete markets equilibrium excess demands

We now prove for the table 3.1, $T=4$, economy that any DE consumption excess demands are also CME consumption excess demands.

Since the DE e^q_{it} are market clearing – that is, satisfy (3.4) – we have to show only that the debt budget constraints are equivalent to (3.3) for some choice of s_{it}; if we can establish that equivalence, then it follows that the DE e^q_{it} are utility maximizing subject to (3.3).

The debt budget constraints for person 1 in the table 3.1, $T=4$, economy can be written

$$\begin{aligned} e^1_{11} &= -d^{11}_{13}(1,1)p^1_{13}(1,1) - d^{21}_{13}(1,1)p^2_{13}(1,1) \\ &\quad - d^{11}_{14}(1,1)p^1_{14}(1,1) - d^{21}_{14}(1,1)p^2_{14}(1,1) \\ e^1_{12} &= -d^{11}_{24}(1,2)p^1_{24}(1,2) - d^{31}_{24}(1,2)p^3_{24}(1,2) \\ &\quad - d^{21}_{14}(1,2)p^2_{14}(1,2) - d^{41}_{14}(1,2)p^4_{14}(1,2) \\ e^1_{13} &= -d^{11}_{13}(1,3) - d^{21}_{13}(1,3) - d^{31}_{14}(1,3)p^3_{14}(1,3) - d^{41}_{14}(1,3)p^4_{14}(1,3) \\ e^1_{14} &= -d^{11}_{24}(1,4) - d^{31}_{24}(1,4) - d^{11}_{14}(1,4) - d^{31}_{14}(1,4) \end{aligned}$$

Let us add and subtract $d^{21}_{13}(1,1)p^1_{13}(1,1)$ on the right-hand side of the first equation, so that the sum $-\{d^{11}_{31}(1,1)+d^{21}_{13}(1,1)\}$ appears. Note that the sum $d^{11}_{13}(1,3)+d^{21}_{13}(1,3)$ appears in the third equation and that these sums are equal to each other because, at any debt prices, debt demands satisfy $d^{11}_{13}(1,1)=-d^{11}_{13}(1,3)$ and $d^{21}_{13}(1,1)=-d^{21}_{13}(1,3)$. Moreover, the sum $d^{11}_{13}(1,1)+d^{21}_{13}(1,1)$ is unconstrained (as to sign). These facts imply that the first and third equations are no more constraining than the single equation that results from substituting for that sum from the third equation into the first to produce

$$\begin{aligned} e^1_{11} + p^1_{13}(1,1)e^1_{13} &= d^{21}_{13}(1,1)\{p^1_{13}(1,1) - p^2_{13}(1,1)\} \\ &\quad - d^{11}_{14}(1,1)p^1_{14}(1,1) - d^{21}_{14}(1,1)p^2_{14}(1,1) \\ &\quad - d^{31}_{14}(1,3)p^3_{14}(1,3)p^1_{13}(1,1) \\ &\quad - d^{41}_{14}(1,3)p^4_{14}(1,3)p^4_{14}(1,3)p^1_{13}(1,1) \qquad (3.A1) \end{aligned}$$

An exactly analogous procedure allows us to combine the second and fourth equations into the following single equation, which is no less constraining than the separate equations:

$$e_{12}^1 + p_{24}^1(1,2)e_{14}^1 = d_{24}^{31}\{p_{24}^1(1,2) - p_{24}^3(1,2)\} - d_{14}^{21}(1,2)p_{14}^2(1,2)$$
$$- d_{14}^{41}(1,2)p_{14}^4(1,2) - p_{24}^1(1,2)\{d_{14}^{11}(1,4) + d_{14}^{31}(1,4)\} \tag{3.A2}$$

Now consider the first term on the right-hand side of (3.A1). If the price difference that multiplies $d_{13}^{21}(1,1)$ is positive, then $d_{13}^{21}(1,1)$ is infinite. Since that cannot be an equilibrium choice, it follows that the DE prices satisfy $p_{13}^1(1,1) \leqslant p_{13}^2(1,1)$; that is, arbitrage is not possible for person 1 in the debts d_{13}^1 and d_{13}^2. Also, since an analogous manipulation of the debt budget constraint for person 2 implies the reverse inequality, it follows that DE prices satisfy $p_{13}^1(1,1) = p_{13}^2(1,1)$. In addition, exactly the same reasoning allows us to conclude that the DE prices satisfy the entire first equality of equation (3.5).

We now proceed to combine (3.A1) and (3.A2) into a single constraint that is no less constraining than both (3.A1) and (3.A2). First, add and subtract $d_{14}^{31}(1,3)p_{14}^1(1,1)$ on the right-hand side of (3.A1) so that the sum $d_{14}^{11}(1,1) + d_{14}^{31}(1,3)$ appears in (3.A1). This sum of demands is equal at any debt prices to $-\{d_{14}^{11}(1,4) + d_{14}^{31}(1,3)\}$, which appears in (3.A2). Moreover, this sum is unconstrained, implying that the equation that results from eliminating it between (3.A1) and (3.A2) is no less constraining than both (3.A1) and (3.A2). This single equation, which we will not write out, has the following form: a linear combination of person 1's excess demands for consumption is equal to a linear combination of person 1's debt demands.

By an argument similar to that used above to establish that DE prices satisfy the first equality of equation (3.5) – an argument that uses the analogs of (3.A1) and (3.A2) for persons 2, 3, and 4 – it follows that the DE prices must be such that the coefficient of each debt demand is zero; that is, intertemporal arbitrage among the various debts must not be possible for anyone. These restrictions on coefficients of debt demands are those needed to be able to choose the s_{it} to satisfy equation (3.6). Also, such choices for the s_{it} imply equivalence between the debt constraints and (3.3).

To summarize, we have indicated how to manipulate the debt budget constraints for the table 3.1, $T=4$, economy so as to establish two results. The first is that security prices in a DE for that economy are constrained so that we can choose s_{it} to satisfy (3.5) and (3.6). Second, with that choice of s_{it}, debt constraints are equivalent to (3.3) so that the e_{it}^h that are utility maximizing subject to the debt constraints are also utility maximizing subject to (3.3). These results imply that any DE is a CME in the table 3.1, $T=4$, economy.

Notes

1 See, for example, Friedman's comments about private bank note issue and unfettered intermediation (Friedman, 1960, pp. 21, 108).

2 For two recent attempts very different from ours, see Bryant (1981) and Diamond and Dybvig (1983).

3 Coexistence of circulating and noncirculating securities can occur even if there is not a coincidence between DEs and CMEs; see Townsend and Wallace (1982) for an example.

References

Bryant, J. (1981) Bank collapse and depression. *Journal of Money, Credit, and Banking* 13, 454–64.

Clower, R. (1967) A reconsideration of the microfoundations of monetary theory. *Western Economic Journal* 6, 1–8.

Debreu, G. (1959) *The Theory of Value*. New York: Wiley.

Diamond, D.W. and Dybvig, P.H. (1983) Bank runs, deposit insurance, and liquidity. *Journal of Political Economy* 91, 401–19.

Friedman, M. (1960) *A Program for Monetary Stability*. New York: Fordham University Press.

Harris, M. (1979) Expectations and money in a dynamic exchange economy. *Econometrica* 47, 1403–20.

Ostroy, J.M. (1973) The informational efficiency of monetary exchange. *American Economic Review* 63, 597–610.

—— and Starr, R.M. (1974) Money and the decentralization of exchange. *Econometrica* 42, 1093–113.

Schelling, T. (1960) *The Strategy of Conflict*. Cambridge, MA: Harvard University Press.

Townsend, R. (1980) Models of money with spatially separated agents. In *Models of Monetary Economies*, eds J. Kareken and N. Wallace. Minneapolis, MN: Federal Reserve Bank of Minneapolis. Reprinted in this volume as chapter 2.

—— and Wallace, N. (1982) A model of circulating private debt. Staff Report 83, Federal Reserve Bank of Minneapolis.

4

Financial Structure and Economic Activity

A recent development in economic science is the attempt to integrate monetary theory with the theory of general economic equilibrium. This work takes as its starting point the idea that money cannot have value in standard general equilibrium models. In these, too much trade can be accomplished in centralized markets (see Clower, 1969, 1971; Hahn, 1973; Wallace, 1980). Thus, to decentralize or break up the structure, either exchange must be made costly or there must be restrictions on who can trade with whom, and thus such choice-theoretic models offer the intriguing possibility that real and monetary phenomena can be understood as intimately related.

This paper continues in the relatively brief choice-theoretic tradition, motivated by real and monetary phenomena associated with economic development and growth.

1 To be noted first is Simon Kuznets's seminal work on national income (Kuznets, 1971). In a cross-section study of 57 countries in 1958, Kuznets shows that the share of the agricultural sector, including forestry, fishing, and hunting, in gross domestic product (GDP) is inversely correlated with per capita GDP. The share of the industrial sector, including transportation and communication, is closely and positively associated with per capita GDP. The share of the service sector tends to be positively but weakly associated with per capita GDP, but the share of banking, insurance, and real estate

Reprinted from *American Economic Review* 73(5), 1983, 895–911. This chapter was motivated by a conversation with Thomas Sargent and has been aided by helpful comments from Robert Barro, Robert E. Lucas, Jr, Dan Peled, Kenneth Singleton, and Neil Wallace. Financial support from the National Science Foundation, the Alfred P. Sloan Foundation, and the Peterkin Symposium on Foundations of Monetary Policy and Government Finance at Rice University, and research assistance from Pramerudee Townsend are all gratefully acknowledged. The author alone assumes full responsibility for any errors and for the views expressed here.

shows a striking rise on shifting from low-income to higher-income countries. Moreover, the evidence suggests that the ratio of industrial prices to agricultural prices is perhaps lower for higher per capita incomes, though the evidence on relative prices for the service sector is inconsistent. Turning to long time series for 13 developed and four less developed countries, Kuznets finds dramatic evidence for a decline of the agricultural sector and a rise in the industrial sector with per capita income, at least in developed countries. Again, results for the service sector are mixed, but Canada, France, and the United States are positive exceptions. The share of a transport–communication subsector rises quite consistently. Turning next to shares of sectors in the labor force, Kuznets finds, on both a cross-sectional and a secular basis, that all the above movements are at least mirrored and in many cases amplified. In particular, both components of the share of the service sector, services and commerce, rise substantially with per capita GDP.

2 To be noted second is the extensive work of Raymond Goldsmith on financial structure and financial intermediation. For the United States, Goldsmith (1958) finds that the activity of intermediaries, as measured by their share in national assets, in tangible assets, and in all claims, has shown a substantial rise from 1860 to 1952. Similarly, Goldsmith (1969) finds that the ratio of financial institutions' assets to gross national product (GNP) rises substantially from 1860 to 1963 in both developed and less developed countries, including Switzerland, the United Kingdom, the United States, Japan, Argentina, and India. In a related manner, the number of households with savings accounts, the number with life insurance policies, and the number with stock ownership expressed as percentages of the population are all low for less developed countries relative to developed countries, and the first two measures tend to increase with per capita income.

3 To be noted third are the cross-sectional and secular studies of (aggregate) asset velocities. McKinnon (1973) shows that the ratio of a broad monetary aggregate M_2 to national income increases on moving from less developed to semi-industrialized countries. Moreover, the ratio of private credit to national income increases roughly with income per capita in cross-country comparisons, but the ratio of currency to income shows no systematic pattern (see section 8). McKinnon also shows that countries such as postwar Japan and Germany, which experienced high and sustained increases in national income over time, also experienced substantial increases in the ratio of M_2 to national income. This is also true of the ratio of private credit to income, though the ratio of currency to national income either remained constant or decreased slightly in these countries (see section 8). A rather substantial secular decline in the ratio of currency to national income is provided by the US experience, 1869–1929, as documented by Cagan (1965). (There has been a subsequent reversal.) The ratio of M_2 to national income increased substantially in this period.[1]

4 To be noted fourth is the long-standing controversy in macroeconomics over the relationship of various monetary aggregates to economic activity and whether the distinction should be made between money and credit. One of the more recent contributions is that of Friedman (1981).

Of course, we do not pretend to offer a model here which might account for the above-mentioned phenomena or settle any controversies. The degree of abstraction is too great. But we do seek to establish that choice-theoretic models can be used to address such observations and provide a useful conceptual framework. The key idea is that the degree of interconnectedness of traders determines both the amount of production and trade and the types of assets which are used to facilitate exchange. Thus real and monetary phenomena are indeed intimately related. Moreover, as we vary the degree of interconnectedness we can generate interesting co-movements, of per capita national income with economy-wide asset holdings, for example.

The basic model used in this chapter in terms of endowments, preferences, and technology is presented in section 1. It builds on Lucas's version of the Cass–Yaari (1966) circle as presented in Townsend (1980, this volume, ch. 2), modified here to allow for variable labor supply. Its key feature is the absence of double coincidence of wants for bilateral pairings, a feature which dates back to Wicksell (1935) at least. In a Robinson Crusoe economy, in which households are completely isolated from one another, each household can consume at most the fruits of its own labor. This autarkic exchange regime is described in section 2. In a structure with spatially separated markets (essentially with bilateral pairings), a highly stylized asset – fiat money – partially overcomes the absence of double coincidence of wants. The decentralized fiat money regime and its equilibrium are described in section 3. Such a regime is consistent with Clower's (1967) dictum that money buys goods and goods buy money, but goods do not buy goods. In a structure with centralized Walrasian markets, another stylized asset – trade credit – delivers Pareto optimal allocations. The centralized trade credit regime and its equilibrium are described in section 4. In it there is a sense in which goods buy goods.

It is next established that the cost of market-produced commodities relative to home-produced commodities is infinite in autarky and is high in the decentralized fiat money regime relative to the centralized trade credit regime. The essential idea is that fiat money from the sale of home-produced commodities is held for one period in the fiat money equilibrium (that is, has unit velocity), whereas trade credit can be used for contemporary purchases in the trade credit equilibrium (that is, has infinite velocity).[2] Thus, on the assumption that substitution effects dominate income effects, labor supply will increase, consumption of home-produced commodities will decrease, consumption of market-produced commodities will increase, trade will increase, and welfare will increase on moving from autarky to the decentralized fiat money regime to the centralized trade credit regime. A formal analysis of these substitution effects is given in section 5.

Finally, by consideration of countries with an internal mix of exchange regimes, we can deliver theoretical cross-country comparisons of the state of economic development. That is, we can examine how per capita consumption of home-produced and market-produced commodities, the volume of trade, the degree of financial intermediation, and per capita asset holdings all move with per capita income. Similarly, we can examine how these variables move in a country which becomes more centralized over time. In effect, this delivers a model of economic growth. In short, following Adam Smith, the specialization (division) of labor, the volume of trade, and the complexity of financial instruments are all limited by the extent of the market; all move in a systematic way with the degree of interconnectedness of the households. These cross-country comparisons and the growth model are discussed in sections 6 and 7 respectively.

The central idea of this chapter, that market fragmentation can play a key role in a theory of economic activity and in a theory of finance, is not new. Gurley and Shaw (1960), Goldsmith (1969), and McKinnon (1973) all accept this idea. Neither is the idea that structural change can cause systematic changes in economy-wide asset holdings new. Tobin (1965) claims that Friedman and Schwartz (1963) should have taken this into account in their explanation of the decline in US velocity, arguing in the spirit of Irving Fisher that

> ... an account of the demand for money [should be] closely tied to its function as means of payment. He [Fisher] would have wished to hear about the frequency and timing of wage payments and bill settlements, the speed and cost of communications, the trend of industrial integration, the scope of the barter and subsistence economy relative to the money economy, the volume of total transactions relative to income generating transactions, and so on. (Tobin, 1965, p. 473)

In fact, several cross-country studies of the demand for money (for example, Doblin 1951; Melitz and Correa, 1970) argue that institutional features should be taken into account. More recently, Bordo and Jonung (1981) offer a time series study of money velocity in five countries, explicitly using measures of the degree of monetization and financial sophistication to account for the typical U-shaped pattern of velocity. In fact, these measures are closely tied to the stylized facts mentioned at the outset, though the model specification is somewhat *ad hoc*. More generally, the work of Bordo and Jonung builds on Wicksell, especially his account of the substitution of credit for currency. What is new about the work in this chapter is that, at the cost of considerable abstraction, it presents an explicit model in the general equilibrium microeconomic tradition; that is, what is offered here is a highly stylized choice-theoretic model which accounts for the relationship between economic activity and financial structure. Again, the model should be regarded as a first step. Some of the obvious caveats are discussed in sections 8 and 9.

1 The underlying structure: preferences, endowments, and technology

Imagine an economy with a countable set of household types, indexed by the positive and negative integers, with a countable set of produced commodities, again indexed by the positive and negative integers, and with labor. Each household of type i can produce commodity i alone at date t by supplying labor at date t; the technology is linear, and so we can let n_{it} denote both labor supplied and produced output of commodity i. Suppose that labor supply is bounded from above. Suppose also that each household of type i cares about units of consumption c_{it} and $c_{i+1,t}$ of commodities i and $i+1$ respectively at date t, as well as units of labor supply n_{it}, and thus has preferences represented by a utility function $U(c_{it}, c_{i+1,t}, n_{it})$ which is strictly concave and continuously differentiable, strictly increasing in the first two arguments, and strictly decreasing in the third. Also, as will be made clear in section 5, the function $U(.,.,.)$ is such that substitution effects of price changes dominate income effects. Each household i discounts the future at rate β; that is, preferences over the infinite horizon of its lifetime are represented by the utility function

$$\sum_{t=0}^{\infty} \beta^t U(c_{it}, c_{i+1,t}, n_{it})$$

Many of the above assumptions can be relaxed, but the current model does allow rather tight characterizations of competitive equilibria in the autarkic, decentralized, and centralized versions of the economy.

2 The autarkic regime

Suppose that households are entirely isolated from one another, as if each were residing on a separate island. Then, in this Robinson Crusoe economy, each household makes a straightforward period-by-period, production–consumption decision: whatever is produced is consumed – there can be no trade. Thus, if we index the choices made by households of type i in parentheses after the variables, the problem confronting each household of type i is as follows.

Problem 4.1

$$\max \sum_{t=0}^{\infty} \beta^t U\{c_{it}(i), c_{i+1,t}(i), n_{it}(i)\} \tag{4.1}$$

by choice of $c_{it}(i), n_{it}(i)$ subject to

$$c_{it}(i) \leqslant n_{it}(i) \tag{4.2}$$

where $c_{i+1,t}(i) \equiv 0$, yielding necessary and sufficient first-order conditions for an interior maximum

$$U_1\{c_{it}(i), 0, n_{it}(i)\} = -U_3\{c_{it}(i), 0, n_{it}(i)\} \tag{4.3}$$

$$c_{it}(i) = n_{it}(i) \tag{4.4}$$

Now we can take the solution to (4.3) and (4.4) to be symmetric across household types i and constant over time, that is,

$$c_{it}(i) = \mathring{c}^1, c_{i+1,t}(i) = \mathring{c}^2 = 0, n_{it}(i) = \mathring{n}$$

for all the produced commodity, the nonproduced commodity, and the labor supply respectively. Note in particular that the consumption of the nonproduced commodity is identically zero. Finally note for subsequent reference that (4.3) and (4.4) can be cast in the form

$$\frac{U_1[\mathring{c}^1, \mathring{c}^2, \mathring{n}]}{U_2[\mathring{c}^1, \mathring{c}^2, \mathring{n}]} = \gamma \tag{4.5}$$

$$\frac{-U_3[\mathring{c}^1, \mathring{c}^2, \mathring{n}]}{U_2[\mathring{c}^1, \mathring{c}^2, \mathring{n}]} = \gamma \tag{4.6}$$

$$\mathring{c}^2 = \mathring{n} - \mathring{c}^1 \tag{4.7}$$

where it is assumed that γ is some positive real number less than the discount rate β and $\mathring{c}^2 = 0$.

3 A decentralized exchange regime with fiat money

A crucial feature that the decentralized regime will explain is the use of fiat money. To ensure this, imagine that, at date t, each household of type i can trade only with a household of type $i+1$ and a household of type $i-1$. Under the assumed preference orderings, the household of type i has no commodity that the household of type $i+1$ wants, and this creates the possibility for exchange of fiat money (see Lucas's version of the Cass–Yaari circle in Townsend (1980, this volume, ch. 2)). Moreover, to rule out private debt or futures contracts in fiat money, it is imagined that there is no chain of pairings or dealings among households such that debt can be redeemed by the issuer.

A timing–location scheme which generates these restrictions is displayed in figure 4.1. Each (representative) household of type i consists of a pair of agents and is imagined to be located on some real line at integer i. There are countably infinite such real lines, indexed by the positive and negative integers, and displayed on top of one another in figure 4.1. The integer i on each line is inhabited by a (representative) household of type i. At each date, each member of household type i is capable of moving horizontally (on the line where the household is located) half the distance to each of the two adjacent integers $i+1$ and $i-1$. Thus, at each date t, each household type i is physically capable of carrying out transactions with a household of type $i-1$ and a household of type $i+1$ in two spatially separated markets, say $(i-1, i)$ and $(i, i+1)$. Between dates, households move about. Each household of type i, i even, is imagined to move vertically downward to the next line, while each household of type i, i odd, stays in its fixed location. Thus, for example, debt issued by a household of type i, i even, can only be passed along to households vertically above the issuer. (See the turnpike exchange model in Townsend (1980, this volume, ch. 2) for a similar construction to prevent the issue of private debt.)

Now let $M_t(i)$ denote the number of units of fiat money carried over by household type i to the beginning of date t, a decision made at date $t-1$. Here again the i in parentheses indicates a decision made by household type i. Note also that here and below all households of type i are to be treated identically, independent of location. Let $M_0(i)$ denote a fixed initial condition at date zero. At the beginning of date t, household type i decides how much of commodity i to produce, surrendering the requisite labor. Then one member of household type i travels to market $(i-1, i)$ with some of commodity i and sells it for fiat money at price p_{it} in terms of fiat money

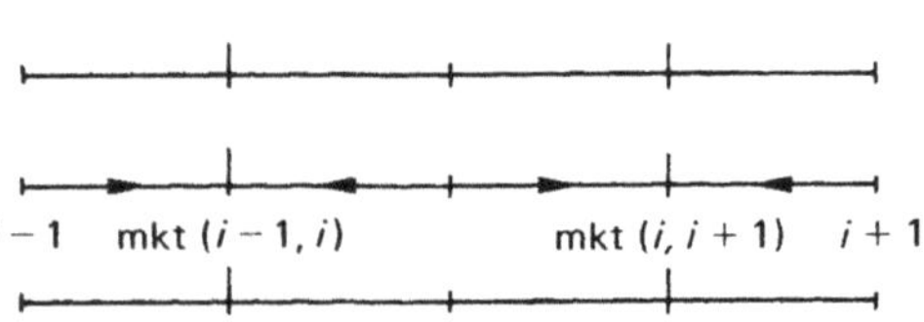

Figure 4.1.

(again, note the symmetry). Similarly, the other member of household type i travels to market $(i, i+1)$ with the beginning-of-period fiat money balances and purchases commodity $i+1$ at price $p_{i+1,t}$. At the end of date t, both members of household type i return to their original location to consume. Thus, taking the price sequence $\{p_{it}, p_{i+1,t}\}_{t=0}^{\infty}$ as given, each household of type i is confronted with the following problem.

Problem 4.2

$$\max \sum_{t=0}^{\infty} \beta^t U\{c_{it}(i), c_{i+1,t}(i), n_{it}(i)\} \tag{4.8}$$

by choice of $c_{it}(i), c_{i+1,t}(i), n_{it}(i), M_t(i)$ subject to

$$p_{i+1,t}c_{i+1,t}(i) + M_{t+1}(i) \leqslant M_t(i) + p_{it}\{n_{it}(i) - c_{it}(i)\} \tag{4.9}$$

$$p_{i+1,t}c_{i+1,t}(i) \leqslant M_t(i) \tag{4.10}$$

given $M_0(i)$. Here (4.9) is the fiat money balance accumulation equation, that is, the date t budget constraint, and (4.10) is the date t constraint that the valuation of consumption of commodity $i+1$ by household type i cannot exceed the beginning-of-period fiat money balances $M_t(i)$. Thus (4.10) is a liquidity constraint generated by the assumed exchange technology of the model. It captures what Clower (1967) has termed a key feature of money.

The above specification leads to the obvious definition of a perfect-foresight competitive equilibrium.

Definition

A fiat money equilibrium is a sequence of finite positive prices p_{it}^* for each commodity i and sequences of decisions for consumptions $c_{it}^*(i), c_{i+1,t}^*(i)$, labor supply $n_{it}^*(i)$, and fiat money balances $M_t^*(i)$ by each household type i such that the following two conditions hold:

- maximization: the sequences $c_{it}^*(i)$, $c_{i+1,t}^*(i)$, $n_{it}^*(i)$, $M_{t+1}^*(i)$ solve problem 4.2 for each household type i given the price sequences $p_{it}^*, p_{i+1,t}^*$;
- market clearing: the sequences $c_{it}^*(i)$, $c_{i+1,t}^*(i)$, $n_{it}^*(i)$ satisfy

$$c_{it}^*(i-1) \leqslant n_{it}^*(i) - c_{it}^*(i) \tag{4.11}$$

  over all commodities i and all dates t.

Note that in market-clearing condition (4.11), only households type i

and $i-1$ consume commodity i and only household type i can produce commodity i. Since, in any market, commodities are exchanged for fiat money, commodity balance (4.11) thus implies equality in demand and supply of fiat money balances as well.

To search for a fiat money equilibrium, consider the first-order conditions for an interior solution of household type i's maximization problem:

$$\beta^t U_1\{c_{it}(i), c_{i+1,t}(i), n_{it}(i)\} - \lambda_t p_{it} = 0 \tag{4.12}$$

$$\beta^t U_2\{c_{it}(i), c_{i+1,t}(i), n_{it}(i)\} - \lambda_t p_{i+1,t} - \phi_t p_{i+1,t} = 0 \tag{4.13}$$

$$\beta^t U_3\{c_{it}(i), c_{i+1,t}(i), n_{it}(i)\} + \lambda_t p_{it} = 0 \tag{4.14}$$

$$-\lambda_t + \phi_{t+1} + \lambda_{t+1} = 0 \tag{4.15}$$

Here λ_t is the positive Lagrange multiplier on the date t budget constraint (4.9), and ϕ_t is the nonnegative Lagrange multiplier on the date t liquidity constraint (4.10). Now suppose that the prices of all commodities are equal at each date and constant over time; that is, $p_{it}=1$ over all commodities i and all dates t. Suppose also that consumption is constant over time for the produced and nonproduced (market-produced) commodities and is the same across household types; that is, $c_{it}(i)=\bar{c}^1, c_{i+1,t}(i)=\bar{c}^2$. Also suppose that labor supply is constant over time and across household types; that is, $n_{it}(i)=\bar{n}$. Then (4.12)–(4.15) yield

$$\frac{U_1[\bar{c}^1, \bar{c}^2, \bar{n}]}{U_2[\bar{c}^1, \bar{c}^2, \bar{n}]} = \beta \tag{4.16}$$

$$\frac{-U_3[\bar{c}^1, \bar{c}^2, \bar{n}]}{U_2[\bar{c}^1, \bar{c}^2, \bar{n}]} = \beta \tag{4.17}$$

Of course, in such a symmetric steady state fiat money equilibrium, market-clearing condition (4.11) at equality is equivalent to

$$\bar{c}^2 = \bar{n} - \bar{c}^1 \tag{4.18}$$

It is assumed that the utility function is such that there exists an interior solution $\bar{c}^1, \bar{c}^2, \bar{n}$ to equations (4.16)–(4.18). To complete the specification of this symmetric steady state fiat money equilibrium, let $M_t(i)=\bar{c}^2 \equiv \bar{M}$ over all dates t and all households type i; thus, all the beginning-of-period fiat money balances are spent on the market-produced commodity each period and are replenished each period with the sale of the produced commodity. (Note that the liquidity constraint (4.10) is always binding.)

It is apparent from its construction that the above specification satisfies the necessary first-order conditions for an interior solution to each household's maximization problem, and that markets clear at each date. This is not quite equivalent to establishing the existence of a monetary equilibrium in the *infinite* horizon economy, but that is readily established by a slight modification of the arguments given in Townsend (1987, this volume, ch. 12) with the utility function bounded (see theorem 12.3 there and the discussion in section 5).

4 A Walrasian centralized exchange regime with trade credit

Now suppose that there is a centralized market for all the households on each of the real lines described in the previous section, that is, one centralized market per line. In each such centralized market at each date, there is an intermediary or Walrasian auctioneer, who may well be one of the households, operating a credit–debit exchange system.[3] In particular, the Walrasian auction description will be taken literally, though it is not standard to do so. Let $r_{i+1,t}$ be the per unit price of commodity $i+1$ in terms of some abstract unit of account, so that $r_{i+1,t}c_{i+1,t}(i)$ denotes the number of units of intraperiod debt incurred by household type i given units of consumption $c_{i+1,t}(i)$ of commodity $i+1$ which household i demands from the intermediary. Similarly, let r_{it} be the per unit price of commodity i in terms of some abstract unit of account, so that $r_{it}\{n_{it}(i)-c_{it}(i)\}$ denotes the number of units of intraperiod credit extended by the intermediary to household type i given units of output $n_{it}(i)-c_{it}(i)$ supplied. Then, taking prices parametrically, the problem confronting household type i is as follows.

Problem 4.3

$$\max U\{c_{it}(i), c_{i+1,t}(i), n_{it}(i)\} \tag{4.19}$$

by choice of $c_{it}(i), c_{i+1,t}(i), n_{it}(i)$ subject to

$$r_{i+1,t}c_{i+1,t}(i) \leqslant r_{it}\{n_{it}(i)-c_{it}(i)\} \tag{4.20}$$

The crucial feature of private debt in this model is that contemporaneous rather than past labor-output decisions are financing contemporaneous consumption decisions. That is, the household need not forgo current consumption – there are no "idle" money balances. In other words, trade credit has infinite as opposed to unit velocity; no stock of that asset is carried over from period to period. Note in this regard that the spatial separation of section 3 might well have been retained; what is crucial here is the existence of a centralized credit–debit system. Thus it might have been supposed that a member of household type i travels to market $(i, i+1)$, buys commodity $i+1$, and writes a check payable to the bearer, in this case household type $i+1$, for a specified number of units of account. Meanwhile a member of household type i travels to market $(i-1, i)$, sells commodity i, and is paid with a check from household type $i-1$. At the end of the period, checks are cleared (somehow) and accounts must balance. Of course, checks *per se* are superfluous in this system; electronically communicated bookkeeping entries will suffice. Such a system would not seem particularly farfetched, given contemporary financial developments. Again, the key idea is that trade credit can be used for within-period purchases, with accounts cleared at the end of the period using credit from within-period sales.

It might be noted also at this point that the centralized credit regime as specified above has active markets at each date. Of course, nothing in the technology of exchange precludes the operation of an initial complete date-contingent commodity market, but, as it turns out, none of the substantive conclusions herein would be altered with that alternative specification. In particular, the equilibrium consumption and labor-supply decisions themselves would not be altered, and the qualitative properties of debt would remain unchanged. It might also have been supposed, despite the existence of centralized credit markets, that all households are endowed with a positive number of units of fiat money, say with a number equal to the initial condition of the fiat money equilibrium in section 3. Under this specification, fiat money would be held but never used in exchange. More formally, we are searching for a trade credit equilibrium in which the price of fiat money is zero.

To continue, then, consider the following definition.

Definition

A date t trade credit equilibrium is a specification of commodity prices r_{it}^* for each commodity i and a specification of decisions for consumptions $c_{it}^*(i), c_{i+1,t}^*(i)$ and labor supply $n_{it}^*(i)$ such that the following two conditions hold:

- maximization: the decisions $c_{it}^*(i)$, $c_{i+1,t}^*(i)$, $n_{it}^*(i)$ solve problem 4.3 for household type i given the prices $r_{it}^*, r_{i+1,t}^*$;
- market clearing: the decisions $c_{it}^*(i)$, $c_{i+1,t}^*(i)$, $n_{it}^*(i)$ satisfy

$$c_{it}^*(i-1) \leqslant n_{it}^*(i) - c_{it}^*(i) \tag{4.21}$$

over all commodities i.

To search for a date t trade credit equilibrium, consider the first-order conditions for an interior solution of household type i's maximization problem:

$$U_1\{c_{it}(i), c_{i+1,t}(i), n_{it}(i)\} - \xi r_{it} = 0 \tag{4.22}$$

$$U_2\{c_{it}(i), c_{i+1,t}(i), n_{it}(i)\} - \xi r_{i+1} = 0 \tag{4.23}$$

$$U_3\{c_{it}(i), c_{i+1,t}(i), n_{it}(i)\} + \xi r_{it} = 0 \tag{4.24}$$

Here ξ is the positive Lagrange multiplier on the budget constraint (4.20). Now suppose that the prices of *all* commodities are set equal to unity; that is, $r_{it} \equiv 1$ over all commodities i. Also, as problem 4.3 does not depend on the date t in any essential way, we can look for a solution which is independent of t, say, $\hat{c}^1$, $\hat{c}^2$, and $\hat{n}$ for produced and nonproduced (market-produced) commodities and labor supply respectively. Thus (4.22)–(4.24) yield

$$\frac{U_1[\hat{c}^1, \hat{c}^2, \hat{n}]}{U_2[\hat{c}^1, \hat{c}^2, \hat{n}]} = 1 \tag{4.25}$$

$$-\frac{U_3[\hat{c}^1, \hat{c}^2, \hat{n}]}{U_2[\hat{c}^1, \hat{c}^2, \hat{n}]} = 1 \tag{4.26}$$

and, from (4.21) at equality,

$$\hat{c}^2 = \hat{n} - \hat{c}^1 \tag{4.27}$$

It is readily verified that, in general, there exists a solution $\hat{c}^1, \hat{c}^2, \hat{n}$ to equations (4.25)–(4.27). In fact, that solution is the unique Pareto optimum among interior allocations which treat households symmetrically. That is, $\hat{c}^1, \hat{c}^2, \hat{n}$ solves the following problem.

Problem 4.4

$$\max_{\{c^1, c^2, n\}} U[c^1, c^2, n]$$

subject to

$$c^2 = n - c^1$$

if one is not driven to some boundary.

Finally, we can take $\hat{D} \equiv \hat{c}^2$ as the measure of credit (per capita) in a trade credit equilibrium.

5 Substitution effects and exchange regime comparisons

Now imagine three countries, one in autarky, one with a decentralized fiat money regime, and one with a centralized trade credit regime. Suppose that we were asked to compare labor supply, output, consumption, trade volume, and welfare levels in the three countries. It turns out that this comparison is straightforward, at least on the assumption that substitution effects dominate income effects. To see why, recall the following: in autarky there is no trade at all; in the decentralized regime, fiat money from the sale of the produced commodity cannot be used immediately in exchange for the nonproduced (market-produced) commodity, that is, fiat money is held for one period; in the centralized regime, credit from the sale of the produced commodity can be used in the same period for consumption of the nonproduced (market-produced) commodity. Of course, in all three regimes the future is discounted by the parameter β, and thus the marginal rate of substitution of future for present consumption equals $1/\beta$ along any constant consumption path. Thus, put somewhat crudely, the cost of consumption of the nonproduced (market-produced) commodity in terms of labor, or in terms of the produced commodity, is infinite in autarky and is high in the decentralized regime relative to the centralized regime. Thus, we would anticipate labor supply to increase, output of the produced commodity to increase, consumption of the nonproduced (market-produced) commodity to increase, consumption of the produced commodity to decrease, trade volume to increase, and welfare levels to increase as we move from autarky to the decentralized regime to the centralized regime.

It is useful to begin with a direct comparison of the decentralized regime with the centralized regime; that is, to compare equations (4.16)–(4.18) with (4.25)–(4.27). These systems are identical apart from the right-hand sides of the first two equations; in effect, the discount rate β is set equal to unity in (4.25) and (4.26). Thus, to compare the specified regimes, it is enough to determine how the solution to system (4.16)–(4.18) moves with parameter β. In short, totally differentiate system (4.16)–(4.18) with respect to parameter β and the solution variables c^1, c^2, and n to yield

$$\begin{bmatrix} U_{11}-\beta U_{21} & U_{12}-\beta U_{22} & U_{13}-\beta U_{23} \\ U_{31}+\beta U_{21} & U_{32}+\beta U_{22} & U_{33}+\beta U_{23} \\ 1 & 1 & -1 \end{bmatrix} \begin{bmatrix} dc^1 \\ dc^2 \\ dn \end{bmatrix} = \begin{bmatrix} U_2 \\ -U_2 \\ 0 \end{bmatrix} d\beta$$

Though it is somewhat tedious to solve, a set of sufficient conditions can be established for the desired result, namely $dn/d\beta > 0$, $dc^1/d\beta < 0$, and $dc^2/d\beta > 0$. These conditions are not vacuous; they are satisfied independent of the value of β if the utility function is separable, for example.[4] Thus, with such an assumption, the labor supply, output, consumption, and trade volume comparisons across the decentralized and centralized regimes are as described earlier. The increase in welfare as we move from the decentralized to the centralized regime follows immediately from the fact also noted earlier that the centralized regime delivers an allocation which is the unique Pareto optimum among allocations which treat households symmetrically.

It is also possible to make labor supply, output, consumption, trade volume, and welfare comparisons between the decentralized regime and autarky. The argument is entirely similar. In particular, consider the solution to system (4.16)–(4.18) as parameter β goes to zero. From the above analysis, it is clear that in such solutions c^1 increases and n decreases, so that $c^2 = n - c^1$ goes to zero from above. Now suppose that the limit is attained when the parameter β equals some positive number γ. Then, the system (4.16)–(4.18) is equivalent to the system (4.5)–(4.7), and so the limit is the equilibrium of the autarkic regime. Again, it is known how the solution to system (4.16)–(4.18) moves with parameter β, and so it is known that labor supply, output, and trade volume all decrease as we move from the decentralized regime to autarky. The decrease in welfare follows from the fact that autarky is a feasible solution in the decision problem of the representative household in the equilibrium of the decentralized regime – a solution not adopted.

6 Some cross-country comparisons on the state of economic development

Let us now consider a country with an internal mix of exchange regimes, in particular with a mix of decentralized and centralized regimes. In terms of the formalism of this chapter, we might suppose, for example, that some fraction λ of household lines are in centralized Walrasian markets. That is, suppose that households are associated with real lines, as in section 3, which are numbered. Every tenth line is centralized, and is part of the "developed" sector. (Here then, $\lambda = 0.10$.) The decentralized sector is as in section 3, but real lines are no longer numbered consecutively; that is, some numbers are missing there. Now, to make labor supply, output, consumption, and trade volume comparisons, find the sector location of the line numbered 0 and determine the per capita variables of households there (recall that households are treated identically). Next, find the location of the line numbered 1 and find the per capita variables of households there. Then determine the *average* per capita variable levels across households in the two lines. Continue in this way for lines numbered 2, 3, and so on, determining the average per capita variable levels at each step. Clearly these averages will approach the appropriate limits, averages of the per capita variables in the decentralized and centralized regimes with specified weights (here 0.9 and 0.1 respectively), as more and more household lines are included in the "sample." Of course, this method of counting is also applicable to countries with a mix of all three exchange regimes.

Now suppose that we were to make comparisons across countries which are more and more centralized, say, to continue with the above example, with higher and higher values of λ. We can take as measures of per capita labor supply, per capita consumption of the home-produced commodity, and per capita consumption of the market-produced commodity

$$n = (1 - \lambda)\bar{n} + \lambda\hat{n} \tag{4.28}$$

$$c^1 = (1 - \lambda)\bar{c}^1 + \lambda\hat{c}^1 \tag{4.29}$$

$$c^2 = (1 - \lambda)\bar{c}^2 + \lambda\hat{c}^2 \tag{4.30}$$

respectively. Thus n and c^2 increase with λ and c^1 decreases with λ under the assumed substitution effects. Also, with prices fixed at unity in equilibrium, n could be taken as a measure of per capita national income y. In contrast, it might be assumed that only market activities are measured in national income accounts, so that c^2 is taken as a measure of per capita national income (or, more aptly, per capita national expenditure). Of course, c^2 is also the measure of trade volume. In practice, adjustments are made for nonmarket activities in national income accounts, and so here we might suppose per capita national income to lie between n and c^2. The important point, though, is that per capita national income would increase as we move across countries which are more and more centralized, as it is the sum of substitution effects which increase labor supply *and* decrease consumption of the home-produced commodity. That is, *measured* national income might increase even if there were no increase in actual labor supply.

We can also consider the per capita share of labor devoted to market-produced commodities, $(1 - \lambda)(\bar{c}^2/\bar{n}) + \lambda(\hat{c}^2/\hat{n})$ in this model. The derivative of this expression with respect to λ is more difficult to sign, but it is more likely to be positive the greater is the substitution effect increasing consumption of market-produced commodities and the less is the substitution effect increasing labor supply. Here, however, measurement problems make the comparison more tenuous. If labor supply is measured only in the production of market-produced goods, then, of course, there will be no effect.

Finally, to continue with the example, we may note that the decentralized regime functions entirely on one asset, outside credit or fiat money, and the centralized regime functions entirely on another, inside money or private credit. Again, depending on the conventions used for initial conditions, fiat money may be held in the centralized regime but is not used in exchange. The important point is that the mix of assets is determined by the degree of centralization λ and thus moves with measures of per capita national income. Here, for example, under the counting conventions described earlier, per capita fiat money balances $M = (1-\lambda)\bar{M}$ or $M = \bar{M}$ should either decrease or stay constant and per capita private credit $D = \lambda\hat{D}$ should increase as we move across countries which are more and more centralized and thus have higher and higher per capita income. Moreover, suppose that we were to examine the inverses of aggregate asset velocities, that is, the ratio of fiat money outstanding to income

$$\frac{M}{y} = \frac{(1-\lambda)\bar{M}}{(1-\lambda)\bar{c}^2 + \lambda\hat{c}^2}$$

or

$$\frac{M}{y} = \frac{\bar{M}}{(1-\lambda)\bar{c}^2 + \lambda\hat{c}^2} \tag{4.31}$$

and the ratio of credit outstanding to income

$$\frac{D}{y} = \frac{\lambda\hat{D}}{(1-\lambda)\bar{c}^2 + \lambda\hat{c}^2} \tag{4.32}$$

on the assumption that y is defined by (4.30) for example. Then it is easy to verify that the former decreases and the latter *increases* as we move across countries which are more and more centralized. The intuition behind the last result seems clear: both per capita income and per capita credit increase with λ, but the marginal household to be "transferred" from the decentralized to the centralized sector, as we move across countries, experiences only an *incremental* increase in consumption $\hat{c}^2 - \bar{c}^2$ though financing its *entire* consumption expenditure with credit $\hat{D}$.

Similarly, suppose that we were to examine the share of claims on intermediaries relative to *all* claims, that is, $D/(M+D)$ in this model. Then, by the above analysis, this measure of intermediation increases with per capita income.

Of course, we can make comparisons across countries which have an autarkic sector as well. It is clear, for example, that if the fraction of households in the centralized sector is held fixed, then the larger is the fraction of households in the decentralized sector relative to the autarkic sector, the higher will be per capita national income and the higher will be per capita holdings of fiat money. In fact, the ratio M/y of fiat money balances to national income would increase under such a comparison. In general, though, the measure of centralization must be two dimensional (since there are three sectors), and this complicates the comparisons. On the incredible assumption that development proceeds sequentially, we might predict, for example, an initial increase in M/y with D/y at zero, and then a decrease in M/y with an increase in D/y, as we move across countries with higher and higher per capita incomes. In practice, we might expect this movement and other movements to be blurred considerably.

7 A theory of economic growth

Now suppose that the model is modified in a way that allows for an increase in the number of households in the intermediated or centralized sector over time (again supposing that the autarkic sector is negligible). In particular, suppose that the event that all households in a specified (numbered) real line are thrown into a centralized credit market at the beginning of date t takes place with probability q. Suppose also that these events are independent across household lines in the decentralized sector at any date and independent over time for any given household line. Also suppose that the probability of financial collapse is zero; once in a centralized sector, there is no movement back to a decentralized sector.

Households may carry beginning-of-period fiat money balances with them in the event that there is an integration into a centralized credit market, but, as noted earlier, the value of such balances there would be zero. Alternatively, such balances can be surrendered in lump-sum fashion to the monetary authority. The important point, though, is that under either specification there are essentially no beginning-of-period state variables over which the household has any control in the event of centralization. In the absence of centralization, it is assumed that fiat money balances remain intact and thus serve the same role as before, as in the fiat money equilibrium. Analytically then, a household in the decentralized sector faces "death" – departure from the decentralized sector – as an independent event with probability q each period. Thus $(1-q)\beta$ becomes the effective discount rate, denoted β^*, and the entire analysis of section 3 for the fiat money equilibrium applies. In particular, there exists a fiat money equilibrium in the decentralized sector, with constant prices as before, characterized by conditions (4.16)–(4.18) with β replaced by β^*. (Note that per capita output in the decentralized sector will be less than in the equilibrium of section 3 because of the lower effective discount rate; that is, β^* is less than β.) Finally, note that equilibrium behavior of households in the centralized credit market remains as before, as in section 4, since households there face a sequence of unconnected static decision problems.

Though financial integration is a random event as far as the individual household is concerned, the movement of economy-wide average time series is deterministic. Independence of integration across the countably infinite number of household lines in the decentralized sector means, by the law of large numbers and the counting convention described earlier, that essentially a fraction q of household lines in the decentralized sector become integrated each period. Thus, beginning with zero integration, the fraction of household lines in the intermediated sector increases from zero to q to $q+(1-q)(q)$ and so on, with a corresponding decrease in the fraction of household lines in the decentralized sector. From the analysis of the previous two sections, this delivers time series which display an increase over time in per capita income, an increase in per capita credit, and a decrease in (or constant level of) per capita fiat money balances. (Of course, the rate of growth of output, for example, will diminish over time, but this diminution will be negligible for a sufficiently small parameter q.) Finally, as before, the ratio of fiat money balances to national income should decrease over time, the ratio of credit to national income should increase over time, and the ratio of claims on intermediaries relative to all claims should also increase over time.[5]

8 The relationship of the theory to observations

To reiterate, the theory presented in this chapter is abstract. No doubt it misses much. Thus any attempt to match the conclusions of the theory with actual observations has to be viewed as somewhat heroic, at best. This effort will be reviewed in this section, with an inclusion of some of the obvious warnings.

First, the key variable of the theory is the degree of centralization of the economy, that is, the degree of interconnectedness among households or the facility with which households can trade with one another. As the degree of interconnectedness increases, both cross-sectionally (across countries) and over time (in a given country), the theory predicts an increase in the specialization (or division) of labor, that is, an increase in the consumption of market-produced commodities. More generally, and more liberally interpreted, more and more labor is devoted to the production of commodities which are not used directly by the household itself. Of course, this increase is associated with a decrease in the relative price of market-produced commodities and an increase in per capita income.

These are the movements which Adam Smith had in mind and which are documented by Kuznets, as noted at the beginning of this chapter. Note again that the share of transportation, communication, and commerce in GDP is positively associated with per capita product. This is direct evidence for the degree of centralization. Further, we can interpret the decline in the share of the agricultural sector and the rise in the shares of the industrial and service sectors as evidence of the specialization of labor. The decline in the price of industrial goods relative to agricultural goods is consistent with that interpretation.

Second, the theory in this chapter predicts an increase in the extent of intermediation or middlemen activities with an increase in the extent of centralization and hence with an increase in per capita income. To some extent, Kuznets's observations on the increasing share of banking and insurance (with real estate) in GDP and the increasing share of the service component are consistent with this, though in the theory in this chapter intermediation *per se* is not resource using and thus would *not* show up in the national income accounts. More consistent with the theory are the observations of Goldsmith that the share of intermediaries in national assets and the ratio of financial institutions' assets to GNP rise over time with increases in per capita GNP. (Recall that in the theory presented here $D/(M+D)$ and D/y both increase with y, as households are shifted from the decentralized to the centralized sector.)

Third, and closely related, the theory of this chapter predicts a change in economy-wide average asset holdings with changes in the underlying structure of the economy, in particular a shift toward trade credit relative to fiat money. No doubt such asset shifts do occur in actual economies,[6] but measuring the shifts is problematic. That is, the highly stylized assets of this chapter must be matched with analogs in the data. Though we can match fiat money with currency in the hands of the public, for example, the association is not straightforward. Currency measures may well include high-velocity circulating *private* debt, such as bank notes in the United States, whereas the fiat money of this chapter is entirely *outside* debt. Of course, the theory presented here offers no basis for a distinction between currency outside banks and high-powered money. Nor does the theory offer any guide as to which monetary aggregate to match with trade credit.

Notwithstanding this criticism, suppose that we do match fiat money with currency in the hands of the public and, for want of a better alternative,[7] trade credit with private credit, generally. Then, following McKinnon (1973), we can plot the ratio of currency to GNP and the ratio of private credit to GNP against per capita income (log scale) for a cross section of countries. This is done in figures 4.2 and 4.3 respectively for the year 1968.[8] As is evident, the ratio of currency to GNP shows no systematic pattern against per capita income.[9] In contrast, however, the ratio of private credit to GNP shows a rough increase as we move from low-income to high-income countries.[10,11] Perhaps more striking are such time series plots for Germany and Japan from 1953 to 1977 (figures 4.4 and 4.5). For both these countries, the ratio of private credit to GNP increased rather dramatically while the ratio of currency to GNP either stayed constant or declined slightly.[12]

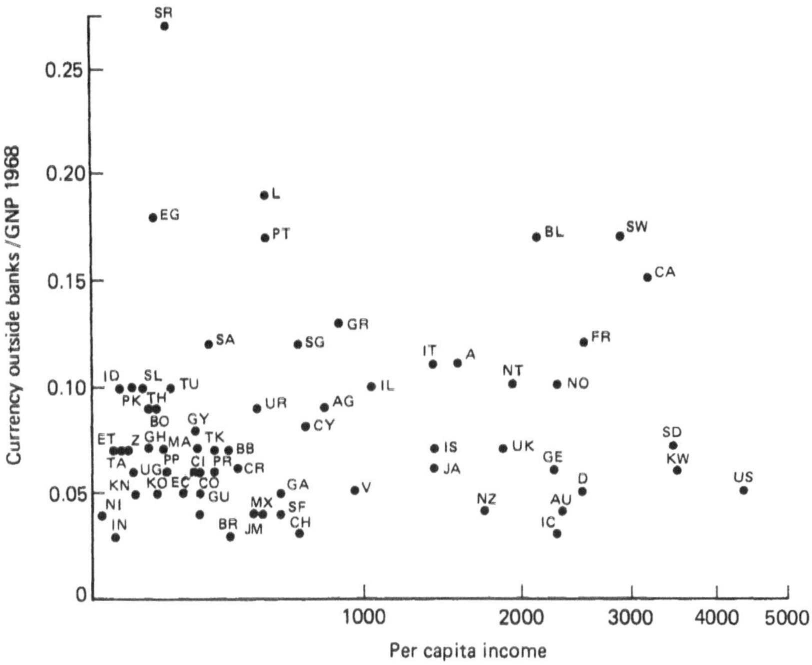

Figure 4.2.

9 Caveats and welfare economics

The theory presented in this chapter does not *explain* economic development or economic growth. The key ingredient – the extent to which households in the economy are centralized – is exogenously manipulated by the modeler, and there is little else. Thus the "theory" of economic development is virtually tautological – countries are not developed because markets are fragmented. Similarly, the theory of economic growth misses much. The key factors which Denison (1967) has singled out as contributing to economic growth, especially growth in factor inputs – the labor force and the capital stock – are absent. Also absent, apparently, is the technological progress which Denison and especially Kuznets have emphasized: growth in output is not explained by growth in factor inputs. There is a sense though in which technological progress *is* doing *all* the work. Suppose that we take consumption expenditures per capita of the *market*-produced good as output y on the assumption that *only* market activities are measured. Then, in the model of economic growth, y/n increases over time, though the underlying production function displays constant returns to scale. Indeed, the model delivers economic growth in this way even if there is no increase in labor supply over time, though labor is

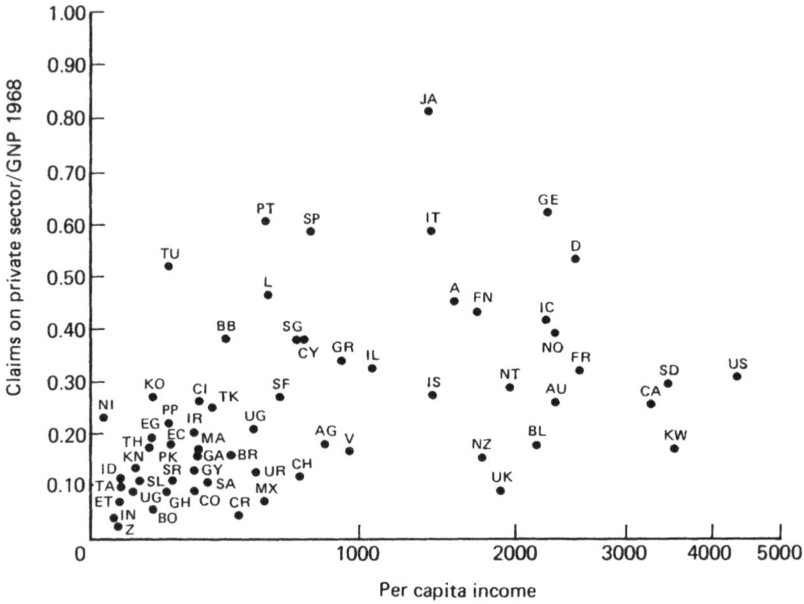

Figure 4.3.

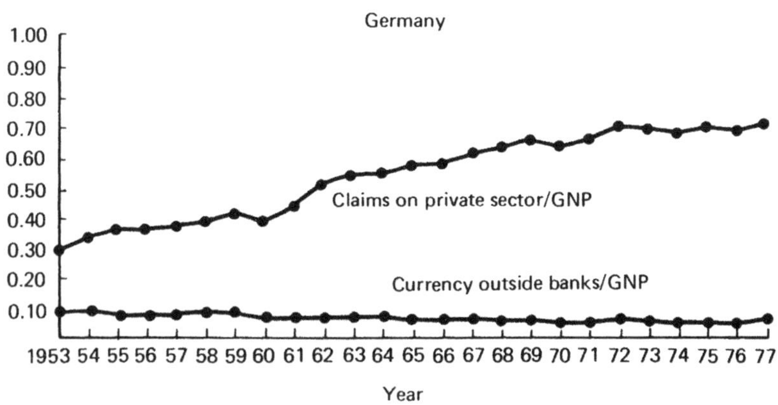

Figure 4.4.

the only factor of production. Thus the measure of centralization λ is the analog of technological progress in other stylized growth models. Still, and more to the point, technological progress is not explained here.[13]

A more satisfactory theory might model the intermediation process in a deeper way. In particular, intermediaries might be viewed as utilizing resources to match households faced with the vagaries of the yield on their

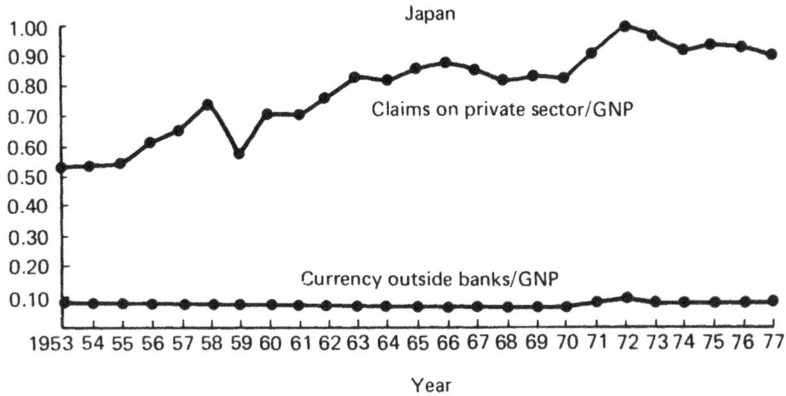

Figure 4.5.

portfolios (see Townsend, 1978, this volume, ch. 10; 1983, this volume, ch. 11). We might envision nontrivial borrowing–lending and capital-formation activities as well. In this more general setting, then, the extent to which households and firms are matched would be endogenous, and we might ask whether more or less intermediation, at a point in time and over time, is a good thing. This chapter has only trivial and perhaps misleading welfare implications in this regard. More intermediation is unambiguously welfare improving. It is associated with growth in one monetary aggregate (private credit) and a decrease in another (fiat money), but there is no real scope for policy in the present model.

There is, however, one policy which might be contemplated in the present model: a deflation in the fiat money regime engineered by beginning-of-period lump-sum taxation of fiat money balances. In Townsend (1980, this volume, ch. 2) such a deflation, with exogenous labor supply, achieves the unique Pareto optimal allocation of resources, whereas the *laissez-faire* competitive equilibrium does not. In effect, with deflation there is increased lending on the part of the government relative to the *laissez-faire* regime, and this lending is precluded among households in the decentralized regime because of spatial separation and limits on communication. Thus we wonder whether this policy implication is misleading, whether in effect the government is given an exogenous advantage over the private sector in coordinating economic activity – a coordination which the agents might well achieve themselves in a more fully specified model. But this is left as an open question.

Notes

1 With regard to cyclical fluctuations, there is the widely cited experience at the outset of the Great Depression, when high-powered money increased though

other monetary aggregates decreased (see Friedman and Schwartz, 1963; Cagan, 1965). Moreover, Cagan argues that countercyclical movements in the currency-to-money ratio and in the currency-to-income ratio obtain more generally, even if episodes associated with financial panics are excluded.

2 It might be assumed a priori, from contemporary observations, that money balance holdings are small and that changes in the trading frictions which account for money balance holdings cannot account for much movement in real variables. Economic history seems to provide some counter-evidence, however. For example, Cameron (1967) argues that "working capital" was significant relative to "fixed capital," and in effect argues that trading frictions and the absence of banks and trade credit were a severe restriction on growth at the beginning of the industrial revolution in England.

3 There may well be more than one intermediary; more generally, the present structure abstracts from the market assignment and price determination process. See Townsend (1983, this volume, ch. 11) for an explicit treatment of intermediaries and an explanation of the competitive outcome.

4 The assumed dominance of substitution effects over income effects is used by Lucas and Rapping (1969) and by Lucas (1972) to ensure that the Phillips curve slopes the "right way." Its use here is entirely similar.

5 We might suppose that, unlike the growth model just examined, the extent to which the economy is centralized or interconnected is random with no central tendency. To accomplish this in the present context, it might be imagined that the events that specified that household lines are thrown into centralized credit markets are not independent of one another. That is, suppose that the movements over household *groupings* are described by a Markov process. With some demanding assumptions on the taxation of fiat money balances, this model will deliver random movements in economy-wide average time series for per capita labor supply, output, consumption, and asset holdings. It may be noted in particular that a relative movement out of the centralized credit markets to the decentralized sector will be associated with a decrease in labor supply per capita, a decrease in national income per capita, a decrease in private credit per capita, and an increase in fiat money balances per capita. Similarly, the ratio of credit to income should move "procyclically" and the ratio of fiat money to income should move "countercyclically." See note 1.

6 Again, see Cameron (1967).

7 One alternative might be some measure of trade credit, as Laffer (1970) has suggested. However, a reading of Laffer also suggests some nontrivial problems in definition.

8 The country code for the figures is as follows: Argentina, AG; Australia, AU; Austria, A; Barbados, BB; Belgium, BL; Bolivia, BO; Brazil, BR; Canada, CA; China, CI; Colombia, CO; Costa Rica, CR; Cyprus, CY; Chile, CH; Denmark, D; Ecuador, EC; Egypt, EG; Ethiopia, ET; Finland, FN; France, FR; Gabon, GA; Germany, GE; Ghana, GH; Greece, GR; Guatemala, GU; Guyana, GY; Iceland, IC; India, ID; Indonesia, IN; Iran, IR; Ireland, IL; Israel, IS; Italy, IT; Jamaica, JM; Japan, JA; Kenya, KN; Korea, KO; Kuwait, KW; Lebanon, L; Malaysia, MA; Mexico, MX; Netherlands, NT; New Zealand, NZ; Nicaragua, NI; Norway, NO; Pakistan, PK; Peru, PR; Philippines, PP; Portugal, PT; Saudi

Arabia, SA; Singapore, SG; South Africa, SF; Spain, SP; Sri Lanka, SL; Sweden, SD; Switzerland, SW; Syria, SR; Tanzania, TA; Thailand, TH; Tunisia, TU; Turkey, TK; Uganda, UG; United Kingdom, UK; United States, US; Uruguay, UR; Venezuela, V; Zaire, Z.

9 But recall that if we allow for an autarkic sector a relative shift from autarky toward the fiat money regime would cause the ratio of currency to GNP to *increase* against per capita income. This effect would confound the decrease discussed in the text.

10 The increase is especially noticeable if countries are grouped into two classes, say less developed versus semi-industrialized and industrialized.

11 The same pattern appears when domestic credit, including claims on the government, is plotted against per capita income. This holds true as well for the individual country comparisons below.

12 Robinson (1961) argues that the shift in the credit-to-income ratio has occurred in the United States as well, though the recent work of B. Friedman, among others, suggests that the postwar experience is mixed.

13 Even more of a burden is placed on the measure of centralization λ in the theory of fluctuations mentioned in note 5; there λ varies over time in an exogenously specified stochastic way. Again, there is no explanation of financial integration or collapse.

References

Bordo, M.D. and Jonung, L. (1981) The long run behavior of the income velocity of money in five advanced countries, 1870–1975: an institutional approach. *Economic Inquiry* 19, 96–116.

Cagan, P. (1965) *Determinants and Effects of Changes in the Stock of Money, 1875–1960.* New York: Columbia University Press.

Cameron, R. (1967) *Banking in the Early Stages of Industrialization.* New York: Oxford University Press.

Cass, D. and Yaari, M. (1966) A re-examination of the pure consumption loans model. *Journal of Political Economy* 74, 353–67.

Clower, R.W. (1967) A reconsideration of the microfoundations of monetary theory. *Western Economic Journal* 6, 1–8.

—— (1969) Introduction. *Monetary Theory.* Harmondsworth: Penguin.

—— (1971) Theoretical foundations of monetary policy. In *Monetary Theory and Policy in the 1970's*, eds G. Clayton, J.C. Gilbert, and R. Sedgwick. New York: Oxford University Press.

Denison, E.F. (1967) *Why Growth Rates Differ.* Washington, DC: Brookings Institution.

Doblin, E.M. (1951) The ratio of income to money supply: an international survey. *Review of Economics and Statistics* 33, 201–13.

Friedman, B.M. (1981) The roles of money and credit in macroeconomic analysis. Presented at the NBER Conference on Business Fluctuations, Chicago, October 1981.

Friedman, M. and Schwartz, A. J. (1963) *A Monetary History of the United States, 1867–1960*. Princeton, NJ: Princeton University Press.

Goldsmith, R. (1958) *Financial Intermediaries in the American Economy*. Princeton, NJ: Princeton University Press.

——(1969) *Financial Structure and Development*. New Haven, CT: Yale University Press.

Gurley, J.G. and Shaw, E.S. (1960) *Money in a Theory of Finance*. Washington, DC: Brookings Institution.

Hahn, F. (1973) On the foundations of monetary theory. In *Essays in Modern Economics*, eds M. Parkin and A.R. Nobay, pp. 230–42. New York: Harper & Row.

Kuznets, S. (1971) *Economic Growth of Nations: Total Output and Production Structure*. Cambridge, MA: Harvard University Press.

Laffer, A.B. (1970) Trade credit and the money market. *Journal of Political Economy* 78, 239–67.

Lucas, R.E., Jr (1972) Expectations and the neutrality of money. *Journal of Economic Theory* 4, 103–24.

——and Rapping, L.A. (1969) Real wages, employment, and inflation. *Journal of Political Economy* 77, 721–54.

McKinnon, R.I. (1973) *Money and Capital in Economic Development*. Washington, DC: Brookings Institution.

Melitz, J. and Correa, H. (1970) International differences in income velocity. *Review of Economics and Statistics* 52, 12–17.

Robinson, M.A. (1961) Debt and economic growth. In *Money and Economic Activity*, ed. L.S. Ritter, 2nd edn. Boston, MA: Houghton Mifflin.

Tobin, J. (1965) The monetary interpretation of history. *American Economic Review* 55, 464–85.

Townsend, R.M. (1978) Intermediation with costly bilateral exchange. *Review of Economic Studies* 45, 417–25. Reprinted in this volume as chapter 10.

——(1980) Models of money with spatially separated agents. In *Models of Monetary Economies*, eds J.H. Kareken and N. Wallace. Minneapolis, MN: Federal Reserve Bank of Minneapolis. Reprinted in this volume as chapter 2.

——(1983) Theories of intermediated structures. *Carnegie–Rochester Conference Series on Public Policy*, vol. 18, *Money, Monetary Policy and Financial Institutions*, pp. 221–72. Supplemental series to *Journal of Monetary Economics*. Reprinted in this volume as chapter 11.

——(1987) Asset return anomalies in a monetary economy. *Journal of Economic Theory* 41(5), 219–47. Reprinted in this volume as chapter 12.

Wallace, N. (1980) The overlapping generations model of fiat money. In *Models of Monetary Economies*, eds J.H. Kareken and N. Wallace. Minneapolis, MN: Federal Reserve Bank of Minneapolis.

Wicksell, K. (1935) *Lectures on Political Economy*. London: Macmillan.

International Monetary Fund (1978) *International Financial Statistics, 1978 Supplement*, p. 31. Washington, DC: International Monetary Fund.

Part III
Private Information as a Key Element in Theories of Contract – Mechanism Design

5

Optimal Contracts and Competitive Markets with Costly State Verification

1 Introduction

The insight of Arrow (1964) and Debreu (1959) that uncertainty is easily incorporated into general equilibrium models is double edged. It is true that it is only necessary to index commodities by the state of nature, and classical results on the existence and optimality of competitive equilibria can be made to apply. Yet it seems that there are few contingent dealings among agents relative to those suggested by the theory. For example, closely held firms issue bonds which pay off a fixed constant, independent of investment project returns, at least if bankruptcy does not occur. More generally, common forms of debt are simple rather than contingent. Similarly, individuals carry insurance policies with deductible portions – small losses are uninsured.

What is needed then is models that explain such phenomena. Arrow (1974) has argued that the observed absence of contingent dealings is closely related to moral hazard and imperfect information. If a contract is contingent on an event, then it must be known whether or not the event occurred. Though this information is likely to be available to only one party of the contract, the range of possible contingent contracts is limited to those which are easily verified by both. Radner (1968) has formalized this concept by exogenously

Reprinted from *Journal of Economic Theory* 21(2), 1979, 265–93 (Orlando, FL: Academic Press). This chapter began as a joint effort with Neil Wallace and reflects that collaboration as well as subsequent comments in many ways. I would also like to thank the participants of the NSF–NBER Conference on Theoretical Industrial Organization at Carnegie–Mellon University, March 1976; my colleagues at Carnegie–Mellon University, especially Artur Raviv and Edward C. Prescott; Edward J. Green, and the referees for helpful comments. Partial support for this research from the Federal Reserve Bank of Minneapolis is gratefully acknowledged. I assume full responsibility for any errors as well as the views expressed here.

limiting contracts between agents to those which are contingent on the events in the information partitions of both agents. Radner also suggests that the information structure of an economy may be costly and endogenous. In this chapter we elaborate on the themes suggested by Arrow and Radner. A model in which agents are asymmetrically informed on the actual state of nature and in which this information can be transmitted to other agents only at some cost is presented. As will be noted, the model is successful in explaining the observations mentioned above, at least subject to some qualifications.

We begin in section 2 with a simple two-agent pure exchange economy in which the endowment of the consumption good of one of the agents, say agent 2, is random. Preferences and endowments are such that there are gains to trading claims contingent on the realization of the random endowment. But any realization is known only by agent 2 unless a verification (auditing) cost is borne. A contract in such a setting is a pre-state agreement as to when there is to be verification and the amount to be exchanged, and a contract is said to be consistent (incentive compatible) if agent 2 submits to verification and honors claims in accordance with the contract. In section 3 Pareto optimal consistent contracts are shown to have familiar characteristics. In particular, there exists a set of realizations over which there is no verification. In the case of insurance this corresponds to the region over which no claims are filed. For closely held firms this corresponds to the region over which bonds pay the stated yield. A verification set is a set of low realizations; insurance claims are settled and firms default.

In the next two sections the robustness of these results is examined by extending the model in several directions. Section 4 introduces a random verification procedure and establishes that the random procedure can dominate, in a Pareto sense, the optimal contract under the assumed deterministic procedure. Though consistent with observations on random audits and the like, this finding represents a major criticism of the deterministic scheme. Section 5 introduces more agents and random variables. Here extensions of the earlier results are established, subject to some *exogenous* restrictions on contingent exchange agreements. One restriction is that the m-agent model is essentially bilateral in nature.

Section 6 proposes a competitive equilibrium concept for the m-agent model. It is established that, under specified assumptions, an equilibrium exists and yields optimal allocations. This section represents an attempt to improve our understanding of general equilibrium competitive models with moral hazard and costly information (see Helpman and Laffont, 1975). It also represents a rigorous analysis of incomplete competitive insurance markets.

Section 7 presents some concluding remarks. The proofs of all lemmas and propositions are contained in an appendix.

The remainder of this introduction deals with the relationship of this chapter to other literature. The characterization of optimal contracts can be viewed in part as an extension of the literature on optimal insurance policies. Arrow (1971, 1973) and subsequently Raviv (1975) have shown that, under certain nonnegativity constraints and in the presence of loading, an optimal insurance contract can have deductibles. It is shown in this chapter that consistency conditions yield the requisite nonnegativity constraints and that it is costly state verification which can make complete risk-sharing suboptimal.

This chapter is also closely related to the literature on imperfect information and principal–agent relationships. In Spence and Zeckhauser (1971), Shavell (1979), and Harris and Raviv (1979) the random output of the consumption good is not exogenous, but rather depends on an action taken by the agent. Spence and Zeckhauser established in this context that the form of an optimal contract depends on the principal's ability to monitor the state of nature, the action taken by the agent, and the output of the consumption good. Subsequently, Shavell and Harris and Raviv focused on the case in which the output of the consumption good is known to both the principal and the agent, in contrast with the model in this chapter, but in which the action of the agent may or may not be observed. Various assumptions can be made on the monitoring technology and the timing of observations. Unlike the model in this chapter, in which verification is perfect when it occurs, these writers allow for observation of the agent's action with error. Shavell further allows observations on care to be costly and to be taken either before or after the realization of output. The model in this chapter also emphasizes the costly nature of observation, but, in contrast, does not deal at all with the timing question.

Retaining the perfect observation assumption, it might have been supposed here that the decision to verify could be made *ex ante* at some fixed cost of the consumption good and that subsequently all realizations would be observed. This then would be the model suggested by Kihlstrom and Pauly (1971), and it has the implication that one agent provides either complete insurance coverage to the other or no coverage at all. Similarly, in Shavell's model, if care is observed perfectly, then an optimal insurance policy offers full coverage. Thus, such an alternative model might explain the complete absence of some dealings, but it could not explain the observations on noncontingent dealings noted at the outset.

If in the model in this chapter verification were imperfect, and if the verification cost were a function of the actual realization of the endowment, then the decision to verify might act as a signal of the realization, and aspects of the signaling incentive literature might be brought to bear. In this regard, we might also weaken the assumption that the probability distribution of the consumption good is known to both agents. In Ross (1977) the financial decision of the manager acts as a signal to uninformed investors of the return stream of the firm. An approach that combines the model in this chapter and that of Ross might suppose that the choice of financial structure signals information that reduces *ex post* auditing costs. In any event, there are many aspects of the present model that could be modified in subsequent work.

2 An economy with two agents and one random variable

It is assumed that each of two agents has an endowment of the single consumption good of the model. The endowment of agent 2, denoted y_2, is a random variable with cumulative probability distribution $F(y_2)$. It is further assumed that y_2 takes on values in the interval $[\alpha, \beta]$, $\alpha > 0$, and is either simple, in which case it has a finite number of realizations, or continuous, in which case it is assumed to have a continuous strictly positive density function $f(y_2)$.[1] The endowment of agent 1, denoted y_1, is not random and $y_1 > 0$.

Each agent j has a utility function U_j over riskless consumption which is continuously differentiable, concave, and strictly increasing. It is assumed moreover that U_2 is strictly concave with $U_2'(0) = \infty$ and $U_2'(\infty) = 0$. We let $c_j(y_2)$ denote the consumption of agent j as a function of y_2; feasibility then requires that $c_1(y_2) + c_2(y_2) \leqslant y_1 + y_2$. Consistent with von Neumann–Morgenstern axioms, each agent j has as objective the maximization of expected utility $\int U_j\{c_j(y_2)\}\, \mathrm{d}F(y_2)$.

The model described thus far can be given various interpretations. For example, agent 2 can be viewed as a firm engaged in an investment project with random return y_2. Agent 2 may issue an asset to agent 1 where the asset is some claim on the returns of the project. The problem is to determine the type of asset that is mutually agreeable to both parties. Alternatively, agent 2 can be viewed as an individual who is to suffer some random loss $\beta - y_2$, and would like to purchase insurance from agent 1. Under either interpretation, exchange is motivated by risk-sharing considerations.

If both agents were always fully informed *ex post* as to the realization (state) of y_2, then they could agree to an exchange contingent on the realization. In general any such *exchange* which results in a (full-information) Pareto optimal allocation will be a nontrivial function of y_2. But the purpose of this chapter to explain the *absence* of such contingent dealings: firms issue bonds which pay out a fixed constant, independent of investment project returns, and individuals hold insurance contracts with deductible portions. Consequently the full-information assumption must be weakened.

Here then it is supposed that the realization of y_2 is known only by agent 2 unless there is verification. If there is verification, y_2 is made known *without error* to agent 1. Verification is costly in that some specified amount of the consumption good is forfeited by agent 2 and disappears from the model. The idea here is that it is costly for a firm to make known its project return to outside investors. Perhaps independent auditors must be hired, and costly state verification can be interpreted as costly auditing. Similarly, it is costly for individuals to establish claimed losses; the extent of damages must be verified.[2]

Resources are allocated in this model in accordance with specified rules on the execution of a contract. First a contract must be defined. Prior to the realization of y_2, agents agree to a contingent exchange. Let $g(y_2)$ denote the actual post-state net transfer of the consumption good from agent 2 to agent 1 as a function of y_2. Then let $\bar{g}$ denote the *pre-state contractual choice* of the function g. Similarly, prior to the realization of y_2, agents agree as to when there is or is not to be verification, contingent on y_2. A verification region S (with complement S') is a set of realizations of y_2 such that there is verification. Then let $\bar{S}$ and $\bar{S}'$ denote the *pre-state contractual choices* of S and S' respectively. Thus, a contract $[\bar{g}, \bar{S}]$ is a pre-state contingent specification of when there is to be verification and the amount to be transferred.

Subsequent to the realization of y_2, agent 2 announces whether there is or is not to be verification. If there is verification, specified amounts of the consumption good are forfeited by agent 2, y_2 is made known to agent 1, and agent 2 transfers what was agreed upon. (In terms of the notation, if $y_2 \in S$, $g(y_2) = \bar{g}(y_2)$.) If there is not verification, then agent 2 can transfer any amount consistent with the prior specification of the amount to be transferred when there was not to be verification. That is, agent 2 can transfer $\bar{g}(x)$ for any x in $\bar{S}'$. Of course, agent 2 will transfer the least amount possible, and so in fact $g(y_2) = \min_{x \in S'} \bar{g}(x)$.[3] Finally, to resolve any indeterminacy, it is assumed that if agent 2 is indifferent between asking for verification or not, then he does not ask for verification.

The cost of verification can be modeled formally in several ways. One natural specification is that the cost of verifying y_2 is some constant, say $\mu > 0$, independent of the actual realization; this specification is pursued further bellow. The cost can also be assumed to depend on y_2, either directly or, alternatively, through the agreed-upon transfer. The latter specification is also pursued below. That is, let $\xi\{g(y_2)\}$ be the cost of verifying the realization y_2.[4] We can argue, for example, that the cost of auditing a firm in bankruptcy proceedings depends on outstanding claims.[5] Finally, note that setting $\xi\{\bar{g}(y_2)\} \equiv \mu$, we obtain the first specification, a constant cost of verification.

With this notation, we can now examine the nature of contracts in this model. A contract $[\bar{g}, \bar{S}]$ is said to be *consistent* if

$$S = \bar{S} \tag{5.1}$$

$$g(y_2) = \bar{g}(y_2) \qquad y_2 \in [\alpha, \beta] \tag{5.2}$$

Thus, under a consistent contract, agent 2 has no incentive to misrepresent, relative to the prior agreement, whether there is or is not to be verification or to not pay off what was agreed upon. It is perhaps obvious that under a consistent contract the agreed-upon transfer from agent 2 to agent 1 cannot depend on information which is known only to agent 2. That is, the function $\bar{g}$ must be identically equal to some constant $\bar{C}$ whenever there is not to be verification: $y_2 \in \bar{S}'$. Similarly, as agent 2 determines whether there is to be verification, he must have an incentive to ask for verification when he is supposed to do so. That is, the transfer plus verification cost must be less than $\bar{C}$ on $\bar{S}$. These conditions are stated formally in the following lemma.

Lemma 5.1
A contract $[\bar{g}, \bar{S}]$ is consistent if and only if $\bar{g}(y_2)$ equals some constant $\bar{C}$ on $\bar{S}'$ and $\bar{g}(y_2) + \xi\{\bar{g}(y_2)\} < \bar{C}$ on $\bar{S}$.

In what follows attention is limited to consistent contracts. But intuitively, at least, this restriction should be without loss of generality; given a contract $[\bar{g}, \bar{S}]$ each agent knows the allocation rules and can determine the actual transfer $g(\bar{g}, \bar{S})$ and verification region $S(\bar{g}, \bar{S})$ implied. Both know that in essence they have agreed to a contract $[\bar{h}, \bar{T}]$ where $\bar{h} = g(\bar{g}, \bar{S})$ and $\bar{T} = S(\bar{g}, \bar{S})$. The implication is summarized in the following lemma.

Lemma 5.2
Given any contract $[\bar{g}, \bar{S}]$ there exists a consistent contract $[\bar{h}, \bar{T}]$ which achieves the same allocation of resources.

Thus the restriction to consistent contracts is without loss of generality. It is in this sense that the problem of "moral hazard" is internalized in this model. It should be noted that this concept of consistency is closely related to the concept of incentive compatibility as discussed by Hurwicz (1972). A contract that is not consistent would require that agent 2 act in a way that is inconsistent with his own (maximizing) inclinations under the rules of the allocation process.

Returning to the interpretations of the model, recall that agent 2 can be viewed as a firm with investment project return y_2. Then a consistent contract $[\bar{g}, \bar{S}]$ can be viewed as a bond which promises to pay some fixed constant $\bar{C}$ unless bankruptcy is declared by agent 2. In that event verification (bankruptcy) costs are incurred, and something less than the fixed yield is paid. (The payment may be negative.) This interpretation offers a simple theory of closely held corporations. In the model a share would be a claim on some proportion of the profits (project return) of the firm. Individuals such as agent 1, who are not "insiders" but who hold shares, must verify claimed profit levels. Publicly held shares thus require more verification than other forms of debt. (Of course, the model in this chapter does not purport to explain the financial structure and bankruptcy decisions of all corporations.)

Alternatively, agent 2 can be viewed as an individual who is to suffer some random loss $\beta - y_2$ and purchases an insurance contract $[\bar{g}, \bar{S}]$ from agent 1 (see Arrow, 1971, 1973; Raviv, 1975). Here $\bar{C}$ is the premium, paid to agent 1 independent of the loss, and $\bar{I}(y_2) = \bar{C} - \bar{g}(y_2)$ is the insurance payment to agent 2 for loss $\beta - y_2$ if a claim is filed, in which case verification costs are incurred. Thus, if $y_2 \in \bar{S}'$, then $\bar{I}(y_2) = 0$. Alternatively, if $y_2 \in \bar{S}$, then consistency requires that $\bar{g}(y_2) + \xi\{\bar{g}(y_2)\} < \bar{C}$ so that $\bar{I}(y_2) - \xi\{\bar{g}(y_2)\} > 0$. This interpretation will motivate some further restrictions on $\xi\{\bar{g}(y_2)\}$ in the analysis that follows.

3 A characterization of optimal contracts

The objective in what follows is to characterize the set of optimal contracts. An allocation of the consumption good is said to be optimal if it is Pareto optimal among the set of allocations which can be achieved by consistent contracts, and any contract which achieves an optimal allocation is itself said to be optimal. It should be noted that the consistency conditions and verification costs require that optimal contracts be defined relative to the initial endowments.[6] It should also be noted that optimal contracts are defined relative to the deterministic verification procedure described above. (Stochastic procedures are discussed in section 4.)

By definition, optimal allocations constitute the contract curve of the two-agent economy. Consistent with the positive intent of this chapter, it is assumed here that agents will enter into an optimal contract and thus end up on the contract curve, though the precise allocation will depend on the bargaining power of the two agents. A competitive equilibrium concept that is Pareto satisfactory relative to optimal allocations is the subject of section 6.

In summary, the objective in what follows is to solve the following problem:[7]

Problem 5.1

Find a function $g(y_2)$, a constant C, and a region S that maximize

$$\int_S U_2[y_2 - g(y_2) - \xi\{g(y_2)\}]\,\mathrm{d}F(y_2) + \int_{S'} U_2(y_2 - C)\,\mathrm{d}F(y_2)$$

subject to

$$\int_S U_1\{y_1 + g(y_2)\}\,\mathrm{d}F(y_2) + \int_{S'} U_1(y_1 + C)\,\mathrm{d}F(y_2) \geqslant K \tag{5.3}$$

$$g(y_2) + \xi\{g(y_2)\} < C \qquad y_2 \in S \tag{5.4}$$

$$y_1 + g(y_2) \geq 0 \qquad \text{for } y_2 \in S \quad \text{and} \quad y_1 + C \geq 0 \qquad \text{for } y_2 \in S' \tag{5.5}$$

Here constraint (5.3) specifies that the expected utility of agent 1 is no less than some constant K. It is further required that $K \geq U_1(y_1)$ so that agent 1 is at least as well off as in autarky. Constraint (5.4) is the consistency requirement that $g(y_2) \equiv C$ on S' has already been imposed by substitution. Constraint (5.5) is the nonnegativity constraint on the consumption of agent 1; by virtue of the assumption $U_2'(0) = \infty$, the analog for agent 2 need not be imposed.

In what follows solutions to problem 5.1 are characterized under classical and nonclassical assumptions on the verification cost function ξ. For the classical approach, ξ is expressed as a continuously differentiable convex function of the transfer function, and necessary Euler conditions for a maximum are utilized. In contrast, with a fixed cost of verification, the analysis is more tedious; a condition shown by Rothschild and Stiglitz (1970) to be equivalent to risk aversion is utilized. Under either approach the important result is that the verification region is a lower interval $[\alpha, \gamma)$, $\gamma \leq \beta$.

The first approach is motivated by the insurance interpretation discussed above.[8] Let $I(y_2) = C - g(y_2)$ where, again, C is viewed as the premium and $I(y_2)$ is the insurance payment. Recall that $I \equiv 0$ on S' and $I > 0$ on S. Then on S let $\xi\{g(y_2)\} = \Psi\{I(y_2)\}$ where $\Psi(I) > 0$. Hence, in this approach the verification cost is assumed to depend only on the size of the insurance payment. It is further assumed that $\Psi(I)$ is convex and continuously differentiable. Moreover, defining $\Psi(0)$ and $\Psi'(0)$ by taking limits as $I \to 0$, it is assumed that $\Psi(0) = 0$ and $\Psi'(0) < 1$. This last condition states that the marginal cost of verification at $I = 0$ is less than the marginal payoff to agent 2 from I. Note that if $\Psi'(0) \geq 1$ and $\Psi(I)$ is convex, then $I - \Psi(I)$ will be everywhere nonpositive, and no insurance will be trivially optimal.

Now consider the following problem.

Problem 5.2
Find a function $I(y_2)$ and a constant C that maximize

$$\int_\alpha^\beta U_2[y_2 + I(y_2) - C - \Psi\{I(y_2)\}]\,\mathrm{d}F(y_2)$$

subject to

$$\int_\alpha^\beta U_1\{y_1 - I(y_2) + C\}\,\mathrm{d}F(y_2) \geq K \tag{5.6}$$

$$I(y_2) \geqslant 0 \tag{5.7}$$

$$y_1 - I(y_2) + C \geqslant 0 \tag{5.8}$$

Under the specified assumptions, if I^*, C^* is a solution to problem 5.2, then g^*, C^*, S^* is a solution to problem 5.1 where $g^*(y_2) = C^* - I^*(y_2)$ and $S^* = \{y_2: I^*(y_2) > 0\}$.[9]

This yields the following proposition.

Proposition 5.1

Any solution I^*, C^* to problem 5.2 with either y_2 simple or y_2 and $I(y_2)$ continuous has the property that $S^* = \{y_2: y_2 < \gamma\}$ for some parameter γ.[10]

Proposition 5.1 would of course be vacuous if the verification region S^* were always either empty or the entire interval. It is shown here by way of an example that S^* can depend on the verification cost in a nontrivial way. For the example, suppose that U_1 is linear, $\Psi(I) = \lambda I$ with $0 \leqslant \lambda < 1$, and y_2 is uniformly distributed on $[\alpha, \beta]$. Agent 1 is constrained to have the same utility as in autarky. A solution to problem 5.2 can be characterized on adjacent intervals. On $[\alpha, \rho]$, constraint (5.8) is binding, and so $I(y_2) = C + y_1$; on $[\rho, \gamma]$, $I(y_2) = (\gamma - y_2)/(1 - \lambda)$; and on $[\gamma, \beta]$ constraint (5.7) is binding and so $I(y_2) = 0$. Hence, for this example, problem 5.2 is equivalent to finding constants γ and C which maximize

$$\frac{1}{\beta - \alpha}\left[\int_\alpha^\beta U_2\{y_2 + y_1 - \lambda(C + y_1)\}\,dy_2 + \int_\rho^\gamma U_2(\gamma - C)\,dy_2 + \int_\gamma^\beta U_2(y_2 - C)\,dy_2\right]$$

subject to

$$\int_\alpha^\rho (C + y_1)\,dy_2 + \int_\rho^\gamma \frac{\gamma - y_2}{1 - \lambda}\,dy_2 = C(\beta - \alpha)$$

where $\alpha \leqslant \gamma \leqslant \beta$, $0 \leqslant C \leqslant \beta$, and $\rho - \gamma - (1 - \lambda)(C + y_1)$. Let γ_λ denote a maximizing γ given the cost parameter λ. If verification is costless, that is, $\lambda = 0$, full insurance is optimal and verification always occurs, that is, $\gamma_\lambda = \beta$. It can also be shown that we approach autarky as $\lambda \to 1$, that is, $\gamma_\lambda \to \alpha$. (If $\lambda = 1$, then there is no role for insurance and the verification region is empty.) In fact, γ_λ can take on any value between α and β by appropriate choice of λ between zero and unity.[11]

Under the specified assumptions, the function Ψ is inconsistent with a fixed cost of verification. Yet it has been argued by some that a fixed cost of acquiring information is typical. It is now established, at least under some further assumptions, that the verification region S will still have the same property.

The analysis is facilitated by the assumption that agent 1 is risk neutral, so that the consumption of agent 2 will equal some constant on S. This is stated formally in the following lemma.

Lemma 5.3

Any solution g^*, C^*, S^* to problem 5.1 with the cost of verification equal to some constant μ, with agent 1 risk neutral, and with nonbinding nonnegativity constraints has the property that the consumption of agent 2 equals some positive constant on S^*.

This lemma enables us to prove the following proposition.

Proposition 5.2

Any solution g^*, C^*, S^* to problem 5.1 with y_2 continuous, with a fixed verification cost μ, with agent 1 risk neutral, and with a nonnegativity condition on the consumption $c_2^*(y_2)$ of agent 2, $\sup c_2^*(y_2) \leqslant y_1 + \mu - \alpha$, has the property that $S^* = \{y_2 : y_2 < \gamma\}$ for some parameter γ.

The contracts characterized in propositions 5.1 and 5.2 have familiar characteristics. If agent 2 is viewed as the insider of a firm financing an investment project, the propositions assert that the firm will default on a bond promising to pay C^* and suffer a costly audit only when the firm performs poorly, that is, when $y_2 < \gamma$. Alternatively, if agent 2 is viewed as a purchaser of insurance, the propositions can be taken as an extension of some results in the insurance literature. Here the insured files a claim only if the loss $\beta - y_2$ exceeds $\beta - \gamma$. Hence $\beta - \gamma$ can be viewed as a deductible. In the insurance literature, nontrivial deductibles ($\gamma \neq \alpha, \beta$) are generated by the assumption that $I(y_2) \geqslant 0$ and by the assumption of loading

$$(1 + \lambda) \int_{\alpha}^{\beta} I(y_2) \, dF(y_2) \leqslant C$$

for some positive constant λ – that is, the actuarial value of the policy must be less than the premium. In this chapter the first constraint is motivated by consistency considerations, and the loading assumption is replaced by an explicit treatment of costly state verification.

4 Stochastic verification

So far attention has been limited to a deterministic verification procedure. That is, verification occurs with probability 1 or 0, depending on whether or not agent 2 asks for verification. This can be contrasted with schemes in which the decision to verify is determined in a random way. We might conjecture that random procedures can lessen the resource cost of verification while the threat of verification induces honesty. Indeed this turns out to be so; in this section we describe a stochastic verification scheme that can dominate the deterministic procedure. It goes without saying that this result limits the force of the results presented in this chapter for deterministic verification.

For the purpose of establishing that stochastic verification schemes can dominate the deterministic procedure, it is enough to provide a simple, but hopefully generic, example. Consequently, it is assumed throughout this section that y_2 is simple with only two realizations $y_2(s)$ and $y_2(t)$, $0 < y_2(s) < y_2(t)$, with probabilities $p(s)$ and $p(t)$ respectively.

The stochastic scheme is as follows. Prior to the realization of y_2, agents 1 and 2 agree to exchange specified amounts contingent on the realization. The amount to be transferred depends on whether or not there is verification, and the latter is determined in a random way. Agent 2 begins by claiming a realization of y_2, either $y_2(s)$ or $y_2(t)$. Let $\pi(w)$ denote the agreed-upon probability that there is verification given that $y_2(w)$ is claimed, $w = s, t$. (Presumably there is some machine (urn) that is known by both agents to generate outcomes with the specified probabilities.) Let $h(w)$ denote the number of units of the consumption good to be transferred from agent 2 to agent 1 given that $y_2(w)$ is claimed by agent 2 and there is no verification. Let $d(w, w')$ denote the amount to be transferred if $y_2(w)$ is realized, $y_2(w')$ is claimed, and there is verification. Let μ denote the fixed cost of verification as incurred by agent 2 if there is verification.

It should be noted that the scheme just described differs in various ways from the allocation procedure of section 2. There agent 2 merely announced whether or not there was to be verification and then, if there was any discretion, determined the transfer. Here agent 2 announces a particular realization of y_2 and, subsequent to his announcement, the transfer is completely determined, albeit in a random way. Yet these schemes are not dissimilar; it is established below that any allocation of resources achievable by the deterministic procedure is achievable here without randomization.

It remains to show that the present scheme can generate a (random) allocation of resources which both agents can count on, that is, that there is some known relationship between actual realizations of y_2 and announced realizations. A condition on the probabilities $\pi(w)$ and transfers $h(w)$, $d(w, w')$ which ensures such a relationship is

$$\{1-\pi(w)\}U_2\{y_2(w)-h(w)\}+\pi(w)U_2\{y_2(w)-d(w,w)-\mu\}$$
$$\geqslant\{1-\pi(w')\}U_2\{y_2(w)-h(w')\}+\pi(w')U_2\{y_2(w)-d(w,w')-\mu\} \tag{5.9}$$

for $w, w'=s, t$. Inequality (5.9) states that, given the realization $y_2(w)$, the expected utility of agent 2 if he claims $y_2(w)$ as a realization is no less than his expected utility if he claims $y_2(w')$. With an indifference convention, then, (5.9) ensures that agent 2 would claim $y_2(w)$ whenever $y_2(w)$ is realized, $w=s, t$.

For the purpose of establishing that the stochastic scheme described above can dominate the deterministic procedure, we can consider the following problem.

Problem 5.3
Find the $\pi(w)$, $h(w)$, and $d(w, w')$ that maximize

$$\sum_{w=s,t} p(w)[\{1-\pi(w)\}U_2\{y_2(w)-h(w)\}+\pi(w)U_2\{y_2(w)-d(w,w)-\mu\}] \tag{5.10}$$

subject to (5.9) and

$$\sum_{w=s,t} p(w)[\{1-\pi(w)\}U_1\{y_1+h(w)\}+\pi(w)U_1\{y_1+d(w,w)\}]\geqslant K \tag{5.11}$$

$$c_1\{y_2(w)\}\geqslant 0 \tag{5.12}$$

$$0\leqslant\pi(w)\leqslant 1 \tag{5.13}$$

Here constraint (5.11) bounds the expected utility of agent 1, (5.12) is the nonnegativity constraint on the consumption of agent 1, and (5.13) restates that the $\pi(w)$ are probabilities.

Now assume that a solution g^*, C^*, S^* to problem 5.1 has the property that there is verification at $y_2(s)$, but not at $y_2(t)$. Then there is a feasible solution to problem 5.3 which achieves the same allocation of resources.[12] For let $\pi(s)=1$, $\pi(t)=0$; that is, verify with probability 1 or 0 at s and t respectively. Also, let $h(t)=C^*$, $d(s,s)=g^*\{y_2(s)\}$, and $d(t,s)=y_2(t)-\mu$. Then by constraint (5.4), $d(s,s)+\mu<h(t)$. It follows that

$$U_2\{y_2(s)-d(s,s)-\mu\}>U_2\{y_2(s)-h(t)\} \tag{5.14}$$

$$U_2\{y_2(t)-h(t)\}>U_2\{y_2(t)-d(t,s)-\mu\} \tag{5.15}$$

where $y_2(t) - h(t) > 0$. With $\pi(s) = 1$ and $\pi(t) = 0$, inequalities (5.14) and (5.15) are consistent with constraint (5.9), and hence the desired allocation can be achieved.

It is now established that this feasible solution to problem 5.3 is not maximizing. In addition to the above specification let $h(s) = g^*\{y_2(s)\}$. Then, keeping $\pi(s) = 1$ and $\pi(t) = 0$, we can rewrite (5.14) and (5.15) as

$$\{1 - \pi(s)\} U_2\{y_2(s) - h(s)\} + \pi(s) U_2\{y_2(s) - d(s, s) - \mu\} > U_2\{y_2(s) - h(t)\} \tag{5.16}$$

$$U_2\{y_2(t) - h(t)\} > \{1 - \pi(s)\} U_2\{y_2(t) - h(s)\} + \pi(s) U_2\{y_2(t) - d(t, s) - \mu\} \tag{5.17}$$

Note that $y_2(t) - h(s) > 0$ and $y_2(t) - d(t, s) - \mu = 0$. It follows that, *ceteris paribus*, $\pi(s)$ can be diminished somewhat without changing the direction of the inequality in (5.17). As for constraint (5.16), note that with $h(s) = d(s, s) = g^*\{y_2(s)\}$ agent 2 is clearly better off without verification at $y_2(s)$ by virtue of the resource savings μ. Hence a diminution of $\pi(s)$ will not cause constraint (5.16) to be violated. With the transfer to agent 1 independent of verification at $y_2(s)$, constraints (5.11) and (5.12) will still be satisfied. Hence there exists a feasible solution to problem 5.3 with $\pi(t) = 0$ and $0 < \pi(s) < 1$ which dominates the (deterministic) solution to problem 5.1.

Given the dominance of stochastic verification, some further comment on problem 5.3 and its solutions would seem to be in order. First, we may question whether the constraints (5.9) can be imposed without loss of generality, as were the consistency conditions in section 2. That is, suppose that the $\pi(w)$, $h(w)$, and $d(w, w')$ are such that both the constraints (5.9) are violated. Then there is a specification of transfers (essentially a relabeling) which achieves the same allocation and satisfies constraints (5.9). If only one constraint is violated, say, for example, agent 2 would always announce that $y_2(s)$ is realized, then there is a modified game in which agent 2 must always announce $y_2(s)$, affecting $h(s)$, $d(s, s)$, or $d(t, s)$. Hence there is a modified, albeit more complicated, version of problem 5.3 which can be imposed without loss of generality.

As to the nature of solutions to problems similar to 5.3, little has been determined.[13] We might conjecture, based on the results for deterministic verification, that the probability of verification should be a nonincreasing function of y_2 and perhaps should be zero in states with high realizations. It may be noted in this regard that, in the example discussed above, resource savings are limited by the extent to which $\pi(s)$ can be diminished without creating an incentive for agent 2 to cheat at $y_2(t)$. If U_2 were unbounded from below, then it seems that the value of the objective function could be made arbitrarily close to the corresponding value with optimal contracts and costless verification by making the $\pi(w)$ arbitrarily close to zero, $w = s, t$. For let $g^*(w)$ denote a maximizing transfer as a function of w with costless verification. Then, ignoring nonnegativity constraints, let $h(w) = d(w, w) = g^*(w)$. Since $U_2(c) \to -\infty$ as $c \to 0$, $\pi(w)$ can be made arbitrarily close to zero by appropriate choice of $d(w, w')$ without violating the constraints (5.9).[14]

In summary, stochastic verification procedures can dominate deterministic procedures. In fact, stochastic procedures are not uncommon. The timing of bank audits by government agencies is somewhat random. Similarly, corporations use stochastic procedures in monitoring internal divisions. It is also said that tax audits by the US Internal Revenue Service are determined in part at random.

5 Constrained optimal contracts in an *m*-agent economy

In this section we return to deterministic verification procedures in an attempt to generalize the earlier results on other dimensions – the number of agents and unobserved random variables. It will be seen that this attempt raises some new and interesting problems with regard to the characterization of optimal contracts.

We begin with a symmetric two-agent economy. That is, the realization of the endowment y_j of each agent j ($j = 1, 2$) is known only by agent j unless a verification cost is borne. Each random variable y_j is associated with a cumulative distribution function $F(y_j)$ and takes on values in the interval $[\alpha_j, \beta_j]$, $\alpha_j > 0$. The y_j are all either simple or continuous. In the latter case each y_j possesses a continuous strictly positive density function f_j. It is assumed moreover that the y_j are independent so that the realization of y_j conveys no information about y_i, $i \neq j$. Each agent j has a utility function U_j over riskless consumption which is continuously differentiable, strictly concave, and strictly increasing with $U_j'(0) = \infty$ and $U_j'(\infty) = 0$.

Prior to the realizations of y_1 and y_2, both agents make exchange and verification plans which are contingent on the realizations. That is, let $g(y_1, y_2)$ denote the actual post-state net transfer of the consumption good from agent 2 to agent 1 as a function of the realizations of y_1 and y_2, and let $\bar{g}(y_1, y_2)$ denote the post-state contractual choice of this transfer function. Also, let S_j denote the set of realizations of y_j under which there actually is verification of y_j, and let $\bar{S}_j$ denote the pre-state contractual choice of this set. Thus a contract in this economy is a specification of $\bar{g}$, $\bar{S}_1$, and $\bar{S}_2$.

Subsequent to the realization of y_j, each agent j announces whether or not there is to be verification. If there is verification, y_j is made known to agent i ($i \neq j$) and $\phi_j(y_j)$ units of the consumption good are forfeited by agent j.[15] It is agreed that, if both agents are verified, then they transfer what was agreed upon, that is, $g(y_1, y_2) = \bar{g}(y_1, y_2)$. If agent 1 is verified but agent

2 is not, then it is agreed that agent 2 can effect any transfer consistent with the known value of y_1 and any y_2 in the agreed-upon nonverification region of y_2, that is, $g(y_1, y_2) = \min \bar{g}(y_1, x)$ where the minimum is over $x \in \bar{S}'_2$. Similarly, if agent 2 is verified but agent 1 is not, then agent 1 determines the transfer, that is, $g(y_1, y_2) = \max \bar{g}(x, y_2)$ where the maximum is over $x \in \bar{S}'_1$. If neither agent is verified, it can be assumed without loss of generality that agent 2 determines the transfer, that is, $g(y_1, y_2) = \min \bar{g}(x_1, x_2)$ where the minimum is over $(x_1, x_2) \in \bar{S}'_1 \times \bar{S}'_2$.[16] Finally, if some agent j asks for verification, but y_j is not in the agreed-upon verification region $\bar{S}_j$, then agent j incurs the verification cost, and the transfer is determined as if agent j had not asked for verification. Note that this effectively precludes such an event, and hereafter we disregard this possibility. (The scheme is easily modified to allow for binding nonnegativity constraints.) Any remaining indeterminacy is resolved by an indifference convention as in section 2.

For agent j the strategy of telling the truth means the post-state announcement of whether he is or is not to be verified in accord with $\bar{S}_j$ and $\bar{S}'_j$. Now we can define a contract $[\bar{g}, \bar{S}_1, \bar{S}_2]$ to be *consistent* if (a) telling the truth is a dominant strategy for each agent j and (b) $g = \bar{g}$. Note that condition (a) implies $S_j = \bar{S}_j$, $j = 1, 2$, and so in this sense the definition of consistency of section 2 has been generalized.

The implications of consistency should not be too surprising. Under a consistent contract the transfer function $\bar{g}$ cannot depend on information that is known only to one agent. That is, the transfer cannot depend on y_j if agent j is not verified. Also, certain incentive inequalities must be satisfied. More formally, we have the following lemma.

Lemma 5.4

A contract $[\bar{g}, \bar{S}_1, \bar{S}_2]$ is consistent if and only if $\bar{g}(y_1, y_2)$ equals some constant $\bar{C}$ on $\bar{S}'_1 \times \bar{S}'_2$, equals some function $\bar{g}^1(y_1)$ on $\bar{S}_1 \times \bar{S}'_2$, and equals some function $\bar{g}^2(y_2)$ on $\bar{S}'_1 \times \bar{S}_2$, and the following inequalities obtain:

$$\bar{g}(y_1, y_2) - \phi_1(y_1) > \bar{g}^2(y_2) \qquad (y_1, y_2) \in \bar{S}_1 \times \bar{S}_2$$

$$\bar{g}^1(y_1) - \phi_1(y_1) > \bar{C} \qquad y_1 \in \bar{S}_1$$

$$\bar{g}(y_1, y_2) + \phi_2(y_2) < \bar{g}^1(y_1) \qquad (y_1, y_2) \in \bar{S}_1 \times \bar{S}_2$$

$$\bar{g}^2(y_2) + \phi_2(y_2) < \bar{C} \qquad y_2 \in \bar{S}_2$$

It may also be noted that, under the dominant strategy equilibrium concept for determining the outcome of a contract $[\bar{g}, \bar{S}_1, \bar{S}_2]$, consistency requirements can be imposed without loss of generality, as in section 2.

We can now proceed with an attempt to characterize optimal contracts. Motivated by the classical approach of section 3, we might hope to formulate an analog of problem 5.2 in which inequality constraints define the space of feasible functions and in which there is no explicit reference to regions. First, define functions $\bar{I}_{21}(y_1)$ and $\bar{I}_{12}(y_2)$ as follows. Let $\bar{I}_{21}(y_1) = \bar{g}^1(y_1) - \bar{C}$ on $\bar{S}_1$, $\bar{I}_{21}(y_1) \equiv 0$ on $\bar{S}'_1$, $\bar{I}_{12}(y_2) = \bar{C} - \bar{g}^2(y_2)$ on $\bar{S}_2$, and $\bar{I}_{12}(y_2) \equiv 0$ on $\bar{S}'_2$. Also, define a function $\bar{K}(y_1, y_2) = \bar{g}(y_1, y_2) - \bar{C} - \bar{I}_{21}(y_1) + \bar{I}_{12}(y_2)$ on $\bar{S}_1 \times \bar{S}_2$ and zero otherwise. Then by substitution into the inequality constraints of lemma (5.4) we obtain the restrictions

$$\bar{I}_{21}(y_1) - \phi_1(y_1) > 0 \qquad y_1 \in \bar{S}_1 \tag{5.18}$$

$$\bar{I}_{12}(y_2) - \phi_2(y_2) > 0 \qquad y_2 \in \bar{S}_2 \tag{5.19}$$

$$\begin{aligned} -\bar{I}_{21}(y_1) + \phi_1(y_1) &< \bar{K}(y_1, y_2) \\ &< \bar{I}_{12}(y_2) - \phi_2(y_2) \qquad (y_1, y_2) \in \bar{S}_1 \times \bar{S}_2 \end{aligned} \tag{5.20}$$

The difficulty with this approach is constraint (5.20) and the appearance of the function $\bar{K}(y_1, y_2)$ on $\bar{S}_1 \times \bar{S}_2$. If, however, $\bar{K}(y_1, y_2)$ is restricted exogenously to be identically zero, then $\bar{g}(y_1, y_2) = \bar{I}_{21}(y_1) - \bar{I}_{12}(y_2) + \bar{C}$ everywhere. We could then postulate that the cost of verification of y_j depends only on the agreed-upon insurance payment $\bar{I}_{ij}$. That is, $\phi_j(y_j) = \Psi_j\{\bar{I}_{ij}(y_j)\}$ with $\Psi_j(0) = 0$. Then, as in section 3, we could formulate an optimization problem with the verification region $\bar{S}_j$ defined by $\bar{S}_j = \{y_j : \bar{I}_{ij}(y_j) > 0\}$. This is done below in greater generality. The maximizing contract is said to be a constrained optimum.

We should consider the implication of the constraint $\bar{K}(y_1, y_2) \equiv 0$.[17] Roughly speaking, this restriction precludes certain risk-sharing arrangements. To get some feel for this suppose that $U_1(c) = c^{\gamma+1}/(\gamma+1)$, $U_2(c) = c^{\rho+1}/(\rho+1)$ with $\gamma = -\frac{1}{4}$ and $\rho = -\frac{1}{2}$. Then the optimal (full-information) transfer function g^* is of the form

$$2g^*(y_1, y_2) = (\lambda^{-4} + 2y_2) \pm \{(\lambda^{-1} + 2y_2)^2 - 4(y_2^2 - \lambda^{-1} y_1)\}^{1/2}$$

where λ is some positive constant. It should be noted that g^* is not separable with respect to y_1 and y_2 as is required by the exogenous restriction. Thus it seems that, among other things, the transfer function is constrained in the region in which both agents are verified.

For the remainder of this section we consider the m-agent generalization of the symmetric two-agent economy. Much of the notation introduced at the outset of this section applied in an obvious way. For example, y_j denotes the endowment of each agent j, where now $j = 1, 2, \ldots, m$. Let $F(y_1, y_2, \ldots, y_m)$ denote the joint distribution of the endowments. Again, independence is assumed. Any realization of y_j is assumed to be known only to agent j unless a verification cost is borne; in that event y_j is made known to *all* agents. Let $g_{ij}(y_1, y_2, \ldots, y_m)$ denote the net transfer of the consumption good from agent i to agent j as a function of the realization of each of the endowments.[18] Then a social contract $\{\bar{g}_{ij}\}_{i,j=1}^{m}, \{\bar{S}_j\}_{j=1}^{m}$ is a pre-state agreement as to the amounts to be transferred and when there is to be verification. Such a contract is said to be consistent if (a) telling the truch is a dominant strategy for each agent j and (b) $g_{ij} = \bar{g}_{ij}$, $i, j = 1, 2, \ldots, m$.

Again, we would like to find an analytically tractable maximization problem whose solutions characterize an optimal social contract. Unfortunately this is done here only after imposing several exogenous restrictions on the exchanges, including that they are bilateral in nature. That is, the agreement $\bar{g}_{ij}$ is restricted to depend at most on y_i and y_j. It bears repeating that this restriction is imposed for analytical convenience and is not motivated by economic considerations.[19] Given this restriction it can be presumed that each pair of agents i and j adopts a resource-allocation procedure virtually identical with the two-agent procedure described above, and, in a similar fashion, restrictions on the transfer function $\bar{g}_{ij}$ analogous to those of the first part of lemma 5.4 can be derived with subscripts i and j where appropriate. When restrictions analogous to $K(\cdot, \cdot) \equiv 0$ are imposed, the $\bar{g}_{ij}$ can be shown to be of the form $\bar{g}_{ij}(y_i, y_j) = \bar{I}_{ij}(y_j) - \bar{I}_{ji}(y_i) + \bar{C}_{ij}$ where $\bar{C}_{ij}$ is some constant and $\bar{I}_{ij}(y_j) \equiv 0$ on $\bar{S}'_j$. Also impose the restrictions that $\bar{I}_{ij}(y_j) \geqslant 0$.

Now suppose that the cost of verifying y_j depends only on the sum of the "insurance payments" from other agents. That is, let the verification cost be $\Psi_j\{\Sigma_i \bar{I}_{ij}(y_j)\}$ where Ψ_j is a continuously differentiable convex function with $\Psi_j(0) \equiv 0$ and $\Psi'_j(0) < 1$.

Motivated by this discussion, then, we restrict a pre-state social contract $\{\bar{g}_{ij}\}_{i,j=1}^{m}, \{\bar{S}_j\}_{j=1}^{m}$ to be of the form

$$\bar{g}_{ij}(y_i, y_j) = \bar{I}_{ij}(y_j) - \bar{I}_{ji}(y_i) + \bar{C}_{ij}$$

$$\bar{I}_{ij}(y_j) \geqslant 0$$

$$\bar{S}_j = \left[y_j\colon \sum_i \bar{I}_{ij}(y_j) - \Psi_j\left\{\sum_i \bar{I}_{ij}(y_j)\right\} > 0 \right]$$

$$\bar{S}'_j = \{ y_j\colon \bar{I}_{ij}(y_j) = 0 \text{ for all } i \}$$

By construction, such a social contract is consistent, and subsequently the bar can be dropped from the notation.

We can now characterize a *constrained optimal social contract* by considering the following problem.

Problem 5.4

Find functions I_{ij} and constants C_j, $i, j = 1, 2, \ldots, m$ that maximize

$$\int U_1\left[y_1\left|\sum_i I_{i1}(y_1)\right|C_1-\sum_i I_{1i}(y_i)-\Psi_1\left\{\sum_i I_{i1}(y_1)\right\}\right]\mathrm{d}F(y_1,y_2,\ldots,y_m)$$

subject to

$$\int U_j\left[y_j+\sum_i I_{ij}(y_j)+C_j-\sum_i I_{ji}(y_i)-\Psi_j\left\{\sum_i I_{ij}(y_j)\right\}\right]$$
$$\times\,\mathrm{d}F(y_1,y_2,\ldots,y_m)\geqslant K_j\qquad j=2,3,\ldots,m\tag{5.21}$$

$$I_{ij}(y_j)\geqslant 0\qquad i,j=1,2,\ldots,m\tag{5.22}$$

$$\sum_{j=1}^{m}C_j=0\tag{5.23}$$

Here S_j is defined by $S_j=\{y_j\colon \Sigma_i I_{ij}(y_j)>0\}$. Here also the constants C_j can be interpreted as a premium received by agent j independent of the realization of the y_i. Note that these completely determine the desired constants C_{ij}.[20] Also impose the better-than-autarky condition $K_j\geqslant\int U_j(y_j)\,\mathrm{d}F(y_i)$.

Finally, we obtain the analog of proposition 5.1 that we have been seeking.

Proposition 5.3
Any solutions I^*_{ij}, C^*_j to problem 5.4 with either the y_j simple or the y_j and the I^*_{ij} continuous has the property that each $S^*_j=\{y_j\colon y_j<\gamma_j\}$ for some parameter γ_j.

6 A Pareto satisfactory competitive equilibrium

The purpose of this section is to analyze the properties of a competitive equilibrium concept for the m-agent economy. In particular it is established that a competitive equilibrium exists and that any equilibrium allocation is a constrained optimum, that is, it can be achieved with a constrained optimal social contract. This result is important in establishing the way in which agents end up on the contract curve and thereby supports the contention that optimal trades will be observed.

For the purpose of this section each y_j will be taken to be simple with n possible realizations.[21] The realization $y_j(s_j)$ occurs with probability $p_j(s_j)$, $s_j=1,2,\ldots,n$. The commodities which are traded in competitive markets prior to the realization of the endowments are claims contingent on the realization of each endowment and unconditional claims.[22] Let $J_{ij}(s_j)$ denote the number of claims contingent on the s_jth realization of y_j purchased by agent i, where one such claim entitles the holder to one unit of the consumption good if $y_j(s_j)$ is realized and zero otherwise. The direction of trade in such contingent claims is restricted. Agent i can purchase claims contingent on his own endowment and issue claims contingent on the endowments of others. That is, $J_{ii}(s_i) \geqslant 0$, and $J_{ij}(s_j) \leqslant 0$, $i \neq j$. Let $q_j(s_j)$ denote the price of a unit claim contingent on $y_j(s_j)$. Let D_i denote the number of unconditional claims on the consumption good purchased by agent i in the market for claims, where one such claim entitles the holder to one unit of the consumption good regardless of the realization of the endowments. There is no direct restriction on the direction of trade in such unconditional claims. Let r denote the price of one such unconditional claim. After the realization $y_i(s_i)$, each agent i must decide whether (or not) to collect the "insurance payment" $J_{ii}(s_i)$, incurring the verification cost $\Psi_i\{J_{ii}(s_i)\}$.

All agents take the prices $q_j(s_j)$ and r as parameters and maximize expected utility subject to the budget constraint. That is, each agent i chooses the $J_{ij}(s_j)$ and D_i to maximize

$$\sum_{s_1=1}^{n} \sum_{s_2=1}^{n} \cdots \sum_{s_m=1}^{n} \{p_1(s_1)p_2(s_2) \ldots p_m(s_m)\}$$

$$\times U_i\left[y_i(s_i) + \sum_{j=1}^{m} J_{ij}(s_j) + D_i - \Psi_i\{J_{ii}(s_i)\} \right] \tag{5.24}$$

subject to

$$\sum_{j=1}^{m} \sum_{s_j=1}^{n} q_j(s_j) J_{ij}(s_j) + rD_i \leqslant 0 \tag{5.25}$$

$$J_{ii}(s_i) \geqslant 0 \qquad J_{ij}(s_j) \leqslant 0 \qquad j \neq i \tag{5.26}$$

$$J_{ii}(s_i) - \Psi_i\{J_{ii}(s_i)\} \geqslant 0 \tag{5.27}$$

$$y_i(s_i) + \sum_{j=1}^{m} J_{ij}(s_j) + D_i - \Psi_i\{J_{ii}(s_i)\} \geqslant 0 \tag{5.28}$$

Here, (5.25) is the budget constraint, (5.26) restricts the direction of trade, as noted, (5.27) ensures that the proceeds of insurance cover verification costs, and (5.28) is the nonnegativity constraint on consumption. Note that these last two constraints could be suppressed.

A *competitive equilibrium* is a set of nonnegative prices $q_j^*(s_j)$ and r^* (not all zero) and commodity demands $J_{ij}^*(s_j)$ and D_i^* for each agent i such that (a) $J_{ij}^*(s_j)$ and D_i^* maximize (5.24) subject to constraints (5.25) and (5.28), and (b) $\Sigma_{i-1}^{m} J_{ij}^*(s_j) \leqslant 0$, $\Sigma_{i=1}^{m} D_i^* \leqslant 0$ (market clearing).

The existence and constrained optimality of such an equilibrium are established.

Proposition 5.4
Under the assumptions of the model there exists a competitive equilibrium.

Proposition 5.5
The allocation of any competitive equilibrium is a constrained optimum.

An equilibrium concept can be said to be Pareto satisfactory if any equilibrium allocation is optimal and if any optimal allocation can be supported as an equilibrium (see Hurwicz, 1972). Proposition 5.5 establishes the first property. As for the second, it is clear that if agents were endowed with the unconditional and contingent claims associated with a constrained optimal allocation, then there would exist an autarkic competitive equilibrium. Hence the equilibrium described in this section is Pareto satisfactory relative to the constrained optimal allocations described in the previous section.

Finally, some unusual characteristics of this equilibrium concept should be noted. The contingent claims which are traded in this model are not anonymous. A contingent claim on y_j is associated with agent j. Though for large m there are many possible sellers of such commodities, there is only one possible buyer, agent j. Hence the assumption that agent j is a price-taker may be troublesome. Ideally, the way to proceed in this context is to formulate a game with endogenous price-setters and with restrictions on trade tied closely to incentive compatibility conditions, and to establish that the equilibrium allocations of such a game approach in the limit those of the competitive equilibrium (as defined above) as the economy is replicated. It would seem crucial in establishing such a result that the "bargaining power" of any agent become negligible in the limit, despite the fact that for any finite economy traders do not have identical initial endowments. Caspi (1978) provides evidence to this effect in a simpler (full-information) context: in a pure exchange economy in which traders have identical preferences and independent but identically distributed random endowments, a *vanishing* fraction of traders receive in the core a claim which differs from the mean of their common endowment as the economy is replicated. The point is that in the context of Caspi's model the monopsony power of each buyer is limited because of the presence of near *ex ante* substitutes. It is strongly suspected that this result will carry over to the limited information context of this model, despite the need for idiosyncratic verification.[23]

7 Concluding remarks

Perhaps one of the more interesting aspects of this chapter is the attempt to explain the financial organization of firms by way of information asymmetries.

As Ross (1977) indicates in taking a similar approach, attempts to reconcile observations on financial structure with the Miller–Modigliani theorem have been less than satisfactory. Yet on this account, at least, this chapter cannot be termed a success. The model as it stands may contribute to our understanding of closely held firms, but it cannot explain the coexistence of publicly held shares and debt. In addition, we would like to model bankruptcy at a deeper level. Thus this chapter can be regarded only as a first step.

The extent to which a model can be said to *explain* economic phenomena depends on the nature of exogenous restrictions on the behavior of agents of the model, that is, restrictions which are not implied by the environment. Perhaps the most troublesome is the restriction to deterministic verification. There are also exogenous restrictions on feasible transfer functions. Risk-sharing arrangements when each of two agents is verified are restricted in a way which is motivated by technical considerations, and mutually advantageous trades contingent on the realized endowment of a third party are also excluded. Clearly here, as in much of the contract literature, more work is needed in multi-agent environments. In this regard we should note again that the existence and optimality of the competitive equilibrium concept of section 6 are established subject to these exogenous restrictions. As is well known, the presence in some settings of exogenous restrictions can affect the existence of equilibrium. It is hoped that the analysis in this chapter will prove useful in subsequent work in characterizing optimal contracts and in establishing the existence of equilibrium when fewer exogenous restrictions are imposed. Of course, the propositions of this chapter will have more force to the extent that the restrictions which have been imposed here can be derived endogenously in environments with more structure, with limitations on multilateral communication for example.

For the most part, the model deals with information in an entirely classical way. There has been some discussion in the literature to the effect that there are increasing returns to scale in the production of information (see, for example, Radner, 1968; Wilson, 1975). Grossman and Stiglitz (1978) have shown that costly information can be revealed completely by the equilibrium prices of competitive markets. In contrast, Hirshleifer (1971) has argued that competitive markets induce the acquisition of too much information. The results of this chapter would seem to illustrate that the nature of information varies with the phenomena of interest to economists and that we should be wary of generalizations.

The model provides an example of the suggestion by Radner (1968) that convexity in the technology of information production is reasonable in situations in which information depends on actions which can be scaled down to any desired size; it is postulated that resources used in state verification vary directly with the size of insurance claims. However, convexity *is* lost under the apparently reasonable specification that there is a fixed cost of verification. It can be argued by way of proposition 5.2 that the characterization of optimal contracts will remain valid even under such a specification. However, nonconvexities can be the source of considerable difficulty in establishing the existence and optimality of a competitive equilibrium. Ongoing research (Prescott and Townsend, 1978) indicates that, in some contexts, these difficulties may be overcome by stochastic schemes. This leads us back again to section 4 and the very real possibility of obtaining existence and welfare results with stochastic verification. However, this must be the subject of another publication.

Appendix

Proof of Lemma 5.1

First, note that, given any contract $[\bar{g}, \bar{S}]$, if y_2 is such that there is not to be verification (that is, $y_2 \in \bar{S}'$), then agent 2 has no incentive to ask for verification. For if agent 2 were not to ask for verification, he would transfer $\min_{x \in \bar{S}} \bar{g}(x)$ to agent 1. Alternatively, if agent 2 were to ask for verification, then $\xi\{\bar{g}(y_2)\}$ would be used in verification and $\bar{g}(y_2)$ would be transferred. Clearly agent 2 can only be made worse off by asking for verification.

Necessity is now established. If a contract $[\bar{g}, \bar{S}]$ is consistent, then $\bar{g}(y_2)$ is identically equal to some constant $\bar{C}$ on $\bar{S}'$. This can be established by contradiction. Let $K = \min_{x \in \bar{S}} \bar{g}(x)$, and suppose for some $y_2 \in \bar{S}', \bar{g}(y_2) > K$. If this y_2 were realized, there would not be verification. Consequently, the actual transfer $g(y_2)$ would be K, which is less than $\bar{g}(y_2)$, contradicting condition (5.2).

If a contract $[\bar{g}, \bar{S}]$ is consistent, then $\bar{g}(y_2) + \xi\{\bar{g}(y_2)\} < \bar{C}$ for all y_2 such that there is to be verification (that is, $y_2 \in \bar{S}$). Again, arguing by contradiction, suppose that this property fails to hold for some $y_2 \in \bar{S}$. Then, if this y_2 were realized, agent 2 would not ask for verification, contradicting condition (5.1).

Sufficiency is now established. If $y_2 \in \bar{S}'$, there will not be verification (so that $y_2 \in S'$) and $\bar{C}$ will be transferred (so that $g(y_2) = \bar{g}(y_2)$). If $y_2 \in \bar{S}$, there will be verification (so that $y_2 \in S$), and $\bar{g}(y_2)$ will be transferred (so that $g(y_2) = \bar{g}(y_2)$).

Proof of Lemma 5.2

The contract $[\bar{h}, \bar{T}]$ as defined in the text is consistent.

Proof of Proposition 5.1

If y_2 is continuous, among the necessary Euler conditions for a maximum are

$$\begin{aligned}[1 - \Psi'\{I^*(y_2)\}]U_2'[y_2 + I^*(y_2) - C^* - \Psi\{I^*(y_2)\}]f(y_2) \\ - \theta_1^* U_1'\{y_1 - I^*(y_2) + C^*\}f(y_2) + \theta_2^*(y_2) - \theta_3^*(y_2) = 0 \quad (5.\text{A}1)\end{aligned}$$

$$\theta_1^* > 0$$

$$\theta_2^*(y_2) \geqslant 0 \qquad I^*(y_2) \geqslant 0 \qquad \theta_2^*(y_2) I^*(y_2) = 0$$

$$\theta_3^*(y_2) \geqslant 0 \qquad y_1 - I^*(y_2) + C^* \geqslant 0 \qquad \theta_3^*(y_2)\{y_1 - I^*(y_2) + C^*\} = 0$$

Let γ be chosen so that

$$\{1 - \Psi'(0)\} U_2'(\gamma - C^*) - \theta_1^* U_1'(y_1 + C^*) = 0 \tag{5.A2}$$

Suppose that $I^*(y_2) = 0$ for some $y_2 \in [\alpha, \gamma)$. Then from (5.A2)

$$\{1 - \Psi'(0)\} U_2'(y_2 - C^*) f(y_2) - \theta_1^* U_1'(y_1 + C^*) f(y_2) > 0 \tag{5.A3}$$

With $I^*(y_2) = 0$, it follows that $\theta_2^*(y_2) \geqslant 0$ and $\theta_3^*(y_2) = 0$, and therefore (5.A3) contradicts (5.A1).

Similarly, suppose that $I^*(y_2) > 0$ for some $y_2 \in [\gamma, \beta]$. Then $I^*(y_2) - \Psi\{I^*(y_2)\} > 0$, and from (5.A2)

$$\begin{aligned}[1 - \Psi'\{I^*(y_2)\}] U_2'[y_2 + I^*(y_2) - C^* - \Psi\{I^*(y_2)\}] f(y_2) \\ - \theta_1^* U_1'\{y_1 - I^*(y_2) + C^*\} f(y_2) < 0\end{aligned} \tag{5.A4}$$

With $I^*(y_2) > 0$ it follows that $\theta_2^*(y_2) = 0$ and $\theta_3^*(y_2) \geqslant 0$, and therefore (5.A4) contradicts (5.A1).

Of y_2 is simple, the proof proceeds as above with obvious changes in notation.

Proof of Lemma 5.3

The proof is rather standard and is not given here for brevity.

Proof of Proposition 5.2

The proof is by contradiction. Suppose that S^* is not a lower interval, that is, $S^* \neq \{y_2 \colon y_2 < \gamma\}$ for any parameter γ. Then, roughly speaking, push the verification region to the left while retaining its mass so that it becomes a lower interval. More precisely, let δ be chosen so that $\text{prob}[\alpha, \delta) = \text{prob}(S^*) > 0$. Then let the verification set be $T = \{y_2 \colon \alpha \leqslant y_2 < \delta\}$ and its complement be $T' = \{y_2 \colon \delta \leqslant y_2 \leqslant \beta\}$. A new consumption path $\tilde{c}_2(y_2)$ will be constructed on T and T' in such a way as to both satisfy constraints (5.3)–(5.5) of problem 5.1 and increase the value of the objective functional, the expected utility of agent 2 (see figure 5.1). This will be the desired contradiction.

By lemma 5.3 and the nonnegativity condition, the initial consumption path $c_2^*(y_2)$ equals some constant K^* on S^*. Of course, $c_2^*(y_2) = y_2 - C^*$ on

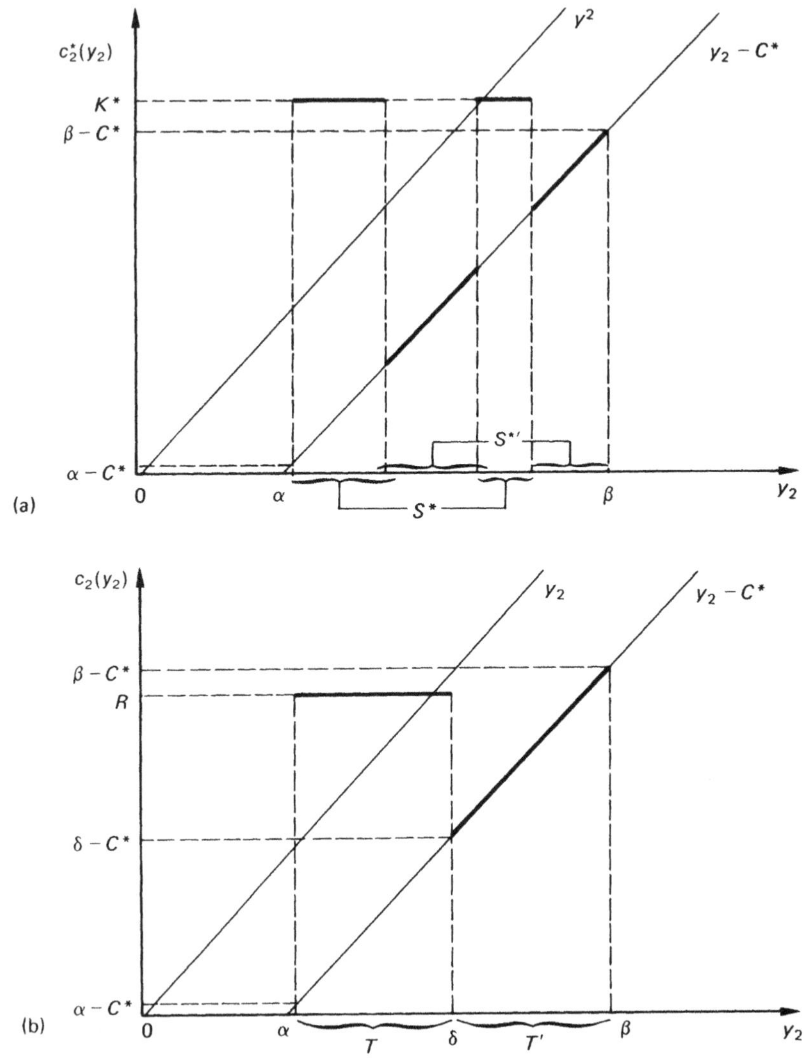

Figure 5.1.

$S^{*\prime}$. For the purposes of this proof it will be assumed that $\alpha - C^* > 0$ and $K^* > \beta - C^*$. The other possible cases can be treated in a similar manner, but this is not done here for brevity. On T' let $\tilde{c}_2(y_2) = y_2 - C^*$. Now given some constant $\tilde{K}$ (with a property to be described below) on T, let $\tilde{c}_2(y_2) = \tilde{K}$ if $\tilde{K} > y_2 - C^*$ and let $\tilde{c}_2(y_2) = y_2 - C^*$ otherwise. The constant $\tilde{K}$ is chosen such that the expected consumption of agent 2 is the same under the partitions $\{S^*, S^{*\prime}\}$ and $\{T, T'\}$. It is assumed that $\delta - C^* < \tilde{K} < \beta < C^*$; again, this is a special case, though other cases are similar. With the same expected cost of verification, the expected consumption of agent 1 will remain unchanged, and so constraint (5.3) is satisfied. With the nonnegativity condition, constraint (5.5) is satisfied. By construction, constraint (5.4) is satisfied.

Let $F^*(x)$ and $\tilde{F}(x)$ denote the cumulative distribution functions of $c_2^*(y_2)$ and $\tilde{c}_2(y_2)$ respectively. That is, $F^*(x) = \text{prob}\{c_2^*(y_2) \leqslant x\}$ and so on. Under the specified assumptions both c_2^* and $\tilde{c}_2$ are bounded between $\alpha - C^*$ and K^*. Then, following Rothschild and Stiglitz (1970), agent 2 with strictly concave U_2 will prefer $\tilde{c}_2$ to c_2^* if

$$\int_{\alpha - C^*}^{z} \{\tilde{F}(x) - F^*(x)\}\,\mathrm{d}x \leqslant 0 \qquad z \in (\alpha - C^*, K^*) \tag{5.A5}$$

with a strict inequality for at least one such z and

$$\int_{\alpha - C^*}^{K^*} \{\tilde{F}(x) - F^*(x)\}\,\mathrm{d}x = 0 \tag{5.A6}$$

Condition (5.A6) holds since $\tilde{c}_2$ and c_2^* are constructed to have the same mean. It remains to verify (5.A5).

Now, roughly speaking, $F^*(x)$ increases at a rate determined by the density $f(y_2)$ as y_2 ranges through $S^{*\prime}$ and remains constant as y_2 ranges through S^*. The mass prob(S^*) is picked up at $x = K^*$ and $F^*(K^*) = 1$. Also, $\tilde{F}(x)$ remains at zero until $x = \delta - C^*$, and then increases at a rate determined by $f(y_2)$ as y_2 ranges through T', with a jump of prob(T) at $x = \tilde{K}$. Note that $\tilde{F}(\beta - C^*) = 1$. (Figure 5.2 is derived from figure 5.1 on the assumption that y_2 is uniformly distributed on $[\alpha, \beta]$.) Thus by construction there exists some $W \in (\delta - C^*, \beta - C^*)$ such that $\tilde{F}(x) \leqslant F^*(x)$ for $\alpha - C^* \leqslant x < W$ and $\tilde{F}(x) \geqslant F^*(x)$ for $W \leqslant x \leqslant \beta - C^*$. It follows that, given (5.A6), (5.A5) must hold also.

Proof of Lemma 5.4

The proof is similar to that of lemma 5.1 and, for brevity, is not included here.

Proof of Proposition 5.3

Proceeding as in the proof of proposition 5.1, let γ_{j1} be chosen such that

$$\begin{aligned}
&\int_{\alpha_2}^{\beta_2} \cdots \int_{\alpha_m}^{\beta_m} \{1 - \Psi_1'(0)\} U_1'\Big[\gamma_{j1} + C_1^* - \sum_i I_{1i}^*(y_i)\Big] f(y_1) \ldots f(y_m)\,\mathrm{d}y_2 \ldots \mathrm{d}y_m \\
&\quad - \theta_j \int_{\alpha_2}^{\beta_2} \cdots \int_{\alpha_m}^{\beta_m} U_j'\Big[y_j + \sum_i I_{ij}^*(y_j) + C_j^* - \sum_{i \neq 1} I_{ji}^*(y_i) \\
&\quad - \Psi_j\Big\{\sum_i I_{ij}^*(y_j)\Big\}\Big] f(y_1) \ldots f(y_m)\,\mathrm{d}y_2 \ldots \mathrm{d}y_m = 0 \qquad j = 2, 3, \ldots, m
\end{aligned} \tag{5.A7}$$

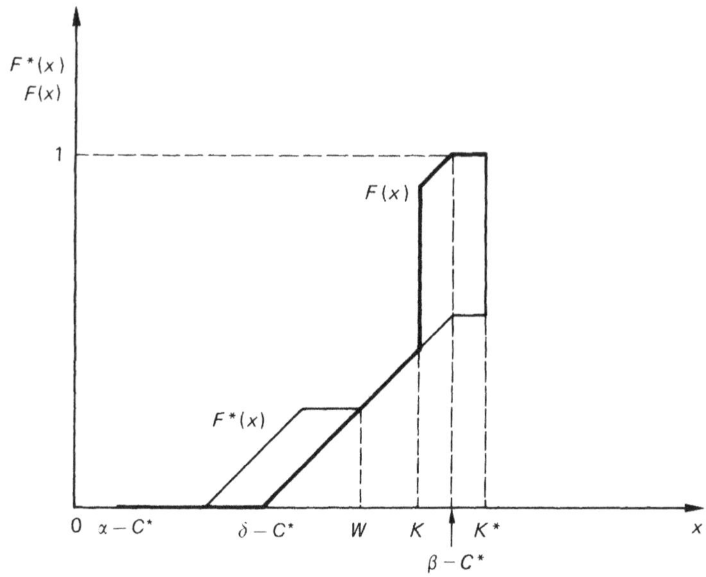

Figure 5.2.

Let $\gamma_1 = \max\{\gamma_{j1}\}_{j=2}^{m}$. Then it can be shown by contradiction that there does not exist any $y_1 \in [\alpha_1, \gamma_1)$ such that $I_{j1}^*(y_1) = 0$ for each j, and there does not exist any $y_1 \in [\gamma_1, \beta_1]$ such that $I_{j1}^*(y_1) > 0$ for some j. The $\{\gamma_j\}_{j=2}^{m}$ can be found in a similar manner.

Proof of Proposition 5.4

Construct an $(nm + 1)$-dimensional commodity space as follows. Let the first n commodities be associated with the excess demand for claims contingent on the realizations $\{y_1(s_1); s_1 = 1, 2, \ldots, n\}$ of the endowment of the first agent as ordered by s_1. Let the commodities $n+1$ to $2n$ be those associated with the excess demand for claims contingent on the realizations $\{y_2(s_2);\ s_2 = 1,\ 2,\ \ldots,\ n\}$ of the second agent with the obvious ordering induced by s_2. Continue in this way through agent m, numbering the first nm elements. Let the $nm + 1$ commodity be associated with the excess demand for unconditional claims.

For each agent $i, i = 1, 2, \ldots, m$, there is associated a set $X_i \subset R^{nm+1}$ of possible consumption vectors (excess demands) defined by (5.26) – (5.28). Thus, for agent 1, for example, given some $x_1 \in X_1$, the first n components of x_1 must be nonnegative, the next $(m - 1)n$ components must be nonpositive, and the last component is unrestricted in sign. Also, by construction, X_i is closed and convex for every i. The endowment of agent i in R^{nm+1} can be taken as the null vector.

For each agent i there is a preference ordering over X_i as defined by

$$V_i(x_i) = \sum_{s_1=1}^{n} \sum_{s_2=1}^{n} \cdots \sum_{s_m=1}^{n} \{p_1(s_1)p_2(s_2) \ldots p_m(s_m)\}$$

$$\times U_i\left[y_i(s_i) + \sum_{j=1}^{m} J_{ij}(s_j) + D_i - \Psi_i\{J_{ij}(s_i)\} \right]$$

for $x_i \in X_i$. As U_i is concave and Ψ_i is convex, and both are continuous, this ordering is closed and convex.

Now by suitably modifying the argument of Arrow and Hahn (1971) it can be established[24] that there exists a price vector $q^* \in R^{nm+1}$, a utility allocation $\{V_i^*\}_{i=1}^m$, and a consumption allocation $\{x_i^*\}_{i=1}^m$ which constitute a *compensated equilibrium* in that $q^* \geqslant 0$, $\Sigma_{i=1}^m x_i^* \leqslant 0$, x_i^* minimizes $q^* x_i$ subject to $V_i(x_i) \geqslant V_i^*$ and (6.26)–(6.28) and $q^* x_i^* = 0$.

Associated with q^* are the prices r^*, $\{q_j^{j*}(s_j)\}$. (Recall the labeling convention adopted above.) It is claimed that, for every j, $\Sigma_{s_j=1}^n q_j^*(s_j) \leqslant r^*$. For suppose the contrary inequality. Then any agent $i \neq j$ could issue claims contingent on the realization of the endowment of agent j and purchase unconditional claims in such a way as to leave relationships (5.27) and (5.28) unaltered and reduce expenditures without limit. This is an obvious contradiction.

Thus $q^* \neq 0$ implies $r^* > 0$. Let $b_i = \min_{s_i} y_i(s_i)$. (Recall that $y_i(s_i) > 0$ for every s_i.) Then the vector $\hat{x}_i = (0, 0, \ldots, -b_i) \in X_i$ is such that $q^* \hat{x}_i < 0$. Hence, by Debreu (1959, section 4.9, equation (1)), x_i^* is a maximal element in X_i subject to $q^* x_i \leqslant 0$. Hence the compensated equilibrium is a competitive equilibrium.

Proof of Proposition 5.5

It is first established that the allocation of a competitive equilibrium is Pareto optimal relative to the commodities $\{D_i\}$ and $\{J_{ij}(s_j)\}$ which are traded. Retaining the notation of the proof of proposition 5.4 note first that, as the U_j are strictly increasing, $q^* > 0$ and hence $\Sigma_{i=1}^m x_i^* = 0$. Therefore the competitive equilibrium is an equilibrium relative to the price system q^* as defined by Debreu (section 6.2) and hence by Debreu (section 6.3, equation (1)) is also an optimum.

Finally, note that any allocation such that $\Sigma_{i=1}^m x_i = 0$ and $x_i \in X_i$ for each i defines a social contract of the restricted form and conversely. For suppose that the commodities $J_{ij}(s_j)$ and D_i are such that $\Sigma_{i=1}^m x_i = 0$ and $x_i \in X_i$ for all i. Then $-J_{ji}(s_i) = \Sigma_{j \neq i} J_{ji}(s_i)$. Let $\bar{I}_{ji}\{y_i(s_i)\} = -J_{ji}(s_i), j \neq i$. Let $\bar{g}_{ij}(y_i, y_j) = I_{ij}(y_i) - I_{ji}(y_i) + C_{ij}$ where the $\bar{C}_{ij}$ are determined in the obvious way from the D_i. Let $\bar{S}_i = \{y_i(s_i): J_{ii}(s_i) > 0\}$. Then from (6.26) and (6.27) $\Sigma_j \bar{I}_{ji}\{y_i(s_i)\} - \Psi_i[\Sigma_j \bar{I}_{ji}\{y_i(s_i)\}] > 0$ on $\bar{S}_i$ and $\bar{I}_{ji}\{y_i(s_i)\} = 0$ on $\bar{S}_i'$ for all j. The converse is similarly established.

Notes

1 In what follows sets of probability zero and properties of functions on sets of probability zero are disregarded, at least where no ambiguity results.

2 Of course there are no independent third parties such as auditors in the model. Also, it may be natural to view insurance companies as bearing the costs of verifying claimed losses. In this regard the assumption that the cost is borne by the insured is not restrictive as these costs may be passed along to the insurer in an optimal exchange.

3 It can be assumed without loss of generality that $\bar{S}'$ is closed.

4 Analytically this will be equivalent to letting the verification cost depend on the actual transfer $g(y_2)$.

5 At this level of abstraction, however, the latter specification of the verification cost may seem somewhat unnatural and is motivated, as will be seen below, by analytic convenience.

6 Here optimal allocations are defined relative to constraints (consistency conditions) derived under the *particular* game described in the text. It is conjectured, however, that these constraints will characterize the outcomes of a large class of alternative games.

7 As consistency conditions are imposed, the bar can be dropped from the notation.

8 The author is much indebted to Artur Raviv, who pointed out the mathematical similarity of a preliminary version of problem 5.1 to a problem in the insurance literature. The method of proof of proposition 5.1 emanated from the method employed by Raviv (1975).

9 To see this, transform problem 5.1 to an equivalent problem by making the substitutions $g(y_2) = C - I(y_2)$ and $\xi\{g(y_2)\} = \Psi\{I(y_2)\}$. Next, in lieu of constraint (5.4), impose on S the apparently weaker restriction that $I(y_2) > 0$. From the nature of this modified problem and the monotonicity of U_j, if $I^* > 0$, then $I^* - \Psi(I^*) > 0$ so that a solution to the modified problem will satisfy constraint (5.4). Next, recalling that $I \equiv 0$ on S' and $\Psi(0) = 0$, enter the expression $I(y_2) - \Psi\{I(y_2)\}$ in the second branch of the objective function of the modified problem and enter $I(y_2)$ in the second branch of constraint (5.3). This yields problem (5.4) with $S = \{y_2 : I(y_2) > 0\}$.

10 The existence and uniqueness of a solution are ensured by the continuity and strict concavity of the objective function and the compactness and convexity of the set of feasible solutions. (If y_2 is continuous, the class of functions $I(y_2)$ is restricted.)

11 It should be mentioned here that risk neutrality on the part of agent 1 is not necessary for a nontrivial verification region. Also, the example suggests that there might be a more general monotone dependence between the verification region and the cost.

12 A similar argument establishes that whatever the relationship between $\pi(s)$ and $\pi(t)$, the allocation achieved in a solution to problem 5.1 is also attainable under the stochastic scheme with nonrandom verification.

13 The difficulty is that constraints (5.9) seem quite messy analytically; examination of the necessary conditions for a maximum, as in the proof of proposition 5.1, has not yet provided much insight. In order to avoid putting measures on measures,

a restriction to simple rather than continuous random variables has been imposed. Yet this seems to make the characterization more difficult.

14 Note that in such cases, problem 5.3 cannot attain its supremum; at $\pi(w)=0$ for all w there are no disincentives to cheating.

15 Here it should be understood that the verification cost $\phi_j(y_j)$ can depend in an exogenous way on the agreed-upon transfer $\bar{g}$, which in turn has y_j as an argument. Thus $\phi_j(y_j)$ should be viewed as a composite function and is not meant to imply that the costs depend in an exogenous way on the realization y_j.

16 Symmetry might suggest that both should determine the transfer, but this leads to an obvious inconsistency. The implication of the present specification will be that the agreed-upon transfer must be some constant on $\bar{S}'_1 \times \bar{S}'_2$, an implication that would also follow if agent 1 determined the transfer. The constant is determined in a solution to a Pareto problem, and thus the process does not favor agent 2 a priori.

17 The intent here and below is to impose sufficient exogenous restrictions to generalize proposition 5.1. It is hoped that the reader finds these restrictions, motivated as they are by technical considerations, as unpleasant as the author does. It should be noted, however, that under these restrictions feasible contracts seem to mimic what we actually observe in some insurance markets; each agent pays a premium independent of the state and receives compensation only as a function of his *own* loss. Additional work should be devoted to finding an environment under which these restrictions are endogenous so that proposition 5.4 and the results of section 6 below have more force.

18 Thus $g_{ji} = -g_{ij}$. Also, it is convenient in what follows to define $g_{ii}=0$ and similarly (except in section 6) for all variables with an identical double subscript.

19 Green (1972), among others, has stressed the need for bilateral models of exchange, but their study here (making the restriction endogenous, perhaps by an explicit treatment of the technology of communication) would constitute a separate chapter. In contrast Wilson (1968) has stressed the collective nature of decisions under risk.

20 The relationship is $\Sigma_i C_{ij} = C_j$, where as usual $C_{jj}=0$ and $C_{ji} = -C_{ij}$.

21 We could easily permit a different number of realizations for each agent.

22 For an earlier discussion of the relationship between insurance contracts and contingent commodity markets in the standard competitive model see Kihlstrom and Pauly (1971).

23 Again it should be noted that competitive insurance markets seem consistent with the imposed restrictions.

24 The assumption that $X_i \subseteq R^l_+$ in Arrow and Hahn is not crucial to their analysis. Here also the set of feasible allocations is convex and compact. Also, the $\hat{x}_i = 1, 2, \ldots, m$ as defined below serve as the feasible allocation associated with the null utility which can be Pareto dominated.

References

Arrow, K.J. (1964) The role of securities in the optimal allocations of risk bearing. *Review of Economic Studies* 31, 91–6.

——(1971) On optimal insurance policies. *Essays in the Theory of Risk Bearing*, pp. 212–19. Chicago, IL: Markham.

——(1973) Optimal insurance and generalized deductibles. Rand Report, Rand Corporation, Santa Monica, CA.

——(1974) Limited information and economic analysis. *American Economic Review* 64, 1–10.

——and Hahn, F. (1971) *General Competitive Analysis*. San Francisco, CA: Holden Day.

Caspi, Y.M. (1978) A limit theorem on the core of an economy with individual risks. *Review of Economic Studies* 45, 267–71.

Debreu, G. (1959) *Theory of Value*. New York: Wiley.

Green, J. (1972) Pre-existing contracts and temporary general equilibrium. Discussion paper 246, Harvard University, Cambridge, MA.

Grossman, S. and Stiglitz, J. (1978) On the impossibility of informationally efficient markets. Technical report 259, Institute of Mathematical Studies of Social Science, Stanford University.

Harris, M. and Raviv, A. (1979) Optimal incentive contracts with imperfect information. *Journal of Economic Theory* 20, 231–59.

Helpman, E. and Laffont, J. (1975) On moral hazard in general equilibrium theory. *Journal of Economic Theory* 10, 8–23.

Hirshleifer, J. (1971) The private and social value of information and the reward to inventive activity. *American Economic Review* 61, 561–74.

Hurwicz, L. (1972) On informationally decentralized systems. In *Decision and Organizations*, eds C.B. McGuire and R. Radner, ch. 14. Amsterdam: North-Holland.

Kihlstrom, R. and Pauly, M. (1971) The role of insurance in the allocation of risk. *American Economic Review* 61, 371–9.

Prescott, E. and Townsend, R. (1979) On competitive theory with private information. Presented at the Econometric Society Summer Meetings, Montreal, 1979.

Radner, R. (1968) Competitive equilibrium under uncertainty. *Econometrica* 36, 31–58.

Raviv, A. (1975) Mathematical models for optimal insurance policy selection. Ph.D. Dissertation, Northwestern University, Evanston, IL.

Ross, S. (1977) The determination of financial structure: the incentive-signaling approach. *Bell Journal of Economics* 8, 23–40.

Rothschild, M. and Stiglitz, J. (1970) Increasing risk. I: A definition. *Journal of Economic Theory* 2, 225–43.

Shavell, S. (1979) On moral hazard and insurance. *Quarterly Journal of Economics* 93, 541–62.

Spence, M. and Zeckhauser, R. (1971) Insurance, information and individual action. *American Economic Review* 61, 380–7.

Wilson, R. (1968) On the theory of syndicates. *Econometrica* 36, 119–32.

——(1975) Informational economies of scale. *Bell Journal of Economics* 6, 184–95.

6

Allocation Mechanisms for Asymmetrically Informed Agents

with Milton Harris

1 Introduction

In this chapter we propose a new approach for predicting both the allocation of resources and the resource-allocation mechanism in certain environments in which agents are asymmetrically informed prior to any trading.[1] We illustrate our approach by applying it to a simple pure exchange environment in which an information asymmetry is present.

The central element of our approach (which is described in more detail below) is to define the concept of an optimal resource-allocation mechanism and to characterize such optimal mechanisms and their allocations for given economic environments. There are two reasons for approaching the problem in this way, that is, searching for optimal resource-allocation mechanisms. The first is simply that we would like to develop a theory which explains observed mechanisms (or processes or institutional arrangements – we use these terms synonymously). For example, we might wish to explain why auctions are used in certain environments but not in others.[2] The second is that we would like to develop a theory which explains the final allocation

This chapter was presented at the NBER–CEME Conference honoring Herbert A. Simon, held at Carnegie–Mellon University, October 1977. It has also provided the basis for presentations at the NBER–CEME Conference on Decentralization held at the University of Minnesota, April 1978, and at workshops at Brown University, University of Chicago, Columbia University, Ohio State University, University of Minnesota, University of Pittsburgh, University of Virginia, the Board of Governors of the Federal Reserve System, and the Federal Reserve Bank of Minneapolis. We would like to thank the participants at these conferences and workshops for numerous helpful suggestions. In addition, we would like to thank our colleagues, Edward C. Prescott and Scott F. Richard, as well as an anonymous referee, for valuable comments.

of resources in environments with asymmetric information, and, to do so, we argue that we must begin with an explicit consideration of mechanisms. To sketch this argument briefly, let us start with the premise that in any economic environment, the observed allocation of resources is actually achieved by some mechanism. We then assert that in some asymmetric information environments there are allocations consistent with the resource constraints (that is, technologically feasible) which, nevertheless, cannot be achieved by any mechanism. That is, we assert that the presence of information asymmetries imposes certain incentive compatibility constraints on achievable allocations.[3] The point here is that these constraints can only be revealed by an explicit consideration of the processes by which allocations are achieved.

Obviously one way of making sure that information constraints are accounted for is simply to analyze the equilibrium of some particular (and explicit) mechanism. This approach is certainly suitable for positive purposes if we believe that the chosen mechanism is a good model of actual arrangements in the environment of interest, and if we are not interested in explaining these arrangements. Yet if we do seek to explain observed arrangements or if we are interested in normative implications, then we would like to establish that the constraints on allocations of the chosen mechanism cannot be circumvented by some alternative process. This leads us to consider a fairly broad class of available mechanisms.[4]

The approach we propose here consists of four steps. First, we define the concept of an allocation mechanism for the environment to be analyzed and specify the class of available mechanisms. Essentially a mechanism is a set of rules which define the game to be played by the agents. Second, we define the concepts of an equilibrium of a mechanism and equilibrium final allocations of a mechanism. Essentially our concept of an equilibrium is the sequential Nash equilibrium in the space of strategies or decision rules with maximizing behavior defined relative to statistical inferences under Bayes's rule. Third, we define preferences over mechanisms and the concept of an optimal mechanism. Here preferences are defined relative to the initial information structure. Fourth, we characterize an optimal mechanism and its equilibrium final allocation.[5]

This approach is very different from those taken in most of the recent literature dealing with the effects of information on the allocation of resources. Essentially this literature has focused on two modeling strategies. In the first, Pareto optimal or core allocations are sought in the space of contingent contracts under the assumption that only those variables observable by all agents can be included as arguments in any contract.[6] In the second, a specific mechanism is imposed on the environment and its equilibrium allocation(s) are investigated.[7] In neither approach is a class of all available mechanisms considered or optimal mechanisms sought.[8] We conclude this section with a brief outline of this chapter in which we sketch our results.

In section 2 we describe the environment in detail and provide some intuition for the result that achievable allocations are constrained by the informational asymmetry. The environment consists of two agents who may trade claims to a single consumption good contingent on two states of nature. One agent is fully informed as to the probabilities of these states before any trade takes place. The other agent knows only the distribution of these probabilities.

In section 3 we define the concept of a mechanism for our environment. The equilibrium concept we employ is discussed in section 4. Section 5 is devoted to showing that certain self-selection constraints must be satisfied by any allocation resulting from any mechanism (see theorem 6.1). Preferences of agents over mechanisms and some optimality concepts for mechanisms are defined in section 6.

In section 7 we show that a certain simple mechanism is optimal and characterize its equilibrium allocation (see theorems 6.2 and 6.3). In this optimal mechanism the uninformed agent proposes a set of feasible allocations and the informed agent chooses the final allocation from among these. The equilibrium final allocation of this mechanism has the property that there may be further gains to trade relative to the final information structure, but agents agree at the outset that such gains will not be exploited. That is, agents end up off the full-information contract curve even though all are fully informed in the end. We also show in section 7 (theorem 6.4) that any mechanism can be dominated by a mechanism which is a slight variant of the optimal mechanism described above.

In section 8 we show that a certain intuitively appealing mechanism can be strictly dominated. Section 9 contains some concluding remarks. To enhance readability, all proofs and some formal definitions are relegated to the appendix.

2 The environment

In the remainder of this chapter we focus on a simple exchange economy consisting of two agents, one consumption good, and two states of nature. There are no agents other than the two just mentioned, for example, no auctioneers, message centers, etc. The informed agent is presumed to know the true probability that each state will occur, and this is known by the uninformed agent. The uninformed agent has a prior distribution over these probabilities, and this prior is known by the informed agent. Both agents are assumed to know all other aspects of the environment.

Endowments of the good for each agent for each state are exogenously fixed. Let x_s denote the total endowment of the good in each state s, $s = 1, 2$, with $x = (x_1, x_2) > 0$. These define the Edgeworth box $B = [0, x_1] \times [0, x_2]$ (see figure 6.1). The endowment of agent 2 is represented by a point $e = (e_1, e_2)$ in the interior of the Edgeworth box. The endowment of agent 1 is $x - e$. Similarly, given a point $c = (c_1, c_2)$ in the Edgeworth box, the consumption bundle of agent 2 is c and that of agent 1 is $x - c$.

Each agent i, $i = 1, 2$, has a von Neumann–Morgenstern utility function u_i defined for all nonnegative consumption r, where u_i is twice continuously differentiable, $u_i'(r) > 0$, $u_i''(r) < 0$ for all $r > 0$ and $u_i'(0) = \infty$. Each agent has as objective the maximization of his expected utility.

Thus if agent i knew the probability of state 1 to be π, he would evaluate the bundle $w = (w_1, w_2)$ consisting of w_j units of the good if state j occurs ($j = 1, 2$) by taking the expectation

$$\pi u_i(w_1) + (1 - \pi) u_i(w_2)$$

Any point c in the Edgeworth box B can be evaluated by each agent in this way given the probability π of state 1. Thus, for any point $c \in B$ and any $0 \leqslant \pi \leqslant 1$ let

$$U_1(c, \pi) = \pi u_1(x_1 - c_1) + (1 - \pi) u_1(x_2 - c_2)$$

$$U_2(c, \pi) = \pi u_2(c_1) + (1 - \pi) u_2(c_2)$$

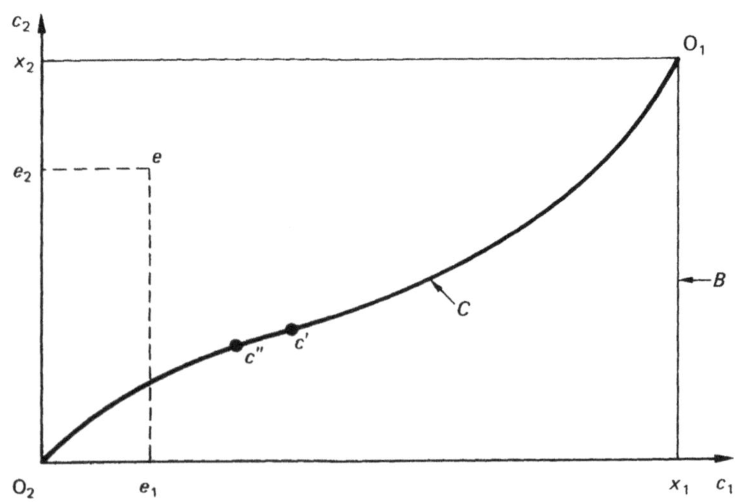

Figure 6.1. Basic concepts

The functions U_1, U_2 then define the preferences of the two agents over points in the Edgeworth box B given some value for the probability of state 1.

The curve labeled C in figure 6.1 is the set of allocations which would be optimal if both agents were informed as to the true value of the parameter π. Under our assumptions, this curve is independent of the actual value of π as long as both agents agree on its value. Thus C is called the consensus contract curve. Formally

$$C = \left\{ c \in B \,\middle|\, \frac{u_2'(c_1)}{u_2'(c_2)} = \frac{u_1'(x_1 - c_1)}{u_1'(x_2 - c_2)} \right\}$$

It should be emphasized here that preferences depend on the parameter π. Geometrically, for each value of π there corresponds a family of indifference curves for each agent. We assume that both agents correctly believe that this parameter can have only one of two values, π_1 or π_2, with $0 < \pi_1 < \pi_2 < 1$. There are then two families of indifference curves for each agent, with the "steeper" curves being associated with $\pi = \pi_2$ (see figure 6.2). Thus for agent 1, for example, the consumption bundle c in figure 6.2 is preferred to c' if $\pi = \pi_2$ and conversely if $\pi = \pi_1$.

We assume now that the actual probability π of state 1 is drawn from a known distribution ϕ_1 defined on $\Pi = \{\pi_1, \pi_2\}$. Thus $\phi_1(\pi_j)$ denotes the probability that $\pi = \pi_j, j = 1, 2$, with $0 < \phi_1(\pi_j) < 1$ and $\phi_1(\pi_1) + \phi_1(\pi_2) = 1$. Agent 2, the uninformed agent, is assumed not to know π initially but to

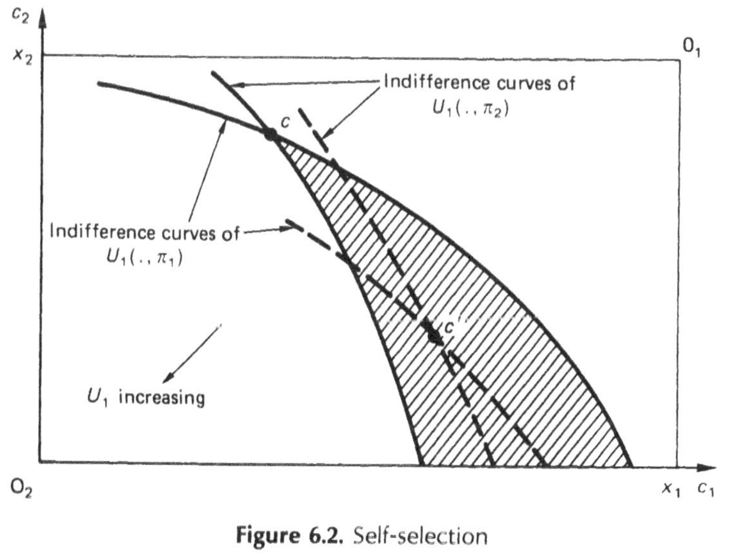

Figure 6.2. Self-selection

have the prior distribution over Π given by ϕ_1. We denote by $\bar{\pi}$ the mean of the distribution ϕ_1. Agent 1, the informed agent, observes the actual realization of π. Again, both agents are assumed to know all other aspects of the environment.

In order to motivate the result that certain allocations are not achievable in this environment because of the informational asymmetry, consider the following mechanism. Agent 1 (informed agent) is asked to name a value of π from the set Π. If he names π_1, then the allocation $c' \in C$ is effected, and if he names π_2, then $c'' \in C$ is effected. This mechanism has some a priori appeal since both c' and c'' are full-information Pareto optimal. However, suppose that $c' \neq c''$, as shown in figure 6.1 for example. In this case, since it is impossible for agent 2 to require agent 1 to name the true value of π, agent 1 will always claim $\pi = \pi_2$, even if $\pi = \pi_1$ (since $x - c'' > x - c'$). Thus the allocation $c = c'$ if $\pi = \pi_1$, and $c = c''$ if $\pi = \pi_2$ is not achievable by this mechanism. (The equilibrium allocation is $c = c''$ for either value of π.) It turns out that, no matter how complicated we make the mechanism, allocations like

$$c = \begin{cases} c^1 & \text{if } \pi = \pi_1 \\ c^2 & \text{if } \pi = \pi_2 \end{cases}$$

are not achievable in this environment unless agent 1 prefers c^1 to c^2 if $\pi = \pi_1$ and vice versa if $\pi = \pi_2$. This condition, which is illustrated in figure 6.2, is called the self-selection condition. The statement that no allocation which fails to satisfy this condition is achievable (even if c^1 and c^2 are random variables) is proved in theorem 6.1 (note that this result would not hold if there were more than one informed agent). Clearly, the allocation $c = c'$ if $\pi = \pi_1$, $c = c''$ if $\pi = \pi_2$ does not satisfy the self-selection condition and is therefore not achievable.

The remainder of this chapter is devoted to characterizing an optimal allocation mechanism for the environment described above and its allocation.

3 Mechanisms

Our concept of a mechanism is simply a set of rules which define the game to be played by the agents. These rules are constraints on what proposals the agents may make at any stage of a bargaining process and a rule for determining the final allocation as a function of the sequence of these proposals.

We have in mind that the constraints on behavior are *not* inherently unenforceable, that is, both agents must have sufficient information to know whether a constraint is being violated. Thus the constraints on strategies at any stage will depend on the information available to both agents at that stage. The information available to the agents at any stage may include, in addition to the initial information, proposals at previous stages and anything which may be inferred from these proposals. Moreover, we assume that, once a mechanism has been adopted, both agents abide by the constraints imposed by the mechanism at all stages. This is the case even if, at some stage, *both* agents would like to abandon the mechanism, that is, violate the constraints. Thus we assume, at least implicitly, that a technology exists for enforcing such agreements.

Before proceeding with a formal definition, it may be helpful first to consider some examples of mechanisms. This will serve to motivate the definitions which follow. As a first example consider the following mechanism (which turns out to be optimal). Agent 2 (the uninformed agent) starts by proposing a pair of possible allocations (a pair of points in the Edgeworth box). Agent 2 may choose this pair randomly from among any finite collection of alternative pairs. After observing agent 2's proposed pair, agent 1 (the informed agent) may then choose either allocation of the pair or he may choose the endowment. Again, agent 1 may make his selection randomly. Agent 1's choice becomes the actual final allocation, that is, no further proposals can be offered after agent 1 chooses and the transaction proposed by agent 1 is effected at that point. This set of rules defines a game that the two agents can play. We denote this optimal mechanism by $\bar{M}$.

As a second example, we can consider a competitive-type mechanism M_C. This game is played as follows. Agent 1 names a value for π from the set Π (he may choose at random and need not name the true value). The final allocation is then determined as the competitive equilibrium allocation of this pure exchange economy when the preferences of agent 2 are defined by his expected utility using his prior on π, that is, $U_2(c, \bar{\pi})$, and agent 1's preferences are defined by his expected utility using the value of π that he just proposed. Note that, given the informational environment, the constraint on agent 1's proposal is enforceable while one which required him to name the true probability would not be. It turns out that this mechanism can be strictly dominated.

Finally, as a third example, consider the following "inference" mechanism M_I. Agent 1 (the informed agent) starts by proposing any feasible allocation (that is, any point in the Edgeworth box). This proposal can be generated by choosing randomly from any finite set of alternative feasible allocations. After observing this proposal, agent 2 may agree to the implied exchange just proposed or he may choose not to trade. He may also choose between these two possibilities at random. We call this an inference mechanism because the uninformed agent may infer the true probability π from the proposal of the informed agent. Naturally, the informed agent will take this possibility into account in choosing his strategy at the first stage. This inference mechanism can also, in general, be strictly dominated. This is shown in section 8.

We now proceed with a more formal definition of a mechanism. A mechanism consists of three objects. First is a specification of the number of stages S which will be involved in the bargaining process (we assume that all mechanisms terminate after a finite number of stages). In each stage, each agent is allowed to make one proposal.[9]

The second object is a specification of the set of all possible proposals P and the subset of P from which each agent i may choose his proposal p_{is} at each stage s. This set depends on all previous proposals $p^{s-1} = (p_0, p_1, \ldots, p_{s-1})$ where $p_t = (p_{1t}, p_{2t})$, $t = 1, 2, \ldots, s-1$, and is denoted $X_{is}(p^{s-1})$. The proposal p_0 is simply for notational convenience. Each mechanism begins with each agent making proposal p_0. Thereafter, an agent can propose p_0 only if required to do so. Being constrained to propose p_0 is equivalent to being required to "sit out" a stage, and observation of p_0 therefore conveys no additional information. At any stage any agent may choose his proposal by choosing at random from a finite number of proposals in his constraint set at that stage.

The third object of a mechanism is a rule F which specifies the distribution of the final allocation as a function of the proposals p^S made in all stages. Thus, for any sequence of proposals p^S, $F(c|p^S)$ is interpreted as the probability that agent 2's consumption bundle is c given that the history of the game is p^S. (Recall that agent 1's consumption bundle will be $x - c$.) Again, we restrict ourselves to simple probability measures so that $F(\cdot|p^S)$ puts positive probability on only a finite number of allocations in the box B.

A specific mechanism, say M, is represented symbolically by the four-tuple $[S, P, X, F]$ where S, P, and F are as defined above,

$$X = \{X_{is} | i = 1, 2, s = 1, \ldots, S\}$$

and p_0 is always taken to be the word "pass." The class of all such mechanisms is denoted $\mathscr{M}$. The trivial mechanism in which the final allocation is always the endowment is denoted M_0.

Although the above definition of a mechanism is quite general, in much of what follows we do not *explicitly* use the full generality. Nevertheless, such an abstract and general concept is required so that our subsequent results will apply to amost anything which we might intuitively think of as a mechanism. The optimal mechanism $\bar{M}$ discussed at the beginning of this section is defined formally in terms of the above definition in section 7. The inference mechanism M_I is defined formally in section 8.[10]

4 Equilibrium of a mechanism

In this section we address the question of what outcomes we would expect to result when the agents are playing the game defined by a given mechanism.

What is required is a concept of equilibrium strategies for any given mechanism. The concept we adopt, which we call sequential Nash equilibrium, is related to Harsanyi's (1967–8) "Bayesian equilibrium" and Selten's (1975) "perfect equilibrium." It also draws on the work of Green (1977), Kydland and Prescott (1977), and Prescott and Visscher (1977).

To motivate our concept of equilibrium, consider agent 1 at some stage s in a mechanism $[S, P, X, F] = M$. At this stage, agent 1 has observed the previous proposals of both agents, that is, the history of the game through stage $s-1$, p^{s-1}, and the actual probability π. He must choose a proposal for stage s from the set $X_{1s}(p^{s-1})$. This, possibly random, choice can depend on p^{s-1} and π. Thus a strategy for agent 1 at stage s of mechanism M is a function σ_{1s} which associates with any history p^{s-1} and either value of π a possibly random choice of a proposal p_{1s} from $X_{1s}(p^{s-1})$. Now we must ask how agent 1 will choose his strategy at stage s. Obviously this choice (assuming maximizing behavior) will depend on what effect the use of various strategies at stage s will have on the final allocation. The strategy he chooses at stage s will affect the outcome in two ways: first directly through the outcome function F, and second indirectly through his own and the other agent's strategies at future stages (unless s is the last stage). Moreover, the way in which 1's current strategy affects the outcome depends on 2's current strategy. Consequently, in order to make agent 1's choice of a strategy at stage s into a well-defined decision problem, we must make some assumption about what he takes future strategies and the current strategy of agent 2 to be. Essentially we assume these beliefs to be correct or self-fulfilling in the Nash sense.

Now consider the choice problem faced by agent 2 at stage s. He has observed the history of the game p^{s-1} but not the actual parameter π. Thus a strategy for agent 2 at stage s of mechanism M is a function σ_{2s} which associates with any history p^{s-1} a possibly random choice of a proposal p_{2s} from $X_{2s}(p^{s-1})$. Again, an optimal choice for agent 2 at stage s will depend on what he takes to be the future strategies of both agents and the current strategy of agent 1, and again we assume these beliefs to be self-fulfilling in the Nash sense. However, there is still a problem in defining agent 2's decision problem in stage s. Clearly his expected utility for the final outcome will depend on his current (at stage s) beliefs about the value of π, both because his preferences depend on these beliefs and because the strategies of agent 1 (and hence the final outcome) depend on the actual value of π. Consequently, we must make some assumption regarding agent 2's (posterior) beliefs about the value of π at stage s. The assumption we adopt is that these beliefs, denoted below by ϕ_s for $s = 1, \ldots, S$, are represented by a posterior distribution obtained by applying Bayes's rule to the prior distribution ϕ_1 and the likelihood that the history of the game would really be p^{s-1} for each value of π given the past strategies of agent 1.[11]

Unfortunately, the equilibrium concept described above cannot be made precise without the introduction of a considerable amount of notation. Since the above intuitive description will suffice for understanding subsequent sections, we relegate the formal definition (and its associated notation) to the appendix. However, we must point out a few important concepts associated with equilibrium for a mechanism. These can be understood without reference to the formal definition.

First, we assume that every mechanism M will have at least one equilibrium set of strategies and outcome. In general, a mechanism may have more than one equilibrium. In what follows, we assume that one particular equilibrium prevails and refer to "the equilibrium" of a mechanism. For the specific mechanisms considered below, the equilibrium assumed to prevail will be clear from the context.

Second, an equilibrium outcome of a mechanism is, in general, a distribution over points in the Edgeworth box B which may depend on the true value of π. The outcome will be random if either some of the equilibrium strategies are random or if the outcome function is random or both. It will be useful to have some notation for the equilibrium outcome. Accordingly let $G(c|M, \pi)$ denote the probability that the equilibrium outcome of mechanism M is c if the true value of the parameter is π for $\pi \in \Pi$, $c \in B$, and $M \in \mathcal{M}$. Our assumptions on allowable random strategies and outcome functions imply that G will be a simple distribution over a finite number of possible allocations for any mechanism M and value $\pi \in \Pi$.

Third, some mechanisms will have equilibrium outcomes which are not random. This will happen if the outcome function is not random and none of the equilibrium strategies is random. We say that a mechanism M is *deterministic* if $G(\cdot|M, \pi)$ is degenerate for each $\pi \in \Pi$. The equilibrium outcome of a deterministic mechanism is simply a function of the true value of the parameter π. Such allocation functions are hereafter referred to as *parameter-contingent allocations*. The fact that an agent chooses his proposal at random from the constraint set cannot be observed by the other agent. Consequently, agents cannot agree to allow only degenerate strategies.[12] Thus, whether a mechanism is deterministic is endogenous, and is a property of the equilibrium of the mechanism.

Finally, we emphasize that the *equilibrium* outcome of a mechanism G should not be confused with the outcome function F. The former describes what the outcome *will be* given various values of π, while the latter indicates what the outcome *would be* given various sequences of proposals.

5 Self-selection constraints

It turns out that the nature of the optimal resource-allocation mechanism for a model of this sort turns on the ability of the informed agent to distort or conceal information for his own gain. That is, agent 1 can direct a mechanism to the equilibrium outcome associated with, say, π_1 independently of the value of π by behaving as though $\pi = \pi_1$ even if $\pi = \pi_2$. Therefore the equilibrium outcome of any mechanism must have the following property: agent 1 prefers the distribution associated with π_1 to that associated with π_2 if $\pi = \pi_1$ and vice versa if $\pi = \pi_2$. This result is stated formally as follows.

Theorem 6.1
For any mechanism M,

$$\sum_c U_1(c, \pi)G(c|M, \pi) \geqslant \sum_c U_1(c, \pi)G(c|M, \pi')$$

for any π, $\pi' \in \Pi$. (The proof is given in the appendix.)

As a special case of theorem 6.1, consider the class of deterministic mechanisms. Let

$$Y(c) \equiv Q_1^{\geqslant}(c, \pi_1) \cap Q_1^{\leqslant}(c, \pi_2)$$

where

$$Q_i^{\geqslant}(c, \pi) = \{c' \in B | U_i(c', \pi) \geqslant U_i(c, \pi)\}$$

is the set of consumption bundles weakly preferred by agent i to the bundle c under the parameter draw π and

$$Q_i^{\leqslant}(c, \pi) = \{c' \in B | U_i(c', \pi) \leqslant U_i(c, \pi)\}$$

is the set of consumption bundles weakly dominated for agent i by the bundle c. ($Q_i^{=}$, $Q_i^{>}$, and $Q_i^{<}$ are defined analogously.) Note that pairs (c', c) such that $c' \in Y(c)$ are "self-selection" pairs for agent 1, that is, he will (weakly) prefer c' to c if $\pi = \pi_1$ and c to c' if $\pi = \pi_2$. The shaded region in figure 6.2 is a graphical representation of $Y(c)$. The deterministic analog of theorem 6.1 states that if the final allocation under some deterministic mechanism is c^j for $\pi = \pi_j$, then (c^1, c^2) must be a self-selection pair. More formally we have the following corollary.

Corollary 6.1
For any deterministic mechanism M with equilibrium outcome c^j if $\pi = \pi_j$ for $j = 1, 2$, $c^1 \in Y(c^2)$.

6 Preferences over mechanisms and optimality

In order to determine optimal mechanisms, we must first define preference orderings over mechanisms for both agents. These preferences are defined using the expected utilities, based on the initial information structure, for the equilibrium outcome of the mechanism.

More precisely, let

$$W_1(M,\pi)=\sum_c U_1(c,\pi)G(c|M,\pi) \qquad \text{for each } \pi\in\Pi$$

$$W_2(M)=\sum_\pi\sum_c U_2(c,\pi)G(c|M,\pi)\phi_1(\pi)$$

Then we can say that, given any two mechanisms M_1 and M_2, M_1 *dominates* M_2 (written $M_1 \geqslant M_2$) if $W_1(M_1,\pi)\geqslant W_1(M_2,\pi)$ for $\pi=\pi_1,\pi_2$ and $W_2(M_1)\geqslant W_2(M_2)$. M_1 *strictly dominates* M_2 (written $M_1 > M_2$) if $M_1 \geqslant M_2$ and $W_1(M_1,\pi)> W_1(M_2,\pi)$ for at least one value of π and/or $W_2(M_1)> W_2(M_2)$. M_1 is equivalent to M_2 (written $M_1\equiv M_2$) if both $M_1 \geqslant M_2$ and $M_2 \geqslant M_1$. Thus, roughly speaking, a dominating mechanism M_2 must yield greater expected utility for agent 2 relative to his initial information about π and greater expected utility for agent 1 for either value of π.

A mechanism M is said to be an *optimal mechanism* if M cannot be strictly dominated by any other mechanism; M is a *core mechanism* if M is optimal and dominates the trivial mechanism M_0. (Recall that M_0 generates the endowment point e for sure. Note that a core mechanism is defined relative to the endowment.)

With regard to our concept of optimality, the specification that a dominating mechanism yields greater expected utility for agent 1 for either value of π may seem strong, since agent 1 knows, for example, that $\pi=\pi_2$. We adopt this specification because we want our optimal mechanism to be independent of π. Ideally we would like to specify a mechanism for choosing mechanisms and refer to an equilibrium choice. However, the choice of a mechanism may reveal information about π, thereby changing the environment for which the mechanisms are defined. In order to avoid this and other problems, we have instead postulated directly an outcome of such a choice process.

7 An optimal mechanism

In this section we construct an optimal mechanism. Under this mechanism agents alternate in making proposals. Agent 2 starts by proposing any pair of feasible allocations. This proposal may be generated randomly. Agent 1 may choose either element of the pair just proposed by agent 2, or he may choose the endowment. Again, this choice may be generated randomly. In any case, agent 1's choice becomes the final allocation. More formally our optimal mechanism $\bar{M} = [\bar{S}, \bar{P}, \bar{X}, \bar{F}]$ is defined by $\bar{S} = 2$, $\bar{P} = B \times B \cup B \cup \{p_0\}$, $\bar{X}_{11}(p_0) = \{p_0\}$, $\bar{X}_{21}(p_0) = B \times B$, $\bar{X}_{12}(p^1) = \{c^1, c^2, e\}$, where $p_{21} = (c^1, c^2)$, $\bar{X}_{22}(p^1) = \{p_0\}$, and $\bar{F}(c|p^2)$ is degenerate on p_{12}. Note that $\bar{M}$ is defined relative to the endowment.

Our next objective is to characterize the equilibrium of $\bar{M}$. As mentioned above, $\bar{M}$ may have more than one equilibrium. In the theorem below, we characterize one equilibrium of $\bar{M}$ (which we thereafter assume prevails). This equilibrium is nonrandom. To see that a nonrandom equilibrium exists (given that some equilibrium exists) consider the optimal strategy of agent 1 at stage 2. By definition of $\bar{F}$, the final allocation will be the proposal at this stage. Therefore agent 1 would randomize optimally only over proposals among which he is indifferent. In this case any degenerate strategy over one of these proposals is also optimal. A similar argument shows that agent 2's optimal strategy at stage 1 may also be taken to be degenerate. Since $\bar{F}$ is degenerate, $\bar{M}$ is a deterministic mechanism.

The equilibrium of $\bar{M}$ is characterized in theorem 6.2. Some additional notation will be helpful (also recall the definition of the consensus contract curve C from section 2). Let

$$C^+ = \left\{ c \in B \left| \frac{u_1'(x_1 - c_1)}{u_1'(x_2 - c_2)} < \frac{u_2'(c_1)}{u_2'(c_2)} \right. \right\}$$

denote the set of allocations to the north of C, and let

$$C^- = (C^+ \cup C)^c$$

denote the set of allocations to the south of C. (Refer to figure 6.3 for a graphical representation of the theorem where $\bar{c}^j$ will be the equilibrium final allocation if $\pi = \pi^j$.)

Theorem 6.2

For any endowment $e \in B$, there exists an equilibrium for mechanism $\bar{M}$, denoted $(\bar{\phi}^2, \bar{p}^2)$ (since the equilibrium strategies are degenerate, they are represented by the corresponding proposals) where $\bar{\phi}_1 = \bar{\phi}_2 = \phi_1$, $\bar{p}_{11} = p_0$, $\bar{p}_{22} = p_0$, and $\bar{p}_{21}$ and $\bar{p}_{12}$ are as follows (see figure 6.3).

Case 1 $e \in C^+$. $\bar{p}_{21}(p_0) = (\bar{c}^1, \bar{c}^2)$ where $\bar{c}^2$ is on the indifference curve of agent 1 under $\pi = \pi_2$ passing through e. Also $\bar{c}^2$ lies in C^+ between e and the consensus contract curve C (the exact location of $\bar{c}^2$ depends on agent 2's prior ϕ_1) moving $\bar{c}^2$ toward e or toward the intersection with G.

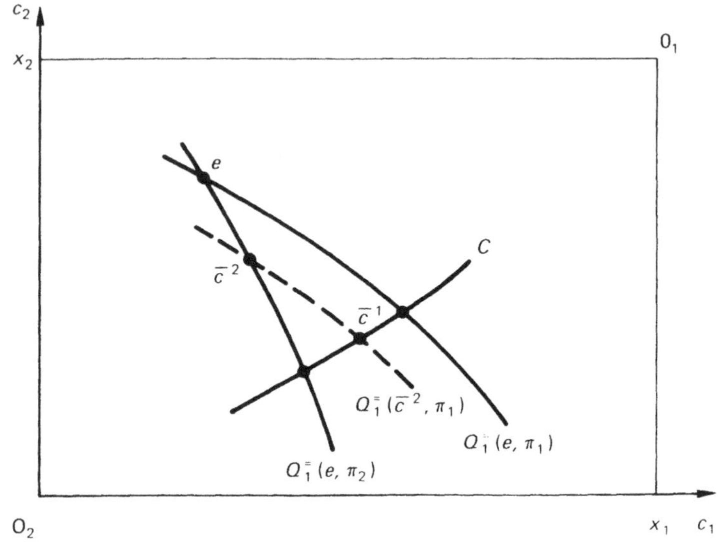

Figure 6.3. Equilibrium allocation of the optimal mechanism

The allocation $\bar{c}^1$ lies at the intersection of C with the indifference curve of agent 1 through $\bar{c}^2$ under $\pi = \pi_1$; $\bar{p}_{12}(\bar{p}^1, \pi_j) = \bar{c}^j$, $j = 1, 2$. In this case $G(c|\bar{M}, \pi_j) = 1$ if and only if $c = \bar{c}^j$ for $j = 1, 2$.

Case 2 $e \in C$. $\bar{p}_{21}(p_0) = (e, e)$, $\bar{p}_{12}(p^1, \pi_j) = e$ for $j = 1, 2$, and $G(c|\bar{M}, \pi_j)$ is degenerate on $c = e$. In this case, agents simply agree not to trade.

Case 3 $e \in C^-$. The results for this case are the same as for case 1 with all subscripts interchanged.

The proof of theorem 6.2, though long and tedious, is not difficult and is outlined in the appendix. The proof depends in part on the observation that, without loss of generality, the pair of allocations proposed by the uninformed agent can be assumed to be a self-selection pair.

In the next theorem we show that mechanism $\bar{M}$ is a core mechanism. To prove this, we first prove that any mechanism can be dominated by a deterministic mechanism. Thus, in the environment assumed here, there are no gains to using mechanisms in which the equilibrium strategies are not degenerate. In particular, any gains to attempting to conceal π by randomizing can also be exploited by a mechanism in which it is not optimal to randomize. This is stated formally in the following lemma.

Lemma 6.1

For any mechanism M, there is a deterministic mechanism M' such that $M' \geqslant M$.

The proof, which relies on Jensen's inequality and the fact that $U_i(c, \pi)$ is linear in π, is given in the appendix.

Next note that we can generate a class of mechanisms all of whose members are slight variations of $\bar{M}$ ($\bar{M}$ is also a member of this class). For any point e' in B, define the mechanism $\bar{M}(e')$ to be the same as $\bar{M}$ except that $X_{12}(p^1) = \{c^1, c^2, e'\}$ (instead of $\{c^1, c^2, e\}$) where $p_{21} = (c^1, c^2)$. Thus $\bar{M} = \bar{M}(e)$. Note that $\bar{M}(e')$ is the same as $\bar{M}$ except that, if the informed agent "rejects" both proposals of the uninformed agent, the final allocation is e' instead of e. We can now prove that any mechanism in the class $\{\bar{M}(e')|e' \in B\}$ is an optimal mechanism.

Theorem 6.3
For any $e' \in B$, $\bar{M}(e')$ is an optimal mechanism for some equilibrium of $\bar{M}(e')$ of the form given in theorem 6.2.

In particular, if $e' = e$, then $\bar{M} = \bar{M}(e)$ is an optimal mechanism. It is also clear that $\bar{M} \geqslant M_0$ since agent 2 may propose (e, e) and agent 1 may always choose e under $\bar{M}$. This result is stated formally as follows.

Corollary 6.2
For the equilibrium of $\bar{M}$ given in theorem 6.2, $\bar{M}$ is a core mechanism.

The next theorem states that any mechanism can be (weakly) dominated by some member of the class $\{\bar{M}(e')|e' \in B\}$. The proof consists in choosing e' in such a way that agent 1 can be no worse off under $\bar{M}(e')$ that under the alternative mechanism. That this is possible follows from theorem 6.1. The choice of e' is illustrated in figure 6.4 (in the figure $(\hat{c}^1, \hat{c}^2)$ is the equilibrium parameter-contingent allocation of the mechanism to be dominated).

Theorem 6.4
For any mechanism M there exists an $e' \in B$ such that $\bar{M}(e') \geqslant M$.

The construction of e' used in the proof of theorem 6.4 (and illustrated in figure 6.4) can be used to show that the competitive mechanism M_C and inference mechanism M_I can be *strictly* dominated by appropriate members of the class $\{\bar{M}(e')\}$. This is done for M_I in section 8. This shows that the optimality results do have content in that two familiar mechanisms can be strictly dominated by mechanisms of the form of $\bar{M}$.

Theorems 6.3 and 6.4 characterize the class of optimal mechanisms. Note that the equilibria of these mechanisms have the property that the pair of allocations proposed by the uninformed agent serves as a self-selection device

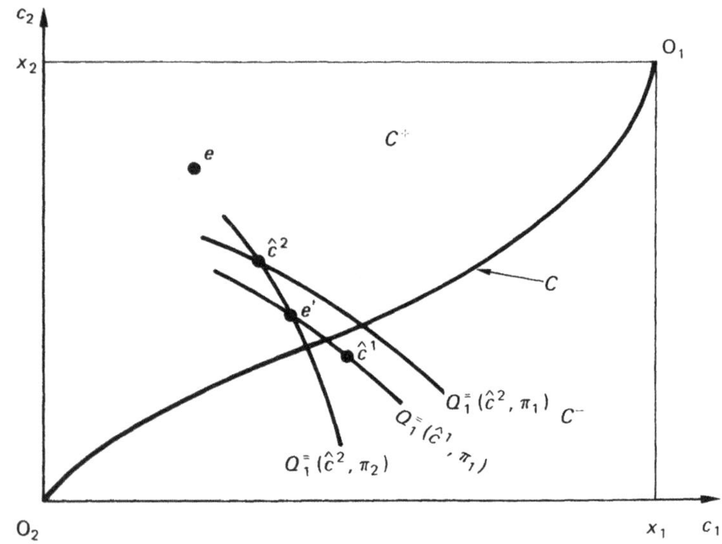

Figure 6.4. Theorem 6.4

for the informed agent. That is, it is optimal for agent 1 to reveal the true value of π by his choice of allocation at the second stage (provided that $e' \notin C$).

Note that $\bar{M}(e')$ is optimal even though the equilibrium final allocation when $\pi = \pi_2$ is not on C and both agents know π at the end of stage 2 (assuming that $e' \notin C$). Thus, although given the situation at the end of stage 2 there may be further gains to trade, it is optimal to agree at the outset that these gains will not be exploited.

8 The inference mechanism

In this section we define and analyze the inference mechanism M_I described in section 3. In particular, we construct an equilibrium of M_I (in a semirigorous fashion) and show how M_I can be strictly dominated by $\bar{M}(e')$ for an appropriate specification of e'.

Recall that the inference mechanism M_I consists of two stages. In the first stage agent 1 can propose any allocation in the box, and in the second stage agent 2 can choose between this proposal and the endowment. More formally the inference mechanism M_I is defined by $S = 2$, $P = B \cup \{p_0\}$, $X_{11} = B$, $X_{21} = \{p_0\}$, $X_{12}(p^1) = \{p_0\}$, $X_{22}(p^1) = \{p_{11}, e\}$, and $F(c|p^2)$ is degenerate on $c = p_{22}$.

One possible equilibrium for this mechanism is shown in figure 6.5. Suppose for the moment that the posterior distribution of agent 2 at the beginning

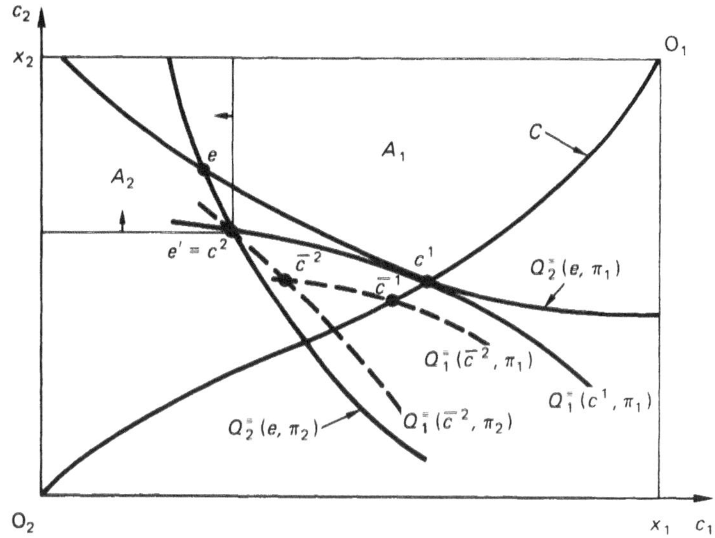

Figure 6.5. Equilibrium of M_{I}

of stage 2, as a function of the proposal of agent 1 at the first stage, is necessarily degenerate. That is, for all possible proposals p^1, agent 2 is sure either that $\pi = \pi_1$ or $\pi = \pi_2$. Then, geometrically, any such posterior partitions the Edgeworth box into two subrectangles A_1 and A_2, where $A_j = \{c \in B \mid \text{agent 2 is sure that } \pi = \pi_j \text{ given } p_{11}\}$. Now assume that those regions are as shown in figure 6.5 determined by point c^2 (the superscript 2 will be explained momentarily): $A_2 = \{c \in B \mid c_1 \leqslant c_1^2, c_2 \geqslant c_2^2\}$ and $A_1 = B - A_2$. Thus if $p_{11} \in Q_2^{<}(e, \pi_j) \cap A_j$, agent 2 will choose the endowment, whereas if $p_{11} \in Q_2^{\geqslant}(e, \pi_j) \cap A_j$, agent 2 likes p_{11} at least as well as the endowment. We thus assume that agent 2 will not randomize and, in the latter situation, will choose p_{11}. It is also clear that agent 1 will not propose an allocation which makes agent 2 better off than necessary for trade, so that

$$p_{11} \in \bigcup_{j=1}^{2} \{Q_2^{=}(e, \pi_j) \cap A_j\}$$

We can also assume that agent 1 will not randomize. Then if $\pi = \pi_j$ agent 1 will propose $\{c^j\}, j = 1, 2$, and moreover this will be the final allocation. Note also that the requirement that beliefs be self-fulfilling is satisfied inasmuch as $c^j \in A_j$.

This equilibrium may shed some light on the result of theorem 6.4. Let $e' = c^2$ as shown in figure 6.5. Then, by continuity of preferences and the nature of the optimal mechanism $\bar{M}(e')$, there exists an initial prior ϕ_1 which puts sufficiently low mass on π_1 that $\bar{c}^2 \neq c^2$ where $\bar{c}^j$ is the equilibrium final allocation of $\bar{M}(e')$ under $\pi = \pi_j$ (see figure 6.5). However, note that if $\bar{c}^1$ were proposed by agent 1 in the inference mechanism, agent 2 would infer that $\pi = \pi_1$ and reject the offer, choosing instead his endowment. Thus $\bar{M}(e')$ allows agents to engage in mutually beneficial exchange on the basis of prior beliefs.

A troublesome aspect of this inference mechanism should also be emphasized. The specification of agent 2's posterior is only one of many possible equilibrium specifications. It can be verified that there is no specification of regions in figure 6.5 which can generate an equilibrium which dominates that given, but the model does not determine uniquely which regions are used (or even that the posterior be degenerate).

9 Conclusions

In this chapter we have argued that, to analyze the allocation of resources in certain types of environments with asymmetric information, we must first consider the process by which allocations are achieved. We have presented a method for such analyses. In applying our approach to a specific abstract environment characterized by asymmetry of information between two agents, we have derived several positive results. With respect to the mechanism, we show that a certain simple deterministic mechanism is undominated by any other mechanism and can dominate any other mechanism provided that the no-trade option is appropriately specified. With respect to the actual resource allocation, we fully characterize the equilibrium final allocation of the optimal mechanism.

Though we believe that the specific method we have presented in this chapter is original to us, we would like to acknowledge the influence of the work of Hurwicz and others (see Hurwicz, 1972; Reiter, 1977) on resource-allocation mechanisms. Hurwicz has stressed that mechanisms should be defined and compared in a precise and rigorous way, and has shown that there need not exist a mechanism (in some environments) which is incentive compatible, is informationally decentralized, and achieves Pareto optimal allocations. Our approach also emphasizes the relationship between incentive compatibility (self-selection) and optimality, but differs from much of the literature on mechanisms in taking a Bayesian or statistical decision-theoretic approach to the information structure and in adopting the sequential Nash equilibrium concept. This leads to a somewhat different concept of optimality than has generally been employed. In consequence, our results are somewhat different from those of Hurwicz and others.

As we have emphasized above, our optimal resource-allocation process is simple and intuitively appealing: the uninformed agent proposes and the informed agent chooses. Thus it seems to have much in common with the well-known "divide-and-choose" process which has intrigued mathematicians and social scientists for some time (see Dubins and Spanier, 1961; Crawford, undated). We would like to note that our mechanism cannot be viewed as a version of the divide-and-choose process as the uninformed agent proposes two specific allocations for the informed agent. Moreover, the choice of the informed agent depends on his information. We also note that the virtue of the divide-and-choose process is its "fairness," at least in environments with symmetric information, whereas the virtue of our mechanism is its optimality in environments with asymmetric information. Finally, we note again the importance of order in our mechanism: it is crucial that the informed agent goes last.

In the remainder of this section, we take up several issues not considered previously. In the process we suggest some directions for further work. First, in our approach, as well as in the signaling literature (see Spence, 1974; Riley, 1975; Rothschild and Stiglitz, 1976; Wilson, 1977), the prior of the uninformed agent plays a key role in determining the allocation of resources. This is not the case, however, in some other attempts at devising mechanisms to allocate resources under asymmetric information, most notably in the public goods literature (see Groves and Ledyard, 1977). We find this difference disturbing and explore it further in the next chapter (Harris and Townsend, 1981, this volume, ch. 7).

Second, we would like to bring up the issue of uniqueness of the core mechanism: although $\bar{M}$ is a core mechanism, it is clear that $\bar{M}$ is not the only core mechanism. In particular, the following mechanism is equivalent to $\bar{M}(e)$: agent 1 proposes first and must choose an allocation from the set $\{\bar{c}^1(e), \bar{c}^2(e)\}$ where $\bar{c}^j(e)$ is the equilibrium final allocation of $\bar{M}(e)$ when $\pi = \pi_j$ for $j = 1, 2$; this is then the final allocation. Thus, to predict the observed mechanism with any greater precision, we must enlarge the theory to take account of other factors. Such factors might include the costs of sending and processing information. This is the direction taken by Hurwicz (1972), Reiter (1977), and others.

Third, we would like to make a comment about testability. Our results with respect to mechanisms have one directly testable implication, that is, the informed trader determines the final allocation by choosing from among some set of alternatives.[13] This seems to be consistent with what we observe in insurance markets and other areas. For example, customers of insurance companies (who are informed as to their own probability of loss) generally choose from among a small set of alternative policies with various coverage specifications. Similarly, purchasers of retirement annuities (who are better informed as to their own probabilities of death at given ages) can typically choose among lump-sum payments and annuities guaranteed for various periods.

With respect to the allocation itself, there is at least one (potentially) testable implication (that is, a restriction on the data which does not depend on the specific utility functions possessed by the agents): the final bundles of the uninformed trader under different values of π will lie along a downward-sloping curve (see figure 6.3). Here there are alternatives against which we can test. These include any model which predicts either a single point, independent of π, or a pair of points, one for each value of π, both of which lie on C (for example, the competitive allocation when the price is a perfect indicator of π). Since C is upward sloping as a relation between consumption in the two states for the uninformed trader, we see that our prediction of the resource allocation is empirically different from either of the two predictions just mentioned.

Admittedly, the data with which to test these implications are difficult to come by. If our results are robust to the addition of agents, insurance contracts issued to customers with various degrees of risk may be a reasonable source of data. Also, data from independent one-on-one bargains in which the probability of some contingency changes across bargains (for example, lawyers and clients with different probabilities of successful litigation) would be suitable if utility functions and endowments were reasonably similar in these bargains. Obviously the degree of abstraction of the environment we assumed here in order to demonstrate the efficacy of our approach limits the seriousness with which we might take any such tests. Nonetheless, it is worth noting that the results do have empirical content.

Finally, it should be clear from the above remarks that one promising direction for further research is to extend our results to similar environments with more agents, more complicated information structure, and production. This is the subject of the next chapter (Harris and Townsend, 1981, this volume, ch. 7).

Appendix

In this appendix we state formally the definition of equilibrium of a mechanism and prove the results stated in the text.

Definition of equilibrium of a mechanism

Before defining an equilibrium, the concept of feasible strategies under a mechanism $M = [S, P, X, F]$ must be made precise. A feasible contingent strategy for agent 1 at stage s is a mapping σ_{1s} from previous proposals p^{s-1} and the actual (known) value of π to a choice of a simple probability measure, which puts positive probability on only a finite number of proposals in $X_{1s}(p^{s-1})$. Let $\Lambda\{X_{1s}(p^{s-1})\}$ denote the set of all such simple measures, and let $\sigma_{1s}(\cdot|p^{s-1}, \pi)$ denote a typical choice of an element in this set as a function of p^{s-1} and π. A feasible contingent strategy for agent 2 at stage s is a mapping

σ_{2s} from previous proposals p^{s-1} into a choice of a simple probability measure on $X_{2s}(p^{s-1})$, with typical choice $\sigma_{2s}(\cdot|p^{s-1})$ in the space $\Lambda\{X_{2s}(p^{s-1})\}$. A feasible sequence of contingent strategies from stages t through S is a sequence $\sigma^{t,S} = (\sigma_t, \ldots, \sigma_S)$ where $\sigma_r = (\sigma_{1r}, \sigma_{2r})$ and σ_{ir} is a feasible contingent strategy for agent i at stage $r \in \{t, t+1, \ldots, S\}$.

Let $\Psi^t(q^{t,S}|p^{t-1}, \sigma^{t,S}, \pi)$ denote the probability of the sequence of proposals from stages t through S being $q^{t,S} = (q_t, \ldots, q_S)$ given the sequence of previous proposals p^{t-1} and the contingent strategies $\sigma^{t,S}$ used in stages t through S, and σ_{1r} is evaluated at π for each stage $r \in \{t, t+1, \ldots, S\}$. More formally Ψ^t is defined by backward recursion as follows:

$$\Psi^S(q^{S,S}|p^{S-1}, \sigma^{S,S}, \pi) = \sigma_{1S}(q_{1S}|p^{S-1}, \pi)\sigma_{2S}(q_{2S}|p^{S-1})$$

$$\Psi^t(q^{t,S}|p^{t-1}, \sigma^{t,S}, \pi) = \Psi^{t+1}(q^{t+1,S}|p^{t-1}, q_t, \sigma^{t+1,S}, \pi)\sigma_{1t}(q_{1t}|p^{t-1}, \pi)\sigma_{2t}(q_{2t}|p^{t-1})$$

Now consider the decision problem of agent 1. At stage t agent 1 takes as given the previous proposals p^{t-1}, the contemporary strategy σ_{2t} of agent 2, the future strategies $\sigma^{t+1,S}$ of himself and agent 2 from stages $t+1$ through S, and, of course, the outcome function F. Thus the problem of agent 1 at stage t is as follows.

Problem 6.1

$$\max_{\lambda \in \Lambda\{X_{1t}(p^{t-1})\}} \sum_{q^{t,S}} \sum_{c} U_1(c, \pi) F(c|p^{t-1}, q^{t,S}) \Psi^t(q^{t,S}|p^{t-1}, \lambda, \sigma_{2t}, \sigma^{t+1,S}, \pi)$$

Now consider the decision problem of agent 2. Suppose that at stage t agent 2 takes as given that the proposals p_s of each previous stage $s \in \{1, 2, \ldots, t-1\}$ were generated under the strategies σ_{1s} and σ_{2s} of agents 1 and 2 respectively. Then let $P^{t-1}(\sigma^{t-1}, \pi)$ denote the set of all previous proposals p^{t-1} which could be generated with positive probability under the strategies $\sigma^{t-1} = (\sigma_1, \sigma_2, \ldots, \sigma_{t-1})$ when the true probability is π. Let $\phi_t(\cdot|p^{t-1})$ denote the posterior probability distribution on π of agent 2 at the beginning of stage t, given previous proposals p^{t-1}. Then, using Bayes's rule, define ϕ_t formally by

$$\phi_t(\pi|p^{t-1}) = \begin{cases} \dfrac{\sigma_{1,t-1}(p_{1,t-1}|p^{t-2}, \pi)\phi_{t-1}(\pi|p^{t-2})}{\sum_{k=1}^{2} \sigma_{1,t-1}(p_{1,t-1}|p^{t-2}, \pi_k)\phi_{t-1}(\pi_k|p^{t-2})} & \text{for } p^{t-1} \in P^{t-1}(\sigma^{t-1}, \pi_1) \cup P^{t-1}(\sigma^{t-1}, \pi_2) \\ \phi_1(\pi) \text{ otherwise} & \end{cases} \tag{6.A1}$$

Thus the decision problem of agent 2 at stage t is as follows.

Problem 6.2

$$\max_{\lambda \in \Lambda\{X_{2t}(p^{t-1})\}} \sum_{\pi} \sum_{q^{t,S}} \sum_{c} U_2(c, \pi) F(c|p^{t-1}, q^{t,S})$$
$$\times \Psi^t(q^{t,S}|p^{t-1}, \sigma_{1t}, \lambda, \sigma^{t+1,S}, \pi)\phi_t(\pi|p^{t-1})$$

Definition

An equilibrium of a mechanism $M = [S, P, X, F]$ is a specification of a feasible sequence, $\hat{\sigma}^S = (\hat{\sigma}_1, \hat{\sigma}_2, \ldots, \hat{\sigma}_S)$ of contingent strategies from stages 1 through S and a specification of a sequence $\hat{\phi}^S = (\hat{\phi}_1, \hat{\phi}_2, \ldots, \hat{\phi}_S)$ of posterior distributions such that the following conditions hold:

1 for each $t = 1, 2, \ldots, S$, each p^{t-1}, and each $\pi \in \Pi$, $\hat{\sigma}_{1t}(\cdot|p^{t-1}, \pi)$ solves problem 6.1 relative to $(\hat{\sigma}_{2t}, \hat{\sigma}^{t+1,S})$ and $\hat{\sigma}_{2t}(\cdot|p^{t-1})$ solves problem 6.2 relative to $(\hat{\sigma}_{1t}, \hat{\sigma}^{t+1,S})$ and $\hat{\phi}_t(\cdot|p^{t-1})$;
2 for each $t = 1, 2, \ldots, S$, each p^{t-1}, and each $\pi \in \Pi$, $\hat{\phi}_t$ satisfies (6.A1) relative to $\hat{\phi}_{t-1}$ and $\hat{\sigma}_{1,t-1}$.

Proof of Theorem 6.1

Let $(\bar{\phi}^S, \bar{\sigma}^S)$ be an equilibrium of M. Let $\hat{\sigma}_1^S$ be the sequence of strategies for agent 1 defined by evaluating his equilibrium strategies at π' regardless of the actual value of π, that is,

$$\hat{\sigma}_{1s}(\cdot|p^{s-1}, y) = \bar{\sigma}_{1s}(\cdot|p^{s-1}, \pi')$$

for any stage $1 \leqslant s \leqslant S$, any parameter value $y \in \Pi$, and any history p^{s-1}. The sequence $(\hat{\sigma}_1^S, \bar{\sigma}_2^S)$ is a feasible sequence of contingent strategies since $\bar{\sigma}^S$ is. To simplify the notation, let $V_1(p^S, \pi)$ be agent 1's expected utility under mechanism M if he observes π and the sequence of proposals is p^S, that is,

$$V_1(p^S, \pi) = \sum_c U_1(c, \pi) F(c|p^S)$$

Now at stage S (the last stage), since $\hat{\sigma}_{1S}$ is feasible, by definition of equilibrium

$$\sum_{q_S} V_1(p^{S-1}, q_S, y)\Psi^S(q_S|p^{S-1}, \bar{\sigma}_S, y)$$
$$\geqslant \sum_{q_S} V_1(p^{S-1}, q_S, y)\Psi^S(q_S|p^{S-1}, \hat{\sigma}_{1S}, \bar{\sigma}_{2S}, y) \tag{6.A2}$$

for any history p^{S-1} and parameter value y. But at stage $S-1$, since $\hat{\sigma}_{1,S-1}$ is feasible, the following chain of inequalities holds (where the first inequality follows from the definition of equilibrium, the two equalities follow from the definition of Ψ^S, and the second inequality follows from (6.A2)):

$$\sum_{q_{S-1}}\sum_{q_S} V_1(p^{S-2}, q_{S-1}, q_S, y)\,\Psi^{S-1}(q^{S-1,S}|p^{S-2}, \bar{\sigma}^{S-1,S}, y)$$

$$\geqslant \sum_{q_{S-1}}\sum_{q_S} V_1(p^{S-2}, q_{S-1}, q_S, y)\,\Psi^{S-1}(q^{S-1,S}|p^{S-2}, \hat{\sigma}_{1,S-1}, \bar{\sigma}_{2,S-1}, \bar{\sigma}_{1S}, \bar{\sigma}_{2S}, y)$$

$$= \sum_{q_{S-1}}\sum_{q_S} V_1(p^{S-2}, q_{S-1}, q_S, y)\,\Psi^S(q_S|p^{S-2}, q_{S-1}, \bar{\sigma}_S, y)$$
$$\times\, \hat{\sigma}_{1,S-1}(q_{1,S-1}|p^{S-2}, y)\bar{\sigma}_{2,S-1}(q_{2,S-1}|p^{S-2})$$

$$\geqslant \sum_{q_{S-1}}\sum_{q_S} V_1(p^{S-2}, q_{S-1}, q_S, y)\,\Psi^S(q_S|p^{S-2}, q_{S-1}, \hat{\sigma}_{1S}, \bar{\sigma}_{2S}, y)$$
$$\times\, \hat{\sigma}_{1,S-1}(q_{1,S-1}|p^{S-2}, y)\bar{\sigma}_{2,S-1}(q_{2,S-1}|p^{S-2})$$

$$= \sum_{q_{S-1}}\sum_{q_S} V_1(p^{S-2}, q_{S-1}, q_S, y)\,\Psi^{S-1}(q^{S-1,S}|p^{S-2}, \hat{\sigma}_1^{S-1,S}, \bar{\sigma}_2^{S-1,S}, y)$$

The above chain of inequalities gives

$$\sum_{q^{S-1,S}} V_1(p^{S-2}, q_{S-1}, q_S, y)\,\Psi^{S-1}(q^{S-1,S}|p^{S-2}, \bar{\sigma}^{S-1,S}, y)$$

$$\geqslant \sum_{q^{S-1,S}} V_1(p^{S-2}, q_{S-1}, q_S, y)\,\Psi^{S-1}(q^{S-1,S}|p^{S-2}, \hat{\sigma}_1^{S-1,S}, \bar{\sigma}_2^{S-1,S}, y) \qquad (6.A3)$$

We can continue with this backward induction until, at stage 1, we have

$$\sum_{q^S} V_1(q^S, y)\,\Psi^1(q^S|p_0, \bar{\sigma}^S, y) \geqslant \sum_{q^S} V_1(q^S, y)\,\Psi^1(q^S|p_0, \hat{\sigma}_1^S, \bar{\sigma}_2^S, y) \quad (6.A4)$$

for any parameter value y. The left-hand side of (6.A4) is agent 1's expected utility for M under parameter value y, that is, $\Sigma_c U_1(c, y)G(c|M, y)$. Since $\hat{\sigma}_1^S$ is just $\bar{\sigma}_1^S$ evaluated at $y = \pi'$, that is,

$$\Psi^1(q^S|p_0, \hat{\sigma}_1^S, \bar{\sigma}_2^S, y) = \Psi^1(q^S|p_0, \bar{\sigma}^S, \pi')$$

the right-hand side of (6.A4) is

$$\sum_{q^S} V_1(q^S, y)\,\Psi^1(q^S|p_0, \bar{\sigma}^S, \pi') = \sum_c U_1(c, y)G(c|M, \pi')$$

Thus, setting $y=\pi$ in (6.A4), we have

$$\sum_{c} U_1(c,\pi)G(c|M,\pi) \geqslant \sum_{c} U_1(c,\pi)G(c|M,\pi')$$

as required.

Proof of Theorem 6.2

It is obvious from the definitions of equilibrium and $\bar{M}$ that $\bar{\phi}_1 = \phi_1, \bar{p}_{11} = p_0$, and $\bar{p}_{22} = p_0$. It is also clear that the equilibrium proposal $\bar{p}_{12}(p_{21},\pi)$ of agent 1 at stage 2 solves, for $\pi \in \Pi$, the following problem.

Problem 6.3

$$\max_{p_{12}\in\{c^1,c^2,e\}} \quad U_1(p_{12},\pi)$$

where $p_{21} = (c^1, c^2)$.

Suppose that agent 2 takes this strategy of agent 1 at stage 2 as given. Then his proposal $\bar{p}_{21} = (\bar{c}^1, \bar{c}^2)$ at stage 1 solves the following problem.

Problem 6.4

$$\max_{p_{21}\in B\times B} \; V_2(p_{21}) \equiv \sum_{j=1}^{2} \bar{\phi}_1(\pi_j)U_2\{\bar{p}_{12}(p_{21},\pi_j),\pi_j\}$$

First we simply note that if, for some $(c^1,c^2)\in B\times B$,

$$c^j \in Q_1^{\geqslant}(c^i,\pi_j) \cap Q_1^{\geqslant}(e,\pi_j) \qquad j=1,2,\; i\neq j$$

that is, agent 1 prefers c^j to c^i and to e when $\pi=\pi_j$, then $\bar{p}_{12}(c^1,c^2,\pi_j)=c^j$, $j=1,2$, is a solution of problem 6.3. Henceforth we consider only equilibria of $\bar{M}$ in which $\bar{p}_{12}$ has this property, that is, $\bar{p}_{12}(c^1,c^2,\pi_j)=c^j$, $j=1,2$, whenever $c^j\in Q_1^{\geqslant}(c^i,\pi_j)\cap Q_1^{\geqslant}(e,\pi_j)$ for $j=1,2$, $i\neq j$.

The next step in the proof is to establish that for $(c^1,c^2)\in B\times B$ there is a pair $(\bar{c}^1,\bar{c}^2)$ which yields the same value of the objective function of problem 6.4 and also satisfies the following additional constraints:

$$\bar{c}^j \in Q_1^{\geqslant}(e,\pi_j) \qquad j=1,2$$

$$\bar{c}^1 \in Y(\bar{c}^2)$$

The first two constraints simply require the proposal $\bar{c}^j$ to satisfy individual rationality for agent 1 under each value of π. That these can be imposed without loss of generality follows from the fact that e is always an available choice for agent 1 at the second stage of $\bar{M}$. The third constraint says that the proposal $(\bar{c}^1, \bar{c}^2)$ satisfies self-selection. To see that this can be imposed without loss of generality we need only examine all possible cases in which it is not satisfied and note that in each case the proposal can be altered so as to satisfy self-selection without changing the final outcome. For example, if agent 1 prefers, say, c^1 to c^2 under either value of π, the proposal (c^1, c^2) can be replaced by (c^1, c^1) without affecting the outcome.

Now, given that agent 2's proposal $\bar{p}_{21} = (\bar{c}^1, \bar{c}^2)$ satisfies the above three constraints, it is clear from the remarks after the statement of problem 6.4 that $\bar{p}_{12}(\bar{p}_{21}, \pi_j) = \bar{c}^j$, $j = 1, 2$. Therefore problem 6.4 can be replaced by the following problem.

Problem 6.5

$$\max_{(c^1, c^2) \in B \times B} \sum_{j=1}^{2} \phi_1(\pi_j) U_2(c^j, \pi_j)$$

subject to

$$c^j \in Q_1^{\geqslant}(e, \pi_j) \qquad j = 1, 2$$
$$c^1 \in Y(c^2)$$

Note that the constraint set of problem 6.5 is compact and the objective function is continuous so that a solution exists.

The remainder of the proof is devoted to characterizing the solution of problem 6.5 in the three cases outlined in the statement of the theorem. First note that, if $(\bar{c}^1, \bar{c}^2)$ solves problem 6.5, then, given $c^2 = \bar{c}^2$, $\bar{c}^1$ solves the following problem.

Problem 6.6

$$\max_{c^1 \in B} U_2(c^1, \pi_1)$$

subject to

$$c^1 \in Y(\bar{c}^2) \cap Q_1^{\geqslant}(e, \pi_1)$$

Case 1 $e \in C^+$. First we claim that $\bar{c}^2 \in C^+$. If this is not true, that is,

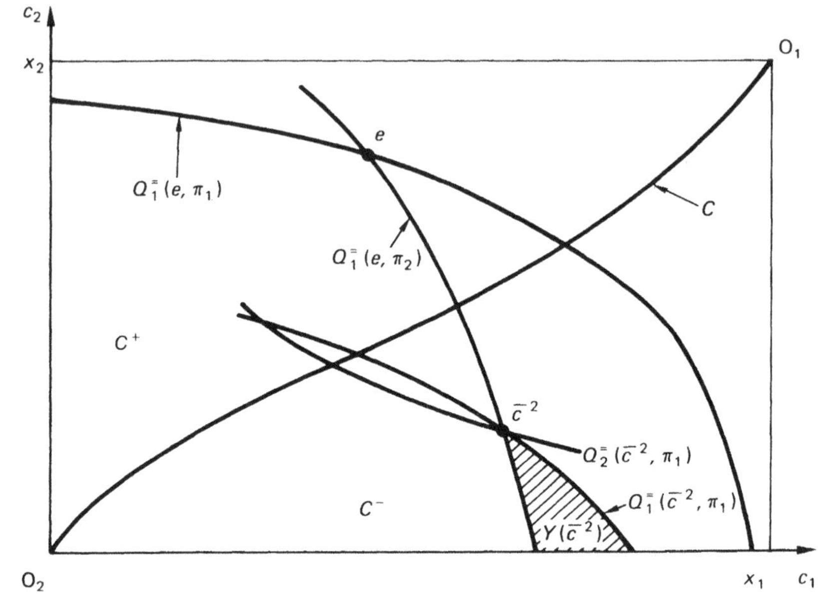

Figure 6.6. Proof of theorem 6.2

$\bar{c}^2 \in C^- \cup C$ (see figure 6.6), it can be shown that, since $\bar{c}^2$ is on or below the consensus contract curve, the solution of problem 6.6 is $\bar{c}^1 = \bar{c}^2$. This can be seen most easily in figure 6.6 where, since $\bar{c}^2$ is below C, $Q_2^=(\bar{c}^2, \pi_1)$ is flatter than $Q_1^=(\bar{c}^2, \pi_1)$ at $\bar{c}^2$. Therefore every point in $Y(\bar{c}^2)$ is inferior to $\bar{c}^2$ relative to $U_2(\cdot, \pi_1)$. (Recall that c^1 is the allocation that will prevail when $\pi = \pi_1$.) A similar argument applies when $\bar{c}^2$ is on C (in which case $Q_2^=(\bar{c}^2, \pi_1)$ is tangent to $Q_1^=(\bar{c}^2, \pi_1)$).

However, we claim that $\bar{c}^1 = \bar{c}^2 = \bar{c} \in C^- \cup C$ cannot solve problem 6.5. To see this, note that $V_2(\bar{c}, \bar{c}) = U_2(\bar{c}, \bar{\pi})$ where $\bar{\pi} = \phi_1(\pi_1)\pi_1 + \phi_1(\pi_2)\pi_2$. Suppose that $\bar{c}^1 = \bar{c}^2 = \bar{c}$ does solve problem 6.5. Then $\bar{c}$ would solve the following problem.

Problem 6.7

$$\max_{c \in B} U_2(c, \bar{\pi})$$

subject to

$$c \in Q_1^{\geqslant}(e, \pi_j) \qquad j = 1, 2$$

The constraint set for this problem is the area on or below the wavy line

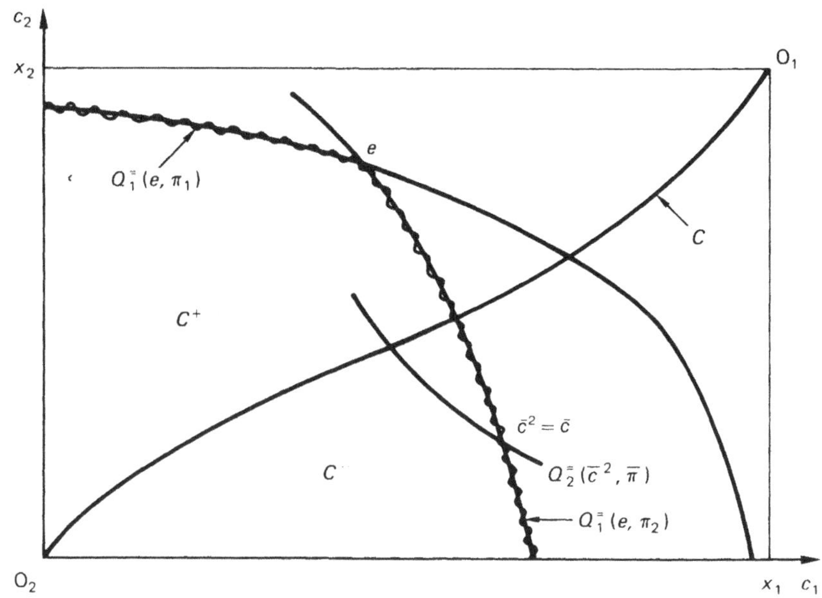

Figure 6.7. Proof of theorem 6.2 (continued)

in figure 6.7. Clearly the solution lies on the wavy line. But since $\bar{c}$ is on or below C, an indifference curve of $U_2(\cdot, \bar{\pi})$ through $\bar{c}$ is flatter than $Q_1^=(e, \pi_2)$ at $\bar{c}$ because $\bar{\pi} < \pi_2$ (see figure 6.7). Therefore there are points c on the wavy line which have $U_2(c, \bar{\pi}) > U_2(\bar{c}, \bar{\pi})$. This contradicts the assertion that $\bar{c}$ solves the above problem. Therefore it cannot be the case that $\bar{c}^2 \in C^- \cup C$. This establishes the claim that $\bar{c}^2 \in C^+$.

It is fairly obvious that $\bar{c}^2$ will lie on the indifference curve of agent 1 passing through e under $\pi = \pi_2$, that is, on $Q_1^=(e, \pi_2)$. This will not be demonstrated rigorously here. There are two remaining possibilities: either $\bar{c}^2$ is above e on $Q_1^=(e, \pi_2)$ or it is between e and C on $Q_1^=(e, \pi_2)$, but not on C. If $\bar{c}^2$ is above e, it is easy to check that the constraint set of problem 6.6 is the shaded region in figure 6.8. Thus by definition of C the solution of problem 6.6 is $\bar{c}^1$ on the consensus contract curve as shown in figure 6.8. However, since $\bar{c}^2$ is above C, $Q_2^=(\bar{c}^2, \pi_2)$ is steeper than $Q_1^=(\bar{c}^2, \pi_2)$ at $\bar{c}^2$ as shown in figure 6.8. Therefore $U_2(e, \pi_2) > U_2(\bar{c}^2, \pi_2)$. But consider problem 6.6 with c^2 fixed at e (instead of above e as in figure 6.8). The constraint set of problem 6.6 would still be the shaded region in figure 6.8, and so the solution would still be at $\bar{c}^1$ as shown in figure 6.8. However, since $U_2(e, \pi_2) > U_2(\bar{c}^2, \pi_2)$,

$$\phi_1(\pi_1)U_2(\bar{c}^1, \pi_1) + \phi_1(\pi_2)U_2(e, \pi_2) > \sum_{j=1}^{2} \phi_1(\pi_j)U_2(\bar{c}^j, \pi_j)$$

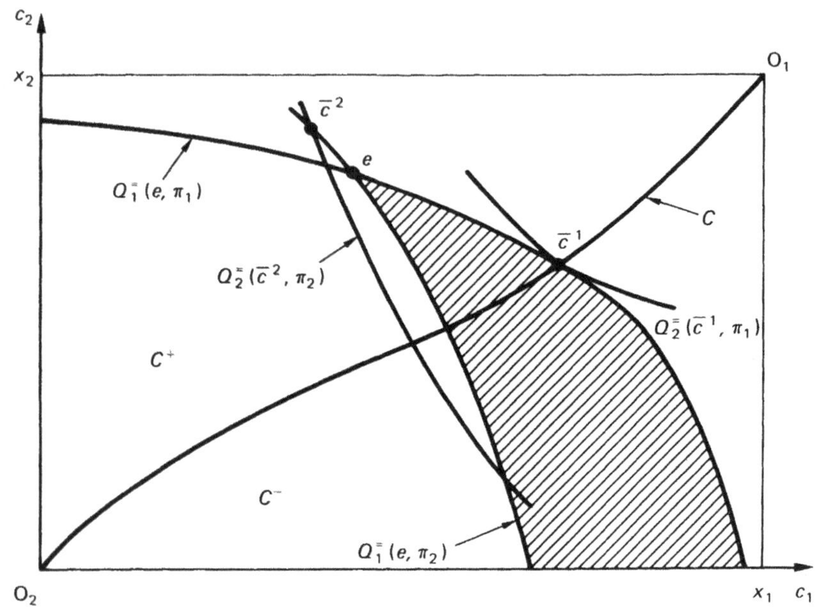

Figure 6.8. Proof of theorem 6.2 (continued)

Therefore $(\bar{c}^1, \bar{c}^2)$ cannot solve problem 6.5 when $\bar{c}^2$ is above e on $Q_1^=(e, \pi_2)$.

We have so far demonstrated that $\bar{c}^2$ must be on $Q_1^=(e, \pi_2)$ between e and C (but not on C). It remains only to show that $\bar{c}^1$ is on $Q_1^=(\bar{c}^2, \pi_1)$ at its intersection with C. To see this recall that $\bar{c}^1$ must solve problem 6.6 given $c^2 = \bar{c}^2$. The constraint set for this problem is shown in figure 6.9 for $\bar{c}^2$ arbitrarily placed on $Q_1^=(e, \pi_2)$ between e and C. Again, it is clear from the definition of C that the solution of problem 6.6 with $c^2 = \bar{c}^2$ is at $\bar{c}^1$ as shown in figure 6.9. This completes the proof of case 1.

Case 2 $e \in C$. For this case we consider the solution to problem 6.5 without imposing the constraint $c^1 \in Y(c^2)$. Denote this problem 6.7. We show that the solution of problem 6.7 is $\bar{c}^1 = \bar{c}^2 = e$, and hence that it (trivially) satisfies $c^1 \in Y(c^2)$. Since the objective function of problem 6.5 is separable in c^1 and c^2, and the constraint $c^j \in Q_1^{\geq}(e, \pi_j)$ does not involve c^i for $i \neq j$, the solution of problem 6.7 can be found by solving the following problem.

Problem 6.8

$$\max_{c^j \in Q_1^{\geq}(e, \pi_j)} U_2(c^j, \pi_j) \qquad j = 1, 2$$

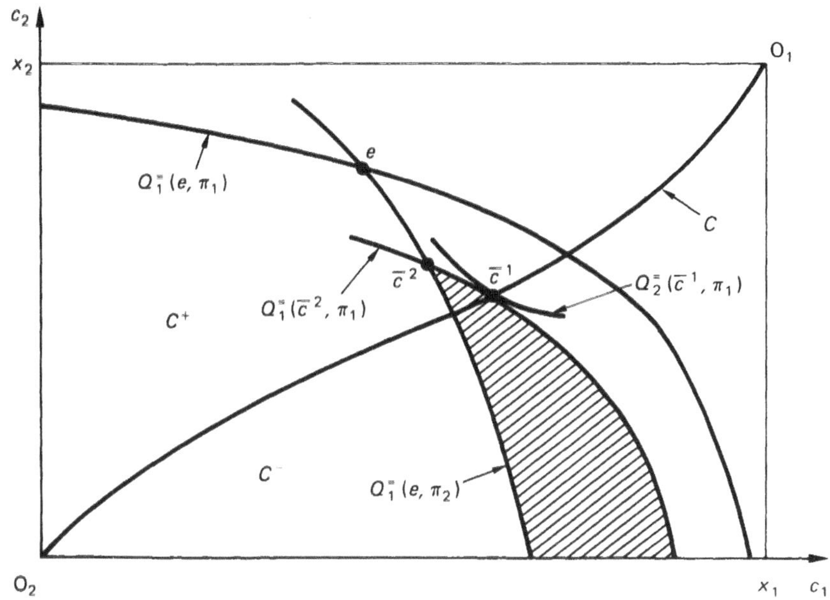

Figure 6.9. Proof of theorem 6.2 (continued)

By definition of C the solution of problem 6.8 is the intersection of $Q_1^{=}(e, \pi_j)$ with C. However, this intersection is e for $j = 1, 2$. Thus e solves problem 6.8 for both $j = 1$ and $j = 2$, and hence e solves problem 6.7 and (e, e) solves problem 6.5. This completes the proof of case 2.

Case 3 This case is the same as case 1 with all subscripts interchanged (including those on π).

We have shown that $\bar{p}_{21} = (\bar{c}^1, \bar{c}^2)$ is as claimed in the statement of the theorem. Since $(\bar{c}^1, \bar{c}^2)$ solves problem 6.5, $\bar{c}^j \in Q_1^{\geq}(e, \pi_j) \cap Q_1^{\geq}(\bar{c}^i, \pi_j)$ for $j = 1, 2$, $i \neq j$. Therefore $\bar{p}_{12}(\bar{p}_{21}, \pi_j) = \bar{c}^j$ for $j = 1, 2$ solves problem 6.3 as noted above. Consequently, the equilibrium allocation will be $\bar{c}^j$ with a probability of unity if $\pi = \pi_j$ for $j = 1, 2$.

Proof of Lemma 6.1

First define the two marginal distributions corresponding to $G(\cdot | M, \pi_j)$:

$$G_1(c_1 | M, \pi_j) = \sum_{c_2} G(c_1, c_2 | M, \pi_j)$$

$$G_2(c_2 | M, \pi_j) = \sum_{c_1} G(c_1, c_2 | M, \pi_j)$$

Then, for any parameter value $y \in \Pi$,

$$\sum_{c} U_1(c, y) G(c \mid M, \pi_j) = y \sum_{c_1} u_1(x_1 - c_1) G_1(c_1 \mid M, \pi_j)$$

$$+ (1 - y) \sum_{c_2} u_1(x_2 - c_2) G_2(c_2 \mid M, \pi_j)$$

Let b_k^j be such that

$$\sum_{c_k} u_1(x_k - c_k) G_k(c_k \mid M, \pi_j) = u_1(x_k - b_k^j) \qquad k = 1, 2$$

(see figure 6.10 for a graphical construction of b_1^j assuming that $G_1(\cdot \mid M, \pi_j)$ puts weight on only two values of c_1 labeled c_1^1 and c_1^2 in the figure). Since u_1 is strictly monotone decreasing and strictly concave in c_k, $b_k^j \geqslant \bar{c}_k^j$ where $\bar{c}_k^j = \Sigma_{c_k} c_k G_k(c_k \mid M, \pi_j)$ is the mean of $G_k(c_k \mid M, \pi_j)$. If G_k is nondegenerate, then $b_k^j > \bar{c}_k^j$. Then, letting $b^j = (b_1^j, b_2^j)$, by construction we obtain

$$U_1(b^j, y) = \sum_{c} U_1(c, y) G(c \mid M, \pi_j) \qquad j = 1, 2 \tag{6.A5}$$

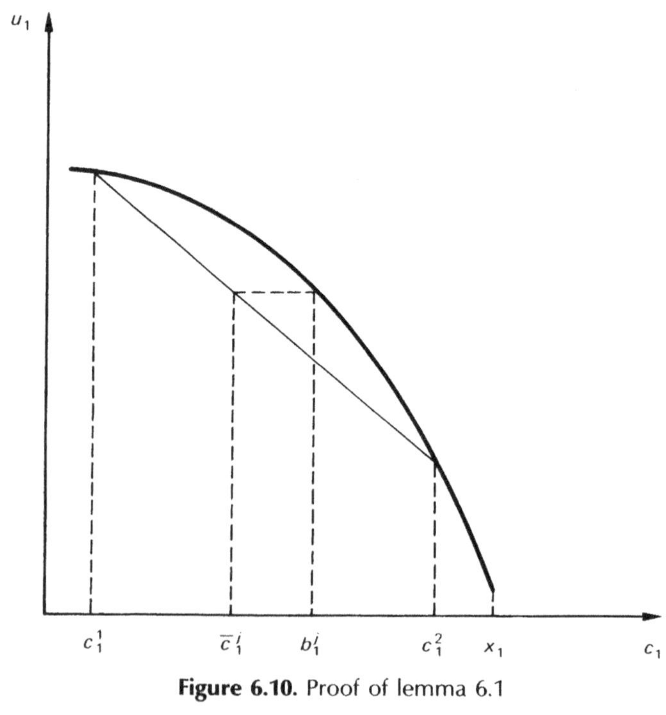

Figure 6.10. Proof of lemma 6.1

Now, by Jensen's inequality,

$$\sum_c U_2(c, y)G(c|M, \pi_j) \leqslant U_2(\bar{c}^j, y) \tag{6.A6}$$

where $\bar{c}^j = (\bar{c}_1^j, \bar{c}_2^j)$ is the mean of $G(c|M, \pi_j)$ as defined above. However, since $b_k^j \geqslant \bar{c}_k^j$, $k = 1, 2$,

$$U_2(\bar{c}^j, y) \leqslant U_2(b^j, y) \tag{6.A7}$$

with strict inequality if G is nondegenerate. Combining the two inequalities (6.A6) and (6.A7) gives

$$U_2(b^j, y) \geqslant \sum_c U_2(c, y)G(c|M, \pi_j) \qquad j = 1, 2 \tag{6.A8}$$

From theorem 6.1,

$$\begin{aligned} W_1(M, \pi_j) &= \sum_c U_1(c, \pi_j)G(c|M, \pi_j) \\ &\geqslant \sum_c U_1(c, \pi_j)G(c|M, \pi_i) \end{aligned} \tag{6.A9}$$

for $i \neq j$. Setting $y = \pi_j$ in (6.A5) and using (6.A9) gives

$$U_1(b^j, \pi_j) \geqslant \sum_c U_1(c, \pi_j)G(c|M, \pi_i) \qquad i \neq j \tag{6.A10}$$

Substituting π_j for y and i for j in (6.A5) gives

$$\sum_c U_1(c, \pi_j)G(c|M, \pi_i) = U_1(b^i, \pi_j) \tag{6.A11}$$

Combining (6.A10) and (6.A11) yields

$$U_1(b^j, \pi_j) \geqslant U_1(b^i, \pi_j) \qquad i \neq j$$

that is, $b^1 \in Y(b^2)$.

Now define M' as follows. Agent 1 (the informed agent) starts by naming a value from π, either π_1 or π_2. If he names π_j, then the allocation is b^j for $j = 1, 2$. Formally, let $S' = 1$, $P' = \Pi \cup \{p_0\}$, $X'_{11}(p_0) = \Pi$, $X'_{21}(p_0) = \{p_0\}$, and for $p_{11} = \pi_j$, $j = 1, 2$,

$$F(c|p^1) = \begin{cases} 1 \text{ if } c = b^j \\ 0 \text{ otherwise} \end{cases}$$

It is easy to check that an equilibrium of this mechanism (ϕ'^1, σ'^1) is given by $\phi'_1 = \phi_1$; $\sigma'_{11}(\cdot|p_0, \pi_j)$ puts all weight on π_j, that is, agent 1 will name the true value of π since $b^1 \in Y(b^2)$. Therefore M' is deterministic and $G(\cdot|M', \pi_j)$ puts all weight on b^j, $j = 1, 2$. We need only check that $M' \geqslant M$. However, by (6.A5) with $y = \pi_j$

$$W_1(M', \pi_j) = U_1(b^j, \pi_j) = W_1(M, \pi_j) \qquad j = 1, 2$$

and by (6.A8) with $y = \pi_j$

$$\begin{aligned} W_2(M') &= \sum_{j=1}^{2} \phi_1(\pi_j) U_2(b^j, \pi_j) \\ &\geqslant \sum_{j=1}^{2} \phi_1(\pi_j) \sum_c U_2(c, \pi_j) G(c|M, \pi_j) \\ &= W_2(M) \end{aligned}$$

Hence $M' \geqslant M$.

Proof of Theorem 6.3

Consider all solutions of problem 6.5 in the proof of theorem 6.2 (with e replaced by e'), that is, solutions of

$$\max_{(c^1, c^2) \in B \times B} \sum_{j=1}^{2} U_2(c^j, \pi_j) \phi_1(\pi_j)$$

subject to

$$c^1 \in Y(c^2),\ c^j \in Q_1^{\geqslant}(e', \pi_j) \qquad j = 1, 2$$

Recall from the proof of theorem 6.2 that if (c^1, c^2) is any solution of problem 6.5, then $U_1(c^2, \pi_2) = U_1(e, \pi_2)$. If problem 6.5 has more than one solution, let $(\bar{c}^1, \bar{c}^2)$ be a solution such that for any other solution, say $(\tilde{c}^1, \tilde{c}^2)$, $U_1(\tilde{c}^1, \pi_1) \leqslant U_1(\bar{c}^1, \pi_1)$. Thus no other solution makes agent 1 better off than $\bar{c}^1$ under $\pi = \pi_1$. Since problem 6.5 has at least one solution and it can be shown that the set of solutions is compact, a solution with this property exists. It is clear from the proof of theorem 6.2 that $(\bar{\phi}^2, \bar{p}^2)$ is an equilibrium of $\bar{M}(e')$ of the form described in the theorem where

$$\bar{\phi}_1 = \bar{\phi}_2 = \phi_1$$

$$\bar{p}_{11} = p_0, \qquad \bar{p}_{21} = (\bar{c}^1, \bar{c}^2), \qquad \bar{p}_{12}(\bar{p}^1, \pi_j) = \bar{c}^j, \qquad \bar{p}_{22}(\bar{p}^1) = p_0$$

To show that $\bar{M}(e')$ (with the equilibrium described above) cannot be strictly dominated, suppose the contrary. Then there is a mechanism M' such that $M' > \bar{M}(e')$. By lemma 6.1, there is a deterministic mechanism M such that $M \geqslant M' > \bar{M}(e')$. Let $\hat{c}^j$ be such that $G(\cdot|M, \pi_j)$ puts all weight on $\hat{c}^j$ for $j = 1, 2$. Since $M > \bar{M}(e')$,

$$U_1(\hat{c}^j, \pi_j) = W_1(M, \pi_j) \geqslant W_1\{\bar{M}(e'), \pi_j\} \geqslant U_1(e', \pi_j) \qquad j = 1, 2$$

Also, by corollary 6.1, $\hat{c}^1 \in Y(\hat{c}^2)$. Therefore $(\hat{c}^1, \hat{c}^2)$ is feasible for problem 6.5. Thus,

$$\begin{aligned} W_2(M) &= \sum_{j=1}^{2} U_2(\hat{c}^j, \pi_j)\phi_1(\pi_j) \\ &\leqslant \sum_{j=1}^{2} U_2(\bar{c}^j, \pi_j)\phi_1(\pi_j) \\ &= W_2\{\bar{M}(e')\} \end{aligned}$$

But since $M > \bar{M}(e')$, $W_2(M) \geqslant W_2\{\bar{M}(e')\}$. Hence $W_2(M) = W_2\{\bar{M}(e')\}$ and $(\hat{c}^1, \hat{c}^2)$ solves problem 6.5. Therefore, if $M > \bar{M}(e')$, we must have $W_1(M, \pi_j) \geqslant W_1\{\bar{M}(e'), \pi_j\}$ with a strict inequality for at least one j. But $W_1(M, \pi_j) = U_1(\hat{c}^j, \pi_j)$ and $W_1\{\bar{M}(e'), \pi_j\} = U_1(\bar{c}^j, \pi_j)$, so that we must have $U_1(\hat{c}^j, \pi_j) \geqslant U_1(\bar{c}^j, \pi_j)$ with a strict inequality for one j. Now since $(\hat{c}^1, \hat{c}^2)$ and $(\bar{c}^1, \bar{c}^2)$ both solve problem 6.5, we have $U_1(\hat{c}^2, \pi_2) = U_1(\bar{c}^2, \pi_2) = U_1(e', \pi_2)$. Therefore we must have $U_1(\hat{c}^1, \pi_1) > U_1(\bar{c}^1, \pi_1)$ which contradicts the definition of $(\bar{c}^1, \bar{c}^2)$.

Proof of Theorem 6.4

Let M be any mechanism and, using lemma 6.1, let M' be a deterministic mechanism such that $M' \geqslant M$. Let $\hat{c}^j$, $j = 1, 2$, be such that $G(\cdot|M', \pi_j)$ puts all weight on $\hat{c}^j$ for $j = 1, 2$. By corollary 6.1, $\hat{c}^1 \in Y(\hat{c}^2)$. Construct e' as shown in figure 6.4, that is, e' is the intersection of $Q_1^=(\hat{c}^1, \pi_1)$ and $Q_1^=(\hat{c}^2, \pi_2)$. Clearly $\bar{M}(e')$ is deterministic since $\bar{M}$ is. Let $(\bar{\phi}^2, \bar{p}^2)$ be an equilibrium of $\bar{M}(e')$ of the form described in theorem 6.2, where $\bar{p}_{21} = (\bar{c}^1, \bar{c}^2)$.

By construction of e', $U_1(e', \pi_j) = U_1(\hat{c}^j, \pi_j)$ for $j = 1, 2$. Since $U_1(\bar{c}^j, \pi_j) \geqslant U_1(e', \pi_j)$ for $j = 1, 2$, $W_1\{\bar{M}(e'), \pi_j\} \geqslant W_1(M', \pi_j)$ for $j = 1, 2$. We need only show that $W_2\{\bar{M}(e')\} \geqslant W_2(M')$.

Now $(\bar{c}^1, \bar{c}^2)$ solves problem 6.5 with e' substituted for e. But by $\hat{c}^1 \in Y(\hat{c}^2)$ and by construction of e', $(\hat{c}^1, \hat{c}^2)$ is feasible for problem 6.5 with e' substituted for e. Therefore

$$\begin{aligned} W_2(M') &= \sum_{j=1}^{2} U_2(\hat{c}^j, \pi_j)\phi_1(\pi_j) \\ &\leqslant \sum_{j=1}^{2} U_2(\bar{c}^j, \pi_j)\phi_1(\pi_j) \\ &= W_2\{\bar{M}(e')\} \end{aligned}$$

as was to be shown.

Notes

1 By asymmetric information, we mean that some agents are better informed about some aspects of the environment and that this fact is known to other agents. This can be contrasted with the case of differential information where agents have different information about the environment but no agent believes any other agent to be better informed.

2 See Harris and Raviv (1978) for a start in this direction.

3 This assertion is proved for the simple environment considered here in theorem 6.1 (section 5). The result can be extended to more complicated environments (see Harris and Townsend, 1981, this volume, ch. 7). A similar result has been obtained by Myerson (1979).

4 The class is broad enough to include most imaginable mechanisms. Of course, we could restrict attention to a few obvious mechanisms, but that restriction would be counter to the spirit of this chapter which is to make as few exogenous restrictions as possible. Our theorems on the existence of an optimal mechanism are "strong" to the extent that the class we consider is "large."

5 A slightly different approach, which turns out to be equivalent to that adopted here, is to characterize *all* the constraints on allocations imposed by the fact that allocations must be achieved by some allocation process. It is then possible to search for optimal allocations in the space of all *achievable* allocations. It turns out that we can then "work backwards" to characterize an optimal mechanism which achieves the optimal allocation. This is the approach adopted in Harris and Townsend (1981, this volume, ch. 7).

6 Examples with everything observable *ex post* include Arrow (1970), Raviv (1977), and Townsend (1978, this volume, ch. 10). Examples with moral hazard in which one or more variables are unobservable by some agents include Spence and Zeckhauser (1971), Ross (1973), Harris and Raviv (1978, 1979), Shavell (1978), and Holmström (1979).

7 This approach has been used for environments more closely related to the one considered here, namely those in which one or more agents are better informed about some aspect of the environment (as opposed to being better informed about an endogenous choice variable as in the moral hazard case). Examples include

Akerlof (1970), Spence (1974), Riley (1975, 1977), Rothschild and Stiglitz (1976), Salop and Salop (1976), Miyazaki (1977), Wilson (1977), and Townsend (1979, this volume, ch. 5) in which the information can be purchased. An important common characteristic of these models is that if an agent is assumed to be informed about something, then only he is informed about it. Models in which there are informed and uninformed agents where the informed agents share common information have been studied by Green (1973) and Grossman (1977) among others. Here the approach is similar but the results are somewhat different. We address this type of environment in Harris and Townsend (1981, this volume, ch. 7).

8 An exception is Myerson (1979) who considers only nonsequential mechanisms. He adopts the Bayesian equilibrium concept, notes that certain self-selection constraints are imposed, and evaluates mechanisms using Bayesian expected utility.

9 Note that any multistage mechanism can also be viewed as a single-stage mechanism in which each agent may propose a sequence of contingent strategies. Each strategy in the sequence would be contingent on the outcome of all previous contingent strategies. Formally, the two mechanisms would be identical, but we find it conceptually simpler to view such a process as evolving sequentially. In what follows we can interpret the term multistage mechanism in either way. A related point is that, since no new information enters the economy during a bargaining process, we might conjecture that any multistage mechanism could be reduced somehow to a one- or two-stage mechanism. Although plausible, this result is far from obvious (considerable attention has been devoted to similar issues in game theory literature; see Ponssard and Zamir (1973) and Kohlberg (1975)). In fact, we show below that there is an optimal mechanism which has only two stages, and in the conclusions we point out how this mechanism can actually be reduced to a one-stage mechanism. Unfortunately, any proof of this result requires explicit consideration of multistage mechanisms and their equilibria. This involves a considerable, but unavoidable, notational burden.

10 The formal definition of M_C is $S = 1$, $P = \Pi \cup \{p_0\}$, $X_{11} = \Pi$, $X_{21} = \{p_0\}$, and $F(c|p^1)$ is degenerate on $c_E(p_{11})$ where $c_E(p_{11})$ is the competitive equilibrium bundle of agent 2 when agent 2's preferences are given by $U_2(\cdot, \bar{\pi})$ and agent 1's preferences are given by $U_1(\cdot, p_{11})$ (here $\bar{\pi} = \phi(\pi_1)\pi_1 + \phi(\pi_2)\pi_2$).

11 An alternative equilibrium concept would require that strategies of a given agent be optimal only for past proposals which can occur with positive probability given the strategies of the other agent. This would not be a "perfect" equilibrium in the sense that this term is used by Selten (1975). The equilibrium concept defined in the text allows fewer equilibria and is therefore preferable from the standpoint of positive theory. We are grateful to Jim Jordan for calling our attention to this alternative equilibrium concept.

12 We are indebted to Ed Prescott for suggesting this last point.

13 Obviously, anyone who engages in an action is choosing from some set of alternatives. The empirical content of the statement is that it is the informed agent who determines the actual allocation. Thus any empirical test of our theory presupposes not only a relatively simple environment but also that the informed agent can be identified.

References

Akerlof, G. (1970) The market for lemons: qualitative uncertainty and the market mechanism. *Quarterly Journal of Economics* 84, 488–500.

Arrow, K.J. (1970) On optimal insurance policies. *Essays in the Theory of Risk Bearing*, pp. 212–19. Chicago, IL: Markham.

Crawford, V.P. A game of fair division. Unpublished manuscript, Massachusetts Institute of Technology, Cambridge, MA.

Dubins, L.E. and Spanier, E.H. (1961) How to cut a cake fairly. *American Mathematical Monthly* 68, 1–17.

Green, E. (1977) Non-cooperative games and equilibrium market strategies. Ph.D. Dissertation, GSIA, Carnegie–Mellon University, Pittsburgh, PA.

Green, J.R. (1973) Information, efficiency, and equilibrium. Discussion Paper 284, Harvard Institute of Economic Research.

Grossman, S. (1977) The existence of futures markets, noisy rational expectations and informational externalities. *Review of Economic Studies* 44(3), 431–9.

Groves, T. and Ledyard, J. (1977) Optimal allocation of public goods: a solution to the "free rider problem." *Econometrica* 45(4), 783–810.

Harris, M. and Townsend, R.M. (1978) Some results on incentive contracts with applications to education and employment, health insurance, and law enforcement. *American Economic Review* 68, 20–30.

—— and —— (1979) Optimal incentive contracts with imperfect information. *Journal of Economic Theory* 20, 231–59.

—— and Townsend, R.M. (1981) Resource allocation under asymmetric information. *Econometrica* 49(1), 33–64. Reprinted in this volume as chapter 7.

Harsanyi, J.C. (1967–8) Games with incomplete information played by "Bayesian" players, Parts I–III. *Management Science* 14, 159–82, 320–34, 481–502.

Holmström, B. (1979) Moral hazard and observability. *Bell Journal of Economics* 10, 74–91.

Hurwicz, L. (1972) On informationally decentralized systems. In *Decision and Organization*, eds C.B. McGuire and R. Radner, ch. 14. Amsterdam: North-Holland.

Kohlberg, E. (1975) The information revealed in infinitely-repeated games of incomplete information. *International Journal of Game Theory* 4(2), 57–9.

Kydland, F. and Prescott, E. (1977) Rules rather than discretion: the inconsistency of optimal plans. *Journal of Political Economy* 85(3), 473–92.

Miyazaki, H. (1977) The rate race and internal labor markets. *Bell Journal of Economics* 8(2), 394–418.

Myerson, R.B. (1979) Incentive compatibility and the bargaining problem. *Econometrica* 47(1), 61–74.

Ponssard, J.P. and Zamir, S. (1973) Zero-sum sequential games with incomplete information. *International Journal of Game Theory* 2(2), 99–107.

Prescott, E.C. and Visscher, M. (1977) Sequential location among firms with foresight. *Bell Journal of Economics* 8(2), 378–93.

Raviv, A. (1977) The design of an optimal insurance policy. GSIA Working Paper 11-76-77, Carnegie–Mellon University, Pittsburgh, PA.

Reiter, S. (1977) Information and performance in the $(\text{new})^2$ welfare economics. *American Economic Review* 67(1), 226–34.

Riley, J.G. (1975) Competitive signalling. *Journal of Economic Theory* 10(2), 174–86.
—— (1977) Informational equilibrium. Rand Corporation Report, Santa Monica, CA.
Ross, S.A. (1973) The economic theory of agency: the principal's problem. *American Economic Review* 63(2), 134–9.
Rothschild, M. and Stiglitz, J. (1976) Equilibrium in competitive insurance markets: an essay on the economics of imperfect information. *Quarterly Journal of Economics* 90, 620–49.
Salop, J. and Salop, S. (1976) Self-selection and turnover in labor markets. *Quarterly Journal of Economics* 90, 619–27.
Selten, R. (1975) Reexamination of the perfectness concept for equilibrium points in extensive games. *International Journal of Game Theory* 4(1), 25–55.
Shavell, S. (1978) Risk sharing and incentives in the principal and agent relationship. Unpublished manuscript, Department of Economics, Harvard University.
Spence, A.M. (1974) Competitive and optimal responses to signals: an analysis of efficiency and distribution. *Journal of Economic Theory* 7, 296–332.
—— and Zeckhauser, R. (1971) Insurance, information and individual action. *American Economic Review* 61(2), 380–7.
Townsend, R.M. (1978) Intermediation with costly bilateral exchange. *Review of Economic Studies* 45(3), 417–25. Reprinted in this volume as chapter 10.
—— (1979) Optimal contracts and competitive markets with costly state verification. *Journal of Economic Theory* 21(2), 265–93. Reprinted in this volume as chapter 5.
Wilson, C. (1977) A model of insurance markets with incomplete information. *Journal of Economic Theory* 16, 167–207.

7

Resource Allocation under Asymmetric Information

with Milton Harris

1 Introduction

The purpose of this chapter is to provide a method for characterizing efficient allocation processes and efficient allocations for a large class of environments in which asymmetric information is an important factor.[1] This method is based on a rigorous application of statistical decision theory and makes explicit both the information available to agents *ex ante* and the way in which information is transmitted during any multistage allocation process.[2] Our approach is illustrated by its application to principal–agent environment, a public goods environment, and a competitive environment with informed and uninformed traders.

In much of the literature on environments with asymmetric information, efficiency is defined with respect to full or symmetric information.[3] Much of the work on public goods, for example, focuses on constructing mechanisms to achieve Samuelson–Lindahl allocations (for example, Groves and Ledyard, 1977). These are allocations which would be Pareto optimal if all agents possessed full information about the *actual* preferences of the agents. We argue that, as an alternative approach to characterizing efficient allocations and mechanisms, we must consider explicitly the restrictions imposed by

---

Reprinted from *Econometrica* 49(1), 1981, 33–64. This paper has formed the basis for presentations at the NBER–CEME Conference on Decentralization (held at the University of Minnesota, April 1978), the Econometric Society meetings (Chicago, August 1978), and Northwestern University (October 1978). We would like to thank the participants at these seminars, and especially J. Jordan, J. Ledyard, E. Maskin, M. Satterthwaite, and C. Wilson for helpful comments. In addition we are grateful for the extremely valuable suggestions of two anonymous referees. Financial support from the National Science Foundation (under grant SOC-7826262) and the Federal Reserve Bank of Minneapolis is gratefully acknowledged. We assume full responsibility for any errors as well as the views expressed here.

asymmetric information.[4] In particular we argue that in environments with asymmetric information, uncertainty about preferences, technology, and endowments may be characterized by probability distributions over unknown shocks or parameters. Then we must take account of this information structure in developing an equilibrium theory of allocation processes or mechanisms and in defining efficient allocations. This results in a different theory of allocation processes and a different definition of optimal allocations from those which would obtain under full information. In particular, both the normative and the positive implications of our approach differ, for some environments, from those of the traditional approach.

The approach which we propose here consists of five steps. First, we carefully specify the economic environment including the information structure. Second, we define the concept of an allocation mechanism for an environment and specify the class of available mechanisms. Third, we define the concepts of equilibrium of a mechanism and equilibrium allocations of a mechanism. Fourth, we define preferences of the agents over mechanisms and the concept of an efficient mechanism. Fifth, and last, we characterize efficient mechanisms and their allocations. Each aspect of the approach is now discussed briefly.

The general class of environments considered in this chapter (see section 3) includes arbitrary sets of agents and production, and a rich set of possible information structures comprising both public and private information. An environment consists of a specification of three objects. First is the set of agents and the technology of production and exchange available to each coalition of agents. Second, the preferences of each agent are specified. These are assumed to depend on a vector of exogenously determined parameters. The information structure is then specified as the set of parameters which is *observed* by each agent together with a prior distribution for each agent describing his information about the parameters he cannot observe. More than one agent may observe the same parameter, that is, some information may be public. These observations are the sole source of all information asymmetries.

Once an environment is specified, the concept of an allocation mechanism for that environment can be defined. Intuitively, an allocation mechanism for a given environment is simply a set of rules which specify the game to be played by the agents in allocating resources and a specification of how the allocation is determined, given the "plays" of the agents during the game. In section 4 this concept is defined formally, together with the class of all available mechanisms.

Next we must have a theory of the outcome of any given mechanism, that is, we must define the concept of equilibrium strategies for a given mechanism. In this context, a *strategy* of an agent is a mapping which determines his play or signal at a given stage of a mechanism as a *function* of the parameters initially observed by him and the sequence of past signals of all agents.

Optimality of a strategy is defined relative to the information that the agent has at the time that the strategy is used. This information will be different from the initial information if the signals of other agents convey information. In particular, agents are assumed to update their beliefs about unobserved parameters using Bayes's rule and the sequence of past signals of other agents. Using this definition of optimal strategies, we define a *perfect Bayesian equilibrium* concept for any mechanism. This concept is related to Harsanyi's (1967–8) "Bayesian equilibrium" and Selten's (1975) "perfect equilibrium."[5] It also draws on the work of Green (1977), Kydland and Prescott (1977), and Prescott and Visscher (1977). Once the equilibrium strategies are determined, the equilibrium allocation of a mechanism is easily defined. The equilibrium concept is discussed more fully in section 5.

As can be seen from the above discussion, equilibrium allocations of mechanisms are allocations which depend on the actual realized values of the parameters of the environment (since equilibrium strategies depend on these values). Such allocations will be referred to as parameter-contingent (PC) allocations. Preference orderings of agents over mechanisms are then naturally defined using expected utilities, based on the initial information structure, over these equilibrium PC allocations. Efficient mechanisms are defined in an obvious way: for example, a core mechanism is one which cannot be improved upon by any coalition of agents, a Pareto optimal mechanism is one which cannot be improved upon by the set of all agents, and so on. These concepts are defined formally in section 7.

Our general results provide a fairly simple way of executing the final step of the approach, namely that of characterizing efficient allocation mechanisms and efficient allocations. Our first major result (see section 6) is that the equilibrium PC allocations of any mechanism must satisfy certain self-selection properties. That is, any agent with private information must prefer (in the sense of expected utility relative to his initial information) the equilibrium allocation which is to result under the actual value of the parameters to the equilibrium final allocation which would result if the parameters observed by him alone took on some other of their possible values. This is because the actual (equilibrium) strategies must be preferred to all other strategies, including the strategy of acting as if our observed parameters took on some other value.

Our first result thus shows that certain technically feasible PC allocations, namely those which do not satisfy self-selection properties, cannot in fact be achieved.[6] Conversely, a second major result (also in section 6) is that any PC allocation which does satisfy self-selection properties can be achieved under a mechanism. Moreover, it is established that we can restrict attention to a mechanism of a particularly simple form – a *direct mechanism* under which each agent reports on the value of each parameter he observes.[7]

These two results suggest that we can define concepts of efficiency directly in the space of PC allocations which exhibit the self-selection property. We do this in section 8 where the equivalence between efficient allocations (in a certain sense) and efficient mechanisms is established. Our third major result is that an allocation is efficient if and only if it is associated with an efficient mechanism. This, then, allows us to convert a problem of characterizing efficient mechanisms into one of characterizing efficient allocations, which can usually be solved using standard mathematical programming techniques. Using the second result outlined in the previous paragraph, we can then easily characterize an efficient direct mechanism which supports the efficient allocations.

An additional result, which is somewhat less general than the three results mentioned above, concerns the relationship between optimal allocations in our sense and full-information optimal allocations. In particular, we show that if there are only two agents and one is fully informed while the other is not, then any PC allocation which is full-information optimal for every parameter value and satisfies self-selection is also optimal in our sense (see section 8). That this result cannot be generalized (without adding other restrictions) is shown via an example (see section 9).

In addition to the general development of sections 3–8 outlined above, we also present three examples. (A fourth example concerned with risk sharing in a pure exchange environment is discussed by Harris and Townsend (1978, this volume, ch. 6), who take a slightly different approach.[8]) The three examples described in sections 2, 9, and 10 respectively are (a) a principal–agent environment, (b) a public goods environment, and (c) a competitive pure exchange environment.

The agency problem presented in section 2, before the general development, introduces several concepts and results central to that development. This environment is essentially that analyzed by Hurwicz and Shapiro (1978) in which the agent has better information about some parameters of a production process than the principal. The example illustrates four important points: (a) an allocation is achievable by a mechanism if and only if it satisfies certain self-selection conditions; (b) not all allocations which are optimal in a full-information sense are achievable (that is, some fail to satisfy the self-selection conditions); (c) there are allocations which are optimal in our sense but which are *not* full-information optimal; (d) which allocations are optimal in our sense depends on prior beliefs of the agents.

In section 9, after the general development, we examine a simple public goods environment in which each agent knows only his own preferences for public and private goods. The main point of this example, apart from further illustrating the power of our approach, is to establish that achievable full-information optimal allocations (namely achievable Samuelson–Lindahl allocations) need to be optimal in our sense.[9] Thus if we take our approach seriously, full-information optimal PC allocations are not necessarily desirable from a normative point of view.

Finally, in section 10 we note, by way of contrast, that in a pure exchange economy with informed and uninformed traders (informed traders are all informed about the same thing) competitive equilibrium allocations in which prices fully reveal all information are core allocations in our sense. This result turns on the standard definition of the core and the fact that with no private information there are no self-selection constraints. Section 11 contains some concluding remarks.

2 A principal–agent environment with technological uncertainty

In this section we consider a principal–agent model motivated by Hurwicz and Shapiro (1978). A principal p has sole access to a technology for transforming labor effort z into output y of the single consumption good of the model in accordance with a production function f. Let $y = f(z, \theta) = \theta z$. Here the parameter θ is drawn from a known distribution. In particular, θ can take one of two values θ^1 or θ^2, with $\theta^1 < \theta^2$, and ϕ denotes the probability that $\theta = \theta^1$. The agent (worker) a knows the actual realization of θ; the principal (manager, landlord) does not. The principal takes the probability that $\theta = \theta^1$ to be ϕ. The agent alone can supply labor, and such effort cannot be observed by the principal.

The principal cares only about consumption. Thus, if r denotes the reward to the agent (his allotment of the consumption good), the utility function of the principal is assumed to be $U_p(y, r) = y - r$. The agent values both leisure and consumption, and his utility function is assumed to be $u_a(r, z) = r - z^2$. Hence with $y = \theta z$ the agent's utility as a function of output, reward, and the productivity parameter θ is $U_a(y, r, \theta) = r - (y/\theta)^2$.

The environment is shown in figure 7.1. The space of feasible allocations is the area below the 45° line through the origin. Indifference curves of the principal are 45° lines with his utility increasing toward the southeast. Indifference curves of the agent depend on θ and are labeled by θ^1 or θ^2. His utility increases toward the northwest. Allocations which would be efficient under full information are shown by the vertical lines labeled C_j (allocations which would be efficient if both parties knew that $\theta = \theta^j$ for $j = 1, 2$). Thus any point on, say, C_1 is such that marginal product of labor equals the agent's marginal rate of substitution between effort and reward if $\theta = \theta^1$.

A PC allocation for this environment is an output quota $y(\theta)$ and reward to the agent $r(\theta)$ which depends on the true realized value of the productivity parameter θ. Such a PC allocation can be denoted (y_j, r_j), $j = 1, 2$, where

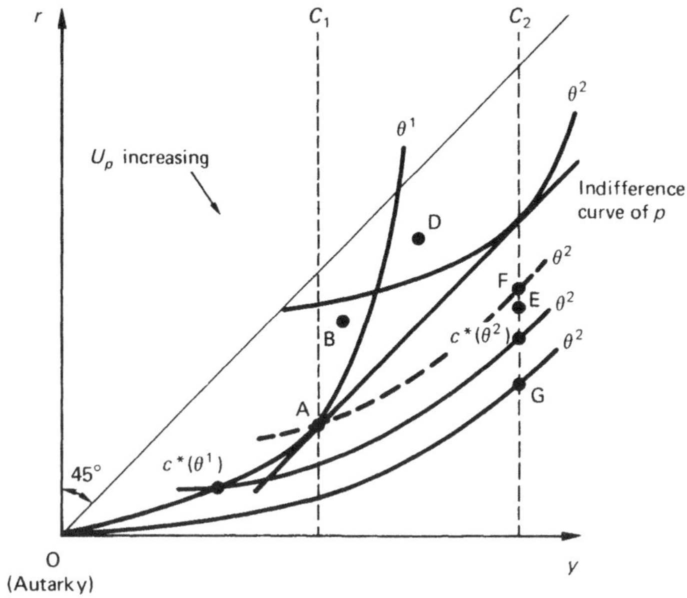

Figure 7.1. Principal–agent environment

$y_j = y(\theta^j)$ and $r_j = r(\theta^j)$. In this environment a PC allocation (y_j, r_j) satisfies self-selection if and only if the agent (worker) prefers the allocation (y_1, r_1) in which he must produce y_1 in return for a reward r_1 to (y_2, r_2) if, in fact, $\theta = \theta^1$, and vice versa if $\theta = \theta^2$. A PC allocation satisfying this property is shown in figure 7.1 as points $B = (y_1, r_1)$ and $D = (y_2, r_2)$. Mathematically, the condition which (y_j, r_j) must satisfy to be a self-selection PC allocation is

$$
\begin{aligned}
r_1 - \left(\frac{y_1}{\theta^1}\right)^2 &\geq r_2 - \left(\frac{y_2}{\theta^1}\right)^2 \\
r_2 - \left(\frac{y_2}{\theta^2}\right)^2 &\geq r_1 - \left(\frac{y_1}{\theta^2}\right)^2
\end{aligned}
\tag{7.1}
$$

The first point we wish to make with this example is that if a PC allocation does not satisfy (7.1) it cannot be achieved by any mechanism, and, conversely, if it does satisfy (7.1) it can be achieved by a very simple mechanism. In this regard, an allocation is achieved by a mechanism if that allocation is an equilibrium allocation of the mechanism. Although the above statement is true for any mechanism, it will be easier to understand if we restrict ourselves to direct mechanisms. In a direct mechanism the agent is asked to name a value for θ (either θ^1 or θ^2), and then some predetermined allocation $\{y(m), r(m)\}$ is effected, where m is the value of θ declared by the agent. To see the first part of the statement, suppose that we have a PC allocation which does not satisfy (7.1), say $(y_1, r_1) = \text{A}$, $(y_2, r_2) = \text{B}$ in figure 7.1. That is, suppose that we wish to achieve the allocation represented by point A (in figure 7.1) when $\theta = \theta^1$ and the allocation represented by point B when $\theta = \theta^2$. Now suppose that, to achieve this allocation, we choose the direct mechanism with

$$\{y(\theta^1), r(\theta^1)\} = \text{A}$$
$$\{y(\theta^2), r(\theta^2)\} = \text{B}$$

Note, however, that A and B do not satisfy self-selection, and in particular the agent prefers B to A regardless of the true value of θ. Thus in the direct mechanism described above, the agent will always declare $m = \theta^2$ even if $\theta = \theta^1$. Thus the equilibrium allocation of this mechanism will be B for either value of θ. In this case A will not be achieved by this mechanism when $\theta = \theta^1$. The only other choice of a direct mechanism which has any chance of resulting in A for $\theta = \theta^1$ and B for $\theta = \theta^2$ is

$$\{y(\theta^2), r(\theta^2)\} = \text{A}$$
$$\{y(\theta^1), r(\theta^1)\} = \text{B}$$

In this case the agent will always declare $m = \theta^1$, and the equilibrium allocation will again be B for either value of θ. Consequently the PC allocation represented by (A, B) cannot be achieved by a direct mechanism.

For the second part of the statement, suppose that we have the PC allocation represented by $(y_1, r_1) = \text{B}$, $(y_2, r_2) = \text{D}$ in figure 7.1. Consider the direct mechanism in which the final allocation as a function of the agent's declared value m of θ is given by $\{y(m), r(m)\} = (y_j, r_j)$ for $m = \theta^j$. Since the pair (B, D) in figure 7.1 satisfies (7.1), the agent will always declare the true value of θ. Thus, if $\theta = \theta^j$, the equilibrium allocation of this mechanism is simply (y_j, r_j). That is, the PC allocation represented by (B, D) can be achieved using a simple direct mechanism in which the agent's equilibrium strategy is to "tell the truth." In sections 3–8, these results are generalized to a large class of environments and mechanisms.

The second point that we wish to illustrate in this example is that there are full-information optimal PC allocations which are not achievable. A full-information optimal PC allocation is simply a PC allocation (y_j, r_j) such that (y_1, r_1) is on C_1 and (y_2, r_2) is on C_2 and both are below the 45° line. For example, consider the PC allocation represented by points A and E in figure 7.1. Note that the agent prefers A to E regardless of the value of θ. Therefore (A, E) does not satisfy (7.1) and, as indicated above, cannot be achieved.

The third point that we wish to make with this example is that there are PC allocations which are optimal in our sense but which are not full-information optimal (this will also serve to illustrate our definition of optimality in section 8). For this environment, a feasible PC allocation (y_j, r_j) is Pareto optimal if (a) it satisfies (7.1), (b) no other feasible PC allocation satisfying (7.1) can make the principal better off (in the expected utility sense, taking expectations over θ using his prior) without making the agent worse off for at least one value of θ, and (c) no other feasible PC allocation satisfying (7.1) can make the agent better off for at least one value of θ without either making him worse off under the other value of θ or making the principal worse off.

Using this definition it is easy to establish that a solution of the following problem is a Pareto optimal PC allocation which is best for the principal subject to the constraint that the agent be no worse off for either value of θ than in autarky, when $(y, r) = (0, 0)$ (the individual rationality constraints are labeled IR):

$$\max_{(y_j, r_j), j=1,2} \quad \phi(y_1 - r_1) + (1 - \phi)(y_2 - r_2)$$

subject to (condition (7.1))

(IR)
$$r_j - \left(\frac{y_j}{\theta^j}\right)^2 \geqslant 0 \qquad \text{for} \qquad j = 1, 2$$

(feasibility)

$$0 \leqslant r_j \leqslant y_j \qquad \text{for} \qquad j = 1, 2$$

In the objective function ϕ is the principal's prior probability that $\theta = \theta^1$. Note that, since any solution must satisfy (7.1), it can be achieved by a direct mechanism as outlined above.

A typical solution (for a particular value of ϕ) is shown as $(y_j^*, r_j^*) = c^*(\theta^j)$, $j = 1, 2$, in figure 7.1. Note that $c^*(\theta^1)$ is not on C_1, thus showing that there are optimal PC allocations which are not full-information optimal.

The fourth and last point we wish to make in this example is that optimal allocations in our sense depend on prior distributions, whereas full-information optimal allocations do not (this fact plays a key role in the public goods example in section 9). To see this imagine that the probability ϕ that the principal places on the event $\theta = \theta^1$ increases. The principal will then seek to increase his utility in this event. This can be accomplished by moving $c^*(\theta^1)$ along the agent's θ^1 indifference curve toward point A. Since self-selection must hold, $c^*(\theta^2)$ must move up C_2 toward point F, that is, p

must give up utility in the event $\theta=\theta^2$. He is willing to make this tradeoff since his probability on $\theta=\theta^1$ has increased. Thus the original values of $c^*(\theta)$ are no longer optimal when the principal's prior changes.

This concludes our discussion of the agency example. We now proceed to the general development.

3 The general environment

The general economic environment consists of a finite set $T\subset R$ of agents and a collection of production technologies associated with coalitions of agents. The agents are defined by their common consumption possibility set $C\subseteq R^l_+$, where the number of commodities l is a fixed integer ($l\geqslant 2$), their preferences, and their initial information.

Preferences are assumed to depend on a vector θ of parameters. Let $N=\{1, \ldots, n\}$ be the set of parameter indices, let $\Theta_k\subset R$, Θ_k finite, be the set of possible values of the kth parameter, $k\in N$, with typical element θ_k, and let $\Theta=\times_{k\in N}\Theta_k$ be the parameter space with typical element θ. Each agent a is assumed to have observed values of the parameters θ_k for k in some subset $N_a\subseteq N$. The set of possible values of parameters observed by agent a is then $\Theta^a=\times_{k\in N_a}\Theta_k$, with typical element θ^a. We assume that each of the n parameters is observed by some agent, that is, $\bigcup_{a\in T}N_a=N$. For any subset of agents $A\subset T$, let $N_A=\bigcup_{a\in A}N_a$ be the set of parameters observed by agents of A. Let $\Theta_A=\times_{k\in N_A}\Theta_k$.

The preferences of each agent are represented by a utility function U_a which depends on his consumption bundle and the parameter vector, that is, $U_a: C\times\Theta\to R$.

We assume that each agent's beliefs concerning parameters not observed by him can be summarized by a nondegenerate prior distribution. This prior for agent a is a mapping ρ_a from $\Theta\times\Theta^a$ into the interval $[0, 1]$ where $\rho_a(\xi|\theta^a)$ is interpreted as a's prior probability that the value of the true parameter vector is ξ given that he observes θ^a.[10] Note that ξ specifies a value for the parameter vector observed by agent a; thus if $\xi^a\neq\theta^a$, $\rho_a(\xi|\theta^a)=0$. We also assume that $\rho_a(\xi|\theta^a)>0$ for all ξ such that $\xi^a=\theta^a$.

An essential ingredient in defining the economic environment is a specification of the allocations achievable by any coalition of agents. Thus, with any subset A of agents of T we associate a nonempty set $\lambda(A)\subseteq C^A$.[11] A typical element of $\lambda(A)$, say c_A, consists of a consumption bundle $c_a\in C$ for each agent $a\in A$. We can think of λ as a mapping which associates with each subset of agents of T its set of achievable allocations. The *technology* is a specification of λ.

We are now ready to define the economic environment. An *environment* E is a vector $[T, l, N, (N_a)_{a\in T}, \Theta, \lambda, U_T, \rho_T, \theta]$, where T is the set of agents, l is the number of goods, N is the set of parameter indices, N_a is the set of parameters observed by agent a, U_a is the utility function of agent a, ρ_a is agent a's prior, and θ is the actual value of the parameter vector. A *subenvironment* E_A of E for a subset of agents $A \subset T$ is a vector $[A, l, N_A, (N_a)_{a\in A}, \Theta_A, \lambda, U_A, \rho_A, \theta_A]$, where λ is restricted to A.

Crucial to our analysis is a specification of what each agent knows before any trade takes place, that is, the *initial information structure.* Given an environment E, each agent in T is assumed to know everything except the values of certain parameters, that is, everything except θ_j for $j \notin N_a$. It should be emphasized that if agent a knows θ_k while agent b does not, then both know that agent a is better informed about parameter k.

This completes our description of the general class of environments. We now turn to developing the concept of a resource-allocation mechanism and proving some general results.

4 Mechanisms

Our concept of a mechanism is simply a set of rules which define an extensive form game to be played by the agents. These rules are constraints on what proposals the agents may make at each stage of a multistage bargaining process and a rule for determining the final allocation as a function of the sequence of these proposals.[12]

The elements of a *mechanism* for a subenvironment E_A for a set of agents $A \subseteq T$ with technology λ (or, for short, a mechanism for A) are as follows. First is an integer τ which is interpreted as the number of stages in the mechanism, that is, signals are sent by the agents sequentially in stages $1, 2, \ldots, \tau$. At each stage, each agent is assumed to have observed all previous signals. Second is a set $\mathscr{S}$ which is the set of all potential signals and an element s^0 which is the null signal (hereafter taken to be the word "pass") introduced mainly for notational convenience. The mechanism is assumed to begin with all agents sending the null signal (at stage 0). Thereafter an agent can send the null signal only if required to do so. Thus observing the null signal provides no new information. Third is a sequence $S_A = \{S_{at} | a \in A, t = 1, \ldots, \tau\}$ of constraint sets which define the set of feasible signals for each agent at each stage. Each of these subsets of $\mathscr{S}$ can depend on all past signals, that is, each S_{at} is a correspondence which associates with each sequence s_A^{t-1} of past signals a subset $S_{at}(s_A^{t-1})$ of the signal space $\mathscr{S}$. Fourth is a function F which determines the final allocation in $\lambda(A)$ as a function of the entire sequence of signals s_A^{τ}.[13]

A mechanism for a set of agents A will be denoted by M_A or by an explicit listing $[\tau, S_A, F]$ of its elements (where $\mathscr{S}$ can be taken to be any set containing all signals consistent with S_A). Note that the only aspect of the environment on which a mechanism depends is the technology λ.

We denote by $\mathscr{M}_A$ the *class of all mechanisms* for the set of agents A.

5 Equilibrium of a mechanism

In this section we define the concept of an equilibrium for a mechanism. The concept we adopt is closely related to Harsanyi's (1967–8) Bayesian equilibrium and Selten's (1975) perfect equilibrium; consequently we call it perfect Bayesian equilibrium. Speaking loosely, we use the term equilibrium of a mechanism to mean a specification of a strategy and a posterior distribution for each agent at each stage of the mechanism such that two properties hold: (a) the specified strategy of each agent at each stage is maximal for him relative to his specified contemporary posterior distribution, taking as given the past signals, the specified contemporary strategies of the other agents, and the specified future strategies of all agents; (b) the specified posterior distribution of each agent at each stage is consistent with Bayes's rule and the specified past strategies of all other agents.

We now make this definition more precise. For what follows we consider a given mechanism $[\tau, S_A, F]$ for a set of agents $A \subseteq T$. A *strategy* at stage t for each agent a is a function σ_{at} mapping previous signals s_A^{t-1} and the vector θ^a of parameters observed by agent a into a signal in $\mathscr{S}$.[14]

It is clear that a specification of strategies for each agent of A determines entirely the sequence of signals which will be sent under the given mechanism as a function of the parameters observed by agents of A. In particular, given some stage r, a sequence of future strategies $\sigma_A^{r+1,\tau}$ from stages $r+1$ through τ for each agent of A, a sequence of past and present signals s_A^r, and a parameter draw θ_A, we can calculate the sequence of induced signals from stages $r+1$ through τ (see the appendix and note 15 for a more formal development).

Now consider the decision problem confronting agent a at stage r. Agent a takes as given the past signals s_A^{r-1}, the contemporary strategies of others $\sigma_{br}(s_A^{r-1}, \xi^b)$, $b \in A - \{a\}$, and the future strategies of all agents $\sigma_A^{r+1,\tau}$. He can then calculate the contemporary signals of the other agents and all future signals as functions of the unobserved (by agent a) parameters and his own present signal. Finally, using this calculation, agent a can calculate his expected utility for the final allocation determined by this sequence of signals as a function of his current signal, that is, $E_{ar}[U_a\{F_a(s_A^\tau), \xi\} | s_A^{r-1}, \sigma_{\bar{a}r}, \sigma_A^{r+1,\tau}, \theta^a]$, where F_a is the allocation assigned by F to agent a, and the expectation is taken using his *current* beliefs about ξ, $\rho_{ar}(\xi | \theta^a, s_A^{r-1})$.[15] Here s_A^{r-1}, $\sigma_{\bar{a}r} = (\sigma_{br})$, $b \in \bar{a} = A - \{a\}$, and $\sigma_A^{r+1,\tau}$ are taken as given. Agent a then chooses his current signal s_{ar} to maximize this expected utility over the set of feasible signals $S_{ar}(s_A^{r-1})$ at stage r.

Agent a's current beliefs about ξ are, however, not arbitrary. Rather, agent

a takes as given the strategy of every other agent b at each previous stage j, $\sigma_{bj}(s_A^{j-1}, \delta^b)$, and eliminates from consideration any parameter vector δ which is not consistent with previously observed signals. The posterior at any stage r is thus the initial prior normalized in this way. We are thus led to the following formal definition of an equilibrium.[16]

Definition

Let A be any subset of agents, and let M_A be any mechanism for A. A *perfect Bayesian equilibrium* of M_A is a sequence of strategies $\sigma_A^{*\tau} = \{\sigma_{Ar}^* | r = 1, \ldots, \tau\}$ for each agent in A, and a set of distribution functions $\rho_A^{*\tau} = \{\rho_{Ar}^* | r = 1, \ldots, \tau\}$ for each agent in A, where $\rho_{ar}^*: \Theta \times \Theta^a \times (\mathcal{S}^A)^{r-1} \to [0, 1]$, which satisfy the following two properties.

1 For any agent $a \in A$, any stage $r = 1, \ldots, \tau$, any parameter vector $\theta^a \in \Theta^a$ and history s_A^{r-1}, and given strategies $\sigma_A^{*\tau}$, let $\Delta_{ar}(s_A^{r-1})$ denote the set of parameter values which are consistent with the observed past signals s_A^{r-1} of agents other than a, given those agents' equilibrium strategy functions. That is,

$$\Delta_{ar}(s_A^{r-1}) = \{\xi \in \Theta | \text{for every } b \in \bar{a}, \text{ and } 1 \leqslant j \leqslant r-1, \ \sigma_{bj}^*[s_A^{j-1}, \xi^b] = s_{bj}\}$$

Then let $K_{ar}(s_A^{r-1}, \theta^a)$ denote the total prior probability assigned by a to such parameter values given that he observes values θ^a for parameters that he can observe. That is,

$$K_{ar}(s_A^{r-1}, \theta^a) = \sum_{\delta \in \Delta_{ar}(s_A^{r-1})} \rho_a(\delta | \theta^a)$$

Then $\rho_{ar}^*(\xi | \theta^a, s_A^{r-1})$ is assumed to satisfy

$$\rho_{ar}^*(\xi | \theta^a, s_A^{r-1}) = \begin{cases} \rho_a(\xi | \theta^a) / K_{ar}(s_A^{r-1}, \theta^a) & \xi \in \Delta_{ar}(s_A^{r-1}) \neq \varnothing \\ 0 & \xi \notin \Delta_{ar}(s_A^{r-1}) \neq \varnothing \\ \rho_a(\xi | \theta^a) & \Delta_{ar}(s_A^{r-1}) = \varnothing \end{cases}$$

2 For any agent $a \in A$, stage $r = 1, \ldots, \tau$, parameter vector $\theta^a \in \Theta^a$, and history s_A^{r-1}, the strategy $\sigma_{ar}^*(s_A^{r-1}, \theta^a)$ is assumed to solve

$$\max_{s_{ar} \in S_{ar}(s_A^{r-1})} \ E_{ar}^*[U_a\{F_a(s_A^\tau), \xi\} | s_A^{r-1}, \sigma_{\bar{a}r}^*, \sigma_A^{*r+1,\tau}, \theta^a]$$

where the expectation E_{ar}^* is taken with respect to $\rho_{ar}^*(\xi | \theta^a, s_A^{r-1})$ taking $\sigma_{\bar{a}r}^*$ and $\sigma_A^{*r+1,\tau}$ as given.

Thus our equilibrium concept is Bayesian in the sense that each agent evaluates strategies and outcomes relative to that agent's prior (or posterior) distribution over unobserved parameters, and perfect in the sense that strategies are required to be optimal for all possible previous histories.

In general, a mechanism may have more than one equilibrium. In what follows, we assume that one particular equilibrium prevails and refer to "the equilibrium" of a mechanism. For the specific mechanisms considered below, the equilibrium assumed to prevail will be clear from the context.

Given any mechanism M_A for a set of agents A, the equilibrium strategies for M_A determine an equilibrium sequence of signals $s_A^{*\tau}(\theta_A)$ for each possible value θ_A of the vector of parameters observed by agents of A. This equilibrium sequence of signals, in turn, determines the *equilibrium allocation* $F\{s_A^{*\tau}(\theta_A)\}$ for M_A as a function of θ_A, which we denote by $c_A(M_A, \theta_A)$. If a mechanism has multiple equilibria, we could denote each one explicitly by including the equilibrium sequence of strategies as an argument in c_A. This notation would allow us to make explicit which equilibrium sequence of strategies is assumed to prevail. However, this would make the notation more cumbersome. In what follows we will rarely need to make explicit which equilibrium sequence of strategies is assumed to prevail. We have therefore chosen to suppress the equilibrium strategies in the notation.

At this point the reader may well wonder why we have not restricted our analysis a priori to games in normal as opposed to extensive form and used the (regular) Bayesian equilibrium notion. This would simplify the notation and proofs considerably. Our answer is that games which are sequential and use the perfect equilibrium notation are of intrinsic interest and seem natural in many economic contexts.[17] Thus, for us, the real question is whether games in extensive form with the perfect Bayesian equilibrium notation are equivalent in some sense to games in normal form with the (regular) Bayesian equilibrium. In this regard we agree with Selten (1975) that "... in the transition from the extensive form to the normal form some important information is lost." In particular, in the asymmetric information environments of this chapter, the (regular) Bayesian equilibrium concept for normal form games allows neither an explicit representation of learning nor the concept of perfectness. That the latter concept has content is well illustrated by noting that the perfect Bayesian equilibrium for our extensive form games admits far fewer equilibria than does the (regular) Bayesian equilibrium for their normal form counterparts.[18]

6 Self-selection theorems

In this section we demonstrate two closely related results. The first result characterizes allocations which result from mechanisms. It is shown that the equilibrium allocation of any mechanism must satisfy certain self-selection properties.[19] The second result is that, conversely, any allocation which satisfies these self-selection properties can be achieved by a mechanism.

These results are important and require some elaboration. First, note that mechanisms result in PC allocations, that is, allocations which depend on the realized values of the parameters. This would suggest that if we are interested in characterizing optimal allocations for this class of environments, we could ignore the mechanisms by which these allocations are achieved and simply search over the set of all technically feasible PC allocations. Our first result shows that certain technically feasible PC allocations, namely those that do not satisfy the self-selection properties, cannot, in fact, be achieved. This implies that, at least, we must eliminate from consideration all PC allocations which do not satisfy these properties. Our second result then shows that only these allocations need be eliminated. The latter result is established by showing that any PC allocation satisfying the self-selection properties can be achieved by a mechanism of a certain simple form. This result itself is important since it implies that the class of mechanisms that need be considered can be reduced to those of this form.

Having emphasized the crucial importance of self-selection properties, it remains to define them precisely and show why they arise. To motivate these, consider an agent, say a, who has private information about, say θ_1 (that is, only this agent observes the value of θ_1). Whatever mechanism is used, say M, agent a can behave as though $\theta_1 = \delta$ even if he has observed θ_1 to be γ (γ and δ are any two elements of Θ_1). That is, he can use the functional form σ_a^* of the equilibrium strategy to generate signals, but evaluate this strategy at the counterfactual realization $\theta_1 = \delta$ instead of at $\theta_1 = \gamma$. This strategy is an alternative to the equilibrium strategy. Since agent a is the only agent who knows θ_1, this alternative strategy will generate the equilibrium allocation for the counterfactual $\theta_1 = \delta$, namely $c_A(M, \delta, \theta_2, \ldots, \theta_n)$. Of course, equilibrium strategies are preferred (maximizing) and so agent a must prefer the allocation $c_A(M, \gamma, \theta_2, \ldots, \theta_n)$ where his parameter draw is $\theta_1 = \gamma$.

It should be pointed out that if more than one agent observes a parameter, that is, the information is public, then the above argument does not hold. This is because the adoption of the Bayesian equilibrium concept for mechanisms precludes collusion. In general, the existence of public information does not constrain the allocations which can be achieved by mechanisms (this point is illustrated by an example in section 10).

We now proceed with a formal treatment of self-selection. For the rest of this section let A be a subset of agents, let M_A be a mechanism for A with $M_A = [\tau, S_A, F]$, and let $(\sigma_A^{*\tau}, \rho_A^{*\tau})$ be an equilibrium of M_A.

Parameters observed only by one agent are private to that agent and, as noted above, play a special role in the analysis. Accordingly, for any vector of parameters θ and for any agent a, we write $\theta = (\theta_{\mathrm{P}}^a, \theta_{\mathrm{H}}^a)$, where θ_{P}^a consists of those components of θ which *only* a observes and θ_{H}^a consists of the remaining components of θ. The vector θ_{P}^a is called the private parameter vector of agent a.

The first main result of this section (discussed above) is as follows.

Theorem 7.1 (Self-selection for mechanisms)
For any mechanism M_A, any agent a, and any value of agent a's observed parameters θ^a,

$$\sum_{\xi\in\Theta} U_a\{c_a(M_A, \xi_A), \xi\}\rho_a(\xi|\theta^a) \geqslant \sum_{\xi\in\Theta} U_a\{c_a(M_A, \delta_{\mathrm{P}}^a, \xi_{\mathrm{H}}^a), \xi\}\rho_a(\xi|\theta^a)$$

for any other possible value of agent a's private parameter vector δ_{P}^a.

The proof is given in the appendix.

As discussed above, a mechanism for the set of agents A results in a PC allocation which is feasible relative to the technology λ, that is, mappings $\tilde{c}_A\colon \Theta_A \to \lambda(A)$. Clearly, we can discuss such PC allocations regardless of whether they are the result of some mechanism (hereafter the term PC allocation will be taken to mean a PC allocation which is feasible relative to the appropriate technology). Accordingly, for an arbitrary PC allocation $\tilde{c}_A$, for any agent a, and any value of his observed parameters θ^a, define a's expected utility for $\tilde{c}_a$ by

$$V_a(\tilde{c}_a, \theta^a) = \sum_{\xi\in\Theta} U_a\{\tilde{c}_a(\xi_A), \xi\}\rho_a(\xi|\theta^a)$$

The PC allocation $\tilde{c}_A$ is said to satisfy self-selection if, for every $a\in A$,

$$V_a(\tilde{c}_a, \theta^a) \geqslant \sum_{\xi\in\Theta} U_a\{\tilde{c}_a(\delta_{\mathrm{P}}^a, \xi_{\mathrm{H}}^a), \xi\}\rho_a(\xi|\theta^a)$$

for any θ^a, and any alternative value of a's private parameter vector δ_{P}^a. Thus theorem 7.1 can be interpreted as saying that all PC allocations achievable by a mechanism must satisfy self-selection. (An allocation is achievable by a mechanism if it is an equilibrium allocation of the mechanism.) Theorem 2 below states that the converse is also true, that is, any PC allocation which satisfies self-selection is achievable by a mechanism. Moreover, the mechanism which can be used to achieve the allocation (referred to below as the direct mechanism D) is of the following simple form: there is only one stage in which each agent reports a value for each parameter he observes; the final allocation is given by a prespecified function of the values reported by each agent. If all information is private, this allocation function is the PC allocation to be achieved.

More formally, a *direct mechanism* is any mechanism in which $\tau = 1$, $S_{a1}(s_A^0) = \Theta^a$, for each agent a.

Theorem 7.2
For any PC allocation $\tilde{c}_A$ which satisfies self-selection, there exists a direct mechanism D_A such that $\tilde{c}_a(\theta_A) = c_A(D_A, \theta_A)$ for any parameter vector θ_A and such that the equilibrium strategies under D_A are truth telling. Furthermore, if all parameters are privately observed, that is, $\theta^a = \theta_P^a$ for each agent a, then the allocation rule F for D_A can be assumed to be the same as the PC allocation $\tilde{c}_A$.

The proof is given in the appendix.

For the case in which all parameters are privately observed, the direct mechanism D_A of theorem 7.2 is Bayesian incentive compatible in the sense of d'Aspremont and Gerard-Varet (1979). Thus the self-selection condition generalizes this concept for mechanisms to environments with public information.

7 Preferences over mechanisms and efficiency

We assume that at the time when each agent a must express a preference over mechanisms he already knows the value of the parameter vector θ^a. Thus preferences over mechanisms are defined using expected utilities, based on the initial information structure, for the final allocation of an equilibrium of the mechanism. Again, if the equilibrium is not unique, one particular equilibrium must be selected. The definitions below rely heavily on this assumption.[20]

More precisely, given a set of agents A, an environment E_A, and a mechanism M_A with equilibrium $(\sigma_A^{*\tau}, \rho_A^{*\tau})$, the expected utility of agent $a \in A$ for the mechanism M_A is defined as

$$W_a(M_A, \theta^a) = \sum_{\xi \in \Theta} U_a\{c_a(M_A, \xi), \xi\} \rho_a(\xi | \theta^a)$$

Given these preferences for mechanisms, we can define the concepts of blocking a mechanism and a core mechanism. A coalition $B \subseteq A$ can block a mechanism M_A if there exists a mechanism M'_B such that $W_b(M'_B, \xi^b) \geq W_b(M_A, \xi^b)$ for every $b \in B$, $\xi^b \in \Theta^b$, with strict inequality for some $b \in B$, $\xi^b \in \Theta^b$. Note that, in this definition, we require that the expected utility for M'_B for each b is at least as great as his expected utility for M_A for each possible draw of b's observed parameters.[21] The reason for this specification is to ensure that efficient mechanisms (defined below) will be independent of the actual parameter draw. That is, the mechanism which we denote as efficient may well depend on the technology, preferences, and general information structure, but we do not want our selection to depend on particular values of parameters. The elements of the environment on which we allow dependence will be referred to as the partial environment. More precisely, the *partial environment* relative to E_A, denoted E_A^0, includes all elements of E_A except the specific parameter draw θ_A.

There are three concepts of *efficient mechanisms* which we wish to consider. First, define a mechanism M_A^* for A to be a core mechanism (relative to the partial environment E_A^0) if no coalition B can block M_A^*. Second, define a mechanism M_A^* to be a Pareto optimal mechanism (relative to E_A^0) if A cannot block M_A^*. Third, define a mechanism M_A^* to be an individually rational Pareto optimal mechanism (relative to E_A^0) if M_A^* is a Pareto mechanism and no single agent in A can block M_A^*. We use the term "efficient mechanism" to refer to any mechanism which satisfies at least one of the above efficiency concepts.

8 Efficient mechanisms and efficient allocations

The results of section 6 suggest that there is an equivalence between PC allocations which satisfy self-selection and allocations generated by mechanisms. This would lead us to conjecture that the search for efficient mechanisms can be accomplished by searching for PC allocations which are efficient in some sense. In this section we define a concept of efficient PC allocations and establish the equivalence between such allocations and allocations generated by efficient mechanisms.

In this section E_A^0 is any fixed partial environment. A coalition $B \subseteq A$ can block a PC allocation $\tilde{c}_A$ satisfying self-selection if there is a PC allocation $\tilde{x}_B$ for B such that $\tilde{x}_B$ satisfies self-selection and $V_b(\tilde{x}_b, \theta^b) \geqslant V_b(\tilde{c}_b, \theta^b)$ for every $b \in B$, $\theta^b \in \Theta^b$, with strict inequality for at least one $b \in B$, $\theta^b \in \Theta^b$. Again, we consider three concepts of efficiency. A PC allocation $\tilde{c}_A$ which satisfies self-selection is a core allocation if, for any $B \subseteq A$, B cannot block $\tilde{c}_A$, a Pareto optimal allocation if A cannot block $\tilde{c}_A$, and an individually rational Pareto optimal allocation if $\tilde{c}_A$ is a Pareto optimal allocation and, for each $a \in A$, $\{a\}$ cannot block $\tilde{c}_A$.

Theorem 7.3

If $\tilde{c}_A$ is a core allocation, then there is a direct core mechanism M_A such that the equilibrium allocation of M_A coincides with $\tilde{c}_A$, that is, $\tilde{c}_A(\theta_A) \equiv c_A(M_A, \theta_A)$

for all θ_A. Conversely, if M_A is a core mechanism, then $c_A(M_A, \cdot)$ is a core allocation. The theorem also holds if "core" is replaced by "Pareto optimal" or "individually rational Pareto optimal."

The proof is given in the appendix.

Theorem 7.3 has the important implication that we need only characterize efficient allocations in order to characterize efficient mechanisms. This is useful because an efficient allocation can often be found as the solution of a constrained optimization problem. Moreover, theorem 7.3 implies that the direct mechanism (in which agents signal values of parameters observed by them) is always efficient if its allocation function F is constructed to generate an efficient allocation. Thus the problem of finding an efficient mechanism can be reduced to finding an efficient allocation, and then constructing F to generate this allocation. In the special case in which all information is private, F can be taken to be the efficient PC allocation. A method for constructing F in other cases is given in the proof of theorem 7.2.

We would like to conclude this section by defining full-information optimal allocations in general and stating a limited result on their relation to optimal allocations in our sense. Intuitively, a PC allocation is full-information optimal if it would be Pareto optimal in the usual sense for any value of the parameter vector. More formally, a PC allocation $\tilde{c}_A$ for a set of agents A is full-information optimal if, for any parameter value θ, there is no other feasible allocation c_A such that

$$U_a(c_a, \theta) \geqslant U_a\{\tilde{c}_a(\theta_A), \theta\}$$

for each agent $a \in A$ with strict inequality for at least one $a \in A$.

Our result is that if there are only two agents and one is fully informed while the other is not, then any full-information optimal allocation which satisfies the self-selection condition is also optimal in our sense. This is stated formally as follows.

Theorem 7.4
If $T = \{a, b\}$, $N_a = N$, $N_b \neq N$, and $\tilde{c}_T^*$ is a full-information optimal PC allocation which satisfies self-selection, then $\tilde{c}_T^*$ is a Pareto optimal PC allocation.

The proof is given in the appendix.

Note that this theorem applies to the principal–agent example of section 2. Thus, in that example, while there are optimal PC allocations which are *not* full-information optimal, any full-information optimal allocation which satisfies self-selection is also optimal in our sense. That the result cannot be generalized to more complicated information structures is shown by an example in the following section on public goods.

9 A public goods environment

Here we describe one of the simplest public goods environments we could think of and the results of applying the general approach of this chapter to that environment. There are two agents labeled a and b, one private good and one public good. The public good can be produced on a one-for-one basis from the private good, but only integer amounts can be produced.[22] Each agent has an endowment of $e < 1$ units of the private good and no public good. Thus neither agent can produce any public good on his own, and together they can produce either zero or one unit. Each agent i has a linear utility function of the form $U_i(x_i, y, \theta_i) = \theta_i x_i + y$, where x_i represents consumption of the private good, y represents consumption of the public good, and θ_i is i's marginal utility for the private good $i = a, b$.

Initially, each agent knows only his own marginal utility for the private good, that is, agent i knows θ_i but not θ_j for $j \neq i$. Moreover, each agent knows that the other agent's parameter (marginal utility) can be one of two possible values θ^1 or θ^2, with $0 < \theta^1 \leqslant 1, \theta^2 > 2$ (the reason for this assumption will be clear shortly). Agent i has a prior probability distribution on the value of agent j's parameter which may depend on his own parameter value θ_i. We denote by α_k agent a's prior probability that $\theta_b = \theta^1$, given that $\theta_a = \theta^k$ for $k = 1, 2$. Naturally, agent a's prior that $\theta_b = \theta^2$, given $\theta_a = \theta^k$, is $1 - \alpha_k$. Similarly, β_k is agent b's prior that $\theta_a = \theta^1$, given that $\theta_b = \theta^k$ for $k = 1, 2$.[23] Thus, typically, knowledge of our own tastes for public and private goods allows us to infer something about the tastes of the other agent. For example, if α_1 were near unity and α_2 were near zero, this would reflect agent a's belief that agent b is likely to be similar in tastes to himself. We assume that $0 < \alpha_k < 1$ and $0 < \beta_k < 1$ for $k = 1, 2$. Finally, each agent knows the production technology for the public good, the endowments of both agents, and the utility functions of both agents (except for the parameter value of the other agent).

This environment is very similar to that studied by Arrow (1977) and d'Aspremont and Gerard-Varet (1979), but, as will be seen below, our results are somewhat different from theirs. Applying theorem 7.1 (section 6), we note first that only PC allocations which satisfy certain self-selection conditions are achievable (as equilibrium final allocations of mechanisms). For this environment there are two parameters θ_a and θ_b, where $\theta_i \in \Theta_i = \{\theta^1, \theta^2\}$ for $i = a, b$. Thus we can represent a PC allocation by $(y_{ij}, a_{ij}, b_{ij}), i, j = 1, 2$, where y_{ij} is the total output of public good if $\theta_a = \theta^i$ and $\theta_b = \theta^j$, a_{ij} is agent a's allocation of private good if $\theta_a = \theta^i$ and $\theta_b = \theta^j$, and b_{ij} is agent b's allocation of private good if $\theta_a = \theta^i$ and $\theta_b = \theta^j$. For convenience, we define Y to be the 2×2 matrix whose (i, j) entry is y_{ij} and similarly for A and B. The self-selection conditions state that if $\theta_a = \theta^1$, agent a's expected utility for $(y_{1j}, a_{1j}), j = 1, 2$ (where the expectation is taken with respect to a's prior on θ_b given $\theta_a = \theta^1$, that is, using the probabilities α_1 and $1 - \alpha_1$) must be greater than his expected utility for (y_{2j}, a_{2j}) and vice versa if $\theta_a = \theta^2$. Also included in the self-selection conditions are similar conditions for agent b. When we use the matrix notation described above, a PC allocation (Y, A, B) satisfies self-selection if

$$(1,0)[Y + \theta^1 A]\begin{pmatrix}\alpha_1\\1-\alpha_1\end{pmatrix} \geqslant (0,1)[Y + \theta^1 A]\begin{pmatrix}\alpha_1\\1-\alpha_1\end{pmatrix} \tag{7.2}$$

$$(0,1)[Y + \theta^2 A]\begin{pmatrix}\alpha_2\\1-\alpha_2\end{pmatrix} \geqslant (1,0)[Y + \theta^2 A]\begin{pmatrix}\alpha_2\\1-\alpha_2\end{pmatrix} \tag{7.3}$$

$$(\beta_1, 1-\beta_1)[Y + \theta^1 B]\begin{pmatrix}1\\0\end{pmatrix} \geqslant (\beta_1, 1-\beta_1)[Y + \theta^1 B]\begin{pmatrix}0\\1\end{pmatrix} \tag{7.4}$$

$$(\beta_2, 1-\beta_2)[Y + \theta^2 B]\begin{pmatrix}0\\1\end{pmatrix} \geqslant (\beta_2, 1-\beta_2)[Y + \theta^2 B]\begin{pmatrix}1\\0\end{pmatrix} \tag{7.5}$$

Second, we note using theorem 7.2 (section 6) that any PC allocation satisfying self-selection, say (Y, A, B), can be achieved using a direct mechanism. In a direct mechanism for this environment, each agent names a value for his parameter from the set $\{\theta^1, \theta^2\}$ (not necessarily the true value). This is done by both agents simultaneously. The two messages, say m_1 and m_2, are then mapped into a final allocation by a function $F(\cdot,\cdot)$. The allocation (Y, A, B) can be achieved simply by setting $F(\theta^i, \theta^j) = (y_{ij}, a_{ij}, b_{ij})$.

Finally, it follows from theorem 7.3 (section 8) that a Pareto optimal PC allocation and a Pareto optimal mechanism can be found by solving

$$\max_{(Y,A,B)} \lambda_1(1,0)[Y + \theta^1 A]\begin{pmatrix}\alpha_1\\1-\alpha_1\end{pmatrix} + \lambda_2(0,1)[Y + \theta^2 A]\begin{pmatrix}\alpha_2\\1-\alpha_2\end{pmatrix}$$
$$+ \lambda_3(\beta_1, 1-\beta_1)[Y + \theta^1 B]\begin{pmatrix}1\\0\end{pmatrix} + \lambda_4(\beta_2, 1-\beta_2)[Y + \theta^2 B]\begin{pmatrix}0\\1\end{pmatrix}$$

subject to (7.2)–(7.5) and

$$Y + A + B \leqslant E = \begin{bmatrix}2e & 2e\\2e & 2e\end{bmatrix}$$

$$A, B \geqslant 0, \qquad y_{ij} \in \{0, 1\}, \qquad i, j = 1, 2$$

In this problem, the objective function is a weighted sum (the λ_i are the weights) of the expected utilities of each agent for each possible marginal utility θ^i. This guarantees that no agent can be made better off for some possible value of his parameter without making him or another agent worse off for some parameter value. The constraints are the self-selection conditions (7.2)–(7.5) and the technological feasibility constraints. In the remainder of this section, we consider the relationship between these Pareto optimal allocations (that is, solutions of the above problem) and full-information Pareto optimal allocations.

Among the full-information optimal allocations for this environment are those that satisfy the familiar Samuelson–Lindahl conditions. Because of the linearity of utility functions and the production technology, these Samuelson–Lindahl conditions are that the public good should be built ($y_{ij} = 1$) if and only if the sum of the marginal rates of substitution of private for public good exceed the marginal cost of building the public good (namely unity), that is,

$$y_{ij} = 1 \qquad \text{if and only if} \qquad 1/\theta^i + 1/\theta^j > 1$$

These allocations are then full-information optimal for any feasible allocation of the private good in this environment. Given our assumption that $0 < \theta^1 \leqslant 1$, $\theta^2 > 2$, these Samuelson–Lindahl conditions reduce to $y_{11} = y_{12} = y_{21} = 1$, $y_{22} = 0$, that is, any feasible PC allocation (Y, A, B) is a Samuelson–Lindahl allocation as long as

$$Y = \begin{bmatrix} 1 & 1 \\ 1 & 0 \end{bmatrix}$$

In addition to these Samuelson–Lindahl allocations, it is sometimes optimal not to build the public good even when $1/\theta^i + 1/\theta^j > 1$. Such an allocation is optimal when the agent with a low value of θ (a high marginal utility for public good) has too little of the private good to compensate the other agent. However, consistent with much of the literature on public goods (for example, Brock, 1976; Groves and Ledyard, 1977) we will focus attention on Samuelson–Lindahl allocations rather than on such corner solutions.

We would like to use the remainder of this section to focus on the following question which is not addressed in the other examples: is it possible for a Samuelson–Lindahl allocation to be achievable but *not* Pareto optimal in our sense? The answer is yes, thus suggesting that Samuelson–Lindahl allocations, even when achievable, may not be desirable from a normative viewpoint. From the positive viewpoint, the affirmative answer means that we might be able to explain public goods allocations which do not fit the Samuelson–Lindahl definition of optimality by using our approach.

To answer the above question in the affirmative, we need only provide an example. Before presenting such an example, however, we would like to understand the result.[24]

A Samuelson–Lindahl allocation requires (only) that the allocation of resources be Pareto optimal for each possible specification of the parameters (θ_a, θ_b). A Samuelson–Lindahl allocation does not take into account any tradeoff between utility under one parameter specification and utility under another parameter specification, whereas all that matters for an optimum in our sense is expected utility of each agent across parameter values he cannot distinguish (that is, those of the other agent). Consequently it may be possible to increase expected utility, for example by giving agent *a* more utility and *b* less utility for some specification of (θ_a, θ_b) while doing the opposite for another specification of (θ_a, θ_b).

To make this verbal argument a little more explicit, suppose that we have an initial Samuelson–Lindahl allocation which we want to improve. Moreover, suppose that we restrict ourselves to a re-allocation which involves *only* the private good (that is, consider only re-allocations which are themselves Samuelson–Lindahl allocations). Let Δa_{ij} be the change in *a*'s allocation of private good in the event that $(\theta_a, \theta_b) = (\theta^i, \theta^j)$, $i, j = 1, 2$. Since we are not changing the allocation of public good, the change in *b*'s allocation of private good is given by $-\Delta a_{ij}$. The corresponding changes in expected utility are given by

$$\Delta U_i^a = \alpha_i \theta^i \Delta a_{i1} + (1 - \alpha_i)\theta^i \Delta a_{i2} \qquad i = 1, 2$$

$$\Delta U_j^b = -\beta_j \theta^j \Delta a_{1j} - (1 - \beta_j)\theta^j \Delta a_{2j} \qquad j = 1, 2$$

where ΔU_i^a is the change in *a*'s expected utility when $\theta_a = \theta^i$ and similarly for ΔU_j^b. If we ignore the fact that the new allocation must satisfy self-selection, manipulation of the above expressions for ΔU_i^a and ΔU_j^b reveals that we can accomplish a Pareto improvement only if

$$\frac{\alpha_2(1 - \alpha_1)}{\alpha_1(1 - \alpha_2)} \neq \frac{\beta_2(1 - \beta_1)}{\beta_1(1 - \beta_2)}$$

This inequality will hold if, for example, $\alpha_2 < \alpha_1$ and $\beta_2 > \beta_1$. In this case, agent *a* believes that agent *b* tends to have preferences for the public good which are similar to his own while agent *b* believes that agent *a* tends to have preferences which are opposite to his own. Thus the improvement exploits the fact that the agents hold different beliefs about the probabilities of the same events.[25]

The above discussion does not constitute a proof that there are achievable Samuelson–Lindahl allocations which can be improved upon. The reasons that it is not a proof are that (a) we have not shown that there are achievable Samuelson–Lindahl allocations in the first place, (b) the construction of the Δa_{ij} ignores the requirement that the new allocation must be achievable, and (c) we restricted ourselves to changing only the private good allocation, that is, we considered only re-allocations which were also Samuelson–Lindahl allocations. As mentioned, however, the proof requires only an example. One such example is the following.[26] The Samuelson–Lindahl allocation

$$Y = Y^S = \begin{bmatrix} 1 & 1 \\ 1 & 0 \end{bmatrix}, \qquad A = \begin{bmatrix} 0.44399 & 0.22898 \\ 0.5 & 0.72487 \end{bmatrix}$$

$$B = \begin{bmatrix} 0.05601 & 0.27102 \\ 0.0 & 0.77513 \end{bmatrix}$$

is achievable and can be strictly dominated by the achievable Samuelson–Lindahl allocation

$$Y = Y^S, \qquad A = \begin{bmatrix} 0.5 & 0 \\ 0 & 1.5 \end{bmatrix}, \qquad B = \begin{bmatrix} 0.0 & 0.5 \\ 0.5 & 0.0 \end{bmatrix}$$

when $\alpha_1 = 0.9$, $\alpha_2 = 0.1$, $\beta_1 = 0.1$, $\beta_2 = 0.9$, $\theta^1 = 1$, and $\theta^2 = 2.1$.

The above example shows that an achievable Samuelson–Lindahl allocation can be dominated by another Samuelson–Lindahl allocation. We have also computed an example in which an achievable Samuelson–Lindahl allocation is dominated by an achievable non-Samuelson–Lindahl allocation (this example is omitted for brevity but is available on request).

10 Competitive allocations and public information

In this section we present one final example which illustrates the important point what when information is public (or common) the set of feasible allocations is not restricted by any self-selection conditions. As a consequence, in the environment of this section – a pure exchange economy – the standard result of welfare economics that competitive allocations are core allocations continues to hold when the term "core" is used in the sense defined in the previous section.

Consider a pure exchange economy with at least three agents and $l \geqslant 2$ commodities. The consumption set is $C = R^l_+$. Each agent t has an initial endowment $e_t \in C$. For any $A \subseteq T$, $\lambda(A) = \{c_A \in C^A | \Sigma_{a \in A} c_a = \Sigma_{a \in A} e_a\}$. There is a single parameter $\theta_1 \in \Theta_1 = \{\theta^1, \theta^2\}$ and, given θ_1, agent t has preferences defined by $U_t(c, \theta_1)$ for $c \in C$ where U_t is concave and monotone increasing in c. There is assumed to be a set of informed traders T_1 (with at least two members) who observe θ_1, that is, $N_t = \{1\}$ for each $t \in T_1$. Let $T_2 = T - T_1$ be the set of uninformed traders, that is, $N_t = \varnothing$ for $t \in T_2$ (we assume $T_2 \neq \varnothing$). We assume that all informed traders have the same endowment and preferences. We further assume that all uninformed traders have the same preferences and endowments, and the same prior distribution on θ_1.[27]

We restrict our attention to competitive allocations which result from the competitive equilibrium concepts discussed by Green (1973) and Grossman (1977) in which all information is revealed in equilibrium. Assume that $c_T(\theta^j)$ is a competitive allocation in the above sense when $\theta_1 = \theta^j$ for $j = 1, 2$. Therefore $c_T(\theta^j)$ is a core allocation relative to preferences defined by $U_t(\cdot, \theta^j)$, for $j = 1, 2$. The proof that the PC allocation $c_T(\cdot)$ is also a core allocation in the sense of section 8 is by contradiction. Assume that $c_T(\cdot)$ is not a core allocation. Then there is a coalition B and a PC allocation $c'_B(\cdot)$ such that, for each $b \in B \cap T_2$,

$$\sum_{j=1}^{2} \phi_j U_b\{c'_b(\theta^j), \theta^j\} \geqslant \sum_{j=1}^{2} \phi_j U_b\{c_b(\theta^j), \theta^j\} \tag{7.6}$$

where ϕ_j is the prior probability of all uninformed agents that $\theta_1 = \theta^j$ $(j = 1, 2)$ and, for each $b \in B \cap T_1$,

$$U_b\{c'_b(\theta^j), \theta^j\} \geqslant U_b\{c_b(\theta^j), \theta^j\} \qquad \text{for} \qquad j = 1, 2 \tag{7.7}$$

with at least one inequality strict. Since all uninformed traders have identical concave preferences, endowments, and priors, we can assume, without loss of generality, that $c'_b(\cdot)$ is the same for all $b \in B \cap T_2$. Now assume that (7.7) is strict for some $b \in B \cap T_1$ and $j = 1$. Since $c_T(\theta^1)$ cannot be blocked relative to θ^1 preferences, we must have $U_b\{c'_b(\theta^1), \theta^1\} < U_b\{c_b(\theta^1), \theta^1\}$ for all $b \in B \cap T_2$. However, by (7.6), this implies that $U_b\{c'_b(\theta^2), \theta^2\} > U_b\{c_b(\theta^2), \theta^2\}$ for all $b \in B \cap T_2$. But since (7.7) holds for $j = 2$, this implies that B can block $c_T(\theta^2)$ relative to θ^2 preferences. This is a contradiction. Clearly, the same argument applies if (7.7) is strict for some $b \in B \cap T_1$ and $j = 2$. The only case left to consider is when (7.7) holds as an equality for all $b \in B \cap T_1$ and $j = 1, 2$. In this case, (7.6) must hold strictly for all $b \in B \cap T_2$. Therefore $U_b\{c'_b(\theta^j), \theta^j\} < U_b\{c_b(\theta^j), \theta^j\}$ for at least one j for all $b \in B \cap T_2$. This again contradicts the fact that $c_T(\theta^j)$ is a core allocation relative to θ^j preferences for this j. This completes the proof.

By theorem 7.3, the above core allocation $c_T(\cdot)$ can be generated using a direct mechanism. To see how this mechanism operates in this environment, consider the following simple example. There are only two informed agents $T_1 = \{1, 2\}$. Suppose that there are two goods and the competitive allocations for the informed agents are given by $c_1(\theta^1) = c_2(\theta^1) = (10, 10)$ and $c_1(\theta^2) = c_2(\theta^2) = (5, 5)$. Note that both informed traders prefer the allocation associated

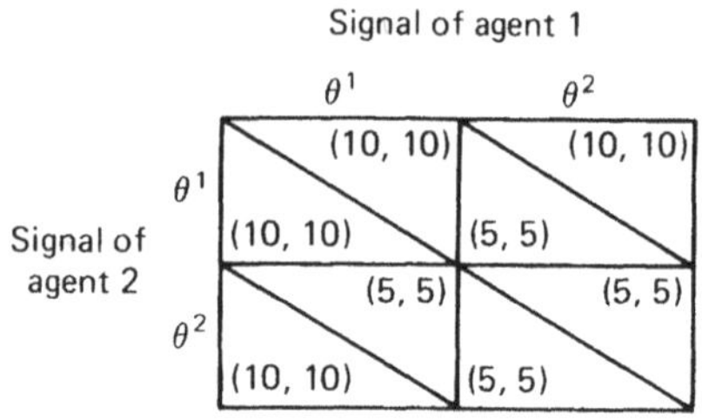

Figure 7.2.

with $\theta_1 = \theta^1$ regardless of the true value of θ_1. In the first stage of the mechanism, each informed trader signals an element of $\{\theta^1, \theta^2\}$. The final allocation as a function of the two signals is shown in figure 7.2 (only the bundles assigned to the informed agents are shown). The upper half of each box shows the final bundle of agent 1 while the lower half shows the final bundle of agent 2. Thus, for example, if agent 1 signals θ^1 and agent 2 signals θ^2, then agent 2 receives (10, 10) and agent 1 receives (5, 5). We claim that a Bayesian equilibrium pair of strategies is for each informed agent to signal θ^j if the true value of θ_1 is θ^j. To see this, suppose that $\theta_1 = \theta^1$. If agent 2 believes that agent 1 will signal θ^1, agent 2 is indifferent as to signaling θ^1 or θ^2 since he receives (10, 10) in either case.[28] He might just as well signal θ^1. Similarly, if agent 1 believes that agent 2 will signal θ^1, it is optimal for agent 1 to signal θ^1 as well. An identical argument holds if $\theta_1 = \theta^2$. Note that the (competitive) allocation (5, 5) for both informed agents is achieved when $\theta_1 = \theta^2$ even though both would prefer the competitive allocation corresponding to $\theta_1 = \theta^1$, that is, (10, 10) for each informed agent. Thus the informed agents would very much like to collude, but collusion is ruled out by the restriction that there be no communication between players prior to the start of a game and by the adoption of a noncooperative equilibrium concept.

11 Conclusion

In this section, rather than summarizing our results, we consider some directions for future research which are suggested by our analysis. These directions include both theoretical extensions and empirical work.

With regard to theoretical extensions, we would like to point out three assumptions whose relaxation may be of interest. The first is the assumption that there are only a finite number of possible values of each parameter. We would hope that our results continue to hold even when some parameters can take on a continuum of values. In this context we note, however, that some results of the signaling literature are not robust to this specification (see Riley, 1979). The second is that the parameters enter the model only through preferences and not through the technology of production and exchange. It is our conjecture that the results will go through without this restriction.[29] Third, we note that our model is essentially static. If the environment involves allocation of resources over time, we could use the Arrow–Debreu device of regarding commodities delivered at different dates as different commodities. The analysis is static, however, in the sense that the mechanism which determines the allocation must be fully played out at the initial date. Thus, although mechanisms may be sequential in nature, we do not allow them to be played out over calendar time with consumption occurring while the mechanism is being played. Relaxing this assumption appears to be difficult and may result in somewhat different conclusions.

With regard to empirical work, we believe that when our general methodology is applied to specific environments modeled in sufficient detail, testable implications will be forthcoming. Since we have not modeled explicitly the process by which mechanisms are chosen, such implications would have to follow from the hypothesis that somehow an "efficient" (core etc.) mechanism is chosen. Unfortunately, this procedure has two drawbacks. First, there may be constraints which limit the ability of the agents to achieve core mechanisms. If we believe that such limitations are important in a specific application, then we must incorporate them into the environment or explicitly model the mechanism choice process. Second, there may be (and usually are) a large number of core mechanisms. This will, of course, reduce the sharpness of any predictions. Explicit modeling of the mechanism choice process may greatly sharpen the predictions. One trivial way of modifying our approach to include a specification of the mechanism choice process is to assume that one agent has the power to choose the mechanism while all other agents are left only with the choice of whether or not to participate. This approach has been taken by Harris and Raviv (1979a, b) to explain various types of observed monopoly marketing schemes. Obviously this modification of the approach is appropriate only in environments in which one agent has monopoly power. More generally applicable approaches to the issue of the mechanism choice process are clearly needed.[30]

Finally, we would like to focus some attention on the role of prior beliefs in our approach. As the foregoing analysis makes clear, such beliefs play an important role in the analysis: which mechanisms and which allocations are efficient in our sense often depend on prior beliefs of agents concerning parameter values that they cannot observe. For the purposes of positive analysis, if priors are not observable by the economist, then the theory may be consistent with a very large class of observed mechanisms and allocations, although some positive implications are robust to the specification of prior beliefs. Thus in order to obtain strong testable implications, it may be necessary for the economist to specify particular priors (or classes of priors) as part of his theory. For some applications, however, this may be no more difficult than specifying other aspects of the environment. For normative purposes, the economist may also need specific information on priors in order to suggest an efficient mechanism. Again, this may or may not be difficult relative to the ever present task of modeling the other aspects of an environment. Finally, we would like to point out that, for some environments (for example, the agency model analyzed above), there are mechanisms which are efficient for any prior beliefs.[31] Such mechanisms have great intuitive appeal, probably for this reason. Indeed, a reasonable hypothesis is that observed mechanisms will be such prior-free efficient mechanisms when they exist. An interesting topic for further theoretical and empirical research is under what conditions will such prior-free efficient mechanisms exist.

Appendix

Before proving the theorems stated in the text, some further notation and a definition are required. As mentioned in the text, if, for some given mechanism for a set of agents A, we know the actual parameter values θ_A and the strategies to be used by each agent at each stage σ_A^τ, then we can compute the implied sequence of signals which will be sent under this mechanism. This can be done recursively as follows. The signals sent at stage 1 are

$$s_{A,1} = \{\sigma_{a,1}(s_A^0, \theta^a)\}_{a \in A} = \sigma_{A,1}(s_A^0, \theta_A)$$

Thus

$$s_A^1 = \{s_A^0, \sigma_{A,1}(s_A^0, \theta_A\} \qquad (7.A1)$$

Similarly

$$s_A^2 = \{s_A^1, \sigma_{A,2}(s_A^1, \theta_A)\}$$

when s_A^1 is given in (7.A1). Clearly, we can continue this process until all the signals s_A^τ have been computed. We denote by $\Psi_A^\tau(\theta_A|\sigma_A^\tau)$ this sequence of signals as a function of θ_A given the strategies σ_A^τ. We also denote by $\Psi_A^t(\theta_A|\sigma_A)$ the sub-sequence consisting of signals for each agent from stage 0 through stage t (for $0 \leqslant t \leqslant \tau$). Note that this sequence of signals depends only on strategies through stage t.

We will also need to define precisely the concept of feasibility (relative to some mechanism) for sequences of signals and strategies. A sequence of signals s_A^τ is feasible for a mechanism $M_A = [\tau, S_A, F]$ if $s_{at} \in S_{at}(s_A^{t-1})$ for each $a \in A$, $t = 1, \ldots, \tau$. A sequence of strategies σ_A^τ is feasible for M_A if, for any $\theta_A \in \Theta_A$, $\Psi_A^\tau(\theta_A|\sigma_A^\tau)$ is a feasible sequence of signals for M_A.

Theorem 7.1 is proved using the following two lemmas.

Lemma 7.A1
Let A be any set of agents, M_A be a mechanism for A with equilibrium $(\sigma_A^{*\tau}, \rho_A^{*\tau})$, and θ_P^a be any possible value of a's vector of private parameters. Then, for any vector of values for those parameters which are not privately observed by a, ξ_H^a, $\Psi_A^\tau(\theta_P^a, \xi_H^a | \sigma_A^{*\tau})$ is a feasible sequence of signals for M_A.

Proof. This is obvious since $\Psi_A^\tau(\theta_P^a, \xi_H^a | \sigma_A^{*\tau})$ is an equilibrium sequence of signals for M_A in any environment in which the parameter values are given by (θ_P^a, ξ_H^a).

Lemma 7.A1 shows that it is always feasible for any agent to evaluate his equilibrium strategy at any value for his vector of private parameters even if this value is different from the true value. Lemma 7.A2 will show that, relative to prior beliefs about the parameter vector ξ, it is always optimal for any agent to use his equilibrium strategy as opposed to any other strategy which, given the equilibrium strategies of the other agents, results in a feasible collection of strategies.

Lemma 7.A2
Suppose that A is any set of agents and $M_A = [\tau, S_A, F]$ is a mechanism for A with equilibrium $(\sigma_A^{*\tau}, \rho_A^{*\tau})$. For any agent $a \in A$, if $(\sigma_{\bar{a}}^{*\tau}, \sigma_a^\tau)$ is a feasible sequence of strategies, then

$$E_a(U_a[F_a\{\Psi_A^\tau(\xi_A | \sigma_A^{*\tau})\}, \xi] | \theta^a) \geq E_a(U_a[F_a\{\Psi_A^\tau(\xi_A | \sigma_{\bar{a}}^{*\tau}, \sigma_a^\tau)\}, \xi] | \theta^a)$$

for any value of the parameter vector θ^a observed by agent a. Here the expectation E_a is taken over the entire parameter vector ξ using a's prior distribution $\rho_a(\xi | \theta^a)$.

Proof. The proof is by backward induction on the stage. We first show that if agent a has used strategies σ_{at} for $t = 1, \ldots, \tau - 1$, it is optimal (relative to his prior) to use $\sigma_{a\tau}^*$ at stage τ. By definition of equilibrium for a mechanism, it is optimal (relative to his posterior at stage τ) for agent a to use $\sigma_{a\tau}^*$ at stage τ for any previous history $s_A^{\tau-1}$. This is true, in particular, if $s_A^{\tau-1}$ is a history generated by the strategies $(\sigma_{\bar{a}}^{*\tau-1}, \sigma_a^{\tau-1})$ for some parameter vector ξ. Let

$$s_A^{\tau-1}(\xi) = \Psi_A^{\tau-1}(\xi | \sigma_{\bar{a}}^{*\tau-1}, \sigma_a^{\tau-1})$$

Also, to streamline the notation, let

$$Q_a^*(s_A^{\tau-1}, \xi) = U_a[F_a\{s_A^{\tau-1}, \sigma_{A\tau}^*(s_A^{\tau-1}, \xi_A)\}, \xi]$$

$$Q_a(s_A^{\tau-1}, \xi) = U_a[F_a\{s_A^{\tau-1}, \sigma_{\bar{a}\tau}^*(s_A^{\tau-1}, \xi_{\bar{a}}), \sigma_{a\tau}(s_A^{\tau-1}, \xi^a)\}, \xi]$$

Thus $Q_a^*(s_A^{\tau-1}, \xi)$ is agent a's utility if the history through stage $\tau-1$ is $s_A^{\tau-1}$, the parameter value is ξ, and each agent uses his equilibrium strategy at the last stage. Similarly, $Q_a(s_A^{\tau-1}, \xi)$ is agent a's utility in the same circumstances except that a is assumed to use the alternative strategy $\sigma_{a\tau}$ at the last stage.

Now for $s_A^{\tau-1} = s_A^{\tau-1}(\xi)$, $\Delta_{a\tau}(s_A^{\tau-1}) \neq \emptyset$ since at least $\xi \in \Delta_{a\tau}(s_A^{\tau-1})$. Thus it follows (from the definition of equilibrium for a mechanism) that

$$\sum_{\delta \in \Delta_{a\tau}\{s_A^{\tau-1}(\xi)\}} \frac{Q_a^*\{s_A^{\tau-1}(\xi), \delta\}\rho_a(\delta|\theta^a)}{K_{a\tau}\{s_A^{\tau-1}(\xi), \theta^a\}} \geq \sum_{\delta \in \Delta_{a\tau}\{s_A^{\tau-1}(\xi)\}} \frac{Q_a\{s_A^{\tau-1}(\xi), \delta\}\rho_a(\delta|\theta^a)}{K_{a\tau}\{s_A^{\tau-1}(\xi), \theta^a\}}$$

or, multiplying both sides by $K_{a\tau}\{s_A^{\tau-1}(\xi), \theta^a\}$,

$$\sum_{\delta \in \Delta_{a\tau}\{s_A^{\tau-1}(\xi)\}} [Q_a^*\{s_A^{\tau-1}(\xi), \delta\} - Q_a\{s_A^{\tau-1}(\xi), \delta\}]\rho_a(\delta|\theta^a) \geq 0 \qquad (7.A2)$$

But (7.A2) must hold for each ξ. Moreover, for any two parameter values ξ and ξ' either $\Delta_{a\tau}\{s_A^{\tau-1}(\xi)\} = \Delta_{a\tau}\{s_A^{\tau-1}(\xi')\}$ or the two sets do not intersect at all, that is, if the two sets intersect, then the two histories $s_A^{\tau-1}(\xi)$ and $s_A^{\tau-1}(\xi')$ must be the same. Therefore if we sum the relation (7.A2) over all parameter values ξ, but eliminate double counting by eliminating one of the values ξ or ξ' whenever $\Delta_{a\tau}\{s_A^{\tau-1}(\xi)\} = \Delta_{a\tau}\{s_A^{\tau-1}(\xi')\}$, we obtain

$$\sum_{\xi \in \Theta} Q_a^*\{s_A^{\tau-1}(\xi), \xi\}\rho_a(\xi|\theta^a) \geq \sum_{\xi \in \Theta} Q_a\{s_A^{\tau-1}(\xi), \xi\}\rho_A(\xi|\theta^a)$$

Recalling the definitions of Q_a^* and Q_a, this shows that it is optimal (relative to his prior) for agent a to use strategy $\sigma_{a\tau}^*$ at stage τ if he has used $\sigma_{a\tau}$ in stages $1, \ldots, \tau-1$, assuming that all other agents are using their equilibrium strategies. It can then be shown (using the same argument) that it is optimal (relative to his prior) for agent a to use $\sigma_{a,\tau-1}^*$ at stage $\tau-1$ given that he used σ_{at} for $t = 1, \ldots, \tau-2$ and that he plans to use $\sigma_{a\tau}^*$ at stage τ. This then shows that (relative to his prior) the sequence of strategies $\sigma_{a1}, \ldots, \sigma_{a,\tau-2}$, $\sigma_{a,\tau-1}^*, \sigma_{a\tau}^*$ dominates the sequence σ_a^τ for agent a. If we proceed with this backward induction we obtain that $\sigma_a^{*\tau}$ dominates σ_a^τ for agent a (relative to his prior) as is claimed in the lemma.

Proof of theorem 7.1

Let θ^a be any vector of values for agent a's observed parameters and let δ_P^a be any (other) values for agent a's privately observed parameters. Let M_A be any mechanism for A (where $a \in A$) with equilibrium $(\sigma_A^{*\tau}, \rho_A^{*\tau})$. Then

$$c_A(M_A, \delta_P^a, \xi_H^a) = F\{\Psi_A^\tau(\delta_P^a, \xi_H^a|\sigma_A^{*\tau})\}$$

for any values ξ_{H}^{a} for the parameters that agent a does not privately observe. For any $t = 1, \ldots, \tau$, any values ξ^{a} of a's observed parameters and any history s_{A}^{t-1} define a strategy σ_{at} for a by

$$\sigma_{at}(s_{A}^{t-1}, \xi^{a}) = \sigma_{at}^{*}(s_{A}^{t-1}, \delta_{\mathrm{P}}^{a}, \xi_{\mathrm{Q}}^{a})$$

where ξ_{Q}^{a} is the subvector of ξ^{a} consisting of those values which a observes but not privately. Thus σ_{at} is the equilibrium strategy of a at stage t but with the values δ_{P}^{a} substituted for a's private parameters regardless of their true values. Then for any parameter vector ξ_{A} observed by agents of A,

$$\Psi_{A}^{\tau}(\xi_{A} | \sigma_{\bar{a}}^{*\tau}, \sigma_{a}^{\tau}) = \Psi_{A}^{\tau}(\delta_{\mathrm{P}}^{a}, \xi_{\mathrm{H}}^{a} | \sigma_{A}^{*\tau})$$

Therefore, by lemma 7.A1, $(\sigma_{\bar{a}}^{*\tau}, \sigma_{a}^{\tau})$ is feasible. The result then follows from lemma 7.A2 and the definition of $c_{A}(M_{A}, \xi_{A})$.

Proof of theorem 7.2

Let $\tilde{c}_{A}$ be any (feasible) PC allocation which satisfies self-selection. Define $\Theta^{A} = \times_{a \in A} \Theta^{a}$ with typical elements $\theta^{A} = (\theta^{a})_{a \in A}$. Note that, in general, $\Theta^{A} \neq \Theta_{A}$ since an element of Θ^{A} will contain repeat values of any parameter which is observed by more than one agent. (For example, suppose that $A = \{a, b\}$, $N = \{1, 2, 3\}$, $N_{a} = \{1, 2\}$, $N_{b} = \{2, 3\}$. Then $\theta^{a} = (\theta_{1}^{a}, \theta_{2}^{a})$ and $\theta^{b} = (\theta_{2}^{b}, \theta_{3}^{b})$ so that $\theta^{A} = (\theta_{1}^{a}, \theta_{2}^{a}, \theta_{2}^{b}, \theta_{3}^{b})$ while θ_{A} would be of the form $(\theta_{1}, \theta_{2}, \theta_{3})$.) Let Z be the subset of Θ^{A} consisting of all those values of θ^{A} such that whenever two agents a and b both observe a parameter, say parameter k, the values θ_{k}^{a} and θ_{k}^{b} agree, that is,

$$Z = \{\theta^{A} \in \Theta^{A} | \text{for any } a, b \in A \text{ and any } k \in N_{a} \cap N_{b}, \theta_{k}^{a} = \theta_{k}^{b}\}$$

For any $k \in N$ and any $\theta^{A} \in Z$, define $z_{k}(\theta^{A})$ to be the common value of θ_{k}^{a} for any agent a who observes parameter k, that is, for any a such that $k \in N_{a}$. Thus z_{k} is a function from Z into Θ_{k}. Finally, let $z = (z_{k}) k \in N_{A}$. (In terms of the above example, Z consists of all those values of θ^{A} for which $\theta_{2}^{a} = \theta_{2}^{b}$. If θ^{A} is such a value, then $z(\theta^{A}) = (\theta_{1}^{a}, \theta_{2}^{a}, \theta_{3}^{b}) = (\theta_{1}^{a}, \theta_{2}^{b}, \theta_{3}^{b})$.)

We wish to construct a mapping F which associates with each value θ^{A} a feasible allocation, that is, $F: \Theta^{A} \rightarrow \lambda(A)$, such that F satisfies the following two constraints:

$$\text{for any } \theta^{A} \in Z, \qquad F(\theta^{A}) = \tilde{c}_{A}\{z(\theta^{A})\} \tag{7.A3}$$

and

$$\hat{V}_{a}(F, \delta^{a}, \gamma^{a}) \leqslant \hat{V}_{a}(F, \gamma^{a}, \gamma^{a}) \tag{7.A4}$$

for any agent a and values δ^a and γ^a of a's observed parameters, where

$$\hat{V}_a(F, \delta^a, \gamma^a) = E_a[U_a\{F_a(\delta^a, \xi^{\bar{a}}), \xi\} | \gamma^a]$$

Here F_a is the bundle assigned by F to agent a, $\xi^{\bar{a}} = (\xi^b) b \in \bar{a}$, and the expectation is taken with respect to a's prior $\rho_a(\xi | \gamma^a)$.

The mapping F will be the allocation rule of the direct mechanism whose equilibrium allocation is $\tilde{c}_A$. Recall that, in this mechanism, there is only one stage in which each agent a reports a value for each parameter he observes. Thus a's signal will be an element θ^a in Θ^a. Condition (7.A3) requires that if the reported parameter values θ^A of all agents agree for jointly observed parameters, that is, $\theta^A \in Z$, then the rule F should give the same allocation as $\tilde{c}_A$ would if it were evaluated at the corresponding value $z(\theta^A)$, that is, after throwing out duplicated parameter values sent in by several agents. Condition (7.A4) requires that, given F, each agent (weakly) prefers to report the true values of his observed parameters γ^a to reporting any other values δ^a, provided that all other agents report their true values. That is, condition (7.A4) requires that F be such that telling the truth is a Nash strategy against F. From this discussion, it is clear if we can find such an F, then the direct mechanism with allocation rule F will be the mechanism required in the statement of the theorem and that the identity maps on Θ^a for each agent a will constitute a set of (Nash) equilibrium strategies for this mechanism. The remainder of the proof consists of constructing such a rule F using the assumption that $\tilde{c}_A$ satisfies self-selection.

First consider the case where all parameters are privately observed, that is, $N_a \cap N_b \neq \varnothing$ for any $a \neq b$. In this case $Z = \Theta^A = \Theta_A$ so any allocation rule F for the direct mechanism is just a PC allocation. Therefore, for any such rule F the above definitions reduce to (note that $\delta^a_{\mathrm{P}} = \delta^a$ in this case)

$$\hat{V}_a(F, \delta^a, \gamma^a) = \sum_{\xi \in \Theta} U_a\{F_a(\delta^a_{\mathrm{P}}, \xi^a_{\mathrm{H}}), \xi\} \rho_a(\xi | \gamma^a)$$

and (see the definition of V_a in section 8)

$$\hat{V}_a(F, \gamma^a, \gamma^a) = V_a(F_a, \gamma^a)$$

Moreover, if we take $F = \tilde{c}_A$, then F satisfies (7.A3) (since $Z = \Theta_A$ and z is the identity in this case). Also, $F = \tilde{c}_A$ satisfies (7.A4) by definition of self-selection for PC allocations (see section 8). This proves the theorem for this case.

For the case in which some parameters are observed by more than one agent, define F as follows. For $\theta^A \in Z$, let

$$F(\theta^A) = \tilde{c}_A\{z(\theta^A)\}$$

so that (7.A3) is satisfied by definition. We must now define F on $Z' = \Theta^A - Z$ such that (7.A4) holds. From the definition of $\hat{V}_a$, it is clear that we need only be concerned with elements of Z of the form $(\delta^a, \xi^{\bar{a}})$ in which all signals agree for jointly observed parameters except that one particular agent a may disagree with the other agents. Accordingly, for any $\theta^A \in Z'$ of the form $(\delta^a, \xi^{\bar{a}})$, define

$$F(\delta^a, \xi^{\bar{a}}) = \tilde{c}_A(\delta^a_{\mathrm{P}}, \xi^a_{\mathrm{H}})$$

Thus F is defined to be $\tilde{c}_A$ evaluated at values reported by a for his privately observed parameters and at values reported by the other agents (assuming that they agree on jointly observed parameters) for all other parameters.

For elements of Z' not of the above form, let F be any feasible allocation, that is, any element of $\lambda(A)$. This completes the construction of F. Given the remarks following the statement of conditions (7.A3) and (7.A4), it only remains to show that F satisfies (7.A4). But

$$\begin{aligned} \hat{V}_a(F, \delta^a, \gamma^a) &= \sum_{\xi \in \Theta} U_a\{\tilde{c}_a(\delta^a_{\mathrm{P}}, \xi^a_{\mathrm{H}}), \xi\} \rho_a(\xi \mid \gamma^a) && \text{by construction of } F \\ &\leqslant V_a(\tilde{c}_a, \gamma^a) && \text{since } \tilde{c}_A \text{ satisfies self-selection} \\ &= \hat{V}_a(F, \gamma^a, \gamma^a) && \text{since } F \text{ satisfies (7.A3)} \end{aligned}$$

Thus F does satisfy (7.A4).

The mechanism $D_A = [1, \Theta^A, F]$ is the required mechanism since under D_A identity maps will be equilibrium strategies (since F satisfies (7.A4)). Therefore the equilibrium signals will be θ^A if the true value of the parameter vector is θ_A. Since all agents will report the same (true) value of jointly observed parameters, $\theta^A \in Z$, so that F evaluated at these equilibrium signals will simply be $\tilde{c}_A(\theta_A)$, that is, $c_A(D_A, \theta_A) = \tilde{c}_A(\theta_A)$ as required.

Proof of theorem 7.3

We prove the theorem only for core mechanism and allocation. The proofs for Pareto and individually rational Pareto mechanism and allocation are exactly analogous.

Suppose that $\tilde{c}_A$ is a core allocation. By definition $\tilde{c}_A$ satisfies self-selection. Using theorem 7.2, let M_A be a mechanism for A such that

$$\tilde{c}_A(\theta_A) = c_A(M_A, \theta_A)$$

We claim that M_A is a core mechanism for E^0_A, for suppose the contrary. Then there is a coalition $B \subseteq A$ and a mechanism M'_B for B such that

$$W_b(M'_B, \theta^b) \geqslant W_b(M_A, \theta^b)$$

for all agents $b \in B$ and $\theta^b \in \Theta^b$ with at least one inequality strict. Let $\tilde{x}_B = c_B(M'_B, \cdot)$. Then

$$V_b(\tilde{c}_b, \theta^b) = W_b(M_A, \theta^b)$$

and

$$V_b(\tilde{x}_b, \theta^b) = W_b(M'_B, \theta^b)$$

But $\tilde{x}_B$ satisfies self-selection (by theorem 7.1), and so B can block $\tilde{c}_A$ (using $\tilde{x}_B$) contrary to the assumption.

Now suppose that M_A is a core mechanism for E^0_A. Let $\tilde{c}_A = c_A(M_A, \cdot)$. Thus $\tilde{c}_A$ satisfies self-selection by theorem 7.1 and the fact that $V_a(\tilde{c}_a, \cdot) = W_a(M_A, \cdot)$. Now suppose that B can block $\tilde{c}_A$ for some coalition $B \subseteq A$. Then there is a PC allocation $\tilde{x}_B$ (feasible for B) such that $\tilde{x}_B$ satisfies self-selection and

$$V_b(\tilde{x}_b, \theta^b) \geq V_b(\tilde{c}_b, \theta^b)$$

for all b and θ^b with at least one inequality strict. Using theorem 7.2, let M'_B be a mechanism for B such that $\tilde{x}_B = c_B(M'_B, \cdot)$. Then $V_b(\tilde{x}_b, \theta^b) \equiv W_b(M'_B, \theta^b)$, and so B can block M_A (using M'_B) in contradiction of the assumption that M_A is a core mechanism.

Proof of theorem 7.4

First note that, since $N_a = N$, for any $\theta \in \Theta$

$$V_a(\tilde{c}_a, \theta^a) = U_a\{\tilde{c}_a(\theta), \theta\} \tag{7.A5}$$

Now suppose that $\tilde{c}^*_T$ is full-information optimal and satisfies self-selection. We need only show that no other $\tilde{c}'_T$ can strictly dominate $\tilde{c}^*_T$ in the sense of section 8. Suppose, to the contrary, that $\tilde{c}'_T$ is a PC allocation which satisfies self-selection and

$$V_t(\tilde{c}'_t, \theta^t) \geq V_t(\tilde{c}^*_t, \theta^t)$$

for each $t \in T$ and $\theta^t \in \Theta^t$ with at least one inequality strict.

Case 1 $V_b(\tilde{c}'_b, \theta^b) > V_b(\tilde{c}^*_b, \theta^b)$ for some $\theta^b \in \Theta^b$. Then for some $\xi \in \Theta$ such that $\xi^b = \theta^b$,

$$U_b\{\tilde{c}'_b(\xi), \xi\} > U_b\{\tilde{c}^*_b(\xi), \xi\}$$

Since $\tilde{c}_T^*$ is full-information optimal, this implies

$$U_a\{\tilde{c}'_a(\xi), \xi\} < U_a\{\tilde{c}_a^*(\xi), \xi\}$$

or, using (7.A5),

$$V_a(\tilde{c}'_a, \xi) < V_a(\tilde{c}_a^*, \xi)$$

This is the desired contradiction.

Case 2 $V_a(\tilde{c}'_a, \theta^a) > V_a(\tilde{c}_a^*, \theta^a)$ for some $\theta \in \Theta$. Using (7.1), this implies that

$$U_a\{\tilde{c}'_a(\theta), \theta\} > U_a\{\tilde{c}_a^*(\theta), \theta\}$$

and, since $\tilde{c}_T^*$ is full-information optimal, we must have

$$U_b\{\tilde{c}'_b(\theta), \theta\} < U_b\{\tilde{c}_b^*(\theta), \theta\} \tag{7.A6}$$

Furthermore, since $V_a(\tilde{c}'_a, \xi^a) \geqslant V_a(\tilde{c}_a^*, \xi^a)$ for every $\xi^a \in \Theta^a$, using (7.A5),

$$U_a\{\tilde{c}'_a(\xi), \xi\} \geqslant U_a\{\tilde{c}_a^*(\xi), \xi\}$$

for every $\xi \in \Theta$. Consequently, since $\tilde{c}_T^*$ is full-information optimal,

$$U_b\{\tilde{c}'_b(\xi), \xi\} \leqslant U_b\{\tilde{c}_b^*(\xi), \xi\} \tag{7.A7}$$

for every $\xi \in \Theta$. But (7.A6), (7.A7), and the definition of V_b imply that

$$V_b(\tilde{c}'_b, \theta^b) < V_b(\tilde{c}_b^*, \theta^b)$$

which is the desired contradiction.

Notes

1 Such environments have recently been the object of considerable and growing attention. Examples include public goods (Groves and Ledyard, 1977), signaling and screening (Spence, 1974; Riley, 1979), agency (Spence and Zeckhauser, 1971; Shavell, 1979), insurance (Rothschild and Stiglitz, 1976; C. Wilson, 1977), competitive markets with some informed traders (Green, 1973; Grossman, 1977), and auction markets (R.B. Wilson, 1977; Holt, 1980). By *asymmetric* information, we mean a situation in which certain agents believe other agents to be *better* informed about some aspect of the economic environment. This is to be distinguished from *differential* information, when agents have different *ex ante*

information but no agent believes any other agent to be better informed than he is.

2 Since writing an earlier version of this chapter we have discovered the work of Myerson (1979) whose approach is similar to our own in several crucial aspects. We also wish to acknowledge the influence of the seminal work of Hurwicz on resource-allocation mechanisms (for example, Hurwicz, 1972). Reiter pioneered in this area as well (for example, Reiter, 1977).

3 Myerson (1979) is a notable exception.

4 Such restrictions have proved quite useful in developing positive theories of economic phenomena (see Prescott and Townsend, 1980).

5 The Bayesian equilibrium concept is used by Arrow (1977), Dasgupta et al. (1979), and d'Aspremont and Gerard-Varet (1979) among others. It is closely related to the rational expectations equilibrium (see Prescott and Townsend, 1980). We would like to thank L. Hurwicz, J. Jordan, and E. Maskin for calling our attention to some of this literature.

6 Myerson (1979) derives similar results for one-stage mechanisms.

7 The terminology "direct mechanism" is borrowed from game theory lierature (for example, Dasgupta et al., 1979).

8 Further applications are described by Harris and Raviv (1979a, b).

9 This complements the results of Arrow (1979) and D'Aspremont and Gerard-Varet (1979) who establish that in some public goods environments there is at least one full-information optimal PC allocation which can be achieved as a Bayesian equilibrium. A related question is whether a full-information optimal PC allocation can be achieved under a mechanism satisfying a budget balance requirement under a dominant strategy (strong Nash) equilibrium for, as Dasgupta et al. (1979) point out, any PC allocation which can be attained as a dominant strategy equilibrium can also be attained as a Bayesian equilibrium. It is well known that there does not exist one mechanism with this property for a fairly rich class of utility functions. (Of course a given mechanism may work for a particular set of utility functions.) This has motivated some to consider a weaker concept of equilibrium, namely the (weak) Nash equilibrium. Under this concept there do exist mechanisms which satisfy both the budget balance and full-information optimal criteria (see, for example, the celebrated work of Groves and Ledyard (1977) and the "demand revelation" literature). Yet here we may question how it is that the weak Nash equilibrium is to be attained; in a weak Nash equilibrium an agent's signal will vary with parameters unobserved by him. Both Groves and Ledyard (1977) and Dasgupta et al. (1979) have noted difficulties with adjustment schemes which are intended to circumvent this problem.

10 For most of our analysis the parameters can be thought of as being drawn from some exogenously specified joint distribution known to all agents with agents' priors being conditional distributions given their observed parameters. We do not require this consistency, however.

11 In general, we use the following notation for Cartesian products of sets. If $A \subseteq T$ and $\{Y_a | a \in A\}$ is any collection of sets, then we denote the product $\times_{a \in A} Y_a$ by Y^A. An element of Y^A is denoted by $(y_a)_{a \in A}$ or by y_A.

12 The definition of a mechanism used here is a straightforward extension of the one used in our earlier paper (Harris and Townsend, 1978, this volume, ch. 6).

The reader is referred to that chapter for a fuller discussion of the issues involved in this concept and some examples which motivate the definition.

13 The formal definition is as follows. Given $A \subseteq T$ and λ_A *a mechanism* for the set of agents A, M_A is (a) an integer $\tau \geqslant 1$, (b) a set $\mathscr{S}$, a designated element $s^0 \in \mathscr{S}$, and a sequence

$$S_A = \{S_{at}: (\mathscr{S}^A)^{t-1} \rightarrow 2^{\mathscr{S}} | a \in A, t = 1, \ldots, \tau\}$$

where

$$(\mathscr{S}^A)^t = \{s_A^0\} \times \mathop{\times}_{r=1}^{r} \mathscr{S}^A \text{ for } t = 1, \ldots, \tau, \; s_A^0 = (s^0)_{a \in A}$$

and $(\mathscr{S}^A)^0 = \{s_A^0\}$ (if $s^0 \in S_{at}(s_A^{t-1})$ for some a, t, and s_A^{t-1}, then $S_{at}(s_A^{t-1}) = \{s^0\}$), and (c) a function $F: (\mathscr{S}^A)^\tau \rightarrow \lambda(A)$.

14 More formally we have a strategy at stage t for agent a, $1 \leqslant t \leqslant \tau$, $a \in A$, which is a function $\sigma_{at}: (\mathscr{S}^A)^{t-1} \times \Theta^a \rightarrow \mathscr{S}$. We assume that strategies and the allocation rule F are deterministic. In general this is inconsistent with the spirit of our approach, because the constraint that a proposal not be chosen in a random way is, in general, unenforceable. In many applications, however, this restriction is not binding, that is, any mechanism whose equilibrium final allocations are random, because either the strategies or the allocation rule are random, can be dominated by one in which they are deterministic (see Harris and Townsend, 1978, this volume, ch. 6).

15 Note the recursive procedure used to define $\Psi_A^\tau(\theta_A|\sigma_A^\tau)$ in the appendix. Then starting at stage r, given past signals s_A^{r-1}, we can similarly define $\Psi_A^{r,\tau}(\theta_A, s_{ar}|s_A^{r-1}, \sigma_{\bar{a}r}, \sigma_A^{r+1,\tau})$, the sequence of signals that will be sent under the given mechanism as a function of the parameter vector θ_A and the contemporary signal s_{ar} of agent a, *given* past signals, contemporary strategies of others, and future strategies of everyone. Thus

$$E_{ar}[U_a\{F_a(s_A^\tau), \xi\}|s_A^{r-1}, \sigma_{\bar{a}r}, \sigma_A^{r+1,\tau}, \theta^a]$$

$$\equiv \sum_{\xi \in \Theta} \rho_{ar}(\xi|s_A^{r-1}, \theta^a) U_a[F_a\{s_A^{r-1}, \Psi_A^{r,\tau}(\xi_A, s_{ar}|s_A^{r-1}, \sigma_{\bar{a}r}, \sigma_A^{r+1,\tau}), \xi\}]$$

16 Note that in the definition $\rho_{ar}^*(\xi|\theta^a, s_A^{r-1}) = \rho_a(\xi|\theta^a)$ for any history s_A^{r-1} which is inconsistent with the equilibrium strategies of agents other than a evaluated at any possible parameter values, that is, for s_A^{r-1} for which $\Delta_{ar}(s_A^{r-1}) = \varnothing$. Also note that, for $r = 1$, $\rho_{a1}^*(\xi|\theta^a, s_A^0) = \rho_a(\xi|\theta^a)$ for any ξ and θ^a and $\Sigma_{\xi \in \Theta} \rho_{ar}^*[\xi|\theta^a, s_A^{r-1}] = 1$ for any θ^a, s_A^{r-1}.

17 See, for example, Green (1977), Kydland and Prescott (1977), and Prescott and Visscher (1977).

18 We are indebted to Jim Jordan for providing us with an example. The example is omitted for brevity but is obtainable from the authors on request. It may well be, however, that every perfect Bayesian equilibrium of an extensive form game (mechanism) is one of the many Bayesian equilibria of its normal form counterpart.

We might well have set out to prove this so that the self-selection theorem (theorem 7.1) would be more easily established (for normal form games). Here we hazard the opinion that such a proof would be similar in many respects to the proof of theorem 7.1 In any event we would still need to consider extensive form games and endure the consequent notational burden.

19 The concept of self-selection has been used extensively in insurance and screening literatures (for example, Rothschild and Stiglitz, 1976; Salop and Salop, 1976; C. Wilson, 1977). This concept is closely related to incentive compatibility as discussed by Hurwicz (1972).

20 An alternative approach would be to define blocking (see below) in terms of the equilibrium allocations of mechanisms instead of the mechanisms themselves. Then we could define a core mechanism to be one with at least one equilibrium which could not be blocked. The results which follow would not be affected by this alteration of the definition.

21 An alternative formulation would be to assume that preferences over mechanisms are expressed prior to the revelation of θ^a to agent a, but the mechanism must be "played out" (as before) subsequent to this revelation. In this case each agent can be imagined to have a prior distribution over the entire parameter vector (say a common joint distribution). The expected utility of each agent for a mechanism would then involve integration relative to this prior.

22 This integer assumption is made only to avoid the subtle issue of how to define "blocking" and the core in a public goods environment. This issue is considered by Rosenthal (1971, 1972), Champsaur et al. (1975), and others. It is peripheral to the points that we wish to make here.

23 In order that these priors are consistent, that is, are conditional distributions derived from the same joint distribution on (θ_a, θ_b), it must be the case that

$$\frac{\alpha_2(1-\alpha_1)}{\alpha_1(1-\alpha_2)} = \frac{\beta_2(1-\beta_1)}{\beta_1(1-\beta_2)}$$

Independence of priors (a stronger condition than consistency) would require that $\alpha_1 = \alpha_2$ and $\beta_1 = \beta_2$. In general, we do *not* assume consistency or independence of these priors.

24 The intuition which follows is due largely to the suggestion of a referee.

25 Note that this is precisely the condition that the agents' priors be inconsistent (see note 22). If we had more general utility functions, say of the form $\theta u(x) + y$ where $u'' \neq 0$, then the condition which the priors must satisfy in order to be able to improve on some Samuelson–Lindahl allocation would involve marginal utilities like $u'(a_{ij})$ as well as the probabilities α_k, β_k. In this case a Pareto improvement could be possible even with consistent priors.

26 We are grateful to Jeffrey Branman for use of his mixed integer–linear computer code and for assistance in implementing it to solve the maximization problem presented in the text. The example presented below was generated using this code.

27 This is consistent with the concept that priors reflect the information of the agents and would be different across agents only if information varied across these agents. Since we are assuming that the information structure is fully described by $N_t = \{1\}$

for $t \in T_1$, $N_t \in \varnothing$ for $t \in T_2$, there is no reason to assign different prior beliefs to different uninformed agents.

28 The method of filling in the entries of the box here corresponds to the construction in the proof of theorem 7.2. It is easy to fill in the entries so that each agent strictly prefers to signal the true value of θ, given that the other agent is also signaling the truth. However, it should be noted that there is an alternative equilibrium for the game in figure 7.2. It is easy to check that the strategy "always signal θ^1 regardless of the true value of θ" is also an equilibrium. Moreover, both informed agents end up better off in this equilibrium when $\theta = \theta^2$ than in the competitive equilibrium. It turns out, however, that, with very mild assumptions on the way preferences depend on θ, it is possible to fill in the "off-diagonal" entries in such a way that "truth-telling" is the only equilibrium and the competitive allocation is the only equilibrium allocation.

29 The problem with allowing the parameters to enter through, say, the production technology instead of through preferences, is that which allocations are feasible may then depend on the particular parameter draw. If so, it may not be possible to specify a mechanism which is independent of the parameters but which still always results in a feasible allocation. In some applications this problem can be finessed, if the model can be formulated so that the set of feasible allocations does not depend on the parameter draw. In the agency model of section 2, for example, the original specification of the model was such that the relevant parameter was associated with the production technology. In that case, however, it was possible to respecify the model in such a way that the parameter entered through preferences.

30 Much of the discussion in this paragraph is due to the suggestion of a referee.

31 For example, in the agency environment the following mechanism is a core mechanism regardless of the principal's prior. (A proof of this statement for a slightly different model is given by Harris and Townsend, 1978, this volume, ch. 6.) The mechanism has two stages. In the first, the principal proposes any pair of feasible allocations. In the second, the agent can choose either of these two allocations or autarky. Naturally, the equilibrium allocation of this mechanism will depend on the principal's prior.

References

Arrow, K.J. (1977) The property rights doctrine and demand revelation under incomplete information. Technical Report 243, Institute of Mathematical Studies of Social Science, Stanford University.

Brock, W.A. (1976) The design of mechanisms for efficient allocation of public goods. Report 7655, Center for Mathematical Studies in Business and Economics, University of Chicago.

Champsaur, P., Roberts, D.J. and Rosenthal, R.W. (1975) On cores in economies with public goods. *International Economic Review* 16, 751–64.

Dasgupta, P., Hammond, P. and Maskin, E. (1979) The implementation of social choice rules: some general results on incentive compatibility. *Review of Economic Studies* 46, 185–216.

D'Aspremont, C. and Gerard-Varet, L.-A. (1979) Incentives and incomplete information. *Journal of Public Economics* 11, 25–45.

Green, E. (1977) Non-cooperative games and equilibrium market strategies. Ph.D. Dissertation, GSIA, Carnegie–Mellon University, Pittsburgh, PA.

Green, J.R. (1973) Information, efficiency, and equilibrium. Discussion Paper 284, Harvard Institute of Economic Research, Cambridge, MA.

Grossman, S. (1977) The existence of futures markets, noisy rational expectations and informational externalities. *Review of Economic Studies* 44, 431–50.

Groves, T. and Ledyard, J. (1977) Optimal allocation of public goods: a solution to the "free rider problem." *Econometrica* 45, 783–810.

Harris, M. and Raviv, A. (1979a) Allocation mechanisms and the design of auctions. GSIA Working Paper 5-78-79, Carnegie–Mellon University, Pittsburgh, PA.

—— and —— (1979b) A theory of monopoly pricing schemes with uncertain demand. GSIA Working Paper, Carnegie–Mellon University, Pittsburgh, PA.

—— and Townsend, R.M. (1978) Allocation mechanisms for asymmetrically informed agents. GSIA Working Paper 35-76-77, Carnegie–Mellon University, Pittsburgh PA. Reprinted in this volume as chapter 6.

Harsanyi, J.C. (1967–8) Games with incomplete information played by "Bayesian" players, Parts I–III. *Management Science* 14, 159–82, 320–34, 481–502.

Holt, C. (1980) Competitive bidding for contracts under alternative auction procedures. *Journal of Political Economy* 88, 433–45.

Hurwicz, L. (1972) On informationally decentralized systems. In *Decision and Organization*, eds C.B. McGuire and R. Radner, ch. 14. Amsterdam: North-Holland.

—— and Shapiro, L. (1978) Incentive structures maximizing residual gain under incomplete information. *Bell Journal of Economics* 9, 180–91.

Kydland, F. and Prescott, E. (1977) Rules rather than discretion: the inconsistency of the optimal plan. *Journal of Political Economy* 85, 473–92.

Myerson, R.B. (1979) Incentive compatibility and the bargaining problem. *Econometrica* 47, 61–74.

Prescott, E.C. and Townsend, R.M. (1980) Equilibrium under uncertainty: multiagent statistical decision theory. In *Bayesian Analysis in Econometrics and Statistics*, ed. A. Zellner, pp. 169–94. Amsterdam: North-Holland.

—— and Visscher, M. (1977) Sequential location among firms with foresight. *Bell Journal of Economics* 8, 378–93.

Reiter, S. (1977) Information and performance in the (new)^2 welfare economics. *American Economic Review* 67, 226–34.

Riley, J.G. (1979) Informational equilibrium. *Econometrica* 47, 331–60.

Rosenthal, R.W. (1971) External economies and cores. *Journal of Economic Theory* 3, 182–8.

—— (1972) Cooperative games in effectiveness form. *Journal of Economic Theory* 5, 88–101.

Rothschild, M. and Stiglitz, J. (1976) Equilibrium in competitive insurance markets: an essay on the economics of imperfect information. *Quarterly Journal of Economics* 90, 629–49.

Salop, J. and Salop, S. (1976) Self-selection and turnover in labor markets. *Quarterly Journal of Economics* 90, 619–27.

Selten, R. (1975) Reexamination of the perfectness concept for equilibrium points in extensive games. *International Journal of Game Theory* 4, 25–55.

Shavell, S. (1979) Risk sharing and incentives in the principal and agent relationship. *Bell Journal of Economics* 10, 55–74.

Spence, A.M. (1974) *Market Signalling*. Cambridge, MA: Harvard University Press.

—— and Zeckhauser, R. (1971) Insurance, information, and individual action. *American Economic Review* 61, 380–7.

Wilson, C. (1977) A model of insurance markets with incomplete information. *Journal of Economic Theory* 16, 176–207.

Wilson, R.B. (1977) A bidding model of perfect competition. *Review of Economic Studies* 44, 511–18.

8

Optimal Multiperiod Contracts and the Gain from Enduring Relationships under Private Information

1 Introduction

The existence and nature of multiperiod contracts is a subject receiving renewed attention from writers interested in aggregative phenomena and industrial organization. Responding in part to the striking conclusions of Sargent and Wallace (1975), Fischer (1977a) and Phelps and Taylor (1977) have developed models in which price or wage (contractual) rigidities give real consequences to the systematic component of monetary policy. More recently, Taylor (1980) has produced a model in which staggered fixed nominal-wage contracts play a key role in explaining persistence and momentum. Of course, this and earlier macroeconomic literature is closely associated with studies on the (cyclical) behavior of industrial prices, and their apparent inflexibility, beginning with Means (1935). Stigler and Kindahl (1970) outline these studies in providing evidence counter to Means's administered-price thesis. More to the point, however, Stigler and Kindahl find that many prices are set by an explicit contract. This finding and the divergent movement of the Bureau of Labor Statistics (BLS) (spot) price index relative to the Stigler–Kindahl (contract) index motivates the work of Carlton (1979).

Reprinted from *Journal of Political Economy* 90(6), 1982, 1166–86 (Chicago, IL: University of Chicago Press). I am especially indebted for helpful comments, insights, and suggestions to Edward C. Prescott, Gerald Faulhaber, Bengt Holmstrom, Dan Peled, Roy Radner, and other participants of seminars at the Bell Laboratories, the Federal Reserve Bank of Minneapolis, Northwestern University, and the University of California at Los Angeles, and the referees. Support from the National Science Foundation, the Federal Reserve Bank of Minneapolis, and the Alfred P. Sloan Foundation is gratefully acknowledged. I accept full responsibility for any errors as well as for the views expressed here.

Most models with multiperiod contracts begin at the level of "descriptive realism," imposing directly (exogenously) the form of observed contracts. It is not the intent of such models to explain the existence and nature of multiperiod contracts. Thus Fischer (1977b) finds common ground with Barro's (1977) criticism of Gray (1976) and Fischer (1977b), noting that "...there is indeed a missing theoretical link in this area... and that is the *explanation* of the form that labor contracts take" (emphasis added). Thus Carlton (1979, p. 1037) argues "that any theory purporting to *explain* price movements must delve into (a) the incentives for contracting, (b) the function performed by contracts, (c) the incentives for contracting for different durations, and (d) the pricing and interrelationship of different-duration contracts" (emphasis added). In this chapter we seek to develop a theory that might be used to begin to explain the existence and nature of some multiperiod agreements. Informational asymmetries play a key role in this theory.[1]

Recent papers have made important advances in explanations of multiperiod agreements, concentrating on contract length. In a microeconomic context, the dynamic labor contract paper of Dye (1979), which builds on the implicit labor contract paradigm of Gordon (1974), Azariadis (1975), and Baily (1977), is one such advance. In a macroeconomic context, the variable contract length paper of Gray (1978) is another. Still, the results of these papers turn on the imposition of arrangements which are incomplete relative to those suggested by the Arrow (1953) and Debreu (1959) treatment of uncertainty – arrangements made possible by indexing commodities by all conceivable states of nature. In Dye (1979), for example, the labor force is fixed for the duration of the contract, independent of the state of demand, and in Gray (1978) wages are indexed to prices but not to real and monetary shocks. In fact Barro (1977) argues that the crucial element in the Keynesian conclusions of the models of Gray (1976) and Fischer (1979) "...is the nonexecution of some perceived mutually advantageous trades."

In this chapter we seek to develop a theory which explains the existence and nature of multiperiod contracts without the imposition of exogenous restrictions – restrictions other than those implied by the economic environment and the information structure. That is, contracts are viewed as Pareto optimal agreements between agents so that no mutually advantageous trades remain. The explanation is accomplished here at the cost of considerable abstraction; the model contains neither money nor competitive markets (prices), and thus it can address neither the policy issues of the macroeconomic literature nor the empirical observations of Stigler and Kindahl (1970). However, it is hoped that a modest conceptual step forward is taken here. In this chapter the motive for multiperiod contracts is the idea that agents attempt to circumvent the incentive information difficulties of single-period one-shot agreements. Under single-period agreements, contingent exchanges that are mutually beneficial when information is complete can be impossible when information is private. If, for example, only one party to a two-party contract observes the outcome of an event upon which the contract depends, then he may be expected always to claim the outcome which is most favorable to himself. That is, the ultimate exchange is noncontingent after all.[2] But even if certain events are observed by only one party period by period, the well-informed agent can be given an incentive to report more honestly than in any one-shot agreement by making future exchanges contingent on present claims.

The idea that mutually beneficial arrangements are possible in the context of private information, with future payments tied to present claims, is closely related to a result in the literature on supergames that agents can achieve a cooperative solution if a game is played repeatedly. In supergames each agent can agree to play his cooperative strategy until the other agent deviates. The one-shot Nash equilibrium strategy can be employed in retaliation. This idea has been applied successfully by Friedman (1977), Green (1980), and Radner (1980) to dynamic oligopoly theory to explain how collusion can be maintained as a noncooperative solution. Each firm agrees to restrict output to the collusion solution until at least one firm dumps, in which case they all dump. Thus the key idea of supergames is that future payoffs to the decision-maker are tied to present actions of the decision-maker. Similarly, in this chapter future transfers to the informed agent depend not only on losses (unobserved by others) claimed in the future but also on present claims.[3] With a limited number of potential claims overall the informed agent will report more honestly than in any single-period agreement. This insight, that conditioning future payoffs on present claims or actions enables agents to do good things in repeated games with private information, is basic. Indeed, we have recently become aware of some work by Rubinstein and Yaari (1980) and Radner (1981) which makes use of the same idea.

As noted, in this chapter we seek to develop a theory which might be used to begin to explain the existence and nature of some multiperiod contracts: it establishes the gain to enduring relationships in a setting with private information. To explain why contracts are of finite length, this gain must be balanced against a cost – some sense in which the contract becomes less suitable over time. This can be accomplished formally by imagining that agents are traveling about on Hotelling's (1929) one-dimensional space. Maintaining a match or pairing can be supposed to become more costly over time; this would capture the cost associated with changing circumstances. To explain why contracts are negotiated at various times, rather than in a planning period, it can be imagined that communication is impossible between agents not in the same location or on Phelps's (1970) island. In this setting we might well imagine that the greater is the gain from enduring relationships the greater is the tendency for longer agreements. However, a deeper explanation of contract length is not pursued in this chapter.

The chapter proceeds as follows. In section 2 we describe the basic environment. There are two agents, one risk averse with a random endowment of the single consumption good of the model which is independent and identically distributed over time and one risk neutral with a constant endowment.[4] A full-information utility possibilities frontier is derived, and it is established that points on the frontier can be achieved by a sequence of one-period contracts; with full information, multiperiod contracts are not needed. Private information is introduced in section 3; it is assumed that the risk-averse agent alone observes his endowment realizations. In the context of this private information there are open issues as to how to define achievable allocations; this is done in this chapter by the derivation and imposition of certain incentive compatibility constraints which arise naturally in a consideration of resource-allocation mechanisms.[5] It is then shown that with private information a restriction to one-period contracts is quite damning – there can be no mutually beneficial exchange. However, it is established in section 4 that mutually beneficial trade is possible in a simple two-period borrowing–lending scheme; thus, with private information, multiperiod contracts are a good thing. Private-information optimal two-period schemes are also defined, and it is shown that the borrowing–lending scheme, though beneficial, is nonoptimal. An example is given which illustrates the optimal use of otherwise inefficient intertemporal tie-ins. It is established generally that in a private-information optimum at least one incentive compatibility condition must be binding; these results parallel some results of Kydland and Prescott (1977) on the inconsistency of optimal plans. Finally in section 5 we argue that every major result of the chapter is valid when agents discount the future (at the same rate), though asymptotic results based on an average-utility criterion, while illustrative of the gain to enduring relationships, are vulnerable.

2 A two-agent economy and full-information optimal allocations

Consider an economy with just two infinitely lived agents, one risk averse with an endowment sequence of the single consumption good of the model that is random and one risk neutral with a constant endowment sequence. Preferences of the risk-averse agent (labeled agent a) over consumption c in any period are described by a utility function $U(c)$, which is strictly concave, strictly increasing, and continuously differentiable with $U'(0)=\infty$ and $U(0)=0$. Let y_t denote the number of units of the consumption good of agent a in period t, where y_t is a random variable which takes on the values y' and y'', $0<y'<y''$, with probabilities Π and $1-\Pi$ respectively. Thus the

sequence $\{y_t\}_{t=1}^{\infty}$ is a very special sequence of independent and identically distributed random variables. Preferences of the risk-neutral agent (labeled agent b) are described by the utility function $V(c)=c$. Let $W>0$ denote the (constant) number of units of the consumption good of agent b in each period t.

In what follows attention will be limited to resource-allocation schemes over finite (but arbitrary) horizons T; of course, these schemes can be spliced together to form an infinite path. As was indicated in section 1, finite-duration schemes arise endogenously if there is a cost of changing circumstances. Attention will also be limited to paths which are stationary; that is, if a particular resource-allocation scheme is employed from periods 1 through T, then that same scheme is employed from periods $T+1$ through $2T$ and so on. Despite these two restrictions, there occasionally arises the need to assign utility values to infinite-horizon paths. To facilitate the exposition this assignment will be made using the average-utility criterion, but, as indicated in section 5, apart from an asymptotic result none of the major conclusions of this chapter depends on the absence of discounting or the average-utility criterion.[6]

Now suppose for the remainder of this section that realizations of the sequence $\{y_t\}_{t=1}^{\infty}$ are fully observed by both agents. Then it is clear that mutually beneficial trade is possible; the risk-neutral agent can absorb all risk. More formally, let $F_t(y_1, y_2, \ldots, y_t)$ denote an endowment-contingent transfer, that is, the number of units of the consumption good transferred from agent b to agent a as a function of the realizations $y^t \equiv (y_1, y_2, \ldots, y_t)$. Suppose also that the horizon over which such contingent trades are possible is fixed at some (finite) real number T. Then a full-information optimal exchange relative to T can be found as a solution to the following problem.

Problem 8.1

$$\max_{\{F_t(y^t)\}_{t=1}^{T}} E \sum_{t=1}^{T} U\{y_t + F_t(y^t)\}$$

subject to

$$E \sum_{t=1}^{T} \{W - F_t(y^t)\} \geqslant KT \tag{8.1}$$

$$y_t + F_t(y^t) \geqslant 0, \quad W - F_t(y^t) \geqslant 0 \qquad t = 1, 2, \ldots, T \tag{8.2}$$

Here the objective function is the expected utility of the risk-averse agent; (8.1) imposes a lower bound on the expected utility of the risk-neutral agent, where K is some constant and T is fixed, and (8.2) is the nonnegativity constraint on consumption.

If we write out the necessary first-order conditions for an interior maximum (and ignore (8.2)), it becomes apparent that

$$U'\{y_t + F_t(y')\} - \lambda = 0 \tag{8.3}$$

at each time t and for each possible y', where λ is a positive Lagrange multiplier. That is, the consumption of the risk-averse agent should be a constant, say c, over both time and endowment realizations. Thus a specification of c determines completely the amount to be transferred as a function of the realization y_t. If $y_t = y'$, so that agent a suffers a loss, then agent a receives a payment d from agent b. If $y_t = y''$ then agent a pays out p. This is so for all periods t, $t = 1, 2, \ldots, T$.

A utility possibilities frontier can now be derived. First, imposing constant consumption in problem 8.1 and noting that the number T enters as a multiplicative constant in the objective function and in constraint (8.1) (and is therefore inessential), we obtain the following problem.

Problem 8.2

$$\max_c U(c)$$

subject to

$$W + E(y_t) - c \geqslant K \tag{8.4}$$

$$c \geqslant 0, \quad W - c + y' \geqslant 0 \tag{8.5}$$

which is the obvious one-period full-information Pareto problem.

Of course, (8.4) can be presumed to hold as an equality. Here, then, the parameter K is the average utility of agent b over the horizon T. If we ignore (8.5), solutions to problem 8.2 depend entirely on this parameter. Using superscripts to denote this dependence, we see that (8.4) as an equality yields

$$c^K = E(y) - K + W \tag{8.6}$$

where $E(y) = E(y_t)$ for all t, so that

$$\bar{U}^K = U(c^K) = U\{E(y) - K + W\} \tag{8.7}$$

$$\bar{V}^K = K \tag{8.8}$$

where the bars denote average utility. Thus a typical concave utility possibilities frontier can be traced out as the parameter K is varied. The nonegativity constraint (8.5) implies

$$E(y) - y' \leqslant K \leqslant E(y) + W \tag{8.9}$$

Hereafter K is restricted to lie in this interval so that the construction above is valid. Finally, it is straightforward to establish that the utility possibilities frontier described above is, in fact, the full-information (average) utility possibilities frontier for the given model with an infinite horizon.

The implication of the discussion above is obvious: any point on the full-information utility possibilities frontier can be obtained by a sequence of one-period agreements. Any such point on the frontier is associated with constant consumption c for the risk-averse agent, which in turn is associated with a transfer of $+d$ or $-p$ for y_t equal to y' or y'' respectively. There is no sense in which this contingent exchange depends on past exchanges. There is no gain to enduring relationships.

3 Private information and a class of incentive-compatible contracts

The model discussed thus far, which assumes full information, has the property that multiperiod contracts are not needed. It is now shown how this conclusion is altered with the introduction of private information. This will make the point that private information can be crucial in an explanation of the existence of multiperiod contracts.

Thus suppose that the endowment y_t of agent a in each period t is never observed by any agent other than a. In this private-information context we are confronted with an obvious question: how are we to define achievable allocations or exchanges so that we can discover the implication of private information for multiperiod contracts?

To begin the discussion, suppose that we are intent on achieving some endowment-contingent transfer $F_t(y_1, y_2, \ldots, y_t)$ if the sequence of realized endowments is $y^t \equiv (y_1, y_2, \ldots, y_t)$. We imagine that we might do this by asking agent a to name a value for y_t in each period t, hoping that he might tell the truth. More formally, let $M_t = \{y', y''\}$ be the message space in period t (possible announcements of y_t) and let $F_t(m_1, m_2, \ldots, m_t)$ be the outcome in period t, a transfer which is a function of previous and current messages $m^t \equiv (m_1, m_2, \ldots, m_t)$. This outcome function F_t is the same as the endowment-contingent transfer function F_t, but its arguments are messages. Now in the last period of a T-period arrangement we want agent a to tell the truth about endowment realizations, that is, to send the message $m_T = y'$, if indeed the endowment is $y_T = y'$, instead of message $m_T = y''$. Clearly he will have an incentive to do this, no matter what message he has sent in the past, if his utility is greater, that is, if the outcome function is such that[7]

$$U\{y' + F_T(m^{T-1}, y')\} \geqslant U\{y' + F_T(m^{T-1}, y'')\} \tag{8.10}$$

for all previous messages m^{T-1}. (A similar expression must hold if $y_T = y''$.) Similarly, in period $T-1$ we want agent a to tell the truth, given that he will tell the truth in the future no matter what he does now. That is, let

$$\begin{aligned} &U\{y' + F_{T-1}(m^{T-2}, y')\} + EU\{y_T + F_T(m^{T-2}, y', y_T)\} \\ &\geqslant U\{y' + F_{T-1}(m^{T-2}, y'')\} + EU\{y_T + F_T(m^{T-2}, y'', y_T)\} \end{aligned} \tag{8.11}$$

for all previous messages m^{T-2}, and so on for $y_{T-1} = y''$. (Here the expectation is over y_T.) Working backward in this way, we derive a series of so-called incentive compatibility conditions which ensure truth telling in each period t, $t = 1, 2, \ldots, T$. That is, if these conditions are satisfied, agent a will tell the truth in periods 1 through T, and the sequence of endowment realizations $(y_1, y_2, \ldots, y_T)$ will be identical with the sequence of messages $(m_1, m_2, \ldots, m_T)$. Thus the transfer $F_t(y_1, y_2, \ldots, y_t)$ is achieved in each period t. This was our objective.

It must now be emphasized that arbitrary endowment-contingent transfers are not always achievable. The incentive compatibility conditions (8.10), (8.11), and so forth impose restrictions on any $F_t(y_1, y_2, \ldots, y_t)$ that we might hope to achieve in this way. Stated differently, only those transfers $F_t(y_1, y_2, \ldots, y_t)$ that satisfy these incentive compatibility conditions can be achieved in the class of announcement games with truth telling, that is, those discussed above.

Before we discuss the generality of this result, a rather striking implication of the incentive compatibility conditions should be noted. As more is preferred to less and there is only one commodity, condition (8.10) and its analog for $y_T = y''$ will be satisfied if and only if

$$\begin{aligned} F_T(m^{T-1}, y') &\geqslant F_T(m^{T-1}, y'') \\ F_T(m^{T-1}, y'') &\geqslant F_T(m^{T-1}, y') \end{aligned} \tag{8.12}$$

for all previous messages m^{T-1}. Thus

$$F_T(m^{T-1}, y') = F_T(m^{T-1}, y'') \tag{8.13}$$

and the last-period transfer cannot depend on the last-period announcement.

That is, the transfer is at most some constant in the last period. This is a severe restriction on trade. In fact, with $T = 1$, so that the last period is the only period, it is clear that mutually beneficial exchange becomes impossible. The implication is summarized as follows: under private information, a sequence of one-period agreements implies no trade. Thus the introduction of private information into this model has fairly damning consequences.[8]

With this result the issue of the generality of the incentive compatibility conditions takes on added importance. That is, these incentive compatibility conditions were derived from the requirement of truth telling in an announcement game. Perhaps these conditions can be circumvented by other schemes. Consider then a more general class of schemes. Let $M_t(m^{t-1})$ be the message space of agent a in period t, now as a function of previous messages $m^{t-1} \equiv (m_1, m_2, \ldots, m_{t-1})$. Here also the message space is arbitrary. Also let $F_t(m^{t-1}, m_t)$ be the outcome as a function of current and previous messages as before. Here, then, any scheme is completely defined by the message spaces $\{M_t(m^{t-1})\}_{t=1}^{T}$ and outcome functions $\{F_t(m^{t-1}, m_t)\}_{t=1}^{T}$.[9] Such a scheme can be thought of as a contract of duration T periods.

Under any such contract, agent a is confronted with the following problem.

Problem 8.3

$$\max_{\{m_t\}_{t=1}^{T}} E \sum_{t=1}^{T} U\{y_t + F_t(m^{t-1}, m_t)\}$$

subject to

$$m_t \in M_t(m^{t-1}) \qquad t = 1, 2, \ldots, T$$

Here the expectation is taken over y_t, $t = 1, 2, \ldots, T$.

A solution to this problem (assuming its existence) can be taken to be a sequence of decision rules $\sigma_t(m^{t-1}, y_t)$, $t = 1, 2, \ldots, T$, mappings from previous messages, and the current endowment realization to a current message. A sequence of decision rules generates a sequence of messages which in turn generates a sequence of transfers as a function of the realized endowments. The issue of generality can now be resolved. Given any contract $\{M_t(m^{t-1})\}_{t=1}^{T}$, $\{F_t(m^{t-1}, m_t)\}_{t=1}^{T}$, and associated optimal decision rules $\{\sigma_t(m^{t-1}, y_t)\}_{t=1}^{T}$, there exists an alternative contract with message space $\hat{M}_t = \{y', y''\}$ and outcome functions $\hat{F}_t(m^{t-1}, m_t)$ under which the truth-telling strategy $\hat{\sigma}_t(m^{t-1}, y_t) = y_t$ is maximal and which achieves the same allocation of resources (see appendix for proof).[10] In this sense the incentive compatibility conditions derived earlier were without loss of generality.[11]

They provide natural constraints on the space of achievable allocations in this environment with private information.

4 Two-period contracts, the gains to trade, private-information optima

In this section we seek to illustrate the gain to multiperiod relationships, even if such relationships are relatively short. Though mutually beneficial trade is impossible with single-period one-shot agreements, mutually beneficial trade is possible with two-period agreements. Moreover, the two-period private-information optima are partially characterized.

To illustrate that mutually beneficial trade is possible with two-period agreements attention is restricted to a simple intuitively appealing scheme. Suppose that agent *a* can ask for whatever transfers he likes in each of two periods, subsequent to his endowment realizations, but that these transfers must sum to zero. This is a type of borrowing–lending scheme in which the risk-neutral agent acts as a banker with zero interest rate. In effect we have a general equilibrium model which rationalizes a two-period version of the consumer savings problem discussed by Schechtman (1976), Yaari (1976), and Bewley (1977) in a partial equilibrium context. Letting $d(y_1)$ denote the first-period transfer to agent *a* as a function of the endowment realization y_1, we see that agent *a* is confronted with the following problem.

Problem 8.4

$$\max_{d(y_1)} U\{y_1 + d(y_1)\} + EU\{y_2 - d(y_1)\}$$

which yields the necessary first-order condition for an interior maximum

$$U'\{y_1 + d(y_1)\} = EU'\{y_2 - d(y_1)\} \qquad y_1 \in \{y', y''\} \tag{8.14}$$

Condition (8.14) states that under a solution the marginal utility of current consumption should equal the expected marginal utility of future consumption. In general, then, the solution $d(y_1)$ is nonzero. (For example, suppose that $y_1 = y'$ though Π is close to zero.) Thus, in general, agent *a* is better off than in autarky. As for agent *b*, he is clearly no worse off; his utility function is linear, and he is therefore indifferent to the timing of receipts. (It is assumed that the environment is such that the nonnegativity constraint on agent *b*'s consumption is not binding.) To reiterate, this two-period scheme allows for mutually beneficial trade because future transfers are tied to present claims; in this case they are equal except for sign.

Granting that this two-period contract is mutually beneficial, we may well ask whether it is not Pareto optimal. That is, does there exist another two-period contract which is better for at least one agent without being worse for the other? This question can be answered affirmatively by making use of the results of the previous section where it was established that the incentive compatibility conditions are natural and unavoidable constraints in the space of endowment-contingent transfers. Thus two-period private-information optimal endowment-contingent transfers can be found as solutions to the following problem.

Problem 8.5

$$\max \Pi[U\{y'+F_1(y')\}+EU\{y_2+F_2(y')\}] \\ +(1-\Pi)[U\{y''+F_1(y'')\}+EU\{y_2+F_2(y'')\}]$$

subject to

$$U\{y'+F_1(y')\}+EU\{y_2+F_2(y')\} \\ \geqslant U\{y'+F_1(y'')\}+EU\{y_2+F_2(y'')\} \tag{8.15}$$

$$U\{y''+F_1(y'')\}+EU\{y_2+F_2(y'')\} \\ \geqslant U\{y''+F_1(y')\}+EU\{y_2+F_2(y')\} \tag{8.16}$$

$$\Pi\{W-F_1(y')+W-F_2(y')\}+(1-\Pi)\{W-F_1(y'')+W-F_2(y'')\} \\ \geqslant 2K \tag{8.17}$$

by choice of first-period transfers $F_1(y')$ and $F_1(y'')$ and second-period transfers $F_2(y')$ and $F_2(y'')$, both as functions of first-period realizations y' and y''.

Here the objective function is the expected utility of agent a, constraints (8.15) and (8.16) are the incentive compatibility constraints implied by truth telling in period 1, and (8.17) is the constraint that the expected utility of agent b is no lower than some constant. (The incentive compatibility condition that $F_2(y_1, y_2)$ does not depend on y_2 is implicit in the notation.) Among the necessary first-order conditions for an (interior) solution to this problem are

$$\Pi U'\{y'+F_1(y')\}+\Psi_1 U'\{y'+F_1(y')\} \\ -\Psi_2 U'\{y''+F_1(y')\}-\Pi\Psi_3=0 \tag{8.18}$$

$$(1-\Pi)U'\{y''+F_1(y'')\}-\Psi_1 U'\{y'+F_1(y'')\} \\ +\Psi_2 U'\{y''+F_1(y'')\}-(1-\Pi)\Psi_3=0 \tag{8.19}$$

$$\Pi EU'\{y_2+F_2(y')\}+\Psi_1 EU'\{y_2+F_2(y')\}$$
$$-\Psi_2 EU'\{y_2+F_2(y')\}-\Pi\Psi_3=0 \tag{8.20}$$

$$(1-\Pi)EU'\{y_2+F_2(y'')\}-\Psi_1 EU'\{y_2+F_2(y'')\}$$
$$+\Psi_2 EU'\{y_2+F_2(y'')\}-(1-\Pi)\Psi_3=0 \tag{8.21}$$

where $\Psi_1 \geqslant 0$, $\Psi_2 \geqslant 0$, $\Psi_3 > 0$.

It is not obvious from inspection of (8.18)–(8.21) that a private-information optimum can be easily characterized. However, it is readily verified that at least one of the incentive compatibility constraints (8.15) or (8.16) must be binding in an optimum. For suppose that $\Psi_1 = \Psi_2 = 0$. Then (8.20) and (8.21) yield $F_2(y') = F_2(y'')$, and (8.18) and (8.19) yield

$$U'\{y'+F_1(y')\}=U'\{y''+F_1(y'')\} \tag{8.22}$$

so that $F_1(y') > F_1(y'')$. However, this specification will violate (8.16).[12]

It is now apparent that the two-period borrowing–lending scheme analyzed at the outset of this section is nonoptimal. From the strict concavity of $U(\cdot)$ and the fact that $d(y')$ and $d(y'')$ are maximal for realizations y' and y'' respectively, $y' \neq y''$,

$$U\{y'+d(y')\}+EU\{y_2-d(y')\}$$
$$>U\{y'+d(y'')\}+EU\{y_2-d(y'')\} \tag{8.23}$$

$$U\{y''+d(y'')\}+EU\{y_2-d(y'')\}$$
$$>U\{y''+d(y')\}+EU\{y_2-d(y')\} \tag{8.24}$$

However, if we let $F_1(y') = d(y')$, $F_2(y') = -d(y')$, $F_1(y'') = d(y'')$, and $F_2(y'') = -d(y'')$, this specification satisfies both incentive compatibility constraints (8.15) and (8.16) as inequalities.

Thus far we have a general proof that the borrowing–lending scheme is nonoptimal. However, there is as yet little intuition as to the cause of nonoptimality or the nature of an optimal contract that Pareto dominates. To provide some intuition, further simplifying assumptions are made, namely that the probability of loss parameter Π equals a half and that the utility function of agent a is quadratic, that is, $U(c) = c - bc^2$.[13] Under these assumptions straightforward algebraic manipulation of condition (8.14) yields the solution to the borrowing–lending scheme: $d(y') = (y'' - y')/4$ and $d(y'') = (y' - y'')/4$. These transfers are half of the full-information optimal transfers and are equal except for sign, a kind of symmetry condition. To find a contract that Pareto dominates, return to problem 8.5 and impose there in addition the latter kinds of symmetry restrictions, that if the transfer to agent a in period 1 for $y_1 = y'$ is $+p_1$, then the transfer to agent a in period 1 for $y_1 = y''$ must be $-p_1$. Similarly, if the transfer to agent a in period 2 for $y_1 = y'$ is $-p_2$, then the transfer to agent a in period 2 for $y_1 = y''$ must be $+p_2$. Finally, let $K = W$ in (8.17) as an equality, consistent with the zero-profit condition of the borrowing–lending scheme. Also note that the symmetry restrictions require that transfers be balanced across first-period states but not necessarily over time as in the borrowing–lending scheme. There is no proof given here that these symmetry restrictions are not binding in an optimum, a solution to problem 8.5; they may well be. But at least this procedure yields a contract that satisfies these restrictions and Pareto dominates the borrowing–lending scheme. Moreover, considerable intuition is provided for the nature of an (unrestricted) optimum.

As a matter of notation it is convenient to let $p_1 = \rho$ and $p_2 = \alpha\rho$. Then the incentive compatibility conditions (8.15) and (8.16) can be written as

$$\begin{aligned} U(y'+\rho) - U(y'-\rho) &\geqslant EU(y_2+\alpha\rho) - EU(y_2-\alpha\rho) \\ &\geqslant U(y''+\rho) - U(y''-\rho) \end{aligned} \tag{8.25}$$

from the left and right inequalities respectively. Under the simplifying assumptions (8.25) is equivalent to

$$\frac{U'(y')}{U'(\bar{y})} \geqslant \alpha \geqslant \frac{U'(y'')}{U'(\bar{y})} \tag{8.26}$$

where $\bar{y} = (y'' + y')/2$. It should be noted that (8.26) is independent of ρ. Also, both sides of (8.26) cannot hold as equalities, and thus only one incentive compatibility condition can be binding. Also note that under the symmetry restrictions (8.17) is satisfied identically and can be dropped as an explicit constraint in problem 8.5; though transfers need not be balanced over time, expected transfers are zero. Finally the objective function can be written

$$\begin{aligned} &\tfrac{1}{2}\{U(y'+\rho) + \tfrac{1}{2}U(y'-\alpha\rho) + \tfrac{1}{2}U(y''-\alpha\rho)\} \\ &\quad + \tfrac{1}{2}\{U(y''-\rho) + \tfrac{1}{2}U(y'+\alpha\rho) + \tfrac{1}{2}U(y''+\alpha\rho)\} \end{aligned} \tag{8.27}$$

Differentiating (8.27) with respect to α subject to both inequalities in (8.26) yields

$$\begin{aligned} &-\tfrac{1}{4}U'(y'-\alpha\rho)\rho - \tfrac{1}{4}U'(y''-\alpha\rho)\rho + \tfrac{1}{4}U'(y'+\alpha\rho)\rho \\ &\quad + \tfrac{1}{4}U'(y''+\alpha\rho)\rho + \mu - \lambda = 0 \end{aligned} \tag{8.28}$$

Under the simplifying assumptions the expression in marginal utilities on the left-hand side of (8.28) is negative; thus the nonnegative Lagrange multipliers λ and μ for the left and right inequalities in (8.26) must satisfy $\mu > 0$, $\lambda = 0$. (Recall that both cannot be positive.) Thus the only binding incentive compatibility constraint in this (restricted) optimum must be (8.16), at the high realization $y_1 = y''$. Thus from (8.26)

$$0 < \alpha = \frac{U'(y'')}{U'(\bar{y})} < 1 \tag{8.29}$$

The transfer ρ can be found by differentiating (8.27) with respect to ρ, which yields the solution

$$\rho = \frac{y'' - y'}{2(1 + \alpha^2)} \tag{8.30}$$

It may now be clearer how the (restricted) optimum dominates the borrowing–lending scheme. The borrowing–lending scheme is of course optimal conditional on the realizations of y_1, but it fails to take into account the *ex ante* risk associated with uncertainty over y_1. Now an obvious first step in the direction of improving the allocation of risk is to maximize *ex ante* expected utility of the risk-averse agent subject to the restriction that $\alpha = 1$, that is, that the transfer be balanced over time as in the borrowing–lending scheme. It turns out, though, that here the solution to that maximization problem, which in general might be termed the *ex ante* modified borrowing–lending scheme, is just the borrowing–lending scheme itself. However, the borrowing–lending scheme is never optimal – (further) movement toward a full-information first-period optimum is called for. That is, parameter ρ should be increased toward $(y'' - y')/2$ and parameter α decreased toward zero. Now this movement in α and ρ in a private-information optimum should not come as a surprise. After all, the borrowing–lending scheme was just a device to allow mutually beneficial trade in the context of private information. Borrowing–lending *per se* is not desirable; the full-information optimum is accomplished completely by risk-sharing arrangements. The movement toward complete first-period risk sharing in a private-information optimum is limited by the incentive of agent a to cheat at $y_1 = y''$. The greater is this incentive, as measured by values of $U'(y'')/U'(\bar{y})$, the greater is α, the more limited is first-period risk sharing, and the greater is the reliance on intertemporal tie-ins (of which borrowing–lending is an extreme case) to overcome incentive problems.

The welfare conclusions above may bring to mind some work on the inconsistency of optimal plans, for example, Kydland and Prescott (1977).

Suppose that in a dynamic context agents necessarily take the best possible action period by period conditioned on beginning-of-period state variables. Thus a global (multiperiod) optimum which requires that agents take nonmaximizing (inconsistent) actions period by period can be viewed as unattainable. To circumvent this problem, at least partially, it may be optimal to devise schemes or institutions under which agents constrain future actions, in effect tie themselves to the mast. Of course, these institutional constraints may well be binding as the future unfolds, but schemes without this property may not be *ex ante* (constrained) optima. Similarly, in this chapter it is natural to impose constraints which require truth telling, and thus a full-information Pareto optimal allocation may be viewed as unattainable. In this context the optimal *ex ante* arrangement is for agents to enter into multiperiod contracts which, in effect, constrain future actions. That is, as the future unfolds, there may well arise an event under which all agents may wish to renege on the arrangement. Simple borrowing–lending schemes which do not have that property are not *ex ante* private-information Pareto optimal.[14]

5 Multiperiod contracts and the discount rate

It has been established thus far that multiperiod contracts are mutually beneficial relative to a sequence of single-period contracts in the context of private information; that is, there is a variety of two-period contracts which Pareto improve upon autarky. However, it is equally clear that no two-period contract, or T-period contract for that matter, can achieve the utility of a full-information optimum; recall the implication of the last-period incentive compatibility condition that the last-period trade be noncontingent. It is in this sense that agents cannot completely overcome the barriers to trade introduced by private information. These results do raise the question, though, of whether agents can approach arbitrarily close to the utility of a full-information optimum as contract length is extended to infinity. It turns out that this question can be answered affirmatively if agents do not discount the future. To see this, take advantage of the trivial insight that as contract length T approaches infinity, approximately a fraction Π of the realizations under the endowment sequence $\{y_t\}$ will be y' and $1-\Pi$ will be y''. Therefore, if the length T is such that ΠT is an integer, give agent a the option of claiming a low realization y', ΠT times in total, with each such claim effecting a transfer $c - y' \equiv d > 0$. If no claim is filed, agent a is to pay $y'' - c \equiv p > 0$. (Here c is determined as the solution to the full-information Pareto problem, problem 8.2.) Under this T-period contract, agent a has an obvious strategy which turns out to be maximal in this case (essentially by Jensen's inequality): claim a low realization whenever it occurs until either there are no claims remaining (in which case no more claims are filed to the end of the contract) or there are as many claims remaining as time periods (in which case a claim is filed in each period to the end of the contract). It can be established formally (see Townsend, 1979*a*) that the average utilities for agents *a* and *b* under this strategy have the desired limits, namely

$$\bar{U} = \Pi U(y' + d) + (1 - \Pi) U(y'' - p)$$

and

$$\bar{V} = W - \Pi d + (1 - \Pi) p$$

respectively.[15]

But what if agents *do* discount the future? Though no formal proof is offered here, it seems likely that such strong asymptotic results are vulnerable. It is revealing to note, for example, that the specified strategy of agent *a* in the contract just described would not be maximizing for sufficiently large T; a better strategy would be to claim that the first ΠT realizations are low, effecting the transfer $c - y' > 0$. (The gain or loss of utility in the last $(1 - \Pi)T$ periods would matter little.) Nor would agent *b* be indifferent to the timing of claims. More generally, the nonexistence of an asymptotically full-information optimal contract would not come as a surprise; in many private-information contexts, full-information optimal allocations cannot be achieved, and here as well discounting might push agents back toward the best one-shot arrangements. Asymptotic results aside, however, the theory of multiperiod contracts being developed here is not vulnerable to discounting. As is now indicated, every major result of the chapter is valid when agents discount the future. In particular, private information can still serve to explain the existence of multiperiod contracts, though the nature of contracts can be affected.

To begin this discussion, suppose that both agents discount future utility at rate β, $0 < \beta < 1$. (More technically, suppose that β^t enters as a multiplicative factor on the t-period utilities of agents *a* and *b* and that time begins at $t = 0$.) Then it is straightforward to establish that the properties of a full-information optimal allocation will remain unchanged: the consumption of the risk-averse agent should be a constant over both time and endowment realizations. Similarly, the full-information utility possibilities frontier will be unchanged essentially, with utilities scaled by the factor $1/(1 - \beta)$, and any point on (a restricted portion of) this frontier could be supported with the same sequence of one-period contracts. Again, the introduction of private information is damning: with one-period contracts there would be no trade (the incentive compatibility conditions remain unchanged apart from the factors β^t – in particular (8.10) has a β^T on both sides of the equation). However, there would still exist gains to trade under a two-period borrowing–lending scheme with interest rate r determined by $1 + r = 1/\beta$; in this case

$$d(y') = \frac{(y'' - y')\beta}{2(1+\beta)}$$

$$d(y'') = \frac{(y' - y'')\beta}{2(1+\beta)}$$

Also, by a proof virtually identical with the one in section 4, such borrowing–lending schemes are not private-information Pareto optimal. In fact, for the quadratic utility example in section 4, a (restricted) private-information optimum, characterized by the parameters ρ and α, takes the form

$$0 < \alpha = \frac{U'(y'')}{\beta U'(\bar{y})} < \frac{1}{\beta}$$

$$\rho = \frac{(y'' - y')}{2(1 + \beta\alpha^2)}$$

Here again the *ex ante* modified borrowing–lending scheme with $\alpha = 1/\beta$ does not produce an increase in welfare over the simple borrowing–lending scheme, but again less extreme intertemporal tie-ins and more complete first-period risk sharing are called for. It is interesting to note, however, that the more the future is discounted (the lower is β), the greater is the incentive to cheat at $y_1 = y''$, that is, the greater is α (though α remains a specified fraction of the rate $1/\beta$), and the less complete is first-period risk sharing, that is, the lower is ρ. Thus the more the future is discounted, the less effective are intertemporal tie-ins in overcoming incentive problems. This alters the nature of the optimal contract.

Appendix

Given some T-period contract $\{M_t(m^{t-1})\}_{t=1}^T$, $\{F_t(m^{t-1}, m_t)\}_{t=1}^T$, let $\{\sigma_t(m^{t-1}, y_t)\}_{t=1}^T$ solve problem 8.3. Let $W_t(m^{t-1})$ denote the total expected utility of agent a from periods t through T, as of the beginning of period t, prior to the realization of y_t, under the maximizing decision rules $\{\sigma_s(m^{s-1}, y_s)\}_{s=t}^T$. The sequence $\{W_t(m^{t-1})\}_{t=1}^T$ must satisfy the functional equation

$$W_t(m^{t-1}) = \sum_{y_t} \Pr(y_t)\left[\max_{m_t \in M_t(m^{t-1})} U\{y_t + F_t(m^{t-1}, m_t)\} + W_{t+1}(m^{t-1}, m_t)\right]$$

with $W_{T+1} \equiv 0$. Then since $\sigma_t(m^{t-1}, y_t)$ is maximizing given the realization y_t, it follows that

$$U[\tilde{y}_t + F_t\{m^{t-1}, \sigma_t(m^{t-1}, \tilde{y}_t)\}] + W_{t+1}\{m^{t-1}, \sigma_t(m^{t-1}, \tilde{y}_t)\}$$
$$\geqslant U[\tilde{y}_t + F_t\{m^{t-1}, \sigma_t(m^{t-1}, \hat{y}_t)\}] + W_{t+1}\{m^{t-1}, \sigma_t(m^{t-1}, \hat{y}_t)] \tag{8.A1}$$

for all m^{t-1} and for all $\tilde{y}_t, \hat{y}_t \in \{y', y''\}$. Note that on the right-hand side of (8.A1) the maximizing decision rule is evaluated at some counterfactual realization $\hat{y}_t$. Thus (8.A1) expresses a crucial incentive compatibility condition: prescribed decision rules for the agent with private information must be consistent with maximization.

The sequence $\{m_t^*(y^t)\}_{t=1}^T$ of messages generated under the specified contract can be defined recursively by

$$m_t^*(y^t) = \sigma_t\{m^{*t-1}(y^{t-1}), y_t\} \tag{8.A2}$$

The sequence of generated trades is then simply $[F_t\{m^{*t}(y^t)\}]_{t=1}^T$. Now (8.A1) can be evaluated along any of these generated paths to yield

$$U(\tilde{y}_t + F_t[m^{*t-1}(y^{t-1}), \sigma_t\{m^{*t-1}(y^{t-1}), \tilde{y}_t\}])$$
$$+ W_{t+1}[m^{*t-1}(y^{t-1}), \sigma_t\{m^{*t-1}(y^{t-1}), \tilde{y}_t\}]$$
$$\geqslant U(\tilde{y}_t + F_t[m^{*t-1}(y^{t-1}), \sigma_t\{m^{*t-1}(y^{t-1}), \hat{y}_t\}])$$
$$+ W_{t+1}[m^{*t-1}(y^{t-1}), \sigma_t\{m^{*t-1}(y^{t-1}), \hat{y}_t\}] \tag{8.A3}$$

for all y^{t-1} and all $\tilde{y}_t, \hat{y}_t \in \{y', y''\}$. Now consider an alternative game. Define $\hat{M}_t(m^{t-1}, m_t) \equiv \{y', y''\}$ and define

$$\hat{F}_t(y^{t-1}, y_t) \equiv F_t[m^{*t-1}(y^{t-1}), \sigma_t\{m^{*t-1}(y^{t-1}), y_t\}] \tag{8.A4}$$

for all possible named values y^{t-1}, y_t. Let $X_t(y^{t-1})$ denote the total expected utility of agent a in this alternative game as of the beginning of time t through time T, prior to the realization y_t, as a function of previous messages y^{t-1} under the truth-telling decision rules $\hat{\sigma}_s(y^{s-1}, y_s) = y_s$, $s = t, t+1, \ldots, T$, with $X_{T+1} \equiv 0$. Now it can be verified using the recursion formulas defining $m_t^*(y^t)$ and the definition (8.A4) that

$$W_{t+1}[m^{*t-1}(y^{t-1}), \sigma_t\{m^{*t-1}(y^{t-1}), \tilde{y}_t\}] = X_{t+1}(y^{t-1}, \tilde{y}_t) \tag{8.A5}$$

and similarly for $\hat{y}_t$. Substituting (8.A5) and (8.A4) into (8.A3) generates

$$U\{\tilde{y}_t + \hat{F}_t(y^{t-1}, \tilde{y}_t)\} + X_{t+1}(y^{t-1}, \tilde{y}_t) \geq U\{\tilde{y}_t + \hat{F}_t(y^{t-1}, \hat{y}_t)\} + X_{t+1}(y^{t-1}, \hat{y}_t) \tag{8.A6}$$

for all y^{t-1} and for all $\tilde{y}_t, \hat{y}_t \in \{y', y''\}$. That is, the truth-telling decision rule is maximizing for agent a in this alternative game (work backward from period T). If this decision rule is applied from $t = 1$ onward, it is clear that the sequence of announced endowment values will equal the sequence of actual realizations. Relationship (8.A4) then guarantees the desired result.

Notes

1 There is of course some literature on multiperiod contracts which does not exploit informational asymmetries: for example, the matching models of Diamond and Maskin (1979), the labor-turnover model of Jovanovic (1979), the limited labor mobility model of Baily (1977), Barro (1977), and Bryant (1979), and the contingency cost models of Riddle (1979) and Dye (1980).

2 Occasionally these considerations are so severe as to rule out any trade or contract whatever (for example Radner, 1968; Arrow, 1974; Townsend, 1979b, this volume, ch. 5).

3 A difference between the approach in this chapter and the approach of supergames should be pointed out, however. In oligopoly contexts, for example, explicit collusion, that is, an agreement to fix outputs, is presumed to be inherently unenforceable even if there is full information. In contrast, in the spirit of this chapter any game or contract which restricts actions is viable if it is consistent with the information structure. But with private information, this is not enough to ensure a full-information optimal allocation. This is where the concept of future retaliation comes into play.

4 The idea here is to produce a model in which there are obvious gains to trade, at least under full information: the risk-neutral agent can absorb all risk. Less extreme (more general) hypotheses could be tolerated in much of what follows, but at the cost of an increase in the complexity of notation, techniques, and exposition. In a way the entire chapter can be viewed as an illustrative example, not as an attempt at maximum generality.

5 Thus in this chapter we extend to a simple dynamic model some earlier results on private information for essentially static environments (Harris and Townsend, 1978, this volume, ch. 6; 1981, this volume, ch. 7; Myerson, 1979). More generally, in this chapter we build on the seminal work of Hurwicz (1972).

6 Typically, the average-utility criterion is used in the literature without discounting.

7 It is assumed, in the case of indifference, that agent a continues to tell the truth. The argument here and below ignores nonnegativity constraints on consumption.

8 Needless to say, this implication need not be so severe; trade may be possible if

there is more than one commodity. The point to be made here is that private information can make a difference in the consideration of contract length.

9 Here m^0 is some fixed number so that $M_1(m^0)$ denotes a fixed message space; similar notation applies at $t = 1$ in what follows.

10 There is some obvious intuition behind the truth-telling theorem for the class of announcement games in a single-period context. Suppose that y' occurs and agent a says y'' and is transferred A, while when y'' occurs agent a says y' and is transferred B. Then just change the payoff so that A is the transfer if y' is reported and B is the transfer if y'' is reported. For additional discussion and general proofs of the truth-telling theorem in static contexts see Harris and Townsend (1978, this volume, ch. 6; 1981, this volume, ch. 7) and Myerson (1979).

11 Of course, this result is limited by the class of games under consideration. Prescott and Townsend (1984, this volume, ch. 17), among others, have shown in other contexts that random exchanges may be beneficial. Whether or not they are here is left as an open question.

12 This is a strong hint that only (8.16) will be binding in an optimum.

13 We are much indebted to Gerald Faulhaber for suggesting the quadratic example which follows. It is assumed, of course, that the utility function is strictly increasing in the relevant range, and for the purpose of the analysis which follows the assumption that $U'(0) = \infty$ is dropped.

14 Here, however, unlike Kydland and Prescott (1977), schemes requiring agents to take arbitrary actions period by period are perfectly enforceable if they are consistent with the information structure (see note 3).

15 The T-period version of the two-period borrowing–lending scheme discussed in the previous section is also asymptotically optimal; again, see Townsend (1979*a*).

References

Arrow, K.J. (1953) Le rôle des valeurs boursières pour la répartition la meilleure des risques. In *Econometrie*, pp. 41–8. Paris: Centre Nationale de la Recherche Scientifique.

—— (1974) Limited knowledge and economic analysis. *American Economic Review* 64, 1–10.

Azariadis, C. (1975) Implicit contracts and underemployment equilibria. *Journal of Political Economy* 83(6), 1183–202.

Baily, M.N. (1977) On the theory of layoffs and unemployment. *Econometrica* 45, 1043–63.

Barro, R.J. (1977) Long-term contracting, sticky prices, and monetary policy. *Journal of Monetary Economics* 3, 305–16.

Bewley, T.F. (1977) The permanent income hypothesis: a theoretical foundation. *Journal of Economic Theory* 16, 252–92.

Bryant, J. (1979) A model of long-term contracts. Staff Report 47, Federal Reserve Bank of Minneapolis, Minneapolis, MN.

Carlton, D.W. (1979) Contracts, price rigidity, and market equilibrium. *Journal of Political Economy* 87(5), 1034–62.

Debreu, G. (1959) *Theory of Value: An Axiomatic Analysis of Economic Equilibrium.* New York: Wiley for Cowles Foundation.

Diamond P.A. and Maskin, E. (1979) An equilibrium analysis of search and breach of contract. I. Steady states. *Bell Journal of Economics* 10, 282–316.

Dye, R.A. (1979) Optimal contract length. Working Paper, Carnegie–Mellon University, Pittsburgh, PA.

—— (1980) Contract span and specification costs. Working Paper, Carnegie–Mellon University, Pittsburgh, PA.

Fischer, S. (1977a) Long-term contracts, rational expectations, and the optimal money supply rule. *Journal of Political Economy* 85(1), 191–205.

—— (1977b) Long-term contracting, sticky prices, and monetary policy: a comment. *Journal of Monetary Economics* 3, 317–23.

—— (1979) Wage-indexation and macroeconomic stability. *Journal of Monetary Economics* 5, 107–47.

Friedman, J.W. (1977) *Oligopoly and the Theory of Games.* Amsterdam: North-Holland.

Gordon, D.F. (1974) A neo-classical theory of Keynesian unemployment. *Economic Inquiry* 12, 431–59.

Gray, J.A. (1976) Wage indexation: a macroeconomic approach. *Journal of Monetary Economics* 2, 221–35.

—— (1978) On indexation and contract length. *Journal of Political Economy* 86(1), 1–18.

Green, E.J. (1980) Noncooperative price taking in large dynamic markets. *Journal of Economic Theory* 22, 155–82.

Harris, M. and Townsend, R.M. (1978) Allocation mechanisms for asymmetrically informed agents. GSIA Working Paper 35-76-77. Carnegie–Mellon University, Pittsburgh, PA. Reprinted in this volume as chapter 6.

—— and —— (1981) Resource allocation under asymmetric information. *Econometrica* 49, 33–64. Reprinted in this volume as chapter 7.

Hotelling, H. (1929) Stability in competition. *Economic Journal* 39, 41–57.

Hurwicz, L. (1972) On informationally decentralized systems. In *Decision and Organization*, eds C.B. McGuire and R. Radner, ch. 14. Amsterdam: North-Holland.

Jovanovic, B. (1979) Job matching and the theory of turnover. *Journal of Political Economy* 87(5), 972–90.

Kydland, F.E. and Prescott, E.C. (1977) Rules rather than discretion: the inconsistency of optimal plans. *Journal of Political Economy* 85(3), 473–92.

Means, G. (1935) Industrial prices and their relative inflexibility. US Congress, Senate, *Document 13*, 74th Congress, 1st session.

Myerson, R.B. (1979) Incentive compatibility and the bargaining problem. *Econometrica* 47, 61–74.

Phelps, E.S. (1970) Introduction: the new microeconomics in employment and inflation theory. In *Microeconomic Foundations of Employment and Inflation Theory*, E.S. Phelps et al. New York: Norton.

—— and Taylor, J.B. (1977) Stabilizing powers of monetary policy under rational expectations. *Journal of Political Economy* 85(1), 163–90.

Prescott, E.C. and Townsend, R.M. (1984) General competitive analysis in an economy with private information. *International Economic Review* 25(1), 1–20. Reprinted in this volume as chapter 17.

Radner, R. (1968) Competitive equilibrium under uncertainty. *Econometrica* 36, 31–58.

—— (1980) Collusive behavior in noncooperative epsilon-equilibria of oligopolies with long but finite lives. *Journal of Economic Theory* 22, 136–54.

—— (1981) Monitoring cooperative agreements in a repeated principal–agent relationship. *Econometrica* 49, 1127–48.

Riddle, W. (1979) A theory of the length of economic contracts. Working Paper, University of Alberta, Edmonton.

Rubinstein, A. and Yaari, M. (1980) Repeated insurance contracts and moral hazard. Research Memorandum 3, Hebrew University, Jerusalem.

Sargent, T.J. and Wallace, N. (1975) "Rational" expectations, the optimal monetary instrument, and the optimal money supply rule. *Journal of Political Economy* 83(2), 241–54.

Schechtman, J. (1976) An income fluctuation problem. *Journal of Economic Theory* 12, 218–41.

Stigler, G.J. and Kindahl, J.K. (1970) *The Behavior of Industrial Prices.* New York: Columbia University Press for National Bureau of Economic Research.

Taylor, J.B. (1980) Aggregate dynamics and staggered contracts. *Journal of Political Economy* 88(1), 1–23.

Townsend, R.M. (1979a) Contract length and the gain from enduring relationships. Working Paper, Carnegie-Mellon University, Pittsburgh, PA.

—— (1979b) Optimal contracts and competitive markets with costly state verification. *Journal of Economic Theory* 21(2), 265–93. Reprinted in this volume as chapter 5.

Yaari, M.E. (1976) A law of large numbers in the theory of consumer's choice under uncertainty. *Journal of Economic Theory* 12, 202–17.

Part IV
Limited Communication as a Key Element in Economic Organization

9
Economic Organization with Limited Communication

In environments that have spatial separation and private information, beneficial multilateral arrangements can depend critically on agents' ability to communicate values of contemporary shocks to one another and to keep track of histories of past transfers or past-announced shocks. In this chapter we formalize this idea and focus on communication-accounting systems. The theory in this chapter allows a formal stylized representation of a variety of systems and allows us to make precise the sense in which various sytems are more or less limited. Oral assignment systems, portable object systems, written message systems, and telecommunication systems are considered.

In its method this chapter follows the literature on contract theory and mechanism design, of Myerson (1979), Harris and Townsend (1981, this volume, ch. 7), and Townsend (1982, this volume, ch. 8), for example, stressing private information and incentives. The idea, essentially, is to specify the agents' endowments and preferences and the production technology available to them, and to be precise about the information structure. Then, rather than imposing a fixed-contract form or fixed-resource-allocation scheme, we consider a broad class of arrangements and determine the constraints implied by private information. We then go on to determine Pareto optimal

Reprinted from *American Economic Review* 77(5), 1987, 954–71. I gratefully acknowledge all helpful comments from the participants of workshops at Carnegie–Mellon University, the University of Chicago, Cornell University, the Federal Reserve Bank of Minneapolis, the University of Iowa, the University of Pennsylvania, the University of Rochester, Stanford University, the University of Virginia, the University of Western Ontario, the University of Wisconsin, and students in Economics 339 at the University of Chicago, the excellent research and computational assistance from Christopher Phelan, and financial research support from the Alfred P. Sloan Foundation and the National Science Foundation grants SES-8406771 and SES-8708242.

arrangements by maximizing weighted sums of the agents' utilities, subject to the obvious resource constraints and these derived, information, incentive compatibility constraints.

In this chapter this method is taken one step further by making explicit both the agents' locations at various times and the technology of communication available to agents over space and time. Exogenous variations in the technology of communication thus cause endogenous variations in the derived incentive constraints and, in this way, in the context of the class of maximization problems, we can capture formally the idea that communication systems matter and that particular systems may be more or less limited. Indeed, oral assignment systems, portable object systems, written message systems, and electronic telecommunication systems can be ordered; these are successively less limited.

The communication-accounting systems considered in this chapter are motivated by observations from "simpler" historical and contemporary economies. Oral communication systems are those in which agents must literally meet each other in order to give instructions to one another or to execute some prespecified arrangement. For example, banking at the beginning of the commercial revolution in Europe took the form of an oral assignment system, as described by Usher (1943). Both the buyer and the seller of a good had to appear before the banker of the seller, and instructions were given to the banker for the transfer of the buyer's account to the seller.

Communication systems with portable tokens are those in which agents receive or surrender tokens at various spatially dispersed locations as evidence of actions taken or claims made under some prespecified arrangement. In the Second World War crucial commodities were apparently rationed in this way, with coupons providing evidence to the seller that the consumer was "entitled" to the good and providing evidence to the government that the seller was in compliance with limited sale provisions. As another instance of the use of tokens, it seems that taverns in England in the 1600s handed out idiosyncratic tokens as small change, entitling the customer, or anyone else, to future purchases. Credit could also be granted with the handing out of such tokens. In an apparently related manner, workers in coal mining towns in West Virginia or in textile mills in South Carolina received company scrip, entitling them to foods and other purchases at the company store. Multiple-token systems may have been in widespread use in some economies at one time. The anthropologists Firth (1939), Malinowski (1953), and Baric (1964) report on ceremonial exchanges in "simpler" economies involving the transfer of prespecified goods for prespecified objects such as shells and fishhooks, perhaps to encourage production and distribution of prespecified goods or to encourage location assignments for certain agents.

Communication systems with writing seem commonplace. A mundane but familiar example is the use of customer pickup orders, which the customer carries from the checkout cashier, where payment is made, to the warehouse department. The papers that a patient hand carries in a hospital as orders for services in various decentralized clinics are related. Similar also are the papers that circulate in firms – written orders for materials from internal stocks. Checks are written messages sent to one's banker, and bills of exchange are written messages to one's trading partner. Telecommunication systems are more familiar recently, with electronic interspatial verification of credit and bank balances.

Unfortunately, real-world examples bring in important complications, such as limited commitment and default possibilities. The theory is not ready for these complications. In fact the theoretical literature that allows us to begin to think about communication-accounting systems, even without these complications, is not large. The purpose of this chapter, then, is to attempt to bring the theory up to speed by consideration of simple prototype environments, starting with the premise of perfect costless enforcement and varying communication technologies exogenously. More limited commitment possibilities, and the interaction of these with communication systems, are then addressed toward the end of the chapter. This leaves more detailed applied work and the requisite modifications of the theory to subsequent research efforts.

The literature related to the research reported here is that on limited communication in resource-allocation mechanisms (for example, Hurwicz, 1972; Mount and Reiter, 1974). However, the formal approaches differ considerably. Here spatial separation is made explicit and the messages are restricted by whether agents can talk to one another and by the objects that agents carry from place to place. Other related literature has to do with the interaction between communication-accounting systems and money. Gale (1980) makes reference to paper assets as accounting devices in a world with a continuum of agents and a limited social planner. However, he focuses on conditions sufficient to ensure that allocations of sequential competitive equilibria with valued money are equivalent to full-information (incentive compatible) Pareto optimal allocations. Here the focus is on private-information Pareto optimal allocations in worlds with spatial separation and explicit limited communication, in which various kinds of financial systems are associated with various kinds of communication systems. No effort is made here to decentralize these optima. Of course the idea that money reflects some decentralization in the exchange process appears frequently in the literature. We should note here in particular the work of Brunner and Meltzer (1971), in which money emerges in a world with an uneven distribution of information by reducing somehow the costs of acquiring information and of constructing transaction chains. Also related to this is the work of Ostroy (1973) and Ostroy and Starr (1974), in which trading rules are said to be decentralized to the extent that they do not depend on past histories. Again, in this chapter we use explicit communication technologies to determine the extent to which agents can use past histories, and contemporary announcements in distinct locations, in their trading rules.

Briefly, the chapter proceeds as follows. Section 1 illustrates the role for communication when there is private information, expositing the contract-theoretic mechanism design approach to the determination of Pareto optimal allocations. This is done in the context of a two-agent one-period pure exchange economy with privately observed shocks to preferences. Section 2 extends the two-agent one-period environment to one with two periods and concentrates on the possible gain from intertemporal links. Section 3 extends the two-agent two-period environment to one with four agents and two locations and delivers examples of beneficial quadrilateral arrangements, at least if there is full communication. Section 4 then begins the analysis of limited communication systems, considering oral assignment systems first. A portable concealable object system is considered in section 5, and multiple portable tokens and written message systems are considered in section 6. Section 7 then analyzes the most powerful technology: costless interspatial electronic telecommunications. Section 8 modifies the basic environment somewhat to show how portable concealable tokens and written messages can serve as location-assignment devices. Section 9 returns to the basic environment, but eliminates explicit randomness to show how portable tokens can serve as a device for enforcement. Section 10 concludes the analysis with some comments on privately observed random endowments.

1 Pareto optimal arrangements with private information but with perfect costless enforcement

For an economy specified at the level of preferences, endowments, and technology, and satisfying a few regularity conditions, we can derive Pareto optimal allocations as solutions to programming problems. That is, if utility functions of agents are concave, if more is preferred to less, and if consumption sets and production-storage technologies are convex, then the utilities possibilities frontier is concave with respect to the origin and contains no "flat" or "horizontal" segments. In that case, any Pareto optimal allocation is associated with a point on the frontier and therefore with some set of weights associated with a supporting hyperplane. Thus the problem of maximizing a particular weighted sum of agents' utilities subject to constraints implied by resources and technology yields, as at least one of its solutions, the Pareto point in question. Any solution to such a programming problem, with arbitrary weights, is necessarily Pareto optimal.

In this chapter we envision the set of institutions of an economy and the allocations that such institutions deliver as being Pareto optimal for the environment of the economy. Thus it is as if all agents of the economy agreed at some initial date to solve one of the programming problems described above, somehow coming to an agreement about what weights to impose. Further, we might assume full commitment, that is, perfect and costless enforcement, so that *ex post* the agents just carry out the socially sanctioned plan. Finally, as Arrow (1953) and Debreu (1959) have emphasized, uncertainty, time and dynamics, and separation of agents in space will not alter this picture of the determination of optimal arrangements if we retain the perfect costless enforcement premise (and do not simultaneously introduce some fundamental nonconvexities).

A feature of this programming approach to the determination of optimal arrangements is that there is nothing for agents to communicate over time. Even the realizations of the random variables of the model need not be communicated because, by assumption, such states of the world are observed by everyone and have been incorporated into the prespecified agreement to allocate labor to production, to transfer goods, and to reallocate agents over space. To allow for communication then, that is, to allow for a discussion of communication-accounting systems, something must be done to alter the model.

The alteration discussed at length in this chapter is the incorporation of private information. That is, in addition to uncertainty, realizations of some of the random variables of the model are presumed to be seen by subsets of agents only. Indeed, this is a natural way to allow for communication, because it is known from the work of Myerson (1979) and Harris and Townsend (1981, this volume, ch. 7) that programs for the determination of Pareto optimal allocations can be utilized if agents are given the opportunity to announce (communicate) values for the subset of random variables, the realizations of which they alone see. That is, we can impose without loss of generality incentive compatibility constraints which ensure that these privately observed realizations are announced truthfully.

Because this idea is at the heart of the analysis, it is best to review it here in the context of a relatively simple environment without any essential dynamics and without any spatial separation. Further, to avoid complications introduced by putting private information on quantities, something which will be contemplated later, it is best to begin by assuming privately observed and unverifiable shocks to preferences. The motive for trade in the planning period is insurance.

Thus imagine an economy with just two agents, a and b, and two time periods, a planning date and a consumption date. Agent a has an endowment e^a in the consumption date, which is a nonnegative vector of goods. Typically, we will consider cases in which there is only one or two goods, but the dimensions of e, and of consumptions below, can be arbitrary if finite. Agent a has preferences in the consumption date over consumption vector c^a as represented by the utility function $U^a(c^a, \theta^a)$. Here θ^a is a shock to a's preferences, observed by agent a alone at the beginning of the consumption date. Also, θ^a takes on values in some set Θ^a. Typically, set Θ^a contains two or three values, and each value is at most two-dimensional, but again the number of values and the dimension can be arbitrary if finite. Agent b has endowment e^b and preferences $U^b(c^b)$ in the consumption period. Utility functions are concave, and there is no production technology. Further, this structure is common knowledge. That is, everything is known up to shocks θ^a, presumed as of the planning period to occur with probabilities $p(\theta^a)$.

In the planning period both agents commit themselves to an allocation of the consumption goods in the consumption period contingent on agent a's announcement in the consumption period of the shocks that he has experienced. That is, both agents precommit to pool their endowments and redistribute the total under a prespecified plan. Further, as a technical matter, this shock contingent allocation rule can be a lottery $\pi(c|\theta^a)$ specifying the probability of consumption bundle $c = (c^a, c^b)$ to agents a and b. This will ensure that the programming problem is concave (actually linear), despite private information, though no essential use will be made of the lotteries in the solutions reported below. Thus if we let $C = \{c = (c^a, c^b); c^a + c^b \leqslant e^a + e^b\}$ denote the space of feasible consumptions, presumed for simplicity to be finite as if there were some indivisibility, the programming problem for the determination of Pareto optimal allocations is as follows.

Program 9.1

Maximize by choice of the $\pi(c|\theta^a)$ the objective function

$$\lambda^a \left\{ \sum_{\theta^a} p(\theta^a) \sum_c \pi(c|\theta^a) U^a(c^a, \theta^a) \right\} + \lambda^b \left\{ \sum_{\theta^a} p(\theta^a) \sum_c \pi(c|\theta^a) U^b(c^b) \right\} \quad (9.1)$$

subject to the incentive compatibility constraints

$$\sum_c \pi(c|\theta^a) U^a(c^a, \theta^a) \geqslant \sum_c \pi(c|\tilde{\theta}^a) U^a(c^a, \theta^a) \qquad \forall \theta^a, \tilde{\theta}^a \in \Theta^a \quad (9.2)$$

We can easily append onto this program *ex ante* participation constraints

$$\sum_\theta p(\theta^a) \sum_c \pi(c|\theta^a) U^a(c^a, \theta^a) \geqslant \sum_\theta p(\theta) U^a(e^a, \theta^a) \quad (9.3)$$

$$\sum_\theta p(\theta^a) \sum_c \pi(c|\theta^a) U^b(c^b) \geqslant U^b(e^b) \quad (9.4)$$

In fact, weights λ^a and λ^b will be chosen implicitly in the examples below by the presumption that the expected utility of agent a is maximized subject to constraint (9.4) for agent b.

Solutions to program 9.1 can be generated as solutions to linear programs, computed numerically. Two examples provide illustrations to be carried through the subsequent analysis. The first has only one consumption good; the second has two.

For the first example, the utility function of agent a is of the form

$$U^a(c, \theta^a) = (c)^{\theta^a}$$

so that agent a is risk averse for each parameter θ^a, with $\theta^a \in (0.4, 0.5, 0.6)$, each possibility occurring with probability 0.33. The utility function of agent b is of the form $U^b(c) = c$, so that b is risk neutral. Also let $e^a = e^b = 5$. Then, if the discrete use of the consumption space is ignored, the full-information solution would allocate the consumption good in such a way as to equate weighted marginal utilities over states. That is, agent a would receive the consumption good when he is urgent, at least at $\theta^a = 0.6$, and give it up when he is patient, at least at $\theta^a = 0.4$. In contrast, with private information the incentive constraints do not allow this dependence, and the solution degenerates to autarky (despite allowance for lotteries). This is natural since there is only one good and more is preferred to less. In this case, then, private information is quite damning to the social arrangement. Though trivial, the full-information and private-information solutions are reported in table 9.1.

For the second example there are two goods, denoted generically x and y, and θ is two dimensional. The utility function of agent a is of the form

$$U^a(c_x, c_y, \theta^a) = (c_x)^{\theta^a_x} + (c_y)^{\theta^a_y}$$

with $(\theta^a_x, \theta^a_y) \in \{(0.4, 0.6), (0.6, 0.4)\}$, and each possibility occurs with probability 0.5. Agent b continues to be linear, now in both goods. Endowments are $e^a_x = e^b_x = e^a_y = e^b_y = 5$. The full-information and private-information solutions are reported in table 9.2.

The full-information and private-information solutions are identical because the incentive constraints (9.2) are not binding; that is, with two commodities,

Table 9.1 Single-period solution, one good

Values for θ^a	c^a *(full information)*	c^a *(private information)*
0.4	2.2	5
0.5	4	5
0.6	8.8	5

Table 9.2 Single-period solution, two goods

Values for θ_x^a, θ_y^a	(c_x^a, c_y^a) *(full information)*	(c_x^a, c_y^a) *(private information)*
(0.4, 0.6)	(2, 8)	(2. 8)
(0.6, 0.4)	(8, 2)	(8, 2)

goods can be assigned optimally in such a way that agent a self-selects. (There is some *ex ante* beneficial insurance associated with the solution.)

Again, there is presumed to be perfect costless enforcement of a selected *ex ante* optimal arrangement. It seems best to take this as given, if only as an approximation, without spelling out the mechanics of the enforcement procedure. Otherwise, without any enforcement mechanism, we must assume full commitment: agents a and b must show up at the consumption date; agents a and b must pool their endowments then as if these had to be placed on preset conveyors, activated by weight; agent a is restricted to announce one value for θ^a in the set Θ^a, as if a computer were programmed to accept one of a prespecified set of values; consumption is re-allocated on the conveyors in accordance with the announced value θ^a and the preset computer program; finally, agents eat in private without redistribution. Such a technology may read more as science fiction than as realistic economics, but it is important to note that in principle there could exist a transfer function, message space technology that would allow a solution to a socially optimal program to be implemented. That is, private information is the only impediment to trade.

2 Multiperiod arrangements and the gain from intertemporal links

The analysis above is easily extended to accommodate some nontrivial dynamics. In particular, suppose agents a and b remained paired with each other over two consumption dates t, $t = 1, 2$. Let preference shocks be experienced by agent a at the beginning of date t. That is, let shock θ_1^a enter into the utility function of agent a at date $t = 1$ and let shock θ_2^a enter into the utility function of agent a at date $t = 2$. However, some persistence in shocks is allowed. That is, $\theta_2^a = f(\theta_1^a, \delta)$, where f is a deterministic function and δ is a nondegenerate random variable, possibly dependent on θ_1^a. This allows, as a special case, no direct intertemporal links in shocks apart from Markov dependence in the probabilities $p(\theta_2^a | \theta_1^a)$. Let e_t^a and e_t^b denote the vectors of endowments of agents a and b at dates t, $t = 1, 2$, assumed for simplicity not to vary with date t. Here and below let β denote the common discount rate for time-separable utilities.[1] Finally, let $\pi_1(c | \theta_1^a)$ denote the allocation rule at date 1 and $\pi_2(c|\theta_1^a, \theta_2^a)$ denote the allocation rule at date 2, both of these specifying probabilities on set $C = \{c = (c^a, c^b), c^a + c^b \leqslant e^a + e^b\}$ as before, still assuming no storage. Then the program for the determination of a private-information Pareto optimal arrangement is as follows.

Program 9.2

Maximize by choice of $\pi_1(c|\theta_1^a)$ and $\pi_2(c|\theta_1^a, \theta_2^a)$ the objective function

$$\begin{aligned}&\lambda^a \left\{ \sum_{\theta_1^a} p(\theta_1^a) \sum_c \pi_1(c|\theta_1^a) U^a(c^a, \theta_1^a) + \beta \sum_{\theta_1^a} p(\theta_1^a) \sum_{\theta_2^a} p(\theta_2^a|\theta_1^a) \right.\\ &\quad \left. \times \sum_c \pi_2(c|\theta_1^a, \theta_2^a) U^a(c^a, \theta_2^a) \right\} + \lambda^b \left\{ \sum_{\theta_1^a} p(\theta_1^a) \sum_c \pi_1(c|\theta_1^a) U^b(c^b) \right.\\ &\quad \left. + \beta \sum_{\theta_1^a} p(\theta_1^a) \sum_{\theta_2^a} p(\theta_2^a|\theta_1^a) \sum_c \pi_2(c|\theta_1^a, \theta_2^a) U^b(c^b) \right\} \end{aligned} \tag{9.5}$$

subject to incentive constraints at date $t = 2$, for all $\tilde{\theta}_1^a$ announcements in the past, for all actual contemporary values θ_2^a, and for all counterfactual announcements $\tilde{\theta}_2^a$,

$$\sum_c \pi_2(c|\tilde{\theta}_1^a, \theta_2^a) U^a(c^a, \theta_2^a) \geqslant \sum_c \pi_2(c|\tilde{\theta}_1^a, \tilde{\theta}_2^a) U^a(c^a, \theta_2^a) \tag{9.6}$$

and subject to incentive constraints at date $t = 1$ for θ_1^a actuals and $\tilde{\theta}_1^a$ counterfactuals,

$$\begin{aligned}&\sum_c U^a(c^a, \theta_1^a) \pi_1(c|\theta_1^a) + \beta \sum_{\theta_2^a} p(\theta_2^a|\theta_1^a) \sum_c U^a(c^a, \theta_2^a) \pi_2(c|\theta_1^a, \theta_2^a)\\ &\geqslant \sum_c U^a(c^a, \theta_1^a) \pi_1(c|\tilde{\theta}_1^a) + \beta \sum_{\theta_2^a} p(\theta_2^a|\theta_1^a) \sum_c U^a(c^a, \theta_2^a) \pi_2(c|\tilde{\theta}_1^a, \theta_2^a)\end{aligned} \tag{9.7}$$

What bears emphasis in this program is the possible dependence of allocation rule at date $t = 2$ on the announcement of parameter θ_1^a at date 1. Indeed, assume that there is only one good, so that beneficial trade under private information is difficult, as the no-insurance autarkic private-information solution of table 9.1 emphasizes. Assume further, to bias the case against intertemporal tie-ins, that there is no functional persistence in the preference shocks and no Markov dependence in probabilities. That is, each shock is drawn with equal likelihood in each period. Still, as shown in table 9.3, for the environment of table 9.1, there is some insurance at date $t = 1$ (but not at date $t = 2$) achieved by intertemporal dependence.

Table 9.3 Multiperiod private-information solution, one good[a]

Values for θ_1^a	c^a *at date 1*	*Values for* θ_2^a	c^a *at date 2*
0.4	3.1	0.4	6.55
		0.5	6.55
		0.6	6.55
0.5	5.1	0.4	4.87
		0.5	4.87
		0.6	4.87
0.6	7.25	0.4	3.1
		0.5	3.1
		0.6	3.1

[a] See note 1.

This dependence does not appear in the full-information full-insurance solution, the full-information solution of table 9.1 reported twice, once for each period. In fact, this dependence would not appear in the full-information solution even with nontrivial Markov probabilities, since the full-information rule remains the same: allocate consumptions so as to equate weighted marginal utilities for every contemporary state. The private-information solution displays dependence because intertemporal tie-ins are used to circumvent the damning effects of the incentive constraints; low consumption at date $t = 1$ is tied to high consumption at date $t = 2$, and conversely. Again, this allows for some insurance.

With two (or more) goods, the date $t = 1$ incentive constraints are not so damning. In fact, as is evident from table 9.2, it is possible to construct examples without binding incentive constraints at date 1 and, if there were no persistence in shocks, intertemporal tie-ins would not be needed. However, persistence in shocks can deliver intertemporal tie-ins. For example, assume that there are two goods at each date. The utility function of agent a at date 1 is of the form

$$U^a(c_x, c_y, \theta_1^a) = (c_x)^{\theta_{1x}^a} + (c_y)^{\theta_{1y}^a}$$

with

$$(\theta_{1x}^a, \theta_{1y}^a) \in \{(0.4, 0.6), (0.6, 0.4)\}$$

each with equal probability, and the utility function at date 2 is of the form

$$U^a(c_x, c_y, \theta_2^a) = (c_x)^{(1-\theta_{1x}^a)\delta_x} + (c_y)^{(1-\theta_{1y}^a)\delta_y} = (c_x)^{\theta_{2x}^a} + (c_y)^{\theta_{2y}^a}$$

with

$$(\delta_x, \delta_y) = \begin{cases} (1,1) & \text{with probability } 0.96 \\ (0.5, 1.5) & \text{with probability } 0.02 \\ (1.5, 0.5) & \text{with probability } 0.02 \end{cases}$$

The solution is reported in table 9.4.[2] It should be noted that the family of allocations available for agent a at date 2 depends on the announced (and actual) parameter draw of agent a at date 1.

Regardless of how the tie-ins are generated, the private-information optimal solution is damaged if tie-ins are nót allowed, that is, if there were no record of preference shock announcements of agent a at date $t = 1$ (so that at most re-announcements are viable). For the one-good example above this is obvious; with no tie-ins there is no trade, and the solution is autarky for both periods. For the two-good example intratemporal re-allocations are still viable, as in the single-period solution of table 9.2. However, the absence of direct tie-ins would be associated with a loss of utility.[3]

It bears repetition that perfect and costless enforcement of the private-information optimal mechanism is still assumed. That is, neither agent can walk away from the agreed-upon arrangement at the end of date 1, and both are committed to comply with the multiperiod message space and transfer function requirements.

3 Optimal multilateral arrangements with spatial separation but full communication

With this investment in mechanism design, we can now extend the two-period model to include four agents and two locations, as a base for discussion of various communication-accounting systems in subsequent sections. This section focuses on the benefit from quadrilateral, rather than bilateral, arrangements.

Table 9.4 Multiperiod private- and full-information solution, two goods

Values for $(\theta^a_{1x}, \theta^a_{1y})$	(c^a_x, c^a_y)	Values for (δ_x, δ_y)	Values for $\theta^a_{2x}, \theta^a_{2y}$	$(c^a_x,$	$c^a_y)$
(0.4, 0.6)	(2, 8)	(1, 1)	(0.6, 0.4)	8.01	2.0
		(0.5, 1.5)	(0.3, 0.6)	1.0	8.0
		(1.5, 0.5)	(0.9, 0.2)	10.0	0.82
(0.6, 0.4)	(8, 2)	(1, 1)	(0.4, 0.6)	2.0	8.0
		(0.5, 1.5)	(0.2, 0.9)	0.82	10.0
		(1.5, 0.5)	(0.6, 0.3)	8.0	1.0

Table 9.5 Agent pairings in the four-agent two-location model

	Location	1	2
Date	1	(a, b)	(a′, b′)
	2	(a, b′)	(a′, b)

The four-agent two-location two-period model is like the two-agent (one-location) two-period model of section 2 except that there are two agents of type a, denoted a and a', and two agents of type b, denoted b and b'. Agent a is presumed to stay at location 1 over the two periods of his lifetime, and agent a' stays at location 2. But agents b and b' switch locations between dates 1 and 2, in accordance with table 9.5.

Agent a experiences privately observed preference shocks at the beginning of each date t, $t = 1, 2$, and similarly for agent a', and, until otherwise specified, the distribution determining shocks for agent a is independent of the distribution determining shocks for agent a'. Agents b and b' experience no shocks. The notation for endowments is as before, and for simplicity these do not vary over agents or over time.

With $\pi_{it}(\cdot)$ as general notation for the allocation rule for the two agents present at location i and date t, $i = 1, 2$, $t = 1, 2$, let $\pi_{11}(c|\theta_1^a)$ and $\pi_{12}(c|\theta_1^a, \theta_2^a)$ denote the probabilities of consumption bundle c in common space C in location 1 at dates 1 and 2 respectively, conditioned on the announcements of agent a and allowing intertemporal tie-ins. Also let $\pi_{21}(c|\theta_1^{a'})$ and $\pi_{22}(c|\theta_1^{a'}, \theta_2^{a'})$ denote the corresponding probabilities of consumption bundle c at location 2, conditioned on the announcements of agent a'. Then the program for the determination of private-information full-communication Pareto optimal allocations is as follows.

Program 9.3
Maximize by choice of the $\pi_{it}(\cdot)$ the objective function

$$\lambda^a \Big\{ \sum_{\theta_1^a} p(\theta_1^a) \sum_c \pi_{11}(c|\theta_1^a) U^a(c^a, \theta_1^a)$$

$$+ \beta \sum_{\theta_1^a} p(\theta_1^a) \sum_{\theta_2^a} p(\theta_2^a|\theta_1^a) \sum_c \pi_{12}(c|\theta_1^a, \theta_2^a)\, U^a(c^a, \theta_2^a) \Big\}$$

$$+ \lambda^b \Big\{ \sum_{\theta_1^a} p(\theta_1^a) \sum_c \pi_{11}(c|\theta_1^a) U^b(c^b)$$

$$+ \beta \sum_{\theta_1^{a'}} p(\theta_1^{a'}) \sum_{\theta_2^{a'}} p(\theta_2^{a'}|\theta_1^{a'}) \sum_c \pi_{22}(c|\theta_1^{a'}, \theta_2^{a'}) U^b(c^b) \Big\}$$

$$
\begin{aligned}
&+\lambda^{a'}\left\{\sum_{\theta_1^{a'}} p(\theta_1^{a'})\sum_c \pi_{21}(c|\theta_1^{a'})U^{a'}(c^{a'},\theta_1^{a'})\right.\\
&\left.+\beta\sum_{\theta_1^{a'}} p(\theta_1^{a'})\sum_{\theta_2^{a'}} p(\theta_2^{a'}|\theta_1^{a'})\sum_c \pi_{22}(c|\theta_1^{a'},\theta_2^{a'})U^{a'}(c^{a'},\theta_2^{a'})\right\}\\
&+\lambda^{b'}\left\{\sum_{\theta_1^{a'}} p(\theta_1^{a'})\sum_c \pi_{21}(c|\theta_1^{a'})U^{b'}(c^{b'})\right.\\
&\left.+\beta\sum_{\theta_1^{a}} p(\theta_1^{a})\sum_{\theta_2^{a}} p(\theta_2^{a}|\theta_1^{a})\sum_c \pi_{12}(c|\theta_1^{a},\theta_2^{a})U^{b'}(c^{b'})\right\} \qquad (9.8)
\end{aligned}
$$

subject to incentive constraints for agent a at date $t = 1, 2$, identical with incentive constraints (9.6) and (9.7), except with $\pi_{1t}(\cdot)$ replacing π_t, and subject to similar incentive constraints for agent a' at date $t = 1, 2$.

Some results are already implicit in this program but deserve elaboration. First, the full-information solution to the program would still equate weighted marginal utilities of the two agents present at each location by appropriate distribution of the total endowment of the two agents present. As only the contemporary preference shock of agent a would enter as a genuine variable into these equations for location 1, and that of agent a' for location 2, full-information optimal rules depend at most on these parameters. In particular, the shock experienced by agent a' at date 1 and location 2 has no bearing on the transfer at date 2 and location 1 even though agent b' is present at both locations. That is, the history experienced by b' would not matter. This argument carries over to the private-information full-communication program in question, as can be deduced by a study of first-order conditions. Similarly, contemporary announcements by agent a' at date 1 and location 2 have no bearing on the transfer at date 1 and location 1. That is, for this pure exchange environment, an interspatial telecommunication technology would not be used for *contemporary* announcements even though it is allowed. (For more on this, see section 7.) However, the private-information full-communication program does allow the announcement of agent a at location 1 and date 1 to enter into the transfer function at location 1 and date 2. Such tie-ins are used because they weaken the damaging effect of incentive compatibility constraints at date 1 for agent a, as can be deduced also by a study of first-order conditions. A similar tie-in is allowed for announcements of agent a' at location 2 across dates 1 and 2.

These tie-ins make the optimal arrangement quadrilateral rather than bilateral. That is, apart from coordination in the choice of allocation rules over the two locations and two dates, as determined by the Pareto weights λ^j, $j = a, a', b, b'$, the solutions to the full-information program (solutions to program 9.3 without the incentive constraints) can be implemented as a sequence of bilateral arrangements, one at each location and date. With tie-ins, however, agent a's announcement at date $t=1$ matters both for agent b at date $t=1$ and for agent b' at date $t=2$. Put crudely, agent a can "borrow" from agent b and promise to "pay" agent b', and similarly for agent a' in his dealings with agents b' and b. In fact, agent b could end up "paying" twice if he were a "lender" to agent a at date $t=1$ and "pays" back a "loan" from agent a' at date 2. But of course these and all other possibilities are weighted optimally *ex ante* in the determination of the social optimum.

An easy way to deliver explicit examples of beneficial quadrilateral arrangements is to trick the relatively complicated program 9.3 into looking like program 9.2. To do this, suppose that agents a and a' have identical utility functions, identical endowments, and suffer the same probability distribution determining preference shocks. Similarly, suppose that agents b and b' have identical utility functions and identical endowments. Finally, restrict attention to Pareto weights λ^j with $\lambda^a = \lambda^{a'}$ and $\lambda^b = \lambda^{b'}$. Then, as can be deduced formally by an examination of the necessary and sufficient first-order conditions, a solution to program 9.2 can be viewed as a double solution to program 9.3, with the probabilities of consumptions to agent a identical with the probabilities of consumptions to agent a', and so on. Thus, tables 9.3 and 9.4 are examples of beneficial quadrilateral arrangements with the understanding, though it does not appear in the notation, that agent a is dealing with agent b at date 1 but dealing with agent b' at date 2, and similarly for agent a' in his dealings with agents b' and b. This will be exploited in what follows.

Perhaps it bears repetition, however, that the perfect costless enforcement premise still underlies the analysis. That is, all agents are required to show up at the locations specified in table 9.5, even though agents b and b' are traveling. Similarly, agents a and b must abide by the prespecified allocation rule at location 1 and date 1, even though neither will deal with the other ever again. We wonder about collusion or default, even though, as before, we can tell a physical story to support the full-commitment program. This subject is of sufficient interest that it is attacked head on in section 9, providing an alternative rationale for communication that is ignored in the intermediate sections which follow.

4 The limitations of oral assignment systems in spatial settings

The next step in the consideration of communication-accounting systems is to retain the entire setup of section 3, but to limit the communication technology. The first technology to be considered is the most primitive of technologies, namely oral assignment. That is, agents a and a' can make announcements at each date and location of contemporary values for preference shocks and, where relevant, past values as well. But no other record-keeping device is available. That is, agents cannot carry commodities or tokens of any kind, cannot carry written messages, and cannot access some centralized telecommunication record-keeping system. Under these circumstances, only the contemporary state matters for the announcement by agent a or agent a', even though announcements of past histories might be permitted. Thus, by familiar relevation principle arguments, agents a and a' can without loss of anything essential be restricted to announcing relevant contemporary values (histories can be announced only to the extent that they help to determine contemporary values).

The effect of course is to preclude direct intertemporal tie-ins of the type already analyzed. That is, program 9.2 reduces to two separate versions of program 9.1 (with identical Pareto weights in each period), and this is obviously Pareto inferior. If agents b and b' are constrained to the utility of autarky, for example, agents a and a' suffer.

In fact, though the analysis is somewhat contrived, we can see from this example how spatial organization itself can depend on communication technologies. In particular, suppose that the motive for travel of agent b to agent a' and of agent b' to agent a at the end of date 1 is that the match between a and b and the match between a' and b' deteriorate over time, mimicked by the assumption in the model that K units of the consumption good disappear from the social endowment available at each location at date 2 if agents remain paired. (Alternatively, in a more elaborate model, imagine that there are gains to specialization and trade if agents move about.) Then there would be a nontrivial choice among organizations: if agents remain paired, the cost of a deteriorated match must be weighed against the gain from direct intertemporal tie-ins. In fact, agents would choose *ex ante* to remain paired for at least some nontrivial values of cost K. Yet they would not remain paired under perfect costless telecommunications, or even under some of the more restricted systems considered below.

5 Portable concealable objects as record-keeping devices

An improved communication technology would allow agents a and a' to carry with them otherwise valueless tokens. In principle, these might be concealed at date 2, but, alternatively, they might be displayed as a record of things past. In particular, if the allocation of tokens at date 1 is under the complete control of the predetermined allocation rules, then past announcements can be indicated, allowing some of the required intertemporal tie-ins.

It is possible, in fact, that just one kind of token can allow recovery of the solution to the full-communication private-information program 9.2 (actually program 9.3). In particular, for the environment generating table 9.3, date 1 consumptions of agent a are ordered by values of θ_1^a, and the families of date 2 consumptions are ordered in reverse by these values. That is, the date 2, $\theta_1^a = 0.6$ branch is uniformly lower than the date 2, $\theta_1^a = 0.5$ branch, which in turn is uniformly lower than the date 2, $\theta_1^a = 0.4$ branch. Thus, if there were no record of first-period announcements, agent a at date 2 would prefer the $\theta_1^a = 0.4$ branch no matter what date 2 shock he experiences, and so on. That is, he would claim the highest branch. With tokens, claims can be limited to branches consistent with agent a's display of tokens. If agent a is given the least amount of tokens at date 1 for $\theta_1^a = 0.6$, and the most for $\theta_1^a = 0.4$, with $\theta_1^a = 0.5$ in between, then no tokens will be concealed and the full-communication solution will be effected.

Interestingly enough, the full-communication solution cannot always be effected with one kind of token, as is illustrated in the next section.[4]

6 Multiple portable tokens and written messages

The example shown in table 9.4 is one for which one kind of token is not enough. To see this, suppose that agent a is given tokens at date 1 for $\theta_1^a = (0.4, 0.6)$ and is given no tokens at date 1 for $\theta_1^a = (0.6, 0.4)$. Then, if at date 1, $\theta_1^a = (0.4, 0.6)$, and at date 2, $(\delta_x, \delta_y) = (0.5, 1.5)$, so that $\theta_2^a = (0.3, 0.6)$, agent a would prefer to show no tokens, would claim he was a $\theta_1^a = (0.6, 0.4)$, and also claim $\theta_2^a = (0.4, 0.6)$. However, if he were given tokens at date 1 under $\theta_1^a = (0.6, 0.4)$, and not otherwise, and if θ_1^a were actually $(0.6, 0.4)$, then he would understate tokens at $\theta_2^a = (0.6, 0.3)$, preferring at date 2 the $\theta_1^a = (0.4, 0.6)$ and $\theta_2^a = (0.6, 0.4)$ outcome.

The intuition behind this result, and the contrast with table 9.3, are instructive. In table 9.3 agent a is either a "borrower" or a "lender" at date $t = 1$, in various degrees, in the sense that the direction of the transaction is reversed at date 2. In table 9.4 there are two goods, and agent a can be a "borrower" or a "lender" in either good. Still, "preference reversal" shocks at date 2 can cause agent a to want to pretend to have been a lender in the commodity he did not lend. This can happen no matter which commodity was lent at date $t = 1$. Of course, two kinds of tokens, one for each commodity which can be lent, circumvent this problem. If green tokens are handed out at date 1 and $\theta_1^a = (0.4, 0.6)$ and red at $\theta_1^a = (0.6, 0.4)$, then a display of red tokens could be required at date 2 when $\theta_1^a = (0.6, 0.4)$ is claimed at date 2, and this is not possible if in fact $\theta_1^a = (0.4\ 0.6)$ was claimed at date 1.

It might seem from this that the number of kinds of tokens needed to support a full-communication optimum is related to the number of commodities

Table 9.6 A complete two-token system

Values of θ_1^a	*No. of red tokens*	*No. of green tokens*
1	1	N
2	2	$N-1$
3	3	$N-2$
⋮	⋮	⋮
N	N	1

or the number of shocks. Actually though, the current environment could be expanded to include any finite number of commodities or shocks, as table 9.6 illustrates.[5] Here, if θ_1^a takes on the second value (in an ordered set) at date 1, for example, then agent a receives at date 1 two red tokens and $N-1$ green tokens. At date 2 he cannot overstate past θ_1^a values, for example claiming the third value, for he would be short of red tokens, and he cannot understate past θ_2^a values, for example claiming the first value, for he would be short of green tokens. Thus two kinds of tokens are enough to distinguish past histories. (We will comment on a related issue, privately observed endowments, in section 10.)

An interesting general issue concerns when a specified number of kinds of tokens will be enough to constitute a full language, that is, enough to achieve a full-communication solution. This issue will not be pursued here, apart from noting that any system with a full set of tokens would be equivalent to a system with unrestricted fully displayed written messages. That is, written message systems are the limit of concealable token systems and as such do not require a separate analysis.[6]

7 Electronic telecommunications – a dominant technology

In the explicit four-agent environment of section 3 there was no gain from electronic telecommunications over space at a point in time. However, modifications of the pure risk-sharing environment can provide a motive for such systems. For example, suppose that the consumption good at date 1 can be stored in direct amount K at date 1, and carried over without depreciation at the same location to date 2. Suppose also that the preference shocks of agents a and a' at date 1 are driven by some common component, with idiosyncratic noise, and that the common component persists to some extent into preference shocks at date 2. Then shock $\theta_1^{a'}$ of agent a' can be used to help forecast the marginal utility of agent a at date 2, and a high marginal utility for consumption at date 2 would motivate relatively high investment K at location 1, date 1. A similar argument applies for shock θ_1^a at location 2 and date 1.

To check this logic, it is useful to go through the formal exercise of writing down a programming problem for the determination of Pareto optimal allocations with electronic interspatial telecommunications and storage. In particular, invoking the kind of symmetry assumptions used earlier to trick the four-agent program to a two-agent program, let $\pi_1(c, K|\theta_1^a, \theta_1^{a'})$ denote the probability of consumption bundle c *and* storage K given announced (and actual) $\theta_1^a, \theta_1^{a'}$ values, where, given K, bundle c lies in the set $\{(c^a, c^b): c^a + c^b \leqslant e^a + e^b - K\}$. Similarly, let $\pi_2(c, K|\theta_1^a, \theta_1^{a'}, \theta_2^a)$ denote the probability of consumption bundle c and storage K given the specified triple of announced (and actual) parameter values, where, for given K, the bundle c lies in $\{(c^a, c^b): c^a + c^b \leqslant e^a + e^b + K\}$. Then the program for the determination of a full-communication private-information optimal arrangement is as follows.

Program 9.4
Maximize by choice of $\pi_1(\cdot)$ and $\pi_2(\cdot)$ the objective function

$$\begin{aligned}
\lambda^a \Bigg\{ & \sum_{\theta_1^a}\sum_{\theta_1^{a'}} p(\theta_1^a, \theta_1^{a'}) \sum_K \sum_c \pi_1(c, K|\theta_1^a, \theta_1^{a'}) U^a(c^a, \theta_1^a) \\
& + \beta \sum_{\theta_1^a}\sum_{\theta_1^{a'}}\sum_{\theta_2^a} p(\theta_2^a|\theta_1^a, \theta_1^{a'}) p(\theta_1^a, \theta_1^{a'}) \sum_K \sum_c \pi_2(c, K|\theta_1^a, \theta_1^{a'}, \theta_2^a) U^a(c^a, \theta_2^{a'}) \Bigg\} \\
& + \lambda^b \Bigg\{ \sum_{\theta_1^a}\sum_{\theta_1^{a'}} p(\theta_1^a, \theta_1^{a'}) \sum_K \sum_c \pi_1(c, K|\theta_1^a, \theta_1^{a'}) U^b(c^b) \\
& + \beta \sum_{\theta_1^a}\sum_{\theta_1^{a'}}\sum_{\theta_2^a} p(\theta_2^a|\theta_1^a, \theta_1^{a'}) p(\theta_1^a, \theta_1^{a'}) \sum_K \sum_c \pi_2(c, K|\theta_1^a, \theta_1^{a'}, \theta_2^a) U^b(c^b) \Bigg\}
\end{aligned} \tag{9.9}$$

subject to consistency in the choice of K; namely for all $\theta_1^a, \theta_1^{a'}, \theta_2^a$

$$\sum_c \pi_2(c, K|\theta_1^a, \theta_1^{a'}, \theta_2^a) \equiv \sum_c \pi_1(c, K|\theta_1^a, \theta_1^{a'}) \tag{9.10}$$

subject to incentive constraints for agent a at date $t = 2$, for all past announcements $\theta_1^a, \theta_1^{a'}$, and for all actual θ_2^a and counterfactual θ_2^a

$$\sum_c \sum_K U^a(c^a, \theta_2^a) \pi_2(c, K|\theta_1^a, \theta_1^{a'}, \theta_2^a) \geqslant \sum_c \sum_K U^a(c^a, \theta_2^a) \pi_2(c, K|\theta_1^a, \theta_1^{a'}, \tilde{\theta}_2^a) \tag{9.11}$$

subject to incentive constraints for agent a at date $t = 1$, and for all actual θ_2^a and counterfactual $\tilde{\theta}_1^a$

$$\sum_{\theta_1^{a'}} p(\theta_1^{a'} | \theta_1^a) \sum_c \sum_K U^a(c^a, \theta_1^a) \pi_1(c, K | \theta_1^a, \theta_1^{a'}) + \beta \sum_{\theta_1^{a'}} \sum_{\theta_2^a} p(\theta_2^a, \theta_1^{a'} | \theta_1^a)$$

$$\times \sum_c \sum_K U^a(c^a, \theta_2^a) \pi_2(c, K | \theta_1^a, \theta_1^{a'}, \theta_2^a)$$

$$\geqslant \sum_{\theta_1^{a'}} p(\theta_1^{a'} | \theta_1^a) \sum_c \sum_K U^a(c^a, \theta_1^a) \pi_1(c, K | \tilde{\theta}_1^a, \theta_1^{a'}) + \beta \sum_{\theta_1^{a'}} \sum_{\theta_2^a} p(\theta_2^a, \theta_1^{a'} | \theta_1^a)$$

$$\times \sum_c \sum_K U^a(c^a, \theta_2^a) \pi_2(c, K | \tilde{\theta}_1^a, \theta_1^{a'}, \theta_2^a) \tag{9.12}$$

The incentive constraints are much as before except that agent a takes as given that agent a' is announcing truthfully at date 1, and agent a learns this parameter announcement *after* the allocation is effected at date 1. Constraint (9.10) ensures that the choice of K is the same whether viewed as determined by the allocation rule $\pi_1(\cdot)$ or the allocation rule $\pi_2(\cdot)$. Alternatively, and more naturally, we could have let the allocation rule $\pi_2(c | \theta_1^a, \theta_1^{a'}, \theta_2^a, K)$ be conditioned on K, but then it would not have been obvious that the essential program is linear.

8 Portable messages as a location assignment device

We have now passed through the gamut of communication technologies in the context of the same four-agent two-location model. Each of the communication technologies considered in the model played a role as a device for keeping track, if possible, of past announcements by the agents with privately observed preference shocks – agents a and a'. No records were needed of the histories experienced by agents b and b'. In contrast, in this section we show how records may be needed for travelers who experience no direct shocks *if* their assignments to locations are endogenous, part of the (optimal) social mechanism.

The model is modified by assuming that there is only one traveler, agent b, who is paired initially at date $t = 1$ with agent a, experiencing preference shock θ_1^a, and then is paired at date $t = 2$ either with an agent d, who is to experience shocks θ_2^d, or with an agent e, who is to experience shocks θ_2^e, but is never paired to both. Further, shocks θ_1^a contain information on forthcoming θ_2^d and θ_2^e, so that an assignment at date $t = 1$ matters. That is, an assignment at date $t = 1$ is a nontrivial function of announced (and actual) θ_1^a. For simplicity, assume that agent a cares about date $t = 1$ consumption only and that agents d and e care about date $t = 2$ consumption only, though agent b, the traveler, cares about consumption at both dates. Then, to ensure some mutual beneficial trade, assume that there are two goods at each date. The notation for endowments e_t^i is as before.

If we let the variable l denote the location assignment of agent b at the end of date 1 to either agent d or e, that is, either $l = d$ or $l = e$, the programming problem for the determination of a *full-communication* private-information optimum is as follows.

Program 9.5
Maximize by choice of date $t = 1$ (potentially random) consumption and assignment rules $\pi_1(c|\theta_1^a)$ and $\pi_1(l|\theta_1^a)$ respectively, and by choice of date $t = 2$ consumption rules $\pi_2(c|\theta_2^d, l = d)$ and $\pi_2(c|\theta_2^e, l = e)$, the objective function

$$\begin{aligned}
&\lambda^a\left\{\sum_{\theta_1^a} p(\theta_1^a)\sum_c \pi_1(c|\theta_1^a)U^a(c,\theta_1^a)\right\} + \lambda^b\Bigg[\sum_{\theta_1^a} p(\theta_1^a)\sum_c \pi_1(c|\theta_1^a)U^b(c) + \beta\sum_{\theta_1^a} p(\theta_1^a)\\
&\quad\times\Bigg\{\pi_1(l = d|\theta_1^a)\sum_{\theta_2^d} p(\theta_2^d|\theta_1^a)\sum_c U^b(c)\pi_2(c|\theta_2^d, l = d)\\
&\quad + \pi_1(l = e|\theta_1^a)\sum_{\theta_2^e} p(\theta_2^e|\theta_1^a)\sum_c U^b(c)\pi_2(c|\theta_2^e, l = e)\Bigg\}\Bigg]\\
&\quad + \lambda^d\Bigg[\sum_{\theta_1^a} p(\theta_1^a)\Bigg\{\pi_1(l = d|\theta_1^a)\sum_{\theta_2^d} p(\theta_2^d|\theta_1^a)\sum_c U^d(c,\theta_2^d)\pi_2(c|\theta_2^d, l = d)\\
&\quad + \pi_1(l = e|\theta_1^a)\sum_{\theta_2^d} p(\theta_2^d|\theta_1^a)U^d(e_2^d,\theta_2^d)\Bigg\}\Bigg]\\
&\quad + \lambda^e\Bigg[\sum_{\theta_1^a} p(\theta_1^a)\Bigg\{\pi_1(l = d|\theta_1^a)\sum_{\theta_2^e} p(\theta_2^e|\theta_1^a)U^e(e_2^e,\theta_2^e)\\
&\quad + \pi_1(l = e|\theta_1^a)\sum_{\theta_2^e} p(\theta_2^e|\theta_1^a)\sum_c U^e(c,\theta_2^e)\pi_2(c|\theta_2^e, l = e)\Bigg\}\Bigg]
\end{aligned} \tag{9.13}$$

subject to incentive constraints for agent a at date $t = 1$, and incentive constraints for agents e and d at date $t = 2$.

Formally, program 9.5 can be converted to a linear program, for example by letting

$$\pi_2(c, l = d|\theta_1^a, \theta_2^d) \equiv \pi_2(c|\theta_2^d, l = d)\pi_1(l = d|\theta_1^a) \tag{9.14}$$

and similarly for $\pi_2(c, l = e|\theta_1^a, \theta_2^e)$, by imposing a linear equation to ensure that the left-hand side of (9.14) is independent of θ_2^d, for example, and by imposing consistency with $\pi_1(l = d|\theta_1^a)$ as in program 9.4, equation (9.10).

With limited communication, an otherwise optimal assignment of agent b to either agent d or agent e may not be assured. Announced shock θ_1^a at date $t = 1$, and, in shorthand notation, assignment $l(\theta_1^a)$ at date $t = 1$, are private to agent b when b meets agent d or agent e at date $t = 2$.

An example helps to make the point. In particular, suppose that agent b has preferences of the form $U^b(c_x, c_y) = c_x + c_y$ at each date, with discount rate $\beta = 0.9$. Preferences of agent a at date 1 are of the form

$$U^a(c_x, c_y, \theta_1^a) = (c_x)^{\theta_x^a} + (c_y)^{\theta_y^a}$$

with $\theta_1^a = (\theta_x^a, \theta_y^a)$ either (0.4, 0.6) or (0.6, 0.4), each drawn with probability 0.5. Preferences of agents d and e at date 2 are of a similar form to agent a's with correlated parameter draws, that is,

$\theta_1^a = (0.4, 0.6)$

$$\Rightarrow \begin{cases} \theta_2^d = (0.7, 0.5) & \text{and} \quad \theta_2^e = (0.3, 0.5) \quad \text{with probability 0.8} \\ \theta_2^d = (0.3, 0.5) & \text{and} \quad \theta_2^e = (0.7, 0.5) \quad \text{with probability 0.2} \end{cases}$$

$\theta_1^a = (0.6, 0.4)$

$$\Rightarrow \begin{cases} \theta_2^d = (0.7, 0.5) & \text{and} \quad \theta_2^e = (0.3, 0.5) \quad \text{with probability 0.2} \\ \theta_2^d = (0.3, 0.5) & \text{and} \quad \theta_2^e = (0.7, 0.5) \quad \text{with probability 0.8} \end{cases}$$

Then the consumption allocations for agents a, d, and e and assignment rule $l(\theta)$ are displayed in Table 9.7.[7]

When $\theta_1^a = (0.4, 0.6)$, agent a is assumed to be assigned to agent d, and when $\theta_1^a = (0.6, 0.4)$, agent a is assumed to be assigned to agent e, each assignment consistent with the likelihood of high marginal utility for agent d or agent e respectively. But agent b, anticipating high transfers under the full communication-assignment rule, wants to go in just the contrary direction.

However, if agent b carries a token of one kind when $l(\theta_1^a) = d$ and a token of another kind when $l(\theta_1^a) = e$, if he must be with agent a at date $t = 1$ and then with agent d or agent e at date $t = 2$, and if he must abide by the

Table 9.7 Optimal location assignment

(θ_x^a, θ_y^a)	(c_x^a, c_y^a)	$l(\theta_1^a)$	(θ_x^d, θ_y^d)	(c_x^d, c_y^d)	(θ_x^e, θ_y^e)	(c_x^e, c_y^e)
(0.4, 0.6)	(2, 6.31)	d	(0.7, 0.5) (0.3, 0.5)	(10, 3) (2, 6.24)		
(0.6, 0.4)	(6, 2)	e			(0.7, 0.5) (0.3, 0.5)	(10, 3) (2, 6.24)

prespecified allocation rule when paired, then a failure to display tokens of the right kind can indicate that agent b is not abiding by the rules. Curiously, two kinds of tokens are needed. For suppose that there was only one kind of token in use and agent b was given it for $\theta_1^a = (0.4, 0.6)$ and not for $\theta_1^a = (0.6, 0.4)$, for example. Then when $\theta_1^a = (0.6, 0.4)$, agent b wants to go to agent d where the likelihood of high transfers is less. But he has no tokens to show, and so he must go to agent e. However, when $\theta_1^a = (0.4, 0.6)$, agent b wants to go to agent e and can do so by concealing his tokens. Again, two kinds of tokens circumvent this problem.

9 Portable messages as a device for enforcement

The structure of section 8 takes as given that agent b must show up and be paired with agent a at date $t = 1$ and must choose to be paired with either agent d or agent e at date $t = 2$. A slight weakening of the commitment premise would allow agent b to choose whether to participate at some dates. In fact, spatial separation alone could then imply private information in the sense that failure of one agent to participate with a second agent at a given location in a given date might not be known by a third party at a subsequent date. That is, communication can be valuable if commitment is limited, even with no underlying uncertainty.

The delicate part of schemes with limited commitment is that the structure of the problem can be undone altogether, so that *ex ante* agreements have no force at all. In that case, there would be nothing to communicate since plans have no content, are known to have no content, and so on. Thus, *some* prior commitment is needed. In this section we start with essentially full commitment, assuming that if agents show up at a prespecified location they *must* abide by the prespecified allocation mechanism in place at that location. Further, at the very last date, agents *must* show up at prespecified locations, no matter what. Hence the (only) aspect of limited commitment which is introduced is the idea that each agent can choose at all dates but the last whether to participate under prespecified allocation rules. The alternative to participation is to eat one's endowment.

For clarity, we return to the basic four-agent two-location two-period model, but eliminate shocks to preferences. Otherwise, the structure is as before. As before, it is best to begin with the full communication record-keeping technology, assuming that actions at locations 1 and 2 at the first date are fully recorded and can be used in the allocation rules at date $t = 2$. The objective in the planning period is to choose (deterministic) allocations c_t^i, $i = a, a', b, b'$, $t = 1, 2$, to maximize a weighted sum of discounted utility streams across the four agents, namely

$$\sum_i \lambda^i \left\{ \sum_{t=1}^{2} \beta^{t-1} U^i(c_t^i) \right\} \tag{9.15}$$

subject to the obvious resource constraints

$$c_t^i + c_t^j = e_t^i + e_t^j \qquad (9.16)$$

and so on for the relevant agent pairing (i,j) at each date t.

The relevant decision for a given agent at the first date is whether to participate as planned at date $t = 1$; participation cannot be assumed and must be induced. However, since constraints which ensure participation at date 1 generally damage the program, relative to the full commitment program, we want such participation constraints to be as weak as possible. This is done by making the "penalty" at date 2 for failure to participate at date 1 as strong as possible. That is, the first-period participation constraint for agent i takes the form

$$U^i(c_1^i) + \beta U^i(c_2^i) \geqslant U^i(e_1^i) + \beta U^i(0) \qquad (9.17)$$

where $c_2^i = 0$ on the right-hand side of (9.17) is the obvious penalty, the lower bound on i's consumption at date 2. Again, the interpretation is that if agent i participates at date 1, receiving c_1^i as planned, then when i shows up at date 2, and he must by assumption do so, he will receive c_2^i as planned, whereas if agent i does not participate at date $t = 1$ and eats his endowment e_1^i, something which cannot be directly thwarted, then when he shows up at date $t = 2$, the fact of default is known and he receives zero. In short, the program for the determination of Pareto optimal allocations is one of maximizing objective function (9.15) subject to four resource constraints (9.16) and four participation constraints (9.17).[8]

To implement a solution to this program *without* costless telecommunicated record-keeping, but with portable concealable objects such as tokens, suppose that if agent i participates at date $t = 1$ he receives c_1^i and a prespecified number of tokens (one will do). Tokens, by assumption, cannot be acquired elsewhere. Then a display of tokens at date 2 effects c_t^i to agent i, and a failure to display tokens effects the penalty – zero consumption. Thus tokens communicate whether or not agent i reneged at date 1, an action which is otherwise unknown to agent i's trading partner at date 2.

This argument can be extended to any T-period finite-horizon model with choice of participation at all dates t but the last. There would be a participation constraint for each agent i at each date t, $t = 1, 2, \ldots, T-1$, and the constraint for agent i at date t would be[9]

$$\sum_{s=t}^{T} \beta^{(s-1)} U^i(c_s^i) \geqslant \sum_{s=t}^{T-1} \beta^{(s-1)} U^i(e_s^i) + \beta^{T-1} U^i(0) \qquad (9.18)$$

With discount rate β less than unity, participation at relative early stages is achieved not by high penalties at the last date T but by the gain from the enduring relationship, that is, from participation at intermediate dates. The number of tokens, or length of written messages, needed to implement the limited commitment solution with otherwise limited communication may become large as T goes to infinity.

10 Privately observed endowments

The analysis above is now easily generalized to incorporate the case of random and privately observed endowments. Indeed, as with tokens, claimed values of endowments can trigger required displays, some of which would prove infeasible for certain actual realizations of endowments.[10] In short, incentive constraints need be imposed only for claimed endowment vectors which are less than or equal to realized endowment vectors, component by component.

More formally, for the two-agent one-consumption period model of section 2, let θ^a denote the vector of endowments of agent a as well as a vector of shocks to the preferences of agent a as before. Also let $\tau = (\tau^a, \tau^b)$ denote a vector of transfers from agents a and b, assuming for simplicity a finite number of possible values for these transfers. Then let $\pi(\tau|\theta^a)$ denote the probability of transfer τ conditioned on announcement θ^a, so that, for each θ^a, $\pi(\tau|\theta^a)$ is a lottery over τ values satisfying $\theta^a - \tau^a \geqslant 0$, $e^b - \tau^b \geqslant 0$, $\tau^a + \tau^b = 0$. The program for the determination of Pareto optimal allocations is then as follows.

Program 9.6
Maximize by choice of the $\pi(\tau|\theta^a)$ the objective function

$$\lambda^a\left\{\sum_{\theta^a} p(\theta^a)\sum_{\tau} U^a[\theta - \tau^a, \theta^a]\pi(\tau|\theta^a)\right\} + \lambda^b\left\{\sum_{\theta^a} p(\theta^a)\sum_{\tau} U^b(e^b - \tau^b)\pi(\tau|\theta^a)\right\} \tag{9.19}$$

subject to incentive constraints, for every $\tilde{\theta}^a \leqslant \theta^a$,

$$\sum_{\tau} U^a[\theta^a - \tau^a, \theta^a]\pi(\tau|\theta^a) \geqslant \sum_{\tau} U^a[\theta^a - \tau^a, \theta^a]\pi(\tau|\tilde{\theta}^a) \tag{9.20}$$

Again, solutions to program 9.6 can require actual displays. For example, with one good, if a high endowment θ^a for agent a is associated with a high marginal utility shock θ^a for agent a, then the *ex ante* optimal insurance solution may have agent a receiving the good when his endowment is high, after it is displayed, and surrendering it otherwise, when his endowment is low.[11] Without pretransfer displays this would not be incentive compatible, for agent a would always claim to have a high endowment in order to receive the higher net transfer.

Generally, though, pretransfer displays cannot completely overcome the incentive problems of private information, and the analysis of communication-accounting systems with privately observed endowment shocks would proceed along the lines of this chapter as for the case of privately observed preference shocks. However, a new and interesting case for analysis now emerges: the case of commodity storage coupled with the presence of *no* intrinsically useless (storable) tokens. In this case, displays of otherwise private stocks can serve in part as worthless tokens did to reveal past histories. But the communication-accounting system with these bona fide commodity tokens would be more limited than the system with intrinsically useless tokens.

Consider the four-agent two-location two-period economy tricked into the two-agent one-location two-period economy by the symmetry conditions, and assume that no communication system is available other than that achieved by direct commodity storage, publicly observed at the time storage decisions are taken but not necessarily observed later. Then let $\pi(\tau, K \mid \theta_1^a)$ denote a lottery over transfers $\tau = (\tau^a, \tau^b)$ and storage in amount K at date 1, conditioned on announcement θ_1^a by agent a at date 1, with transfers τ and storage K satisfying $\theta_1^a - \tau^a \geqslant 0$, $e^b - \tau^b \geqslant 0$, $K = \tau^a + \tau^b$. Also, let $\pi_2(\tau \mid \theta_2^a + K)$ denote a lottery over transfers $\tau = (\tau^a, \tau^b)$ at date 2, conditioned on announcement $\theta_2^a + K$ by agent a at date 2, with $\theta_2^a + K - \tau^a \geqslant 0$, $e^b - \tau^b \geqslant 0$, $\tau^a + \tau^b = 0$.

The point is that the natural state variable at date 2 is $\theta_2^a + K$; only this *sum* can enter into the allocation rule at date 2. Thus if endowment θ_2^a were constant, storage K, in varying with endowment θ_1^a, might allow a complete revelation of past histories, as for the earlier examples with intrinsically useless tokens. But if endowment θ_2^a is not constant, a display of goods may be possible even when commodity storage itself is inadequate. That is, in an effort to achieve the former allocation, agent a may occasionally have the ability to display when formerly he did not, and this would undercut the information revelation role of tokens. However, if storage K were constant, independent of endowment θ_1^a, then allocations can be indexed by θ_2^a. But if K is not constant, and depends on θ_1^a, the θ_2^a-information role of contemporary displays is mitigated. In general, then, neither complete past histories nor contemporary states will enter into the *de facto* allocation rules at date 2. Further constraining the information role of commodity tokens is the fact that commodity storage K as an information variable distorts intertemporal allocations from what they would have been with costless intrinsically useless tokens.

Notes

1 These solutions are computed for $\beta = 0.95$. Also, the solution is reported as deterministic, but in fact the generated solution for a grid of 101 points between 0 and 10 displayed lotteries. For example at $\theta_1^a = 0.6$, the computed solution is 7.2 with probability 0.4872 and 7.3 with probability 0.5128. As this lottery is an artifact of grid size, and would disappear with a continuum of possible consumptions, the reported solution is delivered by linear interpolation. Similar interpolations are performed for the tables that follow.

2 Again endowments are uniformly 5 and $\beta = 0.9$.

3 In the absence of direct tie-ins, that is, in the absence of a record of past announcements, agent a might be required to re-announce date 1 preference shocks and to announce a value for contemporary shocks. In this scheme, re-announcements of date 1 shocks may matter, and in that weak sense there are intertemporal tie-ins. But the solution is worse than if there were a record of past announcements of $\tilde{\theta}_1^a$ in program 9.2.

4 Douglas Diamond has suggested the following ingenious scheme with the idea that even one token might not be needed for the environment of this section and that oral communication might suffice. Suppose all four agents, a, a', b, and b', are to agree a priori to implement a social optimum as if there were full communication. In particular, agents b and b' are to agree a priori, in private, that if agent a reports θ' at date $t = 1$, then agent b is to say some prespecified password, for example "midnight," whereas if agent a reports θ'', agent b is to say some distinct password, for example "high noon." Upon b''s arrival at location 1, area a is to repeat the password, out of countless thousands of possibilities. Agent b' will then know the history of actual past announcements of agent a and is to implement the specified transfer. One problem with this scheme is that the initial agreement between b and b' on passwords as a function of θ announcements must be private between b and b' (if agent a knows the agreement, he will always say the password at date $t = 2$, which allows him to receive the consumption good). Therefore, agents b and b' could just as easily commit themselves to a degenerate password system, always saying the same thing, and planning matters so that a is never to receive the consumption good at date $t = 2$. That is, since the choice of a password function is private, agents b and b' can be assumed to make the best unconstrained choice, and a requirement that a particular function be chosen has no force if it is not consistent with incentives. Something akin to this is assumed in the "revelation principle" literature: requirements that agents tell the truth in an announcement game have no force unless agents have an incentive to do so. This example illustrates, however, the importance of the assumption in this chapter that rules be agreed to publicly and leads to an exploration of enforcement technologies and definitions of reneging. However, this is left as a subject for future research.

5 This example is due to Arthur Kupferman.

6 More generally, a token system is a kind of written message system, a limited one if combinations of tokens cannot adequately convey past history. The idea that tokens are related to writing as "words" are to language may be familiar –

real languages actually evolved from token accounting systems (see Schmandt-Besserat, 1979).

7 Endowments are uniformly 5, and $\lambda^a = \lambda^d = \lambda^e$ with the utility of agent *b* at autarky.

8 More generally, we can write down a program which lets participation or assignment at date 1 be a choice variable, subject to the constraint that if the assignment is not to participate, then agent *i* receives his endowment, and also subject to obedience constraints, that if agent *i* is assigned to participate, then he must prefer to do so, and if he is assigned not to participate, then he must prefer not to do so. It can be established that, for any solution with nonparticipation as the assignment, there is a utility equivalent solution with participation as the assignment; hence the program given above.

9 That this is without loss of generality can be established as in note 8.

10 It should be noted that much of the literature on resource-allocation mechanisms ignores privately observed endowments. Important exceptions are Postlewaite (1979), Hurwicz et al. (1980), and Pithyachariyakul (1982).

11 This example may seem somewhat contrived, but it can be given a more compelling interpretation. Briefly, imagine that agents *a* and *b* each have an investment project and that returns from investment projects at date 1 must be reinvested at date 1 in order to yield an idiosyncratic household-specific nontraded consumption good at date 2. The investment good can be reallocated at date 1, however, and would be reallocated in an *ex ante* optimal arrangement if high investment good returns at date 1 were indicative of high consumption returns at date 2, yielding high marginal return of the *indirect* utility function for contemporary investment. For further details, see Townsend (1986).

References

Arrow, K.J. (1953) Le rôle des valeurs boursières pour la répartition la meilleure des risques. In *Econometrie*, pp. 41–8. Paris: Centre Nationale de la Recherche Scientifique.

Baric, L. (1964) Some aspects of credit, saving, and investment in a nonmonetary economy (Rossel Island). In *Capital, Saving, and Credit in Peasant Societies*, eds R. Firth and B. Yamey. Chicago, IL: Aldine.

Brunner, K. and Meltzer, A.H. (1971) The uses of money: money in the theory of an exchange economy. *American Economic Review* 61, 784–805.

Debreu, G. (1959) *Theory of Value: An Axiomatic Analysis of Economic Equilibrium*. New York: Wiley for Cowles Foundation.

Firth, R. (1939) *Primitive Polynesian Economy*. London: Routledge.

Gale, D. (1980) Money, information and equilibrium in large economies. *Journal of Economic Theory* 23, 28–65.

Harris, M. and Townsend, R.M. (1981) Resource allocation under asymmetric information. *Econometrica* 49, 33–64. Reprinted in this volume as chapter 7.

Hurwicz, L. (1972) On informationally decentralized systems. In *Decision and Organization*, eds C.G. McGuire and R. Radner, ch. 14. Amsterdam: North-Holland.

——, Maskin, E. and Postlewaite, A. (1980) Feasible implementation of social choice correspondences by Nash equilibria. Unpublished manuscript, University of Minnesota.

Malinowski, B. (1953) *Argonauts of the Western Pacific*. New York: Dutton.

Mount, K. and Reiter, S. The informational size of message spaces. *Journal of Economic Theory* 8, 161–92.

Myerson, R. (1979) Incentive compatibility and the bargaining problem. *Econometrica* 47, 61–73.

Ostroy, J.M. (1973) The informational efficiency of monetary exchange. *American Economic Review* 63, 567–610.

—— and Starr, R.M. (1974) Money and the decentralization of exchange. *Econometrica* 42, 1093–113.

Postlewaite, A. (1979) Manipulations via endowments. *Review of Economic Studies* 46, 255–62.

Pithyachariyakul, P. (1982) Exchange mechanism, strategies, and efficiency with private information. Doctoral Dissertation, Northwestern University, Evanston, IL.

Schmandt-Besserat, D. (1979) The earliest precursor or writing. *Scientific American* September, 241.

Townsend, R.M. (1982) Optimal multiperiod contracts and the gain from enduring relationships under private information. *Journal of Political Economy* 90, 1166–86. Reprinted in this volume as chapter 8.

—— (1986) Economic organization with limited communication. Working paper 86-3, Department of Economics, University of Chicago.

Usher, A.P. (1943) *The Early History of Deposit Banking in Mediterranean Europe*. Cambridge, MA: Harvard University Press.

Part V
Core Theories of Intermediation

10

Intermediation with Costly Bilateral Exchange

1 Introduction

This chapter was motivated in part by questions of optimal regulation of financial institutions such as intermediaries. It is believed that an analysis of such questions should take place in a model in which financial institutions emerge endogenously as the choice of agents of the model. Yet there appear to be few models which explain institutions in this way.

The absence of such models is due in part to the acceptance of what are often thought of as necessary conditions for tractable mathematical analysis. In particular, speaking rather loosely, the technologies of production and exchange are usually assumed to be convex. This is true of the standard competitive model as described, for example, by Arrow and Hahn (1971). It is also true of recent attempts to obtain a theory of more limited exchange such as those of Foley (1970), Hahn (1971), and Kurz (1974). In these analyses convexity is used in establishing the continuity of choice functions upon which standard fixed-point theorems rely. Yet, to repeat, convexity prevents the models from explaining specialization.

There have been several attempts to weaken the convexity assumptions.

Reprinted from *Review of Economic Studies* 55(3), 1978, 417–25 (Southampton: Review of Economic Studies Ltd). A version of this chapter appeared in the author's Ph.D. thesis presented at the University of Minnesota, July 1975. I gratefully acknowledge the advice and encouragement of Neil Wallace and the assistance of John Danforth. I would also like to thank the participants of the market organization workshop at Carnegie–Mellon University and the referees for helpful comments. I claim full responsibility for any errors or ambiguities. Financial assistance from the Federal Reserve Bank of Minneapolis is also gratefully acknowledged. The views expressed herein are solely my own and do not necessarily represent the views of the Federal Reserve Bank of Minneapolis or the Federal Reserve System.

In Starr (1969) and in Arrow and Hahn (1971) nonconvex sets are replaced by their convex hulls, standard existence theorems are applied to the convexified economy, and the excess demands of the resulting social-approximate equilibrium are then shown to have limit zero as the number of agents is increased. The thrust of this work is that the competitive equilibrium is a good approximation for nonconvex economies with a large number of agents. This approach has been modified somewhat by Heller (1972) and by Heller and Starr (1972) to allow for various strong nonconvexities associated with setup costs and to explain the use of money.

In this chapter we propose a simple theory of intermediation and, in contrast with the literature described above, we circumvent the difficulties associated with nonconvex technologies by adopting a game-theoretic approach. A model is described in which exchange is motivated by risk-sharing considerations. However, exchange is also resource using; for each bilateral deal there is a fixed cost. This creates the nonconvexity.[1] Then, having specified the set of agents, their preferences, and the technology available to them, we characterize core allocations. As noted by Shapley and Shubik (1966), core allocations are in some sense socially stable; we might expect to observe institutions and exchange arrangements which support such allocations.[2] Indeed, a noncooperative game is proposed for the model, and it is shown that the equilibrium allocations of the game are equivalent to core allocations. In this noncooperative game agents announce strategies under which they are willing to act as intermediaries, buying shares in investment projects and selling shares in the resulting portfolio. In an equilibrium only a subset of agents act as intermediaries, and in this sense the model can be said to explain specialization. These intermediaries emerge endogenously because they are able to economize on the fixed cost of exchange.

The game-theoretic approach adopted here also enables us to dispense with the Walrasian auctioneer. Agents of the model propose the exchange arrangements. Moreover, the strategies of active intermediaries may include per unit prices with fixed fees or a bid–ask spread with minimum purchase requirements. In this sense the equilibrium of the noncooperative game can be viewed as a generalization of the concept of a competitive equilibrium which allows a much richer specification of the terms of trade.

This chapter proceeds as follows. The structure and technology of the model are described in section 2. Then markets, feasible allocations, core allocations, and intermediaries are defined. Core allocations are characterized in section 3. In section 4 a noncooperative game with intermediation strategies is described, and the equivalence of equilibrium allocations and core allocations is established. Section 5 offers some comments on the strengths and limitations of the model.

2 The structure and technology of the model

Let I denote the set of agents. It is assumed that I is countably infinite. Each agent $j \in I$ is endowed with a quantity K^j of the unique factor of production of the model. The endowments of this capital good are identical for all agents and are perfectly divisible. Each agent is also endowed with a stochastic technology which transforms the capital good into a distribution of the unique consumption good of the model. Each of these technologies or investment projects displays constant return to scale. Let λ^j denote the output of the consumption good per unit of the capital input y_j in project j. Each λ^j is a random variable which can take on a finite number of values in R^1_+. Also, the $\lambda^j, j \in I$, are assumed to be independent and identically distributed. A state of the economy subsequent to the realization of the λ^j is a complete specification of the value of each of the $\lambda^j, j \in I$. The set of all possible states will be denoted Ω with typical element ω. Let $\mu(\omega)$ denote the probability that state ω will occur.

The preferences of each agent are assumed to conform to the von Neumann–Morgenstern axioms so that each has an objective function

$$V^j(c^j) = \int_{\omega \in \Omega} \mu(\omega) U^j\{c^j(\omega)\}$$

Here c^j is a random variable with typical element $c^j(\omega) \in R^1_+$, the consumption of agent j in state ω. It is further assumed that the $U^j(\cdot)$ are identical across agents and display constant relative risk aversion. (The superscript j on $U^j(\cdot)$ and $V^j(\cdot)$ will be deleted if no ambiguity results.)

The model is thus constructed in such a way that there are gains to exchange or portfolio diversification. In particular, note that agents are risk averse and the λ^i are independent and identically distributed. In contrast, if the λ^i were perfectly correlated, then no risk spreading could be achieved.

Exchange in the model is assumed to be costly. For each bilateral deal a fixed cost of 2α units of the capital good is incurred, α per agent. Note that this cost is independent of the nature of the exchange. Thus, if there were three agents and each agent were trading with every other agent as in figure 10.1(a), the total transactions costs for the three bilateral exchanges would be 6α. Transactions costs could be reduced to 4α if one agent were to act as a go-between or intermediary for the other two, as indicated in figure 10.1(b).

It remains to describe the set of feasible allocations given this transactions technology. Let $C \subseteq I$ denote a coalition with $\# C$ agents. Let N^j denote the set of agents with whom agent j deals directly. Then a coalition C is said to constitute a *market* if $\# C < \infty$; if for each $j \in C$, $N^j \subseteq C$; and if there exists

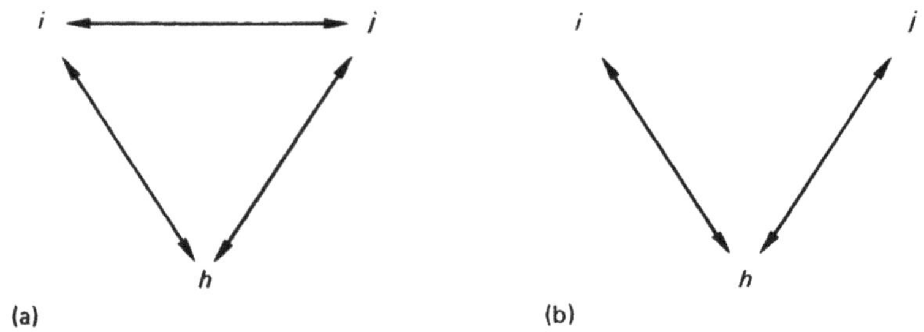

Figure 10.1. (a) Exchange without intermediation; (b) exchange with intermediation

no proper subset A of C such that, for each $j \in A$, $N^j \subseteq A$. Thus a market is defined to be the smallest set of agents for which every agent of the set deals with other agents of the set and with no agent outside the set. Let $\eta(M)$ denote the number of bilateral exchanges in a market M. Hence

$$(\# M - 1) \leqslant \eta(M) \leqslant \frac{(\# M)(\# M - 1)}{2}$$

Then an allocation $\{c^j, y^j; j \in M\}$ is said to be *feasible for a market M* if

$$\sum_{j \in M} (K^j - y^j) \geqslant (2\alpha)\eta(M)$$

and $\Sigma_{j \in M} \lambda^j(\omega) y^j \geqslant \Sigma_{j \in M} c^j(\omega)$, $\omega \in \Omega$. Thus an allocation is said to be feasible for a market if it can be achieved with the resources and technologies of agents of the market, taking into account the resource costs of exchange. An allocation $\{c^j, y^j; j \in C\}$ is said to be *feasible for a coalition C* if there exists a set of markets $\mathscr{A}$ such that $\cup_{M \in \mathscr{A}} M = C$ and the allocation $\{c^j, y^j; j \in M\}$ is feasible for each market $M \in \mathscr{A}$.[3]

The *core* of the economy I is the set of allocations which are feasible for I and which are not blocked by any coalition. An allocation $\{c^j, y^j; j \in I\}$ is said to be *blocked* by a coalition B if there exists an allocation $\{c^j_*, y^j_*; j \in B\}$ which is feasible for B such that $V^j(c^j_*) > V^j(c^j)$ for each agent $j \in B$. Thus an allocation is said to be in the core if there exists no coalition which can do better with its own resources and technology. In a strong sense this definition of the core is standard. However, it may be noted again that core allocations take into consideration the resource costs of exchange. Viewed in another way, this definition takes into consideration the costs of coalition formation.

Finally a formal definition of intermediation is needed. Agent h is said to act as an *intermediary for a market M* if $N^j = h$ for $j \neq h, j \in M$, and $N^h = M - h$.

3 Characterization of the core: a cooperative economy

As has been noted by many researchers, the core can be viewed as a cooperative solution to the resource-allocation problem. This suggests that the search for core allocations can be facilitated by a characterization of the allocations of a cooperative game. Such an approach is adopted in this section. First a cooperative game is described and cooperative allocations are analyzed. These are shown in propositions 10.1–10.3 to be equivalent to core allocations.

In the cooperative economy specified agents are designated as intermediaries. Each intermediary selects a group of agents for projects in his portfolio. These sets are assumed to be disjoint so that in effect intermediaries are forming markets. Each agent in a market agrees to sell shares in his project to the intermediary for a price of 1 in terms of the capital good, and the intermediary sells shares in his portfolio for a price of 1 in terms of the capital good. A share in the output of project j entitles the holder to λ^j units of the consumption good. A share in the portfolio of an intermediary of market M entitles the holder to $\Sigma_{i\in M}\lambda^i/\#M$ units of the consumption good. All transactions costs are shared equally by all agents in a given market. With $\#M-1$ bilateral exchanges in M, these transactions costs will be $(\#M-1)(2\alpha)$. In these circumstances agents in a market will trade shares with the intermediary on a one-to-one basis up to the limits of their initial endowments less transactions costs. Each intermediary determines the number of agents in his market, and each will act to maximize

$$EU\left[\left\{K^j-\frac{(2\alpha)(\#M-1)}{\#M}\right\}\frac{\Sigma_{i\in M}\lambda^i}{\#M}\right] \qquad (10.1)$$

with respect to $\#M$.

Let Γ denote the set of positive integers which maximize (10.1). For example, if $\{1\}\in\Gamma$, there can be an autarkic allocation in which each agent claims the return only on his own project. The set Γ need not be a singleton; hence each market need not have the same number of agents. Also Γ may be empty; that is, there need not exist a positive integer which maximizes (10.1). As the size of the market increases, the marginal gain from increased diversification goes to zero for, by the law of large numbers, $\Sigma_{i=1}^{n}\lambda^i/n\rightarrow E(\lambda^i)$ almost surely as $n\rightarrow\infty$; however, the marginal per capita transactions cost also goes to zero as $2\alpha(n-1)/n\rightarrow 2\alpha$. However, in what follows it will be assumed that $\Gamma\neq\varnothing$, and so it is important to examine the generality of this assumption. It is easily shown that if $K^j\leqslant 2\alpha$, then $\Gamma\neq\varnothing$; otherwise per capita transactions costs would equal or exceed endowments in the limit as the number of agents increases. There also exist economies in which $K^j>2\alpha>0$ and $\Gamma\neq\varnothing$. For example let $U(W)=W^b$. Suppose that for each

$b \in (0, 1)$, $\Gamma = \emptyset$, and consider the sub-sequence $\{n_v\}$ such that (10.1) is strictly increasing. By taking the limit of (10.1) as $v \to \infty$ and then letting $b \to 1$, a contradiction can be obtained.

The equivalence of the core and the allocations of the cooperative economy with $\Gamma \neq \emptyset$ can now be readily established.

Proposition 10.1
If $\Gamma \neq \emptyset$, the allocations of the cooperative economy are in the core.

Proof. Suppose that a coalition B were able to block an allocation of the cooperative economy; without loss of generality B can be taken to be a market. Consider exchange, production, and consumption decisions which result in Pareto optimal allocations for B; an allocation is Pareto optimal for B if it is feasible for B and if no agent of B can be made better off without making some agent of B worse off. As $U(\cdot)$ displays constant relative risk aversion, a necessary condition for a consumption allocation to be optimal for B is that $c^i(\omega) = \theta^i \Sigma_{j \in B} c^j(\omega)$ for each $\omega \in \Omega$ and for each $i \in B$ with $0 \leqslant \theta^i \leqslant 1$, $\Sigma_{i \in B} \theta^i = 1$. Then to determine an optimal production allocation it is sufficient to maximize

$$\int_{\omega \in \Omega} \mu(\omega) U\{c^i(\omega)\} = \gamma_1 + \gamma_2 \int_{\omega \in \Omega} \mu(\omega) U\left\{\sum_{j \in B} c^j(\omega)\right\}$$

for some positive constants γ_1 and γ_2 for any i with $\theta^i \neq 0$. As $U(\cdot)$ is strictly concave, equal amounts should be invested in all projects of B. With total transactions costs minimized at $2\alpha(\# B - 1)$,

$$y^j = K^j - \frac{2\alpha(\# B - 1)}{\# B}$$

for each $j \in B$. Consider a symmetric allocation of the consumption good over states so that $\theta^j = 1/\# B$ for each $j \in B$. Then

$$c^j(\omega) = \left\{K^j - \frac{2\alpha(\# B - 1)}{\# B}\right\} \left\{\frac{\Sigma_{i \in B} \lambda^i(\omega)}{\# B}\right\}$$

By construction this allocation is Pareto optimal for B, and all agents of B have a level of expected utility which is at most equal to the level of the cooperative allocation. Hence the coalition B could not block the cooperative allocation. Note that this establishes that, with $\Gamma \neq \emptyset$, the core is nonempty.

Proposition 10.2
If $\Gamma = \emptyset$, core allocations do not exist.

Proof. Suppose that a core allocation did exist. In any market M of the core allocation, exchange, production, and consumption decisions must result in an allocation which is Pareto optimal for M; otherwise M could block the core allocation, contradicting the definition of the core. Furthermore, as in a core allocation all agents of M have the same level of expected utility,[4] the allocation of the consumption good must be symmetric so that

$$c^j(\omega)=\left\{K^j-\frac{2\alpha(\#M-1)}{\#M}\right\}\left\{\frac{\Sigma_{i\in M}\lambda^i(\omega)}{\#M}\right\}$$

for each j in M. However, as $\Gamma=\varnothing$ there exist some number of agents $n>\#M$ which could form a market with efficient production and exchange and with a symmetric consumption allocation in which all agents are better off than initially. This is the desired contradiction.[5]

Proposition 10.3
If a core allocation exists, then $\Gamma\neq\varnothing$ and the core allocation is an allocation of the cooperative economy.

Proof. That $\Gamma\neq\varnothing$ follows from the contrapositive of proposition 10.2. As in the proof of proposition 10.2, in each market M of the core production and exchange must be efficient with a symmetric consumption allocation. As blocking coalitions do not exist, it follows that $\#M\in\Gamma$.

4 Intermediation strategies and noncooperative equilibria

It is shown in this section that core allocations are equivalent to the equilibrium allocations of a noncooperative game. First the strategies of agents are defined, and the behavior of agents given these strategies is analyzed. The concept of a blocking strategy is then made precise, and an equilibrium for the noncooperative game is defined. The equivalence is established in propositions 10.4 and 10.5.

Prior to the realization of the state, each agent h adopts a strategy under which he is willing to act as an intermediary for some specified market. This strategy is denoted S^h with the following components: the market S_0^h proposed by agent h; the yield S_1^h in terms of the consumption good for one share in the portfolio of agent h; a price S_2^h in terms of the capital good at which agent h is willing to buy an unlimited number of shares in any project j of S_0^h; a fixed fee S_3^{hj} in terms of the capital good for the purchase of shares in the portfolio of agent h by agent j of S_0^h; a price S_4^h in terms of the capital good at which agent h is willing to sell an unlimited number of shares in his portfolio to agents j of S_0^h. Also, let d^{jh} denote the number of shares purchased by agent j in the portfolio of agent h, and let D^{hj} denote the number of shares in project j sold by j to agent h. Also let $A^{jh}=1$ if agent j purchases shares in the portfolio of agent h, and let $A^{jh}=0$ otherwise. (It will also be convenient in what follows to let $d^{jj}=D^{jj}=S_3^{jj}=A^{jj}=0$.)

Agents must act on the strategies S^h prior to the realization of the state; once the state has occurred, agents make the transfers of the consumption good required to honor claims issued. Given that intermediaries have been selected in some way, all other agents regard the strategies S^h as parameters and maximize expected utility. Hence if agent j is not an active intermediary ($d^{ij}=0$ for each $i \in I$) agent j acts to maximize

$$\sum_{h:\, j \in S_0^h} A^{jh}\{EU(d^{jh}S_1^h + y^j\lambda^j - D^{hj}\lambda^j)\} \tag{10.2}$$

with respect to $\{y^j, D^{hj}, d^{jh}, A^{jh}\}$ subject to the following constraints:

$$\left\{\sum_{h:\, j \in S_0^h} A^{jh}(K^j + D^{hj}S_2^h - d^{jh}S_4^h - S_3^{hj} - \alpha - y^j)\right\} \geqslant 0 \tag{10.3}$$

$$c^j(\omega) = \left[\sum_{h:\, j \in S_0^h} A^{jh}\{d^{jh}S_1^h(\omega) + y^j\lambda^j(\omega) - D^{hj}\lambda^j(\omega)\}\right] \geqslant 0 \text{ for each } \omega \in \Omega \tag{10.4}$$

$$A^{jh} = 1 \Rightarrow A^{ji} = 0 \text{ for each } i \text{ such that } j \in S_0^i,\ i \neq h \tag{10.5}$$

Constraint (10.3) is the budget constraint prior to the realization of the state. Constraint (10.4) requires that agent j be able to honor claims on shares which he issues on his project. Constraint (10.5) limits agent j to choosing one intermediary in which to invest.

An intermediary who is active for his proposed market S_0^h will have expected utility

$$EU\left(\sum_{j \in S_0^h} D^{hj}\lambda^j + y^h\lambda^h - \sum_{j \in S_0^h} d^{jh}S_1^h\right) \tag{10.6}$$

It is required that the vector (S^h, y^h) be *feasible* in that S_0^h be finite and the following constraints be satisfied:

$$\left\{K^h + \sum_{j \in S_0^h} d^{jh}S_4^h + \sum_{j \in S_0^h} S_3^{hj} - \sum_{j \in S_0^h} D^{hj}S_2^h - \alpha(\#N^h) - y^h\right\} \geqslant 0 \tag{10.7}$$

$$c^h(\omega) = \left\{ \sum_{j \in S_0^h} D^{hj} \lambda^j(\omega) + y^h \lambda^h(\omega) - \sum_{j \in S_0^h} d^{jh} S_1^h(\omega) \right\} \geqslant 0 \text{ for each } \omega \in \Omega \tag{10.8}$$

Constraint (10.7) is the budget constraint, and (10.8) ensures that claims issued on the strategy S^h can be honored. If there is any discretion, y^h is chosen to maximize (10.6) subject to (10.7) and (10.8).

In the noncooperative game agents do not cooperate explicitly. In particular, the determination of who is to act as an intermediary and under what terms is not exogenous to the model. Each agent is free to announce any intermediation strategy, and it is assumed that each selects a strategy in such a way as to maximize expected utility. In order to define an equilibrium in such a situation, the following definition of a blocking strategy is needed. A strategy S^b with an input choice y^b for some agent $b \in I$ is said to block a consumption allocation $\{c^j; j \in I\}$ if, when (10.2) is maximized for each agent $j \in S_0^b - b$ subject to constraints (10.3)–(10.5) with $A^{jb} = 1$, the vector (S^b, y^b) is feasible and the resulting consumption allocation $\{c_*^j;\ j \in S_0^b\}$ yields $V^j(c_*^j) > V^j(c^j)$ for all $j \in S_0^b$. S^b is a *blocking strategy*.

To be emphasized in this definition is that agent b finds it is in his own interest to announce a blocking strategy. Of course in the process of undercutting an active intermediary of a specified market or in the process of forming a new market, all the agents with whom agent b deals are made better off than initially. Roughly speaking, agent b can be viewed as a firm that is aware of demand curves and seeks to exploit profitable markets. This type of free entry will be crucial in determining the allocation of resources. In particular, an equilibrium will be described in part as an allocation for which there exist no blocking strategies for any agent.

An equilibrium for the noncooperative game is now defined as follows. An *equilibrium* is a set of actions $\{D_*^{ij}, d_*^{ji}, A_*^{ji}, i \in I\}$ and a strategy S_*^j for each agent $j \in I$, an allocation $\{c_*^j, y_*^j; j \in I\}$, and a set of markets $\mathscr{A}$ which satisfy the following conditions:

1 If $d_*^{ij} = 0$ for each $i \in I$, then $\{y_*^j, D_*^{hj}, d_*^{jh}, A_*^{jh}\}$ maximize (10.2) for agent j subject to constraints (10.3)–(10.5) and to $S^h = S_*^h$, $h \neq j$. ($c_*^j(\omega)$ is determined by (10.4).)
2 $\cup_{M \in \mathscr{A}} M = I$. For each $M \in \mathscr{A}$ there exists an $h \in M$ such that $S_{0*}^h = M$. For each $j \in M - h$, $A^{jh} = 1$. For every such h, S^h is feasible, with y^h chosen to maximize (10.6) subject to (10.7) and (10.8). ($c_*^h(\omega)$ is determined by (10.8).)
3 There does not exist a blocking strategy for any agent of I.

Roughly speaking, condition 1 states that any agent who is not an active intermediary maximizes expected utility by choosing an intermediary with whom to trade, the number of shares in his own project to be sold to that intermediary, the number of shares in the portfolio of that intermediary to be purchased, and the amount to invest in his own project, regarding as parameters the announced intermediation strategies of all other agents. Condition 2 states that agents in effect partition themselves into markets. For each market there is one active intermediary with a strategy and a maximizing input choice which support the maximizing choices of inactive agents. The free-entry condition 3 was motivated above.

The equivalence of core allocations and equilibrium allocations can now be established.

Proposition 10.4
If an equilibrium exits, the equilibrium allocation is in the core.

Proof. Clearly an equilibrium allocation $\{c^j_*, y^j_*; j \in I\}$ is feasible for I. Suppose that it were not in the core. Then suppose, as in the proof of proposition 10.1, that there exists a blocking market B in which exchange, production, and consumption decisions result in a Pareto optimal allocation for B. This yields an allocation

$$y^j_{**} = K^j - \frac{2\alpha(\#B - 1)}{\#B}, \; c^j_{**} = \theta^j\{(\#B)(K^j) - (2\alpha)(\#B - 1)\}\left(\frac{\Sigma_{i \in B}\lambda^i}{\#B}\right)$$

where $\Sigma_{j \in B}\theta^j = 1$ and $V^j(c^j_{**}) > V^j(c^j_*)$ for each $j \in B$. Let some agent $b \in B$ adopt the following strategy:

$$S^b_0 = B, \quad S^b_1 = \frac{\Sigma_{i \in B}\lambda^i}{\#B}, \quad S^b_2 = S^b_4 = 1, \quad S^{bj}_3 = \alpha\{2(\#B - 1)\theta^j - 1\} + K^j\{1 - (\#B)\theta^j\}$$

for each $j \in B - b$. If each agent $j \in B - b$ maximizes (10.2) subject to constraints (10.3)–(10.5) with $A^{jb} = 1$, then the allocation $\{c^j_{**}; j \in B\}$ will be achieved. This contradicts property 3 of the equilibrium. Hence the equilibrium allocation must be in the core.

Proposition 10.5
All core allocations can be supported as equilibria.

Proof. By proposition 10.3 any core allocation is also an allocation of the cooperative economy with $\Gamma \neq \varnothing$. The following actions, strategies, and markets support such an allocation.

1 $\mathscr{A}$ is a set of markets with each $M \in \mathscr{A}$ a market of the core allocation. Hence each $M \in \mathscr{A}$ has some $m \in \Gamma$ agents, and $\cup_{M \in \mathscr{A}} M = I$.

2 For each $M \in \mathscr{A}$ there exists some agent $h \in M$ with strategy

$$S_0^h = M, \quad S_1^h = \frac{\Sigma_{i \in M} \lambda^i}{\# M}, \qquad S_2^h = S_4^h = 1$$

$$S_3^{hj} = \begin{cases} 0 & \text{if } \# M = 1 \\ \dfrac{\alpha(\# M - 2)}{\# M} & \text{if } \# M \geqslant 2 \end{cases} \qquad \text{for each } j \in S_0^h$$

3 For each agent $j \in M - h$, $s_0^j = \varnothing$.

4 $d^{jh} = D^{hj} = K^j - \dfrac{2\alpha(\# M - 1)}{\# M}$ for each $j \in M - h$

$$A^{jh} = 1 \text{ for each } j \in M - h$$

$$y^j = K^j - \frac{2\alpha(\# M - 1)}{\# M} \text{ for each } j \in M$$

$$c^j(\omega) = \left\{K^j - \frac{2\alpha(\# M - 1)}{\# M}\right\}\left\{\frac{\Sigma_{i \in M} \lambda^i(\omega)}{\# M}\right\} \text{ for each } \omega \in \Omega \text{ and each } j \in M$$

Equilibrium properties 1 and 2 follow immediately. Note that agents of M will not collude in their dealings with h. If one agent were to act as a conduit for the funds of another to avoid the fixed fee for one of the agents, an additional transactions cost of $\alpha - \{\alpha(\# M - 2)/\# M\}$ would be incurred for the pair.

As the initial allocation is in the core, no market B can be made better off and equilibrium condition 3 is satisfied.

It should be noted that there are othere schemes by which intermediaries can recoup fixed costs. For example let S_5^h denote a minimum purchase requirement for shares in the portfolio of intermediary h. Then, under condition 2 in proposition 10.5 with $\# M > 2$, consider the strategy

$$S_1^h = \frac{\Sigma_{i \in M} \lambda^i}{\# M}, \quad S_2^h = 1, \quad S_3^{hj} = 0$$

$$S_4^h = \frac{K^j - \alpha}{K^j - \{2\alpha(\# M - 1)/\# M\}}, \quad S_5^h = K^j - \frac{2\alpha(\# M - 1)}{\# M}$$

Agent j would like to purchase fewer than S_5^h shares in the intermediary at prices S_4^h greater than unity. However, he is constrained to purchase at least that amount and will not purchase more. Expenditures remain as before and the new strategies will support a core allocation. The quantity $S_4^h - S_2^h$ can be interpreted as a type of bid–ask spread. It is on this margin that the intermediary covers transactions costs.

5 Concluding remarks

In this final section we offer some comments on the strengths and limitations of the model. First, we may wish to determine whether the parametric behavior specified is incentive compatible. Following Hurwicz (1972), a resource-allocation mechanism is said to be individually incentive compatible if the behavior patterns specified are consistent with agents' natural inclinations. If an agent's project were essential to the portfolio offered by an intermediary, then it could be argued that such an agent might not deal passively but attempt to bargain. However, the model is constructed in such a way that each agent acting on his own has no bargaining power. With I countably infinite, the removal of one agent from the model has no effect on the equilibrium allocation.

In a core allocation of the model the number of bilateral exchanges in a market is one less than the number of agents in that market. Though a noncooperative game in which agents propose markets and adopt intermediation strategies will support such core allocations, the form of organization which could emerge in the model may not be unique. An efficient allocation could be achieved if agents were "lined up" on an interval, with each agent trading with adjacent agents. Alternatively, agents could form pyramids. Such hierarchical intermediation structures are common in financial markets. It remains to show that there exist noncooperative games which yield such structures. In principle the form of market organization should also be explained by the model.

The model is particularly elementary. Agents are assumed to have identical tastes which display constant relative risk aversion and identical initial endowments. These facts are known to all agents. An effort to relax the assumption that tastes and endowments are identical would complicate the model. In particular, a restriction to the trading of shares might be binding and hence not satisfactory. Yet, in principle, the kind of analysis suggested above could be carried out. Intermediaries would take into consideration the desires of agents with diverse attitudes toward risk to trade contingent claims. Acting in their own interest, intermediaries may support efficient allocations.

However, if tastes and endowments are not known, there are new difficulties. Though an equilibrium may exist, it may not be both optimal and incentive compatible. Agents may understate their willingness to pay fixed fees to support a given market. This is a problem which has arisen in the context of models for the allocation of public goods. Though the work of Groves and Ledyard (1974) suggests that the problem may not be insuperable, the effect may be to limit the number of agents in a market. A model with imperfect information may also be rich enough to account for the relatively limited number of types of assets which are traded in active markets. This is a subject of further research.

This chapter was motivated in part by questions of optimal regulation of financial institutions. Obviously the analysis remains too abstract to shed much light on any particular set of arrangements. However, the results do suggest that, under some conditions, competitive markets with free entry will support efficient allocations. More work is needed in this area.

Notes

1 Heller (1972) notes that such a transactions technology is quite different from the one assumed in his paper. Heller and Starr (1976) also mention the possibility of a theory of intermediation in a bilateral trade model with costly transactions.

2 This motivates the work of Shapley and Shubik (1966) on the existence of quasi-cores in a model in which nonconvex preferences make the core empty.

3 Clearly the condition that $\# M < \infty$ is not essential to the definition of a market. Yet without this condition, feasible allocations for infinite sets of agents would need to be defined. This might be done, for example, by taking limits in the appropriate way. The alternative adopted here is to find a condition which is sufficient to ensure that such allocations need not be defined.

4 In a core allocation all agents of I must have the same expected utility. For consider some market M of the core and its complement M'. Pick some $i \in M'$. Suppose that $V(c^i) < V(c^j)$ for some $j \in M$. Then agent i could form a blocking coalition by replacing agent j of M. Therefore $V(c^i) \geqslant V(c^j)$ for each $j \in M$. Suppose that $V(c^i) > V(c^j)$ for some j. Then a symmetric counter-argument applies. Hence $V(c^i) = V(c^j)$ for all $j \in M$. Finally note that the selection of $i \in M'$ was arbitrary.

5 This result rests in part on the definition of the core adopted above. In a model in which feasible allocations for infinite markets were defined, we might anticipate that proposition 10.2 would be modified as follows: if $\Gamma = \varnothing$, core allocations with a finite number of agents in each market do not exist.

References

Arrow, K.J. and Hahn, F.H. (1971) *General Competitive Analysis*. San Francisco, CA: Holden-Day.

Foley, D.K. (1970) Economic equilibrium with costly marketing. *Journal of Economic Theory* 2, 276–91.

Groves, T. and Ledyard, J. (1974) An incentive mechanism for efficient resource allocation in general equilibrium with public goods. Discussion Paper 119, Northwestern University, Evanston, IL.

Hahn, F.H. (1971) Equilibrium with transactions costs. *Econometrica* 39, 417–40.

Heller, W.P. (1972) Transactions with set-up costs. *Journal of Economic Theory* 4, 465–78.

—— and Starr, R.M. (1976) Equilibrium with non-convex transactions costs: monetary and non-monetary economies. *Review of Economic Studies* 43, 195–215.

Hurwicz, L. (1972) On informationally decentralized systems. In *Decision and Organization*, eds C.B. McGuire and R. Radner, ch. 14. Amsterdam: North-Holland.

Kurz, M. (1974) Equilibrium with transactions costs and money in a single market exchange economy. *Journal of Economic Theory* 7, 418–52.

Shapley, L.S. and Shubik, M. (1966) Quasi-cores in a monetary economy with non-convex preferences. *Econometrica* 34(4), 805–27.

Starr, R. (1969) Quasi-equilibria in markets with non-convex preferences. *Econometrica* 36, 25–38.

11
Theories of Intermediated Structures

1 Introduction

This chapter is motivated by a series of positive and normative questions concerning intermediation in the economy. More specifically, on the positive side the following questions arise.

1 Why are there mutual funds which intermediate assets and supermarkets which intermediate commodities? More generally, why are there brokers or middlemen?
2 From where do prices come within markets? How are mutual funds priced? What determines bid–ask spreads?
3 What determines the "extent of the market"? Why are some markets said to be "thin"?
4 How do we explain valued assets such as fiat money and circulating private debt – intermediary assets which facilitate exchange? What is the relationship between such assets and highly integrated financial sectors?

On the normative side the following questions arise.

1 Should the government allow unfettered competition among financial intermediaries?

Reprinted from *Carnegie–Rochester Conference Series on Public Policy*, vol. 18, pp. 221–72 (Amsterdam: North-Holland, 1983). This chapter incorporates an earlier working paper "Equilibrium with endogenous marketeers." Helpful comments on this and related research from Edward Green, Milton Harris, Tatsuro Ichiishi, John Long, Allan Meltzer, Scott Richard, Mark Walker, and Neil Wallace, and financial support from the National Science Foundation and the Alfred P. Sloan Foundation are gratefully acknowledged. I assume full responsibility for any errors as well as for the views expressed herein.

2 Should the government attempt to control the quantity of inside money or near-monies?
3 Should the government regulate securities markets?

Of course we do not pretend to offer a definitive answer to any one of these questions in this chapter. The questions do motivate the analysis, and some preliminary answers are provided. In fact, it is hoped that in the end the chapter is suggestive. But our overall intent is to explore methods, conceptual frameworks, and equilibrium constructs to see what might prove useful for subsequent applications. Thus we proceed at a high level of abstraction; the models are highly stylized.

Given that the models in this chapter are highly stylized while the topic discussed is the subject of an extensive literature, some further motivation would seem to be in order.[1] On the positive side, we search for an explanation of intermediaries, an explanation of market structure, and an explanation of money. Obviously, to constitute an explanation, the phenomena in question cannot be assumed a priori. The idea then is to specify the economy at a primitive level – the preferences of households, their endowments, and the technology of production, communication, and exchange – and hope that the phenomena will emerge endogenously. Yet, despite the basic nature of the phenomena mentioned above, research efforts are at a relatively early stage. We are still in search of a deeper understanding of intermediaries (firms) in market economies and the nature of money, to mention just two examples.

In the search for an explanation of phenomena, some structure must be imposed. In effect, this chapter is an open exploration of where we might fruitfully impose the structure, that is, of what might be a useful abstraction. As it turns out, the predictions of the theory are sensitive to where the structure is imposed and, in particular, to how transactions costs and frictions are modeled. Of course, this inevitably indicates directions for future research.

A second closely related reason for specifying the models in this chapter at the level of preferences, endowments, and technology – in effect, a general equilibrium specification – is that it allows us to perform explicit welfare analysis. In particular, we can look at the welfare of households directly, without specifying an *ad hoc* criterion either for intermediaries or for the government. That is, we can analyze the effect of alternative exchange structures and the effect of proposed regulations by using the standard Pareto criterion.

As it turns out, the welfare implications of the theory, and therefore the answers to the policy questions listed above, are sensitive also to where the structure of the model is imposed and to the nature of transactions costs and frictions. Again, this serves to indicate directions for future research.

We proceed as follows. In the next section we outline the chapter in considerable detail. In fact, virtually all the models and substantive results are described there, with references to the appropriate sections which are in turn more formal self-contained treatments. This arrangement allows the reader to explore various aspects of the chapter in more detail, as preferences dictate.

Briefly, in section 3 we describe a pure exchange Edgeworth economy without trading frictions and its Walrasian (competitive) and cooperative (core) allocations. In section 4 we introduce a noncooperative game for the exchange economy and a sequential Nash equilibrium concept for that game, thereby modeling unfettered competition among intermediaries and explaining in one way the determination of market prices. In section 5 we describe the relationship among Walrasian, core, and noncooperative equilibrium allocations when arbitrage by customers across potential intermediaries is allowed. With a large number of households, all these types of allocations are equivalent. In section 6 we describe that relationship when intermediaries alone can compete with one another. Again, with a large number of households, there is an equivalence. In section 7 we present a mutual fund model with explicit trading frictions (costly bilateral exchange). In this model, the core and noncooperative equilibrium allocations are again equivalent, and the model explains in a more satisfactory way the existence and relative number of intermediaries, the "extent of the market," the degree of diversification, and the extent of fixed fees in mutual fund pricing schemes. In section 8 we describe spatial models with explicit dynamics which explain valued currency and circulating private debt – intermediary assets. But here the frictions of distinct spatially separated markets make competitive monetary and debt equilibria Pareto *nonoptimal*. This suggests a role for government in controlling the quantity of currency and inside monies. Finally, in section 9 we describe how pieces of the earlier sections might be fitted together to build a spatial model of financial intermediation. Such a model might explain the coexistence of high-intermediated sectors with "thin" markets and bilateral currency transactions, and how the development of markets goes hand in hand with the development of media of exchange. But again such a model would deliver Pareto nonoptimal allocations and suggests a role for government in coordinating activity across markets or across financial intermediaries. Section 9 can in turn be viewed as an attempt to reveal the source of nonoptimality and offers some caveats for policy analysis. This motivates the directions for future research indicated in section 10.

2 The essence of the chapter

We begin with the simplest possible economy which allows for trade – a pure exchange economy such as that analyzed by Edgeworth (1881), in which households have exogenously specified endowments and preferences over consumption goods and in which there are no trading frictions (see section 3). Time and uncertainty are entirely incorporated by indexing commodities. In this context, then, the standard noncooperative and cooperative equilibrium concepts are the Walrasian equilibrium and the core respectively. The Walrasian equilibrium is the standard competitive equilibrium in which decisions are decentralized by a price system. A core allocation is one which cannot be improved upon by a subset of households with their own resources. These equilibrium concepts are also reviewed in section 3. However, there are some obvious questions. With regard to the competitive outcome, from where do market prices come? More generally, suppose that relatively unfettered competition among intermediaries was allowed. Would the outcome be Pareto optimal, or in the core, or even Walrasian? Indeed, as might be suggested by a reading of Fama (1980), unfettered competition among intermediaries in the pure exchange economy would be like free banking. Thus, following Fama, we can ask whether the decisions of the entire intermediation (banking) sector would be of no consequence for the determination of prices and real activity – those of the Walrasian equilibrium? That is, is there a kind of Modigliani–Miller or neutrality proposition?

These questions are pursued here by making precise one concept of unfettered competition among intermediaries and one concept of the outcome of that competition. This is done in section 4. To be noted first is that in the pure exchange economy we can analyze the simplest form of intermediation – acting as a go-between or broker for the exchange of commodities or claims on commodities (securities). Thus, the economy is given more structure by the (exogenous) imposition of a dynamic two-stage game with such brokers. In the first stage of the game each household is free to announce any vector of prices under which it is willing to act as an intermediary (broker, middleman), offering to buy or sell unlimited quantities of commodities or claims on commodities (securities) at the specified prices.[2] Here a vector of prices is an accounting system, with a specified (potentially abstract) unit of account. In the second stage households take these first-stage price announcements as given in choosing intermediaries with whom to trade and the amount to trade. These latter choices are formalized by a set of decision rules, where a rule is a function of the first-stage announcements. Then, consistent with concepts of dynamic programming, households take these decision rules as given in making announcements in the first stage. In this context the natural equilibrium concept is the sequential Nash equilibrium in the space of first-stage announcements and second-stage decision rules.[3] Again, households are treated symmetrically; anyone who wants may call out a price vector and attempt to attract customers. In effect, there is free entry into the intermediation sector.[4]

Within this general framework, two specific games are considered. In the first, intermediaries cannot restrict the set of potential customers, and customers can deal with more than one intermediary (see section 5). In this game households can resell the commodities (securities) that they have purchased, so that in effect unlimited arbitrage is allowed.[5] Putting this another way, and continuing with the Fama and Modigliani–Miller analogy, in this first game there is open access to the capital market. Thus, as it turns out, with two or more active intermediaries, prices are necessarily competitive and the Walrasian allocation is achieved. Also, with a finite number of households overall, non-Walrasian equilibria, in which there is a single active intermediary, can exist.[6] Such equilibrium allocations are not Pareto optimal. However, the ability of a single intermediary to set non-Walrasian prices is limited by the extent of the market. As his resources become negligible relative to economy-wide aggregates, prices tend to become Walrasian.[7]

In the second game considered here, customers can choose at most one intermediary with whom to trade and intermediaries can restrict the set of potential customers (see section 6). In this game there is no possibility for resale, but intermediaries can compete among themselves. Putting this another way, and continuing again the Fama and Modigliani–Miller analogy, direct access to the capital markets by individuals is limited, but the capital market itself is competitive. Accordingly, with a finite number of households overall, the Walrasian outcome can be achieved, though there may well exist other non-Walrasian equilibria. But again, in the limit economy with an infinity of households, the outcome is necessarily Walrasian. This is one of the more fundamental results of this chapter. All these results for the second game turn on some well-known relationships between core and Walrasian allocations.

Abstracting from dynamic considerations, we find that the equilibrium of the second game has the following properties. First, any household which is not an intermediary maximizes expected utility by choosing an intermediary with whom to trade and the amount to trade. Second, households in effect partition themselves into trading cooperatives.[8] For each cooperative there is an active intermediary or broker who specifies the terms of trade. Third, neither entry by new intermediaries nor change of strategy by existing intermediaries is desired. As noted above, no household can propose an intermediation strategy which, if adopted by households in the named coalition, would make the intermediary and the households in that coalition better off. Thus the equilibrium has both cooperative and noncooperative aspects. A particularly nice feature in the limit economy, with a continuum of households, is that it delivers allocations in the core. In fact an equilibrium allocation cannot be improved upon by a coalition, where allocations of coalitions are restricted to those which can be achieved as Walrasian equilibria for the coalition.[9]

In summary, the sequential Nash equilibria of the two particular noncooperative intermediation games considered here have nice positive and normative characteristics, at least in Edgeworth's pure exchange economy. They deliver properties typically associated with intermediated structures and have the optimality (neutrality) properties described above, at least if the number of households is large.

In other ways, however, the analysis so far is unsatisfactory, in both positive and normative aspects. From the standpoint of positive economics, we may note that some characteristics associated with intermediated structures are missing. First, there need be only one active intermediary (though there may well be more than one – it is the threat of competition which matters). Second, everybody may be in the same market, that is, markets are not thin in any sense. Third, there is nothing which corresponds to fixed fees or to bid–ask spreads with minimum purchase requirements. More generally, it is not clear in what sense we have explained anything, since the games are imposed exogenously by the modeler. Intimately related is the fact that equilibrium allocations can be nonoptimal if there are a finite number of households. Though this outcome is consistent with observations on the inefficiency of monopoly, duopoly, and the like, it is the case nevertheless that there exist alternative schemes which produce Pareto superior outcomes. That is, the source of nonoptimality is the game itself, and (here) the game is not given any deep rationalization.[10]

There are at least two ways out of this dilemma toward a more satisfactory positive and normative theory. These are closely related. One way, following Hurwicz (1959, 1972), is to be more formal about the mechanism which is to achieve the allocation of resources in a given environment. A mechanism is characterized by the set of possible messages which households can send (to a center) at each stage of a resource-allocation process and the outcome function which maps messages into an allocation. For example, we might ask in this context whether there is anything special about the competitive mechanism. Hurwicz (1959) and Jordan (1982) have shown that there is – the competitive mechanism is the unique efficient way of decentralizing the economy. That is, in achieving Pareto optimal allocations, it requires minimal message space. The implication of message space considerations for the noncooperative intermediation games of sections 5 and 6, among others, is left as an open question.

A second related way out of the dilemma, toward a more satisfactory positive theory, is to impose explicit trading frictions in the environment of the economy itself. Indeed, this is the route taken by Townsend (1978, this volume, ch. 10) for a highly stylized economy and further reported here in section 7.

Imagine in particular that each of a (countably infinite) set of household firms is endowed with a quantity of a capital good (the unique factor of production) and with a stochastic technology which transforms the capital good into a distribution of the unique consumption good of the model. Suppose that investment project returns are independent across household firms and that household firms are risk averse. Finally, suppose that each bilateral link between households is *costly*, using a fixed amount of the capital good. In this economy, then, households care very much about the way in which they are linked to one another. In fact, an exchange structure in which everyone is linked to everyone else is generally inefficient – efficient structures minimize the number of bilateral connections. That is, efficient structures necessarily involve intermediation. Moreover, an efficient exchange structure may not have all households linked to one another, even indirectly. As the number of households in a trading coalition increases, there is a gain in terms of (potentially) increased risk sharing but a loss in terms of increased per capita transaction costs.

To be more formal about the outcome we would predict for this economy, an equilibrium concept must be imposed. But what equilibrium concept? A Walrasian equilibrium concept which demands complete decentralization among households would seem to be inappropriate. That is, from what has been said so far, and from the analysis in sections 3–6, the equilibrium concept should take into account what can be achieved by coalitions. Thus it seems that the natural equilibrium notion here is the core. As it turns out, core allocations for this simple economy, with an infinity of virtually identical households, must treat all households symmetrically. This leads in turn to a straightforward maximization problem which has core allocations as its solutions and which makes explicit the tradeoff between increased diversification and increased per capita transaction costs. The important result is that in a core allocation the number of households in a given trading coalition may well be finite. In this sense market size is limited endogenously. Finally, of course, the exchange structure *within* coalitions requires intermediation.

Again, following the lead of sections 3–6, we may ask whether unfettered competition among potential intermediaries leads to core allocations in this model with transaction costs. Again, an equivalence result can be established. That is, suppose that each household firm announces the set of household firms with which it is willing to deal, the yield in terms of the consumption good for one share in its portfolio, a price in terms of the capital good at which it is willing to sell an unlimited number of shares in its portfolio, a fixed fee in terms of the capital good for the purchase of shares in its portfolio, and a price in terms of the capital good at which it is willing to take in an unlimited number of shares on the project of any household firm in its specified set of potential traders. In this context an equilibrium can be defined as a set of mutual funds, a set of consumption–investment decisions, a set of share choices, and a set of intermediation strategies such that the following hold.

1 Any household firm which is not an active intermediary maximizes expected utility by choosing an intermediary with whom to trade, the number of shares in its own project to be sold to the intermediary, the number of shares in the portfolio of that intermediary to be purchased, and the amount to invest in its own project, taking as given the announced intermediation strategies of all other household firms.
2 Household firms in effect partition themselves into mutual funds, and for each mutual fund there is one active intermediary with a strategy and maximizing input choice which support the maximizing choices of inactive household firms.
3 No existing or potential intermediary can find an intermediation strategy which Pareto dominates the consumption–investment allocation.

It can be established formally that the set of equilibrium allocations and set of core allocations are again equivalent. Finally, it can be assumed that the price at which potential intermediaries are willing to buy shares is strictly less than the price at which they are willing to sell shares in their own portfolios, a kind of bid–ask spread. If in addition there is a minimum purchase requirement for shares in the portfolio, again core allocations can be achieved in noncooperative equilibria.

The mutual fund model of section 7 has nice positive and normative properties. It delivers the missing elements mentioned above; the relative number of active intermediaries, the extent of the market, the degree of diversification, and the relative magnitude of fixed fees can all be explained. Moreover, several of these elements come from frictions within the environment itself – the costs of bilateral exchange (the noncooperative game does impose additional structure – otherwise, who acts as an intermediary for whom is not pinned down). Finally, core allocations are Pareto optimal. There seems to be no scope for intervention.

Still, the mutual fund model, like the frictionless Edgeworth economy, is missing observed phenomena. First, there are no active spot markets; all trade or commitments to trade take place in a market organized at the initial date. Second, there are no financial assets which play the role of money – objects which serve as media of exchange (intermediaries of another kind). To capture these phenomena, the economies must be decentralized further. This is done in sections 8 and 9.

To begin the discussion, imagine an Arrow–Debreu model which is specified at a rather general level. Each of a set of household firms is endowed with a vector of consumption goods and a vector of factors of production such as labor and capital, but each vector may have many components which are zero. Each household firm has preferences over consumption and resource vectors in each period of its life, as described by a well-behaved utility function, but, again, not every household firm cares about every commodity or factor of production. Finally, each household firm is endowed with a technology for transforming factors of production into commodity outputs, but these technologies are not all alike.

Now suppose that household firms can form bilateral links in order to trade with one another, as in the mutual fund model, but that these links are costly. Suppose in particular that such links must be formed in any period in which a household firm transfers a consumption good or factor of production to some other household firm or makes a commitment to a transfer at a future date, as if communication were impossible without such links. (In the mutual fund model a fixed cost was incurred which allowed both the making of commitments and the transfer of goods, but here a distinction is made.) It can also be assumed that the cost of such links can vary with both time and the identity of the household firms involved.

Rather extreme but interesting versions of this trading technology suppose that trading links are either completely resource free or infinitely costly. Such versions have the interpretation that household firms are spatially separated, moving from location to location. Household firms in the same location at a given date can trade with one another costlessly; thus, with an infinity of households of each type, we can well assume the existence of a competitive market at that location, motivated by the analysis of sections 5 and 6. Household firms not in the same location at a given date can neither trade with one another nor make commitments to trade in the future. That is, there can be no communication across markets.

These spatial models are proving to be quite successful in explaining phenomena. They are reviewed in more detail in section 8. One such model is Lucas's version of the Cass–Yaari model (Cass and Yaari, 1966), described by Townsend (1980, this volume, ch. 2). Its key feature is the absence of double coincidence of wants among groups of households who meet in bilateral pairings, a feature dating back at least to Wicksell (1935). In this model there exists a monetary equilibrium in which fiat money is valued. That is, currency has a determinate price in terms of other goods. In that sense, money is explained. Also, we can introduce capital and explain rate-of-return dominance and other apparent asset price anomalies (see Townsend, 1987, this volume, ch. 12). Finally, we can introduce a variable labor supply and explain how financial structure and real activity are intimately related (see Townsend, 1987, this volume, ch. 12). Another spatial model is the "turnpike" model of exchange presented by Townsend (1980, this volume, ch. 2) in which valued fiat money facilitates intertemporal transactions; that is, it is a partial substitute for borrowing and lending which is precluded by the spatial separation – the links among households are such that previous commitments cannot be honored. In fact, we may well include some within-group diversity, as Wallace (1980) and Sargent (1987) have suggested, and predict fiat money transactions for households who meet only once and credit transactions for households which have more permanent relationships. Finally, we can alter the "turnpike" exchange structure so that households are more strongly linked with one another, if only indirectly, and explain the existence of high velocity private debt, that is, circulating IOUs (see Townsend and Wallace, 1982).

The success of these spatial models should be contrasted with their suggestive but troublesome normative features. As it turns out (*laissez-faire*) competitive equilibria with fiat money and circulating private debt are generally not Pareto optimal. That is, there exists a redistribution of the consumption goods which is technically feasible and improves the welfare of everyone. These redistributions can be achieved directly with lump-sum taxes and subsidies on commodity endowments or indirectly, in a monetary equilibrium, with lump-sum taxes and subsidies on fiat money. Thus the welfare analysis seems to create some scope for government policy. Indeed, we can replicate the conclusions of the money growth literature on the optimal rate of deflation (see Friedman, 1969). In fact, Townsend (1983, this volume, ch. 4) seems to suggest a more activist policy in the presence of stochastic shocks, and Townsend and Wallace (1982) seem to suggest a coordination problem between markets (multiple equilibria) which might be remedied by restrictions on the issue of private debt. What is not clear is the extent to which this taxation and regulation would violate the decentralization imposed directly on the households a priori, namely that reallocations be achieved by competitively determined exchanges in distinct spatial locations and that there be no communication across such locations. Thus the welfare analysis does not provide definitive conclusions, but it does indicate directions for future research.

At this point we ask the reader to imagine how parts of the earlier sections – the noncooperative intermediation games in sections 3–6, the mutual fund model with costly and endogenous market formation in section 7, and the emergence of media of exchange in the spatial models of section 8 – might be fitted together to build a spatial theory of intermediated financial structures. Imagine in particular that households have some control over their itinerary, that is, they can travel at some cost from exogenously specified locations at any given date. Then we might well imagine that with costly exchange, limited communication, and the absence of double coincidence of wants for certain pairings, fiat money would be valued and would facilitate intermediation.[11] Thus the development of media of exchange would go hand in hand with the development of markets, as Adam Smith (1976) observed. Second, and more generally, we might expect to observe the coexistence of highly intermediated sectors with thin markets and bilateral currency transactions. Third, if commitments can be made only through intermediaries, it seems likely that unfettered competition among intermediaries would *not* deliver core outcomes. In general, core allocations would seem to require some a priori and apparently costless cooperation across intermediaries. The chapter thus concludes with several caveats for policy analysis, and, in section 10, with some suggestions for future research.

3 Structure of a frictionless pure exchange Edgeworth economy

Consider first a pure exchange economy of the type considered by Edgeworth (1881) which is inhabited by a finite number of households. Each of these households has an endowment of each of a finite number of commodities, and each household cares about consumption of these commodities, with preferences represented by a well-behaved utility function. There are no trading frictions. Thus the economy may well be subject to uncertainty and may well evolve over time or even contain diverse locations. However, following Arrow (1953) and Debreu (1959), these aspects are incorporated entirely by indexing commodities by realized states of nature, by time, and by location, assuming that all plans for trade are made at some initial date. In summary, then, the economy is completely determined by a specification of the endowment and utility function for each and every household. In particular, there are no firms or institutions specified a priori.

To be more formal, suppose that there are l possible commodities, so that commodities are labeled by the numbers 1 through l with typical element j. Also, let Ω denote the set of households. Thus Ω is a set of household labels or names. A household labeled a, with $a \in \Omega$, has an endowment e_a, which is a finite but strictly positive l-dimensional vector. Each household a has a utility function U_a, defined over the space of all nonnegative l-dimensional consumption vectors, with typical element f_a. The utility function U_a is assumed to be continuous, strictly increasing, and strictly quasi-concave. (As a technical matter, it is assumed that $U_a(\cdot)$ takes on the value $+\infty$ if any component of the consumption vector is $+\infty$.) We can let V denote the class of all such utility functions. Thus an economy E is a mapping from the set of households Ω into the space of endowment–utility function pairs $R^l_{++} \times V$.

It should be noted that, apart from its name, each household a is completely determined by its endowment and utility function (e_a, U_a). Thus households can be grouped according to types, that is, each household of type i has an endowment–utility function pair (e^i, U^i). There are at most a finite number m of household types, with type i taking on values in the index set $1, 2, \ldots, m$.

A consumption allocation in this Edgeworth economy E is a specification of a consumption vector f_a for each and every household a. That is, an allocation is a function f which assigns to each household a of Ω a consumption vector f_a. A consumption allocation is said to be attainable if it can be achieved with the endowments of the households. In other words, an allocation f for an economy E is attainable if $\Sigma_{a\in\Omega}e_a \geqslant \Sigma_{a\in\Omega}f_a$.

A particularly simple and entirely familiar pure exchange economy is the Edgeworth box economy, where it is assumed that there are two households labeled 1 and 2, and two commodities labeled 1 and 2. Essentially, the set of attainable allocations for the Edgeworth box economy is the set of points in the Edgeworth box.

In what follows we will be very much concerned with how an allocation f is determined for an economy E. We will also want to compare final allocations with those that would be achieved in perfectly competitive markets, on the one hand, and with the allocations that would be achieved if all households behaved cooperatively, on the other hand. Thus competitive and cooperative equilibrium concepts must be formalized.

In the class of pure exchange economies under consideration, a price for a commodity j specifies the number of units of credit which each household receives for each unit of commodity j supplied to the market, and the number of debits incurred for each unit of commodity j demanded from the market. Thus a price system is a nonnegative l-dimensional vector p, with typical element p_j. Of course, the unit of account is somewhat arbitrary here; we can normalize prices by letting p_j equal unity, for example, so that commodity j is the numeraire, or by letting prices sum to unity, $\Sigma_j p_j = 1$, so that a particular market bundle is the numeraire. In *that* sense the price system is indeterminate. Whatever normalization is used, however, each household takes the price system p as given and maximizes utility subject to its budget constraint that the valuation of commodities purchased cannot exceed the valuation of commodities supplied. Of course, in equilibrium the consumption allocations which are determined in this way must clear the market. More formally, an allocation f and a price vector p is called a Walras equilibrium for an economy E if it is attainable and assigns to each household an element which is maximal in the budget hyperplane, $\{x\in R^l_+ : p\cdot e_a = p\cdot x\}$ defined by p. Then an allocation f is called a Walras allocation for E if there exists a price vector p such that (f, p) is a Walras equilibrium for E; here also p can be referred to as a Walras price vector. To avoid trivialities, it is assumed that the economy is such that no Walras equilibrium can be autarkic.

The more or less standard *cooperative* equilibrium concept is the core. It is straightforward to define here. The idea behind the core is that any subset or group of households can combine and reject a proposed economy-wide allocation if that group can do better on its own, that is, with its own resources. More formally, a subset of households C is said to improve upon an allocation f for an economy E if there exists an allocation g which is attainable for C, that is, $\Sigma_{a\in C}g_a \leqslant \Sigma_{a\in C}e_a$, and is such that $U_a(g_a) > U_a(f_a)$ for every household a of C. The set of attainable allocations for E which *no* subset of households can improve upon is called the *core* of E.

The set of core allocations for the Edgeworth box economy is easily deduced. Obviously, an allocation f which is not on the contract curve – the locus of points where indifference curves are tangent – can be improved upon by the set of all households. Also, any allocation which puts one household on an indifference curve below the indifference curve through its endowment can be improved upon by that household itself. Thus, for the two-household Edgeworth box economy, core allocations lie on the portion of the contract curve which is bounded by indifference curves through the endowment. Also, as Edgeworth (1881) argued, the core shrinks to the set of Walras allocations as economy is replicated, with an increasing number n of households of type 1 and type 2 identical with households 1 and 2 respectively. This result is now known to hold for the general class of economies under consideration.

Finally, we can note again the advantage of the general equilibrium structure under consideration – we have at hand an obvious welfare criterion, namely Pareto optimality. That is, an attainable allocation f for an economy E is said to be Pareto optimal if there does not exist an alternative allocation g which is attainable and makes some households better off without making other households worse off. Under the assumptions made here, both the core and the set of Walras allocations are Pareto optimal; we may note, for example, that an allocation which is not Pareto optimal cannot lie in the core. Moreover, as the Edgeworth box economy illustrates, the set of Walras allocations is contained in the core, and these in turn are contained in the set of Pareto optimal allocations (the entire contract curve). Thus the core has more predictive content than the set of Pareto optimal allocations, and less predictive content than Walras allocations, except where the number of traders is large.

4 Unfettered competition among intermediaries in the Edgeworth economy: a class of noncooperative games and a sequential Nash equilibrium concept

In this section we describe a class of noncooperative games. Conceptually it will be convenient to view each of these games as consisting of two stages. In the first stage each household $t \in \Omega$ is free to announce any vector of prices p_t under which it is willing to act as an intermediary in the second stage for a specified set of households A_t. Here it should be understood that, from the point of view of households of A_t, household t is willing to buy or sell unlimited amounts of each of the l commodities at the prices p_t. In particular, there is no possibility of limiting quantities. In general A_t can be chosen from a specified set $\mathscr{C}$ of subsets of Ω. (In particular either $\mathscr{C} = \{\Omega, \varnothing\}$ or $\mathscr{C} = 2^{\Omega}$, the set of all subsets of Ω.) Thus a first-stage strategy for any household t is an announcement $S_t = (p_t, A_t) \in R^l_+ \times \mathscr{C}$.

An announcement $S_t = (p_t, A_t)$ is said to be null if A_t equals the empty set $\varnothing$ and with some abuse of notation we write $S_t = \varnothing$. Under a null announcement, household t forgoes entirely the possibility of acting as an intermediary in the second stage. Also, it is understood that if S_t is nonnull, then household t names itself, that is, $t \in A_t$. Let the function $S: \Omega \rightarrow R^l \times \mathscr{C}$ denote the announcements of all households with typical element S_t for household $t \in \Omega$. We can also write $S = [S_a, a]_{a \in \Omega}$. Also let $S_{\bar{t}}$ denote the announcements of households other than t. That is $S_{\bar{t}} = [S_a, a]_{a \in \bar{t}}$ where $\bar{t} = \Omega - (t)$.

Given that the announcements S of the first stage have been determined in some way, each household in the second stage takes these announcements as given in choosing both intermediaries with whom to trade and the amount to trade, subject to the following restrictions. If for household $t \in \Omega$, $S_t = \varnothing$, then household t must choose intermediaries from among those whose announcements include it in a named coalition. That is, household t chooses a set of intermediaries $D_t(S)$ from the set $M_t(S) \equiv \{a \in \bar{t}: S_a = (p_a, A_a), t \in A_a\}$. The particular games considered below will be characterized in part by further restrictions on the choice of intermediaries from $M_t(S)$. Household t also chooses the amount to trade with each such intermediary, that is, household t chooses a trade vector $Z_t(S) \equiv \{Z_{ta}(S), a \in D_t(S)\}$. It is required that the trade vector $Z_{ta}(S)$ with intermediary a is a member of the budget set $\{z \in R^l: p_a \cdot z = 0\}$ defined by the announced price vector p_a, and that the final consumption of household t is feasible, that is, that $\{\Sigma_{a \in D_t(S)} Z_{ta}(S)\} + e_t \in X$, where $X \subseteq R^l_+$ is some a priori feasible consumption set. Note that, if $M_t(S) = \varnothing$, then $D_t(S) = \varnothing$, and so $Z_t(S)$ is undefined. Note also that so far $D_t(S)$ and $Z_t(S)$ are introduced only as a matter of notation as choice elements; it has not yet been said how particular elements will in fact be chosen.

Now consider a household $t \in \Omega$ with a nonnull announcement $S_t = (p_t, A_t)$. Household t may be either active or inactive under its announcement. Household t is said to be active under S_t if it is chosen by a household in its named coalition, that is, if $t \in D_a(S)$ for some $a \in A_t - (t)$, and it is said to be inactive if it is chosen by no one. If household t is active, then it cannot choose another intermediary with whom to trade, that is, $D_t(S) = \varnothing$. If household t is inactive, it must choose an intermediary with whom to trade from $M_t(S)$, and $D_t(S)$ and $Z_t(S)$ are defined as above for the case $S_t = \varnothing$.[12]

In order to define the decision problem confronting each household at each stage of the game, we must specify what each household takes as given. As is implicit in the discussion above, in the second stage each household takes as given the second-stage choices of all households other than itself, as well as the first-stage announcements S of all households, in choosing intermediaries with whom to trade and the amount to trade. Thus, given S, we can say that some specified second-stage choices $D_t^*(S), Z_t^*(S)$ are maximal for household t relative to some specified choices $[D_a^*(S), Z_a^*(S), a]_{a\in\bar{t}}$ of others if, when there is any discretion, the choices $D_t^*(S)$, $Z_t^*(S)$ maximize U_t. (Recall that there may be no discretion if $S_t \neq \varnothing$ and household t is active given $D_a^*(S)$, $a\in\bar{t}$.) If, for a specified set of choices $[D_a^*(S), Z_a^*(S), a]_{a\in\Omega}$, the specified choices $D_t^*(S)$ and $Z_t^*(S)$ are maximal for each household t, then the set is said to be *maximal*.

It must be noted here that a *finite* maximum will not exist if $X = R^l_+$ and there is an arbitrage possibility. In that even some components of the "maximizing" trade vector will be interpreted as being infinite in absolute value, and the utility function will be interpreted as taking on the value $+\infty$. In general no maximal choices of any kind need exist. However, it will be part of an equilibrium specification (see below) that maximal choices exist.

A *decision rule* for each household t is a function which specifies the maximal choice of intermediaries $D_t^*(S)$ and the maximal trade vector $Z_t^*(S)$ for all possible first-stage announcements S. Thus, from the point of view of household t, its decision rule $D_t^*(\cdot)$, $Z_t^*(\cdot)$ is determined in a maximizing way, given the specified decision rules of $[D_a^*(\cdot), Z_a^*(\cdot), a]_{a\in\bar{t}}$ of others. Again, these decision rules need not be well defined in general, but they must be well defined in equilibrium (see below).

In the first stage of the game each household t takes as given, in choosing its own announcement, specified first-stage announcements $\{S_a^*, a\}_{a\in\bar{t}}$ of all households other than itself, specified second-stage decision rules $[D_a^*(\cdot), Z_a^*(\cdot), a]_{a\in\bar{t}}$ of households other than itself, and its own maximizing decision rule $D_t^*(\cdot), Z_t^*(\cdot)$. Thus, in the view of household t, an announcement $S_t = (p_t, A_t)$ under which it is an active intermediary results in an allocation $\{e_t - \Sigma_a Z_{at}^*(S)\}$, where $S = (S_{\bar{t}}^*, S_t)$, and the summation is over all households a which choose to trade with t, $\{a\in A_t : t\in D_a^*(S)\}$. It is assumed here that the trades $Z_a^*(S)$ are effected. Of course if household t is inactive under S_t, its allocation will be determined by $D_t^*(S), Z_t^*(S)$ as described above. In this context a strategy $S_t = (p_t, A_t)$ can be said to be a *feasible strategy* for household t relative to the specified announcements $\{S_a^*, a\}_{a\in\bar{t}}$ and the specified decisions $[D_a^*(S), Z_a^*(S), a]_{a\in\bar{t}}$ of others if household t is either inactive or active with the vector $[e_t - \Sigma_a Z_{at}^*(S)]\in X$. It is assumed that, given the announcements $[S_a^*, a]_{a\in\bar{t}}$ and decision rules $[D_a^*(\cdot), Z_a^*(\cdot), a]_{a\in\Omega}$, household t varies S_t parametrically over all feasible strategies and, if possible, chooses one which is maximal under U_t.[13] The chosen strategy is said to be maximal relative to the announcements $[S_a^*, a]_{a\in\bar{t}}$ and decision rules $[D_a^*(\cdot), Z_a^*(\cdot), a]_{a\in\Omega}$. Again, maximal strategies need only exist in equilibrium (see below).

A sequential Nash equilibrium of a game is a specification of first-stage announcements and second-stage decision rules such that, for each household t, the specified announcement and decision rule are indeed maximal. More formally we have the following definition.

Definition
A sequential Nash equilibrium is a specification of an announcement S_t^* and decision rule $D_t^*(\cdot), Z_t^*(\cdot)$ for each household $t \in \Omega$ such that (a) for every S, the choices $D_t^*(S), Z_t^*(S)$ are maximal for each household t relative to the choices $[D_a^*(S), Z_a^*(S), a]_{a \in \Gamma}$ of others, and (b) the announcement S_t^* is maximal for each household t relative to the announcements $[S_a^*, a]_{a \in \Gamma}$ of others and the decision rules $[D_a^*(\cdot), Z_a^*(\cdot), a]_{a \in \Omega}$ of everyone.

Hereafter, any reference to an equilibrium of a game for the pure exchange Edgeworth economy will be taken to mean this sequential Nash equilibrium.

Several properties of this equilibrium concept should be noted. First, the equilibrium path is consistent in that the choices of each household are derived as the solution to a dynamic optimization problem. That is, each household t determines its optimal announcement by working backwards from the second stage, taking as given what it and other households will do given (arbitrary) first-stage announcements. In the second stage these second-stage plans will be carried out. Second, it may be noted that, in specifying a particular equilibrium, it is not necessary to specify the choices $[D_a^*(S), Z_a^*(S), a]_{a \in \Omega}$ for *all* possible announcements S. From the point of view of each household t, given the announcements $[S_a^*, a]_{a \in \Gamma}$ of others, the only announcements S which can be generated are of the form $S = (S_t, S_\Gamma^*)$. In addition the rules $D_a^*(\cdot)$, $Z_a^*(\cdot)$ are often clear without elaboration. Third, an equilibrium can be said to be null if in equilibrium all households have adopted the null strategy. Since the environment is such that no Walras equilibrium is autarkic, a null equilibrium cannot exist.[14]

The sequential Nash equilibria of two specific games are characterized in the next two sections.

5 Arbitrage restrictions and the Walrasian outcome in the Edgeworth economy

In game 1 no intermediary can restrict trade to a proper subset of the set of all households Ω. In particular the only nonnull strategies for any household t which are allowed are of the form $S_t = (p_t, \Omega)$, that is, $\mathscr{C} = [\varnothing, \Omega]$. Also, in game 1 any household which is not an active intermediary can choose to trade with any subset of intermediaries from the set with nonnull strategies. In this game, then, intermediaries are relatively restricted in their ability to compete with one another. Finally, attention is limited to environments with the set of all households Ω finite with $\# \Omega \geqslant 3$, and the consumption set $X = R^l_+$.

It is established that any Walras allocation can be achieved in a sequential Nash equilibrium of game 1. Yet the converse need not hold; it is shown by way of an example that there exist equilibria in which a single intermediary exhibits some market power. (If there are two or more active intermediaries, the equilibrium is necessarily competitive.) In the limit, however, as the economy is replicated, the set of equilibria of game 1 shrinks to the set of Walras equilibria. These results turn on the possibility of arbitrage and on the definition of feasible strategies.

First, several obvious characteristics of game 1 are noted. The first of these is essentially that all intermediaries must announce the same price; otherwise, there exists an arbitrage possibility for an inactive household. The second characteristic is that price-taking weakly dominates price-setting at the same price. More formally we have the following remarks.

Remark 11.1 (arbitrage)
Given a set of first-stage announcements S and a set of maximal second-stage choices $[D_a^*(S), Z_a^*(S), a]_{a\in\Omega}$, assume that there exist two households, say 1 and 2, with strategies $S_1 = (p_1, \Omega)$ and $S_2 = (p_2, \Omega)$ such that S_1 is feasible, and there exists a third household, say 3, with either $S_3 = \varnothing$ or $3 \notin D_a^*(S)$, $a \in \Omega - [3]$. Then $p_1 = p_2$.

Remark 11.2 (dominance of price-taking)
Consider household t with a choice between trading with a set of intermediaries M with strategies $S_m = (p, \Omega)$, $m \in M$, that is, choosing from among $[z \in R^l: p \cdot z = 0]$, or being an active intermediary under a feasible strategy $S_t = (p, \Omega)$. Household t cannot prefer the latter alternative.

With these remarks it is now straightforward to establish the following proposition.

Proposition 11.1
Given any Walras equilibrium with allocation–price pair (f, p), the allocation f can also be attained in an equilibrium of game 1 in which there is an active intermediary t with strategy $S_t^* = (p, \Omega)$.

For the proof of proposition **11.1** (given in the appendix), let at least two households announce the strategy (p, Ω) and let one of these households be inactive. Then if any household announces a price vector other than p, there will exist an arbitrage possibility and such a strategy cannot be feasible. Remark 11.2 then establishes the conclusion.

It can be established by way of an example that there exist equilibria of game 1 which are not competitive. For the example let there be three households, two household types, and two commodities. In particular, assume that there are two households of type 2, labeled 2 and 3, and one household of type 1, labeled 1. For the equilibrium let $S_j^* = \emptyset$, $j \neq 1$. Let $S_1^* = (p_m, \Omega)$ where p_m is the monopoly price vector, that is, the maximizing price vector set by household 1 when households 2 and 3 are price-takers. This equilibrium is shown in figure 11.1. There M denotes the maximal position for household 1 relative to the offer curve of households 2 and 3, labeled $O_2 + O_3$. By construction, with $S_j^* = \emptyset$, $j \neq 1$, households 2 and 3 must choose household 1 as an intermediary if $S_1 \neq \emptyset$, that is, $[1] = D_j(S_1^*, S_1)$. Thus S_1^* is the maximal strategy for household 1. By remark 11.1, households 2 and 3 are restricted to the alternative strategies $S_j = (p_m, \Omega)$, $j = 2, 3$; hence by remark 11.2 such strategies cannot dominate.

Our intuition is that the ability of a household to set a price other than a competitive equilibrium price should dissipate with an increase in the number of households. In order to establish this result the following lemma will prove quite useful.

Lemma 11.1
In any equilibrium of game 1 with two or more active intermediaries, each such intermediary names a common Walras price and the corresponding Walras allocation is achieved.

It follows from lemma 11.1 that we can associate with any equilibrium of game 1 the price vector p which prevails. If there are two or more active intermediaries, then p is the common Walras price of their strategies, and if there is only one active intermediary, then p is the price vector of its strategy. If there are no active intermediaries, pick the price vector of one of the

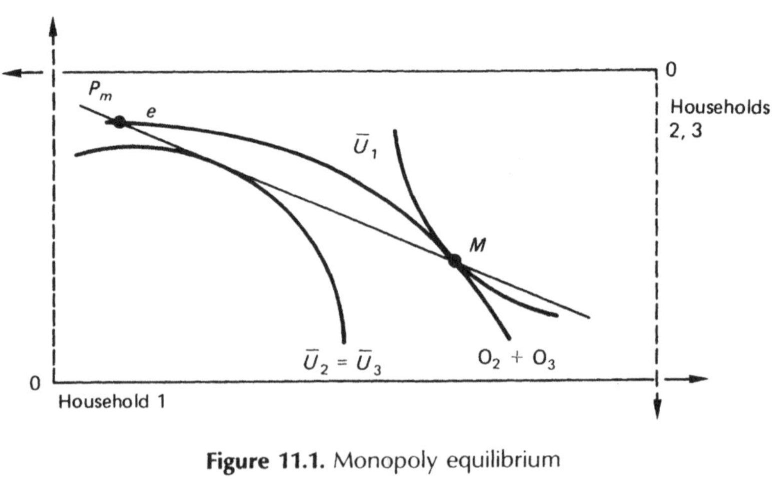

Figure 11.1. Monopoly equilibrium

households with a nonnull strategy. Hence any equilibrium of game 1 is an allocation–price pair, as with the Walras equilibrium.

Armed with lemma 11.1, we can now establish the desired result, namely, the set of equilibria of game 1 shrinks to the set of Walras equilibria as the economy is replicated. More formally we have the following proposition.

Proposition 11.2
Consider a sequence of replica economies $E_n: \Omega_n \to V \times R^l_{++}, n \geqslant 1$, where for every E_n there are m^j households of type i, $i = 1, 2, \ldots, m$. (Each t^j is a positive integer.) For every allocation–price pair (f, p) which is not a Walras equilibrium for the E_n, there exists some N, possibly depending on f and p, such that for every $n \geqslant N$, (f, p) is not an equilibrium of game 1.

Proposition 11.2 turns on the fact that the ability of a *single* active intermediary to set a non-Walras price diminishes as its endowment becomes negligible relative to the economy-wide aggregate endowment. Indeed, this last result can be viewed as a formal justification of the price-taking assumption in large economies.

6 Competition for coalitions and the Walrasian outcome in the Edgeworth economy

It should be reiterated that the results of game 1 turn on the possibility of arbitrage and the inability of a potentially active intermediary to restrict the set of households with which it is willing to trade. That is, intermediaries are relatively restricted in their ability to compete with one another. It may be objected that in some situations an intermediary may specify the set of potential customers in order to gain market power. Moreover, in a more elaborate model in which households are spatially separated and/or exchange is costly, it may be impossible for a household to deal with more than one intermediary. It is our purpose in this section to incorporate these assumptions. In game 2 each household can name a (proper) subset of potential households, that is, $\mathscr{C} = 2^{\Omega}$, and for every a and S, $D_a(S)$ must be at most a singleton.

Despite the radically different nature of game 2 relative to game 1, similar results are obtained. With a finite number of households ($\# \Omega \geqslant 3$), any Walras equilibrium can be supported as an equilibrium of game 2, and in the limit, with a continuum of households, Walras allocations and game 2 equilibrium allocations coincide.

First, an equilibrium of game 2 with allocation f is characterized, in part, by the following remarks.

Remark 11.3

In an equilibrium of game 2 households are partitioned into disjoint coalitions. There may exist a set N_0 of households, each of which is neither active nor named as a potential trader in the strategies of others. Every household of N_0 receives its endowment, that is, for every $a \in N_0$, $f_a = e_a$. The remaining set of households, $\Omega - N_0$, can be further partitioned into a set of pairwise disjoint subsets. In every set N of the partition there exists a household t with strategy $S_t^* = (p_t, A_t)$, $A_t \supset N$, which is an active intermediary for N, that is, for every $a \in N - \{t\}$, f_a is a maximal element of U_a in the set $\{x \in X : p_t \cdot x = p_t \cdot e_a\}$, and $\Sigma_{a \in N} f_a = \Sigma_{a \in N} e_a$.

A second characteristic of an equilibrium of game 2 is best stated and proved in terms of Pareto dominating strategies and effective strategies. These are now defined. A strategy $S_b = (p_b, B)$ for household $b \in \Omega$ is said to *Pareto dominate* an allocation f for an economy E if household b can make all households of B better off, that is, if there exists an allocation g such that $\Sigma_{a \in B}(g_a - e_a) = 0$, $U_a(g_a) > U_a(f_a)$ for every $a \in B$, and g_a is a maximal element under U_a in the budget set $\{x \in X : p_b \cdot x = p_b \cdot e_a\}$ for every household $a \in B - [b]$. A strategy $S_b = (p_b, B)$ is said to be *effective* relative to strategies $S_{\bar{b}}$ and choices $[D_a(S), Z_a(S), a]_{a \in \bar{b}}$, $S = (S_{\bar{b}}, S_b)$ if *all* named households do in fact choose to trade with household b, that is, if $D_a(S) = \{b\}$ for every $a \in B - \{b\}$.

Now let $T_\varnothing$ denote the set of households in an equilibrium with null strategies, and, as before, let f denote the corresponding equilibrium allocation. Then, by the definition of an effective strategy and equilibrium condition (b), we have the following.

Remark 11.4

In an equilibrium of game 2 there does not exist any strategy $S_b = (p_b, B)$ for any household b with $B \subset T_\varnothing$ which Pareto dominates f.

The analog of proposition 11.1 for game 2 now follows readily from the definitions of feasible and effective strategies and the fact that any Walras allocation is necessarily a core allocation.

Proposition 11.3

Given any Walras equilibrium with allocation–price pair (f, p), the allocation f can also be attained in an equilibrium of game 2 in which there is a single intermediary t with strategy $S_t^* = (p, \Omega)$.

For the proof (given in the appendix) let at least three households announce the strategy (p, Ω) and let the rest announce null strategies. Then note that no alternative strategy by any household b can Pareto dominate f since f

is in the core. Thus no strategy can be effective unless household b is not better off, thus establishing that the initial strategies are indeed maximizing.

There can exist equilibria of game 2 which are not Walras equilibria, but again we suspect that such market power dissipates in the limit with a large number of households. Unfortunately, it seems difficult to establish this result by looking at a sequence of replica economies as in game 1. The result that *is* established here is that no market power exists in the limit economy itself, that is, with a continuum of households.[15] We first elaborate on continuum economies.

Let the set of households Ω be the unit interval $[0, 1]$. Given any Lebesgue measurable subset of A of $[0, 1]$, let $\nu(A)$ denote the Lebesgue measure of A. Then $\nu(A)$ can be interpreted as the fraction of households in the population Ω which are members of A. An exchange economy associates with each household a of Ω a utility function U_a, defined on a common consumption set $X \subset R^l_+$, an element of the class V, and a strictly positive endowment e_a, an element of X. Moreover, attention is restricted to environments in which the consumption set X is bounded from above by some vector $\bar{c}$.[16] More formally, an exchange economy E is a measurable function from the probability measure space $(\Omega, \mathscr{A}, \nu)$ into $V \times X$, where $\mathscr{A}$ is the set of Lebesgue measurable subsets of Ω. Then, given an economy E, let A^i denote the set of all households in Ω of type i and assume that $0 < \nu(A^i) < 1$, $i = 1, 2, \ldots, m$, $2 \leqslant m < \infty$. (Note that there are still only a finite number of household types.)

In such an economy attainable allocations, core allocations, and competitive equilibria can be defined for subsets of households. Given an economy E and a subset A ($A \in \mathscr{A}$, $\nu(A) > 0$), a *subeconomy* is a specification of a utility function and an endowment for each household of A, that is, a measurable function E_A from $(A, \mathscr{A}_A, \nu)$ into $V \times X$ where $\mathscr{A}_A \equiv \{C: C = A \cap B, B \in \mathscr{A}\}$. An allocation for a subeconomy E_A is a specification of a consumption vector for every household of A, that is, an integrable function $f: A \rightarrow X$ where f_a is the allocation for household $a \in A$. An allocation f for E_A is said to be *attainable* if it can be achieved with the endowments of households of A, that is, $\int_A f \, d\nu = \int_A e \, d\nu$. A subset C ($C \in \mathscr{A}_A$, $\nu(C) > 0$) is said to improve upon an allocation f for E_A if there is an allocation which is attainable for C and Pareto dominates, that is, if there exists an attainable allocation g for E_C such that $U_a(g_a) > U_a(f_a)$ for almost every (ν) household of C. The set of attainable allocations for E_A that no subset can improve upon is called the *core* of E_A and is denoted $C(E_A)$. Notationally, for the core of the entire economy, let $C(E_\Omega) = C(E)$.

An allocation f for E_A and a price vector $p \in R^l_+$ is called a *Walras equilibrium for the subeconomy* E_A if the allocation is attainable and assigns to amost every (ν) household of A a maximal element of U_a in the budget set $\{x \in X: p \cdot x = p \cdot e_a\}$ defined by p. An allocation f is called a *Walras allocation* for E_A if there exists a price vector $p \in R^l_+$ such that (f, p) is a Walras equilibrium for E_A. p can also be called a *Walras price vector*. Let $W(E_A)$ denote the set of all Walras allocations of E_A. Notationally, for the Walras allocations of the entire economy, let $W(E_\Omega)=W(E)$. Again, it is assumed that no Walras allocation can be autarkic. It is well known, with a continuum of households and under the assumptions made here, that the set of Walras allocations and the core coincide, that is, $W(E_A)=C(E_A)$ for all $A\in\mathscr{A}$.

Various conventions are required for game 2 if it is to be played in an economy with a continuum of households. Each of these conventions is motivated by consideration of economies with Ω finite and the measure v interpreted as the normalized counting measure, that is, given $A\subset\Omega$, $v(A)=\#A/\#\Omega$. First, a first-stage announcement $S_t=(p_t, A_t)$ for household t must be an element of $R^l_+\times\mathscr{A}$ with either $A_t=\varnothing$ or $v(A_t)>0$. Second, a nonnull strategy $S_t=(p_t, A_t)$ is said to be *feasible* for household t given $[S_a, a]_{a\in\Gamma}$ and $[D_a(S), Z_s(S), a]_{a\in\Gamma}$ if p_t is a Walras price vector for the subeconomy $E_{\tilde{A}_t}$ where $\tilde{A}_t=\{a\in A_t: \{t\}=D_a(S)\}$, and household t is interpreted as receiving the consumption vector it would choose as a price taker under p_t (see proposition 11.2 and the subsequent discussion). Similarly, in the definition of a Pareto dominating strategy $S_b=(p_b, B)$, household b will be interpreted as receiving the consumption vector it would choose as a price-taker under p_b. Finally, note that remark 11.4, modified by the conventions, still applies.

Thus, with these conventions, we now have the following proposition.

Proposition 11.4
Given an economy with a continuum of households and a finite number of household types, any equilibrium allocation of game 2 in which the set of inactive intermediaries with nonnull strategies is of measure zero is also a Walras allocation.[17]

It is helpful to sketch a heuristic proof of proposition 11.4 for the special case of two commodities and two household types. If there exists an equilibrium allocation f which is not a Walras allocation, then f is not a core allocation, and there exists an attainable allocation g for a coalition C which treats all its households of type i, denoted C^i, identically and improves upon f. It can be established that $v(C^i)>0$ and $U^i(g^i)\geqslant U^i(e^i)$ for any household of type i. As shown in figure 11.2, the allocation g for C determines a trading line PP through the endowment e with allocation g^i for households of type i. However, if each household of type i were to take that price line with slope $-p$ as given and each were to choose a maximal element in the budget set, this would determine an allocation h^i such that $U^i(h^i)\geqslant U^i(g^i)$, $i=1,2$. Without loss of generality, assume that the distance $d(e,h^1)$ from e to h^1 is no greater than the distance $d(e,h^2)$ from e to h^2 and let $\rho=d(e,h^1)/d(e,h^2)$. Let $\gamma=\min\{v(C^1), v(C^2)\}$. As v is a Lebesgue measure,

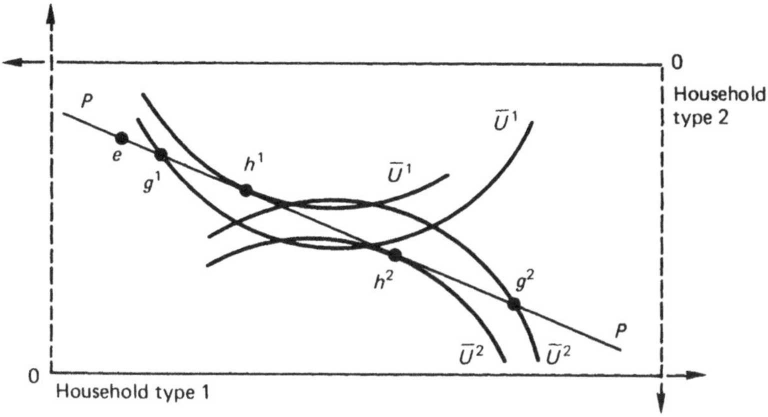

Figure 11.2. A heuristic proof of proposition 11.4

there exist sets $\hat{C}^i \subset C^i$ with $v(C^i) = \gamma$, $i = 1, 2$, and there exists a set $C_*^2 \subset \hat{C}^2$ with $v(C_*^2) = \rho\gamma$. Let $T = \hat{C}^1 \cup C_*^2$. Then allocation h is a Walras allocation for T under the implicit price vector p. Now without loss of generality it can be assumed that $T \subset T_\varnothing$ since by hypothesis $v(T_\varnothing) = 1$. Let household $t \in T$ adopt the strategy $S_t = (p, T)$. By construction this is a Pareto dominating strategy relative to the equilibrium allocation f, and by remark 11.4 this is the desired contradiction.

It should be noted that the allocation g for the coalition C which improves upon f need not constitute a Walras allocation for E_C, and hence cannot necessarily be supported with some price vector. But if g is not a Walras allocation for E_C, then g is not in the core of E_C and there exists an allocation h for a subset T of C which improves upon g and hence also upon f. In the case of two commodities and two households it is obvious how to choose h and T so that h is in the core for E_T, and hence a Walras allocation for E_T, but in general an alternative approach is needed. Continuing with the process outlined above, it is clear that we can construct a sequence of Pareto improving allocation–coalition pairs, and this suggests that perhaps a limiting allocation will have the desired property. Indeed, this is the essence of the proof of proposition 11.4.

It remains to note that in establishing proposition 11.4 an interesting property of core allocations is also established. An allocation can be said to be in a *modified core* if it cannot be improved upon by a coalition of households where allocations of such coalitions are restricted to those which can be achieved as Walras equilibria for the coalition. Apparently, with this restriction it is more difficult for a coalition to improve upon an arbitrary allocation, and so the standard core should be contained in the modified core. However, the proof of proposition 11.4 establishes that if an allocation is not in the core, then it is not in the modified core. Thus the modified core is contained in the standard core, and the two concepts of the core are equivalent.

7 A model of mutual funds with costly bilateral exchange

Following Townsend (1978, this volume, ch. 10) imagine an economy with a set I of household firms, where I is countably infinite. Each household firm is endowed with K units of the unique factor of production of the model. Endowments of this capital good are identical for all household firms and are perfectly divisible. Each household firm is also endowed with a stochastic technology which transforms the capital good into a distribution of the unique consumption good of the model. Each of these technologies or investment projects displays constant returns to scale. Let λ_j denote the output of the consumption good per unit of the capital input y_j in project j. The $[\lambda_j]$ are assumed to be independent and identically distributed across household firms with mean $E(\lambda_j)$. Each household firm j has a strictly concave utility function $U(\cdot)$ over consumption c_j which displays constant relative risk aversion. Generally, consumption c_j can be regarded as a random variable, and each household firm maximizes expected utility.

Now imagine also that exchange is costly. That is, for each bilateral deal between household firms, a fixed cost of $2a$ units of the capital good is incurred, a per household firm. Note that this cost is independent of the nature of the exchange and once incurred allows both pre-state commitments and post-state transfers of the consumption good. Note also that this specification of costly exchange gives a real role to intermediaries. For example, suppose that there were three household firms and each was trading with the other two directly. Then total transactions costs for the three bilateral exchanges would be $6a$. Transactions costs could be reduced to $4a$ if one household firm were to act as a go-between or intermediary for the other two. More generally, with $\#M$ household firms trading with one another, the most efficient number of bilateral exchanges is $\#M - 1$, in contrast with an upper bound of $(\#M)(\#M - 1)/2$ if each household firm trades with everyone.

It remains to describe the set of feasible allocations given this transactions technology. Let $M \subseteq I$ denote a coalition with $\#M$ household firms, and assume initially that $\#M < \infty$. Let N^j denote the set of household firms with which household firm j deals directly. Then a coalition C is said to constitute a market if, for each $j \in M$, $N^j \subseteq M$ and if there exists no proper subset A of C such that, for each $j \in A$, $N^j \subseteq A$. Thus a *market* is defined to be the smallest set of household firms such that every household firm of the set deals with other household firms of the set and with no household firm outside that set. Let $\eta(M)$ denote the number of bilateral exchanges in a market M. As already indicated $(\#M-1)\leqslant\eta(M)\leqslant(\#M)(\#M-1)/2$. Then an allocation $[c_j, y_j]_{j\in M}$ is said to be feasible for market M if $\Sigma_{j\in M}(K-y_j)\geqslant(2\alpha)\eta(M)$, and $\Sigma_{j\in M}\lambda_j(\omega)y_j\geqslant\Sigma_{j\in M}c_j(\omega)$ for every state of the world ω. Thus an allocation is said to be feasible for a market if it can be achieved with the resources and technologies of households of the market, taking into account the resource costs of exchange. If there is an infinity of household firms in a market M, that is, if $\#M=\infty$, an allocation is said to be feasible if it can be achieved as the limit of allocations which are feasible for a nested increasing sequence of finite submarkets contained in M. Finally, an allocation $[c_j, y_j]_{j\in C}$ is said to be feasible for a coalition C if there exists a set of markets $\mathscr{A}$ such that $\cup_{M\in\mathscr{A}}M=C$ and the allocation $[c_j, y_j]_{j\in M}$ is feasible for each market $M\in\mathscr{A}$.

The core for the economy is the set of feasible allocations for the set of all household firms I which are not blocked by any coalition. An allocation $[c_j, y_j]_{j\in I}$ is said to be blocked by a coalition B if there exists an allocation $[c_j^*, y_j^*]_{j\in B}$ which is feasible for B and is such that $U(c_j^*)>U(c_j)$ for each household firm $j\in B$. Thus an allocation is said to be in the core if there exists no coalition which can do better with its own resources and technology.

To determine core allocation, we may note that household firms are faced with an interesting tradeoff. On the one hand, as the number of household firms $\#M$ which trade with one another increases, greater portfolio diversification can be achieved. With risk aversion, this is desirable. On the other hand, even on the assumption that bilateral exchange is as efficient as possible, per capita transactions costs would be $2a(\#M-1)/\#M$, and this also increases with $\#M$. This intuition generates a maximization problem which makes the tradeoff explicit and which determines core allocations as its solutions:

$$\text{maximize } EU\left[\left\{K-\frac{2a(\#M-1)}{\#M}\right\}\frac{\Sigma_{i\in M}\lambda_i}{\#M}\right]$$

with respect to $\#M$, where E denotes the expectations operator and M denotes the set of household firms forming a market or mutual fund.

Here, then, the solution $\#M$ is the optimal number of participants in the mutual fund. Note that with a countably infinite number of household firms, there can be an infinite number of such self-contained funds; therefore in principle each fund can be of any possible size, including infinite. Indeed, the solution $\#M$ may well be infinite, in which case each household firm should receive constant consumption $c=(K-2a)E(\lambda_i)$. This allocation can be achieved (in the limit) by complete diversification. That is, each household firm j should surrender shares in its own project, with each promising to pay λ_j units of the consumption good for shares in a mutual fund, that is, each promising to pay $E(\lambda_j)$. However, it is easy to establish conditions under which there will be a *finite* solution $\# M$ so that market size is limited by transactions costs. In fact, if $K \leqslant 2a$, the solution must be finite, otherwise per capita transactions costs would equal or exceed the capital endowment in the limit. Also, even with $K > 2\alpha$, if $U(c) = c^b$ with b sufficiently close to unity, then the solution must be finite; if household firms are virtually risk neutral, there is little gain to portfolio diversification. Finally, it is easy to show that the solution need not be autarkic, that is, with $\# M = 1$. Thus transactions costs deliver a nontrivial theory of market size.

As noted in section 1, core allocations in this model can be achieved with intermediaries forming mutual funds in a noncooperative way, as in section 6. The reader will be spared the requisite notation. Suffice it to note that every equilibrium allocation is in the core, and all core allocations can be supported as equilibria.

8 Spatial models of media of exchange – intermediary assets

Consider first Lucas's version of the Cass–Yaari model (Cass and Yaari, 1966) described by Townsend (1980, this volume, ch. 2). That is, imagine an economy with a countably infinite number of households and a countably infinite number of perishable commodities. Each (representative) household consists of a pair of agents and is imagined to be located on the real line, say, one household per integer (see figure 11.3). Each household i lives forever and faces an endowment sequence of commodity i (alone) which is constant. Household i cares about commodities i and $i+1$ only and discounts future over present consumption. Thus, if $c_{it}(i)$ and $c_{i+1,t}(i)$ denote the number of units of consumption by household i at time t of commodities i and $i+1$ respectively, the preferences of household i are represented by the utility function $\Sigma_{t=0}^{\infty} \beta^t U\{c_{it}(i), c_{i+1,t}(i)\}$ where $U(\cdot,\cdot)$ satisfies certain regularity properties. In each period t each member of household i is capable of moving half the distance to one of the two adjacent integers, $i+1$ and $i-1$. Consequently, in each period t, each household i is physically capable of carrying out transactions with households $i-1$ and $i+1$ in two spatially

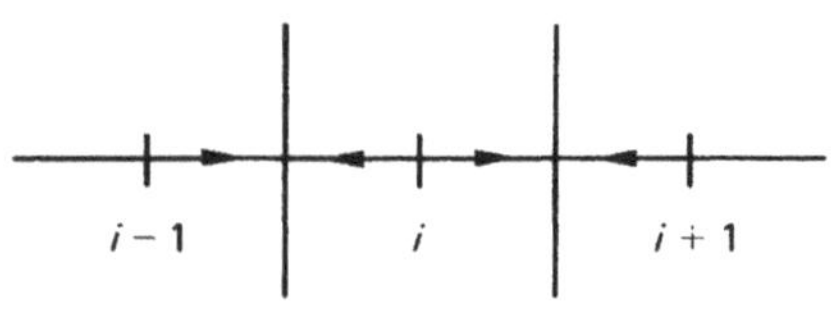

Figure 11.3. Lucas's version of the Cass–Yaari model

separated locations. As a result, the key feature of the model is the absence of double coincidence of wants. At each time t, each household i can trade with household $i+1$, but i has no commodity that $i+1$ wants.

Now suppose that households i and $i+1$ are each representative of a large (infinite) number of households in identical situations following identical itineraries. Suppose also that there is fiat money in the economy – pieces of paper which represent outside indebtedness (there is no redemption possibility). Then, when groups of households i and $i+1$ meet, potential intermediaries can propose the exchange of commodity $i+1$ for fiat money along the lines of the analysis of sections 4–6. In fact, with an infinity of households, we can thus assume the existence of a competitive market in which commodity $i+1$ is exchanged for fiat money at price $p_{i+1,t}$ in terms of fiat money. Of course, there is a market where $i-1$ and i meet, and so on. All these markets are isolated from one another.

As discussed by Townsend (1980, this volume, ch. 2), there does exist a monetary equilibrium for this economy – consumption, money balance, and (positive finite) price sequences such that the consumption and money balances sequences are maximizing for each household given the price sequences, and the commodity and money markets clear. However, that (fixed-price) equilibrium is generally not Pareto optimal and hence is not in the core. In effect, as in Clower (1967), valuation of consumption of commodity $i+1$ is limited by beginning-of-period money balances. That is, money balances must be held for one period before they can be used in exchange, and this creates a distortion. As in Friedman (1969), this distortion can be remedied by lump-sum taxation of fiat money balances, inducing a deflation at the rate $1-\beta$.

The model described above provides a rich setting which we can use to address a variety of economic phenomena. For example, we might assume that commodity i can be stored by household i (alone), so that in effect productive capital accumulation is allowed. Then both capital and fiat money are stores of value, but fiat money alone can effect exchange for the market-produced commodity $i+1$. Hence Townsend (1987, this volume, ch. 12) establishes that in a monetary equilibrium the rate of return on capital can dominate the rate of return on money. In addition, we can allow shocks to technology, preferences, and the money supply (lump-sum injections of fiat money) and produce variable liquidity premiums, that is, Lagrange multipliers on the Clower constraints which move around. This in turn causes conventional intertemporal asset-pricing formulas to be overturned. Again, the monetary equilibria are generally nonoptimal. Thus, with lump-sum injections interpreted as control variables, an activist policy which is responsive to real shocks would seem to be implied.

Alternatively, we can assume that commodity i can be produced by household i each period (but not stored), that is, we can assume the possibility of onerous labor supply. Then we can imagine that the extent to which households are linked to one another is exogenous but variable over time. In fact, three stylized exchange regimes can be considered: autarky, in which households are entirely isolated from one another, a fiat money regime, as described above, and a Walrasian trade–credit regime, in which all households on the real line can trade with one another at each date, as in section 3. Then, as Townsend (1982, this volume, ch. 4) establishes with multiple "household lines," observed comovements of economy-wide average debt and money holdings with real activity can be explained.

All the models described above use an absence of double coincidence of wants in intratemporal consumption. However, we can imagine an absence of double coincidence of wants for intertemporal consumption, so that the relationship of fiat money to borrowing and lending can be examined. Imagine, as in Townsend (1980, this volume, ch. 2), that households are traveling on a highway or turnpike, either east or west, as in figure 11.4. The arrows indicate the direction of travel and the spikes indicate distinct spatial locations where trade can occur. The numbers 0 and 1 index the endowment (of the single consumption good) of a household located at the indicated position. Initially, at $t = 0$, there is one (representative) household at each location and each household moves forward one location each period. Again, these locations are isolated from one another; there can be no transactions or communication among them at any time. The absence of double coincidence of wants is apparent here – if consumption is indexed by location and date, no two (representative) households care about the same two commodities.

Again, we can assume that each household is representative of a large (infinite) number and that intermediaries propose the exchange of the consumption good for fiat money at each location and date. Thus, we can assume the existence of a competitive market at each location and date in which the single commodity can be exchanged for fiat money at price p_t in terms of fiat money. As discussed by Townsend (1980, this volume, ch. 2), a (fixed-price) monetary equilibrium does exist. Again this equilibrium is nonoptimal, and again the inefficiency can apparently be remedied by lump-sum taxes on fiat money balances, but the taxes now require a distinction across household types between those who begin life with a positive endowment and those who do not.

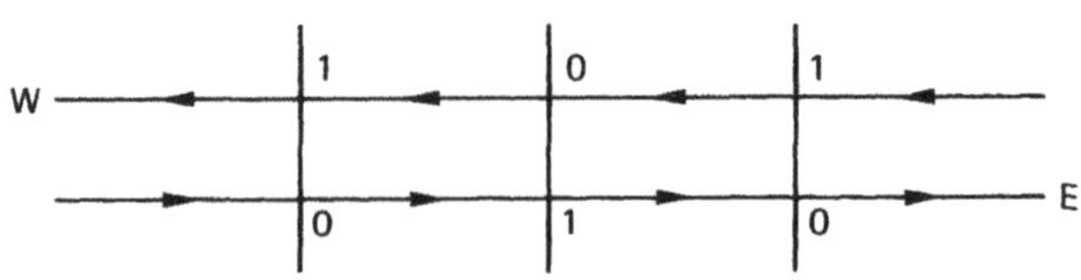

Figure 11.4. The turnpike model

To explain the coexistence of fiat money with borrowing and lending in this turnpike exchange model, we can weaken the representative agent construct and suppose that, along with a group of households which begin life with zero units of the consumption good at a specified location and thus have endowment sequence (0, 1, 0, ...), there is a smaller group following the same itinerary but with endowment sequence (1, 0, 1, ...). As Sargent (1987) and Wallace (1980) have demonstrated, this within-group (within-generation) diversity explains the coexistence. The resulting model has a nice interpretation: the within-group majority uses private credit for transactions with households it meets again, and uses fiat money for transactions with households it meets only once.

Finally, to explain objects like bank notes, bills of exchange, and other forms of *circulating* private debt (inside monies), imagine closing the turnpike exchange model at both ends, forming a circle (following Cass and Yaari (1966) in a different context). Not only would representative households in such a model meet each other repeatedly, allowing the issue of direct (bilateral) IOUs, there would also be chains of household pairings which would allow the redemption of location-specific date-specific IOUs or securities by households other than the original acceptor. Indeed, Townsend and Wallace (1982) establish for a general class of economies (of which the above is an example) the existence of competitive debt equilibria with secondary markets, third-party payment devices, and circulating high velocity private securities. However, it is also established that there can exist a multiplicity of debt equilibria, a class of equilibria unique in consumptions but not in debt issues, and that such equilibria seem to require a coordination of private debt issue across distinct physical locations or markets at specified dates. This coordination would seem to be achieved by a priori restrictions on the issue of some, but certainly not all, circulating securities. Although equilibria with circulating private debt can Pareto improve upon equilibria exogenously restricted to direct bilateral IOUs, the equilibria with circulating private debt are generally not Pareto optimal.

9 Toward a spatial model of intermediated financial structures

Imagine an economy inhabited by a set of H households which live for T periods (both H and T may be infinite). Each household i is endowed with w_t^i units of the single consumption good of the model at date t. Each household i cares about sequences of units of consumption c_t^i as represented by the utility function $\Sigma_{t=0}^{T} \beta^t U^i(c_t^i)$. Here $U^i(\cdot)$ is concave and strictly increasing. Each household i has an itinerary on some spatial plane, say R^2, which specifies its location at date t, say l_t^i, in the absence of any effort (travel cost). In addition, each household can travel in the plane at each date t with a fixed cost of a_t^i and a per unit distance cost of γ_t^i, both in terms of the consumption good. Imagine further that households can trade with one another at date t (pass along specified units of the consumption good) if and only if they are in the same location at date t.[18]

Following the analysis of the mutual fund model, an apparently natural equilibrium concept is the core. To define the core formally we need first to define feasible allocations for arbitrary subsets of households C. Thus we must specify a consumption–location sequence for each household $i \in C$ in such a way that consumptions are feasible given the endowments of households $i \in C$, the locations visited by them, and their travel costs. The core is then a specification of a consumption–location sequence for each household $i \in H$ which is feasible for H and such that there does not exist a set of feasible consumption–location sequences for a subset of household C which can improve upon the original allocation.[19]

We might well imagine that core allocations will generally involve some intermediary or go-between activity to reduce travel costs. Some households may be centrally located, while others may have relatively low travel costs. We might also imagine that, owing to high travel costs or low a priori population densities, there could arise dates t, such that there is little activity (travel or trade) on at least a portion of the spatial plane. In another region, though, "markets" might flourish on the same date.[20]

Again we may ask whether unfettered competition among intermediaries might achieve core allocations. Clearly this depends on how unfettered competition is modeled. Suppose, as seems natural, and following Townsend and Wallace (1982), that any household can issue at date t, in any location where it happens to be, date–location contingent securities. A typical security is a promise to pay specified units of the consumption good at a specified location at some future date s. It is assumed that such a promise must be honored. This in turn implies that a household's location at any date t can be determined (with some effort) by previously issued securities. Now suppose in addition that a household (potential intermediary) at date t can announce the set of households with which it is willing to deal, the set of securities it is willing to exchange, and various associated terms of trade. Here the terms of trade would include the number of units of the date t consumption good that the potential intermediary is willing to surrender for each unit of fiat money or for each security, either issued previously (by someone) and held by a named customer or issued contemporaneously by a named customer. Similarly, the terms of trade would include the number of units of the date t consumption good that the potential intermediary is willing to accept for each unit of fiat money or for each security, either currently held by it (from previous encounters) or issued by it (contemporaneously). We might well imagine that a potential intermediary might be willing to exchange only a subset of potential securities and might announce a schedule of fixed fees as well.

In this setting, then, we can define a multiperiod sequential Nash equilibrium with two stages at each date along the lines of section 4.[21] In such an equilibrium (assuming existence), we might expect to observe active intermediaries. That is, we might assume that centrally located households or households with low travel costs would act as brokers, both taking in the consumption good from "lenders," in exchange for the issue of its own securities (or previously acquired securities), and passing along the consumption good to "borrowers," in exchange for their IOUs (or previously acquired securities).

A multiperiod sequential Nash equilibrium might also illustrate how money, the "extent of the market," and intermediation are all interrelated. Consider the following suggestive (but nonrigorous) scenario, in the spirit of the turnpike exchange model of section 8. Suppose that representative households a and b, a' and b', and so on, are in effect paired at date t as indicated in figure 11.5. That is, a and b are substantially nearer to each other than to an alternative trading partner. At date $t + 1$ household a advances (exogenously) to the previous position of a', and a' advances to the previous position of some a'', and so on. Households b, b', and so on stay put. Suppose also that households a and a' have an endowment which is low and then high at dates t and $t + 1$ respectively, and conversely for households b and b'. Thus it is assumed that households a and b would like to engage in a two-period borrowing–lending agreement (with a borrowing from b), similarly for a' and b', and so on. However, to effect this agreement, not only must a and b travel to some intermediate location at date t (between the points marked a and b), they must do so again at date $t + 1$ (between the points marked b and a') when they are relatively far apart.

If the gains from trade were substantial, they might well make such an arrangement. But if travel costs were sufficiently high, they might not. That is, on another real line, similarly situated but more distant households might not trade. Alternatively, suppose that there is (valued) fiat money in the economy. Then when households a and b meet at date t, at some cost, let a (the potential borrower) exchange fiat money for the consumption good, and similarly for a' and b'. Then at date $t + 1$, let households a and b' meet (at some lesser cost) and let b' surrender fiat money for the consumption good. Thus, we might well expect the monetary economy to Pareto dominate the

Figure 11.5.

nonmonetary economy, and thus money would replace privately issued securities. Further trade pairing which did not occur in the nonmonetary economy might now be effected. In this sense the extent of the market might increase with the advent of fiat money. Moreover, if households *a*, *b*, and so on are each representative of a large number of households, then trade might well be effected with intermediaries, and intermediation might increase with the advent of fiat money.

We now return to the question of whether or not a multiperiod sequential Nash equilibrium allocation would lie in the core. The answer would depend in part on the strategy spaces available to the households. Again we suspect that fixed fees would be needed, and these should vary with a priori customer locations. In addition, a relatively small number of households in a given location a priori might cause problems of imperfect competition, along the lines of those in sections 5 and 6 – the analysis in sections 5 and 6 indicates that this consideration would be mitigated by the extent that (now costly) arbitrage can take place across intermediaries and by the extent to which potential intermediaries compete with one another.

However, even if small numbers and limited strategy spaces do not cause problems, it will generally be the case that multiperiod sequential Nash equilibrium allocations do *not* lie in the core. To see this, note that the noncooperative game described above essentially limits binding commitments – in the nonmonetary economy, at least, transfers of the consumption good must be achieved by security issue, redemption, or trade, and securities can be issued only when households meet (perhaps at some cost) and can travel only with households (perhaps at some cost). Again, a suggestive scenario, similar to the one given earlier, may help to illustrate this point (see also Townsend and Wallace, 1982).

Suppose that there are four households (a, a', b, and b'), two dates (t and $t+1$), and two locations (1 and 2). Suppose that at date t households a and b are paired exogenously at location 1 and households a' and b' are paired exogenously at location 2. Suppose also that at date $t+1$ households a and a' switch locations. Finally, suppose that travel costs are virtually infinite. Then under the security trading rules described above, no security can be redeemed by the issuer at $t+1$. Consequently, no household would relinquish the consumption good for such a security at t. That is, there can be no mutually beneficial exchange. However, it is easy to specify endowments in such a way that autarky can be improved upon by all four households, say by a "borrowing" from b but paying back b', and similarly for a' and b. In fact, any symmetric bilateral arrangement between a and b and between a' and b' can be effected in this way *at no cost*. Thus even if travel costs were sufficiently low that direct symmetric borrowing–lending takes place, such an arrangement would not be Pareto optimal.

Of course, fiat money would help to remedy this situation, but in general we do not expect to overturn the conclusion that multiperiod sequential Nash equilibrium allocations will not lie in the core. The general problem is that the multiperiod sequential Nash equilibrium assumes limited communication and makes it costly to enter into binding agreements, whereas the core takes into account only the cost of exchanging the consumption good itself. A core allocation is in effect a social agreement which *de facto* is "entered into" costlessly. It seems that there are two ways of resolving this conflict. First, we might imagine a model of competition among intermediaries in which securities can be costlessly traded and transferred so that, in effect, there is unlimited communication. However, this attack strategy would, apart from consumption–trading costs, return us to the virtually timeless analysis of Edgeworth and mutual fund models, removing any essential dynamics. Second, we might contemplate altering the definition of the core, somehow taking into account limits on communication and the costs of commitment. However, it is not yet obvious how this ought to be done. We might also note in this regard that the multiperiod sequential Nash equilibrium itself seems to assume some a priori communication and costless commitment, as intermediaries (or customers) somehow coordinate travel and security trades across distinct locations. That is, multiperiod sequential Nash equilibria are almost surely not unique.[22]

As it stands, the divergence between the core and the multiperiod sequential Nash equilibrium indicates that there would be pressures for institutions to emerge which reduce contract costs and facilitate a priori coordination. Clearly, we would like a, b, a', and b' in the example just described to form a syndicate with mutually binding (group) commitments. Alternatively, the core might also be taken as an "ideal" in the evaluation of government policy. In the example just described default rules can be imagined in which a defaults at date $t+1$ on its date t debt to b, but is penalized at date $t+1$, that is, it is forced to pay b'. However, in the absence of a theory of government with costly constitutions or costly regulation, the core as specified here could be a misleading welfare criterion.

10 Directions for research

We should conclude this chapter with some caveats. The idea that trade links are costly *per se* seems to be a useful formalism, presumably capturing the cost of bookkeeping, the cost of enforcement, the cost of monitoring when there is imperfect information, the physical cost of exchange (transportation), the difficulties of communication, and so on. Similarly, Hotelling's spatial plane is a useful formalism, presumably capturing various aspects of diversity and changing circumstance. However, it may well be that for some purposes, both positive and normative, we will want to distinguish these costs and gain a better understanding of the diversity, modeling both at a somewhat deeper level. The divergence between the core and noncooperative equilibrium allocations reinforces that conclusion.

Appendix

Proof of Remark 11.1

The proof is by contradiction. Suppose that $p_1 \neq p_2$. Then household 3 is confronted with an arbitrage possibility. Namely, there exist commodities i and j such that $p_1^i/p_1^j < p_2^i/p_2^j$. (Here the superscript i denotes the ith component of the indicated price vector and so on.) Hence household 3 could exchange commodity j in return for commodity i from intermediary 1 and reverse the transaction with intermediary 2, ending with a surplus of commodity j. With the nonsatiation assumption this exchange would be carried on without limit, and hence the strategy S_1 is not feasible.

Proof of Remark 11.2

As an active intermediary under p, household t attains an allocation on the budget hyperplane $\{x \in R_+^l : p \cdot e_t = p \cdot x\}$, a choice which is available under the first alternative.

Proof of Proposition 11.1

The numbering of households is arbitrary. Let $S_1^* = S_2^* = (p, \Omega)$, $S_j^* = \emptyset$, $j \in \Omega - \{1, 2\}$, $D_a^*(S^*) = \{1\}$ for $a \in \Omega - \{1\}$, and let Z_{a1}^* be the maximal element under U_a in $\{z \in R^l : p \cdot z = 0\}$. Consider first some alternative feasible strategy $S_j = (p_j, \Omega)$ for any household $j \in \Omega - \{1, 2\}$. If this strategy is to strictly dominate S_j^* for j, then j must be active, for if inactive his choice set is as before. Hence $j \in D_a^*(S_j^*, S_j)$ for some $a \in \bar{j}$. In this event there exists a household which can arbitrage between household 3 and one of the households 1 and 2. Since S_j must be feasible, remark 11.1 implies that $p_j = p$, and remark 11.2 implies that such a strategy cannot dominate. With $S_j^* = \emptyset$, $j \in \Omega - \{1, 2\}$, a similar argument establishes that neither 1 nor 2 can find alternative strategies that dominate.

Proof of Lemma 11.1

Note first that with two or more active intermediaries there exists a third household which can arbitrage. Hence by remark 11.1 each active intermediary m has equilibrium strategy $S_m^* = (p, \Omega)$. Consider an intermediary t of type i. Intermediary t cannot be worse off than it would be if it were a price-taker under p, that is, choosing trade Z^{*i} from among $\{z \in R^l : p \cdot z = 0\}$ (given the strict quasi-concavity of U^i, Z^{*i} is unique). Otherwise t would announce the null strategy and plan to trade with one of the active intermediaries in the second stage. Yet by remark 11.2, household t as an active intermediary cannot be better off than as such a price-taker. It follows that each active intermediary of type i achieves the allocation $e^i + Z^{*i}$. Clearly, so do all other households of type i. Of course the choice of type i was arbitrary.

It remains to establish that the allocation $\{e^i + Z^{*i}, i = 1, 2, \ldots, m\}$ and the price vector p constitute a Walras equilibrium. Evidently, for every household a of type i, $e^i + Z^{*i}$ is a maximal element of U_a in $\{x \in R^l_+ : p \cdot x = p \cdot e_a\}$. As for attainability, note that the net trade for any active intermediary of type i is Z^{*i} so that $Z^{*i} = -\Sigma Z^*_{at}(S^*)$ where the summation is over $\{a : t \in D^*_a(S^*)\}$. Then, summing over all active intermediaries yields $\Sigma^m_{i=1} Z^{*i} \# (A^i) = 0$. (Note that the argument here does not require that the second intermediary is active.)

Proof of Proposition 11.2

Consider any allocation–price pair (f, p) which is not a Walras equilibrium for the E_n. Suppose, contrary to the conclusion of the proposition, that (f, p) is an equilibrium of game 1 for infinitely many of the E_n. By lemma 11.1, (f, p) must be attained under a *feasible* strategy for a single intermediary t. A contradiction can now be established. As p is not a Walras price, there exists some commodity h such that $\Sigma^m_{j=1}(f^j_h - e^j_h)r^j > 0$ where f^j_h denotes the maximal choice of commodity h under U^j in the budget set $\{x \in R^l_+ : p \cdot x = p \cdot e^j\}$ and e^j_h denotes the hth component of e^j. But if the intermediary t is of type i, feasibility of its strategy for E_n, $n \geq 2$, requires that

$$e^i_h \geq \sum_{j \neq i} (f^j_h - e^j_h)(nr^j) + (f^i_h - e^i_h)(nr^i - 1)$$

or equivalently

$$f^i_h \geq n \left\{ \sum_{j=1}^{m} (f^j_h - e^j_h)(r^j) \right\}$$

For sufficiently large n this inequality cannot be satisfied for any i, which is the desired contradiction.

Proof of Remark 11.3

That households are partitioned into disjoint coalitions follows from the specification that $D_a(S)$ is at most a singleton for all a and S and that for an active intermediary t, $D_t(S) = \varnothing$. The other statements are obvious.

Proof of Remark 11.4

Suppose the contrary and note that such a strategy would be effective relative to the equilibrium strategies $S_{\bar{b}}^*$ and choices $[D_a^*(S), Z_a^*(S), a]_{a\in\bar{b}}$, $S=(S_{\bar{b}}^*, S_b)$, and hence would be proposed by b. This contradicts equilibrium condition (b).

Proof of Proposition 11.3

Let three households (labeled 1, 2, and 3 without loss of generality) adopt the strategy $S_i^*=(p, \Omega)$, $i=1, 2, 3$, and let all other households, if any, adopt the null strategy, that is, $S_a^*=\varnothing$, $a\neq 1, 2, 3$. Let $D_a(S^*)=\{1\}$, $a\neq 1$. Clearly the Walras allocation can be effected. Now without loss of generality any household b can be restricted to alternative strategies which are either feasible and effective or null. (For, given a feasible strategy $S_b=(p_b, B)$, let $\tilde{B}=\{a\in B: D_a(S_{\bar{b}}^*, S_b)=\{b\}\}$ and consider instead the strategy $S_b=(p_b, \tilde{B}\cup\{b\})$ if $\tilde{B}\neq\varnothing$ or $S_b=\varnothing$ if $\tilde{B}=\varnothing$.) First, consider any alternative nonnull feasible strategy $S_1=(p_b, B)$ by household 1. As f is a Walras allocation for E, f is in the core of E; thus no such alternative strategy can Pareto dominate f. Therefore let F denote the set of households in $B-\{1, 2, 3\}$ who would be no better off relative to f, let $D_a^*(S_{\bar{1}}^*, S_1)=\{2\}$ for $a\in F$, and let $D_a^*(S_{\bar{1}}^*, S_1)=\{1\}$ for a in the complement of F. If $F\neq\varnothing$, S_1 is not effective. If $F=\varnothing$ then some household of $\{1, 2, 3\}$ would be no better off. If $2\in B$ would be no better off, let $D_2^*(S_{\bar{1}}^*, S_1)=\{3\}$ (otherwise let $D_2^*(S_{\bar{1}}^*, S_1)=\{1\}$) so that S_1 could not be effective. Similarly, if $3\in B$ is no better off, let $D_3^*(S_{\bar{1}}^*, S_1)=\{2\}$. Hence the only alternative effective nonnull strategies must be such that 1 would be no better off; hence S_1^* is maximal. If $S_1=\varnothing$, let $D_1^*(S_{\bar{1}}^*, S_1)=\{j\}$ for $j\in\{2, 3\}$ so that again such a strategy cannot dominate S_1^*.

Now assume that 2 considers alternative feasible effective nonnull strategies $S_2=(p_b, B)$. Again let F denote the set of households which would be no better off in $B-\{1, 2, 3\}$ and let $D_a^*(S_{\bar{2}}^*, S_2)=\{1\}$ if $a\in F$. If $F\neq\varnothing$, S_2 is not effective. If $F=\varnothing$ and $1\in B$ would be no better off, let $D_1^*(S_{\bar{2}}^*, S_2)=\{3\}$. If $3\in B$ would be no better off, let $D_3^*(S_{\bar{2}}^*, S_2)=\{1\}$. For $S_2=\varnothing$, let $D_2^*(S_{\bar{2}}^*, S_2)=\{j\}$ for $j\in\{1, 3\}$. A similar argument applies for 3 and for $a\in\Omega-\{1, 2, 3\}$.

Proof of Proposition 11.4

Suppose that there exists some allocation f for E such that f is an equilibrium allocation of game 2 but $f\notin W(E)$. As $W(E)=C(E)$, $f\notin C(E)$. Hence there exists at least one allocation–coalition pair (h, T), where h is an attainable allocation for E_T which improves upon f. Now the following claim is established below.

Claim 11.A1

Given any pair (h, T) which improves upon an allocation f, there exists an allocation–coalition pair (g, C) with $C\subset T$ which also improves upon f and treats all households of any given type identically.

Let $C^i = E^{-1}(U^i, e^i) \cap C$, $i = 1, 2, \ldots, m$. Thus $C^i \in \mathscr{A}$ is the set of households of type i in C. Let M denote the set of integers $\{1, 2, \ldots, m\}$ where m is the number of household types. Let $I(C) = \{i \in M : \nu(C^i) \neq 0\}$. Thus $I(C)$ is the set of indices of household types in C with nonzero measure. Let $\#\{I(C)\}$ denote the number of elements of $I(C)$. Then the pair (g, C) which improves upon f is given utility representation $\tilde{u}$ in $R^{\#\{I(C)\}}$ where $\tilde{u}^i = U^i(g^i)$, $i \in I(C)$ and g^i is the allocation under g to any household of type i. In general, given some set $N \subset M$, let $B^N \subset R^{\#(N)}$ denote the set of all such utility representations associated with (g, C) pairs which improve upon f with $I(C) = N$. Thus a particular (g, C) pair has utility representation in one of $\#(2^M)$ possible sets. (Here 2^M is the set of all subsets of M.) Also, since $f \notin C(E)$, at least one of these sets is nonempty. From the *nonempty* sets pick one of lowest dimension and denote it B^{N^*}. That is, N^* is a set $N^* \subset M$ and $\#(N^*) \leqslant \#(N)$ for every $N \in 2^M$ with $B^N \neq \varnothing$. For notational simplicity let $B^{N^*} \equiv B^*$.

A sequence $[b_k]_{k=1}^{\infty}$ of elements of B^* is said to be *monotone increasing* if for every $k, i, b_k^i \leqslant b_{k+1}^i$. Here the subscript k indicates the element of the sequence and the superscript i indicates the component of the vector. The following claim is established below.

Claim 11.A2

If $[b_k]_{k=1}^{\infty}$ is a monotone increasing sequence in B^* with limit b, then $b \in B^*$.

Now define the set of least upper bounds of B^*, denoted $F(B^*)$ as the set of points $\hat{b} \in R^{\#(N^*)}$ so that the following two conditions hold.

1 There does not exist some $b \in B^*$ such that $b \geqslant \hat{b}$. That is, $F(B^*)$ is a set of upper bounds (here and below the notation $\geqslant$ for vectors means that b exceeds $\hat{b}$ in at least one component and is no less in any component).
2 For every $\delta > 0$ there exists some $b \in 0(\hat{b}, \delta) \cap (\{\hat{b}\} - R^{\#(N^*)}) \cap B^*$. (Here $0(\hat{b}, \delta)$ is the sphere of radius δ centered at $\hat{b}$, and $\hat{b} - R^{\#(N^*)}$ is the nonpositive orthant with origin at $\hat{b}$.)

Now any nonempty subset of k-dimensional Euclidean space R^k which is bounded from above also has a least upper bound. The set B^* is bounded from above since, for any $b \in B^*$, $b^i \leqslant U^i(\bar{c})$ for every $i \in N^*$. Therefore, $F(B^*) \neq \varnothing$.

Given some $\hat{b} \in F(B^*)$, it is possible to construct a monotone increasing sequence of elements of B^* which have $\hat{b}$ as a limit by letting $\delta \to 0$. Hence by claim 11.A2, $\hat{b} \in B^*$.

Let (g, C) denote the allocation–coalition pair associated with the chosen $\hat{b}$. It is now established that $g \in C(E_C)$. For assume the contrary. Then by claim 11.A1 there exists an allocation–coalition pair (g', C') which improves upon g and treats all households of any given type identically. Note that $C' \subset C$. The inclusion here and below is weak. Hence (g', C') improves upon f also. Clearly, $I(C') \subset I(C)$. However, if $I(C')$ is a proper subset of $I(C)$, then (g', C') has utility representation in a space of lower dimension than $\#(N^*)$, in contradiction with the choice of N^*. If $I(C') = I(C)$, then there exists some $b \in B^*$ such that $b > \hat{b}$, since (g', C') improves upon g, in contradiction with the choice of $\hat{b}$ in $F(B^*)$ (see defining property 1 above).

Since $g \in C(E_C)$, g is also a Walras allocation for E_C under a price vector p. Now without loss of generality it can be assumed that $C \subset T_\varnothing$, since $v(T_\varnothing) = 1$. Let some household $t \in C$ adopt the strategy $S_t = (p, C)$. Since g improves upon f for E_C and can be supported with the price vector p, this strategy is Pareto dominant relative to f, and by remark 11.4 this is the desired contradiction.

Proof of Claim 11.1 As h is attainable for E_T,

$$\sum_{i \in I(T)} \left\{ \int_{T^i} h \, \mathrm{d}v - e^i v(T^i) \right\} = 0$$

Therefore, letting

$$\rho^i = \frac{v(T^i)}{\sum_{j \in I(T)} v(T^j)}$$

$$\sum_{i \in I(T)} \rho^i \left| \frac{\int_{T^i} h \, \mathrm{d}v}{v(T^i)} - e^i \right| = 0 \tag{11.A1}$$

Let $Q = \{q \in I(T): h_a$ is not equal to some constant vector for almost every $a \in T^q\}$. Then if $Q = \varnothing$, the claim is trivial. Therefore assume $Q \neq \varnothing$. Then for every $q \in Q$ there exists some set $B^q \subset T^q$, $v(B^q) > 0$ such that, from the strict quasi-concavity of U^q,

$$U^q(h_a) < U^q \left| \frac{\int_{T^q} h \, \mathrm{d}v}{v(T^q)} \right| \quad \text{almost every } a \in B^q \tag{11.A2}$$

Clearly

$$U^i(h_a) = U^i \left| \frac{\int_{T^i} h \, dv}{v(T^i)^q} \right| \qquad \text{almost every } a \in T^i, \ i \in I(T), \ i \notin Q \quad (11.A3)$$

Let $\gamma_1 = \min_{q \in Q} v(B^q)$. Let $\gamma_2 = \min_{i \in Q, i \in I(T)} v(T^i)$. Let $\gamma = \min(\gamma_1, \gamma_2)$. Then as v is a Lebesgue measure, there exist sets $B^q_{**} \subset B^q$ with $v(B^q_{**}) = \gamma$ and sets $B^q_* \subset B^q_{**}$ with $v(B^q_*) = \rho^q \gamma$ for every $q \in Q$. Similarly for $i \in I(T)$, $i \notin Q$, there exist sets $B^i_* \subset T^i$ with $v(B^i_*) = \rho^i \gamma$. Let $C = \cup_{i \in I(T)} B^i_*$ and, for almost every $a \in B^i_*$, let $g_a = \int_{T^i} h \, dv / v(T^i)$, $i \in I(T)$. Then multiplying both sides of (11.A1) by γ it is clear that $\int_C (g - e) \, dv = 0$, so that g is an attainable allocation for C. From (11.A2) and (11.A3), g also improves upon f.

Proof of Claim 11.2 Let (g_k, C_k) denote the allocation–coalition pair associated with b_k which improves upon f. Then for every $i \in N^* = I(C_k)$, $0 \leqslant g^i_k \leqslant \bar{c}$. The left-hand inequality follows from the fact that $g^i_k \in R^l_+$, and the right-hand inequality follows from the boundedness of the consumption set X. Define $\rho^i_k = v(C^i_k) / \Sigma_{j \in N^*} v(C^j_k)$. Then $0 \leqslant \rho^i_k \leqslant 1$, $i \in N^*$. Hence by compactness we can construct from the sequences $[\rho^i_k, g^i_k, i \in N^*]$ sequences $[\rho^i_n, g^i_n, i \in N^*]$ such that $\rho^i_n \to \rho^i \in [0, 1]$ and $g^i_n \to g^i \in [0, \bar{c}]$ as $n \to \infty$. By construction $\int_{C_k} g_k \, dv = \int_{C_k} e \, dv$. That is,

$$\sum_{i \in N^*} (g^i_k - e^i) v(C^i_k) = 0$$

Therefore, dividing through by $\Sigma_{j \in N^*} v(C^j_k)$,

$$\sum_{i \in N^*} (g^i_n - e^i) \rho^i_n = 0$$

for every n. Taking the limit as $n \to \infty$, we obtain

$$\sum_{i \in N^*} (g^i - e^i) \rho^i = 0 \qquad (11.A4)$$

By continuity $U^i(g^i_n) \to U^i(g^i)$ as $n \to \infty$. Also, $U^i(g^i_n) = b^i_n$ and $b^i_n \to b^i$ from below. Therefore $U^i(g^i) = b^i$ and, for every n,

$$U^i(g^i_n) \leqslant U^i(g^i) \qquad i \in N^* \qquad (11.A5)$$

Upon picking an arbitrary n, there is an associated allocation–coalition pair (g_n, C_n) which improves upon f. Define $\gamma = \min_{i \in N^*} v(C_n^i)$. As v is a Lebesgue measure, for every $i \in N^*$ there exists some set $C_*^i \subset C_n^i$ with $v(C_*^i) = \gamma$, and there exists a set $C^i \subset C_*^i$ with $v(C^i) = \rho^i \gamma$. Let $C = \cup_{i \in N^*} C^i \subset C_n$. However, multiplying (11.A4) through by γ we obtain

$$\sum_{i \in N^*} (g^i - e^i) v(C^i) = 0$$

and so g is feasible for C. As (g_n, C_n) improves upon f, it is clear from (11.A5) that (g, C) improves upon f. Moreover, $\rho^i > 0$ for every $i \in N^*$. For suppose that $\rho^i = 0$ for some $i \in N^*$. Then (g, C) improves upon f and has a utility representation in a space of lower dimension than $\#(N^*)$, which is the desired contradiction. Therefore $b \in B^*$.

Notes

1 No attempt is made here to survey the literature on intermediation (or money), although no doubt such a survey would serve a useful purpose. The interested reader is urged to consult Benston and Smith (1976), Wood (1981), and Bhattacharya (1982) who offer critical review much in the spirit of the present paper before presenting their own work.

2 In none of the games for the pure exchange economy do intermediaries impose quantity restrictions (there are, of course, feasibility restrictions). In some sense this is a troublesome feature in the first game and a virtue in the second game (both are described below) – see notes 5 and 9. A general treatment of pricing games with quantity restrictions is beyond the scope of this chapter.

3 The concept of equilibrium in the space of decision rules is related to the perfect equilibrium of Selten (1975), and intimately linked to dynamic programming considerations, as in Bellman (1957). Kydland (1975), Friedman (1977), Kydland and Prescott (1977), Prescott and Visscher (1977), Harris and Townsend (1978, this volume, ch. 6; 1981, this volume, ch. 7), Milgrom and Roberts (1979), Dybvig and Spatt (1980), and Kreps and Wilson (1980) have achieved results of interest using it.

4 This type of free entry is a crucial determinant of the equilibrium allocation. The idea that free entry plays a central role in general equilibrium competitive markets has been emphasized recently in another context by Novshek and Sonnenschein (1980).

5 Unlimited arbitrage would not play a role in the presence of quantity restrictions; thus the propositions for the first game below depend on the absence of such restrictions.

6 With a finite number of households, what is offered here in effect is a general equilibrium model of imperfect competition. In such a model price-setters emerge endogenously in the sense that they are not specified a priori but instead are determined in equilibrium. Given the criticism of Roberts and Sonnenschein (1977)

of the standard general equilibrium approach to imperfect competition (described by Arrow and Hahn, 1971), such models might be taken seriously.

7 Edgeworth (1881) noted that there could be an indeterminacy of final settlements on the contract curve of his economy if there were a finite number of households but that such an indeterminacy would dissipate as the number of households increased (that is, as the economy is replicated). He also noted that if by custom or convenience households were restricted to trade at fixed rates of exchange, then the indeterminacy of final settlements would abide, but by way of demand curves, not the contract curve. In this chapter we establish that in the limit such an indeterminacy also dissipates.

8 Two other papers dealing explicitly with the connectedness of traders are those of Myerson (1977) and Kalai et al. (1978). See also note 22.

9 Thus we establish that the core will not be enlarged if allocations are restricted in this way, and thereby contribute to the literature which argues that various restrictions on coalition formation are inessential to the definition of the core (for example, Mas-Colell, 1978). Note also that, if intermediaries could name prices with quantity limits, there would be fewer restrictions on the allocations achievable by coalitions and the result would be weakened. Naming prices with quantity limits (or imposing fixed fees) may be helpful in some contexts in overcoming nonconvexities (see below).

10 The equivalence between competitive equilibrium allocations and the allocations of *alternative* noncooperative games is addressed by Shubik (1973), Pazner and Schmeidler (1975), Hurwicz (1976, 1979), Schmeidler (1976), Shapley and Shubik (1976), Postlewaite and Schmeidler (1978, 1979), and Wilson (1978).

11 The importance of this trade-enhancing role for money has been emphasized to the author by Allan Meltzer (see also Brunner and Meltzer, 1971).

12 Here the set of feasible choices (strategies) for any household depends on the selected choices (strategies) of the other households. In a sequential Nash equilibrium, defined below, this specification causes no difficulty, but it is not conventional in formal game-theoretic terms. In conventional game theory, feasible strategies should be independent of chosen strategies of others; if not, the game is not well defined *out of equilibrium*. To be more formal we might imagine an extended or multi-round second stage (that is, an n-stage game) in which households are numbered exogenously and select from among potential intermediaries in order. For a similar caveat, see note 13.

13 Here each household t is restricted exogenously to feasible strategies. Clearly, given that a specified game is actually played, it is well known *ex post* whether or not a strategy was feasible, and it is in this sense that the exogenous restriction is warranted. Note also that in an equilibrium, as defined below, the decision rules which household t takes as given will be those actually used, and that a specified game need not generate feasible allocations out of equilibrium. This is a common property of the noncooperative games mentioned earlier; see Postlewaite and Schmeidler (1979) for a further discussion.

14 The proof is by contradiction. In a null equilibrium there is no trade. Therefore at least one household would gain under the announcement (p, Ω) where p is a Walras price vector.

15 The author is well aware of the asymmetric treatment of the two games.

16 The author is unhappy with this additional restriction. It seems to be needed for technical reasons to exclude allocations which are arbitrarily large for a set of households of a given type which is arbitrarily small in measure. See the proof of proposition 11.4.

17 It is clear from remark 11.3 that the set of active intermediaries is at most countable and hence of Lebesgue measure zero. Thus, under the hypothesis, the set of households with null strategies is of measure unity. That the set of active intermediaries is of measure zero, so that intermediaries in effect vanish in the limit economy, is consistent with the concept of the invisible hand.

18 This economy is rather easy to describe, but an analysis of it would not be straightforward since multiple within-period movements are allowed. To further simplify matters, we might assume, for example, that prior to any trade at a given date, each household must specify some *ex post* location m_t^i, possibly distinct from l_t^i, that movements to these new locations occur simultaneously, and that no subsequent movements at date t are allowed. It might also be assumed that there are at most a finite number of possible locations on the plane, a finite number of households, and a finite number of dates. However, we might well have imagined that there are multiple commodities, variable factor supplies, and nontrivial production technologies, along the lines of the first class of spatial models described in section 8.

19 More formally, for the more restricted economy described in note 18, given a subset of households C, let $C_t(m)$ denote the subset of C which ends up at location m at date t. That is, $C_t(m) = \{i \in C : m_t^i = m\}$. Then consumption–location sequences $[c_t^i, m_t^i]_{t=0}^T$, $i \in C$, are said to be feasible for C if

$$\sum_{C_t(m)} c_t^i \leqslant \sum_{C_t(m)} w_t^i - \gamma_t^i(|l_t^i - m|) - \sum_{\{i: l_t^i \neq m\}} a_t^i$$

for all feasible locations m and for all dates t, with

$$c_t^i \geqslant 0$$

$$a_t^i + \gamma_t^i(|l_t^i - m|) \leqslant w_t^i \qquad \text{if } l_t^i \neq m$$

A consumption–location sequence $[c_t^i, m_t^i]_{t=0}^T$ for all households $i \in H$ is said to be in the *core* if there does not exist a subset of households C with a feasible consumption–location sequence $[c_t^{i*}, m_t^{i*}]$ such that

$$\sum_{t=0}^{T} \beta^t u^i(c_t^{i*}) > \sum_{t=0}^{T} \beta^t u^i(c_t^i) \qquad \text{for all } i \in C$$

20 Having said this, though, it is apparent that, even for the more restricted economy described in note 18, core allocations would not be easy to determine. It might be necessary to use a computer for parametric specifications.

21 If T is finite, one could determine maximizing strategies by working backward from the last date. Here, following Prescott and Visscher (1977), it may be especially

useful to suppose that choices at the second stage of each date are made sequentially (as if households were ordered).

22 There are some links here to multiplicities in the search and matching literature which the author is exploring elsewhere. See, for example, Diamond (1982) and Mortensen (1974).

References

Arrow, K.J. (1953) Le rôle des valeurs boursières pour la répartition la meilleure des risques. In *Econometrie*, pp. 41–8. Paris: Centre Nationale de la Recherche Scientifique.

—— and Hahn, F.H. (1971) *General Competitive Analysis*. San Francisco, CA: Holden-Day.

Bellman, R. (1957) *Dynamic Programming*. Princeton, NJ: Princeton University Press.

Benston, G.J. and Smith, C.W., Jr (1976) A transaction cost approach to the theory of financial intermediation. *Journal of Finance* 31, 215–31.

Bhattacharya, S. (1982) Aspects of monetary and banking theory and moral hazard. *Journal of Finance* 37, 371–84.

Brunner, K. and Meltzer, A.H. (1971) The uses of money: money in the theory of exchange. *American Economic Review* 61, 784–805.

Cass, D. and Yaari, M. (1966) A re-examination of the pure consumption loans model. *Journal of Political Economy* 74, 353–67.

Clower, R.W. (1967) A reconsideration of the microfoundations of monetary theory. *Western Economic Journal* 6, 1–8.

Debreu, G. (1959) *The Theory of Value*. New Haven, CT: Yale University Press.

Diamond, P. (1982) Aggregate demand management in search equilibrium. *Journal of Political Economy* 90, 881–94.

Dybvig, P. and Spatt, C. (1980) Does it pay to maintain a reputation? Unpublished manuscript, Carnegie–Mellon University, Pittsburgh, PA.

Edgeworth, F.Y. (1881) *Mathematical Psychics* London: Kegan Paul.

Fama, E.F. (1980) Banking and the theory of finance. *Journal of Monetary Economics* 6, 39–57.

Friedman, J.W. (1977) *Oligopoly and the Theory of Games*. Amsterdam: North-Holland.

Friedman, M. (1969) *The Optimum Quantity of Money and Other Essays*. Chicago, IL: Aldine.

Harris, M. and Townsend, R.M. (1978) Allocation mechanisms for asymmetrically informed agents. Working Paper 35-76-77, Carnegie–Mellon University, Pittsburgh, PA. Reprinted in this volume as chapter 6.

—— and —— (1981) Resource allocation under asymmetric information. *Econometrica* 49(1), 33–64. Reprinted in this volume as chapter 7.

Hurwicz, L. (1959) Optimality and efficiency in resource allocation processes. In *Mathematical Methods in the Social Sciences*, eds K.J. Arrow, S. Karlin, and P. Suppes, pp. 27–48. Stanford, CA: Stanford University Press.

—— (1972) On informationally decentralized systems. In *Decision and Organization*, eds C.B. McGuire and R. Radner, ch. 14. Amsterdam: North-Holland.

—— (1976) Outcome functions yielding Walrasian and Lindahl allocations at Nash equilibrium points. Mimeograph. University of Minnesota.

—— (1979) On allocations attainable through Nash equilibrium. *Journal of Economic Theory* 21(1), 140–65.

Jordan, J.S. (1982) The competitive allocation process is informationally efficient uniquely. *Journal of Economic Theory* 28, 1–18.

Kalai, E., Postlewaite, A., and Roberts, J. (1978) Barriers to trade and disadvantageous middlemen: non-monotonicity of the core. *Journal of Economic Theory* 19(1), 200–9.

Kreps, D. and Wilson, R. (1980) On the chain-store paradox and predation: reputation for toughness. Unpublished manuscript, Stanford University.

Kydland, F. (1975) Noncooperative and dominant player solutions in discrete dynamic games. *International Economic Review* 16, 321–35.

—— and Prescott, E.C. (1977) Rules rather than discretion and the inconsistency of optimal plans. *Journal of Political Economy* 85, 475–96.

Mas-Colell, A. (1978) A note on the core equivalence theorem: how many blocking coalitions are there? *Journal of Mathematical Economics* 5, 207–15.

Milgrom, P. and Roberts, J. (1979) Equilibrium limit pricing doesn't limit entry. Discussion Paper 399, Northwestern University, Evanston, IL.

Mortensen, D. (1974) Search equilibrium and the core in a decentralized pure exchange economy. Unpublished manuscript, Northwestern University, Evanston, IL.

Myerson, R.B. (1977) Graphs and cooperation in games. *Mathematics of Operations Research* 2, 225–9.

Novshek, W. and Sonnenschein, H. (1980) Small efficient scale as a foundation for Walrasian equilibrium. *Journal of Economic Theory* 22(2), 243–55.

Pazner, E. and Schmeidler, D. (1975) Non-Walrasian Nash equilibria in Arrow–Debreu economies. Mimeograph, University of Illinois, Urbana-Champaign, IL.

Postlewaite, A. and Schmeidler, D. (1978) Approximate efficiency of non-Walrasian Nash equilibria. *Econometrica* 46, 127–35.

—— and —— (1979) Notes on optimality and feasibility of informationally decentralized allocation mechanisms. Working Paper 583, University of Illinois.

Prescott, E.C. and Visscher, M. (1977) Sequential location among firms with foresight. *Bell Journal of Economics* 8, 373–93.

Roberts, J. and Sonnenschein, H. (1977) On the foundations of the theory of monopolistic competition. *Econometrica* 45, 101–13.

Sargent, T.J. (1987) *Macroeconomic Theory*, 2nd edn. New York: Academic Press.

Schmeidler, D. (1976) A remark on microeconomic models of an economy and on a game theoretic interpretation of Walras equilibria. Discussion Paper 76-68, Center for Economic Research. University of Minnesota.

Selten, R. (1975) Reexamination of the perfectness concept for equilibrium points in extensive games. *International Journal of Game Theory* 4, 25–55.

Shapley, L. and Shubik, M. (1976) Trade using one commodity as a means of payment. Discussion Paper R-1851-NSF, Rand Corporation, Santa Monica, CA.

Shubik, M. (1973) A theory of money and financial institutions: commodity money, oligopoly, credit, and bankruptcy in a general equilibrium model. *Western Economic Journal* 11, 24–8.

Smith, A. (1976) *The Wealth of Nations.* Chicago, IL: University of Chicago Press. (Originally published in 1776.)

Townsend, R.M. (1978) Intermediation and costly bilateral exchange. *Review of Economic Studies* 45, 417–25.

—— (1980) Models of money with spatially separated agents. In *Models of Monetary Economies*, eds J.H. Kareken and N. Wallace, pp. 265–303. Minneapolis, MN: Federal Reserve Bank of Minneapolis. Reprinted in this volume as chapter 2.

—— (1983) Financial structure and economic activity. *American Economic Review* 73(5), 895–911. Reprinted in this volume as chapter 4.

—— (1987) Asset return anomalies in a monetary economy. *Journal of Economic Theory* 41(5), 219–47. Reprinted in this volume as chapter 12.

—— and Wallace, N. (1982) A model of circulating private debt. Staff Report, Federal Reserve Bank of Minneapolis, Minneapolis, MN.

Wallace, N. (1980) The overlapping generations model of fiat money. In *Models of Monetary Economics*, eds J.H. Kareken and N. Wallace, pp. 49–78. Minneapolis, MN: Federal Reserve Bank of Minneapolis.

Wicksell, K. (1935) *Lectures on Political Economy.* New York: Macmillan.

Wilson, R.A. (1978) A competitive exchange model. *Econometrica* 46, 577–85.

Wood, J. (1981) Financial intermediaries and monetary control. *Journal of Monetary Economics* 8, 145–63.

Part VI
Limited Asset Markets with Spatial Separation

12
Asset Return Anomalies in a Monetary Economy

1 Introduction

In an insightful and provocative article, Hicks (1935) calls for an integration of the theory of value with the theory of money. By the theory of value, Hicks means the dictum that the relative value of two commodities depends on their relative marginal utilities. But, for Hicks, marginal utility analysis was taken as nothing other than a general theory of choice. Thus Hicks finds that the central monetary observation to be explained by choice theory is the preference for holding barren money rather than interest bearing securities or capital goods.

The purpose of this chapter, then, is to offer one explanation for such rate-of-return dominance and, more generally, to integrate the theory of value with the theory of money. Alternatively, the chapter is motivated by the obvious questions: how are we to incorporate money into a general equilibrium model in such a way as to explain such asset return anomalies, and what are the implications more generally for asset-pricing formulas?

In this endeavor, we are faced with the now familiar complaint of such diverse authors as Brunner and Meltzer (1971), Clower (1971), Hahn (1973a), Wallace (1980), and Cass and Shell (1983) that the standard general equilibrium Arrow–Debreu model, in assuming unlimited market participation

---

Reprinted from *Journal of Economic Theory* 41(5), 1987, 219–47 (Orlando, FL: Academic Press). Helpful comments from Lars Peter Hansen, Robert E. Lucas Jr, Edward C. Prescott, Thomas J. Sargent, Kenneth J. Singleton, Neil Wallace, and the participants of the NBER Conference on Intertemporal Puzzles in Macroeconomics, Cambridge, July 1982, financial support from the National Science Foundation and the Alfred P. Sloan Foundation, and programming assistance from Riccardo Revelli are all gratefully acknowledged. I assume full responsibility for any errors as well as for the views expressed here.

and no trading frictions, does not allow a role for money. Thus the standard model must be altered in some way, but at the moment we do not have many tightly specified alternatives. One class of models which comes to mind is the class of overlapping generations models based on the construct of Samuelson (1958). In these models money seems to flow naturally from the assumed demographic structure, that is, from a structure which generates missing markets, and for these models we now have well-worked-out theorems establishing the existence of monetary equilibria and associated optimality properties (see, for example, Balasko and Shell, 1983a). Unfortunately, however, as is indicated by Wallace (1980), monetary equilibria in these models are inconsistent with the existence of dominating assets, a complaint voiced by Hahn (1973a) and Tobin (1980), among others.

There are a variety of possible responses to this complaint. On the one hand, we might become discouraged about the possibility of constructing choice-theoretic models of money, preferring perhaps to start with the anomalies rather than explaining them. On the other hand, we might take issue with the anomalies themselves, arguing perhaps that rate-of-return dominance is, in general, the product of exogenously imposed legal restrictions; this seems to be close to the position of Wallace (1983). An intermediate response, however, would be to search for alternative choice-theoretic models of money. Again, in such models money would not enter via exogenously imposed restrictions, say that certain goods can only be acquired with money, but rather would emerge naturally in some way from an underlying exchange structure.

In this chapter we take the intermediate route. In particular, we follow Hicks's suggestion and introduce some frictions, specifically the friction of spatial separation. That is, it is assumed that there is an absence of double coincidence of wants among households which meet with one another at distinct spatial locations.[1] Thus, without a common medium of exchange, competitive market exchange is quite limited; in effect, in the spatial model considered here, households can consume only the commodities they produce. However, with a common medium of exchange, the commodities produced by the household in a given period can be traded for money in one market in a given period, money which in turn can be traded for a market-produced commodity in another market in a subsequent period. Thus money plays a role in providing liquidity, enabling the household to purchase commodities which it does not own. This gives it an advantage over other assets. Indeed, the model delivers Clower's (1967) dictum *endogenously* and thus is formally close to the Clower constraint models of Grandmont and Younes (1972, 1973) and Lucas (1980, 1982, 1984) among others.[2] The underlying exchange model is described in more detail in section 2, and the resulting Clower constraint model is the subject of section 3.

Of course, telling such exchange stories is not enough. In a choice-theoretic model of money a central task is to prove the existence of a competitive monetary equilibrium in which money has value. But how are we to do this? On the face of it, we might hope to follow the tradition of neoclassical growth theory, for example, Cass (1965), Koopmans (1965), Brock and Mirman (1972), Sargent (1979), and Lucas and Stokey (1984), first establishing the existence of an optimum and then, following Debreu (1954), establishing that an optimum can be supported as a competitive equilibrium with suitably chosen prices. Here, though, the endogenously induced finance constraint severs the link between competitive equilibria and Pareto optima, as in Grandmont and Younes (1972), Lucas (1984), and Townsend (1980, this volume, ch. 2), and we are faced with the task of establishing the existence of a competitive monetary equilibrium directly. This is a nontrivial undertaking, since, as is noted by Hahn (1965), the general equilibrium theorems of Debreu (1959), McKenzie (1959), and others are not immediately applicable owing to discontinuity.

Existence of a monetary equilibrium for the model in this chapter, which allows for return dominance and for shocks to technology, endowments, preferences, and the money supply, is established in section 4, building on the insightful papers of Bewley (1980) and Heller (1974).[3]

After all this investment, we can return to the observations that motivated the chapter – the dominance of the rate of return of capital and interest-bearing securities over money – and ask whether these and other anomalies are displayed, in general, in monetary equilibria. As is established in section 5, neither the money asset nor a privately owned capital asset seem to be priced efficiently in monetary equilibria – the returns on both generally violate standard intertemporal valuation relationships. Indeed, this is what delivers rate-of-return dominance. These results are apparent from the first-order conditions of the maximum problem of a "representative" consumer, and, as the product of a positive and stochastically varying Lagrange multiplier on the finance constraint, can be viewed as extensions of the results obtained earlier by Grandmont and Younes (1973), Lucas (1980), and Townsend (1980, this volume, ch. 2). Further, with some additional work, we can derive asset-pricing formulas for arbitrary market securities and deliver dominance of the nominal return of one-period money loans over individually held "idle" money balances. More generally, we can examine the extent to which the standard asset-pricing formulas of the real general equilibrium models of Lucas (1978), Breeden (1979), Brock (1980), and Prescott and Mehra (1980),[4] for example, as applied to data in the empirical work of Grossman and Shiller (1981), Hall (1981), Hansen and Singleton (1982, 1983), and Mankiw et al. (1982), for example, are equivalent to the asset-pricing formulas of the economy considered here – an economy in which money is essential. As it turns out, the monetary economy considered here has sufficient structure that we can obtain rather sharp nonstandard results. Of course, the idea more generally is that the market imperfections or trading difficulties which give rise to money may well have implications for asset prices.

2 The economy

In this section we describe one underlying exchange environment which generates the Clower constraint monetary model of section 3. Of course the entire *analysis* of this chapter takes the Clower constraint model as a starting point; in that sense the analysis of this chapter is general, and nothing hinges on the particular story given in this section. However, given the motivation for the chapter, we do want to describe at least one explicit general equilibrium stylized environment which rationalizes the Clower constraint setup.

The stylized environment given here is a blend of the Lucas–Cass–Yaari model and the "turnpike" model described in sections 4 and 2 respectively of Townsend (1980, this volume, ch. 2). The reader who finds the following description somewhat cryptic is urged to consider these sections more closely.

Briefly, imagine that there is a countable set of household types and a countable set of commodities, both indexed by the positive and negative integers. Each household of type i consists of a pair of agents and is imagined to be located on some real line at integer i (see figure 12.1). There is a countable infinity of such real lines, arranged horizontally in figure 12.1, and again the integer i on each line is inhabited by a (representative) household of type i. At each date t, each member of household i is capable of moving horizontally (on the line where it is located) half the distance to each of the two adjacent integers $i+1$ and $i-1$. Thus, at each date t, each household i is physically capable of carrying out transactions with a household of type $i-1$ and a household of type $i+1$ in two spatially separated markets, say $(i-1, i)$ and $(i, i+1)$. Between dates, households can move about. Each household of type i, i even, is imagined to move vertically downward to the next line, while each household of type i, i odd, stays in its fixed location. Thus, for example, debt issued by a household of type i, i even, can only be passed along to households vertically above the issuer; this construction prevents the issue of private debt. Each household of type i, whatever its location at a given date, should be taken as representative of a large (infinite)

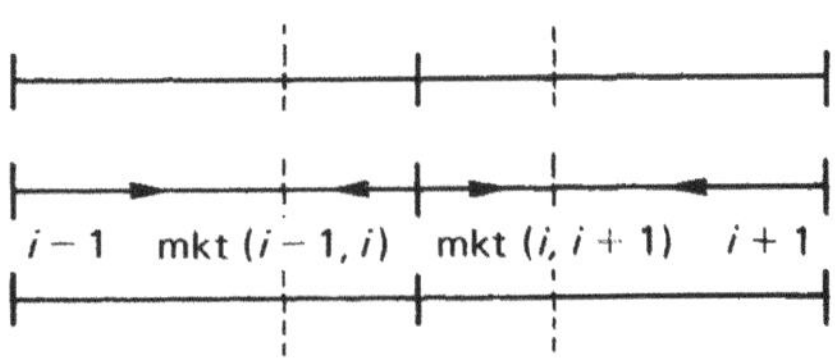

Figure 12.1. A spatial pattern of trade

number of households in an identical situation following an identical itinerary. This rationalizes the existence of a competitive market when two representative households meet.

Each household of type i is endowed with $w_t(i, s_t)$ units of commodity i (only) at date t, depending possibly on the state s_t but not on date t itself. Here, however, $w_t(i, s_t)$ is a constant with respect to the index i. That is, household i has $w_t(s_t)$ units of commodity i, household $i+1$ has $w_t(s_t)$ units of commodity $i+1$, and so on. (Further, this kind of symmetry across households is continued below.) It is assumed that $w_t(s_t) > 0$. Here there is a finite set A of possible states s_t at each date t; see Bewley (1980) for a similar formulation of uncertainty. Each household of type i also possesses a technology for transforming commodity i (only) at date t into commodity i at date $t+1$, namely a function $f: R^1_+ xA \rightarrow R^1_+$. That is, commodity i can be either consumed (by some household) at date t or invested by household i, say I_{t+1} units, to produce $f(I_{t+1}, s_{t+1})$ units of commodity i at date $t+1$ in state s_{t+1}. It is assumed that, for every $s_t \epsilon A$, $f(\cdot, s_t)$ is strictly concave, strictly increasing, and continuously differentiable with $f(0, s_t) = 0$, $f'(\infty, s_t) = 0$, $f'(0, s_t) = \infty$; this is the usual putty–putty version of the capital accumulation models cited in section 1. As a matter of notation, let $h_t = (s_0, s_1, \ldots, s_t)$ denote the entire history of states through date t. Then investment by household type i at date t may depend on that history, and we write $I_{t+1}(h_t)$.

Each household of type i cares about units of consumption c_t^1 of commodity i, the so-called home-produced good, and consumption c_t^2 of commodity $i+1$, the so-called market-produced good, both at date t, and has preferences represented by the utility function $U(c_t^1, c_t^2, s_t)$ which is strictly concave, strictly increasing, and continuously differentiable in consumptions. Further, to ensure interior solutions, it is assumed that, for any $c_t^2 > 0$ and any s_t, $\lim_{c_t^1 \rightarrow 0} U_1(c_t^1, c_t^2, s_t) = \infty$; that for any $c_t^1 > 0$ and any s_t, $\lim_{c_t^2 \rightarrow 0} U_2(c_t^1, c_t^2, s_t) = \infty$; and that, for any nonzero finite price vector $p = (p_1, p_2)$, the induced indirect utility function over nominal income y, namely $V(y; p_1, p_2, s_t)$, has the property that, for any s_t, $\lim_{y \rightarrow 0} V_y(y; p_1, p_2, s_t) = \infty$. Note that preferences can be random at date t, a function of the state s_t. In principle, household type i's consumption of commodities i and $i+1$ can depend on the entire history h_t at date t. Therefore let $c_t^1(h_t)$ and $c_t^2(h_t)$ denote the number of units of consumption of commodities i and $i+1$ respectively by household i at date t under history h_t. (Again, note the imposed symmetry across households.) Thus preferences of each household of type i over the $T+1$ periods of its lifetime are represented by the utility function

$$E_0 \sum_{t=0}^{T} \beta^t U\{c_t^1(h_t), c_t^2(h_t), s_t\}$$

Here the expectation E_0 is over states s_t, given s_0, and the discount rate β

satisfies $0 < \beta < 1$. Also T may be either finite or infinite; it will be clear from the context below which assumption is made.

There is also fiat money in this economy, that is, pieces of paper which represent outside indebtedness. Let M_0 denote the number of units of fiat money held by household i at date zero, a fixed initial condition, and again the same across all households. In addition, each household of type i is endowed with $z_t(h_t)$ units of fiat money at the beginning of each date t, possibly depending on the history h_t. These endowments can be viewed as random lump-sum injections by a monetary authority or, more generally, monetary instability variables. If $z_t(h_t)$ is negative, it is interpreted as a lump-sum tax. However, if there is a tax, it is assumed that the sequence of previous transfers is such that household i can pay the tax without engaging in trade, that is, $M_0 + \Sigma_{\tau=0}^{t} z_\tau(h_\tau) > 0$ for each t; this avoids bankruptcy problems. (It will also be equivalent to the condition that in *equilibrium* per household money balances will always be strictly positive.) Moreover, if the horizon is finite with T as the last date, then net injections of money are necessarily taxed away in the end, in effect at date $T+1$. This is accomplished by imposing the terminal condition $M_0 + \Sigma_{\tau=0}^{T} z_\tau(h_\tau) = M_{T+1}(h_T)$, where $M_{T+1}(h_T)$ is the number of units of fiat money held at the end of date T under history h_T (in effect, the tax at $T+1$). It may be noted, following Lerner (1947), that a coupling of fiat money issue with promised taxation is not unusual; see Hepburn (1924) for a discussion of its use in the American colonial period, for example. This device also has a long history in the monetary economics literature, culminating with the recent efforts of Balasko and Shell (1983a,b).

It should be noted now that preferences, technology, endowments, and monetary policy are all potentially random in this model. In fact, by specifying finite-state-space stochastic processes on each of these, we can induce a stochastic process on states of the world s_t. Thus the formulation is quite general and allows statistical independence as a special case. It will be supposed that the process s_t is Markov, that is the probability that $s_{t+1} = b$ given $s_t = a$ does not depend on t. The state s_t is known by all households at the beginning of date t.

We might note now the absence of double coincidence of wants when households meet. For example, in markets $(i, i+1)$, a household type i has no commodity a household of type $i+1$ wants, and this creates the possibility for monetary exchange. (Again, see Lucas's version of the Cass–Yaari (1966) circle in Townsend (1980, this volume, ch. 2, section 4).) Indeed, at market $(i, i+1)$ given history h_t, we can assume the existence of a competitive market in which commodity $i+1$ can be purchased with money (by a household i) at monetary price $p_t(h_t)$. Similarly, at market $(i-1, i)$, we can assume that commodity i is sold (by a household i) for money at price $p_t(h_t)$. Again note the imposed symmetry on prices of commodities $i, i+1$, and so on. We might also note, then, that in this setup, money from the sale of commodity i cannot be used *contemporaneously* by household i for the purchase of commodity $i+1$. Of course, having completed purchases and sales, agents of household i return home to consume and invest. As a matter of notation, let $M_{t+1}(h_t)$ denote the number of units of fiat money carried over to the beginning of date $t+1$.

3 Decision problems and the definition of a monetary equilibrium

If we again limit attention to outcomes which are symmetric across households, the problem of each household i is now the problem of a "representative" household, namely, taking the price sequence $p_t(h_t)$ and the tax sequence $z_t(h_t)$ parametrically, as follows.

Problem 12.1

$$\max E_0 \sum_{t=0}^{T} \beta^t U\{c_t^1(h_t), c_t^2(h_t), s_t\} \tag{12.1}$$

by choice of $c_t^1(h_t), c_t^2(h_t), I_{t+1}(h_t), M_{t+1}(h_t)$ all $t \geqslant 0$, all h_t, subject to

$$\begin{aligned} &p_t(h_t)c_t^1(h_t) + p_t(h_t)c_t^2(h_t) + M_{t+1}(h_t) + p_t(h_t)I_{t+1}(h_t) \\ &\quad \leqslant M_t(h_{t-1}) + p_t(h_t)w_t(s_t) + p_t(h_t)f\{I_t(h_{t-1}), s_t\} + z_t(h_t) \\ &\qquad\qquad\qquad \text{all } t \geqslant 0, \text{ all } h_t \end{aligned} \tag{12.2}$$

$$p_t(h_t)c_t^2(h_t) \leqslant M_t(h_{t-1}) + z_t(h_t) \qquad \text{all } t, \text{all } h_t \tag{12.3}$$

given $M_0 + z_0(s_0) > 0, I_0 \geqslant 0, M_{T+1}(h_T) \geqslant M_0 + \Sigma_{\tau=0}^{T} z_\tau(h_\tau)$. Then this yields the following definition.

Definition
A symmetric monetary equilibrium is a sequence of finite positive prices $p_t^*(h_t)$ and sequences of consumptions $c_t^{1*}(h_t), c_t^{2*}(h_t)$, money balances $M_{t+1}^*(h_t)$, investments $I_{t+1}^*(h_t)$, and lump-sum injections $z_t^*(h_t)$ such that the following two conditions hold.

- *Maximization*: the sequences $c_t^{1*}(h_t), c_t^{2*}(h_t), M_{t+1}^*(h_t), I_{t+1}^*(h_t)$ solve problem 12.1 given the price sequence $p_t^*(h_t)$ and lump-sum injections $z_t^*(h_t)$.

- *Market clearing*: the sequences $c_t^{1*}(h_t), c_t^{2*}(h_t), I_{t+1}^*(h_t)$ satisfy

$$c_t^{2*}(h_t) + c_t^{1*}(h_t) \leq w_t(s_t) + f\{I_t^*(h_{t-1}), s_t\} - I_{t+1}^*(h_t) \qquad \text{all } t, h_t \tag{12.4}$$

Note that in the market-clearing condition (12.4) only households type i and $i-1$ consume commodity i, and only household type i is endowed with or can invest commodity i. Also, since in any market commodities are exchanged for money, commodity balance (12.4) implies equality in the demand and supply of money balances. Thus in equilibrium the representative household's decisions about $M_{t+1}(h_t)$ are coincident with aggregate money balances available, namely $M_0 + \Sigma_{\tau=0}^t z_\tau(h_\tau)$.

It may also be noted that in a symmetric monetary equilibrium there is only one maximization problem to evaluate and, in particular, market clearing is defined relative to the choice variables of the representative household. But from the point of view of the household, the economy is decentralized. For an arbitrary price vector $p_t(h_t)$, choices satisfying its budget constraint do not necessarily satisfy the market-clearing condition. In particular, the amount of money it supplies in the market $(i, i+1)$ need not equal the amount it purchases in the market $(i-1, i)$. The task is to find a price vector which implies market clearing. In fact, the next section contains a proof of the existence of a symmetric monetary equilibrium for the finite-horizon and infinite-horizon cases.

4 Existence of a symmetric monetary equilibrium

The strategy adopted to prove the existence of a symmetric monetary equilibrium is to use the more or less standard existence arguments of Debreu (1959) for the finite-horizon economy, which allow for diversity among agents. This is precisely the tack taken by Heller (1974) for proving the existence of equilibrium in an economy with fiat money, and fortunately, as far as its use here is concerned, Heller's model allows for capital accumulation. Unfortunately, Heller's model also exploits the properties of an exogenously specified (nontrivial) transactions cost technology, which has no analog here. However, it is established that a modified Heller-style proof can be applied to our case.

The proof relies heavily on the taxation of fiat money in the last period T. In effect, this tax allows the price of money to be an arbitrary positive number in period T, and, with this, the price of money can be shown to be positive in earlier periods, no matter what the realized history.[5] Therefore, Debreu's (1959) continuity and fixed-point arguments can be applied. It can be established, moreover, under specified assumptions, that money is traded in any such monetary equilibrium, that is, money does facilitate exchange. The existence of such a nontrivial monetary equilibrium for finite-horizon economies is a major result of this chapter. It is summarized here and proved in the appendix.

Theorem 12.1

For every horizon $T < \infty$ and every terminal price of money $p_T(h_T) = \alpha/(1-\alpha)$ there exists a symmetric monetary equilibrium.

Still, we may feel uncomfortable that the end-of-horizon tax is an artificial device. To counter this, two more theorems are established. First, under specified assumptions, the monetary equilibrium prices and allocations for the finite-horizon economies converge to well-defined feasible limits (at least along some sub-sequence and, for examples, along the entire sequence) as the horizon is driven to infinity. Again, this is summarized here and proved in the appendix.

Theorem 12.2

There exists a sub-sequence of horizons T, say T_n, such that individual choices $\{c_t^1(h_t), c_t^2(h_t), I_{t+1}(h_t), M_{t+1}(h_t)\}^{T_n}$, $t = 0, 1, \ldots, T_n$, and prices $\{p_t(h_t)\}^{T_n}$, $t = 0, 1, \ldots, T_n$, converge to well-defined limits denoted $\{c_2^1(h_t), c_t^2(h_t), I_{t+1}(h_t), M_{t+1}(h_t)\}^{\sim}, t = 0, 1, \ldots, \infty$, and $\{p_t(h_t)\}^{\sim}, t = 0, 1, \ldots, \infty$, respectively. Moreover the choices indicated by the tilde are feasible for the individual given the prices indicated by the tilde and satisfy market clearing as well.

The interpretation is that the behavior of households is unaffected in the limit by a tax in the arbitrarily distant future. Thus, in principle, we might hope to use the behavior and prices of a sufficiently long-lived economy as predictions of the model.

Second, we can replace the tax in Heller's setup with utility for end-of-horizon money balances (as well as end-of-horizon capital), following Bewley (1980). However, the previous arguments need little modification to establish existence of equilibrium for such T-period economies. Again, we can take a limit and, in this case, establish conditions under which the limiting behavior is maximal in the infinite-horizon economy. Thus, sufficient conditions are given for the existence of a monetary equilibrium in the infinite-horizon economy. Again, this is summarized here and proved in the appendix.

Theorem 12.3

Consider an artificial finite-horizon economy with no taxes on money balances at the last date T but with preferences modified at date T, in effect adding a date $T+1$ term

$$E_0\beta^{T+1}M_{T+1}(h_T)+E_0\beta^{T+1}f\{I_{T+1}(h_T),s_{T+1}\}$$

Then there exists a symmetric monetary equilibrium with individual choice vector $\{c_t^1(h_t), c_t^2(h_t), M_{t+1}(h_t), I_{t+1}(h_t)\}^T$, $t=0, 1, \ldots, T$, and price vector $\{p_t(h_t)\}^T$, $t=0,1,\ldots,T$, for every horizon $T<\infty$. Moreover, there exists a sub-sequence of horizons, say T_n, such that the T_n sequences above converge to limits $\{c_t^1(h_t), c_t^2(h_t), M_{t+1}(h_t), I_{t+1}(h_t)\}^\sim$, $t=0, 1, \ldots, \infty$, and $\{p_t(h_t)\}^\sim$, $t=0, 1, \ldots, \infty$, respectively for all dates t and all histories h_t. If the $U(\cdot, s_t)$ are uniformly bounded from above by some $\bar{u}<\infty$ and below by zero, the $f(\cdot, s_t)$ are uniformly bounded from above by some $f<\infty$, and

$$\lim_{T\to\infty} E_0\beta^T\left\{\sum_{t=0}^{T} z_t(h_t)+M_0\right\}=0$$

then the choices and prices indicated by tildes constitute an equilibrium in the infinite-horizon economy.

5 Properties of equilibria: the anomalies

A nice aspect of the model under study is that the first-order conditions for the solution to the representative household's maximization problem (12.1) readily deliver interesting properties of monetary equilibria – unconventional intertemporal valuation of assets, rate-of-return dominance, and nonstandard asset-pricing formulas. The key is that the period-by-period liquidity constraints can bear positive Lagrange multipliers, that is, shadow prices or "liquidity premia," which must be taken into account in the standard value relationships of choice theory.[6]

To proceed, note that the choice variables $c_t^1(h_t), c_t^2(h_t), M_{t+1}(h_t)$, and $I_{t+1}(h_t)$ enter into at most a finite number of terms. Thus we may use the methods of Lagrange to deliver necessary first-order conditions for an interior maximum:

$$\beta^t\text{prob}(h_t|s_0)U_1\{c_t^1(h_t), c_t^2(h_t), s_t\}-\lambda_t(h_t)p_t(h_t)=0 \tag{12.5}$$

$$\beta^t\text{prob}(h_t|s_0)U_2\{c_t^1(h_t), c_t^2(h_t), s_t\}-\lambda_t(h_t)p_t(h_t)-\phi_t(h_t)p_t(h_t)=0 \tag{12.6}$$

$$-\lambda_t(h_t)+\sum_{s_{t+1}}\phi_{t+1}(h_t, s_{t+1})+\sum_{s_{t+1}}\lambda_{t+1}(h_t, s_{t+1})=0 \tag{12.7}$$

$$-p_t(h_t)\lambda_t(h_t)+\sum_{s_{t+1}}\lambda_{t+1}(h_t,s_{t+1})p_{t+1}(h_t,s_{t+1})f'\{I_{t+1}(h_t),s_{t+1}\}=0 \tag{12.8}$$

where $\lambda_t(h_t)$ is the (positive) Lagrange multiplier on budget constraint (12.2), in effect the marginal utility gain of a marginal increase in income (in terms of money), and $\phi_t(h_t)$ is the (nonnegative) Lagrange multiplier on constraint (12.3), in effect the marginal gain from a marginal weakening of the liquidity constraint. We might note in particular that equation (12.7) is the relationship among Lagrange multipliers implied by a marginal transaction in $M_{t+1}(h_t)$, shifting income from t to $t+1$; $M_{t+1}(h_t)$ provides income in state s_{t+1} and weakens the liquidity constraint in $t+1$ for all s_{t+1}.

Conditions (12.5)–(12.8) must hold in any monetary equilibrium. That is, they must hold when evaluated at equilibrium choices and prices. First, note that in equilibrium the per household money balances $M_{t+1}(h_t)$ chosen must equal per household money balances available, $M_0+\Sigma_{\tau=0}^{t}z_\tau(h_\tau)$, a number which by assumption is strictly positive. Thus in equilibrium the constraint that $M_{t+1}(h_t)\geqslant 0$ is nonbinding and (12.7) must hold at equality. Second, note that with strictly positive (finite) prices $p_t(h_t)$ at date t and history h_t, $p_t(h_t)w_t(s_t)+M_t(h_{t-1})>0$ and there is thus a source of positive nominal income for nominal expenditure $y_t(h_t)$. Then, with $V_y\{0;p_t(h_t),p_t(h_t),s_t\}=\infty$, nominal expenditures can never be zero in equilibrium. Further, the Inada conditions $U_1(0,c^2,s)=\infty$ and $U_2(c^1,0,s)=\infty$ and the strict positivity of the upper bound on $c_t^2(h_t)$, namely $\{M_t(h_{t-1})+z_t(h_t)\}/p_t(h_t)$, then imply that consumptions $c_t^1(h_t)$ and $c_t^2(h_t)$ are always strictly positive as well. Finally with $f'(0,s_{t+1})=\infty$, the constraint $I_{t+1}(h_t)\geqslant 0$ can be ignored as well, and (12.8) must hold as an equality.

Again, the first-order conditions (12.5)–(12.8) are rich in their implications for asset returns, as is now argued.

5.1 *Unconventional intertemporal valuation for the money asset and for the privately owned capital good*

Equations (12.5)–(12.8) and the $t+1$ counterparts of (12.5) and (12.6) can be manipulated to yield

$$U_1\{c_t^1(h_t),c_t^2(h_t),s_t\}=\frac{\beta E_t U_1\{c_{t+1}^1(h_t,s_{t+1}),c_{t+1}^2(h_t,s_{t+1}),s_{t+1}\}p_t(h_t)}{p_{t+1}(h_t,s_{t+1})}+\frac{\Sigma_{s_{t+1}}\phi_{t+1}(h_t,s_{t+1})p_t(h_t)}{\beta^t\text{prob}(h_t|s_0)} \tag{12.9}$$

$$U_2\{c_t^1(h_t), c_t^2(h_t), s_t\} = \frac{\beta E_t U_2\{c_{t+1}^1(h_t, s_{t+1}), c_{t+1}^2(h_t, s_{t+1}), s_{t+1}\} p_t(h_t)}{p_{t+1}(h_t, s_{t+1})} + \frac{\phi_t(h_t) p_t(h_t)}{\beta^t \text{prob}(h_t | s_0)} \quad (12.10)$$

Equations (12.9) and (12.10) display the unusual valuation relationships for the money of this model; the money asset as a store of value will generally not seem to be "priced efficiently" relative to either the home-produced or the market-produced good; that is, a marginal increase in money holdings will not have the marginal loss in utility from deferred (current) consumption equaling the expected marginal gain in utility from increased future consumption. To see why, consider (12.9). Suppose that $c_t^1(h_t)$ is marginally decreased and converted by sale to an increase in money holdings $M_{t+1}(h_t)$ which is carried over to date $t+1$. Now the consequent increase in income might be spent directly on $c_{t+1}^1(h_t, s_{t+1})$, but if money was constraining consumption at $t+1$ and s_{t+1}, a more efficient transaction is to readjust consumption levels, marginally increasing $c_{t+1}^2(h_t, s_{t+1})$ as well. Thus, there is an "extra" gain, the added term on the right-hand side of (12.9). Similar interpretations apply in the other equation. Obviously, we must take into account the special role played by money in contemplating intertemporal substitution of consumption bundles.

Further manipulation of (12.5)–(12.8) yields

$$U_1\{c_t^1(h_t), c_t^2(h_t), s_t\} = \beta E_t U_1\{c_{t+1}^1(h_t, s_{t+1}), c_{t+1}^2(h_t, s_{t+1}), s_{t+1}\} f'\{I_{t+1}(h_t), s_{t+1}\} \quad (12.11)$$

$$U_2\{c_t^1(h_t), c_t^2(h_t), s_t\} = \beta E_t U_2\{c_{t+1}^1(h_t, s_{t+1}), c_{t+1}^2(h_t, s_{t+1}), s_{t+1}\} f'\{I_{t+1}(h_t), s_{t+1}\} + \frac{\phi_t(h_t) p_t(h_t)}{\beta^t \text{prob}(h_t | s_0)} - \frac{\Sigma_{s_{t+1}} p_{t+1}(h_t, s_{t+1}) \phi_{t+1}(h_t, s_{t+1}) f'\{I_{t+1}(h_t), s_{t+1}\}}{\beta^t \text{prob}(h_t | s_0)} \quad (12.12)$$

It is seen from (12.11) that investment levels and capital asset holdings will be efficient relative to the home-produced commodity. Equation (12.11) must hold, after all, since consumptions $c_t^1(h_t)$ and $c_t^1(h_t, s_{t+1})$ can be reallocated by the investment $I_{t+1}(h_t)$. However, capital asset holdings will generally *not* be efficient relative to the market-produced commodity. To see why, consider (12.12). Suppose that $c_t^2(h_t)$ is marginally decreased, releasing income so that $I_{t+1}(h_t)$ is marginally increased, and this in turn finances a marginal increase in the $c_{t+1}^2(h_t, s_{t+1})$. As before, the decrease in $c_t^2(h_t)$ is less costly than might be supposed with $\phi_t(h_t) > 0$; however, the increase in $c_{t+1}^2(h_t, s_{t+1})$ is less beneficial with $\phi_{t+1}(h_t, s_{t+1}) > 0$. Again, money as an asset has a special role to play in facilitating consumption, and this can alter conventional valuation relationships for *other* assets.[7]

5.2 Rate-of-return dominance

It is now apparent that the real rate of return on privately owned capital dominates the real return on money. From (12.9) and (12.11), for example, if any of the $\phi_{t+1}(h_t, s_{t+1})$ are positive, then

$$\beta E_t U_1\{c_{t+1}^1(h_t, s_{t+1}), c_{t+1}^2(h_t, s_{t+1}), s_{t+1}\}\left[f'\{I_{t+1}(h_t), s_{t+1}\} - \frac{p_t(h_t)}{p_{t+1}(h_t, s_{t+1})}\right] > 0 \tag{12.13}$$

Similarly, from (12.10) and (12.12),

$$\beta E_t U_2\{c_{t+1}^1(h_t, s_{t+1}), c_{t+1}^2(h_t, s_{t+1}), s_{t+1}\}\left[f'\{I_{t+1}(h_t), s_{t+1}\} - \frac{p_t(h_t)}{p_{t+1}(h_t, s_{t+1})}\right] > 0 \tag{12.14}$$

Thus the marginal return on capital, expressed in terms of expected marginal utility of consumption, exceeds the marginal return on money. The paradox is explained by noting that money plays a role in loosening the date $t+1$ liquidity constraint.

To express return dominance in a more dramatic way, imagine an economy without uncertainty, that is, suppose that there is no movement in the state variables s_t, so that these can be suppressed in the notation. It can then be established that in a steady state the marginal return on capital is $f'(I_{t+1}) = 1/\beta > 1$, and it thus exceeds the return on money $p_t/p_{t+1} = 1$.[8] Again, the explanation seems apparent: in the steady state, money held at date i is spent entirely on consumption of the market-produced good at date $t+1$. But capital invested at date t must be converted to money at date $t+1$ if it is to be spent on consumption of the market-produced good. Thus there is a one-period difference in consumption dates between money and capital holdings; hence the return to capital is discounted by the one-period discount rate β, that is $f'(I_{t+1})\beta = 1$.[9]

5.3 *Nonstandard asset-pricing formulas for market securities*

So far we have considered two assets, the money asset, which is actively traded, and the capital asset, which is privately held though it does enter into the production process. But what about the wide variety of securities which are traded in actual market economies? What can we say about the standard asset-pricing formulas which have been taken to date from actual market economies on the assumption, if only implicit, that money is inessential, just another asset? Under what conditions would such formulas continue to apply to the monetary economy under consideration here?

To proceed, recall that we have taken each household of type i, whatever its location at a given date, as representative of a large (infinite) number of households in an identical situation following an identical itinerary, in effect cohort households. (The mathematics has assumed that there is only one household.) Thus, as in standard representative consumer asset-pricing models, we can contemplate the potential sale and purchase of a variety of assets among cohort households which, when priced at the monetary equilibrium consumptions and Lagrange multipliers, using the obvious marginal rate of substitution formulas, are never traded in equilibrium.[10]

For example, the within-cohort price of the market-produced commodity at date $t+1$ under history h_t and state s_{t+1} relative to the market-produced commodity at date t under history h_t is

$$\frac{\beta\,\mathrm{prob}(s_{t+1}|h_t)U_2\{c^1_{t+1}(h_t, s_{t+1}), c^2_{t+1}(h_t, s_{t+1}), s_{t+1}\}}{U_2\{c^1_t(h_t), c^2_t(h_t), s_t\}} \equiv \frac{1}{1 + r^2_{t+1}(h_t, s_{t+1})} \tag{12.15}$$

where $r^2_{t+1}(h_t, s_{t+1})$ is a within-cohort contingent real rate of interest. Of course, with this real rate of interest,

$$U_2\{c^1_t(h_t), c^2_t(h_t), s_t\} = \{1 + r^2_{t+1}(h_t, s_{t+1})\}\beta\,\mathrm{prob}(s_{t+1}|h_t) \times U_2\{c^1_{t+1}(h_t, s_{t+1}), c^2_{t+1}(h_t, s_{t+1}), s_{t+1}\} \tag{12.16}$$

and a conventional intertemporal asset-pricing formula holds trivially.

Similarly, suppose that one of the (representative) households in some cohort were given the possibility of trading (with some other member of the cohort) beginning-of-period money balances for end-of-period consumptions, with all other cross-island market possibilities intact. It can be verified directly from the first-order conditions of an extended maximization problem that

$$\frac{\beta^t \text{prob}(h_t|s_0) U_1\{c_t^1(h_t), c_t^2(h_t), s_t\}}{\lambda_t(h_t) + \phi_t(h_t)} \tag{12.17}$$

$$\frac{\beta^t \text{prob}(h_t|s_0) U_2\{c_t^1(h_t), c_t^2(h_t), s_t\}}{\lambda_t(h_t) + \phi_t(h_t)} \tag{12.18}$$

are the appropriate within-cohort money prices at date t under history h_t for the home-produced and market-produced consumption goods respectively. We can also deliver these prices in a more direct way, noting from problem 12.1 and from (12.2) and (12.3) that $\lambda_t(h_t) + \phi_t(h_t)$ is the obvious "marginal utility of money" at date t (from the point of view of date zero). Now it is apparent from (12.18) and (12.6) that the implicit within-cohort money price of the market-produced commodity is equal to the explicit cross-island monetary equilibrium money price of the market-produced commodity. But, from (12.17) and (12.5), this is not true of the home-produced commodity. (We will return to this observation below.)

In the same way, we might assume that the representative consumer could borrow and lend beginning-of-period money balances in a within-cohort market. For example, the within-cohort price of money at date $t+1$ under history h_t and state s_{t+1} relative to money at date t would be

$$\frac{\lambda_{t+1}(h_t, s_{t+1}) + \phi_{t+1}(h_t, s_{t+1})}{\lambda_t(h_t) + \phi_t(h_t)} \equiv \frac{1}{1 + r_{t+1}(h_t, s_{t+1})} \tag{12.19}$$

where $r_{t+1}(h_t, s_{t+1})$ is a contingent money rate of interest. Of course, we can also consider a within-cohort unconditional claim on money at date $t+1$, valid for all states s_{t+1}, as such an asset is merely a bundle of individual contingent money claims. Its price in terms of date t money is thus just

$$\frac{\Sigma_{s_{t+1}}\{\lambda_{t+1}(h_t, s_{t+1}) + \phi_{t+1}(h_t, s_{t+1})\}}{\lambda_t(h_t) + \phi_t(h_t)} \equiv \frac{1}{1 + r_t(h_t)} \tag{12.20}$$

where $r_t(h_t)$ is the nominal rate of interest. Moreover, by virtue of (12.7),

$$\frac{1}{1 + r_t(h_t)} = \frac{\lambda_t(h_t)}{\lambda_t(h_t) + \phi_t(h_t)} \tag{12.21}$$

so that the within-cohort nominal rate of interest is never negative and is positive whenever ϕ_t is positive. Thus the theory has interesting natural implications for the nominal rate of interest.

We may also note in passing that, from (12.5) and (12.21), the within-cohort money price of the home-produced commodity at date t is now just

$$\frac{p_t(h_t)}{1 + r_t(h_t)} \tag{12.22}$$

Intuitively, money from the (cross-island) sale of the home-produced commodity should be discounted by the nominal rate of interest, since it takes one period to purchase the market-produced consumption good with that money. In contrast, we may recall that the within-cohort price of the market-produced commodity is equal to $p_t(h_t)$ without adjustment.

Using the within-cohort nominal rate of interest and the within-cohort money prices, we can establish that within-cohort unconditional one-period money loans will be priced efficiently, again in accord with standard asset-pricing formulas. For, again, within-cohort prices are just marginal rates of substitution, and we can easily trace out a sequence of transactions (of goods now for money now, money now for money later, and money later for goods later) and show that some identity is satisfied, trivially. Of course in equilibrium no such loans are effected. Rather, we see another kind of apparent asset return dominance: money is held in "idle" balances, even though, in general, with $\phi_t(h_t) > 0$, there is a positive rate of interest. But of course money is needed for within-period transactions.

Indeed, we are now ready to consider the purchase and sale of (arbitrary) securities which are priced in terms of money at the purchase date and yield returns in terms of money at the sale date. Suppose in particular that one unit of the market-produced commodity is sold in some cohort for money at date t, that the money is used for the purchase of the security in question, and that the monetary returns from the security at date $t + 1$ and state s_{t+1} are used to purchase the market-produced consumption good at date $t + 1$ and state s_{t+1}. However, since the within-cohort money price of the market-produced consumption good is equal to the explicit cross-island monetary equilibrium price we have

$$\begin{aligned} &U_2\{c_t^1(h_t), c_t^2(h_t), s_t\} \\ &\quad = R_{t+1}(h_t, s_{t+1})\beta \operatorname{prob}(s_{t+1} | h_t) U_2\{c_{t+1}^1(h_t, s_{t+1}), c_{t+1}^2(h_t, s_{t+1}), s_{t+1}\} \end{aligned} \tag{12.23}$$

where $R_{t+1}(h_t, s_{t+1})$ is the real gross contingent rate of return on the asset in question, with prices at the purchase date and redemption date deflated by the nominal cross-island price level. As noted, formulas of this kind, or more specifically the stochastic analogs which also hold here, have been taken to date. However, repeating this experiment with respect to the home-produced consumption good yields a nonstandard formula, if monetary prices and returns are deflated in the same way using the cross-island prices. That is, consistent with (12.22), we should use instead an interest-rate-deflated nominal price level at the purchase and sale date. Alternatively, we should be careful to use the within-cohort nominal price level.

In concluding this subsection we should note that the key element in pricing assets seems to be the time when money proceeds from the sale of consumption goods or resources are available for expenditures on other consumption goods, and to that extent the analysis in this chapter should carry over to more elaborate models. For example, if a "household-produced" good such as labor is not used immediately for consumption of leisure, then it seems that, relative to the marginal utility of leisure, standard asset-pricing formulas are in jeopardy.

6 Concluding remarks

In this chapter we have tried to make some progress on two fronts. First, motivated by observations, we have tried to enlarge the class of well-defined choice-theoretic models that we have at our disposal, developing further some of the spatial models of earlier literature. The proof of existence of a competitive monetary equilibrium can be viewed in this light. Of course we hope that the proof is not special to the particular spatial model considered here, and that at least part of it will be applicable more generally. Additional evidence that this is indeed the case is the proof of existence of a competitive equilibrium for circulating private debt in the model of Townsend and Wallace (1987, this volume, ch. 3), a proof which follows in part the one given here, building upon Debreu, with suitable modifications.

The second front on which we have tried to make some progress is our ability to explain observed phenomena. In this regard, the spatial model considered here appears highly stylized, and, as an explanation of money and related asset return anomalies, quite restricted. After all, there is only one (actively traded) *financial* asset, and the payments lag which generates the finance constraint is of a particularly simple and rigid form. However, we do not seem to have many formal models yet which capture a general yet intuitive notion of liquidity. Apparently, production technologies which limit our ability to retrieve investments, as in Diamond and Dybvig (1983), are not enough *alone*; in their model costless intermediation in claims on capital can support an optimum. Neither are costly transportation technologies enough, apparently, when considered in isolation in an Arrow–Debreu setting. What does seem crucial is some form of limited market participation, as captured here in a formal, albeit brutal, way with distinct market locations and exogenously imposed itineraries. In any event, the present model does capture some of our intuition, and we may hope that it will spur future formal efforts.

Appendix: spaces and theorems

The economy of section 2 is first mapped into a modified version of Heller's (1974) model. First, we want to treat money as a separate commodity and to distinguish purchases from sales. Therefore let $x_{0t}(h_t)$, $x_t^1(h_t)$, $x_t^2(h_t)$ denote the (nonnegative) purchases in date t under history h_t of money, home-produced goods, and market-produced goods respectively by the representative household. Similarly, let $y_{0t}(h_t)$ and $y_t^1(h_t)$ denote (nonnegative) sales of money and the home-produced commodity respectively. Note that, in this formulation, each household believes that it can purchase additional units of the home-produced commodity but knows that it cannot sell the market-produced commodity, which it does not have. Of course, in equilibrium purchases of the home-produced commodity will also be zero. Let $w_{0t}(h_t) = z_t(h_t)$ denote the "endowment" of money for each date t and let $w_t^1(s_t) = w_t(s_t)$ denote the endowment of the home-produced commodity. (Note that the "endowment" of money may be negative if there is a tax.) Let $\tilde{s}_{0t}(h_t)$ and $\tilde{s}_t^1(h_t)$ denote the (nonnegative) number of units of money and the home-produced commodity respectively coming out of "storage" at date t under history h_t, and $r_{0t}(h_t)$ and $r_t^1(h_t)$ denote the analogously defined (nonnegative) quantities put into "storage" at date t. Thus at date $t = 0, \tilde{s}_{00}(h_0) = M_0 > 0$ and $\tilde{s}_0^1(h_0) = f(I_0, s_0)$. Thus at date T finite, $r_{0T}(h_T) \geqslant M_0 + \Sigma_{\tau=0}^{T} z_\tau(h_\tau)$. Finally, let $x_t(h_t)$ denote the relevant vector of purchases, and so on for the other variables $y_t(h_t), \tilde{s}_t(h_t), r_t(h_t)$, with the relevant subscripts and superscripts deleted.

Following Heller, we can define a storage technology $S_t(h_t)$ for the representative household. That is, for storage input and output vectors to be feasible it is required that

$$\{r_t(h_t), \tilde{s}_{t+1}(h_{t+1})\} \in S_{t+1}(h_{t+1}) \tag{12.A1}$$

where $S_t(h_t)$ is a closed convex set. Clearly the strict concavity of $f(\cdot, s_t)$ with free disposal, the linear nature of storage in fiat money with free disposal, and the fixed terminal condition on fiat money holdings are all consistent with this specification. For example, $S_{t+1}(h_{t+1}) = [r_{0t}(h_t) \geqslant 0, r_t^1(h_t) \geqslant 0, \tilde{s}_{0,t+1}(h_{t+1}) \geqslant 0,\ \tilde{s}_{t+1}^1(h_{t+1}):\ \tilde{s}_{0,t+1}(h_{t+1}) \leqslant r_{0t}(h_t)$, and $\tilde{s}_{t+1}^1(h_{t+1}) \leqslant f\{r_t^1(h_t), s_{t+1}\}]$.

If we let $c_{0t}(h_t)$, $c_t^1(h_t)$, and $c_t^2(h_t)$ denote the number of (nonnegative) units of consumption of money and commodities respectively by the representative household at date t under history h_t, it is clear that

$$c_{0t}(h_t) = w_{0t}(h_t) + x_{0t}(h_t) - y_{0t}(h_t) + \tilde{s}_{0t}(h_t) - r_{0t}(h_t) \geqslant 0 \tag{12.A2a}$$

$$c_t^1(h_t) = w_t^1(s_t) + x_t^1(h_t) - y_t^1(h_t) + \tilde{s}_t^1(h_t) - r_t^1(h_t) \geqslant 0 \qquad (12.A2b)$$

$$c_t^2(h_t) = x_t^2(h_t) \geqslant 0 \qquad (12.A3)$$

Note also that, in equilibrium, money will not be consumed, that is, $c_{0t}(h_t) \equiv 0$. Finally, let c denote the relevant vector of consumptions, that is, with components running over commodities, over dates t, and over histories h_t. Then preferences are described by the utility function $u(c) = E_0 \Sigma_{t=0}^T \beta^t U\{c_t^1(h_t), c_t^2(h_t), s_t\}$.

Now let $p_t'(h_t)$ denote the price of any commodity in terms of some abstract unit of account at date t under history h_t (recall that we are searching for a symmetric monetary equilibrium). Also let $p_{0t}(h_t)$ denote the corresponding price of money. Prices are normalized so that $p_{0t}(h_t) + p_t'(h_t) = 1$ with $p_{0t}(h_t) \geqslant 0$, $p_t'(h_t) \geqslant 0$. Call this simplex $P_t(h_t)$. Here, then, $p_t(h_t) \in P_t(h_t)$ is a two-dimensional vector, unlike previous notation. However, once an equilibrium is discovered with prices in the simplex, we can take the ratio $p_t'(h_t)/p_{0t}(h_t)$ as the price of commodities $p_t(h_t)$ as before. In what follows, the price of money at date T will be fixed at some α, where $0 < \alpha < 1$ for all histories h_T, that is, $p_{0T}(h_T) = \alpha$, $p_T'(h_T) = 1 - \alpha$, all h_T. Let $P_T(h_T)$ denote the set consisting of this unique vector. Then let P^α be the cross-product space of the $P_t(h_t)$ and $P_T(h_T)$ with the generic price system p.

Following Heller, the fact that all trade involves money is written as

$$p_{0t}(h_t) x_{0t}(h_t) \leqslant p_t'(h_t) y_t^1(h_t) \qquad (12.A4)$$

$$p_{0t}(h_t) y_{0t}(h_t) \geqslant p_t'(h_t) x_t^1(h_t) + p_t'(h_t) x_t^2(h_t) \qquad (12.A5)$$

In words, constraint (12.A4) says that money purchases cannot exceed in value commodity sales, and constraint (12.A5) says that purchases of commodities cannot exceed in value money sales. Note that constraints (12.A4) and (12.A5) imply the usual budget constraint

$$p_{0t}(h_t) x_{0t}(h_t) + p_t'(h_t) x_t^1(h_t) + p_t'(h_t) x_t^2(h_t) \leqslant p_{0t}(h_t) y_{0t}(h_t) + p_t'(h_t) y_t^1(h_t) \qquad (12.A6)$$

Finally we have the following liquidity constraint not included in Heller's model:

$$x_t^2(h_t) p_t'(h_t) \leqslant p_{0t}(h_t) \tilde{s}_{0t}(h_t) + p_{0t}(h_t) w_{0t}(h_t) \qquad (12.A7)$$

Now define the vector of choice variables $b_t(h_t) = \{x_t(h_t), y_t(h_t), r_t(h_t), \tilde{s}_t(h_t)\}$ and let b be the relevant vector of the $b_t(h_t)$. Then define $B(p)$ as the set of

bs which satisfy (12.A1)–(12.A7) under the price system p. Thus the representative household maximizes $u(c)$ over $B(p)$. Let the set of maximizing bs be denoted $\gamma(p)$. With this notation we can now repeat the definition of a symmetric monetary equilibrium.

Definition
A symmetric monetary equilibrium is a strictly positive price vector p^* and choice vector b^* such that the following two conditions hold:

- maximization: vector $b^* \in \gamma(p^*)$.
- market clearing: $x_{0t}^*(h_t) = y_{0t}^*(h_t)$ all t, all h_t for money

$$x_t^{1*}(h_t) + x_t^{2*}(h_t) - y_t^{1*}(h_t) = 0 \qquad \text{all } t, \text{ all } h_t \text{ for commodities.}$$

Finally we obtain the following theorem.

Theorem 12.A1
For every horizon $T < \infty$ and for every terminal price of money α, $0 < \alpha < 1$, there exists a symmetric monetary equilibrium.

Proof. First, as in Heller (1974), it can be established that if the $p_{0t}(h_t)$, $p_t'(h_t)$ are all strictly positive, then $B(p)$ has an interior point. The addition of constraint (12.A7) does not alter the essential part of the argument: for the representative household we can find a sequence of the $b_t(h_t)$ with all components strictly positive, with all the components of c strictly positive, with constraints (12.A4)–(12.A7) all at strict inequality, and with storage input–output vectors all in the interior of the $S_t(h_t)$. This sequence is the interior point. Second, as in Heller, it can be established that the budget set $B(p)$ is a closed convex set for all $p \in P^\alpha$ and is a continuous correspondence for all $p \in P^\alpha$ satisfying $p_{0t}(h_t) > 0$, $p_t'(h_t) > 0$, for all dates t and all histories h_t.

Now following Debreu (1959), consider a cube K, of the same dimensions as $B(p)$, which contains the set of attainable choice vectors for the representative household in its interior. This is possible since for any date t and any history h_t resources are finite and aggregate money holdings are finite; thus purchases, sales, and storage input–output vectors are bounded. Take $\bar{B}(p)$ to be the intersection of $B(p)$ with K.

Let $\bar{\gamma}(p)$ denote the set of utility-maximizing elements in $\bar{B}(p)$. Clearly $\bar{\gamma}(p)$ is nonempty, bounded, and convex, and, by a theorem of Berge (1963) and the second result above, is upper semicontinuous and hence closed for $p_{0t}(h_t) > 0$, $p_t'(h_t) > 0$. Now, following Heller again (closely), consider the correspondence $\hat{\gamma}(p)$ obtained from $\bar{\gamma}(p)$ by taking the union of $\bar{\gamma}(p)$ and the set of limit points of the graph of $\bar{\gamma}(p)$. Then $\hat{\gamma}(p)$ is upper semicontinuous for all $p \in P^\alpha$ since its graph is closed and $\hat{\gamma}(p) = \bar{\gamma}(p)$ for $p_{0t}(h_t) > 0$, $p_t'(h_t) > 0$

since $\bar{\gamma}(p)$ is upper semicontinuous there. Finally, let $\bar{\delta}(p)$ be the convex hull of $\hat{\gamma}(p)$.

Now let

$$\mu_t\{b_t(h_t)\} = \{p_t(h_t) \in P_t(h_t) | p_{0t}(h_t)\{x_{0t}(h_t) - y_{0t}(h_t)\}$$
$$+ p_t'(h_t)\{x_t^1(h_t) + x_t^2(h_t) - y_t^1(h_t)\} \text{ is maximal in } P_t(h_t), t < T\}$$

$$\mu_T\{b_T(h_T)\} = p_T^\alpha$$

where P_T^α is a fixed vector. Let $\mu(b)$ denote the associated cross-product of the μ_ts. Now consider the correspondence $\phi(b, p) = \bar{\delta}(p) x \mu(b)$ defined on $K \times P^\alpha$. All the properties of Kakutani's fixed-point theorem are satisfied, and so there exists some p^*, b^* such that $p^* \in \mu(b^*)$ and $b^* \in \bar{\delta}(p^*)$.

Now the budget inequality (12.A6) at prices p^* yields the first inequality in

$$0 \geqslant p_{0t}^*(h_t)\{x_{0t}^*(h_t) - y_{0t}^*(h_t)\} + p_t^{*\prime}(h_t)\{x_t^{1*}(h_t) + x_t^{2*}(h_t) - y_t^{1*}(h_t)\}$$

$$\geqslant p_{0t}(h_t)\{x_{0t}^*(h_t) - y_{0t}^*(h_t)\} + p_t'(h_t)\{x_t^{1*}(h_t) + x_t^2(h_t) - y_t^{1*}(h_t)\} \qquad t < T \tag{12.A8}$$

The second inequality in (12.A8) holds for all $p_t(h_t) \in P_t(h_t)$, including the endpoints, from the definition μ_t. Thus each of the terms in braces in (12.A8) is nonpositive; there is (positive) excess demand in neither money nor commodities. Therefore assume that some $p_{0t}^*(h_t)$ is zero for $t < T$. With $p_{0t}^*(h_t) \equiv \alpha > 0$ there would be excess demand for money, which is a contradiction. Similarly, assume that $p_t^{*\prime}(h_t) = 0$. Then there would be excess demand for commodities, which is a contradiction. Thus prices are all strictly positive. Finally, the budget constraints (12.A6) will hold at equality yielding an equality in the first line of (12.A8) with strictly positive prices. Thus excess demand cannot be negative and markets clear for $t < T$. For date T, consider (12.A2a) and $t = T$. Then, with zero consumption of money at date T (since b^* is maximizing) and with the specified end-of-horizon terminal condition on money balances, there is zero excess demand for money at date T for all h_T. Again, the budgets at equality and the imposed positive price of commodities at T yield zero excess demand for commodities at T. Thus the existence of an equilibrium for the bounded economy has been established.

Now it is claimed that b^* must also be maximizing in the unbounded economy, that is, that $b^* \in \gamma(p^*)$. From market clearing and the choice of k, $b^* \in \bar{\gamma}(p^*)$ is in the interior of $\bar{B}(p^*)$. Suppose that there exists some $\hat{b} \in \gamma(p^*)$ which performs better than b^* under the utility function $u(c)$. Then $b(\lambda) = \lambda \hat{b} + (1 - \lambda) b^*$ is utility improving, also by the convexity of preferences, and is in $\bar{B}(p^*)$ for sufficiently small λ. This contradicts $b^* \in \tilde{\gamma}(p^*)$, and this completes the proof.

Remark. It is reassuring that there exist nontrivial monetary equilibria, that is, with active trade in money. It is fairly easy to construct examples. For, assume that the utility function is separable, that is, of the form $U(c_t^1, c_t^2, s_t) = V(c_t^1, s_t) + W(c_t^2, s_t)$ with $W'(0, s_t) = \infty$. Then some of the market-produced commodity will be purchased with money at any positive price, and of course prices are positive by construction in a monetary equilibrium.

The monetary equilibria of theorem 12.A1 depend on the terminal price of money, which is fixed at an arbitrary constant α, $0 < \alpha < 1$, and on the length of the horizon T. To remove the latter indeterminacy, at least, a limit result is now established. Let p^T and b^T denote the price system and choice vector of a monetary equilibrium for the T-period economy, $T < \infty$ with $p_{0T}(h_t) \equiv \alpha$. Clearly, we can generate a sequence of monetary equilibria as the horizon T goes to infinity. It is somewhat reassuring that there exists a sub-sequence of these monetary equilibria which converges to some limit and that the limiting behavior is feasible under the limiting price system. This is stated formally in the following theorem.

Theorem 12.A2
There exists a sub-sequence of horizons T, say T_n, such that the $b_t^{T_n}(h_t)$ and the $p_t^{T_n}(h_t)$ converge to some limits, say $\tilde{b}(h_t)$ and $\tilde{p}_t(h_t)$ for all dates t and histories h_t as $n \to \infty$. Moreover, $\tilde{b}$ satisfies (12.A1)–(12.A7) under $\tilde{p}$ and the market-clearing condition defined above.

Proof. First, note that $p_t^T(h_t) \in P_t(h_t)$ for every T, and thus $p_t^T(h_t)$ is uniformly bounded with respect to T. Similarly, as in the proof of theorem 12.A1, we can take $b_t^T(h_t)$ to be in some bounded set for every T. Now there are countably many of these components $p_t^T(h_t), b_t^T(h_t)$ as $T \to \infty$. Following Bewley's Cantor diagonal argument (Bewley, 1980, p. 194) we can find a sub-sequence of T such that all these components converge. Inequality constraints (12.A2)–(12.A7), the market-clearing condition, and storage feasibility (12.A1) (where the $S_{t+1}(h_{t+1})$ are closed) are all satisfied at every T (sufficiently large) and thus passage to the limit is immediate. This completes the proof.

Theorem 12.A2 does not establish that the limiting prices and allocations constitute a monetary equilibrium in the infinite-horizon economy. To obtain sufficient conditions for this, the finite-horizon economies are altered somewhat by changing preferences in period T. In addition, it is supposed that the $U(\cdot, s_t)$ are uniformly bounded from above and below, the production functions $f(\cdot, s_t)$ are uniformly bounded from above, and the growth rate of monetary injections is bounded in mean by the discount rate. More formally, consider the following theorem.

Theorem 12.A3 (Existence of a monetary equilibrium for the infinite-horizon economy)
Consider an artificial finite-horizon economy with no taxes on money balances at the last date T, but with preferences modified at T, adding the term $E_0\beta^{T+1}\tilde{s}_{0,T+1}(h_{T+1}) + E_0\beta^{T+1}\tilde{s}^1_{T+1}(h_{T+1})$. There exists a symmetric monetary equilibrium (p^T, b^T) in the artificial economy for every horizon $T < \infty$. Moreover, there exists a sub-sequence of horizons T_n such that the $b_t^{T_n}(h_t)$, $p_t^{T_n}(h_t)$ converge to some limits $\tilde{b}_t(h_t)$, $\tilde{p}_t(h_t)$ for all dates t and histories h_t. If the $U(\cdot, s_t)$ are uniformly bounded from above by some $\bar{u} < \infty$ and from below by zero, the $f(\cdot, s_t)$ are uniformly bounded from above by some $\bar{f} < \infty$ and $\lim_{T\to\infty} E_0\beta^T\{\Sigma_{t=0}^T z_t(h_t) + M_0\} = 0$, then $(\tilde{p}, \tilde{b})$ constitutes a monetary equilibrium in the infinite-horizon economy.

Proof. First, follow the proof of theorem 12.A1 to establish the existence of a symmetric monetary equilibrium in the artificial economy, but with prices at date T, $p_T(h_T)$, unrestricted, except for the requirement $p_T(h_T) \in P_T(h_T)$, the unit simplex. Define the mappings μ_t as before, now with a similar construction of μ_T. At the fixed point there can be excess demand for neither money nor commodities, as before. Note that $p^*_{0T}(h_T) \neq 0$ now, given the direct utility for money balances at date T. This implies in turn that the maximizing demands satisfy market clearing.

Now, as in theorem 12.A2, the sequence of equilibrium prices and choice vectors converges to some feasible limit $\tilde{p}_t(h_t)$, $\tilde{b}_t(h_t)$ for some sub-sequence of horizons T_n going to infinity. As before, these limits are in $B(\tilde{p})$ and satisfy the market-clearing condition in the infinite-horizon economy. It will be argued that $\tilde{p}_t(h_t) \gg 0$ and that $\tilde{b}$ is maximizing in the infinite-horizon economy. This will complete the proof.

It is first established that $\tilde{p}_{0t}(h_t) > 0$ and $\tilde{p}'_t(h_t) > 0$ for all dates t and all histories h_t. For, suppose that $p'_t(h_t) = 0$ for some date t and some history h_t. Then, for sufficiently large T_n, by definition, $p_t'^{T_n}(h_t)$ would be arbitrarily close to zero. But then to suppose $x_t^{1T_n}(h_t) \equiv 0$ is to contradict maximization for sufficiently large T_n, and otherwise there is a contradiction to equilibrium (market clearing in commodities). Similarly, suppose that $\tilde{p}_{0t}(h_t) = 0$ for some date t under some history h_t. But then for sufficiently large T_n, $p_{0t}^{T_n}(h_t)$ would be arbitrarily close to zero. It follows that the $p_{0\tau}^{T_n}(h_t, s_{t+1}, \ldots, s_\tau)$ must also have limits of zero for all dates $\tau > t$ and all histories $h_t, s_{t+1}, \ldots, s_\tau$. For suppose that $\tilde{p}_{0\tau}(h_t, s_{t+1}, \ldots, s_\tau) > 0$ for at least one date τ under at least one history $h_t, s_{t+1}, \ldots, s_\tau$. Then, to suppose that $\tilde{s}_{0t}^{T_n}(h_t) \leqslant \{M_0 + \Sigma_{u=0}^t z_u(h_u)\}$ is to contradict maximization for sufficiently large T_n, and otherwise there is a contradiction to equilibrium – market clearing in money balances. That the $p_{0\tau}^{T_n}(h_t, s_{t+1}, \ldots, s_\tau)$ all have limits of zero implies in turn that the consumptions $c_\tau^{2T_n}(h_t, s_{t+1}, \ldots, s_\tau)$ all have limits of zero, by constraints (12.3). Finally, it can be established directly from the first-order conditions for a maximum (see (12.4)–(12.8)) that the $p_t^{T_n}(h_t)$ can be defined recursively by

$$p_t^T(h_t) = \frac{\beta^t \operatorname{prob}(h_t|s_0)U_1\{c_t^{1T}(h_t), c_t^{2T}(h_t), s_t\}}{\lambda_t(h_t)}$$

$$\lambda_t^T(h_t) = \sum_{s_{t+1}} \frac{\beta^{t+1} \operatorname{prob}(h_t, s_{t+1}|s_0)U_2\{c_{t+1}^{1T}(h_t, s_{t+1}), c_{t+1}^{2T}(h_t, s_{t+1}), s_{t+1}\}}{p_{t+1}^T(h_t, s_{t+1})}$$

for all $T = T_n$, where the superscript T indexes the length of the horizon T and here, for the moment, $p_t(h_t) = p_t'(h_t)/p_{0t}(h_t)$. This, with the consumption limits derived above and $U_2\{c_t^1, 0, s_t\} = \infty$, implies $\lim_{T_n \to \infty} p_t^{T_n}(h_t) = 0$, a contradiction of $\tilde{p}_{0t}(h_t) = 0$.

Now let V denote the value of the infinite-horizon objective function of the representative household under $\tilde{b}$ with prices $\tilde{p}$. Also, let F denote the supremum of the objective function under all feasible policies, that is, all $b \in B(\tilde{p})$. Clearly, $V \leqslant F$. We want to argue that $V \geqslant F$ as well.[11] Therefore, let G^{T_n} denote the maximal value of the objective function by choice of $b \in B(\tilde{p})$ but with utility functions $U(\cdot, s_t)$ fixed at their upper bounds for all states s_t at all dates $t > T_n$. Clearly, $G^{T_n} \geqslant F$, so that $\lim_{n \to \infty} G^{T_n} \geqslant F$ (taking the sub-sequence of n if necessary). Now let H^{T_n} denote the value of the objective function of the representative household in a monetary equilibrium for the artificial economy with finite horizon T_n under prices $p_t^{T_n}(h_t)$. Suppose that it can be established that $\lim_{n \to \infty} H^{T_n} = V$ and $\lim_{n \to \infty} |G^{T_n} - H^{T_n}| = 0$. Then $V \geqslant F$ and the proof is complete.

That $\lim_{n \to \infty} |H^{T_n} - V| = 0$ is easy to establish. First, pick some $\varepsilon > 0$. Then choose n sufficiently large that

$$\sum_{t=T_n+1}^{\infty} \beta^t \bar{u} < \frac{\varepsilon}{3}$$

$$E_0 \beta^{T_n+1} \sum_{t=0}^{T_n} \{z_t(h_t) + M_0\} < \frac{\varepsilon}{6}$$

$$\beta^{T_n+1} \bar{\jmath} < \frac{\varepsilon}{6}$$

Thus the utility value of the tail of the objective function for the programming problem determining V is arbitrarily small and the utility values of beginning-of-period $T_n + 1$ money balances and commodity storage respectively in the programming problem determining H^{T_n} are arbitrarily small. Then, by continuity of the $U(\cdot, s_t)$ and convergence of the $b_t^{T_n}(h_t)$ to $\bar{b}_t(h_t)$, n can be chosen, still larger if necessary, such that

$$\left| E_0 \sum_{t=0}^{T_n} \beta^t U\{c_t^{T_n}(h_t), s_t\} - E_0 \sum_{t=0}^{T_n} \beta^t U\{\tilde{c}_t(h_t), s_t\} \right| < \frac{\varepsilon}{3}$$

Thus $|H^{T_n} - V| < \varepsilon$ for sufficiently large n.

That $\lim_{n \to \infty} |H^{T_n} - G^{T_n}| = 0$ is established as follows. As before, for $\varepsilon > 0$, choose n sufficiently large that

$$\sum_{t=T_n+1}^{\infty} \beta^t \bar{u} < \frac{\varepsilon}{3}$$

$$E_0 \beta^{T_n+1} \sum_{t=0}^{T_n} \{z_t(h_t) + M_0\} < \frac{\varepsilon}{6}$$

$$\beta^{T_n+1} \bar{f} < \frac{\varepsilon}{6}$$

Then it only remains to show that the utility values of the objective function over the first T_n periods, under the programs defining H^{T_n} and G^{T_n}, can be made arbitrarily close. First, note that the prices $\tilde{p}_t(h_t)$ and $p_t^{T_n}(h_t)$ are all strictly positive. Now pick the solution $b \in B(\tilde{p})$ which yields the value G^{T_n}. Since $\lim_{n \to \infty} p^{T_n}(h_t) = \tilde{p}_t(h_t)$, b can be modified slightly to make it a feasible choice for the problem defining H^{T_n}, namely the T_n-period problem of the representative household in a monetary equilibrium under $p_t^{T_n}(h_t)$. In fact, for sufficiently large n, no more than $\varepsilon/3$ utility units need be lost in this modification in the first T_n periods. Therefore

$$H^{T_n} - E_0 \beta^{T_n+1} \tilde{s}^*_{0, T_n+1}(h_{T_n+1}) - E_0 \beta^{T_n+1} \tilde{s}^{1*}_{T_n+1}(h_{T_n+1})$$

is at most $\varepsilon/3$ units below

$$G^{T_n} - \sum_{t=T_n+1}^{\infty} \beta^t \bar{u}$$

Similarly,

$$G^{T_n} - \sum_{t=T_n+1}^{\infty} \beta^t \bar{u}$$

is no more than $\varepsilon/3$ units below

$$H^{T_n} - E_0\beta^{T_n+1}\tilde{s}^{*}_{0,T_n+1}(h_{T_n+1}) - E_0\beta^{T_n+1}\tilde{s}^{1*}_{T_n+1}(h_{T_n+1})$$

Therefore

$$|H^{T_n} - G^{T_n}| \leqslant \left| H^{T_n} - E_0\beta^{T_n+1}\tilde{s}^{*}_{0,T_n+1}(h_{T_n+1}) - E_0\beta^{T_n+1}\tilde{s}^{1*}_{T_n+1}(h_{T_n+1}) - G^{T_n} \right.$$

$$\left. + \sum_{t=T_n+1}^{\infty} \beta^t \bar{u} \right| + |E_0\beta^{T_n+1}\tilde{s}^{*}_{0,T_n+1}(h_{T_n+1})| + |E_0\beta^{T_n+1}\tilde{s}^{1*}_{T_n+1}(h_{T_n+1})|$$

$$+ \left| \sum_{t=T_n+1}^{\infty} \beta^t \bar{u} \right| < \varepsilon$$

for sufficiently large n.

Notes

1 Spatial separation is at least implicit in the decentralized exchange models of Niehans (1963), Feldman (1973), Ostroy (1973), Ostroy and Starr (1974), and Harris (1979) and in the "costly trips" models of Baumol (1952), Tobin (1956), and, more recently, Jovanovic (1982). In the present chapter we build directly on Lucas's version of the Cass–Yaari circle (Cass and Yaari, 1966), as presented by Townsend (1980, this volume, ch. 2).

2 Idle balances and rate-of-return dominance are also explained in a sense in the transactions costs, general equilibrium, monetary literature (for example, Hahn, 1971, 1973a; Kurz, 1974a,b; Heller and Starr, 1976; Heller, 1980). There money is given an exogenous (less costly) advantage in facilitating exchange. Here money emergies from an exogenous specification of endowments, preferences, technology, and especially spatial frictions. Of course, market participation can be limited as in Lucas (1982, 1984) by the (exogenous) specification that beginning-of-period asset markets be centralized but that within-period commodity markets be decentralized, requiring the use of money. But again, the effort here is to specify (exogenously) who can trade with whom and then to let both asset and commodity trades be determined endogenously. Finally, it should be noted that Stockman (1981) allows capital accumulation in a Clower constraint model and achieves rate-of-return dominance without noting the result.

3 Existence of a temporary monetary equilibrium and of a stationary perfect foresight monetary equilibrium for a Clower constraint type model is established directly by Grandmont and Younes (1972). But as Hool (1976) notes, their analysis does not cover the case of $k = 0$, which corresponds to the usual version of a Clower constraint model, and the case which is applicable here. Hool (1976) extends the analysis for temporary equilibrium only. Both Grandmont and Younes and Hool rule out capital accumulation and uncertainty. Lucas (1980) establishes

the existence of a monetary equilibrium in a Clower constraint model with essentially one (market-produced) commodity, allowing for uncertainty at the level of individual preferences (there is no aggregate uncertainty).

4 See the references cited by Lucas (1982) for earlier versions of the real theory.

5 Here, and throughout the chapter, positive everywhere means positive with probability unity relative to the underlying (finite) event space A for states s_t with histories $h_t = (s_0, s_1, \ldots, s_t)$ and relative to the specified Markov transition probabilities, $\text{prob}(s_{t+1}|s_t)$, s_0 given.

6 An earlier draft of this chapter contains numerical examples of monetary equilibria in which Lagrange multipliers are strictly positive and which therefore display the anomalies described below. For further details see Townsend (1982).

7 There is a more conventional investment relationship in terms of the market-produced commodity which does hold in this model:

$$
\begin{aligned}
E_t U_2\{c^1_{t+1}(h_t, s_{t+1}), c^2_{t+1}(h_t, s_{t+1}), s_{t+1}\} & \frac{p_t(h_t)}{p_{t+1}(h_t, s_{t+1})} \\
= \beta E_t U_2\{c^1_{t+2}(h_t, s_{t+1}, s_{t+2}), & c^2_{t+2}(h_t, s_{t+1}, s_{t+2}), s_{t+2}\} \\
\times \frac{p_{t+1}(h_t, s_{t+1}) f'\{I_{t+1}(h_t), s_{t+1})\}}{p_{t+2}(h_t, s_{t+1}, s_{t+2})} & \qquad (1)
\end{aligned}
$$

The rationale behind (1) is straightforward: suppose that it is given that an incrementally small amount of $c^1_t(h_t)$ is to be sacrificed at time t. This amount can be sold for money at date t, which in turn can be sold at date $t+1$ under any state s_{t+1} for the market-produced commodity. Alternatively, this amount can be invested from dates t to $t+1$, then sold for money which in turn can purchase $c^2_{t+2}(h_t, s_{t+1}, s_{t+2})$. What is striking about (1) is its relationship to the usual formula

$$
\begin{aligned}
U_2\{c^1_t(h_t), c^2_t(h_t), s_t\} = \beta E_t U_2\{c^1_{t+1}(h_t, s_{t+1}), c^2_{t+1}(h_t, s_{t+1}), s_{t+1}\} \\
\times f'\{I_{t+1}(h_t), s_{t+1}\} \qquad (2)
\end{aligned}
$$

Relative to (2), consumption in (1) is updated one period (so an adjustment is made for uncertainty) and real returns are adjusted by rates of inflation.

8 To do this, consider first an artificial finite-horizon economy in which money balances and investment give direct utility in date T, as in theorem 12.3. Now the necessary and sufficient first-order conditions for an interior maximum are the nonstochastic analogs of (12.5)–(12.8) for $t = 0, \ldots, T$:

$$\beta^t U_1(c^1_t, c^2_t) - \lambda_t p_t = 0 \qquad (3)$$

$$\beta^t U_2(c^1_t, c^2_t) - \lambda_t p_t - \phi_t p_t = 0 \qquad (4)$$

$$-\lambda_t + \phi_{t+1} + \lambda_{t+1} = 0 \qquad (5)$$

$$-p_t \lambda_t + p_{t+1} \lambda_{t+1} f'(I_{t+1}) = 0 \qquad (6)$$

with the extra conditions for M_{T+1} and I_{T+1} at date T

$$\beta^T - \lambda_T = 0 \tag{7}$$

$$\beta^T - \lambda_T p_T = 0 \tag{8}$$

Now suppose that the money price of commodities is some constant, say $p_t = 1$ for all dates t. Suppose also that consumption is constant, say $(c_t^1, c_t^2) = (\bar{c}^1, \bar{c}^2)$ for all dates t. Then, if this is so, investment will be constant to satisfy (3) and (4), that is,

$$-\beta^t U_1(\bar{c}^1, \bar{c}^2) + \beta^{t+1} U_1(\bar{c}^1, \bar{c}^2) f'(\bar{I}) = 0 \tag{9}$$

Thus the steady state I is determined by the condition $f'(\bar{I}) = 1/\beta$. Then, from equation (5)

$$\phi_{t+1} = \beta^t (1 - \beta) U_1(\bar{c}^1, \bar{c}^2) \tag{10}$$

and from (3), (4), and (10),

$$U_1(\bar{c}^1, \bar{c}^2) = \beta U_2(\bar{c}^1, \bar{c}^2) \tag{11}$$

that is, the marginal rate of substitution equals β. Condition (11) with the steady state market-clearing condition

$$c_t^1 + c_t^2 = w + f(\bar{I}) - \bar{I} \tag{12}$$

determines $\bar{c}^1$ and $\bar{c}^2$. Now let the initial condition $I_0 = \bar{I}$ and let date T choice $I_{T+1} = \bar{I}$. Also let initial condition $M_0 = \bar{c}^2$ and the date T choice $M_{T+1} = \bar{c}^2$. Thus, with an inconsequential normalization of the utility function, namely $U_1(\bar{c}^1, \bar{c}^2) = 1$, conditions (3)–(8) are all satisfied and all markets clear. Thus a steady state monetary equilibrium for the T-period artificial economy has been constructed. Now note that the above construction is valid for arbitrary finite T. Therefore, taking a limit as $T \to \infty$, we have a sequence of monetary equilibria which, by construction, has the same steady state price and choice vectors as limits. Therefore, by theorem 12.3, the limit prices and choice vectors constitute an equilibrium in the infinite horizon-economy.

9 As one referee has noted, this example may be too dramatic inasmuch as it relies on a discount rate β strictly less than unity. Rate-of-return dominance is possible in the economy *with uncertainty* even if β equals unity. Additionally, it might be noted here that there *may* exist "steady state" inflationary or deflationary equilibria in the economy without uncertainty if the money supply is growing or shrinking over time. However, a deflation greater than the rate of discount would seem to be inconsistent with equilibrium.

10 The fact that these assets are not traded in equilibrium is not a virtue of the monetary economy under consideration, but then neither is the nontrading outcome a virtue in the *real* asset-pricing models of the literature.

11 This idea and part of the argument which follows were suggested by E.C. Prescott.

References and Bibliography

Baumol, W.J. (1952) The transactions demand for cash: an inventory theoretic approach. *Quarterly Journal of Economics* 66, 545–56.

Balasko, Y. and Shell, K. (1981) The overlapping generations model II: The case of pure exchange with money. *Journal of Economic Theory* 24, 112–42.

—— and —— (1983a) Lump-sum taxation: the static economy. CARESS Working Paper 83-08RR, University of Pennsylvania.

—— and —— (1983b) Lump-sum taxes and transfers: the overlapping generations model with money. CARESS Working Paper 83-06R, University of Pennsylvania.

Berge, C. (1963) *Topological Spaces.* New York: Macmillan.

Bewley, T. (1980) The optimum quantity of money. In *Models of Monetary Economies*, eds J.H. Kareken and N. Wallace, pp. 169–210. Minneapolis, MN: Federal Reserve Bank of Minneapolis.

Breeden, D.T. (1979) An intertemporal asset pricing model with stochastic consumption and investment opportunities. *Journal of Financial Economics* 7, 265–96.

Brock, W.A. (1980) Asset prices in a production economy. In *The Economics of Uncertainty*, ed. J.J. McCall. Chicago, IL: University of Chicago Press.

—— and Mirman, L. (1972) Optimal economic growth and uncertainty: the discounted case. *Journal of Economic Theory* 4, 479–513.

Brunner, K. and Meltzer, A.H. (1971) The uses of money: money in the theory of an exchange economy. *American Economic Review* 61, 784–805.

Bryant, J. (1982) Are money and capital "separable"? Unpublished manuscript, Rice University, Houston, TX.

Cass, D. (1965) Optimal growth in aggregate model of capital accumulation. *Review of Economic Studies* 32, 233–40.

—— and Shell, K. (1983) Do sunspots matter? *Journal of Political Economy* 91, 193–227.

—— and Yaari, M. (1966) A re-examination of the pure consumption loans model. *Journal of Political Economy* 74, 353–67.

Clower, R.W. (1967) A reconsideration of the microfoundations of monetary theory. *Western Economic Journal* 6, 1–8.

—— (1971) Theoretical foundations of monetary policy. In *Monetary Theory and Monetary Policy in the 1970's*, eds G. Clayton, J.C. Gilbert, and R. Sedgwick. London: Oxford University Press.

Debreu, G. (1954) Valuation equilibrium and Pareto optimum. *Proceedings of the National Academy of Sciences of the USA* 40, 500–92.

—— (1959) *The Theory of Value.* New York: Wiley.

Diamond, D. and Dybvig, P. (1983) Bank runs, deposit insurance, and liquidity. *Journal of Political Economy* 91, 401–19.

Feldman, A.M. (1973) Bilateral trading processes, pairwise optimality, and Pareto optimality. *Review of Economic Studies* 40, 463–74.

Friedman, M. (1969) *The Optimum Quantity of Money and Other Essays.* Chicago, IL: Aldine.

Grandmont, J.M. and Younes, Y. (1972) On the role of money and the existence of a monetary equilibrium. *Review of Economic Studies* 39, 355–72.

—— and—— (1973) On the efficiency of a monetary equilibrium. *Review of Economic Studies* 40, 149–66.

Grossman, S.J. and Shiller, R.J. (1981) The determinants of the variability of stock market prices. *American Economic Review* 71, 222–7.

Hahn, F.H. (1965) On some problems of proving existence of an equilibrium in a monetary economy. In *The Theory of Interest Rates*, eds F.H. Hahn and F.P.R. Brechling, pp. 126–35. London: Macmillan.

—— (1971) Equilibrium with transactions costs. *Econometrica* 39, 417–40.

—— (1973a) On the foundations of monetary theory. In *Essays in Modern Economics*, eds M. Parkin and A.R. Nobay, pp. 230–42. New York: Harper & Row.

—— (1973b) On transaction costs, inessential sequence economies, and money. *Review of Economic Studies* 40, 449–62.

Hall, R.E. (1981) Intertemporal substitution in consumption. Mimeograph, Hoover Institution and the Department of Economics, Stanford University.

Hansen, L.P. and Singleton, K.J. (1982) Generalized instrumental variables estimation of nonlinear rational expectations models. *Econometrica* 50, 1269–86.

—— and —— (1983) Stochastic consumption, risk aversion, and the temporal behavior of stock market returns. *Journal of Political Economy* 91, 249–65.

Harris, M. (1979) Expectations and money in a dynamic exchange economy. *Econometrica* 47, 1403–19.

Heller, W.P. (1974) The holding of money balances in general equilibrium. *Journal of Economic Theory* 7, 93–108.

—— and Starr, R.M. (1976) Equilibrium with nonconvex transactions costs: monetary and nonmonetary economies. *Review of Economic Studies* 43, 195–216.

Helpman, E. (1981) Optimal spending and money holdings in the presence of liquidity constraints. *Econometrica* 49, 1559–70.

Hepburn, A.B. (1924) *A History of Currency in the United States*. New York: Macmillan.

Hicks, J.R. (1935) A suggestion for simplifying the theory of money. *Econometrica* 1–19. Reprinted in *Readings in Monetary Theory*, Homewood, IL: Irwin, 1951.

Hool, B. (1976) Money, expectations, and the existence of a temporary equilibrium. *Review of Economic Studies* 43, 439–46.

Jovanovic, B. (1982) Inflation and welfare in the steady state. *Journal of Political Economy* 90, 561–77.

Kohn, M. (1981) In defense of the finance constraint. *Economic Inquiry* 19, 177–95.

Koopmans, T. (1965) On the concept of optimal economic growth. *Pontificia Academia Scientiarum* 28, 225–300.

Kurz, M. (1974a) Equilibrium in a finite sequence of markets with transactions costs. *Econometrica* 42, 1–20.

—— (1974b) Equilibrium with transaction costs and money in a single market exchange economy. *Journal of Economic Theory* 7, 418–52.

Lerner, A.P. (1947) Money as a creature of the state. *Proceedings of the American Economic Association* 37, 312–17.

Lucas, R.E. Jr (1978) Asset prices in an exchange economy. *Econometrica* 46, 1426–46.

—— (1980) Equilibrium in a pure currency economy. In *Models of Monetary Economies*, eds J.H. Kareken and N. Wallace. Minneapolis, MN: Federal Reserve Bank of Minneapolis.

——(1982) Interest rates and currency prices in a two-country world. *Journal of Monetary Economics* 10, 335–59.

——(1984) Money in a theory of finance. In *Carnegie–Rochester Conference Series on Public Policy*, vol. 21, pp. 9–45.

——and Stokey, N.L. (1984) Optimal fiscal and monetary policy in an economy without capital. *Journal of Monetary Economics* 12, 55–93.

McKenzie, L.W. (1959) On the existence of general economic equilibrium for a competitive market. *Econometrica* 27, 54–71.

Mankiw, N., Rotemberg, J., and Summers, L.H. (1982) Intertemporal substitution in macro-economics. Working Paper 898, National Bureau of Economic Research, Cambridge, MA.

Mehra, R. and Prescott, E.C. (1982) A test of the intertemporal asset pricing model. Unpublished manuscript.

Niehans, J. (1969) Money in a static theory of optimal payment arrangements. *Journal of Money, Credit, and Banking* 1, 706–26.

Ostroy, J.M. (1973) The informational efficiency of monetary exchange. *American Economic Review* 63, 597–610.

——and Starr, R.M. (1974) Money and the decentralization of exchange. *Econometrica* 42, 1093–113.

Prescott, E.C. and Mehra, R. (1980) Recursive competitive equilibrium: the case of homogeneous households. *Econometrica* 48, 1365–80.

Robertson, D.H. (1940) Saving and hoarding. In *Essays in Monetary Theory*. London: P.S. King.

Samuelson, P.A. (1958) An exact consumption-loan model of interest with or without the social contrivance of money. *Journal of Political Economy* 66, 467–82.

Sargent, T.J. (1979) Tobin's q and the rate of investment in general equilibrium. In *On the State of Macroeconomics*, eds K. Brunner and A. Meltzer. Amsterdam: North-Holland.

Shiller, R.J. (1982) Consumption, asset markets and macroeconomic fluctuations. *Carnegie–Rochester Conference Series on Public Policy*, vol. 17, 203–38.

Stockman, A.C. (1981) Anticipated inflation and the capital stock in a cash-in-advance economy. *Journal of Monetary Economics* 8, 387–94.

Tobin, J. (1955) A dynamic aggregative model. *Journal of Political Economy* 63, 103–115.

——(1956) The interest-elasticity of the transactions demand for cash. *Review of Economics and Statistics* 38, 241–7.

——(1965) Money and economic growth. *Econometrica* 33, 671–84.

——(1980) Discussion. In *Models of Monetary Economies*, eds J.H. Kareken and N. Wallace, pp. 83–90. Minneapolis, MN: Federal Reserve Bank of Minneapolis.

Townsend, R.M. (1980) Models of money with spatially separated agents. In *Models of Monetary Economies*, eds J.H. Kareken and N. Wallace, pp. 265–303. Minneapolis, MN: Federal Reserve Bank of Minneapolis.

——(1982) Asset prices in a monetary economy: explaining rate of return dominance and other apparent anomalies. Working Paper, Carnegie–Mellon University.

——and Wallace, N. (1987) Circulating private debt: an example with a coordination problem. In *Contractual Arrangements for Intertemporal Trade*, eds E.C. Prescott and N. Wallace. Minneapolis MN: University of Minnesota Press. Reprinted in this volume as chapter 3.

Tsiang, S.C. (1980) Keynes's finance demand for liquidity, Robertson's loanable funds theory, and Friedman's monetarism. *Quarterly Journal of Economics* 14, 467–92.

Wallace, N. (1983) A legal restriction theory of the demand for "money" and the role of monetary policy. *Federal Reserve Bank of Minneapolis Quarterly Review* 1–7.

—— (1980) The overlapping generations model of fiat money. In *Models of Monetary Economies*, eds J.H. Kareken and N. Wallace, pp. 49–78. Minneapolis, MN: Federal Reserve Bank of Minneapolis.

Wicksell, K. (1935) *Lectures on Political Economy*. New York: Macmillan.

Part VII
Equilibrium Theories of Volatile Markets with Rational Learning and Optimal Signal Extraction

13

Market Anticipations, Rational Expectations, and Bayesian Analysis

1 Introduction

Muth (1961), Lucas and Prescott (1971), and Lucas (1975a) have stressed that the concept of rational expectations is an *equilibrium* concept and that rational expectations can be regarded as the outcome of some unspecified process of learning and adapting on the part of economic agents. Hence attempts to make such processes explicit can be viewed as analyses of the stability of rational expectations equilibria. In particular we can pose the following stability question: what tendency is there in a model for convergence to a self-fulfilling equilibrium if initially agents have imperfect information concerning the environment in which they must make decisions but use Bayes's rule in accordance with past observations to infer the values of unknown parameters? Several writers including Cyert and DeGroot (1970), Arrow and Green (1973), Crawford (1973), Grossman (1975), and Kihlstrom and Mirman (1975) have addressed this or related questions.

To answer the question in the context of a particular model we must specify precisely what is known by agents at the outset. In this regard two approaches can be distinguished. In the first approach each agent is assumed to have in mind a relatively simple model which expresses the relationships among the variables of concern to him. In this formulation there is imperfect information in that some parameters of the simple model are regarded as unknowns, and learning in that each agent revises over time his estimates of those parameters

---

Reprinted from *International Economic Review* 19(2), 1978, 481–94. I am much indebted to Edward C. Prescott for collaboration on this chapter. I would also like to thank my other colleages at Carnegie–Mellon for helpful comments. I assume full responsibility for any errors or ambiguities. A preliminary version of this chapter was presented at the meetings of the Econometric Society, Madison, WI, June 1976.

on the basis of past observations, but the simple model may *not* be consistent, at least at the outset, with the reduced form equations of the actual model. However, these equations may change over time with the actions of agents, and eventually there *may* be convergence to a situation in which the parameters of the simple model are identified and consistent with the actual model. To the extent that there is convergence, such a result is comforting to rational expectations theorists. However, it can be argued that the lack of convergence need only indicate that agents were doomed at the outset by the modeler who imposed on them an incorrect view of the world and an apparently limited statistical procedure.[1]

In the second approach, which is the one adopted here, there is an attempt to move away from an *ad hoc* specification of the initial models used by agents by postulating that agents know at the outset the reduced form equations of the actual model, though they may be uncertain as to the values of some unknown parameters. This raises the following problem. To correctly estimate the relevant parameters, agents need to have knowledge of the way in which the reduced form equations evolve over time. But the time path itself may depend on the way in which all agents solve the inference problem. This problem is particularly acute if agents do not share common beliefs, for then parameters representing *market* beliefs become state variables of the model.[2] Of course the problem is made more difficult if the parameters representing market beliefs are also unknowns, for then there is an infinite regress problem in which decisions depend on what agents believe the market believes, on what agents believe the market believes the market believes, and so on. It turns out that both these problems can be resolved in the space of agents' strategies with a Nash equilibrium concept.

In his introductory remarks Muth only asserts that under rational expectations the *average* of subjective distributions of agents of the model equals the objective distribution of the model. He also observes that expectations data reveal considerable cross-sectional differences of opinion. To these last remarks may be added the observation made by Keynes (1965) and others that in actual market situations agents do seem to take the beliefs of others into consideration. In particular, Keynes draws an analogy between those who purchase shares on stock markets and those in a contest who select from among many photographs the one which they believe that others will select. Of course, implicit in Keynes's remarks is the view that this is unfortunate. The activity of forecasting the choice of others is termed *speculation*, while the activity of forecasting the prospective yield of assets over their whole life is termed *enterprise*. Keynes also wrote that "Americans are apt to be unduly interested in discovering what average opinion believes average opinion to be."[3] In contrast it is argued in this chapter that a concern with the beliefs of others is consistent with rationality, though economic considerations may dominate in the limit. In effect what is described is a model with maximizing agents in which the psychology of the market plays an explicit role.

In this chapter we proceed as follows. The general structure of the models is described in section 2. A linear partial equilibrium framework is adopted in which risk-neutral profit-maximizing firms face an exogenous stochastic demand. In this context a self-fulfilling equilibrium is defined. The problem confronting a firm is then formulated in the space of agents' strategies, and a Nash equilibrium is defined. The latter allows for diverse initial prior distributions and learning. Section 3 presents a simple application of the equilibrium concept and establishes convergence to a self-fulfilling equilibrium. Section 4 generalizes the example and resolves the infinite regress problem of beliefs. Section 5 discusses the relationship between a Nash equilibrium in the strategy space and the general concept of a rational expectations equilibrium in these models with Bayesian learning. In section 6 an attempt is made to relax the specification that agents initially know the reduced form equations of the model up to some unknown parameters without imposing an inconsistent model. Firms are assumed to be completely ignorant of the way other firms *form* expectations but receive noisy and biased signals of market beliefs. The equilibrium of this model converges over time to a self-fulfilling equilibrium in the more general sense that Muth had in mind. Section 7 offers some concluding remarks on the stability of rational expectations equilibria and theories of market psychology with rational agents.

2 Structure of the models and equilibrium concepts

Following Muth (1961) a linear partial equilibrium framework is adopted. Each of a set of firms maximizes expected profit, a function which is quadratic in output. This produced commodity is sold in a competitive market with stochastic demand. Production decisions must be made prior to the realization of the demand. Subsequent to the realization of demand, the market-clearing price is the one which would be determined by a Walrasian auctioneer. There are no contingent commodity markets. Under these assumptions the production decision of each firm is a linear function of the expected price. In terms of generality, neither the linearity nor the partial equilibrium approach nor the exogenous restriction of markets nor the risk neutrality is satisfactory. Yet it is hoped that the results of this chapter could be obtained in a more general framework.

The set of firms I is assumed to be the closed unit interval $[0, 1]$. Let q_{it} denote the output of firm i at time t. Let P_t denote the market price of this commodity at time t. Output q_{it} must be chosen prior to the realization of P_t. Prior to its realization, each firm i believes that P_t is a real-valued random variable with mean $E_{it}(P_t)$. Note that $E_{it}(\cdot)$ is indexed by i so that the subjective expectations may differ among firms. Each firm i acts to maximize $E_{it}(P_t)q_{it}-(1/2a)(q_{it})^2$ $(a>0)$ with respect to q_{it}. This yields the linear decision rule $\tilde{q}_{it}=aE_{it}(P_t)$. It is assumed that $E_{it}(P_t)$ is a Lebesgue measurable function of $i\in[0,1]$ so that $\int_0^1 E_{jt}(P_t)\,\mathrm{d}j$ exists and represents what may be termed the market-anticipated price at time t. Let S_t denote the quantity of output supplied at time t. Then $S_t=a\int_0^1 E_{jt}(P_t)\,\mathrm{d}j$. As each firm is of Lebesgue measure zero, each regards the market-anticipated price and market output as invariant with respect to its own beliefs and actions.[4]

Let D_t denote the demand for the produced good at time t. It is assumed that $D_t=-bP_t+\theta+\varepsilon_t$ where $b>0$, and $\{\varepsilon_t, t=1,2,\ldots\}$ is a sequence of independent and identically distributed random variables, each of which is normally distributed with zero mean and variance σ_ε^2. The parameter θ may or may not be known. Let $P_t(\varepsilon_t)$ denote the market-clearing price at time t as a function of ε_t so that (with negative prices permitted)

$$P_t(\varepsilon_t)=\frac{\theta+\varepsilon_t-a\int E_{jt}(P_t)\,\mathrm{d}j}{b} \tag{13.1}$$

In a self-fulfilling equilibrium[5]

$$E_{jt}(P_t)=E\{P_t(\varepsilon_t)\} \qquad \text{for each } j\in I \tag{13.2a}$$

The expectation on the right is taken with respect to the distribution of ε_t, and so condition (13.2a) requires that the common expectation of price equals the mean of the statistical distribution which is generated by the model. It follows that in a self-fulfilling equilibrium $E_{jt}(P_t)=\theta/(a+b)$, $j\in I$, $P_t(\varepsilon_t)=\theta/(a+b)+\varepsilon_t/b$, and $S_t=a\theta/(a+b)$. As noted in section 1, Muth has in mind the somewhat weaker condition

$$\int E_{jt}(P_t)\,\mathrm{d}j=\frac{\theta}{a+b} \tag{13.2b}$$

The problem confronting a firm in this framework is now formulated in the space of agents' strategies, and a Nash equilibrium is defined. This approach will allow for diverse initial beliefs, for learning, and for an analysis of the stability question posed earlier. In all the subsequent models in this chapter each firm is assumed to know the model up to some unknown parameters and to have beliefs concerning such parameters. These initial beliefs of firm i are represented by a normal probability distribution which is characterized by a vector of parameters $W_{i1}\in\Omega$. Each firm observes at each time t a vector of variables y_t. Then a decision rule $d_{it}(\cdot)$ for firm i at time t is a function which maps W_{i1} and the history of observables $\{y_1, y_2, \ldots, y_{t-1}\}$ to an output choice q_{it}. That is, $\tilde{q}_{it} = d_{it}(W_{i1}; y_1, y_2, \ldots, y_{t-1})$. A set of decision rules $\{d^*_{it}(\cdot), i \in I\}$ is said to constitute a *Nash equilibrium* at time t if, for each firm i, $\tilde{q}_{it} = d^*_{it}(W_{i1}; y_1, \ldots, y_{t-1})$ is a maximizing choice of q_{it} given the $d^*_{jt}(\cdot), j \neq i$. Note that a Nash equilibrium at time t requires that each firm know the decision rules $d^*_{jt}(\cdot), j \neq i$, but not necessarily the output choices $\tilde{q}_{jt}, j \neq i$. It should also be noted that the $d^*_{it}(\cdot)$, $i \in I$, with $D_t = -bP_t + \theta + \varepsilon_t$ and $S_t = D_t$ completely determine the motion of the system over time.

The objective in what follows is to find a specification for the $\{d_{it}(\cdot), i \in I\}$ which constitutes a Nash equilibrium in each period. Clearly, the nature of such rules will depend on the information structure of the model. In this regard it should be noted that if the parameters a, b, and θ and the distribution of ε_t are known, then the supply decisions of the self-fulfilling equilibrium are Nash equilibrium strategies. Suppose that $\tilde{q}_{jt} = a\theta/(a+b)$ for each $j \neq i$. Then $\int \tilde{q}_{jt}\,dj = a\theta/(a+b)$ so that $bP_t = \theta + \varepsilon_t - a\theta/(a+b)$. Consequently $E_{it}(P_t) = \theta/(a+b)$ so that $\tilde{q}_{it} = a\theta/(a+b)$.

It should also be emphasized that by positing that the model is known by firms up to some unknown parameters and that there exists a Nash equilibrium in each period, the class of models which can be used to analyze learning and convergence is restricted. For example, consider the following model analyzed by Cyert and DeGroot (1974). Each firm believes that

$$P_t = \rho P_{t-1} + v_t \tag{13.3}$$

where the $\{v_t; t = 1, 2, \ldots\}$ is a sequence of independent but identically distributed normal variates with known zero mean and (known) variance $1/r = \sigma_\varepsilon^2/b^2$. Each firm regards ρ as a fixed but unknown parameter. If the beliefs of the representative firm concerning ρ at the beginning of period t are represented by a normal distribution when mean m_t and variance $1/h_t$, then, having observed P_t, the representative firm will have beliefs on ρ at the beginning of period $t+1$ represented by a normal distribution with mean m_{t+1} and variance $1/h_{t+1}$ where

$$m_{t+1} = \frac{h_t m_t + rP_{t-1}P_t}{h_t + rP_{t-1}^2}, \qquad h_{t+1} = h_t + rP_{t-1}^2 \tag{13.4}$$

It follows from (13.3) and (13.4) that, for the representative firm,

$$E_t(P_t) = m_t P_{t-1} \tag{13.5}$$

However, if we assume that, for the model of section 2, $\theta = 0$ and $v_t = \varepsilon_t/b$, equation (13.1) yields the actual reduced form equation

$$P_t = -\frac{aE_t(P_t)}{b} + v_t \tag{13.6}$$

Thus, substituting (13.5) into (13.6) and using the relationships of (13.4) with h_1, m_1, and P_0 specified exogenously, we obtain

$$P_t = -\frac{a\varphi_t(\sigma_\varepsilon^2; h_1; m_1; P_0, P_1, \ldots, P_{t-1})P_{t-1}}{b} + v_t \tag{13.7}$$

Equation (13.7) is inconsistent with the view that ρ is a fixed parameter. Moreover, assume that a single firm were to become enlightened as to the actual mechanism generating prices, that is, equation (13.7), whereas other firms continue to use equation (13.3). Then if $E_t(\rho) \neq 0$ and $P_{t-1} \neq 0$, the choice of output of the enlightened firm would differ from the output choice of all other firms. In short, if all firms were enlightened, the decision rules which map h_1, m_1, and $\{P_0, P_1 \ldots, P_{t-1}\}$ into output choices in accordance with (13.3)–(13.5) would not in general constitute Nash equilibrium strategies.[6]

3 Convergence with Nash equilibrium decision rules

It is assumed in this section that the parameters a and b and the distribution of ε_t are known by all firms but that the parameter θ is unknown. Each firm i has an initial prior distribution on θ which is normal with mean $m_1(i)$ and variance σ_1^2. The parameter θ is regarded by each firm as independent of ε_t. Let $W_{i1} = [m_1(1), \sigma_1^2]$. It is further assumed that the $\{W_{i1}, i \in I\}$ are known by all firms. P_t is observed each period; S_t and ε_t are unobserved.

The search for Nash equilibrium decision rules for this model is facilitated by the following observation. For firm i the state of the model subsequent to the realization of P_t is completely specified by its own mean beliefs $m_t(i)$ about θ, and (if known) by the mean beliefs $\int m_t(j)\,dj$ of others. $\tilde{q}_{it}$ should increase with $m_t(i)$; *ceteris paribus*, a high expected demand is equivalent to a high expected price. In contrast, $\tilde{q}_{it}$ should decrease with $\int m_t(j)\,dj$; *ceteris paribus*, market supply should increase with optimism about demand, lowering the price expected by firm i. This leads to the following proposition.

Proposition 13.1

Suppose that the $\{m_t(i), i \in I\}$ are functions of $\{W_{i1}; P_1, P_2, \ldots, P_{t-1}\}$ and that $\int m_t(j)\,dj$ is known at time t. Then there exist Nash equilibrium decision rules at time t of the form $d_{it}(W_{i1}; P_1, P_2, \ldots, P_{t-1}) = \alpha_0 m_t(i) + \alpha_1 \int m_t(j)\,\mathrm{d}j$ with constants $\alpha_0 > 0, \alpha_1 < 0$.

Proof. Suppose that

$$\tilde{q}_{jt} = \alpha_0 m_t(j) + \alpha_1 \int m_t(k)\,\mathrm{d}k \tag{13.8}$$

Then

$$\int \tilde{q}_{jt}\,\mathrm{d}j = (\alpha_0 + \alpha_1) \int m_t(k)\,\mathrm{d}k$$

Firm i knows that $D_t = \theta - bP_t + \varepsilon_t$ and the market-clearing condition $S_t = D_t$. Hence

$$bE_{it}(P_t) = m_t(i) - (\alpha_0 + \alpha_1) \int m_t(j)\,\mathrm{d}j$$

Therefore

$$\tilde{q}_{it} = \frac{a}{b}\left\{ m_t(i) - (\alpha_0 + \alpha_1) \int m_t(j)\,\mathrm{d}j \right\} \tag{13.9}$$

Equations (13.8) and (13.9) are consistent with $\alpha_0 = a/b$ and $\alpha_1 = -a^2/b(a+b)$. Hence

$$\tilde{q}_{it} = \frac{a}{b}\left\{ m_t(i) - \frac{a}{a+b} \int m_t(j)\,\mathrm{d}j \right\} \tag{13.10}$$

It remains to show that the hypotheses of proposition 13.1 are satisfied. At time 1 $\int m_1(j)\,\mathrm{d}j$ is known. Then q_{i1} is chosen in accordance with (13.10). The supply decisions of other firms are unobserved, but firm i believes that all such decisions are made in accordance with (13.10); it is on the basis of this belief that the choice of q_{i1} is rationalized. Firm i then observes the market-clearing price P_1 of period 1 and regards $bP_1 + S_1$ as a realization of $\theta + \varepsilon_1$. Then a posterior normal distribution on θ is formed by firm i with parameters $W_{i2} = [m_2(i), \sigma_2^2]$ where

$$m_2(i) = \frac{\sigma_\varepsilon^2 m_1(i) + \sigma_1^2(bP_1 + S_1)}{\sigma_1^2 + \sigma_\varepsilon^2}, \qquad \frac{1}{\sigma_2^2} = \frac{1}{\sigma_\varepsilon^2} + \frac{1}{\sigma_1^2}$$

In a similar manner firm i can compute $\{W_{j2}, j \in I\}$. The entire process is then repeated.

Under these assumptions $m_t(i) \to \theta$ as $t \to \infty$ for each $i \in I$ with probability 1. Hence $S_t \to a\theta/(a+b)$, $P_t \to \theta/(a+b) + \varepsilon_t/b$ and $E_{it}(P_t) \to \theta/(a+b)$, $i \in I$. The limiting equilibrium is the self-fulfilling equilibrium.

4 On the existence of Nash equilibrium decision rules and the problem of infinite regress

In this section we analyze a generalized version of the model presented in section 3 which allows for less initial information on the beliefs of others. Conditions sufficient to ensure the existence of Nash equilibrium decision rules are presented, and in the process a problem of infinite regress is solved; each firm is shown to make decisions based on what it believes, what it believes that the market believes, what it believes that the market believes that the market believes, and so on. The motion of the system over time is also analyzed.

For the model in this section firms are again assumed to know the parameters a and b and the distribution of ε_t. As before, P_t is observed at time t, and ε_t and S_t are unobserved. Also as before, each firm has an initial prior on the unknown parameter θ. In contrast, the means of the prior beliefs of others may be unknown. But each firm is assumed to have a well-specified distribution on the mean beliefs of others. To describe these beliefs the following notation and terminology are useful. Let $\theta_{0t} = \theta$ for all t. Let the prior of firm i on θ at time t be termed its zero-order belief on θ with expectation $m_{0t}(i)$. Let $\theta_{1t} = \int m_{0t}(j)\,\mathrm{d}j$; θ_{1t} is regarded as another parameter of the model. Let the prior of firm i on θ_{1t} at time t be termed its first-order belief on θ with expectation $m_{1t}(i)$. Let $\theta_{2t} = \int m_{1t}(j)\,\mathrm{d}j$. θ_{2t} is another parameter of the model. Let the prior of firm i on θ_{2t} be termed its second-order belief on θ with expectation $m_{2t}(i)$. Continuing in this manner, let $\theta_{nt} = \int m_{n-1,t}(j)\,\mathrm{d}j$ for all integers $n \geqslant 1$. Let $\theta_t = \{\theta_{nt}; n \geqslant 0\}$. Let $m_t(i) = \{m_{nt}(i); n' \geqslant 0\}$. Let $\Sigma(\theta_t)$ denote the covariance matrix of θ_t for firm i with $(k+1)$th row, $(n+1)$th column element $\sigma_{kn}(\theta_t)$.

It is assumed that firm i's prior on θ_1 is distributed normally with mean vector $m_1(i)$ and covariance matrix $\Sigma(\theta_1)$. The latter is held in common by all firms, and this is known by all firms. Parameter θ_1 is regarded as independent of ε_1 for all i. It should be noted that if θ_{n1} is known then θ_{m1} is known by all $m \geqslant n$. In such cases the prior of each firm i on θ_1 will have finite dimensions. In general, $W_{i1} = [m_1(i), \Sigma(\theta_1)]$ for this model.

Following the results of section 3 it is natural to postulate that a consistent decision rule for firm i at time t will be a linear function of its zero-, first-, second-, and possibly higher-order mean beliefs on θ. That is, the choice of output of firm i will depend on its mean belief of θ, its mean belief of the mean beliefs of others, its mean belief of the mean beliefs of the mean beliefs of others, and so on. This structure may appear to lead to the problem of infinite regress, but under specified assumption the infinite series converges.[7] In particular consider the following proposition.

Proposition 13.2
Suppose that the $\{m_{nt}(i); n \geqslant 0\}$ are functions of $\{W_{i1}; P_1, P_2, \ldots, P_{t-1}\}$. Suppose also that, as $N \to \infty$, $\Sigma_{i=0}^{N}\Sigma_{j=0}^{N}\alpha_i\alpha_j\sigma_{ij}(\theta_t)$ converges and $\Sigma_{n=0}^{N}\alpha_n m_{nt}(j)$ converges uniformly where $\alpha_n = (a/b)^{n+1}(-1)^n$. Then there exist Nash equilibrium decision rules at time t of the form $\tilde{q}_{it} = \Sigma_{n=0}^{\infty}\alpha_n m_{nt}(i)$.

Proof. Suppose that

$$\tilde{q}_{jt} = \sum_{n=0}^{\infty} \alpha_n m_{nt}(j) \tag{13.11}$$

where $\alpha_n = (a/b)^{n+1}(-1)^n$. Then $\int \tilde{q}_{jt}\,\mathrm{d}j = \Sigma_{n=0}^{\infty}\alpha_n\theta_{n+1,t}$. (Note that the summation and integration operators can be interchanged.) For each firm i, the sequence $\Sigma_{n=0}^{N}\alpha_n\theta_{n+1,t}$ converges in distribution to a normal random variable with mean $\Sigma_{n=0}^{\infty}\alpha_n m_{n+1,t}(i)$ and variance $\Sigma_{i=0}^{\infty}\Sigma_{j=0}^{\infty}\alpha_i\alpha_j\sigma_{(i+1)(j+1)}(\theta_t)$. Hence $E_{it}\int \tilde{q}_{jt}\,\mathrm{d}j = \Sigma_{n=0}^{\infty}\alpha_n m_{n+1,t}(i)$. By market clearing $bE_{it}(P_t) = m_{0t}(i) - \Sigma_{n=0}^{\infty}\alpha_n m_{n+1,t}(i)$ so that

$$\tilde{q}_{it} = \frac{a}{b}\left\{m_{0t}(i) - \sum_{n=0}^{\infty}\alpha_n m_{n+1,t}(i)\right\} \tag{13.12}$$

Equations (13.11) and (13.12) are in the same form.

It is interesting to note that the second hypothesis of proposition 13.2 is satisfied if $a < b$ and if the $\{m_{nt}(i); i \in I, n \geqslant 0\}$ and the $\{\sigma_{kn}(\theta_t); k \geqslant 0, n \geqslant 0\}$ are uniformly bounded. The standard cobweb model is also stable if the slope of the supply curve (of the function $q_{i,t+1} = aP_t$) is less in absolute value than the slope of the inverse demand curve. If $a \geqslant b$, alternative conditions may ensure the convergence of the relevant infinite series. The following result can also be established.

Proposition 13.3
Suppose that the $\{m_{nt}(i); n \geqslant 0\}$ are functions of $\{W_{i1}; P_1, P_2, \ldots, P_{t-1}\}$. Then there exist Nash equilibrium decision rules (of dimension k) of the form $\tilde{q}_{it} = \Sigma_{n=0}^{k}\alpha_n m_{nt}(i)$ if and only if $m_{kt}(i)$ is a known constant over $i \in I$.

Proof. The proof follows an obvious modification of the proofs of propositions 13.1 and 13.2.

Proposition 13.3 can be viewed as a generalization of proposition 13.1; if θ_{1t} is known, then $m_{1t}(i)=\theta_{1t}$ for all $i\in I$.

It remains to analyze the motion of the system over time and to establish in particular that $m_{nt}(i)$ is a well-defined function of $(W_{i1}; P_1, P_2, \ldots, P_{t-1})$ for all i, n, and t.[8] Our ability to say anything in this regard depends on finding a solution to an apparently nontrivial fixed-point problem, for, having observed P_t, firm j must convert his posterior beliefs on θ_t, what the market believed last period, to prior beliefs on θ_{t+1}, what the market believes now. Yet the way that the parameters move over time will be determined by the way in which other firms are solving the same problem. Fortunately the recursive way in which θ_t is defined enables us to find a solution to this fixed-point problem in a recursive manner.

In general, given the existence of Nash equilibrium decision rules at time t, $bP_t=\theta_{0t}+\varepsilon_t-\Sigma_{n=0}^{\infty}\alpha_n\theta_{n+1,t}$ where $\alpha_n=(a/b)^{n+1}(-1)^n$. Then, subsequent to the realization of P_t, firm i will have a posterior normal distribution on θ_t with means

$$m_{0,t+1}(i)=m_{0t}(i)+C_0\left\{bP_t-m_{0t}(i)+\sum_{n=0}^{\infty}\alpha_n m_{n+1,t}(i)\right\} \quad (13.13)$$

$$\alpha_{k-1}E_{i,t+1}(\theta_{kt})=\alpha_{k-1}m_{kt}(i)+C_k\left\{bP_t-m_{0t}(i)+\sum_{n=0}^{\infty}\alpha_n m_{n+1,t}(i)\right\} \quad k\geq 1 \quad (13.14)$$

where

$$C_k=\sum_{n=0}^{\infty}\left(\frac{a}{b}\right)^k\left(\frac{a}{b}\right)^n\sigma_{kn}(\theta_t)\times\left\{\sum_{k=0}^{\infty}\sum_{n=0}^{\infty}\left(\frac{a}{b}\right)^k\left(\frac{a}{b}\right)^n\sigma_{kn}(\theta_t)+\sigma_\varepsilon^2\right\}^{-1} \quad k\geq 0$$

with covariance matrix of terms

$$\begin{aligned}\left(\frac{a}{b}\right)^k\left(\frac{a}{b}\right)^n\sigma^*_{kn}(\theta_t)&=\left(\frac{a}{b}\right)^k\left(\frac{a}{b}\right)^n\sigma_{kn}(\theta_t)\\&-\left\{\sum_{j=0}^{\infty}\left(\frac{a}{b}\right)^k\left(\frac{a}{b}\right)^j\sigma_{kj}(\theta_t)\right\}\left\{\sum_{j=0}^{\infty}\left(\frac{a}{b}\right)^j\left(\frac{a}{b}\right)^n\sigma_{jn}(\theta_t)\right\}\\&\times\left\{\sum_{k=0}^{\infty}\sum_{n=0}^{\infty}\left(\frac{a}{b}\right)^k\left(\frac{a}{b}\right)^n\sigma_{kn}(\theta_t)+\sigma_\varepsilon^2\right\}^{-1}\end{aligned}$$

Integration over (13.13) yields

$$\theta_{1,t+1} = \gamma_{10} P_t + \sum_{n=1}^{\infty} \gamma_{1n} \theta_{nt} \tag{13.15}$$

for suitably chosen constants $\{\gamma_{1n}; n \geqslant 0\}$ in terms of the parameters a, b, σ_ε^2, and $\sigma_{kn}(\theta_t)$. Taking the expectation for firm i in (13.13) with respect to the posterior distribution of θ_t and substituting from (13.14) yields

$$m_{1,t+1}(i) = \gamma_{20} P_t + \sum_{n=0}^{\infty} \gamma_{2,n+1} m_{nt}(i) \tag{13.16}$$

Integration over (13.16) yields

$$\theta_{2,t+1} = \gamma_{20} P_t + \sum_{n=1}^{\infty} \gamma_{2n} \theta_{nt} \tag{13.17}$$

which is of the same form as (13.15). Proceeding recursively in this manner, we obtain

$$\theta_{k,t+1} = \gamma_{k0} P_t + \sum_{n=1}^{\infty} \gamma_{kn} \theta_{nt} \qquad k \geqslant 1 \tag{13.18}$$

Hence the prior distribution of θ_{t+1} at time $t+1$ is well defined with means and covariance matrix determined from (13.14), (13.18), and $\sigma_{kn}^*(\theta_t)$. It follows that, under appropriate regularity conditions, $m_{t+1}(i)$ is a well-defined function of $\{W_{i1}; P_1, P_2, \ldots, P_t\}$.[9]

It is conjectured that $m_{nt}(i) \to \theta$ as $t \to \infty$ with probability 1 for all $i \in I$ and $n \geqslant 0$. Such a conjecture is easily proved in a model in which S_t is also observed each period, for then the equation

$$bP_t + S_t = \theta + \varepsilon_t \tag{13.19}$$

can be used to update priors about θ, and the equation

$$S_t = \sum_{n=0}^{\infty} \alpha_n \theta_{n+1,t} \tag{13.20}$$

can be used in conjunction with (13.19) in a now familiar recursive manner to form a prior distribution on the $\theta_{n,t+1}$. It is clear from (13.19) that $m_{0t}(i) \to \theta$ as $t \to \infty$ with probability 1 regardless of θ_1. Consequently $m_{nt}(i) \to \theta$ as $t \to \infty$.

5 On the relationship between Nash and rational expectations equilibria

The concept of a Nash equilibrium in the strategy space may be a natural way to extend the concept of a self-fulfilling equilibrium to situations in which agents have different beliefs. But such an extension is not unique. For suppose in the model described in section 4, for example, that all firms act as if

$$\begin{aligned} bP_t &= \theta + \varepsilon_t - \sum_{n=0}^{\infty} \left(\frac{a}{b}\right)^{n+1} (-1)^n \theta_{n+1,t} && t = 1 \\ bP_t &= \theta + \varepsilon_t - \sum_{j=1}^{t-1} \beta_{jt} P_{t-j} - \sum_{n=0}^{\infty} \delta_{nt} \theta_{n+1,1} && t = 2, 3, \ldots \end{aligned} \qquad (13.21)$$

By virtue of the existence of a Nash equilibrium there exist values for the β_{jt} and δ_{nt} in terms of the parameters a, b, σ_ε^2, and $\sigma_{kn}(\theta_1)$ such that equation (13.20) is self-fulfilling in each period. That is, expectations will be correct if, at time t before the choice of q_{jt}, each firm j takes the expectation in (13.21) with respect to the distribution of ε_t and, if $t = 1$, the prior distribution of θ_1, or if $t > 1$, the posterior distribution of θ_1 conditional on $\{P_1, P_2, \ldots, P_{t-1}\}$ using equation (13.21) for the previous periods. Each firm need not be concerned with the strategies followed by others if all correctly perceive the way that prices move over time. This is in keeping with the concept of a rational expectations equilibrium as described, for example, by Lucas and Prescott (1971). (It should be noted in passing that in models with Bayesian learning a state of the economy is a specification of the history of all observables.)

In this chapter we have focused on the concept of a Nash equilibrium in the strategy space because the consequent analysis makes it clear that it *is* rational for agents to be concerned with the beliefs of others.[10] Moreover, such an analysis may clarify how it is that agents perceive the correct reduced from equation for price; it is clear from (13.21) that the distribution of P_t is nonstationary, and so the usual stories may seem less convincing here. However, there remains the question of whether a set of Nash equilibrium strategies could be attained by a process of learning. In this regard an alternative equilibrium concept only leads to an old question in a new guise.

6 Convergence with noisy and biased market signals: an alternative approach

In this section we present an alternative approach to convergence to the self-fulfilling equilibrium. A model is proposed in which firms receive noisy and biased signals of market anticipations. Under apparently weak conditions firms eventually identify with some noise the true reduced form equation for the price.

It is assumed that each firm knows the parameters a and b and the distribution of ε_t. Each firm is completely ignorant of the way that other firms form expectations. However, before the output decision q_t each firm observes $\int E_{jt}(P_t)\,\mathrm{d}j$ with some bias and some noise. In particular let

$$I_{it} = \int E_{jt}(P_t)\,\mathrm{d}j + \Psi_i + \xi_{it} \tag{13.22}$$

where $\xi_{it} \sim N(0, \sigma_\xi^2)$. Parameters Ψ_i and θ are unknown. Firm i has a prior distribution on (Ψ_i, θ) at time t which is bivariate normal with mean $[E_{it}(\Psi_i), E_{it}(\theta)]$ and covariance matrix with kth row, nth column element σ_{knt}. ε_t, ξ_{it}, and (θ, Ψ_i) are all independent. P_t and I_{it} are observed. S_t, ξ_{it}, and ε_t are unobserved. From (13.22), $S_t = a(I_{it} - \Psi_i - \xi_{it})$. Market clearing yields

$$bP_t = \theta + \varepsilon_t - a(I_{it} - \Psi_i - \xi_{it}) \tag{13.23}$$

Then, for firm i,

$$E_{it}(P_t) = \frac{E_{it}(\theta) - aI_{it} + aE_{it}(\Psi_i)}{b} \tag{13.24}$$

so that $\tilde{q}_{it} = (a/b)\{E_{it}(\theta) - aI_{it} + aE_{it}(\Psi_i)\}$. It is assumed that (13.24) is consistent with (13.22) in that integration over firms in (13.24) yields the term $\int E_{jt}(P_t)\,\mathrm{d}j$ appearing on the right-hand side of (13.22).

From (13.23) the random variable $bP_t + aI_{it}$ is viewed by firm i as drawn from a normal distribution with unknown mean $\theta + a\Psi_i$ and specified variance $\sigma_\varepsilon^2 + a^2\sigma_\xi^2$. The prior of firm i on the unknown mean is normal with mean $m_{it} = E_{it}(\theta) + aE_{it}(\Psi_i)$ and variance $\sigma_{22t} + a^2\sigma_{11t} + 2a\sigma_{12t}$. It follows that $m_{it} \to \theta + a\Psi_i$ as $t \to \infty$ for each $i \in I$. Over time each firm learns the true value of $\theta + a\Psi_i$. Hence $bE_{it}(P_t) \to \theta - a\int E_{jt}(P_t)\,\mathrm{d}j - a\xi_{it}$ as $t \to \infty$. Then, under some regularity conditions, as $t \to \infty$

$$\int E_{jt}(P_t)\,\mathrm{d}j \to \frac{\theta}{a+b} + \frac{a\int \xi_{jt}\,\mathrm{d}j}{a+b}$$

On average, in the limit, the self-fulfilling equilibrium (13.26) is attained.

It should be stressed that convergence in this sense does not require that the values of θ and Ψ_i each be known. For example, firm i may overestimate the value of the parameter θ and underestimate the value of the supply signal bias Ψ_i in such a way as to yield the true value of the linear combination

$\theta + a\Psi_i$. In the limit, firm i can correctly estimate the relevant reduced form equation

$$bP_t + aI_{it} = \theta + \varepsilon_t + a\Psi_i + a\xi_{it} \tag{13.25}$$

though the structural equations (13.22) and $D_t = \theta - bP_t + \varepsilon_t$ remain underidentified. Of course $E_{it}(P_t)$ as determined from (13.25) completely determines the action of firm i.

7 Concluding remarks

This chapter can be regarded in part as an attempt to contribute to an understanding of the stability of rational expectations equilibria. In particular the stability of a self-fulfilling equilibrium in a class of models has been examined. Consistent extended models have been constructed, and the sequences of Nash equilibria of these extended models have been analyzed. In focusing on consistent extended models and the Nash equilibrium concept, it became natural to examine the amount and nature of information required by agents in order for their decision problems to be well defined and for the sequence of Nash equilibria to converge to a self-fulfilling equilibrium. An analysis of the stability of a self-fulfilling equilibrium should naturally involve such questions.

Thus the stability of the self-fulfilling equilibrium is established, at least for some models. However, in a larger sense, questions concerning the stability of the more general concept of rational expectations equilibria may be ill posed. We can of course analyse the sequence of equilibria of an extended model and perhaps establish convergence. But if the extended model is well defined its equilibria will necessarily be rational. Thus Cyert and DeGroot (1974) note that what they refer to as consistent models necessarily display rational expectations. In section 5 of this chapter we make the point that Nash equilibria in the strategy space can also be viewed as rational expectations equilibria with respect to price distributions conditioned on past observations.

This chapter can also be regarded as an attempt to incorporate various psychological theories of economic behavior into a model in which agents are rational. It is argued that a concern with the beliefs of others is consistent with rationality, but economic considerations are also important. In section 3 the terms $m_t(i)$ and $\int m_t(j)\,dj$ both enter into a maximizing decision rule for agent i. In section 4 agents are concerned with expectations of all orders! Economic considerations may dominate in that in the limit agents learn the true value of θ and acquire uniform beliefs. In section 6, I_{it} as a noisy and biased signal of $\int E_{jt}(P_t)\,dj$ is crucial to agent i. Again, in the limit, economic considerations dominate though the noise of the signals persists.

The model also points to an explanation for market surveys of intentions or anticipations. Such signals, even if noisy and biased, provide information as to the beliefs of others. This information may be crucial in making the decision problem of the individual well defined, in reducing uncertainty, and in establishing the speed of convergence to a stationary state. (In a more elaborate model, the quantity and quality of information to be disseminated would be determined endogenously.) Moreover, the results of section 6 establish that convergence to a self-fulfilling equilibrium is possible even if agents are not very well informed. Firms may be completely ignorant of the way that others form expectations, and the bias $|\Psi_i|$ and noise σ_ξ^2 may be large. Though agents never identify the underlying structural relations of the model, they can learn the correct reduced form equation for price – the crucial variable in their decision problem – by simple Bayesian procedures.

Notes

1 The statistical procedure is limited in that there is no hypothesis testing of the *model* being used; in particular the actual model is not provided as an alternative. An example of this approach is given in section 2.

2 For a simple resolution of this problem where there is one representative firm (so that implicitly agents share common beliefs) see Cyert and DeGroot (1974). Lucas (1975b) notes the difficulties which can arise when information sets differ among agents but successfully circumvents the problem by postulating a certain pooling arrangement.

3 Keynes also argued that third-order expectations schemes in which agents act on the basis of beliefs of what others believe others believe were also an important determinant of behavior.

4 Subsequently $\int x_i\,di$ will denote Lebesgue integration of the function x_i on $[0, 1]$. It will be assumed that the model is specified in such a way that x_i is indeed a Lebesgue integrable function. Also any reference in the text to *all* firms should be understood to mean all $i \in [0, 1]$ except for a set of measure zero.

5 The term self-fulfilling equilibrium is used here in contradistinction to the more general concept of a rational expectations equilibrium as defined, for example, by Lucas (1975b). See also the discussion in section 5.

6 If $m_t \to 0$ as $t \to \infty$, then there is a convergence to a self-fulfilling equilibrium. Cyert and DeGroot (1974) present the results of several Monte Carlo runs of this model for various specifications of a/b, m_1, and P_0 (holding $r = 1$ and $h_0 = 0$). Though the model apparently converges under some specifications, it is also reported that for $a/b = 1.5$, $P_0 = m_1 = 1$ the model diverges for five of 10 runs in that P_t begins oscillating wildly, increasing in absolute value, and for $a/b = 1.75$, $m_1 = 1$, and $P_0 = 10$ the model explodes for all 10 runs. It should also be noted that with a diffuse prior ($h_1 = 0$) the estimates $E_t(\rho)$ are those of ordinary least

squares. Thus the failure of the model to converge cannot be attributed to Bayesian analysis.

7 This approach to the problem of infinite regress is also adopted in part by Cyert and DeGroot (1970).

8 Proposition 13.3 may suggest the possibility that if $m_{kt}(i)$ is a known constant over $i \in I$, then $m_{k\tau}(i)$ will be a known constant for all $\tau > t$. Unfortunately this need not be so.

9 Certain regularity conditions are needed to ensure the existence of Nash equilibria in each period. It has also been assumed implicitly in the text that all terms involved in the Bayesian updating procedure are well defined.

10 From a technical point of view the search for a rational expectations equilibrium is facilitated by the formulation of the problem in the strategy space. However, the equivalence of the two equilibrium concepts is not established, for suppose that θ were known by each agent and that $a > b$. Then there exists a rational expectations equilibrium – it is the trivial self-fulfilling equilibrium. However, equation (13.11) is not well defined.

References

Arrow, K.J. and Green, J.R. (1973) Notes on expectations equilibria in Bayesian settings. Working Paper 33, Institute for Mathematical Studies in the Social Sciences, Stanford University.

Crawford, R.G. (1973) Implications for learning for economic models of uncertainty. *International Economic Review* 14, 587–600.

Cyert, R.M. and DeGroot, M.H. (1970) Bayesian analysis and duopoly theory. *Journal of Political Economy* 78, 1168–84.

—— and —— (1974) Rational expectations and Bayesian analysis. *Journal of Political Economy* 82, 521–36.

Grossman, S.J. (1975) Rational expectations and the econometric modeling of markets subject to uncertainty: a Bayesian approach. *Journal of Econometrics* 3, 255–72.

Keynes, J.M. (1965) *The General Theory of Employment, Interest, and Money*. New York: Harcourt Brace and World. (Originally published in 1936.)

Kihlstrom, R.E. and Mirman, L.J. (1975) Information and market equilibrium. *Bell Journal of Economics* 6, 357–76.

Lucas, R.E., Jr (1975a) Asset prices in an exchange economy. Unpublished manuscript, University of Chicago.

—— (1975b) An equilibrium model of the business cycle. *Journal of Political Economy* 83(6), 1113–44.

—— and Prescott, E.C. (1971) Investment under uncertainty. *Econometrica* 39, 659–81.

Muth, J.F. (1961) Rational expectations and the theory of price movements. *Econometrica* 29, 315–35.

14

Forecasting the Forecasts of Others

1 Introduction

That economic decision-makers do not share the same beliefs concerning the time series of economic variables relevant to their decisions is a key part of the writings of such diverse authors as Pigou (1929), Keynes (1965), and Lucas (1972, 1975). In his explanation of industrial fluctuations, Pigou emphasizes that in modern industry businessmen are partially but not completely interconnected, possessing only limited information on what others are doing. Pigou then argues that these interconnections tend to promote the mutual generation of forecast errors, both within and across industries. Further, such forecast errors can be mutually generated over time, leading to serial correlation and waves of optimism and pessimism. Similarly, it was Keynes's view that with the opening of stock exchanges investors shift from a concern with long term determinants of profitability or yield to a concern with short term movements in market prices themselves. Thus conventional valuation would be liable to change violently as the result of sudden fluctuations in opinion owing to factors which do not really make much difference to prospective yield, and even relatively informed investors

---

Reprinted from *Journal of Political Economy* 91(4), 1983, 546–88 (Chicago, IL: University of Chicago Press). I am extraordinarily indebted to Lars Peter Hansen, Thomas J. Sargent, Edward C. Prescott, and Ian Bain for instruction and insights, and I would like to thank Robert E. Lucas, Jr, Edmund S. Phelps, Carl Futia, and participants of seminars at Carnegie–Mellon University, the University of Chicago, Columbia University, the Federal Reserve Bank of Minneapolis, and the NBER Conference on Business Fluctuations, Chicago, October 1981, for helpful comments. I accept full responsibility for errors and the views expressed herein. Support for this research from the National Science Foundation and the Alfred P. Sloan Foundation and programming assistance from Riccardo Revelli and Lakshmi Subramanian are also gratefully acknowledged.

would be concerned with average opinion. More recently, Lucas (1972) has emphasized the role of confusion between relative and absolute price movements in his explanation of the positive correlation between prices and economy activity, and Lucas (1975) has used economy-wide average beliefs as a state variable, along with money and capital, to explain certain stylized facts of business cycles, especially persistence and cumulation in response to serially uncorrelated economic shocks.

In this chapter we attempt to develop further an equilibrium account of some of the qualitative observations which motivate Pigou (1929) and Keynes (1965) as well as Lucas (1972, 1975). That is, we follow Muth (1961), Lucas and Prescott (1971), and Lucas (1972, 1975) in adopting the "rational expectations" hypothesis, with the following assumptions: (a) decision-makers act as if they were solving explicit inference and dynamic decision problems with well-specified information sets and objective functions, taking as given the aggregate laws of motion of observed and unobserved state variables, including perhaps the laws describing the inferences of other decision-makers; (b) these laws of motion are in turn those actually generated in the model by the inferences and decisions of the decision-makers.[1] The important aspect of this formulation is that it can accommodate learning and disparate expectations across decision-makers and can handle information structures in which decision-makers forecast the forecasts of others.[2]

In this chapter we emphasize four qualitative characteristics of economic time series which equilibrium models of this kind can generate. The first is the "learning mechanism" for the propagation of economic shocks. That is, learning alone can convert serially uncorrelated economic shocks into serially correlated movements in economic decision variables.[3] This result is not particularly novel – it is clear from the earlier work of Lucas (1975) and Crawford (1979), for example – but perhaps this propagation mechanism has not yet received the attention it deserves.[4] Second, because decision-makers have limited *a priori* information on underlying economic shocks, they may well respond to variables generated by the decisions of others and to the noise in such decisions, even if there are no real economic links among such decision-makers. Thus time series can display certain cross-correlation properties and may appear more noisy than if decision-makers acted in isolation. Third, models with disparate but rational expectations, in which decision-makers forecast the forecasts of others, can lead to some rather new and exciting dynamics. In particular, we show how serially uncorrelated economic shocks can induce a certain volatility – relatively rapid oscillations in forecasts and decision variables in response to economic shocks, and not the usual exponential decay. Fourth, and more generally, we argue that forecasts and forecast errors can be serially correlated in a certain crucial sense. That is, economic shocks which are innovations relative to the underlying driving stochastic processes of the model, and hence are serially uncorrelated, are not necessarily the innovations of the information sets of decision-makers. Thus forecasts of the economic innovations and forecast errors of the driving stochastic processes can display certain cross-correlation and serial correlation properties when expressed in terms of the economic innovations themselves. This is one way to understand the first three properties.

We might well ask at this point whether these results are easily obtained. After all, models in which decision-makers forecast the forecasts of others have a reputation for being difficult to formulate and analyze.[5] Indeed, this chapter was originally motivated by a search for solution techniques which would prove useful in a variety of applications under a variety of information structures. To that end, we adopt a highly stylized model and focus attention on what problems arise and what formulation–solution techniques are needed as the information structure is varied. As it turns out, all the information variants examined here *are* easy to analyze. That is, techniques do vary somewhat across information variants but, in one form or another, all techniques make use of standard formulas for conditional means and variances of normal random variables.

With interesting economic time series and tractable solution techniques, we can proceed to ask whether the models studied here have content in a more formal econometric sense. That is, suppose that an econometrician were confronted with data generated from one of the information variants of the basic model, and suppose that market beliefs are unobserved latent variables. Would he be able to make sense of such time series, that is, interpret the time series relative to theory?[6] More specifically, would he be able to fit the data to the theoretical model and identify key underlying parameters?[7] As it turns out, in the linear-quadratic normal random variable model under consideration, many of the questions can be answered in the affirmative.[8]

To summarize, we proceed as follows. In section 2 we describe the basic model, which is a partial equilibrium model of investment, following Lucas and Prescott (1971), with unobserved permanent and transitory shocks to demand, so that there is a nontrivial signal-extraction problem with the costly adjustment of capital (Lucas, 1967; Gould, 1968; Treadway, 1969; Mortensen, 1973; Sargent, 1979), following Haavelmo (1960), Eisner and Strotz (1963), and Jorgenson (1963), so that a natural propagation mechanism is already present, and with dispersed markets or islands restricting information flows, following Phelps (1970) and the business cycle literature (for example, King, 1978; Barro, 1980; Grossman and Weiss, 1980), so that the "forecasting the forecasts" problem can be analyzed. In section 3 we describe the dynamic stochastic maximization problem confronting the individual (representative) firm in each market and derive the best decision rule. In section 4 we describe precisely the definition of equilibrium employed throughout the chapter – a dynamic linear equilibrium with rational but disparate expectations. In section 5 we generate a law of motion for the aggregate capital stock in each market which allows us to focus attention entirely on inference problems. In section 6 we describe a "hierarchical" information variant, in which one market receives price but not quantity information from an informationally self-contained market lower in the hierarchy. This hierarchical system is easily solved with a recursive use of Kalman filtering techniques. The important point is that any firm sees a filtered version of (endogenous) time series generated by linear laws of motion of a finite number of state variables.

In section 7 we present the time series dynamics for the hierarchical structure with some numerical examples, and in section 8 we describe a symmetric but disparate information structure in which firms in each market see an economy-wide average price contaminated with measurement error. Here there is a confounding of the laws of motion of observed and unobserved state variables with the inference problems of firms. But a method of undetermined coefficients, a nonlinear but tractable procedure, is developed (see also King, 1978; Chari, 1979; Sargent, 1979; Barro, 1980; Futia, 1981). Moreover, two procedures for forecasting in this setting are described, at least on the assumption that there is full information after a finite number of periods. One procedure makes use of the entire relevant history, and the other utilizes the distinction between moving-average representations in the space of economic disturbances and representations in the space of disturbances which are innovations relative to agents' information sets (motivated by Hansen and Sargent, 1989). In section 9 we describe the time series dynamics for the symmetric structure, again with numerical examples. Finally, in section 10 we discuss how the model might, in principle, be fitted to data. In this section we extend the techniques of Sargent (1978, 1981) and Hansen and Sargent (1980a, b), and we discuss the possibilities and limitations of more conventional econometric procedures, as well as the procedures of Sims (1980a, b) and Kydland and Prescott (1982).

2 The basic model

Imagine an economy in which a single commodity can be produced in each of a set of local "islands." At the level of abstraction adopted here, these islands can be interpreted as local markets within an industry, separate markets within a country, and so on. The essential aspect of the specification is that the commodity itself cannot be moved across islands or markets. Thus we might even assume that the commodity itself varies across islands as if there were separate industries, with all variables expressed in common units. However, information can flow among islands, at least to a limited extent, consistent with Phelps's (1970) island paradigm.

More formally, then, assume that there is a set of markets indexed by i, $i = 1, 2, \ldots, I$. (Subsequently I may be either finite or infinite.) There is a continuum of firms (on the unit interval) in each market i, and each firm has a production function of the form

$$y_t^i = f_0 k_t^i \qquad f_0 > 0 \tag{14.1}$$

where y_t^i is the output of the produced good of the (representative) firm in market i at time t and k_t^i is the capital stock of the firm, chosen at time $t-1$. Thus output is linear in the capital stock. Summing over all firms in market i, let Y_t^i and K_t^i denote the corresponding aggregates of market i.

Each market i is confronted with an exogenous linear demand schedule for the produced good which is buffeted by relatively persistent shocks and completely transitory shocks. The transitory shocks are independent across markets and the persistent component is common. Thus, to the extent that the persistent component is unobserved, markets are informationally linked. That is, economic time series in one market may contain information on the persistent component which is of interest to firms in another market.

More formally, then, under market clearing

$$P_t^i = -b_i Y_t^i + z_t^i \qquad b_1 > 0 \tag{14.2}$$

where P_t^i is the price of the produced good in market i at time t and z_t^i is a shock to market i demand at time t. Here z_t^i is the sum of a persistent economy-wide component θ_t and a completely transitory market-specific component ε_t^i, that is,

$$z_t^i = \theta_t + \varepsilon_t^i \tag{14.3}$$

The common shock θ_t follows a first-order autoregressive process

$$\theta_t = \rho\theta_{t-1} + v_t \qquad 0 < |\rho| < 1 \tag{14.4}$$

where v_t and ε_t^i are jointly normally distributed and independent among themselves and over time, with mean zero and covariances σ_v^2 and σ_ε^2 respectively.

Note that in the formulation above a trend in economic variables is precluded. In fact, the system as specified has a steady state with mean zero. In what follows, however, all variables can be interpreted more generously as deviations from (unspecified) mean values.

3 Individual firm maximization

The decision problem confronting each firm in market i at time 0 is to choose a sequence of contingent plans for capital stocks k_t^i so as to maximize discounted expected profits, that is,

$$\max_{\{k_t^i\}_{t=1}^{\infty}} E_0^i \sum_{t=0}^{\infty} \beta^t \left\{ P_t^i f_0 k_t^i - \frac{f_1}{2}(k_t^i)^2 - \frac{f_2}{2}(k_{t+1}^i - k_t^i)^2 \right\}$$

$$f_0, f_2 > 0, \quad f_1 \geqslant 0 \tag{14.5}$$

Here E_0^i denotes the expectation of (future) prices conditioned on information available to the firm in market i at time $t = 0$, Ω_0^i, parameter β is the discount rate, $0 < \beta < 1$, the term $P_t^i f_0 k_t^i$ represents revenue from sales at time t, the price sequence $\{P_t^i\}_{t=0}^{\infty}$ is taken parametrically and is bounded in mean, the term $(f_1/2)(k_t^i)^2$ induces a kind of "long run" decreasing return to scale (constant return to scale if $f_1 = 0$), and the term $(f_2/2)(k_{t+1}^i - k_t^i)^2$ represents a cost of adjustment, thereby linking the period-by-period decisions of the firm.[9] Such adjustment-cost formulations capture the idea that firms do not respond immediately to perceived movements in market demand, giving explicit dynamics to the "static" long run adjustment stories of standard price theory (see Lucas, 1967). Again, a typical firm in market i is to choose a sequence of contingent plans or decision rules

$$k_{t+1}^i = k_{t+1}^i(\Omega_t^i) \tag{14.6}$$

where Ω_t^i is the information available to the representative firm at time t in market i and includes, among other things, current past market i aggregate capital stocks and current and past market i prices. Various versions of the model will be considered below by altering these information sets Ω_t^i. Of crucial importance will be the inclusion of *some* series in other markets.

To solve this decision problem, we can make substantial use of certainty equivalence, as in Holt et al. (1960), following Hansen and Sargent (1980a) and described in more detail in the working paper by Townsend (1981). The end result is a decision rule of the form

$$k_{t+1}^i = \lambda_1 k_t^i + \frac{f_0 \beta \lambda_1}{f_2} \sum_{j=0}^{\infty} (\beta \lambda_1)^j E(P_{t+1+j}^i | \Omega_t^i) \tag{14.7}$$

where $E(\cdot | \Omega_t^i)$ denotes the expectation conditioned on the information set Ω_t^i. (Note that k_t^i is included in Ω_t^i.) Thus, as we might expect, the capital stock decision of the representative firm in market i is a linear function of the beginning-of-period capital stock and the expectation of all future market-specific prices. As we will see, the latter expectations are often expressed in terms of a finite number of state variables.

4 A definition of equilibrium

The sequence of expected future prices, which each firm in market i takes as given, is of course determined in an equilibrium with market-clearing condition (14.2). Moreover, this sequence will be required to have the rational expectations property that the firms' expectations be consistent with the statistical distribution of prices which the model generates. Note that these expectations across markets need not be identical, as information sets across markets need not be identical. However, each firm's expectations are required to be statistically correct in the sense of minimizing the mean square forecast error given the model. Thus, to accommodate rational but disparate expectations, the equilibrium is specified at the level of decision rules. That is, firms act as if they know that prices are determined at each date by market-clearing considerations, that the demand at each date is determined by schedule (14.2), and that the supply at each date is determined by a law of motion describing the evolution of the market-wide average capital stock. More formally, consider then (with some repetition of earlier equations) the following definition.

Definition

A dynamic linear equilibrium with rational but possibly disparate expectations is a law of motion for the aggregate capital stock in each market i:

$$K_{t+1}^i = h_1 K_t^i + h_2 M_t^i \qquad i = 1, 2, \ldots, I \tag{14.8}$$

where $M_t^i = E(\theta_t | \Omega_t^i)$ and there is a law of motion for the parameter θ

$$\theta_{t+1} = \rho\theta_t + v_{t+1} \tag{14.9}$$

(linear) forecasting formulas for the θ_{t+s} in each market i

$$E(\theta_{t+s} | \Omega_t^i) = \rho^s M_t^i \qquad s = 0, 1, \ldots, \infty, \quad i = 1, 2, \ldots, I \tag{14.10}$$

firm-specific laws of motion for the capital stock in each market i

$$k_{t+1}^i = g_1 k_t^i + g_2 K_t^i + g_3 M_t^i \qquad i = 1, 2, \ldots, I \tag{14.11}$$

and a price equation in each market i

$$P_t^i = \theta_t + \varepsilon_t^i - b_1 f_0 K_t^i \qquad i = 1, 2, \ldots, I \tag{14.12}$$

such that (a) for each firm in market i the individual law of motion (14.11) is maximizing, that is, is derived from (14.7) given the aggregate law of motion (14.8) and market-clearing condition (14.12) for i and parameter motion (14.9), under the forecasting formulas (14.10) for i;[10] (b) for all firms in market i the individual law of motion (14.11) generates the aggregate law (14.8), that is, $g_3 = h_2$, $g_1 + g_2 = h_1$; and (c) for each firm in market i the forecasting formulas (14.10) are statistically correct, that is, based on all available information in market i at time t given the aggregate capital laws and market-clearing conditions (14.8) and (14.2) over all i and parameter law (14.9) and given the forecasting formulas (14.10) over all i.

It must be remarked here that this definition remains somewhat imprecise until the information sets Ω_t^i are specified. It is assumed that Ω_t^i contains *at least* $(M_t^i, M_{t-1}^i, \ldots, K_t^i, K_{t-1}^i, \ldots, P_t^i, P_{t-1}^i, \ldots)$. (Note here that M_t^i denotes common *market* i forecasts, a state variable from the point of view of the individual firm in market i since it describes the beliefs of other firms.) Equilibrium condition (c) allows the possibility that firms in market i see prices and/or capital stocks in other markets, for example, and so statistically correct forecasts must use the laws of motion of these variables. Note that these laws may involve the forecasts in other markets, which, under the definition, must have the same statistically correct property. We will concentrate on this simultaneity in what follows and examine the extent to which it can cause difficulties.

5 A law of motion for market aggregates

The definition of an equilibrium given above may appear somewhat forbidding in a computational sense. However, we can make use of an insight of Sargent (1979) that the law of motion of the aggregate capital stock in each market i can be derived without directly calculating firm-specific laws of motion. Moreover, the aggregate law can be computed without being at all specific about the information sets and forecasting. The details of this procedure are described in the working paper by Townsend (1981). The important result is

$$K_{t+1}^i = \gamma_1 K_t^i + \frac{f_0 \gamma_1 \beta \rho}{f_2(1 - \gamma_1 \beta \rho)} M_t^i \tag{14.13}$$

which has the form of (14.8) in the definition of equilibrium.

Given statistically correct forecasts determining M_t^i and the law of motion (14.13), we can work backward to compute the firm-specific decision rule (14.11). However, this is never done in what follows. Instead, advantage is taken of the insight that statistically correct forecasts along with (14.13) completely determine an equilibrium. Having already computed (14.13), finding an equilibrium here is equivalent to finding statistically correct forecasts if the resulting price sequences are bounded in mean. These forecasts will be functions of the information structure, as is illustrated in the following sections.

6 Equilibrium in a hierarchical information structure

This section[11] focuses on a highly stylized structure in order to illustrate the interplay of forecasts across markets. It is assumed in particular that there are two markets, one which is informationally self-contained and one which receives price but not quantity information from the other. As we shall see in section 7, this structure induces a special kind of volatility in the second market. The present section is devoted to formulation–analysis issues and makes the point that Kalman filtering techniques easily handle the inference problems of decision-makers when the information structure is hierarchical, even if observed time series are endogenous. It will also set the stage for understanding the difficulties which emerge later on when the information structure is symmetric.

More formally, then, assume that there are just two markets, so that $I = 2$. Assume also that the first market is informationally self-contained, so that $\Omega_t^1 = (K_t^1, K_{t-1}^1, \ldots, P_t^1, P_{t-1}^1, \ldots, M_t^1, M_{t-1}^1, \ldots)$. Finally, assume for now that $t = 0$ is a starting date, so that histories extend back to $t = 0$, and that firms in market 1 have an initial prior on the parameter θ_0, at the beginning of date $t = 0$, in particular that θ_0 is regarded as normally distributed with means ρM_{-1}^1 and variance $\sigma^2(\theta_0)$. Thus, with prices *and* quantities known at the end of each period t, the entire history of local shocks $(z_0^1, z_1^1, \ldots, z_t^1)$ is completely deducible at the end of each period t. Thus each firm in market 1 can make direct use of that history to form beliefs on θ_t at the end of period t, that is, to form the distribution of θ_t conditioned on that history. As we will now indicate, there are two ways of deriving these conditional distributions.

One way is to make direct explicit use of the entire history at each date t. Note, in particular, that at the end of period t the representative firm in market 1 has seen

$$\begin{aligned} z_0^1 &= \theta_0 + \varepsilon_0^1 \\ z_1^1 &= \rho\theta_0 + v_1 + \varepsilon_1^1 \\ &\vdots \\ z_t^1 &= \rho^t\theta_0 + \rho^{t-1}v_1 + \ldots + \rho v_{t-1} + v_t + \varepsilon_t^1 \end{aligned}$$

Thus the representative firm can form a posterior distribution on the parameter vector $x' = [\theta_0\, v_1 \ldots v_t]$, conditional on the vector $y' = [z_0^1\, z_1^1 \ldots z_t^1]$ given noise vector $w' = [\varepsilon_0^1\, \varepsilon_1^1 \ldots \varepsilon_t^1]$, via standard formulas for (conditional) means and variances of normal random variables. That is, suppose that we are given that

$$y = Cx + w, \qquad y, w \in R^l, \qquad x \in R^n \tag{14.14}$$

and that the prior normal distribution on x and w is characterized by means and variances

$$E(x) = \bar{x}, \qquad E(w) = \bar{w} \tag{14.15}$$

and

$$\begin{aligned} E\{(x-\bar{x})(x-\bar{x})'\} &= \Sigma_{xx} \\ E\{(w-\bar{w})(w-\bar{w})'\} &= \Sigma_{ww} \end{aligned} \tag{14.16}$$

respectively. Then the posterior distribution of x, conditional on y, has means and variances

$$\hat{x}(y) = \bar{x} + \Sigma_{xx}C'(C\Sigma_{xx}C' + \Sigma_{ww})^{-1}(y - C\bar{x} - \bar{w}) \tag{14.17}$$

and

$$E_y[\{x - \hat{x}(y)\}\{x - \hat{x}(y)\}'] = \Sigma_{xx} - \Sigma_{xx}C'(C\Sigma_{xx}C' + \Sigma_{ww})^{-1}C\Sigma_{xx} \tag{14.18}$$

respectively (see Bertsekas, 1976). Here, then,

$$\bar{x}' = [\rho M_{-1}^1\, 0 \ldots 0] \qquad \bar{w}' = [0\, 0 \ldots 0]$$

$$\Sigma_{xx} = \begin{bmatrix} \sigma^2(\theta_0) & 0 & \ldots & 0 \\ 0 & \sigma_v^2 & \ldots & 0 \\ \vdots & \vdots & \ddots & \vdots \\ 0 & 0 & \ldots & \sigma_v^2 \end{bmatrix} \qquad \Sigma_{ww} = \begin{bmatrix} \sigma_\varepsilon^2 & 0 & \ldots & 0 \\ 0 & \sigma_\varepsilon^2 & & \vdots \\ \vdots & & \ddots & \vdots \\ 0 & & \ldots & \sigma_\varepsilon^2 \end{bmatrix}$$

We might note in passing that in this formulation the firm is learning about the parameter θ_0 at each date $t \geqslant 0$, and thus with more and more observations the posterior distribution on θ_0 should tend to become degenerate with mean θ_0 and variance zero. (In this regard the updating can be viewed as sequential, with only the most recent observations employed explicitly.) Similarly, the firm is learning about the parameter v_1 at each date $t \geqslant 1$, and so on. Thus, in general, the firm should learn parameters in the arbitrarily distant past arbitrarily well. But the variable of interest, $\theta_t = \Sigma_{j=0}^{t-1} \rho^j v_{t-j} + \rho^t \theta_0$, is constantly buffeted by new shocks v_t which are not well understood. Indeed, the posterior distribution for θ_t can now be computed directly, at the end of period t, since it is just a linear combination of a finite number of unknown parameters $(v_t, v_{t-1}, \ldots, \theta_0)$. We might expect that posterior to have a variance which reflects the degree of uncertainty mentioned above and a mean which moves around with the realized history of the shocks v_t.

Finally, we might note that in substituting for y in (14.17) from (14.14) it becomes clear that the mean forecast $\hat{x}(y)$ of x is a linear function of the random variables x and w. In the application here, then, the mean forecast of the parameter v_t is a linear function of the random variables $(v_t, v_{t-1}, \ldots, v_1)$ and $(\varepsilon_t^1, \varepsilon_{t-1}^1, \ldots, \varepsilon_0^1)$. It is already apparent, then, that his learning mechanism is the cause of some persistence. It converts serially uncorrelated economic shocks, the v_t and ε_t^1, into serially correlated forecasts of the shocks v_t. That is, $E(v_t | \Omega_t^1)$ is correlated with $E(v_{t-1} | \Omega_{t-1}^1)$ as both contain v_{t-1}, for example, except in the special case of full information when $\sigma_\varepsilon^2 = 0$. By the same token, then, we anticipate that the mean forecasts of the variables θ_t – say $E(\theta_t | \Omega_t^1)$, $E(\theta_{t-1} | \Omega_{t-1}^1)$ and so on – will be serially correlated with a persistence over and above that present in θ_t itself. That is, the forecast error $E(\theta_t | \Omega_t^1) - \theta_t$ will be serially correlated, and will be a moving average of past random variables v_t and ε_t^1. This will be made clear below.

A distinct disadvantage of the method described above for computing the conditional distribution of θ_t is that the state vector x_t increases in dimension with the length of the history (back to $t = 0$) – there are more and more innovations. An alternative way of computing the conditional distribution of θ_t exploits a recursive algorithm developed by Kalman (1960). That is, suppose that we have under consideration a finite-dimensional state vector x_t, following a linear law of motion

$$x_{t+1} = Ax_t + v_{t+1} \qquad v_t, x_t \in R^n \tag{14.19}$$

with period-by-period observations

$$y_t = Cx_t + w_t \qquad w_t, y_t \in R^l \tag{14.20}$$

Thus the information set Ω_t is $(y_0, y_1, \ldots, y_t)$. Suppose also that

$$E(v_t) = 0, \quad E(w_t) = 0, \quad E[v_t v_t'] = M, \quad E[w_t w_t'] = N \tag{14.21}$$

where w_t and v_t are independent normal random variables. Then, by using the fact that

$$E(x_t|\Omega_t) = E(x_t|\Omega_{t-1}) + E[x_t|\{y_t - E(y_t|\Omega_{t-1})\}] \tag{14.22}$$

standard formulas for conditional means and variances of normal random variables, like (14.17) and (14.18), deliver a law of motion for conditional forecasts

$$E(x_t|\Omega_t) = AE(x_{t-1}|\Omega_{t-1}) + \Sigma_{t|t}C'N^{-1}\{y_t - CAE(x_{t-1}|\Omega_{t-1})\} \tag{14.23}$$

and a law of motion for the variance–covariance matrix

$$\Sigma_{t|t-1} \equiv E[\{x_t - E(x_t|\Omega_{t-1})\}\{x_t - E(x_t|\Omega_{t-1})\}'|\Omega_{t-1}]$$

namely

$$\Sigma_{t+1|t} = A\{\Sigma_{t|t-1} - \Sigma_{t|t-1}C'(C\Sigma_{t|t-1}C' + N)^{-1}C\Sigma_{t|t-1}\}A' + M \tag{14.24}$$

The matrix $\Sigma_{t|t}$ in (14.23) is defined by

$$\begin{aligned}\Sigma_{t|t} &\equiv E[\{x_t - E(x_t|\Omega_t)\}\{x_t - E(x_t|\Omega_t)\}'|\Omega_t] \\ &= \Sigma_{t|t-1} - \Sigma_{t|t-1}C'(C\Sigma_{t|t-1}C' + N)^{-1}C\Sigma_{t|t-1}\end{aligned} \tag{14.25}$$

Moreover, under specified regularity conditions, the variance–covariance matrix $\Sigma_{t|t-1}$ in (14.24) converges to some constant Σ independent of the variance of the initial prior. In this case we can define a constant matrix $\bar{\Sigma}$ from (14.25) by substituting Σ for $\Sigma_{t|t-1}$, and thus coefficients in the linear law of motion (14.23) are no longer time dependent. Moreover, we can interpret this solution as having assumed an *infinite* history so that the steady state has been obtained at $t = 0$. This assumption is useful for analytic and econometric purposes. To reiterate, then, under the Kalman filtering algorithm contemporary mean beliefs can be updated from past mean beliefs and the contemporary observation y_t alone – mean beliefs capture all that is necessary for forecasting from the infinite history.

Returning to the present application, the inference problem faced by firms in the first market, note again that

$$z_t^1 = \theta_t + \varepsilon_t^1 \tag{14.26}$$

and

$$\theta_{t+1} = \rho\theta_t + v_{t+1} \tag{14.27}$$

Thus let $x_t = \theta_t$, $y_t = z_t^1$, $A = \rho$, $C = 1$, $M = \sigma_v^2$, and $N = \sigma_\varepsilon^2$. Therefore, with appropriate substitutions and manipulations, (14.23) yields

$$M_t^1 = \alpha_0 M_{t-1}^1 + \alpha_1 z_t^1 \tag{14.28}$$

where $\alpha_0 = \rho(1 - \bar{\Sigma}/\sigma_\varepsilon^2)$ and $\alpha_1 = \bar{\Sigma}/\sigma_\varepsilon^2$. (Note here that the coefficients α_0 and α_1 can be expressed entirely in terms of ρ and variances σ_ε^2 and σ_v^2.)

Now we can also note that, with an infinite past,

$$M_t^1 = E(\theta_t|\Omega_t^1) = \frac{\alpha_1 v_t}{(1-\alpha_0 L)(1-\rho L)} + \frac{\alpha_1 \varepsilon_t^1}{1-\alpha_0 L} \tag{14.29}$$

and

$$E(\theta_t|\Omega_t^1) - \theta_t = \frac{\alpha_1 v_t}{(1-\alpha_0 L)(1-\rho L)} + \frac{\alpha_1 \varepsilon_t^1}{1-\alpha_0 L} - \frac{v_t}{1-\rho L} \tag{14.30}$$

Thus the forecast error of θ_t is a linear combination of current and past v_t and ε_t^1 and is serially correlated, as was anticipated above.

With this artillery we now turn to the inference problem of firms in a second market. Suppose in particular that firms in some market 2 see price P_t^1 in market 1 in addition to the shock z_t^2 to their own market. That is, suppose $\Omega_t^2 = (K_t^2, K_{t-1}^2, \ldots, P_t^2, P_{t-1}^2, \ldots, M_t^2, M_{t-1}^2, \ldots, P_t^1, P_{t-1}^1, \ldots)$. Thus firms in market 2 do *not* see the aggregate capital stock (output) in the first market and thus do not obtain a second direct observation on θ_t. But firms in market 2 do see a filtered version of the vector of state variables in market 1: the shock θ_t, the mean forecast M_t^1 in market 1, and the capital stock K_t^1 in market 1. That is, letting $x_t' = [K_t^1 \; M_t^1 \; \theta_t]$, note that

$$\begin{bmatrix} K_{t+1}^1 \\ M_{t+1}^1 \\ \theta_{t+1} \end{bmatrix} = \begin{bmatrix} h_1 & h_2 & 0 \\ 0 & \alpha_0 & \alpha_1\rho \\ 0 & 0 & \rho \end{bmatrix} \begin{bmatrix} K_t^1 \\ M_t^1 \\ \theta_t \end{bmatrix} + \begin{bmatrix} 0 \\ \alpha_1 v_{t+1} + \alpha_1 \varepsilon_{t+1}^1 \\ v_{t+1} \end{bmatrix} \tag{14.31}$$

or

$$x_{t+1} = A x_t + v_{t+1}^0 \tag{14.32}$$

Then firms in market 2 see

$$\begin{bmatrix} P_t^1 \\ z_t^2 \end{bmatrix} = \begin{bmatrix} -b_1 f_0 & 0 & 1 \\ 0 & 0 & 1 \end{bmatrix} \begin{bmatrix} K_t^1 \\ M_t^1 \\ \theta_t \end{bmatrix} + \begin{bmatrix} \varepsilon_t^1 \\ \varepsilon_t^2 \end{bmatrix} \tag{14.33}$$

or

$$y_t = Cx_t + w_t^0 \tag{14.34}$$

The point is that (14.34) and (14.32) represent a system to which the Kalman filtering algorithm can again be applied directly. In this application, then, firms in market 2 attempt to keep track of the capital stock and mean forecasts in the first market, as well as the persistent shock θ_t. Again, all these variables are unobserved.

Now, in this case a less trivial Kalman filtering theorem[12] ensures the convergence of the variance–covariance matrix of the conditional distribution of the state vector x_t, defined in (14.31) and (14.32), with means satisfying the recursive relationship of (14.23) or

$$E\left(\begin{bmatrix} K_{t+1}^1 \\ M_{t+1}^1 \\ \theta_{t+1} \end{bmatrix} \middle| \Omega_{t+1}^2\right) = (A - \bar{\Sigma}C'N^{-1}CA)E\left(\begin{bmatrix} K_t^1 \\ M_t^1 \\ \theta_t \end{bmatrix} \middle| \Omega_t^2\right)$$
$$+ \bar{\Sigma}C'N^{-1}\left(\begin{bmatrix} P_{t+1}^1 \\ z_{t+1}^2 \end{bmatrix}\right) \tag{14.35}$$

(Note that here the matrices of coefficients weighting the prior mean and the current observation depend on the parameters of technology and demand, through the definitions of A and C in (14.31)–(14.32) and (14.33)–(14.34) respectively.) Substituting (14.33) at $t+1$ and then (14.31) into (14.35) yields

$$E\left(\begin{bmatrix} K_{t+1}^1 \\ M_{t+1}^1 \\ \theta_{t+1} \end{bmatrix} \middle| \Omega_{t+1}^2\right) = (A - \bar{\Sigma}C'N^{-1}CA)E\left(\begin{bmatrix} K_t^1 \\ M_t^1 \\ \theta_t \end{bmatrix} \middle| \Omega_t^2\right)$$
$$+ \bar{\Sigma}C'N^{-1}CA\begin{bmatrix} K_t^1 \\ M_t^1 \\ \theta_t \end{bmatrix} + \bar{\Sigma}C'N^{-1}Cv_{t+1}^0 + \bar{\Sigma}C'N^{-1}w_{t+1}^0 \tag{14.36}$$

Moreover, substitution of (14.31)–(14.32) into (14.36) and the obvious manipulation yield

$$E\left(\begin{bmatrix} K_t^1 \\ M_t^1 \\ \theta_t \end{bmatrix} \Big| \Omega_t^2 \right) - \begin{bmatrix} K_t^1 \\ M_t^1 \\ \theta_t \end{bmatrix}$$

$$= \{I-(A-\bar{\Sigma}C'N^{-1}CA)L\}^{-1}\{\bar{\Sigma}C'N^{-1}CA(I-AL)^{-1}v_{t-1}^0$$

$$+\bar{\Sigma}C'N^{-1}Cv_t^0+\bar{\Sigma}C'N^{-1}w_t^0\}-(I-AL)^{-1}v_t^0 \tag{14.37}$$

This is the market 2 analog of (14.30), and it is again apparent that the forecast error in market 2 will be serially correlated as a moving average of shocks $\varepsilon_t^1, \varepsilon_t^2$, and v_t. Note also that forecast errors will be serially correlated across markets 1 and 2 owing to the influence of the v_t and the ε_t^1 terms.

In summary, then, this economy with two markets has laws of motion

$$\begin{bmatrix} K_{t+1}^2 \\ E(K_{t+1}^1 | \Omega_{t+1}^2) \\ E(M_{t+1}^1 | \Omega_{t+1}^2) \\ M_{t+1}^2 \\ K_{t+1}^1 \\ M_{t+1}^1 \\ \theta_{t+1} \end{bmatrix} = \begin{bmatrix} h_1 & (0 \;\; 0 \;\; h_2) & 0 \\ 0 & A-\bar{\Sigma}C'N^{-1}CA & \bar{\Sigma}C'N^{-1}CA \\ 0 & 0 & A \end{bmatrix}$$

$$\times \begin{bmatrix} K_t^2 \\ E(K_t^1 | \Omega_t^2) \\ E(M_t^1 | \Omega_t^2) \\ M_t^2 \\ K_t^1 \\ M_t^1 \\ \theta_t \end{bmatrix} + \begin{bmatrix} 0 \\ \bar{\Sigma}C'N^{-1}Cv_{t+1}^0+\bar{\Sigma}C'N^{-1}w_{t+1}^0 \\ v_{t+1}^0 \end{bmatrix} \tag{14.38}$$

The recursive manner in which this hierarchical system is determined is apparent from (14.38): apart from the shocks, motion in the first market determines beliefs in the second market which determine motion in the second market. Note also that this system is stable because the matrices along the diagonal are stable. Therefore all variables are bounded in mean. Thus, prices in each market are bounded in mean, and the existence of an equilibrium is established.

7 Time series dynamics for the hierarchical structure

Now suppose that an econometrician were given time series of capital stocks and prices in both markets. We might ask what implications the theory has for these series, at least for various possible parameter values. One way to answer that question is to look at the implied covariance structure of the data, and indeed that route will be taken in the discussion of formal estimation in section 10. Here we wish to characterize the data, perhaps in a more revealing way, by examining the response of the system from an initial steady state (of zero) to a positive one-standard-deviation impulse in specified economic shocks at date 1, holding all other economic shocks at zero, following the suggestions of Lucas (1975) and Sims (1980a, b).

Consider first the capital stock series in the first market. Note in particular that (14.31) can be written after repeated substitutions as

$$(1-\rho L)(1-h_1 L)(1-\alpha_0 L)K_{t+1}^1 = h_2\alpha_1\sigma_v v_t^* + h_2\alpha_1(1-\rho L)\sigma_\varepsilon \varepsilon_t^{*1} \tag{14.39}$$

where the shocks indicated by an asterisk are normalized to have unit variance. Equation (14.39) completely describes the statistical properties of the capital stock in market 1. These properties become especially clear when a comparison is made with the model with no learning (full information), namely

$$(1-\rho L)(1-h_1 L)K_{t+1}^1 = h_2\sigma_v v_t^* \tag{14.40}$$

In both (14.39) and (14.40), intrinsic persistence will be higher and the capital stock series will be smoother the higher is the serial correlation parameter ρ in the driving stochastic process θ_t, since demand stays high longer, and the higher is the ratio of adjustment costs to revenue (high h_1 is associated with high f_2/f_0) because it is costly to adjust more quickly. The effects of economic shocks can not only persist in (14.39) and (14.40), they can also cumulate in the sense of Lucas (1975). That is, the full effect of the shock is not immediate – there can be a rising portion in the response function (see figure 14.1). However, we might note that in (14.39), relative to (14.40), there is additional persistence induced by the learning which varies directly with the noise in current observations (a high ratio of variances $\sigma_\varepsilon/\sigma_v$ is associated with high α_0). However, (14.39) allows a response to entirely transitory

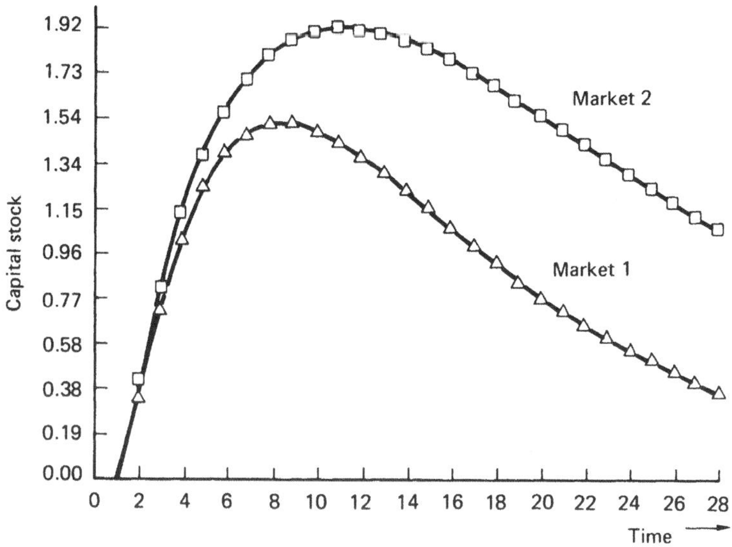

Figure 14.1. Hierarchical structure response to persistent common shock (high adjustment costs)

shocks, the ε_t^1, as these are partially mistaken for relatively persistent shocks v_t. This adds more volatility to the capital stock series.

The statistical process for price in the first market is linearly related to the statistical process for the capital stock via the market-clearing hypothesis. There is in addition a stochastic intercept, representing the period-by-period shocks to demand. That is,

$$P_t^1 = \sum_{j=0}^{\infty} \rho^j v_{t-j} + \varepsilon_t^1 - b_1 f_0 K_t^1 \tag{14.41}$$

The statistical process for the capital stock in the second market is more complicated than in (14.39) since, as noted, (14.41) is taken into account in the inference problems of firms in the second market.[13] It may be noted again that firms in the second market will respond to the relatively persistent shocks v_t as well as to the transitory shocks ε_t^1 and ε_t^2 in both markets. In this sense, the second market is more volatile than the first. But, as they possess more observations, firms in the second market are relatively better informed. Thus market 2 responds more readily to persistent common shocks (see table 14.1 and figure 14.1) and less readily to transitory local shocks in the first market (see table 14.2 and figure 14.2). In this sense, then, the statistical process for

Table 14.1 Hierarchical structure response to persistent common shock (high adjustment costs)

	Mean beliefs		*Capital stock*		
Time	*In island 1*	*In island 2*	*In island 1*	*In island 2*	*Price in island 1*
1	0.597406781	0.723919251	0.000000000	0.000000000	1.000000000
2	0.754126830	0.830056978	0.344032644	0.416888227	0.831193471
3	0.757145206	0.815213292	0.715557441	0.818848934	0.666888512
4	0.709848917	0.786750604	1.021045993	1.138934858	0.524790801
5	0.649160913	0.759951506	1.243569749	1.384238931	0.407386050
6	0.587975734	0.734319136	1.390551374	1.569361062	0.312379725
7	0.530529996	0.708619299	1.475485134	1.705951679	0.236343973
8	0.477966812	0.682456960	1.511843409	1.802825166	0.175928218
9	0.430347608	0.655889972	1.511299207	1.866960475	0.128207369
10	0.387377153	0.629113683	1.483431489	1.904096755	0.090734191
11	0.348662738	0.602335458	1.435901784	1.919038704	0.061498083
12	0.313804907	0.575738991	1.374747835	1.915833951	0.038861029
13	0.282427475	0.549478622	1.304675924	1.897897531	0.021494352
14	0.254185836	0.523681405	1.229317171	1.868110381	0.008323149
15	0.228767654	0.498450495	1.151441842	1.828901060	−0.001520444
16	0.205891034	0.473868351	1.073134982	1.782314506	−0.008735864
17	0.185301983	0.449999559	0.995938937	1.730070100	−0.013885769
18	0.166771804	0.426893300	0.920968428	1.673610764	−0.017421869
19	0.150094631	0.404585512	0.849003123	1.614144522	−0.019705989
20	0.135085170	0.383100788	0.780561909	1.552679721	−0.021027210
21	0.121576654	0.362454051	0.715962309	1.490054926	−0.021615807
22	0.109418989	0.342652015	0.655367885	1.426964325	−0.021654588
23	0.098477090	0.323694470	0.598825928	1.363979332	−0.021288095
24	0.088629381	0.305575409	0.546297307	1.301567008	−0.020630080
25	0.079766443	0.288284008	0.497680019	1.240105746	−0.019769561
26	0.071789799	0.271805480	0.452827655	1.179898682	−0.018775732
27	0.064610819	0.256121823	0.411563805	1.121185137	−0.017701942
28	0.058149737	0.241212463	0.373693200	1.064150407	−0.016588903
29	0.052334763	0.227054816	0.339010256	1.008934138	−0.015467288
30	0.047101287	0.213624767	0.307305551	0.955637496	−0.014359000

Assigned parameters: $\rho = 0.900$; $b_1 = 1.000$; $\beta = 0.960$; $f_0 = 0.200$; $f_1 = 0.000$; $f_2 = 0.800$; $\sigma_v^2 = 1.000$; $\sigma_\varepsilon^2 = 1.000$; $\sigma_\eta^2 = 1.000$. Computed parameters: $h_1 = 0.818$; $h_2 = 0.576$; $\alpha_0 = 0.362$; $\alpha_1 = 0.597$.

Σ matrix (island 1)	Σ matrix (island 2)		
0.597406781	1.362374115	0.312149664	0.169669081
	0.312149664	0.616612548	0.265536615
	0.169669081	0.265536615	0.378926534

K_t^2 moves away from the limited-information system (14.39) toward the full-information system (14.40).

There are, however, some interesting dynamics in the second market which have no parallel in either the full-information system (14.40) or the self-contained system with learning (14.39). Consider the response of the second market to transitory shocks in the first market. Under high adjustment costs (see table 14.3), the best forecast in the second market of the parameter θ_t

Table 14.2 Hierarchical structure response to transitory market 1 shock (low adjustment costs)

Time	*Mean beliefs* In island 1	*Mean beliefs* In island 2	*Capital stock* In island 1	*Capital stock* In island 2	*Price in island 1*
1	0.597406781	0.275942299	0.000000000	0.000000000	1.000000000
2	0.216460727	−0.029342976	0.486052485	0.224507730	−0.388841988
3	0.078431059	−0.012405283	0.276674876	0.022575855	−0.221339901
4	0.028418231	−0.005139347	0.121054325	−0.005422166	−0.096843460
5	0.010296888	−0.004498733	0.048166658	−0.005303209	−0.038533326
6	0.003730912	−0.003886124	0.018343005	−0.004757391	−0.014674404
7	0.001351836	−0.003262932	0.006830551	−0.004146043	−0.005464441
8	0.000489816	−0.002739521	0.002513062	−0.003512528	−0.002010450
9	0.000177477	−0.002301869	0.000918455	−0.002955607	−0.000734764
10	0.000064306	−0.001934158	0.000334419	−0.002484308	−0.000267535
11	0.000023300	−0.001625151	0.000121509	−0.002087628	−0.000097207
12	0.000008442	−0.001365512	0.000044097	−0.001754148	−0.000035277
13	0.000003059	−0.001147353	0.000015992	−0.001473909	−0.000012794
14	0.000001108	−0.000964049	0.000005797	−0.001238435	−0.000004638
15	0.000000402	−0.000810030	0.000002101	−0.001040580	−0.000001681
16	0.000000146	−0.000680617	0.000000761	−0.000874334	−0.000000609
17	0.000000053	−0.000571880	0.000000276	−0.000734648	−0.000000221
18	0.000000019	−0.000480515	0.000000100	−0.000617278	−0.000000080
19	0.000000007	−0.000403747	0.000000036	−0.000518660	−0.000000029
20	0.000000003	−0.000339243	0.000000013	−0.000435798	−0.000000011
21	0.000000001	−0.000285044	0.000000005	−0.000366173	−0.000000004
22	0.000000000	−0.000239505	0.000000002	−0.000307673	−0.000000001
23	0.000000000	−0.000201241	0.000000001	−0.000258518	−0.000000000
24	0.000000000	−0.000169090	0.000000000	−0.000217216	−0.000000000
25	0.000000000	−0.000142076	0.000000000	−0.000182513	−0.000000000
26	0.000000000	−0.000119377	0.000000000	−0.000153354	−0.000000000
27	0.000000000	−0.000100305	0.000000000	−0.000128854	−0.000000000
28	0.000000000	−0.000084280	0.000000000	−0.000108268	−0.000000000
29	0.000000000	−0.000070815	0.000000000	−0.000090971	−0.000000000
30	0.000000000	−0.000059502	0.000000000	−0.000076437	−0.000000000

Assigned parameters: $\rho = 0.900$; $b_1 = 1.000$; $\beta = 0.960$; $f_0 = 0.800$; $f_1 = 0.000$; $f_2 = 0.200$; $\sigma_v^2 = 1.000$; $\sigma_\varepsilon^2 = 1.000$; $\sigma_\eta^2 = 1.000$. Computed parameters: $h_1 = 0.207$; $h_2 = 0.814$; $\alpha_0 = 0.362$; $\alpha_1 = 0.597$.

Σ matrix (island 1)	Σ matrix (island 2)		
0.597406781	0.490756468	0.316838956	0.211021629
	0.316838956	0.689790614	0.347483817
	0.211021629	0.347483817	0.444759602

(which remains zero) first increases, then goes negative, then becomes positive again, and then seems to decrease toward zero. Thus forecast errors on θ_t display (sharply) damped oscillations around the steady state. This "volatility" can be contrasted with the usual exponential decay of forecast errors in the first market under (14.39). Clearly, firms in the second market are drawing inferences from the price in the first market, which is first positive and then negative. However, the negative inferences are eventually corrected.

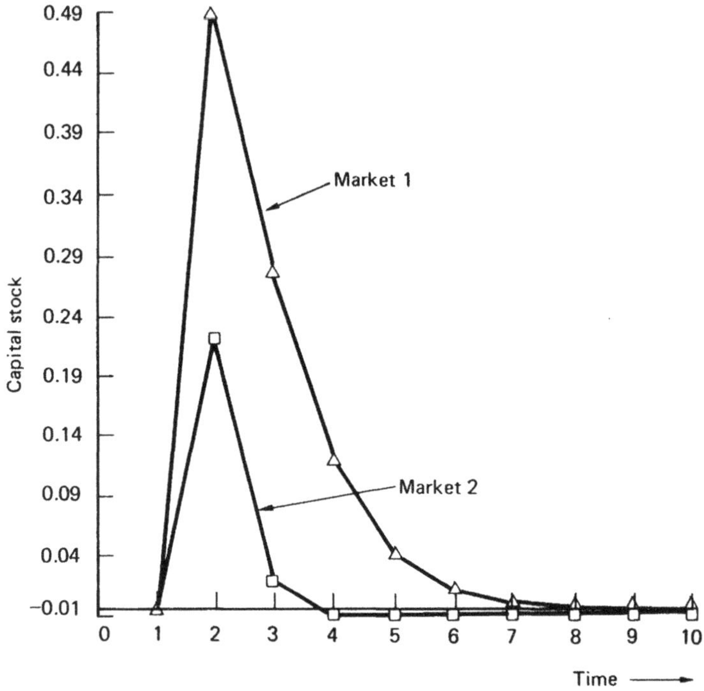

Figure 14.2. Hierarchical structure response to transitory market 1 shock (high adjustment costs)

(Recall that all variables should be interpreted as variations from steady state values.)

When adjustment costs are low (see table 14.2), we again observe the strikingly different behavior forecasts in the two markets (see figure 14.3). Here forecasts in the second market remain negative enough to pull the capital stock in the second market below its steady state value (see figure 14.2).

As between tables 14.2 and 14.3, the qualitatively different nature of the response to a transitory shock for low and high adjustment costs respectively can be attributed in part to the different steady state covariance matrix of the conditional distribution of beliefs in the second market, reported in the tables as the $\bar{\Sigma}$ matrix, which is quite sensitive to the adjustment cost parameters f_0 and f_2. In neither case, however, are there any zero entries in that matrix. In particular, under the assumed parameter specifications, firms in market 2 never learn with certainty the capital stock in market 1. This is what generates the interesting dynamics. That is, the space spanned by current and past prices in market 1 is not equivalent to the space spanned by the current and past market 1 shocks z_t^1.

Table 14.3 Hierarchical structure response to transitory market 1 shock (high adjustment costs)

Time	*Mean beliefs* *In island 1*	*In island 2*	*Capital stock* *In island 1*	*In island 2*	*Price in island 1*
1	0.597403342	0.344998702	0.000000000	0.000000000	1.000000000
2	0.216461330	0.064259251	0.344030663	0.198676713	−0.068806133
3	0.078431947	0.005355471	0.405926789	0.199439029	−0.081185358
4	0.028418796	−0.002231772	0.377043768	0.166140967	−0.075408754
5	0.010297181	−0.001425525	0.324628249	0.134547903	−0.064925650
6	0.003731050	−0.000429915	0.271338681	0.109182420	−0.054267736
7	0.001351897	0.000000616	0.223989043	0.089017519	−0.044797809
8	0.000489842	0.000131948	0.183906943	0.072779082	−0.036781389
9	0.000177488	0.000157482	0.150640280	0.059578531	−0.030128056
10	0.000064310	0.000153722	0.123262325	0.048800761	−0.024652465
11	0.000023302	0.000143964	0.100813547	0.039986932	−0.020162709
12	0.000008443	0.000133894	0.082436314	0.032775325	−0.016487263
13	0.000003059	0.000124516	0.067402943	0.026873477	−0.013480589
14	0.000001108	0.000115860	0.055108896	0.022042857	−0.011021779
15	0.000000402	0.000107841	0.045056436	0.018088467	−0.009011287
16	0.000000146	0.000100389	0.036837362	0.014850828	−0.007367472
17	0.000000053	0.000093456	0.030117485	0.012199516	−0.006023497
18	0.000000019	0.000087002	0.024623410	0.010027870	−0.004924682
19	0.000000007	0.000080994	0.020131559	0.008248664	−0.004026312
20	0.000000003	0.000075401	0.016459115	0.006790565	−0.003291823
21	0.000000001	0.000070194	0.013456605	0.005595235	−0.002691321
22	0.000000000	0.000065346	0.011001819	0.004614961	−0.002200364
23	0.000000000	0.000060834	0.008994840	0.003810720	−0.001798968
24	0.000000000	0.000056633	0.007353980	0.003150592	−0.001470796
25	0.000000000	0.000052722	0.006012449	0.002608467	−0.001202490
26	0.000000000	0.000049081	0.004915643	0.002162985	−0.000983129
27	0.000000000	0.000045691	0.004018920	0.001796672	−0.000803784
28	0.000000000	0.000042536	0.003285779	0.001495232	−0.000657156
29	0.000000000	0.000039599	0.002686379	0.001246963	−0.000537276
30	0.000000000	0.000036864	0.002196323	0.001042293	−0.004392646

Assigned parameters: $\rho = 0.900$; $b_1 = 1.000$; $\beta = 0.960$; $f_0 = 0.200$; $f_1 = 0.000$; $f_2 = 0.800$; $\sigma_v^2 = 1.000$; $\sigma_\varepsilon^2 = 1.000$; $\sigma_\eta^2 = 1.000$. Computed parameters: $h_1 = 0.818$; $h_2 = 0.576$; $\alpha_0 = 0.362$; $\alpha_1 = 0.597$.

Σ matrix (island 1)

0.597403342

Σ matrix (island 2)

1.361775834	0.312092067	0.169608920
0.312092067	0.616601903	0.265529661
0.169608920	0.265529661	0.378920486

8 Equilibrium in a symmetric information structure with confounding

In the hierarchical structure, firms in the second market are forming inferences on the basis of an endogenous time series – prices in the first market. These prices depend on the aggregate capital stock in the first market, which the firms do not see. The law of motion of this capital stock is known, however, though it depends on beliefs in the first market, which the firms in the second

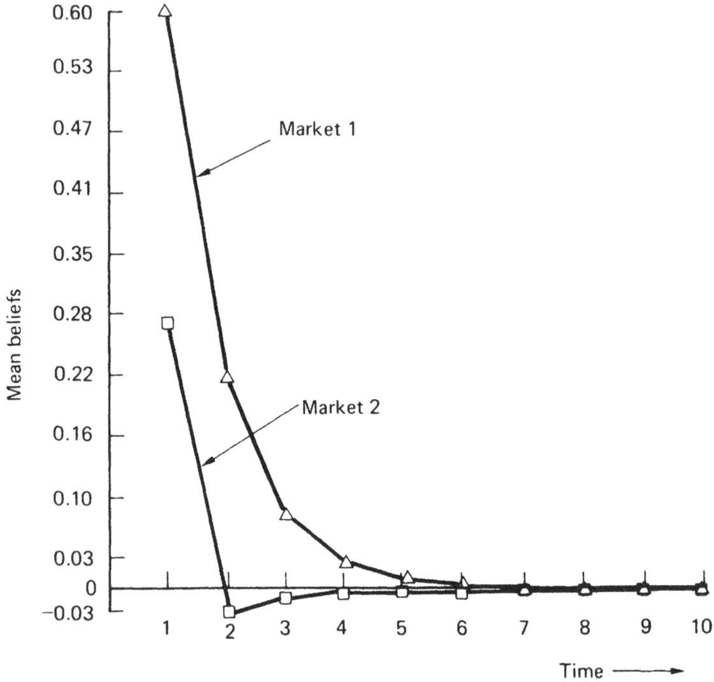

Figure 14.3. Hierarchical structure response to transitory market 1 shock (low adjustment costs)

market do not see. The law of motion of these beliefs is known, however, and depends on the underlying demand shock θ_t, with known law of motion. In summary, firms in the second market are forming expectations on the expectations in the first market, but the laws of motion of the market 1 expectations are well defined and can be expressed in terms of a finite number of state variables. Thus the Kalman filter can be applied. In fact, we could well add another layer on to the hierarchical information structure, supposing that firms in some third market see prices in the second market and so on, building on system (14.38).

We might well ask, though, what would happen in a symmetric rather than a hierarchical information structure. Thus, suppose that firms in market 1 (firms 1) see P_t^2. Then, to make inferences, firms 1 must have expectations on M_t^2, say $E_t^1(M_t^2)$. But firms in market 2 (firms 2) see P_t^1 also. Therefore firms 2 must have expectations on M_t^1. But M_t^1 is related to $E_t^1(M_t^2)$. Thus firms 2 need to have expectations on M_t^1 *and* $E_t^1(M_t^2)$, say $E_t^2(M_t^1)$ and $E_t^2E_t^1(M_t^2)$. Returning to market 1, it becomes apparent that there is an infinite regress problem here (see also Townsend, 1978, this volume, ch. 13).

In the space of mean beliefs, at least, we seem to have need of an infinite number of state variables, but then it is no longer possible to make use of *standard* Kalman filtering formulas. This section is devoted to a discussion of this problem and possible solutions.

The infinite regress problem also emerges in a model with an infinity of markets where it is somewhat easier to analyze. Suppose that firms in each market see an economy-wide average price $\bar{P}_t$ with error η_t, that is, see $P_t = \bar{P} + \eta_t$ where $\bar{P}_t = \lim_{I \to \infty} \Sigma_{i=1}^{I} (P_t^i/I)$, and η_t is distributed normally with mean zero and variance σ_η^2, independent of v_t and of ε_t^i, for all i. Of course, averaging over markets, $\bar{P}_t = -b_1 f_0 K_t + \theta_t$ where the economy-wide average capital stock is $\bar{K}_t = \lim_{I \to \infty} \Sigma_{i=1}^{I} (K_t^i/I)$ and the economy-wide average local shock is zero, that is, $\lim_{I \to \infty} \Sigma_{i=1}^{I} (\varepsilon_t^i/I) = 0$ by the law of large numbers. Then firms in each market i attempt to make inferences about the economy-wide common demand shock θ_t on the basis of noisy economy-wide price data P_t and the market-specific shocks z_t^i. But to do this they must in effect make inferences about the economy-wide average capital stock (output) which they do not see. The law of motion of the latter is known to depend on economy-wide average mean beliefs. Therefore firms in each market would need to make inferences about such beliefs, and the infinite regress is started.

The general problem is that laws of motion are needed for the inference problems, but the inferences in turn determine the laws of motion. In this section we capture this simultaneity by returning to the space of contemporary and past economic innovations. The model is then written down in the form of moving-average representations, and the method of undetermined coefficients is used to handle the simultaneity.

To begin, let $\bar{M}_t = \lim_{I \to \infty} \Sigma_{i=1}^{I} (M_t^i/I)$ denote economy-wide average mean beliefs. Now suppose that economy-wide average mean beliefs follow

$$\bar{M}_t = C(L)v_t + D(L)\eta_t \tag{14.42}$$

where $C(L)$ and $D(L)$ are polynomials in the lag operator with coefficients yet to be determined. These polynomials need not be of finite order. Then, averaging across markets, the law of motion for the economy-wide average capital stock is

$$\bar{K}_t = h_1 \bar{K}_{t-1} + h_2 \bar{M}_{t-1} \tag{14.43}$$

Substitution of (14.42) at $t-1$ into (14.43) and the obvious manipulation yield

$$\bar{K}_t = \frac{h_2 C(L) L}{1 - h_1 L} v_t + \frac{h_2 D(L) L}{1 - h_1 L} \eta_t \tag{14.44}$$

on the assumption of an infinite past. Thus we can write the observations of firms in market i at time t as

$$z_t^i = \frac{v_t}{1-\rho L} + \varepsilon_t^i \tag{14.45}$$

$$P_t = \left\{\frac{1}{1-\rho L} - \frac{b_1 f_0 h_2 C(L) L}{1-h_1 L}\right\} v_t + \left\{1 - \frac{b_1 f_0 h_2 D(L) L}{1-h_1 L}\right\} \eta_t \tag{14.46}$$

As in section 6, we might hope to make use of the observer equations (14.45)–(14.46) at $t, t-1$, and so on with formulas for conditional means and variances of normal random variables to form posterior distributions at date t on the innovations $v_t, v_{t-1}, \ldots$, with means $E(v_t|\Omega_t^i)$, $E(v_{t-1}|\Omega_t^i), \ldots$, and so on. These means might in turn be expressed in terms of current and past economic innovations $v_t, v_{t-1}, \ldots, \eta_t, \eta_{t-1}, \ldots, \varepsilon_t^i, \varepsilon_{t-1}^i, \ldots$. Then these means might be used to form conditional mean forecasts of θ_t at time t, that is, $M_t^i = R(\theta_t|\Omega_t^i) = \Sigma_{j=0}^{\infty} \rho^j E(v_{t-j}|\Omega_t^i)$. We might then average over markets i and deliver an equation of the form (14.42). We might then hope that the coefficients in $C(L)$ and $D(L)$ could be determined.

A potential problem with this approach is the appearance of an infinite number of innovations. To circumvent this problem, we might assume an initial starting date, an initial prior distribution, and an appropriate (and possibly time-dependent) specification of (14.42). However, this approach is awkward at best, and there remains the problem of increasing dimensionality over time, as in section 6.

An alternative approach, which keeps the dimensionality finite but allows the advantage of an infinite past, is to alter the information structure somewhat. Suppose that all economic innovations dated $t-j$ and backward are known at date t (see also Chari, 1979). For example, suppose that $j = 2$. Then

$$\Omega_t^i = \{P_t^i, P_{t-1}^i, \ldots, K_t^i, K_{t-1}^i, \ldots, M_t^i, M_{t-1}^i, \ldots, P_t, P_{t-1}, \ldots, \\ \eta_{t-2}, \eta_{t-3}, \ldots, v_{t-2}, v_{t-3}, \ldots, \varepsilon_{t-2}^i, \varepsilon_{t-3}^i, \ldots\}$$

Then there are a *finite* number of observation variables in market i at date t containing information on the unknown innovations, namely

$$z_t^{i*} = v_t + \rho v_{t-1} + \varepsilon_t^i \tag{14.47}$$

$$z_{t-1}^{i**} = v_{t-1} + \varepsilon_{t-1}^i \tag{14.48}$$

$$P_t^* = v_t + \rho v_{t-1} - b_1 f_0 h_2 D_0 \eta_{t-1} - b_1 f_0 h_2 C_0 v_{t-1} + \eta_t \tag{14.49}$$

$$P_{t-1}^{**} = v_{t-1} + \eta_{t-1} \tag{14.50}$$

where the variables indicated by single and double asterisks on the left-hand side of (14.47)–(14.50) are defined implicitly and include all past *known* innovations. (Note here from (14.43) that $\bar{K}_{t-1}$ and $\bar{K}_{t-2}$ are known at time t.) Thus we can make use of the standard formulas for conditional means and variances.[14] In (14.17)–(14.18), for example, let

$$x' = [v_t \;\; v_{t-1}] \qquad \bar{x}' = [0 \;\; 0]$$

$$y' = [z_t^{i*} \;\; z_{t-1}^{i**} \;\; P_t^* \;\; P_{t-1}^{**}] \qquad w' = [\varepsilon_t^i \;\; \varepsilon_{t-1}^i \;\; \eta_t - b_1 f_0 h_2 D_0 \eta_{t-1} \;\; \eta_{t-1}]$$

and so on. Then (14.17) delivers $E(v_t|\Omega_t^i)$ and $E(v_{t-1}|\Omega_t^i)$ as linear functions of $v_t, v_{t-1}, \varepsilon_t^i, \varepsilon_{t-1}^i, \eta_t$, and η_{t-1}. That is,

$$M_t^i = E(v_t|\Omega_t^i) + \rho E(v_{t-1}|\Omega_t^i) + \sum_{j=2}^{\infty} \rho^j v_{t-j} \tag{14.51}$$

which takes on the form

$$M_t^i = \psi_0 v_t + \psi_1 v_{t-1} + \phi_0 \eta_t + \phi_1 \eta_{t-1} + \Lambda_1 \varepsilon_t^i + \Lambda_1 \varepsilon_{t-1}^i + \sum_{j=2}^{\infty} \rho^j v_{t-j} \tag{14.52}$$

Averaging over markets i then yields

$$\bar{M}_t = \psi_0 v_t + \psi_1 v_{t-1} + \phi_0 \eta_t + \phi_1 \eta_{t-1} + \sum_{j=2}^{\infty} \rho^j v_{t-j} \tag{14.53}$$

This is of the same form as (14.42) and so we can hope to match coefficients, namely

$$\psi_0 = C_0, \quad \phi_0 = D_0 \tag{14.54}$$

We will return to (14.54) below.

Of course, the procedure just described can be applied to any finite full-information lag specification, that is, with economic innovations dated $t-j$ and backward known at date t, j finite. However, it is also apparent that the dimensionality problem begins to re-emerge as j increases; a matrix of dimensions $2j$ must be inverted.

This observation alone might motivate the search for an alternative more recursive procedure. As it turns out, there exists an alternative procedure which is of intrinsic interest, given the topic of this chapter, since it makes clear and exploits the distinction between shocks to driving stochastic processes, economic shocks, and shocks which are innovations relative to decision-makers' information sets.

To begin to describe the alternative procedure, assume that we have under consideration a system of the form

$$y_t = M(L)\xi_t \tag{14.55}$$

where $M(L)$ is a polynomial which is one-sided in nonnegative powers of L. Then the observation variables y_t are just moving averages of past observable shocks ξ_t (the ξ_t are assumed to be serially uncorrelated and to have an identity variance–covariance matrix). Then we make use of the powerful Wiener–Kolmogorov prediction formulas, namely

$$E_t(y_{t+1}) = \left|\frac{M(L)}{L}\right|_+ \xi_t \tag{14.56}$$

and

$$E_t(y_{t+2}) = \left|\frac{M(L)}{L^2}\right|_+ \xi_t \tag{14.57}$$

and so on, where the subscript + means that negative powers of L should be ignored. Clearly, these predictions are easily calculated.

Returning to equations (14.47) and (14.49) and assuming full information at $t-2$, for example, we can write

$$\begin{bmatrix} v_{t-2} \\ z_t^{i*} \\ P_t^* \end{bmatrix} = \begin{bmatrix} L^2 & 0 & 0 \\ (1+\rho L) & 1 & 0 \\ (1+\alpha L) & 0 & (1-\delta L) \end{bmatrix} \begin{bmatrix} v_t \\ \varepsilon_t^i \\ \eta_t \end{bmatrix} \tag{14.58}$$

where $\alpha = \rho - b_1 f_0 h_2 C_0$ and $\delta = b_1 f_0 h_2 D_0$. System (14.58) is similar in appearance to (14.55), that is, it can be written as $y_t = M(L)\xi_t$, but there is an obvious problem: the shocks on the right-hand side of (14.58) are *not* observable or deducible (note that, in (14.58), $M(L)$ does not have an inverse which is one-sided in nonnegative powers of L). Equivalently, the moving-average system (14.58) is not fundamental relative to the information sets of firms in market i. To make use of the Wiener–Kolmogorov prediction formulas, we must express the variables on the right-hand side of (14.58) in terms of observable or deducible shocks.[15] That is, we must find a representation which is fundamental relative to the information sets of firms.

To motivate the search for this fundamental moving-average representation, consider the covariance generating function for the y_t in (14.58), namely

$g(z)=\Sigma_{h=-\infty}^{+\infty}\gamma(h)z^h$, where $\gamma(h)=E[y_t y'_{t+h}]$, a function which thus describes the entire variance–covariance structure of the observables y_t. On the assumption of unit variances, $\sigma_\varepsilon^2=\sigma_\eta^2=\sigma_v^2=1$, which is not essential, and following Sargent (1979), the function $g(z)$ can be written

$$g(z)=M(z)M(z^{-1})' \tag{14.59}$$

or, alternatively,

$$g(z)=M(z)WB(z)\hat{W}B(z)B(z^{-1})'\hat{W}'B(z^{-1})'W'M(z^{-1})' \tag{14.60}$$

where

$$B(z)B(z^{-1})'=1 \qquad WW'=I \qquad \hat{W}\hat{W}'=I \tag{14.61}$$

Here $B(z)$ is the Blaschke factor discussed by Hansen and Sargent (1981). Thus the variance–covariance structure of the data does not pin down a unique moving-average representation. The idea, then, from (14.60) is to convert the representation (14.58) to a fundamental representation

$$y_t=M^{**}(L)\xi_t^{**} \tag{14.62}$$

that is, with known innovation ξ_t^{**} where

$$M^{**}(L)=M(L)WB(L)\hat{W}B(L) \tag{14.63}$$

$$\xi_t^{**}=B(L^{-1})'\hat{W}'B(L^{-1})'W'\xi_t \tag{14.64}$$

The reader is referred to the appendix for details of the calculations. Again, the Wiener–Kolmogorov prediction formulas are

$$E\left(\begin{bmatrix} v_{t-1} \\ z_{t+1}^{i*} \\ P_{t+1}^{*} \end{bmatrix} \middle| \Omega_t^i\right)=\left\{\frac{M^{**}(L)}{L}\right\}_+ \xi_t^{**} \tag{14.65}$$

$$E\left(\begin{bmatrix} v_{t} \\ z_{t+2}^{i*} \\ P_{t+2}^{*} \end{bmatrix} \middle| \Omega_t^i\right)=\left\{\frac{M^{**}(L)}{L^2}\right\}_+ \xi_t^{**} \tag{14.66}$$

for the one-step-ahead and two-step-ahead forecasts. Therefore, to forecast

v_t and v_{t-1}, we need only the first row of $M^{**}(z)$:

$$\frac{1}{\sqrt{3}}\hat{W}_{11}+\frac{2z}{\sqrt{6}}\hat{W}_{21}\frac{z}{\sqrt{3}}\hat{W}_{12}+\frac{2z^2}{\sqrt{6}}\hat{W}_{22}\frac{2z^2}{\sqrt{6}}\hat{W}_{23}$$

Thus

$$E(v_{t-1}|\Omega_t^i)=\frac{2\hat{W}_{21}}{\sqrt{6}}\xi_{1t}^{**}+\frac{\hat{W}_{12}}{\sqrt{3}}\xi_{2t}^{**}+\frac{2\hat{W}_{22}}{\sqrt{6}}\xi_{2,t-1}^{**}+\frac{2\hat{W}_{23}}{\sqrt{6}}\xi_{3,t-1}^{**} \tag{14.67}$$

and

$$E(v_t|\Omega_t^i)=\frac{2\hat{W}_{22}}{\sqrt{6}}\xi_{2t}^{**}+\frac{2\hat{W}_{23}}{\sqrt{6}}\xi_{3t}^{**} \tag{14.68}$$

These prediction formulas are linear in the ξ^{**} with coefficients linear in the $\hat{W}_{ij}$.

To search for the undetermined coefficients C_0 and D_0, (14.67) and (14.68) must be cast in terms of the economic innovations v_t, η_t, and ε_t^i. The relationship is expressed in (14.64). For example,

$$\xi_{1t}^{**}=\left(\frac{2}{\sqrt{6}}\hat{W}_{21}L+\frac{1}{\sqrt{3}}\hat{W}_{11}L^2\right)v_t+\left(\frac{1}{\sqrt{2}}\hat{W}_{31}L+\frac{1}{\sqrt{6}}\hat{W}_{21}L-\frac{1}{\sqrt{3}}\hat{W}_{11}L^2\right)\varepsilon_t^i$$
$$+\left(-\frac{1}{\sqrt{2}}\hat{W}_{31}L+\frac{1}{\sqrt{6}}\hat{W}_{21}L-\frac{1}{\sqrt{3}}\hat{W}_{11}L^2\right)\eta_t \tag{14.69}$$

We can thus see how the information set innovations are linear functions of current and past economic shocks. Substituting expressions like (14.69) into (14.67) and (14.68) yields the forecasts $E(v_{t-1}|\Omega_t^i)$ and $E(v_t|\Omega_t^i)$ as linear functions of v_t, v_{t-1}, ε_t^i, ε_{t-1}^i, η_t, and η_{t-1}, with coefficients which are quadratic in the W_{ij}. This again solves the forecasting problem.[16]

We turn now to the problem of finding the undetermined C_0 and D_0 from equation (14.54). We might note in particular that C_0 and D_0 enter on the left-hand side of (14.54) in the parameters ψ_0 and ϕ_0. That is, parameters C_0 and D_0 were taken as given by the firms in solving their inference problems. But these inferences in turn determine the law of motion in (14.42) and thus affect the parameters ψ_0 and ϕ_0. This is the confounding problem. We may note, moreover, the fundamentally nonlinear nature of this problem. The parameters C_0 and D_0 determine (in part) the coefficients $\hat{W}_{ij}$, and ψ_0 and ϕ_0 are quadratic functions of the latter. Still, equations (14.54) turn out to be not all that awesome. The existence and uniqueness of solutions are established in the appendix, making use of the Blaschke procedure.

The mapping described in the appendix also suggests a scheme for computing solutions to (14.54): the method of successive approximations. Though there is no formal basis for supposing that solutions can be computed by this method – that is, the mapping is not shown to be a contraction – in practice this method generates the solution quickly for a broad range of initial parameter values (for example, accurate to eight decimal places after ten iterations). The economics behind this method is somewhat reassuring. Suppose that firms were to take as given some (arbitrary) moving-average representation for economy-wide average forecasts of the common demand shock. Then the inference problem in each market becomes well defined and produces a best forecast in each market of the common shock. Averaging over markets, we arrive at a new moving-average representation. Repeating the process, there is convergence to a situation in which average forecasts in the population are consistent with best forecasts based on that average.[17] (This is reminiscent of a convergence result in Lucas (1978).)

In concluding this section, it should be noted from (14.52) that the response of M^i_{t+j} to innovations η_t, ε^i_t, and v_t is determined entirely by the coefficient ρ^j on v_t after j periods for j sufficiently large. Thus M^i_t is stable, and so K^i_t and P^i_t are stable and therefore bounded in mean. Thus the existence of an equilibrium has been established.

9 Time series dynamics for the symmetric structure

Now suppose that an econometrician were to observe economy-wide average capital stock and price series for the economy of section 8. To characterize the restrictions which the theory puts on these series, we will examine responses to measurement errors and to innovations in economic shocks at date 1 for various possible parameter values.

To begin, note from (14.42) and the law of motion for economy-wide average capital stock that

$$(1-h_1L)\bar{K}_{t+1}=h_2\{C(L)v_t+D(L)\eta_t\} \tag{14.70}$$

with economy-wide average price determined by

$$\bar{P}_t=-b_1f_0\bar{K}_t+\sum_{j=0}^{\infty}\rho^j v_{t-j} \tag{14.71}$$

The response of system (14.70)–(14.71) to shocks v_t in the common demand component is very much as expected with the extent of cumulation and persistence varying directly with the magnitude of the autocorrelation parameter ρ and the degree of costly capital adjustment f_2/f_0. More interesting experiments concern the response of the system to measurement errors η_t. Though there are no oscillations in forecast errors (or output), a somewhat surprising feature is the magnitude and extent of the response to such bogus shocks, as displayed in figure 14.4. For the case of relatively high adjustment costs, the capital stock cumulates and takes considerable time to slide back toward its steady state value. This is so even if firms are given full information after two periods ($j = 2$). In fact the response patterns are not very different for the case of the longer information lags; the case $j = 20$ is computed here using Subramanian's (1982) program and displayed in figure 14.4. For the case of relatively low adjustment costs, the response patterns are again not very different. There is more persistence when the lag to full information increases, the $j = 20$ case (see figure 14.5). However, the initial response to the measurement error in the $j = 20$ case is now slightly *less* than in the $j = 2$ case, though firms have relatively less information overall. Again, the steady state variance–covariance matrix of beliefs is sensitive to the adjustment cost parameters f_0 and f_2.

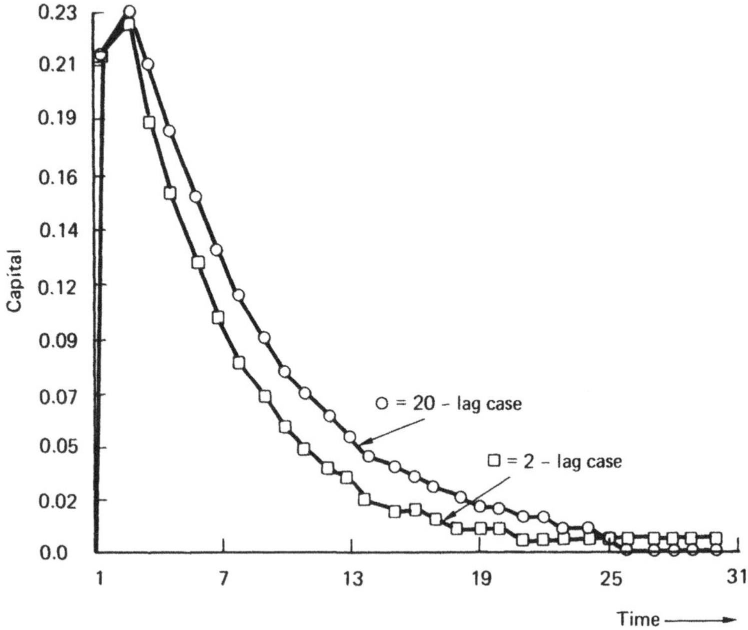

Figure 14.4. Symmetric structure response to measurement error (high adjustment costs)

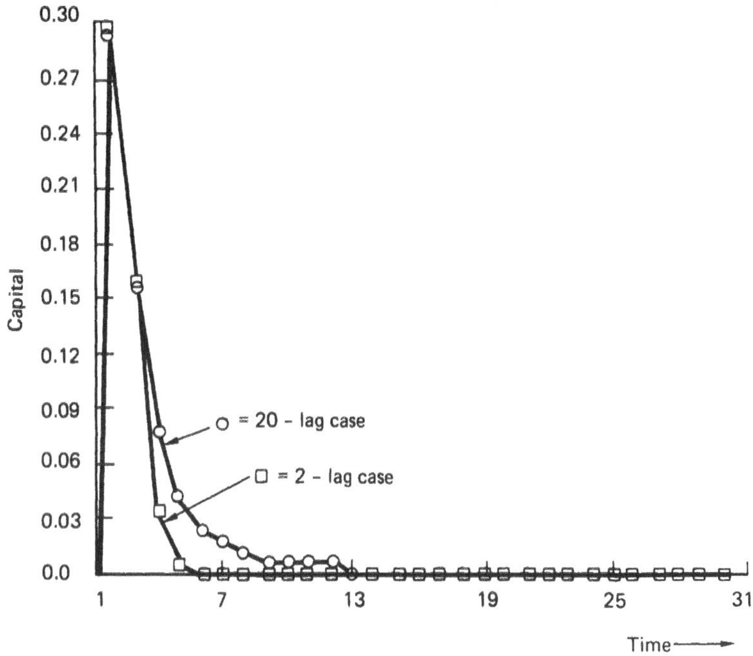

Figure 14.5. Symmetric structure response to measurement error (low adjustment costs)

10 Fitting the theory to data (in principle)

We now ask if an econometrician could determine in principle whether the theories with learning and somewhat sophisticated expectation formation being proposed in this chapter are consistent with actual data. One way we might hope to do this, consistent with the time series dynamics already presented and with the work of Sims (1980a, b), is to look in the data for patterns of response to economic shocks or innovations and to try to match these with response patterns predicted by the theory. We will comment on this procedure at the end of this section. For now, however, we merely note that these response patterns are a convenient way, but not the only way, of describing the variance–covariance structure of the variables observed by the econometrician. Formal estimation or "fitting" procedures try to match directly the variance–covariance structure of observables with the variance–covariance structure of corresponding variables of the theory.

To be more precise, we will adopt here, with suitable modifications, a technique of Sargent (1978, 1981) and Hansen and Sargent (1980a, b) which lets the theory deliver the entire econometric model including the error term.

The econometric model is not exact, because the econometrician treats both forecasts and underlying economic shocks as unobservable latent variables. Here, as in the Hansen–Sargent papers, the theory implies certain cross-equation restrictions on the coefficients of the econometric model and certain lag (zero) restrictions on its errors terms as well. We then use these restrictions to estimate and identify the underlying parameters of the theory – the parameters of preferences, technology, and driving stochastic processes. There follows a caveat on the "exact" nature of such error term models. This will provoke a discussion of the possibilities and limitations of more standard econometric procedures, on the one hand, and a suggestion of Kydland and Prescott (1982), on the other. As noted, this section concludes with some comments on Sims's suggestion for summarizing data and a caveat on that method.

To begin, suppose that an econometrician had available time series on the capital stock and price in the first market in the hierarchical structure of section 6. (We will focus on the first market alone in order to concentrate on method.) Suppose, however, that the underlying shocks v_t and ε_t^1 are unobserved by the econometrician. Thus market beliefs M_t^1 and these shocks play the role of unobserved variables and, following Hansen and Sargent, deliver the error term in the vector time series, which is a mixed autoregressive moving-average (ARMA) process:

$$\begin{bmatrix} (1-\rho L)(1-h_1 L)(1-\alpha_0 L) & 0 \\ 0 & (1-\rho L)(1-h_1 L)(1-\alpha_0 L) \end{bmatrix} \begin{bmatrix} K_{t+1}^1 \\ P_t^1 \end{bmatrix}$$

$$= \begin{bmatrix} h_2\alpha_1\sigma_v & h_2\alpha_1(1-\rho L)\}\sigma_\varepsilon \\ \{(1-h_1L)(1-\alpha_0L)-b_1f_0h_2\alpha_1L\}\sigma_v & \{(1-h_1L)(1-\rho L)(1-\alpha_0L)-b_1f_0h_2\alpha_1L(1-\rho L)\}\sigma_\varepsilon \end{bmatrix} \begin{bmatrix} v_t^* \\ \varepsilon_t^{*1} \end{bmatrix} \quad (14.72)$$

System (14.72) is the econometric model. We note immediately the various zero restrictions on the coefficients of the lag structure and the cross-equations restrictions on coefficients in terms of the parameters of the model: $f_0, f_1, f_2, \rho, \beta, \sigma_\varepsilon^2, \sigma_v^2, b_1$. (Note that these parameters determine h_1, h_2, α_0, and α_1.)

Now suppose that an econometrician were given data over T periods, $K^1(T)' = [K_1^1 K_2^1 \ldots K_T^1]$ and $P^1(T)' = [P_0^1 P_1^1 \ldots P_{T-1}^1]$. On the assumption (consistent with the theory) that these data are generated from a normal distribution, the likelihood function is

$$l(T) = -\tfrac{1}{2}(2T)\log(2\pi) - \tfrac{1}{2}\log\det\{\Gamma(T)\} - \tfrac{1}{2}[K^1(T)'P^1(T)']\Gamma(T)^{-1}\begin{bmatrix} K^1(T) \\ P^1(T) \end{bmatrix} \tag{14.73}$$

where

$$\Gamma(T) = E\begin{bmatrix} K^1(T) \\ P^1(T) \end{bmatrix}[K^1(T)'P^1(T)']$$

is the variance–covariance matrix and is determined by the theory and the parameters of the model. Maximum likelihood estimates are derived by maximizing $l(T)$ with respect to various feasible values for these parameters.

It is instructive to see how $\Gamma(T)$ is determined by theory and the parameters of the model. For convenience, system (14.72) can be rewritten as

$$H_1(L)\begin{bmatrix} K^1_{t+1} \\ P^1_t \end{bmatrix} = H_2(L)\begin{bmatrix} v^*_t \\ \varepsilon^{*1}_t \end{bmatrix} \tag{14.74}$$

Now note that under this stationary structure $\Gamma(T)$ is completely determined by the covariance matrices

$$\gamma(h) = E\begin{bmatrix} K^1_{t+1} \\ P^1_t \end{bmatrix}[K^1_{t+1+h}P^1_{t+h}] \qquad h = 0, \pm 1, \pm 2, \ldots$$

and the $\gamma(h)$ are completely determined by the covariance generating function $g(z) = \Sigma_{h=-\infty}^{+\infty}\gamma(h)z^h$, where $g(z) = H_1(z)^{-1}H_2(z) \times H_2(z^{-1})'H_1(z^{-1})^{-1\prime}$. As noted, the matrices of coefficients in $H_1(z)$, $H_2(z)$ have already been determined by theory and can be expressed in terms of the underlying parameters of the model.

It is of interest to ask whether these underlying parameters can be identified, that is, whether there is any indeterminacy in the estimates for large (infinite) samples. Suppose that we were armed with the true variance–covariance structure of the bivariate process K^1_{t+1}, P^1_t so that the $\gamma(h)$ and hence $g(z)$ were actually known. We ask first whether the coefficients in the matrices of $H_1(z)$, $H_2(z)$ would be known and then whether the underlying parameters can be determined from these coefficients.

The first question can be posed another way. Given some $H_1(z)$, $H_2(z)$ pair, is there another $H_1(z)$, $H_2(z)$ pair consistent with the same $g(z)$? Writing $g(z) = H_1(z)^{-1}H_2(z)B(z)B(z^{-1})'H_2(z^{-1})'H_1(z^{-1})^{-1\prime}$, where $B(z)$ is orthogonal, that is, $B(z)B(z^{-1})' = I$, it seems that the answer may be no; apparently $H_2(z)$ is only unique up to orthogonal matrices $B(z)$. Here again, $B(z)$ is the Blaschke factor discussed in section 8. However, now invoke the restrictions implied by theory on the matrices of $H_2(z)$, in particular the zero restrictions. It can be shown that $H_1(z)$ and $H_2(z)$ are indeed identified.[18]

The second part of the identification question is whether we can uncover the underlying parameters from the coefficients in $H_1(z)$ and $H_2(z)$. It is claimed that this can be done, if the econometrician has prior knowledge of the discount rate β, by making use of the cross-equation restrictions.[19] Thus the vector time series from the first market will effectively recall all parameter values.[20]

In the technique described above for estimation and identification it is assumed that the data really are generated by the model of the theory. Note, for example, that the error term in a vector autoregression of price and capital stock in the first market is a linear combination of current and past unobserved economic shocks which constitute part of the model itself; in the model these shocks have effects on observables either directly, as on contemporary prices, or indirectly through their effect on decision-makers' forecasts. Thus, movement in the error term plays a key role in identifying the underlying parameters of the model, and the variance of the error term is not necessarily small relative to the variance of observables. Consider the model of capital stock movements in the econometric model (14.72). There is no reason a priori to believe that uncertainty is not a fundamental part of the problem confronting decision-makers (as it would be if both σ_v^2 and σ_ε^2 were small) or that current observations are unimportant in learning (as they would be if α_1 were small).

Unfortunately, though, this wedding of theory and econometrics is not without difficulties. The technique mentioned above leaves no room for errors which result from theory as an abstraction or approximation. That is, all the rich detail of the data is forced on the free parameters of the model. Viewed as an observable–unobservable index model – as described, for example, by Sargent and Sims (1977) – the model is exact; there are no own-error terms (with, we hope, small variances).

This leads us to a discussion of perhaps a more standard econometric procedure, deriving an exact model from theory and tacking on error terms as dictated by discretion and by the data. We will now examine in what sense this is or is not possible if agents of the model themselves have incomplete information on exogenous driving processes and thus are engaged in learning.

Suppose, first, that the econometrician has *direct* observations, along with the agents of the model, on the stochastic processes being forecast. Then the econometrician could potentially estimate the parameters of those stochastic processes, and, with guesses about agents' initial priors, the Kalman filtering algorithm could be used to compute agents' forecasts period by period. With these constructed forecast series and the other observables, part of the theoretical model may be exact. Thus, we might consider tacking on error terms for purposes of estimation. This is virtually the procedure adopted by

Crawford (1979); it could be applied here to the model of the first market if the econometrician were to obtain direct observations on z_t^1.

Without such direct observations, though, this recursive procedure cannot be applied. With data on the capital stock and price only, the pricing equation in the first market alone will not yield the parameters ρ, σ_v^2, and σ_ε^2; that is, the parameter b must be estimated jointly. But to do this consistently, we need to make explicit use of the evolution of the capital stock series. Thus, even if the econometrician and the agents of the model see the same time series, the agents, knowing the structure, can deduce more period by period. Thus, from the point of view of the econometrician, the model delivered by theory is not exact. This leads us back toward the first estimation strategy of Hansen and Sargent discussed above.

In some contexts it may be possible to loosen the Hansen–Sargent procedure directly by tacking error terms onto the econometric model derived from theory. This is especially true if the model from theory displays stochastic singularities, as the one here apparently does. Then we might hope to retain identification. In general, though, identification becomes an open question.

Another approach which takes theory seriously and which avoids tacking on error terms is that of Kydland and Prescott (1982). Rather than asking theory to explain the entire variance–covariance structure of the data, as in maximum likelihood techniques, these authors concentrate on key moments or "on certain statistics for which the noise introduced by approximations and measurement errors is likely to be small relative to the statistic." Under this approach, we try to match specified sample moments from runs of the model under various possible parameter specifications with the specified moments from actual data. Thus, we again make direct use of the Kalman filtering algorithm in computing agents' forecasts.

If we are unable or unwilling to focus on a subset of moments, then we are again faced with the problem of fitting the theory to the entire variance–covariance structure of the data. Sims (1980a, b) has suggested that a nice way to summarize this structure is to estimate the coefficients in relatively unrestricted vector autoregressions and examine the response of the system to innovations in the error terms of these regressions. This brings us back to the response to economic shocks in section 7 as one way of summarizing the implications of the theory. A caveat is in order here, however: the error term in the theoretical model (14.72), for example, has no natural economic interpretation as it is a linear combination of current and *past* economic shocks. That is, the theoretical model (14.72) can be inconsistent with the assumptions that Sims makes on error terms in his vector autoregressions (in other models, of course) and with his interpretation of error terms as surprises or forecast errors. Putting this another way, the error term in a vector autoregression can be sensitive to the assumed information structure for decision-makers in the model itself. The error term in the full-information model (14.40) has a ready interpretation as a permanent shock. The error term in the learning model (14.39) is some mongrel. The full implication of this for (highly desirable) exploratory data analysis is left as a subject for future research.

Appendix

An algorithm for uncovering the fundamental moving-average representation
Note first that the matrix $M(z)$ is lower triangular and hence has a determinant of $z^2(1-\delta z)$ with two zeros at $z=0$. Thus $M(z)$ has two zeros inside the unit circle, and this is precisely why it does not have a one-sided inverse in nonnegative powers of L. We will search for matrices W, $\hat{W}$, and $B(z)$ consistent with the orthogonality conditions (14.61) which "flip" these zeros outside the unit circle.

The algorithm is as follows. First, evaluate the matrix $M(z)$ at $z=0$. Next, postmultiply by some matrix W in such a way as to put zeros in the first column of the product matrix. In this case

$$W=\begin{bmatrix} \dfrac{1}{\sqrt{3}} & \dfrac{2}{\sqrt{6}} & 0 \\ -\dfrac{1}{\sqrt{3}} & \dfrac{1}{\sqrt{6}} & \dfrac{1}{\sqrt{2}} \\ -\dfrac{1}{\sqrt{3}} & \dfrac{1}{\sqrt{6}} & -\dfrac{1}{\sqrt{2}} \end{bmatrix}$$

Next, remove the zeros in the first column by using the Blaschke matrix

$$B(z)=\begin{bmatrix} z^{-1} & 0 & 0 \\ 0 & 1 & 0 \\ 0 & 0 & 1 \end{bmatrix}$$

That is, let $M^*(z)=M(z)WB(z)$, so that

$$M^*(z)=\begin{bmatrix} \dfrac{z}{\sqrt{3}} & \dfrac{2z^2}{\sqrt{6}} & 0 \\ \left(\dfrac{1+\rho z}{\sqrt{3}}-\dfrac{1}{\sqrt{3}}\right)z^{-1} & \dfrac{(1+\rho z)2}{\sqrt{6}}+\dfrac{1}{\sqrt{6}} & \dfrac{1}{\sqrt{2}} \\ \left(\dfrac{1+\alpha z}{\sqrt{3}}-\dfrac{1-\delta z}{\sqrt{3}}\right)z^{-1} & \dfrac{(1+\alpha z)2}{\sqrt{6}}+\dfrac{1-\delta z}{\sqrt{6}} & \dfrac{-(1-\delta z)}{\sqrt{2}} \end{bmatrix}$$

We have, in effect, flipped one of the zeros outside the unit circle. However, note that the determinant of $M^*(z)$ still has a zero at $z=0$. Therefore apply the same procedure, again starting from $M^*(z)$. This time the matrix analog of W is $\hat{W}$ defined by terms like

$$\hat{W}_{11}=\left(\frac{18}{18+k_1^2+3k_2^2}\right)^{1/2}$$

and so on, where $k_1=\rho+\alpha+\delta$ and $k_2=\rho-\alpha-\delta$, so that the $\hat{W}_{ij}$ are nonlinear functions of α and δ. The relevant Blaschke matrix is the same $B(z)$ as before. This procedure yields $M^{**}(z)=M^*(z)\hat{W}B(z)$. Thus the fundamental moving-average representation has been achieved with moving-average coefficients $M^{**}(z)$ as defined in (14.63) and with innovations ξ_t^{**} as defined in (14.64).

Existence and uniqueness of solutions for the undetermined coefficients

Consider first the following mapping. Start with arbitrary parameters C_0 and D_0. These determine numbers α and δ, and these in turn determine numbers k_1 and k_2. The numbers k_1 and k_2 determine the $\hat{W}_{ij}$, but it is important to note that the matrix $\hat{W}$ must be orthogonal. Thus each $\hat{W}_{ij}$ is bounded in absolute value by unity, for all initial parameters C_0 and D_0. From system (14.54), the computed C_0, D_0 values on the left-hand side of (14.54) must satisfy

$$C_0=\frac{2\hat{W}_{22}^2}{3}+\frac{2\hat{W}_{23}^2}{3}+\frac{2\rho\hat{W}_{12}\hat{W}_{22}}{\sqrt{18}}$$

$$D_0=\frac{2\hat{W}_{22}}{\sqrt{6}}\left(\frac{1}{\sqrt{6}}\hat{W}_{22}-\frac{1}{\sqrt{2}}\hat{W}_{32}\right)+\frac{2\hat{W}_{23}}{\sqrt{6}}\left(\frac{1}{\sqrt{6}}\hat{W}_{23}-\frac{1}{\sqrt{2}}\hat{W}_{33}\right)$$
$$+\rho\frac{\hat{W}_{12}}{\sqrt{3}}\left(\frac{1}{\sqrt{6}}\hat{W}_{22}-\frac{1}{\sqrt{2}}\hat{W}_{32}\right) \tag{14.A1}$$

Thus computed C_0 and D_0 take on values in a nonempty compact convex space. Moreover, the mapping defined above is well defined, assuming $\rho\neq 0$, and continuous on this space. Therefore by the Brouwer fixed-point theorem, there exists a solution to equations (14.54).

It remains to formally establish the uniqueness of solutions to (14.54). Substitution into (14.A1) and cancellation of like terms yields

$$C_0=\frac{12+4\rho^2-2\rho b_1 f_0 h_2(C_0-D_0)+2(b_1 f_0 h_2)^2(C_0-D_0)^2}{4\rho^2-4\rho b_1 f_0 h_2(C_0-D_0)+4(b_1 f_0 h_2)^2(C_0-D_0)^2+18} \tag{14.A2}$$

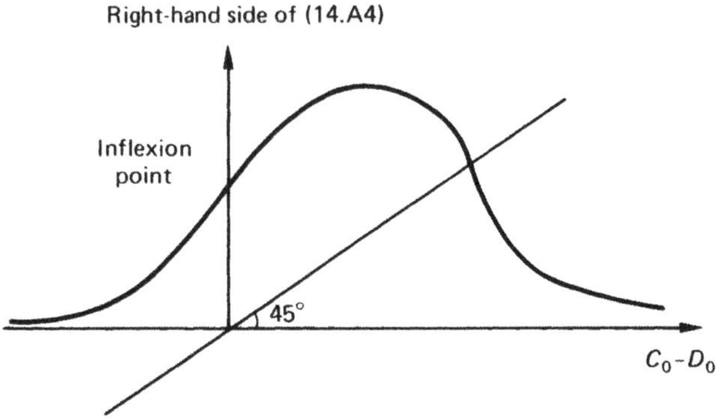

Figure 14.6.

$$D_0 = \frac{6 + 2\rho^2 - 2\rho b_1 f_0 h_2 (C_0 - D_0) + 2(b_1 f_0 h_2)^2 (C_0 - D_0)}{4\rho^2 - 4\rho b_1 f_0 h_2 (C_0 - D_0) + 4(b_1 f_0 h_2)^2 (C_0 - D_0)^2 + 18} \quad (14.\text{A}3)$$

$$C_0 - D_0 = \frac{6 + 2\rho^2}{4\rho^2 - 4\rho b_1 f_0 h_2 (C_0 - D_0) + 4(b_1 f_0 h_2)^2 (C_0 - D_0)^2 + 18} \quad (14.\text{A}4)$$

Plotting the right-hand side of equation (14.A4) in figure 14.6, we see clearly that there is a unique solution to (14.A4) in C_0–D_0 space. Then C_0 and D_0 are determined from (14.A2) and (14.A3) respectively. (Unfortunately, attempts to sign the slope of the function in figure 14.6 have been unsuccessful, foiling attempts to formally establish why computing solutions by the method of successive approximations works.)

Notes

1 The equilibrium definition employed here builds on Townsend (1978, this volume, ch. 13), Sargent (1979), and Prescott and Townsend (1980), among others, and is related to ongoing work in the theory of general economic equilibrium by Green (1977), Jordan (1977), Kreps (1977), Radner (1979), and Allen (1981), among others. Unlike the general equilibrium literature, however, here prices do not simultaneously clear markets and convey information.

2 Again, the learning takes place in a rational expectations equilibrium way, as in Townsend (1978, this volume, ch. 13) and Bray and Kreps (1981). In Arrow and Green (1973), Cyert and DeGroot (1974), DeCanio (1979), Blume and Easley (1982), and Bray (1982), learning can produce convergence to rational expectations equilibrium, but the learning process itself need not be rational. See also Friedman (1979).

3 As Lucas and Sargent (1978) note, the distinction between sources of impulses

and propagation mechanisms is stressed by Frisch (1933) in a classic paper. Lucas and Sargent also identify three propagation mechanisms in the literature. One stems from costs of adjustment, a second from optimal asset accumulation, and a third from the frictions of search theory.

4 See also Jovanovic (1979), Brunner et al. (1980), and Kydland and Prescott (1982). A more comprehensive discussion of the relationship between economic models with uncertainty and statistical decision theory is given by Prescott and Townsend (1980).

5 In Lucas (1975) agents with different histories have different forecasts and, in effect, these forecasts themselves become an object of speculation. But to simplify this complex picture, Lucas pools the forecasts and makes the average common knowledge. Futia has taken up models with disparate but rational expectations in two papers and emphasizes that Lucas's problem is one of making inferences from *endogenous* time series. Futia (1981) has solved such a problem in a hierarchical structure with informed and uninformed traders. But in general the problem is nonlinear and seems difficult to solve. It is avoided in Futia's (1980) work on capturing what are believed to be the key elements of Lucas's model; agents are endowed with exogenous distinct information sets but with more information than they can capture from endogenous time series. Chari (1979) studies models with dispersed information and turns up more difficulties. If agents do not see economy-wide output, then there cannot be a finite list of state variables; agents must be concerned with the infinite past in an explicit way. Of course, in this chapter we do not propose a way out of *all* the difficulties associated with the above-mentioned models. However, we do seek to identify a broad class of models under which such difficulties can be either handled or avoided.

6 This chapter delivers on Sargent's (1981) call for econometric analysis of models in which there are information discrepancies across agents.

7 The need for this type of analysis, to overcome Lucas's (1976) critique of conventional econometric practice, is eloquently described by Sargent (1981).

8 There are some caveats on identification, however.

9 Suppose that there is a linear technology which maps the amount of capital adjustment $(k^i_{t+1} - k^i_t)^2$ into a labor requirement $(f_2/2)(k^i_{t+1} - k^i_t)^2$. Suppose also that the labor can be hired at a fixed wage $\bar{w}$ in any period t. Then $(\bar{w}f_2/2)(k^i_{t+1} - k^i_t)^2$ is the appropriate cost term in the objective function. There is a similar interpretation for the capital maintenance term $(f_2/2)(k^i_t)^2$. Then, on dividing through by $\bar{w}$, P^i_t can be interpreted as the relative price of the produced good in terms of labor.

10 On the right-hand side of (14.7) is the sequence of expected future prices $E(P^i_{t+1}|\Omega^i_t)$, $E(P^i_{t+2}|\Omega^i_t)$, and so on. Substituting (14.8) into (14.12) at $t+1$, we obtain $P^i_{t+1} = \theta_{t+1} + \varepsilon^i_{t+1} - b_1 f_0(h_1 K^i_t + h_2 M^i_t)$. Thus $E(P^i_{t+1}|\Omega^i_t) = \rho M^i_t + 0 - b_1 f_0 h_1 K^i_t - b_0 f_0 h_2 M^i_t$. Similarly, $P^i_{t+2} = \theta_{t+2} + \varepsilon^i_{t+2} - b_1 f_0 h_1 h_1 K^i_t - b_1 f_0 h_1 h_2 M^i_t - b_1 f_0 h_2 M^i_{t+1}$. Since $M^i_{t+1} = E(\theta_{t+1}|\Omega^i_{t+1})$, $E(M^i_{t+1}|\Omega^i_t) = E(\theta_{t+1}|\Omega^i_t)$ by the law of iterated expectations. Thus $E(P^i_{t+2}|\Omega^i_t) = \rho^2 M^i_t + 0 - b_1 f_0 h_1^2 K^i_t - b_1 f_0 h_1 h_2 M^i_t - b_1 f_0 h_2 \rho M^i_t$. Substituting expressions like these into (14.7) delivers (14.11).

11 That hierarchical structures should be tractable with Kalman filtering was suggested to the author by Thomas Sargent. See also Prescott and Townsend (1980).

12 This theory (see Kwakernaak and Sivan 1972, p. 535) requires that the variance–covariance matrix M be written $M = GM^*G'$, where $M^* \geqslant \alpha I$, $N \geqslant \beta I$, M^* positive definite, where α, β are positive constants, and the rows of

$$\begin{bmatrix} C \\ CA \\ CA^2 \\ \vdots \\ CA^{n-1} \end{bmatrix}$$

and columns of $(G, AG, A^2G, \ldots, A^{n-1}G)$ span the n-dimensional space. For the application here, let G and M^* be defined by

$$G = \begin{bmatrix} 0 & 0 \\ 1 & 0 \\ 0 & 1 \end{bmatrix} \qquad M^* = \begin{bmatrix} \alpha_1^2\sigma_v^2 + \alpha_1^2\sigma_\varepsilon^2 & \alpha_1\sigma_v^2 \\ \alpha_1\sigma_v^2 & \sigma_v^2 \end{bmatrix}$$

where C, A, and N are defined implicitly in the text.

13 From system (14.35), let $D = A - \bar{\Sigma}C'N^{-1}CA$ and $F = \bar{\Sigma}C'N^{-1}$. Then $M_t^2 = E(\theta_t|\Omega_t^2)$ is determined by the third row of (14.35), namely, $E(x_t|\Omega_t^2) = (I - DL)^{-1}F(P_t^1 z_t^2)'$. The law of motion (14.13) for K_t^2 then completes the picture.

14 This procedure was suggested by Ian Bain and Edward C. Prescott as an alternative to the procedure described below. The *entire* chapter is now written in a way which, it is hoped, makes the present procedure obvious and straightforward.

15 The author would like to thank Lars Hansen for suggesting systems like (14.58) and the use of Wiener–Kolmogorov prediction formulas, and for teaching him about Blaschke factors (see below). Since η_{t-2} is in the information set of firms at time t, it may appear that system (14.58) should be augmented to include η_{t-2} in the vector on the left-hand side. However, the procedure described in the text below can be applied to the augmented system with the result that the predictions of v_t and v_{t-1} remain unaltered. It might also seem that parameter δ must be less than unity to justify the procedure described in the text but the augmented system makes clear that this need not be the case. (The author is indebted to Lars Hansen for this insight.)

16 As Subramanian (1982) has established, the Blaschke procedure described above is numerically tractable for any finite full-information lag system with innovations known at $t - j$. (Lags up to $j = 50$ have been computed.) The dimension of the matrices remains at $2 + 1 = 3$ and does not increase with j. Of course, the Blaschke algorithm requires more and more iterations; that is, more and more matrices W, $\hat{W}$, and so on must be computed. But there is a sense in which the procedure is recursive, as is apparent from (14.63) and (14.64). The reader is urged to consult Subramanian for a more detailed account.

17 Subramanian (1982) has established that this procedure converges to apparently unique solutions for arbitrarily large information lag j systems.

18 The argument is due to Lars Hansen, and is available from the author on request.

19 From the second-row first-column and second-column elements of $H_2(L)$, it is evident that σ_v and σ_ε are determined. From the first-row second-column element of $H_2(L)$, $h_2\alpha_1\sigma_\varepsilon$ and $\rho h_2\alpha_1\sigma_\varepsilon$ are determined, and so ρ is known. Then $\bar{\Sigma}$ can be computed from (14.24) and (14.25), and thus α_0 and α_1 are determined. Thus, from $h_2\alpha_1$, h_2 is determined. From $H_1(L)$, the three parameters h_1, α_0, and ρ are known up to labeling. But with ρ and α_0 known, h_1 is determined. Therefore from the second-row first-column element, $b_1 f_0$ is determined. Now recall from (14.13) that $h_1 = \gamma_1$, $h_2 = (f_0\gamma_1\beta\rho)/\{f_2(1-\gamma_1\beta\rho)\}$. With γ_1, β, and ρ known, f_0/f_2 is determined. Then, since $\gamma_1\gamma_2 = 1/\beta, \gamma_1 + \gamma_2 = (f_1/f_2) + \{(1+\beta)/\beta\} + (b_1 f_0 f_0/f_2)$, f_1/f_2 is determined. Thus the parameters of technology are determined up to some normalization, say $f_2 = 1$, as expected, since multiplying the objective function through by a constant cannot change the implications of the theory. With $f_2 = 1$, f_0, f_1, and b_1 are determined.

20 Perhaps a more interesting question to ask is whether identification would be possible if parameter values of technology and demand were allowed to vary across markets. Data from the first market would allow us to determine the coefficients in the matrices C, A, M, and N, and thus $\bar{\Sigma}$ would be determined. These could then be used to identify the parameters in the second market from the analog of system (14.72). The point is that the recursive structure can be exploited.

To proceed with more formal econometrics for the symmetric information structure, system (14.70)–(14.71) can be expressed as an ARMA process, and thus the maximum likelihood techniques of Hansen and Sargent can again be used for estimation. Under such techniques the parameters C_j, D_j must be computed, say by successive approximations. But these computations are no more burdensome than those used in solving the recursive equation (14.24) of the Kalman filter. Needless to say, numerical methods must be used in any event under any estimation procedure. One caveat is in order, though: here identification of the parameters in technology and demand *may* be a problem because there is no recursive way to attack the cross-equation restrictions, as in the two-market hierarchical structure. This is left as an open question.

References and Bibliography

Allen, B.E. (1981) Generic existence of completely revealing equilibria for economies with uncertainty when prices convey information. *Econometrica* 49, 1173–99.

Arrow, K.J. and Green, J.R. (1973) Notes on expectations equilibria in Bayesian settings. Working Paper 35, Institute of Mathematical Studies of Social Science, Stanford University.

Barro, R.J. (1980) A capital market in an equilibrium business cycle model. *Econometrica* 48, 1393–417.

Bertsekas, D.P. (1976) *Dynamic Programming and Stochastic Control.* New York: Academic Press.

Blume, L.E. and Easley, D. (1982) Learning to be rational. *Journal of Economic Theory* 26, 340–51.

Bray, M. (1982) Learning, estimation, and the stability of rational expectations. *Journal of Economic Theory* 26, 318–39.

—— and Kreps, D.M. (1981) Rational learning and rational expectations. Unpublished manuscript, Graduate School of Business, Stanford University.

Brunner, K., Cukierman, A., and Meltzer, A.H. (1980) Stagflation, persistent unemployment and the permanence of economic shocks. *Journal of Monetary Economics* 6, 467–92.

Chari, V.V. (1979) Linear stochastic models with decentralized information. Unpublished manuscript, Graduate School of Industrial Administration, Carnegie-Mellon University, Pittsburgh, PA.

Crawford, R.G. (1979) Expectations and labor market adjustments. *Journal of Econometrics* 11, 207–32.

Cyert, R.M. and DeGroot, M.H. (1974) Rational expectations and Bayesian analysis. *Journal of Political Economy* 82, 521–36.

DeCanio, S.J. (1979) Rational expectations and learning from experience. *Quarterly Journal of Economics* 93, 47–57.

Eisner, R. and Strotz, R.H. (1963) Determinants of business investment. In *Impacts of Monetary Policy*, eds Commission on Money and Credit. Englewood Cliffs, NJ: Prentice-Hall.

Friedman, B.M. (1979) Optimal expectations and the extreme information assumptions of "rational expectations" macromodels. *Journal of Monetary Economics* 5, 23–41.

Frisch, R. (1933) Propagation problems and impulse problems in dynamic economics. In *Economic Essays in Honor of Gustav Cassel*. London: Allen & Unwin. Reprinted in *Readings in Business Cycles*, eds R.A. Gordon and L.R. Klein. Homewood, IL: Irwin for the American Economic Association, 1965.

Futia, C.A. (1980) Stochastic business cycles. Unpublished manuscript, Bell Laboratories, Murray Hill, NJ.

—— (1981) Rational expectations in stationary linear models. *Econometrica* 49, 171–92.

Gould, J.P. (1968) Adjustment costs in the theory of investment of the firm. *Review of Economic Studies* 35, 47–55.

Green, J.R. (1977) The non-existence of informational equilibria. *Review of Economic Studies* 44, 451–63.

Grossman, S.J. and Weiss, L. (1980) Heterogeneous information and the theory of the business cycle. Unpublished manuscript, Department of Economics, University of Chicago.

Haavelmo, T. (1960) *A Study in the Theory of Investment*. Chicago, IL: University of Chicago Press.

Hansen, L.P. and Sargent, T.J. (1980a) Formulating and estimating dynamic linear rational expectations models. *Journal of Economic Dynamics and Control* 2, 7–46.

—— and —— (1980b) Linear rational expectations models for dynamically interrelated variables. In *Rational Expectations and Econometric Practice*, eds R.E. Lucas Jr and T.J. Sargent. Minneapolis, MN: University of Minnesota Press.

—— and —— (1989) Exact rational expectations models: specification and estimation (revised). In *Underground Classics in Economics*. Boulder, CO: Westview Press.

Holt, C.C., Modigliani, F., Muth, J.F. and Simon, H.A. (1960) *Planning Production, Inventories, and Work Force*. Englewood Cliffs, NJ: Prentice-Hall.

Jordan, J.S. (1977) Expectations equilibrium and informational efficiency for stochastic environments. *Journal of Economic Theory* 16, 354–72.

Jorgenson, D.W. (1963) Capital theory and investment behavior. *AER Papers and Proceedings* 53, 247–59.

Jovanovic, B. (1979) Job matching and the theory of turnover. *Journal of Political Economy* 87(5), 972–90.

Kalman, R.E. (1960) A new approach to linear filtering and prediction problems. *Journal of Basic Engineering* 82, 35–45.

Keynes, J.M. (1965) *The General Theory of Employment, Interest and Money.* New York: Harcourt Brace. (Originally published in 1936.)

King, R.G. (1978) Asset markets and the neutrality of money. Unpublished manuscript, Department of Economics, University of Rochester, Rochester, NY.

Kreps, D.M. (1977) A note on "fulfilled expectations" equilibria. *Journal of Economic Theory* 14, 32–43.

Kwakernaak, H. and Sivan, R. (1972) *Linear Optimal Control Systems.* New York: Wiley.

Kydland, F.E. and Prescott, E.C. (1982) Time to build and aggregate fluctuations. *Econometrica* 50, 1345–70.

Lucas, R.E., Jr (1967) Adjustment costs and the theory of supply. *Journal of Political Economy* 75(4), 321–24.

—— (1972) Expectations and the neutrality of money. *Journal of Economic Theory* 4, 103–24.

—— (1975) An equilibrium model of the business cycle. *Journal of Political Economy* 83, 1113–44.

—— (1976) Econometric policy evaluation: a critique. In *The Phillips Curve and Labor Markets*, eds K. Brunner and A.H. Meltzer, Carnegie–Rochester Conference Series on Public Policy, vol. 1. Amsterdam: North-Holland.

—— (1978) Asset prices in an exchange economy. *Econometrica* 46, 1429–45.

—— and Prescott, E.C. (1971) Investment under uncertainty. *Econometrica* 39, 659–81.

—— and Sargent, T.J. (1978) After Keynesian macroeconomics. In *After the Phillips Curve: Persistence of High Inflation and High Unemployment*, Federal Reserve Bank of Boston Conference Series 19. Boston, MA: Federal Reserve Bank of Boston.

Mortensen, D.T. (1973) Generalized costs of adjustment and dynamic factor demand theory. *Econometrica* 41, 657–65.

Muth, J.F. (1961) Rational expectations and the theory of price movements. *Econometrica* 29, 315–35.

Phelps, E.S. (1970) Introduction: the new microeconomics in employment and inflation theory. In *Microeconomic Foundations of Employment and Inflation Theory*, E.S. Phelps et al. New York: Norton.

Pigou, A.C. (1929) *Industrial Fluctuations*, 2nd edn. London: Macmillan.

Prescott, E.C. and Townsend, R.M. (1980) Equilibrium under uncertainty: multiagent statistical decision theory. In *Bayesian Analysis in Econometrics and Statistics*, ed. A. Zellner. Amsterdam: North-Holland.

Radner, R. (1979) Rational expectations equilibrium: generic existence and the information revealed by prices. *Econometrica* 47, 655–78.

Sargent, T.J. (1978) Estimation of dynamic labor demand schedules under rational expectations. *Journal of Political Economy* 86, 1009–44.

—— (1979) *Macroeconomic Theory*. New York: Academic Press.

—— (1981) Interpreting economic time series. *Journal of Political Economy* 89, 213–48.

—— and Sims, C.A. (1977) Business cycle modeling without pretending to have too much *a priori* economic theory. In *New Methods in Business Cycle Research: Proceedings from a Conference*, ed. C.A. Sims, Minneapolis. MN: Federal Reserve Bank of Minneapolis.

Sims, C.A. (1980a) Macroeconomics and reality. *Econometrica* 48, 1–48.

—— (1980b) International evidence on monetary factors in macroeconomic fluctuations. Unpublished manuscript, Department of Economics, University of Minnesota.

Subramanian, L. (1982) Summer Paper II, Graduate School of Industrial Administration, Carnegie–Mellon University, Pittsburgh, PA.

Townsend, R.M. (1978) Market anticipations, rational expectations, and Bayesian analysis. *International Economic Review* 19, 481–94. Reprinted, revised and modified in this volume as chapter 13.

—— (1981) Forecasting and forecasts of others. Unpublished manuscript, Graduate School of Industrial Administration, Carnegie–Mellon University, Pittsburgh, PA.

Treadway, A.B. (1969) On rational entrepreneurial behavior and the demand for investment. *Review of Economic Studies* 36, 227–39.

15

Equilibrium Theory with Learning and Disparate Expectations: Some Issues and Methods

1 Introduction

Motivated by certain stylized facts or observations, and perhaps by a desire to develop models that offer a reliable guide for policy, economists have developed equilibrium models that are more and more sophisticated in their treatment of time and imperfect information. The profession has witnessed a movement from static models to dynamic models with perfect foresight and, more recently, with the advances of Muth (1961), Lucas and Prescott (1971), and Lucas (1972, 1975), among others, to dynamic models with uncertainty and rational expectations.[1] Muth's work was motivated by two major conclusions from studies of expectations data: "1. Averages of expectations in an industry are more accurate than naive models and as accurate as elaborate equation systems, although there are considerable cross-sectional differences of opinion. 2. Reported expectations generally underestimate the extent of changes that actually take place." Muth goes on to invoke his rational expectations hypothesis, "that the expectations of firms (or, more generally, the subjective probability distribution of outcomes) tend to be distributed, for the same information set, about the prediction of the theory (or the 'objective' probability distributions of outcomes)," and to establish that both the periodic movement of time series displayed in so-called corn–hog cycles and the second preceding observation can be explained using that hypothesis. Similarly, the work of Lucas and Prescott was motivated by econometric considerations – a desire to develop a guide as to how

Reprinted from *Individual Forecasting and Aggregate Outcomes*, eds E.S. Phelps and R. Frydman (New York: Cambridge University Press, 1983). Helpful comments from Lars Peter Hansen, Thomas J. Sargent, John Taylor, Roswell G. Townsend, and the participants of the conference in New York and a seminar at the University of Pennsylvania, and support from the National Science Foundation and the Alfred P. Sloan Foundation are all gratefully acknowledged. I assume full responsibility for any errors, as well as for the views expressed here.

variables measuring anticipated future demand should be placed in industry investment rules. In making forecasting considerations explicit, they invoked the more general rational expectations hypothesis that the entire subjective and objective probability distributions be equal. Finally, Lucas's work on business cycles was motivated by the desire to explain certain key cross-correlation and serial-correlation properties of prices, unemployment, and output, and to develop models with implications about the way in which reduced form equations might change with changes in the systematic component of stabilization policy. Thus Lucas developed formal equilibrium analysis consistent with rational but disparate expectations across decision-makers.

Despite these advances, there remains some concern regarding the use of the rational expectations hypothesis. It is perhaps unwise to attempt to speak for others, but this concern itself may be motivated by economic observations. Rational expectations, it is thought, require essentially uniform beliefs at some level and imply more stationarity or stability of time series than is consistent with even casual observations. Put rather crudely decision-makers do not agree about things that keep moving around. Indeed, it is easy to read Keynes (1965) on the role of expectations in stock markets and Pigou (1929) on the role of expectations in industrial fluctuations and sustain the view that equilibrium analysis is inappropriate. It was Keynes's view that, with the opening of stock exchanges, investors shift from a concern with long term determinants of profitability or yield to a concern with short term movements in the market prices themselves. Thus conventional valuation will be "established as the outcome of the mass psychology of a large number of ignorant individuals which is liable to change violently as the result of a sudden fluctuation in opinion due to factors which do not really make much difference to prospective yield." In this environment, Keynes believed that even expert professionals "possessing judgment and knowledge beyond that of the average private investor" would be forced to concern themselves with average opinion. Similarly, Pigou (1929) argued that the key feature of cycles is that decision-makers are unaware of what others are doing and are thus bound to make mistakes, that is, to make forecast errors; of course, this is also a key idea in Lucas (1975). Further, Pigou argued that these errors can be mutually generated, that is, with errors of optimism generated by errors of pessimism, and so on.

The research program of which this chapter is a part continues in the tradition of enriching equilibrium theory, extending it to the point that it might begin to address some of the observations that Keynes and Pigou had in mind. Thus, it follows Muth, Lucas, and Prescott, among others, adopting a strategy described by Hayek (1939) and offering precise equilibrium constructs to explain relatively complicated dynamic phenomena. Of course, the equilibrium constructs of this chapter should not be taken as literal descriptions of the way the world works; as in Muth, it is not asserted here that the system of equations resembles the scratchwork of entrepreneurs in any way. Moreover, we can argue, as did Muth (1961), that rationality of expectations is a logical (albeit somewhat extreme) specification to examine, an assumption that can be modified: "Systematic biases, incomplete or incorrect information, poor memory, etc. can be examined with analytical methods based on rationality."

For this research program to be successful, equilibrium models with learning and with disparate but rational expectations must be tractable. Unfortunately, such models are not currently regarded as tractable by many in the economics profession, perhaps for a variety of reasons. First, models with learning are frequently used to address the question of whether or not there will be convergence to rational expectations equilibria. Indeed, Muth (1961) and Lucas and Prescott (1971) suggested that rational expectations should be regarded as the natural outcome of some unspecified process of learning and adapting on the part of decision-makers. However, attempts to model that process have produced mixed conclusions (see Arrow and Green, 1973; Cyert and DeGroot, 1974; Townsend, 1978, this volume, ch. 13; DeCanio, 1979; Bray and Kreps, 1981; Frydman, 1981; Blume and Easley, 1982; Bray 1982). In general, convergence to (strong form) rational expectations seems problematical, and there remain many open questions concerning how best to model learning processes and to pose stability questions. Second, equilibrium models with rational but disparate expectations often seem to require that decision-makers not only forecast underlying economic state variables but also forecast the forecasts of others. This can be viewed as quite demanding (see also Friedman, 1979). Third, economy-wide average forecasts can become an object of speculation in these models, and this in turn can lead to an infinite regress problem in which decision-makers forecast the forecasts of forecasts of others, and so on. Finally, and related, Lucas (1975), Chari (1979), and Futia (1981) have indicated analytical difficulties in solving for closed form solutions in models in which decision-makers forecast from *endogenous* time series, encountering the infinite regress problem, nonlinear equations, or an infinite number of state variables.[2]

Thus on the one hand there is the hope that we might explain the movement of economic time series in equilibrium models with learning and with disparate but rational expectations, and on the other hand there is the view that such models are difficult to solve. In this chapter we take a step toward resolving this dilemma by devoting much of our attention to the formulation–analysis issue. That is, the basic intent of the research of which this chapter is a part is to find constructs and techniques that will prove useful in a variety of economic models. In this regard, these efforts have been rather successful; it is argued here that the class of linear dynamic models with learning and with disparate but rational expectations is indeed tractable under a wide variety of information specifications. Moreover, these models do deliver qualitatively interesting time series, as hoped. In particular, even in a simple setting they deliver waves of optimism and pessimism and cyclical fluctuations in output.

We proceed by fixing a simple partial equilibrium industry model that might be suggested by a reading of Muth (1961): a basic structure with shocks to demand that are the sum of a (relatively) permanent component and a transitory component. We follow this with an investigation of the problems that arise and the formulation–solution techniques that are needed as the information structure is varied in the simple model. With arbitrary prior beliefs on the initial demand shock, there *is* an infinite regress problem in forecasts. However, that problem has a natural solution, at least in principle, in an infinite-dimensional space (see section 3). Moreover, statistical decision theory can frequently be used to pin down the source of prior beliefs, and in that way we can return to finite-dimensional state space methods, such as the Kalman filtering algorithm – Bayes's rule for linear dynamic systems (see sections 4, 5, and 6). In particular, recursive structures with informed and uninformed traders are tractable. Even when simple Kalman filtering is inapplicable, the infinite regress problem can be solved by a nonlinear technique in a finite-dimensional space, that is, the space of undetermined coefficients for moving-average representations of economy-wide average forecasts (see section 7).

In all these information specifications, decision-makers take as given linear laws of motion of state variables, such as shocks and forecasts, that they do and/or do not see, and more often than not these laws have time-invariant coefficients. That is, as in Muth's (1961) early formulation, state variables take on period-by-period realizations as if generated from well-defined stationary stochastic processes. These "self-fulfilling" stochastic processes are the analogs of the "self-fulfilling" price distributions in relatively static rational expectations models. It should be noted also that, to the extent that the state variables are unobserved, the information specifications here contain unobserved components or latent variables. Such latent variable constructs have become increasingly useful to economists studying social phenomena; see, for example, Friedman (1957) and Muth (1960) on permanent income, Crawford (1976) and Jovanovic (1978) on labor turnover and job match, and Kydland and Prescott (1981) and Meltzer (1981) on fluctuations. For a more comprehensive discussion of the relationship between economic models with uncertainty and statistical decision theory see Prescott and Townsend (1980).

Finally, it should be emphasized again that in this chapter the interest in equilibrium models with learning and with disparate but rational expectations is motivated by the search for abstractions with testable implications, that is, abstractions capable of explaining the movement of economic time series. In this respect, dynamic linear equilibrium models show some promise, and on this account (but certainly not others) the issue of whether or not there is convergence to strong form rational expectations outcomes loses some of its interest (see section 5). In particular, there can be convergence in such models to a steady state suitable for econometric purposes – the variance–covariance matrices of beliefs settle down, so that coefficients in the laws of motion are time invariant. However, in such a steady state, means of beliefs are subject to economic and measurement error shocks and thus move around in an interesting way that is not predicted in strong form rational expectations equilibrium (of the same model). In fact, as noted earlier, such shocks can induce oscillations and the waves of optimism and pessimism that Pigou (1929) had in mind. More generally, the research program of which this chapter is a part builds on the work of Hansen and Sargent (1980a, b, 1981) and Sargent (1978, 1981a) on the formulation and estimation of dynamic linear rational expectations models, incorporating learning and information discrepancies across decision-makers. Of course, all this work is designed to circumvent Lucas's critique (1976) of conventional econometric policy evaluation.

2 The basic model

Following Muth (1961), a linear partial equilibrium framework is adopted. Each of a set of firms maximizes expected profit, a function that is quadratic in output. This produced commodity is sold in a competitive market with stochastic demand. Production decisions must be made prior to the realization of the demand. Subsequent to the realization of demand, the market-clearing price is the one that would be determined by a Walrasian auctioneer. There are no contingent commodity markets. Under these assumptions, the production decision of each firm is a linear function of the expected price. In terms of generality, neither the linearity nor the partial equilibrium approach nor the exogenous restriction on markets nor the risk neutrality is satisfactory.

It is assumed that there are many firms, so that each regards his own contribution to market output and his influence on market beliefs as negligible. Formally, this is accomplished by supposing that the set of firms I is the unit interval. That is, firm i has label $i \in [0, 1]$. Let q_{it} denote the output of firm i at time t. Let P_t denote the market price of the commodity output at time t. Output q_{it} must be chosen prior to the realization of P_t. Prior to its realization, suppose that each firm i believes that P_t is a real-valued random variable with mean $E_{it}(P_t)$. Each firm acts to maximize $E_{it}(P_t)q_{it} - (1/2a)(q_{it})^2$, where $a > 0$, with respect to q_{it}. This yields the linear decision rule $q_{it} = aE_{it}(P_t)$. Also, let $Q_{it} = \int q_{it}\, di$ denote aggregate or average output at time t, where it is assumed, both here and later, that such Lebesgue integration is well defined.

In conjunction with market clearing (that is, supply equals demand), price P_t is determined by the linear demand schedule $P_t = \theta_t + \varepsilon_t - bQ_t$, where $b > 0$. Here $\{\varepsilon_t\}$ is a sequence of independent and identically distributed (i.i.d.) random variables – completely transitory shocks – each of which is normally distributed with mean zero and variance σ_ε^2. Parameter θ_t, the relatively permanent shock, follows the first-order Markov process $\theta_{t+1} = \rho\theta_t + v_{t+1}$, where $|\rho| < 1$ and $\{v_t\}$ is a sequence of independent and identically distributed random variables, each with mean zero and variance σ_v^2, independent of the $\{\varepsilon_t\}$. Finally, it should be noted that the basic model and all its information variants that follow have steady states of zero. Thus variables should be interpreted as deviations from means both here and later.

3 Arbitrary prior beliefs and the infinite regress problem in expectations: a solution[3]

Now assume that at the end of each period t, firms see P_t but do not (directly) see aggregate output Q_t. Assume also that the relatively permanent and transitory components of demand, θ_t and ε_t, are both unobserved. Then, in choosing output $q_{i,t+1}$ at the beginning of period $t+1$, firm i will attempt to forecast P_{t+1}, which, under market clearing, is a linear combination of the forecast of θ_{t+1} and Q_{t+1}, namely $E_{i,t+1}(P_{t+1}) = E_{i,t+1}(\theta_{t+1}) - bE_{i,t+1}(Q_{t+1})$. But how does the firm forecast Q_{t+1}? Taking account of the symmetry of the situation, we might assume that each firm recognizes that all the other firms are attempting to solve a similar forecasting problem. Hence, if firm i's output decision $q_{i,t+1}$ depends at least on $E_{i,t+1}(\theta_{t+1})$, the aggregate output Q_{t+1} must depend at least on market anticipations of θ_{t+1}, namely $\int E_{j,t+1}(\theta_{t+1})\,dj$. Therefore firm i will attempt to forecast this market anticipation $E_{i,t+1}\int E_{j,t+1}(\theta_{t+1})\,dj$. But again, by the symmetry of the situation, other firms form such anticipations. Therefore again, to be one step ahead of the market, so to speak, firm i will attempt to forecast these latter forecasts $E_{i,t+1}\int E_{j,t+1}\int E_{k,t+1}(\theta_{t+1})\,dk\,dj$, and so on. Thus we have described an infinite regress problem in expectations.

It is argued in this section that this infinite regress problem necessarily emerges in the basic model if we are only willing to specify arbitrary initial prior beliefs on the part of firms about the parameter θ_t and about the beliefs of other firms. However, perhaps contrary to appearance, the infinite regress problem does have a solution, at least in principle, in an infinite-dimensional space. That is, there exists a dynamic competitive equilibrium with rational but disparate expectations. In the next section we take up a discussion of how to resolve the infinite regress problem, perhaps in a more natural way, by truncating the infinite regress.

The discussion in this section will be aided considerably by a small investment in notation. Therefore let $\phi_{0t} = \theta_t$ for all t. Let the prior of firm i on θ_t at time t be termed its zero-order belief on θ_t with expectation $m_{0t}(i)$. Regard the economy-wide average $\int m_{0t}(j)\,\mathrm{d}j$ of these forecasts as another variable ϕ_{1t}. Let the prior of firm i on ϕ_{1t} at time t be termed its first-order belief on θ_t with expectation $m_{1t}(i)$. Regard the economy-wide average $\int m_{1t}(j)\,\mathrm{d}j$ of these forecasts as another variable ϕ_{2t}. Let the prior of firm i on ϕ_{2t} be termed its second-order belief on θ_t with expectation $m_{2t}(i)$. Continuing *recursively* in this manner, let $\phi_{nt} = \int m_{n-1,t}(j)\,\mathrm{d}j$ for all integers $n \geqslant 1$.

Now define an infinite-dimensional vector of variables $\phi_t = [\phi_{nt}, n \geqslant 0]$. Let $m_t(i) = [m_{nt}(i), n \geqslant 0]$ be an infinite-dimensional vector of expectations on ϕ_t, and let $\Sigma(\phi_t)$ denote a doubly infinite-dimensional matrix of covariances with $(k+1)$th row and $(n+1)$th column element $\sigma_{kn}(\phi_t)$. We will assume that firm i's beliefs about θ_t and about the beliefs of other firms are completely described by the infinite-dimensional normal distribution with mean $m_t(i)$ and covariance matrix $\Sigma(\phi_t)$. The covariance matrix is common knowledge. Thus, in this specification, means can vary across firms i but covariances cannot. However, both means and covariances can evolve over time. Beliefs at $t = 0$ are taken as an initial condition.

With this notation, the definition of a competitive equilibrium is now relatively straightforward.

Definition

A dynamic competitive equilibrium with rational but disparate expectations is a specification of a decision rule for each firm $i \in I$

$$q_{it} = \sum_{n=0}^{\infty} \alpha_n m_{nt}(i) \tag{15.1}$$

a rule for economy-wide average output

$$Q_t = \sum_{n=0}^{\infty} \beta_n \phi_{n+1,t} \tag{15.2}$$

laws of motion for the variables ϕ_t

$$\phi_{0,t+1} = \rho\phi_{0t} + v_{t+1} \tag{15.3}$$

$$\phi_{k,t+1} = \delta_{k0}(t)P_t + \sum_{n=1}^{\infty} \delta_{kn}(t)\phi_{nt} \qquad k \geqslant 1 \tag{15.4}$$

laws of motion for the forecasts of the ϕ_t for each firm $i \in I$

$$m_{k,t+1}(i) = \gamma_{k+1,0}(t)P_t + \sum_{n=0}^{\infty} \gamma_{k+1,n+1}(t)m_{nt}(i) \geqslant 0 \qquad k \geqslant 0 \quad (15.5)$$

and the market-clearing equation

$$P_t = \phi_{0t} + \varepsilon_t - bQ_t \qquad (15.6)$$

such that the following hold.

1 Maximization: the decision rule (15.1) is maximizing for each firm i given the average output rule (15.2) and the market-clearing condition (15.6).
2 Statistically correct forecasting: the laws of motion for forecasts (15.5) are statistically correct for each firm i given the average output rule (15.2), the market-clearing condition (15.6), and the parameter laws (15.3) and (15.4).
3 Consistent aggregation in output: the average output rule (15.2) is consistent with the individual decision rules (15.1), that is, $\alpha_n = \beta_n$, $n \geqslant 0$.
4 Consistent aggregation in forecasts: the laws of motion for forecasts (15.5) over all i generate the laws of motion for variables (15.4), that is,

$$\gamma_{kn}(t) = \delta_{kn}(t) \qquad k \geqslant 1, n \geqslant 0$$

The definition is self-explanatory in large part, but some additional comments seem appropriate. In particular, the separation between individual and average laws, both in output and in forecasts, should be noted. That is, each firm i takes the average output rule (15.2) and laws of motion of parameters (15.3) and (15.4) as given in determining its own output and in making its own forecast. This keeps strategic interaction at a minimum. In fact, substituting (15.2) into (15.6) completely removes the dependence of the output decision of firm i on the average decision Q_t; just as in a standard rational expectations equilibrium, there is a kind of self-fulfilling distribution in prices.

An equilibrium may seem difficult to compute, but it is not. Essentially, all we need to do is make the substitutions suggested in consistency requirements 3 and 4, and then search for the undetermined coefficients $\{\alpha_n\}$ in (15.1) and (15.2) and the undetermined coefficients $\{\gamma_{kn}(t)\}$ in (15.4) and (15.5). Moreover, these searches can be conducted recursively, as is now indicated. First, use (15.1), (15.2), and (15.6) to determine the $\{\alpha_n\}$. Under some mild regularity conditions, there exists a solution of the form $\alpha_n = (-1)^n a(ab)^n$, $n \geqslant 0$ (see Townsend, 1978, this volume, ch. 13, proof of proposition 13.2). Second, consider the updating problem of firm i. Using (15.2) and (15.6) again, we find that the posterior of firm i on the variables

ϕ_t at the end of period t is a weighted average of its prior and the observation P_t (see Townsend (1978, this volume, ch. 13, equations (13.2) and (13.3)), for a similar calculation). The weights are determined by ratios of linear combinations of covariances, all in terms of the (known) parameters of $\Sigma(\phi_t)$, σ_v^2, σ_ε^2, a, and b. Now attack the system recursively. The law of motion for ϕ_{0t} is given in (15.3). Therefore the posterior on ϕ_{0t} (just determined) and the law (15.3) give the updating formula of firm i for $\phi_{0,t+1}$, that is, (15.5) at $k = 0$. Averaging over firms i produces the law of motion for $\phi_{1,t+1}$, that is, (15.4) at $k = 1$. Now take the expectation of firm i over $\phi_{1,t+1}$ and substitute the posterior formulas for all the ϕ_t. This yields (15.5) at $k = 1$. Then average over all firms i to produce (15.4) at $k = 2$. We can proceed in principle to compute all the infinite laws in this manner.

Thus the infinite regress problem has a direct solution, at least in principle. However, various potential drawbacks of this setup and its solution should be noted. First, it must be verified that the many infinite sums are well defined. Second, and related, in computing a solution we have to hope for closed form solutions or hope that iterative procedures can be truncated after some point. Third, the coefficients in the equilibrium representation vary over time, an aspect that can only complicate econometric work; it is hoped that these converge to constants over time. Fourth, and related, it is hoped that the influence of the initial priors dissipates over time. In subsequent sections, all these hopes are fulfilled with alternative setups and solution techniques.

4 Truncating the infinite regress: the gain from statistical decision theory

As noted, we might be happier for conceptual and computational reasons if the regress of the previous section could be truncated after some point. (Even Keynes (1965) stopped with third-order expectations in his observations on the stock market.) A sufficient way of truncating is for there to be common knowledge of expectations at some (finite) order. In this section we discuss various ways in which such common knowledge might occur.

To begin the discussion, imagine in the setup of the previous section that there is diversity at the beginning of period t regarding the forecasts of θ_t, that is, that the $m_{0t}(i)$ vary over i. But suppose for some reason or other that there is agreement on the extent of the disagreement, that is, that the average of these forecasts is known, is known to be known, and so on, that is, $\int m_{0t}(j)\,\mathrm{d}j$ is common knowledge. Then it can be established as a special case of the previous analysis that there exist equilibrium decision rules of the form

$$q_{it} = am_{0t}(i) - \frac{a(ab)}{1+ab}\int m_{0t}(j)\,\mathrm{d}j$$

Moreover, in this case, because the economy-wide output Q_t is known, statistical updating produces the result that $\int m_{0t}(j)\,\mathrm{d}j$ will remain common knowledge in every period (see Townsend (1978, this volume, ch. 13, section 3) for details).

It is problematical how common knowledge of some finite-order forecasts might be achieved. Surveys of expectations would surely help, but of course there are sampling and survey errors. In general, this is an area for future research efforts (Townsend, 1978, this volume, ch. 13, section 6).

This brings us to perhaps the most compelling *modeling strategy* for truncating the infinite regress: statistical decision theory. Imagine that each decision-maker's beliefs are not arbitrary but rather are the result of conditioning on a joint distribution on some specific observations. Then decision-makers do not necessarily share common forecasts (conditional distributions). However, they will have common knowledge of the way that others are making their own forecasts (that is, the statistical updating formulas), and in some contexts this can be enough to truncate the infinite regress. The following three sections, each of which is intended to illustrate a separate point, illustrate this gain to statistical decision theory in successively more complicated information structures.

5 Learning, convergence to rational expectations, and the existence of steady state distributions: some conceptual issues

In introducing and developing the concept of rational expectations, Muth (1961) and Lucas and Prescott (1971) have argued that the concept of rational expectations is an *equilibrium* concept and should perhaps be regarded as the outcome of some unspecified process of learning and adapting on the part of economic decision-makers. Recently, various authors have taken up this issue, asking whether or not models with learning converge to the rational expectations equilibrium outcome. In this section we address the convergence question.

To pose the issue of learning here, a limiting special case of the general model is considered first. Imagine that each of the parameters θ_t is equal to some constant θ, that is, that $\rho = 1$ and $\sigma_v^2 = 0$. In this context, a rational expectations equilibrium is a self-fulfilling price distribution; that is, a distribution of prices that, if taken as given by firms and used in their maximum problems, implies output decisions that, in turn, with market clearing under the random demand schedule, imply the initial distribution of prices. More specifically,

$$P_t(\varepsilon_t) = \frac{\theta}{1 + ab} + \varepsilon_t \qquad (15.7)$$

is such a self-fulfilling distribution. We may now ask whether or not there will be convergence to this distribution over time if, for some reason, initial guesses about the distribution are wrong but learning is allowed.

One way to proceed is to imagine that decisions-makers, firms in this instance, have in mind a relatively simple model that they use to make decisions and update beliefs, that is, to learn about one or a number of parameters. Suppose, borrowing here and later from Cyert and DeGroot (1974), that each firm believes that

$$P_t = \rho P_{t-1} + \varepsilon_t \tag{15.8}$$

where $\{\varepsilon_t\}$ is a sequence of i.i.d. variables, each with mean zero and variance $\sigma_\varepsilon^2 = 1/r$. Each firm regards ρ as a fixed but unknown parameter about which it attempts to learn. That is, ρ is regarded as a normal random variable, with mean m_t and variance $1/h_t$ at the beginning of each period t. Thus, with contemporary observations on price P_t,

$$m_{t+1} = \frac{h_t m_t + rP_{t-1}P_t}{h_t + rP_{t-1}^2}, \qquad h_{t+1} = h_t + rP_{t-1}^2 \tag{15.9}$$

from standard statistical updating formulas (DeGroot, 1970). To close the model, note that for the representative firm, from (15.8),

$$E_t(P_t) = m_t P_{t-1} \tag{15.10}$$

However, from the actual market-clearing equation with $\theta = 0$ (as is now assumed),

$$P_t = -abE_t(P_t) + \varepsilon_t \tag{15.11}$$

Thus, substituting (15.10) into (15.11),

$$P_t = -abm_t P_{t-1} + \varepsilon_t \tag{15.12}$$

Here, then, the relatively simple model used by firms, namely (15.8), is not generally consistent with the actual distribution of prices (15.12); in the learning process, m_t moves around, and so parameter ρ in (15.8) is not fixed.

We might hope for consistency in the limit. In fact, if $m_t \to 0$, then we would have convergence to a strong form rational expectations equilibrium. However, the results reported by Cyert and DeGroot (1974) using their model are not comforting in this regard; the model oscillates and even explodes under some reasonable parameter specifications in various Monte Carlo runs.

What inferences can be drawn from the failure of Cyert and DeGroot's model to converge? Perhaps little. The failure to converge might be taken to indicate that decision-makers were doomed at the outset by an incorrect view of the world and a limited statistical procedure. The model firms used was wrong and was never tested by them. This, of course, raises the question of how best to model inconsistent learning processes and to conduct stability analysis. As noted, a number of writers are attacking these issues.

An alternative to postulating relatively simple (incorrect) models that decision-makers use in learning is to assume that decision-makers' models are consistent with the structure of the economy. It must be emphasized immediately that this is not as demanding an assumption as it might first seem, for we can still entertain all the rich variety of information structures and learning that statistical decision theory allows. There can be uncertainty about the nature of demand, the information and expectations of other agents, the decisions taken by them, and so on.

In the context of such a consistent structure, the convergence question can again be posed. In fact, it might be asked whether or not the period-by-period price distributions of the model of section 3, with the equilibrium definition proposed there, would converge to the self-fulfilling price distribution described at the outset of this section. That is, would there be convergence to a (strong form) rational expectations equilibrium? This question was answered affirmatively by Townsend (1978, this volume, ch. 13) for the special case when industry output is observed period by period. More recently, Bray and Kreps (1981) have indicated that convergence (if not existence) results may be quite general. However, it is argued here, as in Bray and Kreps (1981), that this particular convergence question is no longer of interest as a potential justification for rational expectations given that rational expectations are imposed in the learning process. To put it as bluntly as possible, such an imposition is tantamount to assuming what we want to prove. The failure of the model to converge to a special configuration would seem to indicate little.

Of what use, then, are rational expectations models with rational learning? Again, the hope is that such models might mimic certain key features or stylized facts of the data. That is, do rational expectations models with learning have potentially testable implications, and, if so, are they consistent with data? This alternative issue leads in turn to yet another convergence question that *can* be answered in many contexts.

It seems unlikely a priori that a model with fixed shocks or parameter values can explain much of the interesting movement in economic time series even if there is learning and an absence of convergence. Thus, the model in this section, with θ_t shocks to demand fixed at θ for all t, loses its appeal. Therefore we return to the more general structure in which demand is perpetually buffeted by new shocks v_t. That is, with $\theta_t = v_t + \rho v_{t-1} +$

$\rho^2 v_{t-2} + \ldots + \rho^t \theta_0$, firms attempt to learn at the end of period t about the parameter θ_0 *and* past parameters $v_1, v_2, \ldots, v_t$. Equivalently, firms attempt to learn about the random variable θ_t at the end of each period t. See Townsend (1983, this volume, ch. 14) for a more detailed discussion of this equivalence.

Imagine that initially at $t=0$ each firm has a common normal prior on the variable θ_0 with mean m_0 and variance Σ_0. Moreover, this prior belief is common knowledge. In addition, at the end of each period t each firm sees the market-clearing price P_t *and* the observation u_t, which is linearly related to noise to the demand shocks θ_t, namely

$$u_t = \theta_t + w_t$$

where w_t is an i.i.d. normal random variable with mean zero and variance σ_w^2. In this context, we might hope to find an equilibrium that is consistent with considerable and interesting movement in economic time series and that is potentially testable.

The discussion will be aided considerably by redefining an equilibrium for this particular information structure. In doing so, it will prove helpful to let q_t and m_t denote the output decision and mean forecast of the representative firm, with Q_t and M_t the corresponding economy-wide averages.

Definition

A dynamic competitive equilibrium with rational and homogeneous expectations is a law of motion for θ_t

$$\theta_{t+1} = \rho\theta_t + v_{t+1} \tag{15.13}$$

an observer equation

$$u_t = \theta_t + w_t \tag{15.14}$$

a decision rule for the representation firm

$$q_t = \alpha_0 m_t + \alpha_1 M_t \tag{15.15}$$

a rule for economy-wide average output

$$Q_t = \beta M_t \tag{15.16}$$

a law of motion for the mean forecast of the representative firm

$$m_{t+1} = \gamma_0 m_t + \gamma_1 P_t + \gamma_2 M_t + \gamma_3 u_t \tag{15.17}$$

a law of motion for the economy-wide average mean forecast

$$M_{t+1} = \delta_1 P_t + \delta_2 M_t + \delta_3 u_t \tag{15.18}$$

and a market-clearing equation

$$P_t = \theta_t + \varepsilon_t - bQ_t \tag{15.19}$$

such that the following hold.

1 Maximization: the decision rule (15.15) is maximizing given the average output rule (15.16) and market-clearing equation (15.19).
2 Statistically correct forecasting: the law of motion (15.17) is statistically correct given the law of motion (15.13), the observer equation (15.14), the market-clearing equation (15.19), the average output rule (15.16), and the average forecasting rule (15.18).
3 Consistent output aggregation: rules (15.15) and (15.16) are consistent.
4 Consistent forecast aggregation: rules (15.17) and (15.18) are consistent.

It is hoped that what is striking about this definition is its apparent simplicity. In particular, we have here a finite number of state variables and time-invariant coefficients. Both these specifications are warranted; that is, an equilibrium with these properties can be constructed, as is now indicated.

First, note from (15.18) that because M_0 is assumed to be known, and P_t and u_t are common observations, M_1 is known, and so on. This is what keeps the dimensionality finite. Then it only remains to compute the undetermined time-invariant coefficients. Now equations (15.15), (15.16), and (15.19) are easily solved as before to yield $\alpha_0 = a$, $\alpha_1 = -a(ab)/(1+ab)$, $\beta = \alpha_0 + \alpha_1$. To compute the coefficients in (15.17), use is made of the extremely powerful Kalman filtering algorithm (for example, Bertsekas, 1976).[4] The system described here is a special case of a model with a linear law of motion for state variables

$$x_{t+1} = Ax_t + \bar{v}_{t+1}$$

and observer equations

$$y_t = Cx_t + \bar{w}_t$$

Here $x_t = \theta_t$, $A = \rho$, $\bar{v}_t = v_t$,

$$\bar{w}_t = \begin{bmatrix} \varepsilon_t \\ w_t \end{bmatrix}, \quad y_t = \begin{bmatrix} P_t + b\beta M_t \\ u_t \end{bmatrix}, \quad C = \begin{bmatrix} 1 \\ 1 \end{bmatrix}$$

where

$$E\bar{v}_t = 0, \quad E(\bar{w}_t) = \begin{bmatrix} 0 \\ 0 \end{bmatrix}, \quad E\bar{v}_t\bar{v}_t' = M = \sigma_v^2, \quad E\bar{w}_t\bar{w}_t' = N = \begin{bmatrix} \sigma_\varepsilon^2 & 0 \\ 0 & \sigma_w^2 \end{bmatrix}$$

Under the mild regularity conditions that are satisfied here (Bertsekas, 1976; Kwakernaak and Sivan, 1977), for arbitrary prior distributions on x_0 with mean $E_0(x_0)$ and variance $\Sigma_{0|-1}$, the updated posterior distributions converge, so that the means satisfy the recursive relationship

$$E_t(x_t) = AE_{t-1}(x_{t-1}) + \bar{\Sigma}C'N^{-1}\{y_{t-1} - CAE_{t-1}(x_{t-1})\} \tag{15.20}$$

and the covariance matrices satisfy the recursive relationship

$$\Sigma_{t|t-1} = A\{\Sigma_{t-1|t-2} - \Sigma_{t-1|t-2}C'(C\Sigma_{t-1|t-2}C' + N)^{-1}C\Sigma_{t-1|t-2}\}A' + M \tag{15.21}$$

where

$$\Sigma_{t|t-1} = E_t[\{x_t - E_t(x_t)\}\{x_t - E_t(x_t)\}']$$

and $\Sigma_{t|t-1}$ converges termwise to a time-invariant matrix Σ. Then $\bar{\Sigma}$ in (15.20) satisfies

$$\bar{\Sigma} = \Sigma - \Sigma C'(C\Sigma C' + N)^{-1}C\Sigma \tag{15.22}$$

and its terms are variances and covariances of beliefs on the state vector x_t at the end of date t. Clearly, (15.20)–(15.22) can be used to deliver the time-invariant coefficients in (15.17). Then (15.18) is determined by $\delta_1 = \gamma_1$, $\delta_3 = \gamma_3$, and $\delta_2 = \gamma_0 + \gamma_2$. Finally, it should be noted that (15.20) can be viewed as in place even at $t = 0$ on the assumption that the system has an infinite past. This device of assuming an infinite past as the limiting case will be used again in a subsequent section. It is highly convenient for analytic and econometric purposes.

It is clear, of course, that the steady state matrix $\bar{\Sigma}$ will not in general converge to zero, its value in a period-by-period strong form rational expectations equilibrium, with θ_t known at the end of period t, so that $E_{t+1}(\theta_{t+1}) = \rho\theta_t$. At best, we can estimate or learn past innovations v_τ, $\tau < t$, arbitrarily well if τ is arbitrarily far in the past. However, contemporary θ_t is continually buffeted by new shocks v_t about which little is known. The additional information in u_t will help in forecasting (that is, reduce $\bar{\Sigma}$) but will not cause a degeneracy unless $\sigma_w^2 = 0$.

Thus the failure of the system to converge to a period-by-period strong form rational expectations equilibrium should not come as a surprise and is certainly not damning. In fact, the freedom that the model allows in specifying indirectly the steady state forecasting variance $\bar{\Sigma}$ may be useful for econometric purposes, because in principle it allows a better fit of the model to actual date. It determines the extent to which forecasts respond to contemporary observations, and this in turn determines the extent to which the system itself moves around, say in response to relatively permanent shocks. In addition, a nontrivial forecasting variance $\bar{\Sigma}$ allows the system to respond to completely transitory shocks ε_t and to measurement errors u_t. Finally, it should be emphasized that this linear-normal system can, in principle, be taken to data by the methods described in detail by Townsend (1982, this volume, ch. 13, section 10).

6 Exploiting recursive structures with finite state space methods

The information structure of the previous section allowed no diversity in forecasts; equilibrium was characterized by rational and homogeneous expectations. This section and the next consider progressively more complicated information structures that do allow diversity.[5] In this section we have a group of informed firms and a group of uninformed firms. It is established that such structures can be successfully attacked with statistical decision theory and the use of recursive procedures. Yet, despite the diversity, and in contrast with the analysis of section 3, there is no infinite regress problem. Moreover, such structures can produce interesting time series.

To begin, imagine that at the beginning of period 0, all firms have a common normal prior on the variable θ_0, with mean $E(\theta_0)$ and variance $\mathrm{var}(\theta_0)$. This prior is common knowledge. Now, at the end of each period t, $t \geqslant 0$, each of a set I of informed firms, fraction ρ_I of the set of all firms, observes a random variable $u_t = \theta_t + w_t$, where w_t is an i.i.d. normal random variable with mean zero and variance σ_w^2. Each of a set U of uninformed firms, fraction ρ_U, does not observe u_t. However, *all* firms see the market-clearing price P_t at the end of each period t. Industry output, however, is not observed directly, though it may be inferred by some.

To attack this structure, we will first uncover a finite list of state variables that will allow us to write down the decisions of firms and the evolution of their beliefs. All these state variables will be known in each period to the informed firms, but uninformed firms will know only a subset. Of course, θ_t remains unknown to all.

To begin, let $E_{It}(\theta_t)$ and $\Sigma_{It}(\theta_t)$ denote the beginning-of-period prior mean and variance on θ_t of informed firms. Now, for uninformed firms, $E_{It}(\theta_t)$ is unknown, because the u_t are not observed by them. However, we can assume that they regard $E_{It}(\theta_t)$ as an unknown variable π_t that is jointly normally distributed with the unknown variable θ_t; that is, $[\theta_t, \pi_t]$ is normally distributed, with mean $[E_{Ut}(\theta_t), E_{Ut}(\pi_t)]$ and covariance matrix $\Sigma_{Ut}(\theta_t, \pi_t)$. Then the state variables mentioned earlier are π_t, $\Sigma_{It}(\theta_t)$, $E_{Ut}(\theta_t)$, $E_{Ut}(\pi_t)$, and $\Sigma_{Ut}(\theta_t, \pi_t)$. Finally, note that $\Sigma_{It}(\theta_t)$ and $\Sigma_{Ut}(\theta_t, \pi_t)$ are assumed to be common knowledge.

We are now in a position to redefine an equilibrium with this state space.

Definition

A dynamic competitive equilibrium with rational but disparate expectations is a law of motion for θ_t

$$\theta_{t+1} = \rho\theta_t + v_{t+1} \tag{15.23}$$

an observer equation

$$u_t = \theta_t + w_t \tag{15.24}$$

a low of motion for π_t

$$\pi_{t+1} = \xi_{1t}\pi_t + \xi_{2t}\theta_t + \xi_{3t}w_t + \xi_{4t}\varepsilon_t \tag{15.25}$$

a decision rule for uninformed firms

$$q_{Ut} = \alpha_1 E_{Ut}(\theta_t) + \alpha_2 E_{Ut}(\pi_t) \tag{15.26}$$

a decision rule for informed firms

$$q_{It} = \beta_0 E_{It}(\theta_t) + \beta_1 E_{Ut}(\theta_t) + \beta_2 E_{Ut}(\pi_t) \tag{15.27}$$

laws of motion for forecasts and covariance matrix of beliefs of uninformed firms

$$E_{U,t+1}(\theta_{t+1}) = \gamma_{1t}E_{Ut}(\theta_t) + \gamma_{2t}E_{Ut}(\pi_t) + \gamma_{3t}P_t \tag{15.28}$$

$$E_{U,t+1}(\pi_{t+1}) = \gamma_{4t}E_{Ut}(\theta_t) + \gamma_{5t}E_{Ut}(\pi_t) + \gamma_{6t}P_t \tag{15.29}$$

$$\Sigma_{U,t+1}(\theta_{t+1}, \pi_{t+1}) = \psi[\Sigma_{Ut}(\theta_t, \pi_t), \sigma_v^2, \sigma_w^2, \sigma_\varepsilon^2] \tag{15.30}$$

laws of motion for forecasts and variance of beliefs of informed firms

$$E_{I,t+1}(\theta_{t+1}) = \delta_{1t}E_{It}(\theta_t) + \delta_{2t}P_t + \delta_{3t}u_t + \delta_{4t}E_{Ut}(\theta_t) + \delta_{5t}E_{Ut}(\pi_t) \tag{15.31}$$

$$\Sigma_{I,t+1}(\theta_{t+1}) = \Phi[\Sigma_{It}(\theta_t), \sigma_v^2, \sigma_w^2, \sigma_\varepsilon^2] \tag{15.32}$$

and a market-clearing equation

$$P_t = \theta_t + \varepsilon_t - b(\rho_I q_{It} + \rho_U q_{Ut}) \tag{15.33}$$

such that the following hold.

1 Maximization: the decision rules (15.26) and (15.27) are each maximizing given the rules (15.26) and (15.27) and the market-clearing equation (15.33).
2 Statistically correct forecasting for informed firms: the laws of motion (15.31) and (15.32) are statistically correct given the decision rules (15.26) and (15.27), the market-clearing equation (15.33), the parameter law (15.23), and the observer equation (15.24).
3 Statistically correct forecasting for uninformed firms: the laws of motion (15.28), (15.29), and (15.30) are statistically correct given the decision rules (15.26) and (15.27), the market-clearing equation (15.33), the parameter laws of motion (15.23) and (15.25), and the observer equation (15.24).

One comment is immediately in order. Unlike previous definitions, there is no distinction here between individual and aggregate decisions and forecasts. However, it should be understood that the representative informed firm takes as given that the output decisions and forecasts of other informed forms are identical with its own, and similarly for uninformed firms.

An equilibrium is not difficult to compute. First, the coefficients α_1, α_2, β_0, β_1, and β_2 in (15.26) and (15.27) are computed by the method of undetermined coefficients, using property 1 of the equilibrium.[6] Second, the forecasting formulas (15.31) and (15.32) for informed firms are readily computed by Bayesian considerations; essentially, each informed firm is obtaining two independent observations on θ_t at the end of period t, through u_t and $P_t - b(\rho_{It} q_{It} + \rho_{Ut} q_{Ut})$, and the law of motion (15.23) is known. For this purpose it is important to remember that q_{Ut} (and q_{It}) is expressed in terms of state variables that informed firms know. Now (15.25) follows immediately from (15.31), with $\pi_t = E_{It}(\theta_t)$. Finally, we have to attack the forecasting formulas for the uninformed firms. Using (15.33) with (15.31) and (15.27) (and (15.26)), uninformed firms are obtaining one observation θ_t and π_t through P_t – recall again $\pi_t = E_{It}(\theta_t)$. Therefore the posterior $E_{U,t+1}(\theta_t)$ and $E_{U,t+1}(\pi_t)$ can be formed in the usual Bayesian way. Now the parameter laws of motion (15.23) and (15.25) for θ_{t+1} and π_{t+1} are known; therefore priors on π_{t+1} and θ_{t+1} at the beginning of period $t+1$ are readily calculated. This yields (15.28)–(15.30).

An unfortunate aspect of the foregoing definition is the presence of time-varying coefficients – the coefficients are functions of period-by-period covariances that are allowed to move around. As it turns out, this is not a problem. First, steady state Kalman filtering considerations can be used to remove the time dependence of Σ_{It}. This removes time dependence from (15.31) and hence from (15.25). It then becomes apparent that the inference problem of uninformed firms can be cast as a classical optimal observer problem as well. To see this, consider the state vector $x_t = [\theta_t, \pi_t]'$. Then uninformed firms see $y_t = P_t + b\rho_U q_{Ut} + b\rho_I \beta_1 E_{Ut}(\theta_t) + b\rho_I \beta_2 E_{Ut}\pi_t) = \theta_t + \varepsilon_t - b\rho_I \beta_0 \pi_t$, so that

$$y_t = Cx_t + \bar{w}_t \tag{15.34}$$

where $C = 1 - b\rho_I \beta_0$ and $\bar{w}_t = \varepsilon_t$. Of course, x_t has the linear law of motion

$$x_{t+1} = Ax_t + \bar{v}_{t+1} \tag{15.35}$$

from (15.23) and (15.25), where

$$A = \begin{bmatrix} \rho & 0 \\ \xi_2 & \xi_1 \end{bmatrix}, \qquad \bar{v}_{t+1} = \begin{bmatrix} v_{t+1} \\ \xi_3 w_t + \xi_4 \varepsilon_t \end{bmatrix}$$

In the optimal observer system (15.34) and (15.35), the measurement error noise $\bar{w}_t$ and state excitation noise $\bar{v}_{t+1}$ are correlated. However, Kalman filtering can handle this correlation – the covariance matrix of beliefs for uninformed firms converges to some constant, removing the time dependence from Σ_{Ut} and hence from (15.28) and (15.29).

It may now be noted how the hierarchical information structure and statistical decision theory allow a recursive attack on the system. First, it is assumed that there is a common prior distribution that is common knowledge. Informed firms know that the forecast of uninformed firms is the mean of their conditional distribution – the common distribution conditioned on variables that the uninformed firms *and* the informed firms see. Therefore informed firms know the forecast of uninformed firms. Uninformed firms do not know the actual forecast of informed firms. But they do know that the forecast of informed firms is the mean of their conditional distribution – the common distribution conditioned on variables that the informed firms see, but that uninformed firms do not see completely. By Bayes's rule, then, uninformed firms know how the unobserved forecast of informed firms moves period by period, namely, as a function of the underlying unobserved state variables, observed and unobserved information variables, and the forecast of uninformed firms, which, of course, uninformed firms know. Therefore uninformed firms can forecast the forecast of informed firms. There is no infinite regress problem: *recursive structures are tractable by finite state space methods.*

As a final note, we might remark on the potential of recursive structures to generate interesting time series as displayed in table 15.1 and figures 15.1 and 15.2. Suppose, for example, that the industry is in a steady state at time t ($t=0$) and is subjected to a unit variance shock ε_t, holding all other contemporary and future shocks at zero. All firms' forecasts of θ_t (which actually remains zero) will increase, thereby increasing industry output. Sustained increases of output (above the steady state of zero) for the first three periods keep prices low (below zero) for the first three periods, and uninformed firms come to believe that θ_t is actually negative. Consequently, uninformed firms reduce output (below zero), causing prices to become positive for periods 4–7. As a result, their forecasts become positive again for periods 8–10 and prices become negative. This oscillatory pattern continues for some time, eventually converging to zero. Now, if we take the differences between θ_t and $E_{Ut}(\theta_t)$ as a forecast error, then in this scenario forecast errors oscillate, delivering the waves of optimism and pessimism that Pigou (1929) had in mind. This can be contrasted with the more conventional exponential decay of forecasts of informed firms (which figure out that the shock is zero within five periods, virtually).

It should be emphasized here that uninformed firms *do* take into account their own quantity movements in forecasting, but they remain uncertain

Table 15.1 Response to a transitory ε_t shock

t	P_t	q_{It}	q_{Ut}	θ_t	$\pi_t = E_{It}(\theta_t)$	$E_{Ut}(\theta_t)$	$E_{Ut}(\pi_t)$
1	−0.30353	0.05970	0.31636	0.00000	0.36322	0.61102	0.17714
2	−0.26419	−0.16979	0.28703	0.00000	0.09439	0.56990	0.48685
3	−0.08535	−0.06082	0.09305	0.00000	0.02453	0.19823	0.44104
4	0.06403	0.07040	−0.07110	0.00000	0.00637	−0.12748	0.16707
5	0.10680	0.10845	−0.11813	0.00000	0.00166	−0.22883	−0.08042
6	0.06504	0.06547	−0.07191	0.00000	0.00043	−0.14487	−0.16611
7	0.00235	0.00246	−0.00260	0.00000	0.00011	−0.01026	−0.11149
8	−0.03357	−0.03354	0.03710	0.00000	0.00003	0.07003	−0.01330
9	−0.03282	−0.03281	0.03628	0.00000	0.00000	0.07142	0.04884
10	−0.01237	−0.01237	0.01367	0.00000	0.00000	0.02858	0.05319
11	0.00643	0.00643	−0.00710	0.00000	0.00000	−0.01243	0.02311
12	0.01284	0.01281	−0.01419	0.00000	0.00000	−0.02739	−0.00754
13	0.00853	0.00853	−0.00942	0.00000	0.00000	−0.01889	−0.01979
14	0.00095	0.00095	−0.00105	0.00000	0.00000	−0.00269	−0.01444
15	−0.00380	−0.00380	0.00420	0.00000	0.00000	0.00787	−0.00268
16	−0.00409	−0.00409	0.00452	0.00000	0.00000	0.00887	0.00542
17	−0.00175	−0.00175	0.00194	0.00000	0.00000	0.00400	0.00657
18	0.00060	0.00060	−0.00067	0.00000	0.00000	−0.00112	0.00319
19	0.00153	0.00153	0.00169	0.00000	0.00000	−0.00325	−0.00062
20	0.00111	0.00111	0.00122	0.00000	0.00000	−0.00244	−0.00233

$\sigma_v^2 = 1.00000$; $\sigma_\varepsilon^2 = 1.00000$; $\sigma_w^2 = 1.00000$; $\rho = 0.95000$; % inf $= 0.05000$; $a = 1.00000$; $b = 1.00000$.

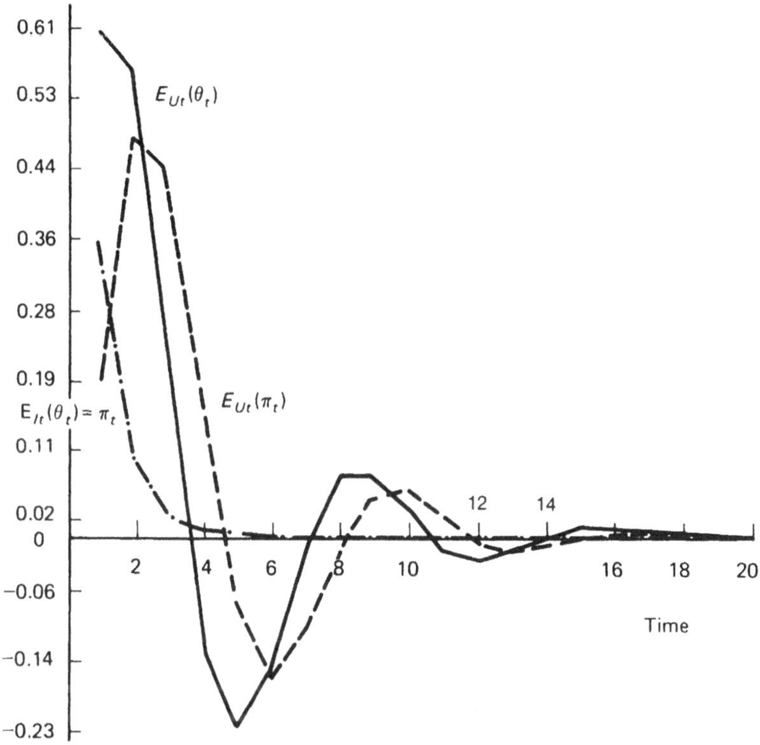

Figure 15.1. Response to transitory shock: forecasts

about the outputs of *informed* firms. Therefore a series of low prices can cause them to put weight on θ_t's being low. Of course, these forecasts themselves *are* the best possible given the uninformed firms' information set and their knowledge of the economy; that is, the forecast error of θ_t that uninformed firms expect or forecast at the beginning of period t given their information then *is* zero. It should also be emphasized in this regard that the scenario described here is not the only possible sequence of events that can take place in the economy, and uninformed firms, as good Bayesians, put positive weight on other possible scenarios' generating the random variable they see (in fact, innovation accounting experiments like the one described take place with probability zero, though they serve us well in characterizing the time series, here picking up a degree of volatility, for example).

Despite its simplicity, the present industry model can thus be used to begin an analysis of some of the observations made by Keynes (1965). In particular, factors that make no real difference to prospective profitability, such as completely transitory shocks, trigger oscillations in less informed opinion,

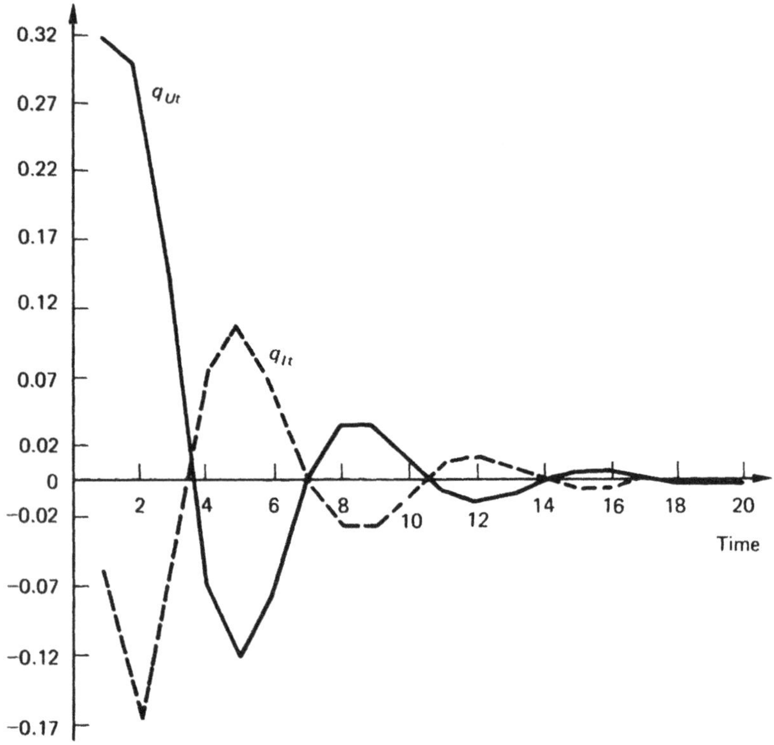

Figure 15.2. Response to transitory shock: outputs

and this in turn causes fluctuations in the market price. Moreover, informed firms do take less informed opinion into account, though in this industry setting the latter influence is stabilizing. This can be seen from table 15.1 and figure 15.2. Again, after four periods, informed firms know that the shock is completely transitory, but they continue to respond in a negative way to output decisions of the uninformed firms, ending up on the other side of the steady state as it were.

7 Equilibrium in a symmetric but disparate information structure: the infinite regress problem again with a new solution

As noted, the information structure of the previous section allows a recursive attack on the system. But imagine a symmetric information structure in which *each* firm receives its own information on the underlying state variable of interest, namely θ_t. That is, suppose that, in addition to P_t, each firm i sees at the end of period t a random variable

$$u_{it} = \theta_t + w_{it} \tag{15.36}$$

where the w_{it} are regarded as normally distributed random variables, independent both across firms and over time, each with mean zero and variance $\sigma_w^2 \neq 0$. With industry output unobserved, each firm is obtaining observations on θ_t that are confounded through P_t with the forecasts that other firms made on θ_t last period, which under (15.36) will not be known. Thus, to correctly forecast θ_t, each firm must forecast the economy-wide average forecasts of θ_t last period. Thus, each firm's forecast of θ_t depends on its forecast of the economy-wide average forecast of θ_t last period. Thus, the economy-wide average forecast of θ_t depends on the economy-wide average forecast of the economy-wide average forecast of θ_t last period. Now the economy-wide average forecast of θ_t last period must have a similar property. Thus, to correctly forecast θ_t, each firm must forecast the economy-wide average forecast last period of the economy-wide average forecast of θ_t two periods ago, and so on. It is apparent that there is an infinite regress problem here, despite the use of statistical decision theory.

In this section[7] we describe a technique for overcoming this difficulty – a technique of undetermined coefficients, as in Townsend (1983, this volume, ch. 14). It is argued, moreover, that the information specification here, like the one in the previous section, has interesting implications for economic time series.

We begin by setting out the definition of equilibrium for this section in rather general terms. For notation, let Ω_{it} denote the information set of firm i at the beginning of period t. Let Ω_{it} contain at least past prices $P_{t-1}, P_{t-2}, \ldots$ and past information variables $u_{i,t-1}, u_{i,t-2}, \ldots$. Also, let $E(P_t|\Omega_{it})$ denote firm i's forecast of price P_t conditioned on the information set Ω_{it}, and let $\bar{P}_t$ denote the economy-wide average of these forecasts. This yields the following definition.

Definition

A dynamic competitive equilibrium with rational but possibly disparate expectations is a law of motion for the parameter θ_t

$$\theta_{t+1} = \rho\theta_t + v_{t+1} \tag{15.37}$$

an observer equation for each firm i

$$u_{it} = \theta_t + w_{it} \tag{15.38}$$

a decision rule for each firm i

$$q_{it} = aE(P_t|\Omega_{it}) \tag{15.39}$$

a rule for economy-wide average output

$$Q_t = a\bar{P}_t \tag{15.40}$$

a forecasting formula for each firm i

$$E(P_t|\Omega_{it}) = C(L)v_{t-1} + D(L)\varepsilon_{t-1} + E(L)w_{i,t-1} \tag{15.41}$$

a specification of the economy-wide average forecast $\bar{P}_t$

$$\bar{P}_t = A(L)v_{t-1} + B(L)\varepsilon_{t-1} \tag{15.42}$$

and a market-clearing equation

$$P_t = \theta_t + \varepsilon_t - bQ_t \tag{15.43}$$

such that the following hold.

1 Statistically correct forecasting: the forecast (15.41) is statistically correct given the parameter law (15.37), the observer equation (15.38), the information set Ω_{it}, the market-clearing equation (15.43), the average output rule (15.40), and the rule for economy-wide average forecast (15.42).
2 Consistent aggregation in forecasts: formulas (15.41) and (15.42) are consistent, that is, the one-sided polynomials in the lag operator $A(L)$, $B(L)$, $C(L)$, $D(L)$, $E(L)$ satisfy $C(L) = A(L)$ and $D(L) = B(L)$.

Some comments are immediately in order. First, individual firm maximization and consistent aggregation in output have already been imposed, as is clear from (15.39) and (15.40). Second, the main task in the construction of an equilibrium is the simultaneous and consistent determination of individual and average forecasts. Note, in particular, that the average rule (15.42) is used by individual firms in the determination of (15.41).

The general procedure for the determination of an equilibrium is the method of undetermined coefficients. We begin with an arbitrary specification of (15.42), that is, with coefficients in $A(L)$ and $B(L)$ unknown to the modeler but assumed to be known to the firms. Then, in some manner, the forecasting problems of individual firms are solved. This yields (15.41) in terms of the undetermined coefficients. Then (15.41) is averaged over firms, with the w_{it} disappearing (for this purpose, we should view the set of firms as countably infinite). The average is then matched up with (15.42) to determine the undetermined coefficients.

There is a potential dimensionality problem with the foregoing procedure. To see this, u_{it} and P_t can be written in terms of the economic innovations ε_t and v_t, as well as the measurement error w_{it}, namely

$$u_{it} = \sum_{j=0}^{\infty} \rho^j v_{t-j} + w_{it} \tag{15.44}$$

$$P_t = \sum_{j=0}^{\infty} \rho^j v_{t-j} - abA(L)v_{t-1} - abB(L)\varepsilon_{t-1} + \varepsilon_t \tag{15.45}$$

Cast in this form, it appears that each firm should be forecasting *all* current and past shocks to demand. Therefore, to simplify the problem, following Chari's (1979) solution to his own (infinite) dimensionality problem, assume in addition that the entire history of shocks and measurement errors from $t-j$ on is known at time t. For example, let $j=2$; then $v_{t-2}, v_{t-3}, \ldots, \varepsilon_{t-2}, \varepsilon_{t-3}, \ldots$ are included in Ω_{it}. Then equations (15.44) and (15.45) can be written as

$$u_{it}^* = v_t + \rho v_{t-1} + w_{it} \tag{15.46}$$

$$P_t^* = v_t + \rho v_{t-1} - abA_0 v_{t-1} - abB_0 \varepsilon_{t-1} + \varepsilon_t \tag{15.47}$$

where the variables with asterisks are defined implicitly.

Two methods can be used to forecast the innovations v_t, v_{t-1}, ε_t, and ε_{t-1} from (15.46) and (15.47). Both are described by Townsend (1983, this volume, ch. 14) and summarized here. For the first method, write out all current and past observables that contain information on the unknown innovations; that is, write out (15.46) and (15.47) at t and $t-1$. Then use standard formulas for conditional means and variances of normal random variables. This delivers the forecasts of the innovations in terms of observables and hence, by substitution, in terms of the innovations themselves. This method is straightforwrd, but it is not recursive; a dimensionality problem begins to arise as the lag to full information increases, that is, as $j \to \infty$.

For the second method, the observer system (15.46) and (15.47) for each firm i can be written as

$$\begin{bmatrix} \varepsilon_{t-2} \\ v_{t-2} \\ u_{it}^* \\ P_t^* \end{bmatrix} = \begin{bmatrix} 0 & 0 & L^2 \\ L^2 & 0 & 0 \\ (1+\rho L) & 1 & 0 \\ (1+\alpha L) & 0 & (1-\delta L) \end{bmatrix} \begin{bmatrix} v_t \\ w_{it} \\ \varepsilon_t \end{bmatrix} \tag{15.48}$$

or

$$y_t = M(L)\xi_t \tag{15.49}$$

where $\alpha = \rho - abA_0$ and $\delta = abB_0$. It is from this system that each firm i will attempt to forecast v_t, v_{t-1}, ε_t, and ε_{t-1} at the end of period t. (Note that only two undetermined coefficients, A_0 and B_0, are being carried into this forecasting problem.)

System (15.48) cannot be used for forecasting because the representation is not fundamental relative to firm i's information set. That is, the variables on the right-hand side are not in the space spanned by the current and past values of variables on the left-hand side. To see this, note that $M(z)$ is not of full rank at $z = 0$, which is a point inside the unit circle. However, but it is possible to convert (15.49) to a moving-average representation that is fundamental, say

$$y_t = M^{**}(L)\xi_t^{**} \tag{15.50}$$

where

$$M^{**}(L) = M(L)WB(L)\hat{W}B(L) \tag{15.51}$$

$$\xi_t^{**} = B(L^{-1})'\hat{W}'B(L^{-1})'W'\xi_t \tag{15.52}$$

and the matrices W, $\hat{W}$, and $B(z)$ are orthogonal. This procedure is described in detail by Townsend (1983, this volume, ch. 14) and can be applied directly here. In fact, the matrices W, $\hat{W}$, and $B(z)$ are identical with those of Townsend. System (15.50) can be used directly for forecasting via the Wiener–Kolmogorov formulas. This delivers forecasts of v_t, v_{t-1}, ε_t, and ε_{t-1} as linear functions of current and past ξ_t^{**}. Then (15.52) can be used to deliver these forecasts in terms of the unobserved shocks ξ_t. We can then proceed as indicated earlier.

It should be noted that this procedure does not eliminate the infinite regress in expectations. Forecasts of $\bar{P}_t$ will vary across firms, and thus we could compute an economy-wide average of these latter forecasts, and so on, perhaps indefinitely. However, it is no longer necessary to determine these forecasts to compute the equilibrium.

A nice aspect of the foregoing procedure is that we can guarantee the existence of solutions for the undetermined coefficients via a fixed-point argument even though the equations in the undetermined coefficients are nonlinear. It is hoped, from Townsend (1983, this volume, ch. 14), that such solutions are unique and can be computed quickly via an iterative procedure. Arbitrary coefficients in the moving-average representation (15.42) produce coefficients for firms' forecasts that in turn can be averaged to yield another set of coefficients in the representation (15.42). For Townsend (1983, this volume, ch. 14), such a procedure converged quickly to a unique solution, though the model was somewhat different.

As a special case of the model here, let $\sigma_\varepsilon^2 = 0$, so that there is no transitory component to demand. Still, with economy-wide average output unobserved, at least not directly, firms face an apparently nontrivial signal extraction problem. However, on the assumption of an infinite past, we can search for a moving-average representation for the economy-wide average price forecast of the form (15.42). In fact, we can solve for the undetermined coefficients in the representation, namely $A_j = \rho^{j+1}/(1 + ab)$, $B_j = 0$, for all j. With these coefficients, the space spanned by current and past P_ts is identical with the space spanned by current and past v_ts; therefore the entire (infinite) history of the v_ts, and thus θ_t, is known to all firms at the end of period t (the observer equations (15.38) are redundant). It is easy to verify then that this information specification yields a period-by-period strong form rational expectations equilibrium, with $E(P_t) = \rho\theta_{t-1}/(1 + ab)$.

More generally, though with $\sigma_\varepsilon^2 \neq 0$ and of course $\sigma_w^2 \neq 0$, there will be diversity in forecasts, and economy-wide average output will not be inferred. Then the effect of ε_t shocks can produce interesting time series.

8 Concluding remarks

We began this chapter with the premise that equilibrium models with learning and with disparate but rational expectations will prove to be useful in describing aspects of reality. Of course, no model should pretend to describe reality completely. Thus, rather than being deterred by assumptions that can cause analytical difficulties, the emphasis here has been on specification strategies and solution techniques that make these models tractable. It turns out that the time series of these models do display interesting oscillations and can in principle be fitted to data. Therefore, consistent with the basic premise, an empirical application may soon be warranted.

One caveat is in order: economic policy issues have not been considered. When considering the effect of a "new" policy, we must confront the "change of regime" issue and ask what determines decision-makers' expectations (see Phelps, 1980; Sargent, 1981b). To the extent that decision-makers' expectations are arbitrary, we are led to an infinite regress problem. However, it may well be that statistical decision theory will prove to be a useful construct here as well, with priors of decision-makers linked to government policy announcements, general political sentiment, and past experience.

Notes

1 Needless to say, in this chapter we do not attempt to trace the development of the rational expectations equilibrium concept or to tie together the microeconomic and macroeconomic literature.

2 This reference is somewhat misleading, because in one way or another these authors *do* solve their respective problems. The solution procedures offered here are not unrelated.

3 In this section we build on the work of Townsend (1978, this volume, ch. 13), where the solution procedure was first described. However, the discussion here is marked by a strikingly simpler and more conventional definition of equilibrium that removes strategic considerations among decision-makers (as described later). With this definition, it is easier to describe the solution algorithm which handles the added generality here of a Markov process on θ_t.

4 Again, we could write out the entire history of observables and use standard formulas for conditional means and variances of normal random variables to forecast the entire history of innovations, and hence forecast θ_t. The Kalman filter is a recursive procedure that circumvents the dimensionality problems associated with this alternative.

5 This specification was considered by Prescott and Townsend (1980). But again, the discussion here is marked by an alternative definition of equilibrium in the more general setting in which the θ_t move around. Here, also, new Kalman filtering results are obtained, and a general method for attaching such structures is described.

6 These undetermined coefficients are determined by the equations

$$\beta_0 = a(1 - b\rho_I\beta_0)$$
$$\beta_1 = a(-b\rho_U\alpha_1 - b\rho_I\beta_1)$$
$$\beta_2 = a(-b\rho_I\beta_2 - b\rho_U\alpha_2)$$
$$\alpha_1 = a(1 - b\rho_I\beta_1 - b\rho_U\alpha_1)$$
$$\alpha_2 = a(-b\rho_I\beta_0 - b\rho_I\beta_2 - b\rho_U\alpha_2)$$

It can be verified directly that these linear equations do have a solution.

7 In this section we draw heavily on some recently developed techniques described by Townsend (1983, this volume, ch. 14). They are applied here to a model with within-market interactions, a feature missing from the work of Townsend. Helpful comments from Lars Hansen on the procedures of this section are gratefully acknowledged.

References

Arrow, K.J. and Green, J.R. (1973) Notes on expectations equilibria in Bayesian settings. Working Paper 33, Institute for Mathematical Studies in the Social Sciences, Stanford University.

Bertsekas, D.P. (1976) *Dynamic Programming and Stochastic Control.* New York: Academic Press.

Blume, L.E. and Easley, D. (1982) Learning to be rational. *Journal of Economic Theory* 26, 340–51.

Bray, M. (1982) Learning, estimation and the stability of rational expectations. *Journal of Economic Theory* 26, 318–39.

—— and Kreps, D.M. (1981) Rational learning and rational expectations. Research Paper 616, Graduate School of Business, Stanford University.

Chari, V.V. (1979) Linear stochastic models with decentralized information. Unpublished manuscript, Carnegie–Mellon University, Pittsburgh, PA.

Crawford, R.G. (1976) An empirical investigation of a dynamic model of labor turnover in U.S. manufacturing industries. Dissertation, Carnegie–Mellon University, Pittsburgh, PA.

Cyert, R.M. and DeGroot, M.H. (1974) Rational expectations and Bayesian analysis. *Journal of Political Economy* 82, 521–36.

DeCanio, S. (1979) Rational expectations and learning from experience. *Quarterly Journal of Economics* 93, 47–57.

DeGroot, M.H. (1970) *Optimal Statistical Decisions.* New York: McGraw-Hill.

Friedman, B. (1979) Optimal expectations and the extreme information assumptions of "rational expectations" macro-models. *Journal of Monetary Economics* 5, 23–42.

Friedman, M. (1957) *A Theory of the Consumption Function.* Princeton, NJ: Princeton University Press for the NBER.

Frydman, R. (1981) Towards an understanding of market processes: individual expectations, market behavior and convergence to rational expectations equilibrium. Unpublished manuscript, New York University.

Futia, C.A. (1981) Rational expectations in stationary linear models. *Econometrica* 49, 171–92.

Hansen, L.P. and Sargent, T.J. (1980a) Formulating and estimating dynamic linear rational expectations models. *Journal of Economic Dynamics and Control* 2, 7–46.

—— and —— (1980b) Linear rational expectations models for dynamically interrelated variables. In *Rational Expectations and Econometric Practice*, eds R.E. Lucas Jr and T.J. Sargent, pp. 127–56. Minneapolis, MN: University of Minnesota Press.

—— and —— (1981) Exact rational expectations models: specification and estimation. Staff Report 71, Federal Reserve Bank of Minneapolis.

Hayek, F.A. (1939) Price expectations, monetary disturbances and malinvestments. In *Profits, Interest, and Investment.* London: Routledge. Reprinted in *Readings in Business Cycle Theory*, pp. 351–65. Philadelphia: American Economic Association, 1944.

Jovanovic, B. (1978) Job matching and the theory of turnover. Ph.D. Dissertation, University of Chicago.

Keynes, J.M. (1965) *The General Theory of Employment, Interest, and Money.* New York: Harcourt Brace and World. (Originally published in 1936.)

Kwakernaak, H. and Sivan, R. (1977) *Linear Optimal Control Systems.* New York: Wiley.

Kydland, F. and Prescott, E.C. (1981) Time to build an equilibrium persistence of unemployment. Unpublished manuscript, Carnegie–Mellon University, Pittsburgh, PA.

Lucas, R.E., Jr (1972) Expectations and the neutrality of money. *Journal of Economic Theory* 4, 103–24.

——(1975) An equilibrium model of the business cycle. *Journal of Political Economy* 83, 1130–44.

——(1976) Econometric policy evaluation: a critique. In *The Phillips Curve and Labor Markets*, eds K. Brunner and A.H. Meltzer, Carnegie–Rochester Conference Series on Public Policy, vol. 1. Amsterdam: North-Holland.

——and Prescott, E.C. (1971) Investment under uncertainty. *Econometrica* 39, 659–81.

Meltzer, A.H. (1982) Rational expectations, risk, uncertainty, and market responses. In *Crises in the Economics and Financial Structure*, ed. P. Wachtel. Lexington, MA: Lexington Books.

Muth, J.F. (1960) Optimal properties of exponentially weighted forecasts. *Journal of the American Statistical Association* 55, 299–306.

——(1961) Rational expectations and the theory of price movements. *Econometrica* 29, 315–35.

Phelps, E.S. (1980) The trouble with "rational expectations" and the problem of inflation stabilization. Unpublished manuscript, Columbia University, New York.

Pigou, A.C. (1929) *Industrial Fluctuations*, 2nd edn. London: Macmillan.

Prescott, E.C. and Townsend, R.M. (1980) Equilibrium under uncertainty: multiagent statistical decision theory. In *Bayesian Analysis in Econometrics and Statistics*, ed. A. Zellner, pp. 169–94. Amsterdam: North-Holland.

Sargent, T.J. (1978) Estimation of dynamic labor demand schedules under rational expectations. *Journal of Political Economy* 86, 1109–44.

——(1981a) Interpreting economic time series. *Journal of Political Economy* 89, 213–48.

——(1981b) Stopping moderate inflations: the method of Poincaré and Thatcher. Unpublished manuscript, University of Minnesota and Federal Reserve Bank of Minneapolis.

Townsend, R.M. (1978) Market anticipations, rational expectations, and Bayesian analysis. *International Economic Review* 19(2), 481–94. Reprinted in this volume as chapter 13.

——(1983) Forecasting the forecasting of others. *Journal of Political Economy* 91(4), 546–87. Reprinted in this volume as chapter 14.

Part VIII
Equilibrium Theory with Competitive Markets in Complete, Information-constrained Contracts

16
Pareto Optima and Competitive Equilibria with Adverse Selection and Moral Hazard

with Edward C. Prescott

1 Introduction

The purpose of this chapter is to explore the extent to which standard general equilibrium analysis of Pareto optima and of competitive equilibria can be applied to economies with moral hazard and adverse selection problems. In these economies the information structure is *explicit* but *private*. Of particular interest are the Rothschild and Stiglitz (1976) and Wilson (1977) insurance economy, in which each agent observes a parameter indicating the probability of suffering a loss, that is, whether he is a high risk or low risk agent, a Spence (1974) signaling economy, in which each agent observes a parameter indicating his inherent productivity as well as the direct or indirect disutility of some unproductive activity, a moral hazard insurance economy in which agents can take an unobserved action determining the probability of suffering a loss, and a private-information labor market economy in which households suffer unobserved shocks to preferences (or to an underlying household production function).

We proceed by showing in section 2 that, despite the apparent diversity among the economies mentioned above, each can be viewed as a special case of a simple general structure with convex constraints and preferences. This is accomplished by considering consumption lotteries indexed by time and

---

Reprinted from *Econometrica* 52(1), 1984, 21–45. Earlier drafts of this paper have been presented at the NBER Conference on Theoretical Industrial Organization, Montreal, October 1979, the 4th World Congress Meetings of the Econometric Society, Aix-en-Provence, August 1980, and the Summer Meetings of the Econometric Society, San Diego, CA, June 1981. Helpful comments from Ted Groves, Roy Radner, John Roberts, Charles Wilson, our colleagues, the participants of these seminars, and a referee are all gratefully acknowledged. We also thank the National Science Foundation and the Alfred P. Sloan Foundation for financial support.

by privately observed shocks and agent types. The constraint set then naturally includes certain incentive compatibility conditions, following the seminal work of Hurwicz (1971); these ensure that it is not in the interest of agents to misrepresent their private information.

In section 3 we establish that Pareto optimal allocations can be determined as solutions to the problem of maximizing weighted averages of the agent-type utilities subject to the incentive compatibility conditions and resource constraints – a concave programming problem. This result is then used to characterize the optima for both the adverse selection insurance and the private-information labor market economy. It is established as a by-product that the Rothschild–Stiglitz separating equilibrium is optimal in the space of lotteries under exactly the same conditions which make it optimal in the space of (apparently) deterministic allocations. For the private-information labor market economy it is established, generally, that optima are inefficient in the *ex post* full-information sense, being consistent with unemployment or overemployment of labor and even with a random allocation of labor though all households are averse to risk. The latter results complement the findings of Green and Kahn (1983) and Grossman and Hart (1983) on *ex post* inefficiencies in labor contracts and especially those of Chari (1983) in the use of lotteries.

Section 4 begins an attack on the question of the applicability of classical competitive analysis to economies which can be mapped into our general structure. Previously, Prescott and Townsend (1984, this volume, ch. 17) established that standard competitive analysis could be applied to a Fisherian dynamic securities economy with private information. For that economy competitive equilibria were shown to exist and to be optimal, in contrast with the problems that have been encountered for other private-information economies that also fall within our general structure. With the approach employed by Spence (1974) in his studies of signaling economies, for example, there is a multiplicity of equilibria and they generally are not optimal. With the approach employed by Rothschild and Stiglitz (1976), an equilibrium may fail to exist, and again, if one does exist, it may be nonoptimal. We find that the key property upon which standard existence and optimality theorems depend has to do with only one aspect of the information structure of the economy, whether or not agents with characteristics which are distinct and privately observed at the time of initial trading enter the resource constraints in a homogeneous way; preferences, technology, other kinds of *ex ante* diversity, and *ex post* diversity are not critical. An implication of this result for economies with signaling opportunities is that nonoptimality, multiplicity, or nonexistence problems do not arise if there is a market for contracts prior to agents knowing their (still privately observed) types. Neither are there problems for the moral hazard insurance economy, nor for the private-information labor market economy.

In section 4 we illustrate how the private-information labor market economy optimum can be supported in a competitive equilibrium. Each household chooses a contract which maximizes its expected utility subject to its budget constraint. The contract entails options which can be exercised at the discretion of the household and involves commitments to supply labor in return for the consumption good. Firms in our labor market economy are viewed as producer intermediaries which make commitments to hire labor and produce the consumption good. Again, the commitments are priced in a competitive market and firms maximize profits. The implication of this section is that unemployment, overemployment, and random assignments, being consistent with optimal contracts, are also consistent with competitive equilibrium allocations. We have, in effect, taken a step toward a synthesis of the implicit labor contract paradigm of Gordon (1974), Azariadas (1975), and Baily (1977) with standard competitive analysis.

In the final section of the chapter we briefly report on our efforts to secure standard existence and optimality theorems for all economies consistent with the general structure and offer an instructive contrast with our results for the private-information labor market economy (among others). Apparently, there can be a fundamental (unavoidable) adverse selection problem if agents with characteristics which are distinct and privately observed at the time of initial trading enter the economy-wide resource constraints in a heterogeneous way, as is the case for the adverse selection insurance and the signaling economies.

2 The economies

2.1 *Basic mathematical structure*

There are a finite number of agent types $i = 1, \ldots, I$ and a continuum of each type. The fraction of agents of type i is denoted by λ_i. The commodity space is a linear space L and the common consumption possibility set $\bar{X} \subset L$ for each agent type is closed and convex. The utility function $u_i: \bar{X} \to R$ of each agent of type i is concave (and frequently linear). The endowment of each agent is $\xi \in L$, and is the same for all agent types. Each agent's type is private information. The commodity space, consumption set, utility functions, and endowment will all be given more precise interpretations in the example economies which follow.

Let $x_i \in L$ be a consumption allocation to each agent of type i. Let r_{ik} be a real-valued linear function on L $(k = 1, 2, \ldots, K; i = 1, 2, \ldots, I)$. Then society is subject to resource constraints of the form

$$\sum_i \lambda_i r_{ik}(x_i - \xi) \leqslant 0 \qquad k = 1, \ldots, K$$

Note that we allow there to be more than one constraint; the private-information securities economy of Prescott and Townsend (1984, this volume, ch. 17) provides an example.

An I-tuple $x=(x_i)$ of elements belonging to L is *implementable* if

$$x_i \in \bar{X} \qquad \text{all } i \tag{16.1}$$

$$u_i(x_i) \geqslant u_i(x_j) \qquad \text{all } i, j \tag{16.2}$$

$$\sum_i \lambda_i r_{ik}(x_i - \xi) \leqslant 0 \qquad \text{all } k \tag{16.3}$$

The first requirement is that the consumption vector belongs to the individuals' consumption possibility set. The second is that each individual of type i weakly prefers x_i to all the other x_j. Thus it is not in the interest of any agent to claim to be of some other type. These are the *ex ante* incentive compatibility constraints. Certain *ex post* incentive compatibility constraints arise naturally in consideration of the set of all allowable contracts (see below) and thus help to determine the common consumption possibility set $\bar{X}$. Justification for restricting attention to the class of allocations satisfying the incentive compatibility constraints is given by Harris and Townsend (1978, this volume, ch. 6; 1981, this volume, ch. 7) and Myerson (1979), building on the seminal work of Hurwicz (1971). The third condition is again the set of resource constraints.

In much of this chapter L is assumed to have finite dimensions. This assumption simplifies the presentation without the loss of anything essential. Then, if both the $u_i(\cdot)$ and $r_{ik}(\cdot)$ are linear, we use the dot product to represent them, that is,

$$u_i \cdot x_i \equiv u_i(x_i) = \sum_l u_{il} x_{il}$$

and similarly

$$r_{ik} \cdot x_i \equiv r_{ik}(x_i) = \sum_l r_{ikl} x_{il}$$

where l indexes components of $x_i \in L$. (Limiting arguments such as those used by Prescott and Townsend (1984, this volume, ch. 17) might well be used to establish the results of this chapter if L is not finite dimensional.)

We now demonstrate how the well-known adverse selection insurance, moral hazard insurance, and signaling economies as well as a private-information labor market economy can all be represented in this framework.

2.2 Adverse selection insurance economy: E_1

Consider the following insurance environment that was examined by Rothschild and Stiglitz (1976) and Wilson (1977). There is a continuum of agents; say the set of agents is the unit interval. Each agent of type i receives a random endowment z:

$$z = \begin{cases} z_0 & \text{with probability } \theta_i \\ z_1 & \text{with probability } 1-\theta_i \end{cases}$$

Here $0 < z_0 < z_1$, so that when $z = z_0$ an agent is said to suffer a loss. This is public information. There are two types of agents by risk class, $i = 1, 2$, where $0 < \theta_1 < \theta_2 < 1$. Thus the θ_1 type agents are the low risk people and the θ_2 type agents are the high risk people. Each agent's type is private information. Of people of type i, θ_i is also the fraction that will suffer a loss. Thus there is no aggregate uncertainty as the fractions of the various types λ_i are known.[1]

Each agent has preferences on $C \subset R_+$ as defined by the utility function $U: R_+ \to R$ where U is strictly concave, strictly increasing, and continuously differentiable with $U'(0) = \infty$. The points z_0 and z_1 belong to C. Suppose that a consumer is assigned c_0 if a loss is suffered and c_1 if there is no loss. The expected utility for an agent of type i is then

$$\theta_i U(c_0) + (1-\theta_i) U(c_1)$$

where $c_0, c_1 \in C$.

This environment can be cast in terms of the basic mathematical structure. One approach is to let L be R^2. Then let x_i be a consumption allocation to agents of type i with the first component being c_{i0} and the second c_{i1}. The common endowment is $\xi = (z_0, z_1)$. Then $\bar{X}$ corresponds to $C \times C$ and is closed and convex provided that C is closed and convex. The single linear resource constraint is

$$\sum_i \lambda_i \{\theta_i (c_{i0} - z_0) + (1-\theta_i)(c_{i1} - z_1)\} \leqslant 0$$

The incentive compatibility constraints are

$$\theta_i U(c_{i0}) + (1-\theta_i) U(c_{i1}) \geqslant \theta_i U(c_{j0}) + (1-\theta_i) U(c_{j1}) \qquad \text{all } i, j$$

However, the space of consumption allocations (x_i) restricted by such constraints is not convex given the strict concavity of U.

An alternative approach which results in the utility function being linear, and therefore avoids the nonconvexities associated with the incentive compatibility constraints, is to consider lotteries on C. In order that the space L be finite dimensional, the set C is assumed to be finite with n elements. The lotteries are n-dimensional vectors specifying the probability of each point in C, say $\mu = \{\mu(c)\}_{c \in C}$ where $\Sigma_c \mu(c) = 1$ and $\mu(c) \geqslant 0$, all $c \in C$. Let μ_0 be the lottery if a loss is suffered and μ_1 if there is no loss. The expected utility of (μ_0, μ_1) for a type i individual is then

$$W_i(\mu_0, \mu_1) = \theta_i \sum_c U(c)\mu_0(c) + (1-\theta_i)\sum_c U(c)\mu_1(c)$$

It is also assumed here that fraction $\mu_0(c)$ of agents of type i who suffer a loss receive the allocation c and similarly for $\mu_1(c)$, so that lotteries introduce no aggregate randomness. The endowment ξ is a pair of probability distributions on C: the first of these assigns probability 1 to $z_0 \in C$ and the second assigns probability 1 to $z_1 \in C$.

This latter economy can be put into the general mathematical structure as follows. Let $L = R^{2n}$. Let the first n elements of a consumption vector x, denoted x_0, be the $x_{0c} = \mu_0(c)$ defined above for $c \in C$, and let the second n elements of x, denoted x_1, be the $x_{1c} = \mu_1(c)$ for $c \in C$. The consumption possibility set then requires that x_0 and x_1 are probability distributions, that is,

$$\bar{X} = \left\{ x \in L : \sum_c x_{0c} = 1, \ \sum_c x_{1c} = 1, x \geqslant 0 \right\}$$

Let the first n elements of the utility function u_i be the $\theta_i U(c)$ for $c \in C$, and let the second n elements be the $(1-\theta_i)U(c)$ for $c \in C$. With these definitions

$$u_i(x) = u_i \cdot x = W_i(\mu_0, \mu_1)$$

which is just the expected utility to an i type of lottery μ_0 if a loss is suffered and to a lottery μ_1 if there is no loss.

The common endowment ξ is an element of L. The resource constraint is that the average consumption is less than or equal to the average endowment:

$$\sum_i \lambda_i \left\{ \theta_i \sum_c x_{i0c} c + (1-\theta_i) \sum_c x_{i1c} c \right\} \leqslant \sum_i \lambda_i \left\{ \theta_i \sum_c \xi_{0c} c + (1-\theta_i) \sum_c \xi_{1c} c \right\}$$

As there is a single resource constraint, the subscript k on the resource constraint function r_{ik} can be dropped. The first n components of r_i are the

$\theta_i c$ for $c \in C$ and the next n components are the $(1 - \theta_i)c$. Thus the resource constraint can be put in the form

$$\sum_i \lambda_i r_i \cdot (x_i - \xi) \leqslant 0$$

as required by the general formulation.

2.3 Signaling economy: E_2

A particularly interesting class of economic environments are those with signaling opportunities. We consider the following simple signaling economy. The set C is a subset of R^3_+. The first component c_1 is consumption of goods, the second component c_2 is the signal, and the third component c_3 is consumption of leisure. The utility function for individuals of type i is linear in c, and of the form

$$U_i(c) = \theta_i c_1 - c_2$$

where the θ_i have been ordered so that $\theta_1 < \theta_2 < \ldots < \theta_I$. The fraction of type i is $\lambda_i > 0$. Again, agent types are private information.

The output of an individual is not observed. A finite fraction, albeit small, of the continuum of individuals is required to produce any output and the resulting productivity of a group is the average of the productivities of the group's members. These assumptions imply that it is impossible to deduce anything about an individual's productivity by observing the output of his group. Let π_i denote the output of the consumption good per unit of labor of individuals of type i. Individuals with larger θ_i are more productive, so that $\pi_I > \pi_{I-1} > \ldots > \pi_1 \geqslant 0$. The assumption that the signal does not affect output is not crucial and was made for simplicity. The endowment of leisure time is unity.

Because agents are risk neutral, we need not consider lotteries; that is, the utility functions are already linear. If they were not risk neutral, following the previous example, it would be necessary to consider lotteries on C.

To represent this economy within our basic structure, the commodity space L is R^3 with component x_1 as consumption, component x_2 as signal, and component x_3 as leisure consumed. The consumption possibility set is

$$\bar{X} = \{x \in L: x \geqslant 0, x_3 \leqslant 1\}$$

and the utility function for an i type is

$$u_i(x) = \theta_i x_1 - x_2$$

The endowment $\xi \in L$ is the vector $(0, 0, 1)$.

The resource constraint is

$$\sum_i \lambda_i \{x_{i1} + \pi_i(x_{i3} - \xi_3)\} \leqslant 0$$

This states that the average consumption $\Sigma_i \lambda_i x_{i1}$ must be less than average production $\Sigma_i \lambda_i \pi_i(\xi_3 - x_{i3})$. As for the previous example, there is a single resource constraint, characterized by the vectors $r_i \in R^3$ where $r_i = (1, 0, \pi_i)$. With this definition the resource constraint can be put in the form

$$\sum_i \lambda_i r_i \cdot (x_i - \xi) \leqslant 0$$

as required by the general formulation.

2.4 *A moral hazard insurance economy: E_3*

The adverse selection insurance economy E_1 is modified as follows. There is only one type of agent, and so we can ignore the λ_i in what follows, but the probability of loss depends upon a costly private action of the agent. More precisely, each agent receives a random endowment $z \in Z = \{z_0, z_1\}$ with $0 < z_0 < z_1$ and the probability of z given that the agent's action $a \in A = \{a_1, a_2, \ldots, a_m\}$ is $\theta_{z|a}$. The realization of z is public; the action taken is not. Also, the larger is action a, the smaller is the probability of loss $\theta_{z_0|a}$. The interpretation here is that a larger action corresponds to an agent's being more careful. This is a standard setup.

Each agent has preferences on the finite set $C \times A$, where C is a finite subset of R_+ and has n elements. Preferences are defined by a utility function $U(c, a)$ where U is increasing in c, decreasing in a, and concave. For $(c, a) \in C \times A$, let $U_{ca} = U(c, a)$.

In terms of our basic mathematical structure, let the linear space L be the Euclidean space of dimension $n2m$. A consumption vector x is a triply indexed element (x_{cza}) for $c \in C$, $z \in Z$, and $a \in A$. The interpretation is as follows. A lottery with probabilities x_a first determines an action a for each agent. Number x_a is also the fraction of agents in the population who are to take action a. Conditional on this action a, a second lottery with probabilities $x_{cz|a}$ determines consumption c and endowment z of the agent. Of course, nature plays a role in this second lottery since the conditional probabilities $\theta_{z|a}$ are technologically determined constraints. In fact it is required that

$$\sum_c x_{cz|a} = \theta_{z|a}$$

for consistency. Finally, the marginal and conditional distributions x_a and $x_{cz|a}$ determine the joint distribution x_{cza} specified above.

Agents have preferences on $\bar{X}$ where

$$\bar{X} = \left\{ x \in L_+ : \sum_{c,z,a} x_{cza} = 1;\ \theta_{z|a} \sum_{c,z} x_{cza} = \sum_{c} x_{cza} \text{ all } a, z; \right.$$

$$\left. \sum_{c,z} U_{ca} x_{cza} \geqslant \sum_{c,z} U_{ca'} x_{cza} \frac{\theta_{z|a'}}{\theta_{z|a}} \text{ all } a, a' \right\}$$

The first constraint is that the probabilities sum to unity. The second is that the probability distribution of z given a (if defined for that probability distribution) equals the technologically determined probability $\theta_{z|a}$. The third constraint is to ensure incentive compatibility. This is not obvious and is derived as follows. The commodity point x must be structured such that, if a occurs, it is not in the interest of the agent to choose some other action a', that is

$$x_a \sum_{c,z} U_{ca} x_{cz|a} \geqslant x_a \sum_{c,z} U_{ca'} \operatorname{prob}\{c, z \mid a'\}$$

Here $\operatorname{prob}\{c, z \mid a'\}$ is the probability of the pair (c, z) given that the agent is subject to lottery x_{cza} but chooses action a'. Thus, under x_{cza}

$$\operatorname{prob}\{c, z \mid a'\} = x_{c|za} \theta_{z|a'} = \frac{x_{cz|a}}{\theta_{z|a}} \theta_{z|a'}$$

By substitution, the above expression holds if and only if

$$\sum_{c,z} U_{ca} x_{cz|a} x_a \geqslant \sum_{c,z} U_{ca'} x_{cz|a} x_a \frac{\theta_{z|a'}}{\theta_{z|a}}$$

As $x_{cza} = x_{cz|a} x_a$, the third constraint indeed ensures incentive compatibility. This particular representation makes clear that set $\bar{X}$ is convex.

Of course, there is also a resource constraint that average consumption be no greater than average endowment, or

$$\sum_{c,z,a} x_{cza}(c - z) \leqslant 0$$

This constraint corresponds to constraint (16.3) in the basic structure, with the endowment ξ being the zero vector in L. Here the single resource constraint takes on a special form,

$$r \cdot (x - \xi) \leqslant 0$$

with $r_{cza} = c - z$. The vector r is not indexed by i.

2.5 *Private-information labor market economy: E_4*

Imagine an economy in which households have preferences over some market-produced consumption good c and over the labor supply l as represented by a utility function $U_\theta(c, l)$ which is continuous, concave, increasing in c, and decreasing in l. Here c and l are nonnegative real numbers, with a maximal labor supply of l. Here also $\theta \in \Theta = \{1, 2\}$ is interpreted as one of two possible shocks to the household's preferences at the time of consumption and labor supply.[2] Each household's shock is private information to the household in the consumption period. It *is* known that a fraction λ_θ of households in the population will suffer shock θ in the consumption period. Thus, from the standpoint of a prior planning period, each household regards λ_θ as the probability of suffering shock θ in the consumption period.

There are a finite number of firms in the economy, each with a technology for transforming labor l into output q of the consumption good in a linear way, namely $q = al, a > 0$; think of a fixed number of industrial projects or a fixed number of plots of land in an agrarian economy. Firms are owned by households with predetermined profit shares in the population. With the assumption of constant returns to scale, however, profits are necessarily zero in a competitive equilibrium and thus will be disregarded in what follows. By the same token, we may act as if there were only one firm.

The natural commodity bundle for households in this model is a consumption–labor supply pair (c, l). The space of such bundles would be used if trade were restricted to take place subsequent to the realization of household shocks θ. However, trade *can* take place in the prior planning period. Therefore, following Arrow (1964) and Debreu (1959), it is natural to index the (c, l) bundle by household-specific shocks. Shocks are private to the household, however, and therefore to circumvent incentive problems, we assume that each individual household is assigned a *contract* which specifies consumption–labor supply pairs (c, l) under a variety of individually effected contingencies or options. For example, the contract might allow "sick" leaves, voluntary overtime, and so on, in addition to the "work as usual" option. (There is no monitoring of underlying circumstances.) The point is that the household itself chooses which option to effect subsequent to its underlying circumstance, its shock θ. Now under any contract an individual household will act in its own best interest, inducing a natural ordering on outcomes, (c, l) pairs relative to its θ-contingent utility function.

Thus, we can adopt a more abstract canonical representation for any contract, following Harris and Townsend (1978, this volume, ch. 6; 1981, this volume, ch. 7) and Myerson (1979), and assume, without loss of generality, that households make direct announcements of their shocks θ and that contracts are such that these announcements are made truthfully. Finally, we assume the further possibility that a contract specifies a *random* (c, l) bundle, conditional on an announcement θ. For example, laborers may report to work under some circumstances, but there need be no guarantee of employment.

More formally, then, the labor market economy with planning period contracts is cast in terms of the basic mathematical structure as follows. First, to ensure that the commodity space is finite dimensional, restrict attention to a finite number n of consumption–labor supply pairs (c, l). Then let the commodity space L be R^{2n}. The first n components of a consumption vector $x \in L$, with typical elements $x_1(c, l)$, assign probability to consumption–labor supply pairs conditional on the announcement $\theta = 1$, with a similar interpretation for the second n components and $\theta = 2$. Households are alike *ex ante* in the planning period (but not *ex post*), and so the λ_i and i can be dropped from the notation. The expected utility of the representative household is then

$$u(x) = \sum_{\theta} \lambda_\theta \sum_{(c,l)} x_\theta(c, l) U_\theta(c, l)$$

Thus the consumption possibilities set is

$$\bar{X} = \Bigg\{ x \in L: x \geqslant 0, \sum_{(c,l)} x_\theta(c, l) = 1 \text{ for } \theta = 1, 2 \text{ and}$$

$$\sum_{(c,l)} x_\theta(c, l) U_\theta(c, l) \geqslant \sum_{(c,l)} x_\phi(c, l) U_\theta(c, l) \text{ for } \theta, \phi \in \Theta \Bigg\}$$

This ensures both that the x_θ are probability measures for each θ and that in the consumption period each household will truthfully reveal its shock θ.

The endowment $\xi \in L$ is the element for which $\xi_\theta(c, l) = 0$ unless $(c, l) = (0, 0)$, that is, ξ_θ puts all probability on the zero point in the underlying commodity space. The resource constraint is that average consumption does not exceed average production, that is

$$\sum_{\theta} \lambda_\theta \sum_{(c,l)} x_\theta(c, l) c \leqslant \sum_{\theta} \lambda_\theta \sum_{(c,l)} x_\theta(c, l) a l$$

Here $x_\theta(c, l)$ is interpreted as the fraction of agents of type θ who are assigned the consumption–labor supply pair (c, l). Thus the resource constraint has the form

$$r \cdot (x - \xi) \leqslant 0$$

where component $r_\theta(c, l) = \lambda_\theta(c - al)$.

3 Pareto optima

Pareto optimal allocations for the general structure can be obtained by maximizing weighted averages of the utilities of the agent types. Let the set of possible weights be

$$\Gamma = \left\{ \gamma \in R^I : \gamma_i \geqslant 0 \quad \text{and} \quad \sum_i \gamma_i = 1 \right\}$$

For $\gamma \in \Gamma$, let $\phi(\gamma)$ denote the set of consumption allocations which are solutions to the program

$$\max_{x=(x_i)} \sum_i \gamma_i u_i \cdot x_i$$

subject to $x_i \in \bar{X}$, all i, $u_i \cdot x_i \geqslant u_i \cdot x_j$, all i and j, and $\Sigma_i \lambda_i r_{ik} \cdot (x_i - \xi) \leqslant 0$, all k. Thus $\phi(\gamma)$ is a subset of the I-cross-product space of L. Finally, let

$$\Phi = \bigcup_{\gamma \in \Gamma} \phi(\gamma)$$

Lemma 16.1
The set Φ contains all the Pareto optima. If $\gamma > 0$ (that is, $\gamma_i > 0$ all i), then all allocations belonging to $\phi(\gamma)$ are optima. Finally, if an I-tuple $x = (x_i)$ belongs to $\phi(\gamma)$ and if x is not Pareto dominated by another element belonging to $\phi(\gamma)$, then x is an optimum.

Proof. The constraints are convex and the objective function is linear. Consequently, the utility possibility set is convex. Let γ define a supporting hyperplane at the point on the utility possibilities frontier associated with the Pareto optimal allocation x^*. Such a hyperplane exists by the separation theorem. For this $\gamma^* \in \Gamma$, x^* is a solution to the program. This proves the first statement of the lemma.

To prove the second statement consider some $\gamma > 0$ and some allocation $x \in \phi(\gamma)$. Suppose that x can be Pareto dominated. Then x cannot be a solution to the γ program. This contradiction establishes that solutions to such programs are Pareto optima.

To prove the last statement of the lemma, let x be a solution to some γ program with the specified nondominance property, but suppose that x is not an optimum. Then there exists an allocation x' which Pareto dominates x. By assumption, x' does not belong to $\phi(\gamma)$. But the value of x' for the γ program is at least as great as the value for x, and thus x' must be a solution to the γ program, which is the desired contradiction.

Theorem 16.1
If the set $\bar{X}$ is compact and contains ξ, the set of Pareto optimal allocations is nonempty.

Proof. A feasible solution exists, namely $x_i = \xi$ for all i, and so the constraint set is nonempty. The objective function is linear and therefore continuous. As the resource and incentive constraints are closed, a continuous function is being maximized on a compact set. Consequently, for any $\gamma \in \Gamma$, a solution to the program exists. By the lemma, a solution to a γ program is necessarily an optimum if $\gamma > 0$.

Our examples with lotteries all assume that the underlying consumption possibilities set C has a finite number of points. This is sufficient to ensure that set $\bar{X}$ is compact, a result that is used in the existence argument. There is a straightforward extension of the result to the case when C is a compact separable metric space, for example, a closed and bounded subset of R^n with the Euclidean metric; with the weak topology, the set of probability measures on the Borel subsets of C is compact (under these weaker conditions) and the functions defining the objective and constraints are continuous. When the constraint set is defined by the finite set of linear inequalities (other than the nonnegativity constraints), a stronger version of lemma 16.1 holds; then every Pareto optimal allocation is the solution to a program with all components of γ positive.[3]

3.1 *Pareto optima for the adverse selection insurance economy*

Rothschild and Stiglitz (1976) demonstrate, under certain conditions, that their separating equilibrium both exists and is an optimum within a more limited class of allocations than the one we consider. One question that will be answered is whether that allocation is an optimum within our larger class of allocations. The principal result, however, is the complete specification of the set of Pareto optima for this insurance economy.

Let $\bar{z}$ be the *ex post* per capita endowment, so that

$$\bar{z} = \sum_i \lambda_i \{\theta_i z_0 + (1 - \theta_i) z_1\}$$

Per capita consumption is constrained by this quantity. With this definition, the program for determining the Pareto optima for $\gamma \in \Gamma$ is the *linear* program

$$\max \sum_i \gamma_i \sum_c U(c)\{x_{i0c}\theta_i + x_{i1c}(1-\theta_i)\}$$

$$x_1, x_2 \geqslant 0$$

where x_{i0c} is the probability of a type i consuming $c \in C$ conditional on a loss and x_{i1c} is the probability of a type i consuming c conditional on no loss, $i = 1, 2$. The constraints are as follows:

$$\sum_c U(c)\{(x_{10c} - x_{20c})\theta_2 + (x_{11c} - x_{21c})(1-\theta_2)\} \leqslant 0 \qquad (16.4)$$

(agents of type 2 weakly prefer x_2 to x_1);

$$\sum_c U(c)\{(x_{20c} - x_{10c})\theta_1 + (x_{21c} - x_{11c})(1-\theta_1)\} \leqslant 0 \qquad (16.5)$$

(agents of type 1 weakly prefer x_1 to x_2);

$$\sum_{i,c} \lambda_i c\{x_{i0c}\theta_i + x_{i1c}(1-\theta_i)\} \leqslant \bar{z} \qquad (16.6)$$

(this is the single-resource constraint);

$$\sum_c x_{10c} = 1 \qquad (16.7)$$

$$\sum_c x_{11c} = 1 \qquad (16.8)$$

$$\sum_c x_{20c} = 1 \qquad (16.9)$$

$$\sum_c x_{21c} = 1 \qquad (16.10)$$

(the probabilities sum to unity).

If we let μ_k denote the Lagrange multiplier associated with constraint (16.k) differentiating with respect to the x_{10c} yields the first-order conditions,

$$\gamma_1 U(c)\theta_1 - \mu_1 U(c)\theta_2 + \mu_2 U(c)\theta_1 - \mu_3 c\theta_1\lambda_1 + \mu_4 \leqslant 0 \qquad (16.11)$$

for all $c \in C$. Analogous first-order conditions hold for the x_{20c}, the x_{11c}, and the x_{21c}.

Constraint (16.11) must hold with equality for some $c \in C$. Otherwise all the x_{10c} would be zero and that would violate constraint (16.7). The left-hand side of (16.11) can be viewed as a function of c. Thus the Lagrange multipliers must be such that this function has a maximum (of zero) at points at which condition (16.11) holds as an equality. Now suppose that the set C has an arbitrarily large number of elements, so that the maximal distance between any point and its nearest neighbor is arbitrarily small. Also recall that $u(\cdot)$ is strictly concave. Then if

$$\gamma_1\theta_1 - \mu_1\theta_2 + \mu_2\theta_1 \leqslant 0 \tag{16.12a}$$

the left-hand side of (16.11) is a strictly decreasing convex function of c and so attains a maximum at $c = 0$. If

$$\gamma_1\theta_1 - \mu_1\theta_2 + \mu_2\theta_1 > 0 \tag{16.12b}$$

the left-hand side of (16.11) is a strictly concave function of c and so attains a maximum at a single point (on the assumption that the set C can be made arbitrarily large). In summary, the result is that x_{10c} equals unity for some $c \in C$ and zero otherwise. By precisely the same argument, probability measures x_{11}, x_{20}, and x_{21} place all their mass on single points denoted by c_{11}, c_{20}, and c_{21} respectively. These points depend upon the weights γ chosen.

One implementable allocation is for everyone to consume $\bar{z}$ independent of their realized endowment. The utility for this allocation is $U(\bar{z})$ for everyone. If one agent type realizes expected utility exceeding $U(\bar{z})$, that type's expected consumption must exceed $\bar{z}$, by Jensen's inequality. This implies, via the resource constraint, that the expected consumption of the agents of other types is less than $\bar{z}$ and, by Jensen's inequality, their expected utility is less than $U(\bar{z})$.

We divide the Pareto optima into three sets. The first is for everyone to consume $\bar{z}$ with certainty. The second set contains those optima for which the expected utility of type 1 agents exceeds $U(\bar{z})$, and the third set contains those for which the expected utility of type 1 agents is less than $U(\bar{z})$.

It can be established that for set 2 there is no uncertainty in consumption for type 2 agents (that is, $c_{20} = c_{21} = c_2$). Suppose the contrary. By eliminating uncertainty in the consumption of type 2 agents (if there is any), while preserving their expected consumption, the utility of type 2 agents is increased, the resource constraint continues to be satisfied, and slack is introduced into constraint (16.4). Note that constraint (16.5) continues to be satisfied: the expected consumption of type 2 agents is less than $\bar{z}$ in set 2 so that the type 1 agents strictly prefer their allocation x_1 which yields expected utility greater than $U(\bar{z})$ to the no-uncertainty x_2 allocation. This also establishes that $\mu_2 = 0$ in set 2. In addition, $c_{10} \neq c_{11}$, for otherwise (16.4) would be violated.

Actually constraint (16.4) is binding in set 2 for otherwise c_{10} and c_{11} could be made more nearly equal while preserving the expected consumption of type 1. This increases expected utility of type 1. Resource constraint (16.6) is also binding for, if it were not, by increasing c_2 a little, the expected utility of type 2 agents could be increased without violating any constraint. Since (16.4) and (16.6) are binding, c_{10} and c_{11} must satisfy

$$\theta_2 U(c_{10}) + (1-\theta_2)U(c_{11}) = U(c_2) \tag{16.13}$$

and

$$\lambda_1\{\theta_1 c_{10} + (1-\theta_1)c_{11}\} + \lambda_2 c_2 = \bar{z} \tag{16.14}$$

for elements of Pareto optima set 2. To find the solution to (16.13) and (16.14), consider the space of (c_{10}, c_{11}) pairs. The point c_2 lies in this space on the 45° line below the negatively sloped line (16.14) (recall $c_2 < \bar{z}$). Thus this line intersects the indifference curve for which (16.13) is satisfied at two points. The better of the solutions for agents of type 1 is the one for which $c_{10} < c_2 < c_{11}$. Subsequently, c_{10} and c_{11} are functions of c_2 as the better solution to (16.13) and (16.14).

This nearly completes the specification of the allocations in Pareto optima set 2. However, there is the condition that the Lagrange multipliers μ_1 and μ_3 are positive. We exploit this condition with the additional assumption that all the optimal allocations are interior points of the set C which is sufficiently large to insure that such allocations satisfy the appropriate conditions for maxima as if C were a continuum. Thus, given that $\mu_2 = 0$ and that $c_{20} = c_{21} = c_2$, from (16.11) and the analogous first-order conditions,

$$\begin{aligned}
&\left\{\gamma_1 - \frac{\mu_1\theta_2}{\theta_1}\right\}U'(c_{10}) = \mu_3\lambda_1 \\
&\left\{\gamma_1 - \frac{\mu_1(1-\theta_2)}{1-\theta_1}\right\}U'(c_{11}) = \mu_3\lambda_1 \\
&\{\gamma_2 + \mu_1\}U'(c_2) = \mu_3\lambda_2 = \mu_3(1-\lambda_1) \\
&\gamma_1 + \gamma_2 = 1
\end{aligned} \tag{16.15}$$

Given c_2, these are four linear equations in the unknowns μ_1, μ_3, γ_1, and γ_2. (Remember that c_{10} and c_{11} are functions of c_2, which is the better solution to (16.13) and (16.14).) An additional requirement is that the solution to (16.15) (which exists) is nonnegative. This requirement, which is tedious to establish, is that

$$\frac{\lambda_2}{\lambda_1}\frac{\theta_2-\theta_1}{\theta_1(1-\theta_1)} \geqslant \frac{U'(c_2)\{U'(c_{10})-U'(c_{11})\}}{U'(c_{10})U'(c_{11})} \tag{16.16}$$

As c_2 approaches $\bar{z}$, the distance between c_{10} and c_{11} goes to zero. Therefore, given that U is continuously differentiable for c_2 sufficiently near $\bar{z}$, this inequality is satisfied. Thus Pareto optima set 2 is nonempty. Finally, let $\bar{c}_2$ be the minimal level for which inequality (16.16) is satisfied. Then it holds for all $\bar{c}_2 \leqslant c_2 < \bar{z}$. If this were not the case, the utility possibility set would not be convex.

The argument for characterizing optima set 3 is symmetric with respect to the agent types with some obvious exceptions necessitated by the fact that $\theta_2 > \theta_1$. To characterize optima for set 3 interchange subscripts for the two agent types with the exception that the solution to (16.13) and (16.14) for which $c_{20} > c_{21}$ is used and the direction of inequality (16.16) is reversed.

As conditions (16.13), (16.14), and (16.16), along with the additional requirement that the contracts be actuarially fair, are just those for the optimality of the Rothschild–Stiglitz separating equilibrium allocation, this allocation is also Pareto optimal in our larger class of allocations.

Randomness in consumption is used to separate the agents. The agent type realizing the higher expected utility incurs the uncertainty. The cost of this uncertainty is less to agents of that type and they are more than compensated for it by higher expected consumption.

3.2 *Pareto optima for the private-information labor market economy*

In this section we make the point that the introduction of private information alone into an otherwise standard environment can produce not only apparent inefficiencies such as labor unemployment but also a random assignment of labor supplied in a world where all households are averse to risk. The key to this conclusion is that *ex post* full-information inefficiencies and randomness are both consistent with *ex ante* private-information optimal allocations.

The program for determining the optima for the private-information labor market economy is the linear program

$$\max_{x_\theta(c,l)} \sum_\theta \lambda_\theta x_\theta(c,l) U_\theta(c,l)$$

subject to

$$\sum_{(c,l)} x_1(c,l)U_1(c,l) \geqslant \sum_{(c,l)} x_2(c,l)U_1(c,l) \tag{16.17}$$

$$\sum_{(c,l)} x_2(c,l)U_2(c,l) \geqslant \sum_{(c,l)} x_1(c,l)U_2(c,l) \tag{16.18}$$

$$\sum_{\theta} \lambda_\theta \sum_{(c,\,l)} x_\theta(c, l) al \geqslant \sum_{\theta} \lambda_\theta \sum_{(c,\,l)} x_\theta(c, l) c \tag{16.19}$$

$$\sum_{(c,\,l)} x_1(c, l) = 1 \tag{16.20}$$

$$\sum_{(c,\,l)} x_2(c, l) = 1 \tag{16.21}$$

Here (16.17) and (16.18) are the relevant incentive compatibility constraints, which will cause a household of type θ to truthfully announce that it is of type θ. Constraint (16.19) is the resource constraint, and (16.20) and (16.21) require that the probabilities sum to unity.

In this section, attention is restricted to economies in which the utility functions are separable and have the form

$$U_\theta(c, l) = V(c) - W_\theta(l)$$

The function $V(\cdot)$ is strictly increasing and strictly concave with $V'(0) = \infty$. The functions W_θ are strictly increasing and convex. Agents of type 2 are assumed to be uniformly more risk averse with respect to labor supply; that is, $W_1''(l) < W_2''(l)$ for all $0 \leqslant l \leqslant \bar{l}$. It is also assumed for simplicity that $\lambda_1 = \lambda_2 = \frac{1}{2}$.

An upper bound for the value of the program is obtained when the program without the incentive constraints is solved. This solution is easily obtained because an optimum exists in the space of deterministic allocations (degenerate lotteries). An interior solution for this less constrained program satisfies

$$V'(c_1) = V'(c_2)$$

$$W_\theta'(l_\theta) = aV'(c_\theta) \qquad \theta = 1, 2$$

Here c_θ and l_θ are the deterministic consumption and labor supply for type θ. Thus at an interior solution to the less constrained program the marginal utility of consumption and the marginal rate of substitution of consumption for labor supply are equal across agent types, with the latter equal to the marginal product of labor a. Of course, the resource constraint will be satisfied at equality: $c_1 + c_2 = al_1 + al_2$.

An interior solution to the unconstrained program will not generally satisfy the incentive constraints. To see this, note that in such a solution consumptions are necessarily equal across agent types, say, equal to c. Therefore, to satisfy the incentive constraints labor supplied must be equal as well, say equal to l. Then from the resource constraint, $c = al$. However, the points at which

$W'_\theta(l) = aV'(al)$ will generally differ for the two θ types. Thus, with incentive constraints imposed, the best deterministic allocation yields value strictly less than the optima when they are not imposed. We now introduce lotteries into labor supply and make the point that, with differences in risk aversion, such lotteries can lessen the impact of incentive constraints.

This is well illustrated by the following parametric specification. Suppose that $V(c) = \ln c$, $W_1(l) = l$, and $W_2(l) = l^2/3$. Thus, households of type 1 *ex post* are risk neutral in labor supply. Without the incentive constraints, the solution to the program would be $c_1 = c_2 = a$, $l_1 = \frac{1}{2}$, and $l_2 = \frac{3}{2}$. This allocation violates the incentive constraints, for type 2 would claim to be of type 1. However, randomness can be introduced into the labor supply of type 1. This does not affect the utility of type 1 households as they are risk neutral in labor supply. This randomness does make the allocation to type 1 less attractive to type 2. Consider the following allocations. With certainty, set $c_1 = c_2 = a$ and $l_2 = \frac{3}{2}$. Set $l_1 = 0$ with probability $1 - \alpha$ and set $l_1 = l$ with probability α, where α satisfies $(1 - \alpha) \cdot \alpha \bar{l} = \frac{1}{2}$. This allocation satisfies *all* the constraints and yields the same value as the program without the incentive constraints for sufficiently large $\bar{l}$.

The example just described illustrates in a dramatic way the gain to lotteries; the utility of a full-information optimum can be achieved here, though, in general, we believe that full-information optimality is an inappropriate welfare criterion. However, the example is unsatisfactory for this section in that labor supply is not *ex post* inefficient; despite the randomness, the marginal rate of substitution of consumption for labor supply for all households equals the marginal product of labor.

We now establish that there must be randomness in labor supply for economies sufficiently close to this special economy with all types strictly risk averse in labor supply. We also establish that there can be no randomness in consumption for either type. With randomness in a type's labor supply, otherwise identical agents supply different quantities of labor. Thus, with constant consumption, the *ex post* marginal rate of substitution between consumption and labor supply cannot equal the corresponding marginal rate of transformation for all agents of that type.

We first establish that, for an optimum, the lottery on consumption is degenerate. Among the first-order conditions for the above program are

$$(\lambda_1 + \mu_1 - \mu_2)V(c) - \mu_3 \lambda_1 c - (\lambda_1 + \mu_1)W_1(l) + \mu_2 W_2(l) + \mu_3 \lambda_1 al + \mu_4 \leqslant 0 \tag{16.22}$$

for all (c, l) where the Lagrange multipliers are numbered in accord with constraints (16.17)–(16.21). This condition must hold with equality for some (c, l) pair. To discover where equality is achieved, it is convenient to view the left-hand side of (16.22) as a function of c and l. If $\lambda_1 + \mu_1 - \mu_2 \leqslant 0$, the left-hand side of (16.22) would be a convex strictly decreasing function of c, and so would achieve a maximum with respect to c, holding l fixed, at $c = 0$. Thus consumption would be deterministic at $c = 0$, but this cannot be a solution with $V'(0) = \infty$. Thus $\lambda_1 + \mu_1 - \mu_2 > 0$ and the left-hand side of (16.22) achieves a unique maximum with respect to c at some $c_1 > 0$ independent of l (on the assumption that the distance between adjacent cs can be made arbitrarily small). By a similar argument, consumption of type 2 households is deterministic at some $c_2 > 0$.

We now establish that for some economies there must be randomness in labor supply for some agent type. We assume $V(c) = \ln c$, $W_2(l) = l^2/3$, and $W_1(l) = l^{\beta}$, $1 \leqslant \beta$. The limit as β approaches unity is the parametric example considered previously. For the limit $\beta = 1$, we have shown that the best deterministic allocation yields an expected utility that is strictly less than the value of the optimum in the space of lotteries. It can be established by a careful continuity argument that this must also be true for all β in some open right-neighborhood of unity. This establishes the need for lotteries on labor supply for some economies with all types strictly risk averse.

The randomness in labor supply requires that, at the deterministic optimum, the agent supplying less labor is sufficiently less risk averse in labor supply. Then, by introducing randomness in that type's labor supply and reducing differences in consumption between types, the incentive problems can be lessened and expected *ex ante* utility increased.

4 Competitive contract markets in economies with moral hazard

In this section we define a standard competitive equilibrium in our commodity space. That is, we define the price system on the linear space L, and optimal actions are defined relative to that price system. In equilibrium, consumption choices are maximal in the budget set, a production choice maximizes profits in the production possibilities set, and markets clear. Thus the economy is decentralized in the usual way. As it turns out, such a competitive equilibrium construct is successful in the moral hazard insurance economy, the private-information labor market economy, and virtually any other economy in which the coefficients r_{ik} of the resource constraint (16.3) do not depend on i, that is, $r_{ik} = r_k$ for all i. That is, in such environments competitive equilibria exist, are optimal, have a natural market interpretation, and yet are capable of explaining apparent non-market-clearing phenomena. We illustrate this success in the context of the private-information labor market economy.

We should perhaps reiterate here that we are following the Arrow–Debreu treatment of time and uncertainty. Our competitive contract markets operate at some initial date, and the contracts or commodities which are traded are commitments to take specified, possibly random, actions under various possible contingencies. As time evolves and observed and unobserved states of nature are realized, these commitments (contracts) are honored. Thus there are no *ex post* spot markets, though here these might be mutually beneficial *ex post*. We do not pretend to offer here a theory of the determination of market structure or legally enforceable agreements.

We begin by following Prescott and Townsend (1984, this volume, ch. 17) and define a production–intermediation set Y in such a way that $y \in Y$ and a standard market-clearing condition $\Sigma_i \lambda_i (x_i - \xi) = y$ imply the resource constraint (16.3). Namely we let

$$Y = \{y \in L : r_k(y) \leqslant 0 \text{ all } k\} \tag{16.23}$$

This production–intermediation set can be interpreted as an exchange technology where negative (positive) components correspond to a commitment to take in (distribute) resources. These commitments can be indexed by agent types; in effect, commitments can vary across agents with observable characteristics or with unobservable but declared characteristics. But the weights that agent types receive, the r_k, are fixed by the exchange technology Y beyond the control of the firm–intermediary. (We will give a more detailed interpretation of the production–intermediation set for the private-information labor market economy in what follows.) In summary, then, we use the following definition.

Definition

A competitive equilibrium is an $(I + 1)$-tuple $((x_i^*), y^*)$ of elements of L and a price vector $p^* \in L$ for which (a) each i element x_i^* maximizes $u_i(x)$ over the set $\{x \in X : p^* \cdot x \leqslant p^* \cdot \xi\}$, (b) element y^* maximizes $p^* \cdot y$ over the set Y, and (c) $\Sigma_i \lambda_i x_i^* = y^* + \xi$.

Existence and optimality of competitive equilibria can be established quite generally. Prescott and Townsend (1984, this volume, ch. 17) established in some detail the existence of a competitive equilibrium for a private-information securities economy. Moreover, the proof given there, which relies heavily on the now standard existence arguments as in McKenzie (1959), Debreu (1962), Arrow and Hahn (1971), and others, is applicable to other economies. In what follows, we will give a more direct proof of the existence of a competitive equilibrium for the private-information labor market economy, emphasizing the economic interpretation and taking advantage of the representative agent construct. (We might well have chosen the moral hazard insurance economy.) However, we reiterate that *ex ante* diversity of the kind illustrated in the securities economy is not a problem for existence of competitive equilibria. As for optimality, we note that in the space of lotteries, consistent with our general environment, preferences and the consumption set are convex. Thus, by Debreu (1954), competitive equilibrium allocations are Pareto optimal. Again, this will be established directly in what follows for the private-information labor market economy. Again, more general arguments are given by Prescott and Townsend (1984, this volume, ch. 17).

To begin the discussion for the private-information labor market economy, let a generic point in the (underlying) commodity space be an output–labor pair denoted (c, l) and assume, as before, that there are a finite number of such pairs. Now suppose that prior to the resolution of uncertainty, that is, in the planning period market, each of the finite number of firms is allowed to make commitments to the market (say, to brokers or marketeers) to supply any number of units of any such (c, l) pair. More formally, let $y_\theta(c, l)$, if positive, denote the number of commitments to produce c units of output for and to hire l units of labor from households which announce that they are of type θ (such announcements are public information). Each of the firm–intermediaries, then, is constrained by a production–intermediation possibilities set Y defined by

$$Y = \left\{ y = \{y_\theta(c, l)\} : \sum_\theta \lambda_\theta \sum_{(c,\,l)} y_\theta(c, l)(al - c) \geqslant 0 \right\} \tag{16.24}$$

In effect (16.24) states that each firm–intermediary cannot plan to distribute on average more of the consumption good than it produces on average. (Note that each firm–intermediary takes the coefficients or weights in Y as given, beyond its control.) The actions of the firm–intermediary are priced in competitive markets and these prices are taken as given. That is, let $p_\theta(c, l)$ be the per unit price of the $y_\theta(c, l)$ commitment in terms of some abstract unit of account. Then the firm–intermediary acts to maximize profits:

$$\sum_\theta \sum_{(c,\,l)} y_\theta(c, l) p_\theta(c, l) \tag{16.25}$$

subject to $y \in Y$. Recall that we are assuming that firm–intermediaries are owned by households, but again, with the assumption of constant returns to scale, profits will be zero and profit shares are disregarded. Again we can act as if there were only one firm–intermediary.

Households also make commitments to the market over output–labor pairs but with a different interpretation. Households are imagined to choose *ex ante*, in the planning period market, a contract with options indexed by $\theta \in \Theta$. Each option is a (possibly degenerate) lottery over consumption–labor supply pairs, and the household can also choose the terms of the lottery. However, the options are such that a household of type θ *ex post* will choose *ex post* the option indexed by θ if indeed it suffers shock θ. Again, see the motivating remarks in section 2. Finally, of course, all the contracts are priced in a competitive market. More formally, let the consumption set $\bar{X}$ and endowment $\{\xi_\theta(c,l)\}$ be as defined in section 2. Then the objective of the representative household is to maximize *ex ante* the expected utility

$$\sum_{\theta} \lambda_\theta \sum_{(c,l)} x_\theta(c,l) U_\theta(c,l) \tag{16.26}$$

by choice of $x \in \bar{X}$ subject to the budget constraint

$$\sum_{\theta} \sum_{(c,l)} p_\theta(c,l) x_\theta(c,l) \leqslant \sum_{\theta} \sum_{(c,l)} p_\theta(c,l) \xi_\theta(c,l) \tag{16.27}$$

To reiterate, each household purchases a contract as a package, and does not really purchase the individual components separately. However, the valuation of a contract is determined by the sum of the valuations of its individual components.

To be noted again is that the economy here is decentralized by the price system in the usual way. Thus to ensure consistency of the actions taken by households and the first-intermediary, a market-clearing condition is needed:

$$y_\theta(c,l) = x_\theta(c,l) - \xi_\theta(c,l) \qquad \text{all } \theta \in \Theta, \text{ all } (c,l) \text{ pairs} \tag{16.28}$$

Note that condition (16.28), when substituted into the production–intermediation set (16.24), yields the resource constraint.

It is now easily established that a competitive equilibrium exists and is optimal. First note from the profit maximization hypothesis and the condition of constant returns to scale that

$$p_\theta^*(c,l) = \lambda_\theta(c - al) \qquad \text{all } \theta \in \Theta, \text{ all } (c,l) \text{ pairs}$$

is the only possible candidate for the equilibrium price system up to some arbitrary normalization. (We have, in effect, let the consumption good be the numeraire.) This price system on bundles (c, l) has a natural interpretation. From the standpoint of the firm–intermediary, prices of bundles increase with higher output c at rate λ_θ (that is, revenue increases) and prices decrease with higher labor input l at rate $\lambda_\theta a$ (that is, cost increases). Moreover, under this price system the tradeoff between labor and output is the parameter a, so that in effect we have marginal productivity pricing. We note of course that bundles for use by different household types can be priced differently. From the standpoint of households' budget constraints, increases in consumption c raise expenditures while increases in labor supplied l raise income. The price of a (c, l) bundle for use under the θ option is $\lambda_\theta(c - al)$ while the price of a (c, l) bundle with probability α is $\alpha\lambda_\theta(c - al)$; that is, the price system is linear in lotteries.[4]

Substitution of the $p_\theta^*(c, l)$ into the budget constraint for the household yields the linear program which determines Pareto optima. Thus a solution exists and is Pareto optimal, and competitive equilibrium condition (a) is satisfied. Then if we set $y_\theta^*(c, l) = x_\theta^*(c, l) - \xi_\theta(c, l)$, market-clearing condition (c) is satisfied. Finally, substitution of $p_\theta^*(c, l)$ into profits (16.25) makes it clear that profits are nonpositive. But the budget constraint (16.27) is satisfied as an equality, so that in fact profits are zero under $y_\theta^*(c, l)$. Thus condition (b) is satisfied.

How will the competitive equilibrium allocation be effected? As is standard in general equilibrium competitive analysis, the market assignment process and the price determination process are unspecified. To be more specific though, we might suppose that there are a finite number of marketeers or labor brokers which make up the planning period market. Each broker has called out the competitive equilibrium price vector and has attracted a representative pool of workers and one firm–intermediary (the brokers are really households themselves). Each household in the pool of the broker has entered into the contract $\{x_\theta^*(c, l)\}$. The firm has committed itself to an input–output vector $\{y_\theta^*(c, l)\}$. Next, in the consumption period, each household truthfully announces its shock θ. If $\{x_\theta^*(c, l)\}$ is not degenerate in labor supply, then the broker uses some random sorting device to select workers from its pool in the proper proportions. These are directed to the firm consistent with planning period demand. The consumption good is then produced and distributed by the broker to *all* workers in the pool in accordance with $\{x_\theta^*(c, l)\}$, as if under a wage benefit or insurance package. We are assuming, of course, that planning period contracts are honored (or costlessly enforced by a legal system); that is, there can be no collusion in labor supply among households (say, to eliminate risk) and no *ex post* spot markets.

Now suppose that an outside observer were to see the realized outcome of a competitive equilibrium allocation. We have just established that such an allocation is optimal, and so we know its properties from section 3. However, these properties might lead the outside observer to conclude that the realized outcome is inconsistent with the competitive market paradigm: if labor and output are fully observed, then the constant marginal product of labor might be inferred. That then might naturally be taken as the wage rate. If households were asked to indicate whether they would like to work more at that wage rate, some would so indicate. Thus there would be measured unemployment (non-market clearing). Moreover, the outside observer might see disparities in employment among households who indicate that they are otherwise identical, as if employment were capricious or random. Conceivably, some households might be completely unemployed, while others might work up to maximum capacity. But, again, such outcomes are not inconsistent with the competitive market paradigm if the objects which are traded are carefully defined. As we have indicated, such outcomes can be optimal from the *ex ante* point of view of the representative household, and can be achieved in competitive markets for labor contracts with appropriately specified options. We have, in effect, taken a step toward a synthesis implicit labor contract theory with standard competitive analysis.

5 Standard competitive equilibria in economies with adverse selection: the difficulties of price decentralization

Unlike the moral hazard insurance and private-information labor market economies, the resource constraints in the adverse selection insurance and signaling economies are of the form

$$\sum_i \lambda_i r_{ik} \cdot (x_i - \xi) \leqslant 0 \qquad k = 1, \ldots, K \tag{16.29}$$

rather than of the less general form

$$\sum_i \lambda_i r_k \cdot (x_i - \xi) \leqslant 0 \qquad k = 1, \ldots, K \tag{16.30}$$

This turns out to be a very important difference, for production and consumption activities cannot be separated as before.[5] To see this, let

$$Y = \left\{ y \in L\colon \sum_i \lambda_i r_{ik} \cdot y \leqslant 0, k = 1, \ldots, K \right\} \tag{16.31}$$

be the candidate for the production–intermediation possibilities set. If $r_{ik} = r_k$ for all i, then the production–intermediation set (16.31) is the production–intermediation set (16.23) used previously. In this case market clearing, that is,

$$y = \sum_i \lambda_i (x_i - \xi) \tag{16.32}$$

and y belonging to Y imply the resource constraint. However, in general, (16.29), (16.31), and (16.32) are inconsistent.

As it turns out, three natural ways to circumvent this adverse selection problem all fail to decentralize the economy in the usual way. In this section we summarize what we have learned in these attempts. For a more detailed discussion, the reader is referred to Prescott and Townsend (1981).

One attack on the inconsistency (adverse selection) problem is to ignore it, with the hope that it fails to occur in equilibrium, that is, in a standard competitive equilibrium, in which decisions are completely decentralized by a price system. Thus, we might make use of the production–intermediation set (16.31) in the obvious commodity spaces. For the adverse selection insurance economy, the obvious commodity space is the space of loss–no-loss consumption bundles. However, that with (16.31) implies the *same* budget line for all household types, the (average) market odds line of Rothschild and Stiglitz (1976), and that with diversity across household types implies the nonexistence of a standard competitive equilibrium. For the Spence signaling economy, the obvious commodity space is the space of commodity triplets specifying consumption, signal, and labor supply. However, that with (16.31) implies a zero price for the signal, with labor priced in terms of the consumption good at the average productivity. Thus a standard competitive equilibrium exists for the Spence signaling economy, but it involves no signaling – the phenomenon that the model was intended to explain.

Motivated by these considerations we might hope to allow different agent types to choose different commodity bundles in equilibrium. Hence we expanded the commodity space in an obvious way. Namely, for the Spence signaling economy we assumed that different signals could be treated as different commodities, each with a potentially distinct price in terms of the consumption good. We also introduced a production–intermediation set with coefficients in the technology which firms treat parametrically but which in fact are functions of the households' equilibrium consumption choices. We then defined a standard competitive equilibrium with production externalities and established that all the Spence signaling equilibria are examples of equilibria of this kind, including the no-signaling equilibria, the minimal-signaling equilibria, and the oversignaling equilibria. Of course, many of these are Pareto nonoptimal; indeed, many can be Pareto ranked. We also established that an analogous procedure could be applied to the adverse selection insurance economy to support a bewildering variety of standard competitive equilibria (with production externalities). Thus equilibria of this kind fail to provide much predictive content and also have undesirable normative properties.

We also expanded the commodity space in a different way, in the spirit of Arrow (1969), with the intent of removing externalities. More specifically, we index the original commodity point in the general structure by i, thereby increasing the dimensionality by a factor I. Again, the new commodity point has the interpretation of a contract with options which are effected by the individual households. In this expanded space there *is* a specification of the production–intermediation set (without externalities) which is *always* consistent with market clearing and the resource constraints. Thus we can consider an extension of the standard support theorem for Pareto optimal allocations. In fact, we established that there *is* a price system such that every Pareto optimum can be supported in a kind of competitive equilibrium. However, the competitive equilibrium is restricted in that the assignment in the optimum to other agent types must be taken into account in each household's maximization problem. In effect, then, there are externalities in consumption. Moreover, the same support theorem can be used to establish that unrestricted competitive equilibria in the indexed commodity space generally do not exist for the signaling and adverse selection insurance economies.

We conclude that there do seem to be fundamental problems for the operation of competitive markets for economies or situations which suffer from adverse selection. We have not discovered a standard competitive equilibrium construct which would predict well in such situations.

Notes

1 As noted by Prescott and Townsend (1984, this volume, ch. 17), both here and below we proceed from an aggregate distribution to individual uncertainty rather than the other way in order to avoid certain well-known mathematics problems associated with measurability (see Bewley and Radner, 1980).

2 The introduction of shocks to preferences may seem somewhat artificial. But the economy is readily given a deeper more satisfactory interpretation. Suppose in particular that labor can also be supplied to a household production function, that is, there is a technology for transforming labor input into output of an idiosyncratic home-produced good which cannot be transferred among households. Suppose also that the household production function is subject to privately observed technology shocks θ. Finally, suppose that households have preferences over consumption of the market-produced good, the home-produced good, and the total labor supply. Then this specification delivers an *indirect* utility function (as in the text) over consumption of the market-produced good and over market labor supply.

3 We would like to thank an anonymous referee for pointing out this result.

4 Evidently the price system is linear in underlying commodities c and l for fixed θ, but may vary with λ_θ and in that sense is nonlinear.

5 There would be separation in the signaling economy if markets opened prior to individuals knowing their types. Thus, signaling opportunities *per se* are not the cause of failure. Similarly, this failure *would* have arisen in the environment of Prescott and Townsend (1984, this volume, ch. 17) if there were some statistical dependence in the θ shocks and the initial specification of i types. There would also be a problem in the moral hazard insurance economy *if* it were combined with the adverse selection insurance economy.

References

Arrow, K.J. (1964) The role of securities in the optimal allocation of risk bearing.

Review of Economic Studies 31, 91–6.
——(1969) The organization of economic activity: issues pertinent to the choice of market vs. nonmarket allocation. In *The Evaluation and Analysis of Public Expenditures: The PBB System*, Joint Economic Committee Compendium, 91st Congress 1st Session, Vol. 1. Washington, DC: US Government Printing Office.
—— and Hahn, F. (1971) *General Competitive Analysis*. San Francisco, CA: Holden Day.
Azariadas, C. (1975) Implicit contracts and underemployment equilibria. *Journal of Political Economy* 83 1183–202.
Baily, M.N. (1977) On the theory of layoffs and unemployment. *Econometrica* 45, 1043–64.
Bewley, T. and Radner, R. (1980) Stationary monetary equilibrium with a continuum of independently fluctuating consumers. Working Paper, Northwestern University, Evanston, IL.
Chari, V. (1983) Involuntary unemployment and implicit contracts. *Quarterly Journal of Economics* 98, 107–22.
Debreu, G. (1954) Valuation equilibrium and Pareto optimum. *Proceedings of the National Academy of Science* 40, 588–92.
——(1959) *The Theory of Value*. New York: Wiley.
——(1962) New concepts and techniques for equilibrium analysis. *International Economic Review* 3, 257–73.
Gordon, D. (1974) A neo-classical theory of Keynesian unemployment. *Economic Inquiry* 12, 431–59.
Green, J. and Kahn, C. (1983) Wage employment contracts. *Quarterly Journal of Economics* 98, 173–88.
Grossman, S. and Hart, O. (1983) Implicit contracts under asymmetric information. *Quarterly Journal of Economics* 98, 123–56.
Harris, M. and Townsend, R.M. (1978) Allocation mechanisms for asymmetrically informed agents. GSIA Working Paper 35-76-77, Carnegie–Mellon University, Pittsburgh, PA. Reprinted in this volume as chapter 6.
—— and ——(1981) Resource allocation under asymmetric information. *Econometrica* 49, 33–64. Reprinted in this volume as chapter 7.
Hurwicz, L. (1971) On informationally decentralized systems. In *Decision and Organization*, eds R. Radner and B. McGuire. Amsterdam: North-Holland.
McKenzie, L. (1959) On the existence of general equilibrium for competitive markets. *Econometrica* 27, 54–71.
Myerson, R. (1979) Incentive compatibility and the bargaining problem. *Econometrica* 47, 61–74.
Prescott, E.C. and Townsend, R.M. (1981) Optima and competitive equilibria with adverse selection and moral hazard. Working Paper, Carnegie–Mellon University, Pittsburgh, PA.
—— and ——(1984) General competitive analysis in an economy with private information. *International Economic Review* 25(1), 1–20. Reprinted in this volume as chapter 17.
Rothschild, M. and Stiglitz, J. (1976) Equilibrium in competitive insurance markets: an essay on the economics of imperfect information. *Quarterly Journal of Economics* 90, 629–49.

Spence, A.M. (1974) *Market Signaling: Information Transfer in Hiring and Related Screening Processes.* Cambridge, MA: Harvard University Press.

Wilson, C. (1977) A model of insurance markets with incomplete information. *Journal of Economic Theory* 16, 176–207.

17

General Competitive Analysis in an Economy with Private Information

with Edward C. Prescott

1 Introduction

The last decade has witnessed a virtual explosion in the economics of private information and moral hazard. Models using private information constructs have now gained prominence in many of the substantive areas of economics, including monetary economics, industrial organization, finance, and labor economics. Yet despite these advances, or indeed because of them, we believe that there is a need for an alternative complementary approach – the extension of modern general equilibrium theory to such environments. In this chapter, therefore, we extend the theory of general economic equilibrium of Arrow (1953), Debreu (1959), and McKenzie (1959), among others, to a prototype class of environments with private information and examine again the role of securities in the optimal allocation of risk-bearing. We consider in particular pure exchange economies with the usual multiple commodity (intratemporal), borrowing–lending (intertemporal), and insurance (uncertainy) motives for trade but assume that households experience privately observed period-by-period shocks to preferences (see section 2). For that class of economies, we establish the existence of Pareto optimal allocations (in section 3) and the existence of competitive equilibria in markets for securities

---

Reprinted from *International Economic Review* 25(1), 1984, 1–20. This chapter is a revised version of "On competitive theory with private information" presented at the University of Chicago, Columbia University, Cornell University, Northwestern University, and Yale University, the Summer Meetings of the Econometric Society in Montreal, and the NBER Conference–Seminar on the Theory of General Equilibrium at Berkeley in February 1980. Helpful comments from Truman Bewley, Charles Wilson, the participants of these seminars, and anonymous referees are gratefully acknowledged. We also thank the National Science Foundation and the Federal Reserve Bank of Minneapolis for financial support and accept full responsibility for any errors as well as for the views expressed herein.

of a certain kind (in section 4). We also establish (in section 5) the first fundamental welfare theorem – that competitive equilibrium allocations are Pareto optimal. The second fundamental welfare theorem – that the optima can be supported as competitive equilibria – does not hold, suggesting difficulties of price decentralization in economies with *ex ante* private information.

The class of economies that we consider in this chapter is large. That is, we consider economies in which the distribution of (privately observed) shocks in the population is the same as the probability distribution of shocks for each individual household. We also require that households with the same shocks be treated *ex ante* in the same way.[1] That is, following the Arrow (1953) and Debreu (1959) treatment of uncertainty, we index a household's allocation by that household's shock (type). In this way, there is no aggregate uncertainty, and the general equilibrium feasibility constraint is a simple vector of linear inequalities. But since shocks are privately observed, not all shock-contingent allocations that satisfy the feasibility constraint are achievable. In addition, the allocations must be such that it is not in the interest of households to misrepresent their types. That is accomplished by the imposition of additional conditions which, following Hurwicz (1971), we term incentive compatibility constraints.[2] Still, the space of allocations that specify achievable consumptions contingent upon privately observed shocks proves to be an inappropriate commodity space for general competitive analysis. Even though the underlying utility functions are concave, the space of shock-contingent consumption allocations restricted by the incentive compatibility constraints is not generally convex, and there can be gains from introducing lotteries. Consequently, the linear commodity space employed in the analysis here is the space of shock-contingent signed measures, which is a linear space containing the required shock-contingent lotteries.

Lotteries have been used in game theory to make spaces convex, following the seminal contribution of von Neumann and Morgenstern (1947). They have been used extensively in the social choice field for similar reasons, and they have been used in various economic models to discriminate among agents with private information. However, to the best of our knowledge, lotteries have not been used in classic general equilibrium competitive analysis. This is surely because the natural spaces are already convex, and there is no need for them.[3]

Though this exercise is abstract, we believe that it may prove useful in the positive economics of private information. The highly abstract Arrow–Debreu state-contingent analysis has proved to be an invaluable tool in the study of economies with publicly observed shocks. It has proved to be particularly useful in determining whether a highly limited set of security and spot markets is sufficient to exploit all the gains from trade. When this is the case, we are certain that the results do not hinge upon arbitrary exclusions of security markets but rather only upon assumptions concerning preferences, endowments, technologies, and the information structure. In any event, we gain a better understanding of existing arrangements. In an analogous way, the constructs of the chapter may prove useful in verifying for a particular set of contractual or institutional arrangements and economic environments that there are no potential gains from instituting other arrangements. We also hope these constructs might help us to better interpret reality.

As noted, our general analysis allows for more than one underlying consumption good and more than one consumption date, and thus allows the usual intratemporal and intertemporal motives for trade. We recognize, though, this level of generality may make it difficult to interpret the constructs we have developed in this chapter.[4] Thus, in section 6 we present a simple example economy with one consumption good and one consumption date and focus entirely on uncertainty and the insurance motive for trade. For this economy, the competitive equilibria are characterized by insurance contracts with options, the exercise of which is private information dependent. In addition, the equilibrium contracts incorporate contrived randomness, even though all agents have convex preferences. We argue that such contrived randomness is not unusual, being consistent with casual observations on security markets and the state-contingent analysis of Arrow and Debreu. We also show that a simple institutional arrangement with random allocation of "excess demand" achieves the competitive equilibrium allocation, suggesting that at least some apparent disequilibrium phenomena can be interpreted as institutional or contractual arrangements that support equilibrium allocations. (Section 6 is virtually self-contained and can be read before the more general analysis in the chapter.)

2 The general securities model

Imagine an economy with a continuum of agents and l commodities. Each of the agents has an endowment vector $e_t \geqslant 0$ in each period t, $t = 0, 1, \ldots, T$. Let c_t denote the nonnegative consumption vector in period t; then each agent has preferences over consumption sequences as described by the utility function

$$E \sum_{t=0}^{T} U(c_t, \theta_t)$$

Here E is the expectation operator with respect to the random variables c_t and θ_t (the latter random variables will be described below). Each single-period utility function $U(\cdot, \theta_t)$ is continuous, concave, and increasing, and is defined for $c_t \geqslant 0$. The parameter θ_t is interpreted as a shock to individual preferences at the beginning of period t, observed only by the individual agent. For simplicity, parameter θ_t is assumed to take only a finite number of values; that is, for each t, $\theta_t \in \Theta$ where Θ has n elements. Fraction $\Pi_{t=0}^{T} \lambda(\theta_t)$ of the population have shock realization $(\theta_0, \theta_1, \ldots, \theta_T)$. The individual agents at the beginning of time 0 know their own θ_0 but have no basis for forecasting their future θ_t, except that they know the fractions of the population that will realize each shock sequence. Consequently, by symmetry, the predictive probability distributions of all given agents for their future preference shocks are identically and independently distributed, with $\lambda(\theta)$ for $\theta \in \Theta$ being the probability that $\theta_t = \theta$.[5] We note that the class of economies under study is quite similar to those studied by Gale (1980) and Lucas (1980).

What is the appropriate commodity space for a given economy? One approach is to follow Arrow (1953) and Debreu (1959) and index consumption c_t for each individual by the individual's specific history $(\theta_0, \ldots, \theta_t)$. There is a problem with this approach, however. There may be incentives (gains) for agents to enter into lotteries even though they are all risk averse. In the example in section 6, lotteries are needed for optimal and equilibrium allocations. This arises because the space of shock-contingent consumption allocations restricted by the incentive constraints is not convex. The following simple version of the model demonstrates this nonconvexity.

Suppose that $T = 1$, $e_0 = 0$, and $l = 1$, so that there is consumption of the single good only in period $t = 1$. Suppose also that the set $\Theta = \{1, 2\}$. For the shock-contingent indexing approach, let $c(\theta)$ for $\theta = 1, 2$ denote consumption in period 1 of a θ-type agent. The expected utility of allocation $\{c(1), c(2)\}$ in period 0 is then

$$\lambda(1)U\{c(1), 1\} + \lambda(2)U\{c(2), 2\}$$

There will be truthful revelation of shock (types) only if

$$U\{c(1), 1\} \geqslant U\{c(2), 1\} \tag{17.1}$$

$$U\{c(2), 2\} \geqslant U\{c(1), 2\} \tag{17.2}$$

These are the appropriate incentive compatibility constraints; they insure that a type 1 agent weakly prefers $c(1)$ to $c(2)$ and a type 2 agent weakly prefers $c(2)$ to $c(1)$. To see that (17.1) and (17.2) do not define a convex set, consider allocations $\{c(1), c(2)'\}$ and $\{c(1), c(2)''\}$ that both satisfy constraint (17.1) with equality, that satisfy constraint (17.2), and that have $c(2)' \neq c(2)''$. Given the strict concavity of $U(\cdot, 1)$, any convex combination of these two allocations violates constraint (17.1).

With consumption lotteries contingent on θ, the nonconvexity is overcome. Suppose for simplicity that the underlying commodity space is finite; that is,

c can be one of a finite number of possible bundles in C. Then let the vector $x(\theta)$ be a *random* assignment to each agent of type θ, where $x(c, \theta)$ is the probability of bundle c. Then a shock-contingent random allocation $\{x(1), x(2)\}$ can be achieved in a direct revelation mechanism with truth telling only if

$$\sum_{c \in C} U(c, 1)x(c, 1) \geqslant \sum_{c \in C} U(c, 1)x(c, 2)$$

$$\sum_{c \in C} U(c, 2)x(c, 2) \geqslant \sum_{c \in C} U(c, 2)x(c, 1)$$

These conditions are the random analogs of (17.1) and (17.2). These conditions are linear in the $x(c, \theta)$ and therefore constitute convex constraints. Finally, the expected utility of the shock-contingent lotteries $x = \{x(1), x(2)\}$ is

$$W(x, \theta) = \lambda(1) \sum_{c \in C} U(c, 1)x(c, 1) + \lambda(2) \sum_{c \in C} U(c, 2)x(c, 2)$$

It is linear in x and so the utility function is concave in that argument. This, incidentally, is true whether the underlying utility functions $U(\cdot, \theta)$ are or are not concave.

With classical general equilibrium analysis (in finite-dimensional spaces) there is no need for lotteries, for the constraint sets are convex and the utility functions are concave. Relaxing either of these assumptions results in the possibility of gains from lotteries.

We now return to the more general model and prepare to establish the existence of Pareto optimal and competitive equilibrium allocations and the optimality of competitive equilibria using a commodity space that contains consumption lotteries. To simplify the notation, however, we assume $T = 2$; this is the smallest T that fully illustrates the nature of the analysis. Also, for technical reasons, we assume $e_t \gg 0$, that consumption is bounded, $0 \leqslant c_t \leqslant b$, and that the $U(\cdot, \theta_t)$ are strictly increasing. Finally, for notational convenience, let $\Theta = \{1, 2, \ldots, n\}$ and denote θ_0 by i. We can now refer to agents of type i, $i = 1, \ldots, n$, classified by their initial shock.

There are obvious generalizations to the model we analyze. There can be statistical dependence in the θ_t, $t \geqslant 1$, as long as there is independence from the initial parameter θ_0. There can be non-time-additive-separable utility functions, discounting, observable heterogeneous characteristics, and non-trivial production technologies. We did not seek generality in order to focus on private information and how general competitive analysis can be extended to include it.

To begin the formal analysis, denote the underlying consumption possibilities set by $C=\{c\in R^l: 0\leqslant c\leqslant b\}$. Let the commodity space L be the space of $(1+n+n^2)$-tuples of finite real-valued countable-additive set functions on the Borel subsets of C. For element $z=[z_0, \{z_1(\theta_1)\}_{\theta_1\in\Theta}, \{z_2(\theta_1,\theta_2)\}_{\theta_1,\theta_2\in\Theta}]$, z_0 is the measure on the period 0 consumption good vector, the $z_1(\theta_1)$, of which there are n, are measures on the period 1 consumption vector conditioned on θ_1, and $z_2(\theta_1,\theta_2)$, of which there are n^2, are measures on the period 2 consumption vector conditioned on both θ_1 and θ_2. The space L is linear, a property which is needed for standard general competitive analysis. Further, the space L contains the space P of $(1+n+n^2)$-tuples of probability measures or lotteries on Borel subsets of C, which are needed for the reasons noted above.

The consumption set and preferences are defined first. For $x\in P$, the utility functional for a type i is the expected utility

$$W(x,i)=\int U(c,i)x_0(dc)+\sum_{\theta_1}\lambda(\theta_1)\int U(c,\theta_1)x_1(dc,\theta_1)$$
$$+\sum_{\theta_1}\lambda(\theta_1)\sum_{\theta_2}\lambda(\theta_2)\int U(c,\theta_2)x_2(dc,\theta_1,\theta_2) \qquad (17.3)$$

Not all $x\in P$ satisfy the incentive compatibility conditions, and so these functionals are defined only upon a subset of P. At period $t=2$, an agent must weakly prefer $x_2(\theta_1,\theta_2)$ if the agent is type θ_2 and announced type θ_1 at $t=1$. Thus

$$\int U(c,\theta_2)x_2(dc,\theta_1,\theta_2)\geqslant\int U(c,\theta_2)x_2(dc,\theta_1,\theta_2') \qquad \theta_1,\theta_2,\theta_2'\in\Theta \quad (17.4)$$

is a necessary condition for a point to be in the consumption possibility set. Given (17.4), the period $t=1$ incentive compatibility requirement is

$$\int U(c,\theta_1)x_1(dc,\theta_1)+\sum_{\theta_2}\lambda(\theta_2)\int U(c,\theta_2)x_2(dc,\theta_1,\theta_2)$$
$$\geqslant\int U(c,\theta_1)x_1(dc,\theta_1')+\sum_{\theta_2}\lambda(\theta_2)\int U(c,\theta_2)x_2(dc,\theta_1',\theta_2) \qquad \theta_1,\theta_1'\in\Theta$$
$$(17.5)$$

If asked in period $t=1$ to choose a member of $\{x_1(\theta_1),\{x_2(\theta_1,\theta_2)\}\}$, an agent would weakly prefer the pair $(x_1(\theta_1),\{x_2(\theta_1,\theta_2)\})$ if that agent's shock is actually θ_1. Let $X\equiv\{x\in P: x \text{ satisfies (17.4) and (17.5)}\}$. The set $X\subset L$ is the consumption set of the representative agent. Given any $x\in X$, preferences of type i are ordered by $W(x, i)$. A point $x^0 \in X$ is a satiation point in X for agent i if $W(x, i) \leq W(x^0, i)$ for all $x \in X$.

The endowment of agent i in each period t is an l-dimensional vector $e_t \gg 0$, $e_t \in C$. Therefore let ξ be that element of P such that ξ_0 puts all mass on e_0, $\xi_1(\theta_1)$ puts all mass on e_1 for each $\theta_1 \in \Theta$, and $\xi_2(\theta_1, \theta_2)$ puts all mass on e_2 for $\theta_1, \theta_2 \in \Theta$.

We now have a pure exchange economy defined by the population fractions $\lambda(i)$, $i \in \Theta = \{1, 2, \ldots, n\}$, the linear space L, the common consumption set $X \subset L$, the common endowment $\xi \in L$, and preferences $W(\cdot, i)$ defined on X for every agent of type i, $i \in \Theta$.

An implementable allocation for this economy is an n-tuple (x_i) with $x_i \in X$ for every i which satisfies the resource constraints in each period t, $t = 0, 1, 2$,[6]

$$\sum_i \lambda(i) \int c x_{i0}(\mathrm{d}c) \leq e_0 \tag{17.6}$$

$$\sum_i \lambda(i) \sum_{\theta_1} \lambda(\theta_1) \int c x_{i1}(\mathrm{d}c, \theta_1) \leq e_1 \tag{17.7}$$

$$\sum_i \lambda(i) \sum_{\theta_1} \lambda(\theta_1) \sum_{\theta_2} \lambda(\theta_2) \int c x_{i2}(\mathrm{d}c, \theta_1, \theta_2) \leq e_2 \tag{17.8}$$

and which satisfies a prior self-selection constraint

$$W(x_i, i) \geq W(x_j, i) \qquad i, j \in \Theta \tag{17.9}$$

Thus we assume that a fraction $x_{i0}(B)$ of the agents of type i in period 0 are assigned an allocation in Borel set B in period 0, and similarly for $x_{i1}(B, \theta_1)$, $x_{i2}(B, \theta_1, \theta_2)$. Here, then, all agents of type i have chosen lottery x_{i0} in period 0 and so on. The prior self-selection constraint captures the idea that an allocation (x_i) can actually be implemented only if all agents of type i reveal their true type by the choice of the bundle x_i from among the n-tuple (x_i).

An implementable allocation (x_i) is said to be a Pareto optimum if there does not exist an implementable allocation (x_i') such that

$$W(x_i', i) \geq W(x_i, i) \qquad i = 1, 2, \ldots, n \tag{17.10}$$

with a strict inequality for some i.

3 Existence of a Pareto optimum

To establish the existence of a Pareto optimum for our economy, it is enough to establish the existence of a solution to the problem of maximizing a weighted average of the utilities of the agent types; that is, maximize

$$\sum_i w(i) W(x_i, i)$$

where

$$0 < w(i) < 1, \qquad \sum_i w(i) = 1$$

by choice of the n-tuple (x_i), $x_i \in X$, subject to the resource constraints (17.6)–(17.8) and the prior self-selection constraint (17.9). To establish the existence of a solution to the problem, we make use of the theorem that continuous real-valued functions on nonempty compact sets have a maximum.

To do this, we use the weak topology on the space of signed measures. Let the topology on L be the weak topology. The underlying commodity space C is a compacted subset of R^l, which is a separable metric space, and so the set of probability measures $P \supset X$ is compact with respect to this topology (see Parthasarthy, 1967, ch. 2, theorem 6.4). Since the resource constraints (17.6)–(17.8), the prior self-selection constraint (17.9), and the constraints (17.4) and (17.5) are all defined relative to integrals of bounded continuous functions, the constraint set is closed. Therefore it is compact because it is a closed subset of the compact set P. The constraint set is nonempty because $x_i = \xi$ for all i is feasible. Since continuous real-valued functions on nonempty compact topological spaces achieve a maximum, a Pareto optimum is guaranteed to exist.

The above argument relies heavily on the compactness of C.[7] In fact, this assumption is crucial. By modifying the example of section 6 where C is not compact, we have produced an environment in which we can approach arbitrarily close to but not attain the utility of a full-information optimum; for that environment, then, a Pareto optimum does not exist.

4 Existence of a competitive equilibrium

In this section we establish that our economy can be decentralized with a price system, that is, that there exists a competitive equilibrium. We accomplish this task by introducing a firm into the analysis, with a judiciously chosen (aggregate) production set. We then follow the spirt of the proofs used by Bewley (1972) and Mas-Colell (1975) for establishing the existence of a competitive equilibrium with a continuum of commodities. Various approximate economies are considered, with a finite number of commodities. Existence of a competitive equilibrium for these economies is established using a theorem of Debreu (1962). We then take an appropriate limit.

Let there be one firm in our economy with production set $Y \subset L$, where $Y = \{y \in L$: (17.11), (17.12), and (17.13) below are satisfied$\}$:

$$\int c y_0(\mathrm{d}c) \leqslant 0 \tag{17.11}$$

$$\sum_{\theta_1} \lambda(\theta_1) \int c y_1(\mathrm{d}c, \theta_1) \leqslant 0 \tag{17.12}$$

$$\sum_{\theta_1} \lambda(\theta_1) \sum_{\theta_2} \lambda(\theta_2) \int c y_2(\mathrm{d}c, \theta_1, \theta_2) \leqslant 0 \tag{17.13}$$

It should be noted here that the components of the $y \in Y$ are signed measures and thus each is a way of adding. A negative weight corresponds to a commitment to take in resources and a positive weight corresponds to a commitment to distribute resources. Thus, in (17.11), for example, we term $\int c_j y_0(\mathrm{d}c)$ should be interpreted as the net trade (sale) of the jth consumption good in period 0. Inequality (17.11) states that, as a clearinghouse or intermediary, the firm cannot supply more of the consumption good than it acquires. When indexed by the parameter θ, a component of y should be interpreted as a commitment to agents who announce that they are of type θ. It should be noted that the production set Y contains the zero element of L and also displays constant returns to scale.

Following Debreu (1954), we define a state of our economy as an $(n+1)$-tuple $\{(x_i), y\}$ of elements of L. A state $\{(x_i), y\}$ is said to be attainable if $x_i \in X$ for every $i \in \Theta$, $y \in Y$, and $\Sigma_{i=1}^{n} \lambda(i) x_i - y = \xi$. Now suppose that a state $\{(x_i), y\}$ is attainable. Then, setting $y = \Sigma_i \lambda(i) x_i - \xi$ in (17.11)–(17.13), we obtain the resource constraints (17.6)–(17.8). Similarly, given any n-tuple (x_i), $x_i \in X$, satisfying the resource constraints (17.6)–(17.8), define y by $y = \Sigma_i \lambda(i) x_i - \xi$, and then $y \in Y$. Thus there is a one-to-one correspondence between attainable states in the economy with production and allocations in the pure exchange economy satisfying the resource constraints. An attainable state $\{(x_i), y\}$ is said to be a Pareto optimum if the n-tuple (x_i) satisfies (17.9) and there does not exist an attainable state $\{(x_i'), y'\}$ which satisfies (17.9) and Pareto dominates, that is, satisfies (17.10). Again, there is a one-to-one correspondence between optimal states and optimal allocations.

A price system for our economy is some real-valued linear functional on L, that is, some mapping $v: L \to R$. More will be said about price systems v in what follows, but we may note here that v will have $1+n+n^2$ components, each of which is a continuous linear functional relative to the weak topology (see also Mas-Colell, 1975). That is, given some $z \in L$,

$$v(z) = \int f_0(c) z_0(dc) + \sum_{\theta_1} \int f_1(c, \theta_1) z_1(dc, \theta_1) + \sum_{\theta_1} \sum_{\theta_2} \int f_2(c, \theta_1, \theta_2) z_2(dc, \theta_1, \theta_2)$$

where the functions $f_0(\cdot)$, $f_1(\cdot, \theta_1)$, and $f_2(\cdot, \theta_1, \theta_2)$ are (bounded) continuous functions on C (see Dunford and Schwartz, 1957, p. 421, theorem 9).

We now make the following definition.

Definition

A competitive equilibrium is a state $\{(x_1^*), y^*\}$ and a price system v^* such that (a) for every i, x_i^* maximizes $W(x_i, i)$ subject to $x_i \in X$ and $v^*(x_i) \leqslant v^*(\xi)$, (b) y^* maximizes $v^*(y)$ subject to $y \in Y$, and (c) $\Sigma_{i=1}^{n} \lambda(i) x_i^* - y^* = \xi$.

An outline of our proof for the existence of a competitive equilibrium for our economy is as follows. First, the underlying commodity space C is restricted to a finite number of points, the nodes of a mesh or grid on C. In this restricted economy a countably additive real-valued set function is completely defined by an element of a Euclidean space with dimensions equal to the dimensions of the restricted C. The linear space of these restricted economies is the $1+n+n^2$ cross-product of the Euclidean space. Consumption sets, preferences, endowments, and a production set can be defined on this space in the obvious way. The existence of a competitive equilibrium for the restricted economy is then established using a theorem of Debreu (1962). Then, letting the grid become finer and finer, we can construct a sequence of competitive equilibria for economies which are less and less restricted. A sub-sequence of these competitive allocations and prices converges, and the limiting allocations and prices are shown to be a competitive equilibrium for the unrestricted economy. We now give a more detailed argument.

The first restricted economy can be constructed in any essentially arbitrary way by subdividing each of the l coordinate axes of the commodity space C into intervals, subject to the following restrictions. First, each endowment point e_t, $t = 0, 1, 2$, must be one of the nodes of the consequent grid. Second, if we let

$$c_0^* > \max_i \left\{ \frac{e_0}{\lambda(i)} \right\}, \qquad c_t^* > \max \left\{ \frac{e_t}{\lambda(\theta_t)} \right\} \qquad t = 1, 2 \tag{17.14}$$

each point c_t^*, $t = 0, 1, 2$, must be one of these nodes. (We thus assume that the upper bound b of C is such that $0 < c_t^* \leq b$.) Third, the element zero must be an element of the consequent grid. The first of these restrictions will mean that the endowment points lie in each of the restricted consumption sets, and the second will mean that no agent type can be satiated in the attainable consumption sets, given the resource constraints.

The second restricted economy is obtained from the first by equal subdivision of the original intervals of the l coordinate axes. The third is obtained by equal subdivision of the second, and so on. In what follows, we let the subscript k be the index number of the sequence of restricted economies.

For the kth restricted economy, let C^k be the restricted underlying commodity space and L^k be the finite-dimensional subspace of L for which the support of each of the $n^2 + n + 1$ measures is C^k. That is, let $x_0(c)$, the $x_1(c, \theta_1)$, and the $x_2(c, \theta_1, \theta_2)$ for $c \in C^k$ each be the measure of the set $\{c\}$ containing the single point c. Then the space L^k is finite dimensional, and a point is characterized by the vector $\{x_0(c), x_1(c, \theta_1)$, and $x_2(c, \theta_1, \theta_2)\}$, $c \in C^k, \theta_1, \theta_2 \in \Theta$. Note that the integral of an integrable function $f: C \to R$ with respect to a measure x on C^k is

$$\int_C f(c) x(dc) = \sum_{c \in C^k} f(c) x(c) \tag{17.15}$$

The consumption and production possibility sets for the kth restricted economy are $X^k = X \cap L^k$ and $Y^k = Y \cap L^k$ respectively. The integrals used in the definition of X, Y, and W, namely in (17.4) and (17.5), (17.11)–(17.13), and (17.3), respectively, have representations as finite sums over the elements of C^k. As e_0, e_1, and e_2 belong to C^k, the endowment for economy k is $\xi^k = \xi \in L^k$.

As our linear space for the kth restricted economy is a subset of Euclidean space, the price system is also an element of the Euclidean space. Thus, we can define a price system $p^k = [\{p_0^k(c)\}, \{p_1^k(c, \theta_1)\}, \{p_2^k(c, \theta_1, \theta_2)\}]$, $c \in C^k$, $\theta_1, \theta_2 \in \Theta$, where each component is an element of R.

Now let m be the least common denominator of the $\lambda(i)$, $i = 1, 2, \ldots, n$, and consider the kth restricted finite economy containing number $\lambda(i)m$ agents of type i and production set mY^k.[8] Now restrict attention to an m-agent economy in which all agents of any given type i must be treated identically. Then, following Debreu (1962), we have the following definition.

Definition

A quasi-equilibrium of the kth restricted finite economy is a state (x_i^{k*}, y^{k*}) and a price system p^{k*} such that

(i) for every i, x_i^{k*} is a greatest element $\{x_i \in X^k: p^{k*} \cdot x_i \leqslant p^{k*} \cdot \xi^k\}$ under $W(\cdot, i)$ and/or $p^{k*} \cdot x_i^{k*} = p^{k*} \cdot \xi^k = \min p^{k*} \cdot X^k$
(ii) $p^{k*} \cdot my^{k*} = \max p^{k*} \cdot mY^k$
(iii) $\Sigma_i m\lambda(i) x_i^{k*} - my^k = m\xi^k$
(iv) $p^{k*} \neq 0$

A quasi-equilibrium is a competitive equilibrium if the first part of condition (i) holds. In what follows we will establish the existence of a quasi-equilibrium using a theorem of Debreu (1962) and then establish directly that it is also a competitive equilibrium. It is immediate that a competitive equilibrium for the kth restricted finite economy is also a competitive equilibrium for the original kth restricted economy with a continuum of agents (m cancels out of conditions (ii) and (iii)).

We make use of the following theorem, as a special case of Debreu (1962).

Theorem 17.1 (Debreu)

The kth restricted finite economy has a quasi-equilibrium if

1(a) $$A(mX^k) \cap \{-A(mX^k)\} = \{0\}$$

1(b) $$X^k \text{ is closed and convex;}$$

for every i,

2(a) for every consumption x_i in $\hat{X}_i^k$, there is a consumption in X^k preferred to x_i

2(b) for every x_i' in X^k, the sets

$$\{x_i \in X^k: W(x_i, i) \geqslant W(x_i', i)\}$$

$$\{x_i \in X^k: W(x_i, i) \leqslant W(x_i', i)\} \text{ are closed in } X^k$$

2(c) for every x_i' in X^k, the set $\{x_i \in X^k: W(x_i, i) \geqslant W(x_i', i)\}$ is convex;

3(a) $$(\{m\xi^k\} + mY^k) \cap mX^k \neq \varnothing$$

3(b) $$(\{\xi^k\} + A(mY^k)) \cap X^k \neq \varnothing;$$

4(a) $$0 \in mY^k$$

4(b) $$A(mX^k) \cap A(mY^k) = \{0\}$$

where $A(H)$ is the asymptotic cone of set H, $mH = \{s: s = mh, h \in H\}$, and $\hat{X}_i^k$ is the attainable consumption set for the type i consumer in the kth restricted economy.

Each of these conditions holds for our restricted finite economy (see Prescott and Townsend (1979) for the tedious but straightforward argument). Thus the existence of a quasi-equilibrium is established. We now verify that the first part of condition (i) must hold. In a quasi-equilibrium, condition (ii) holds, that is, there exists a maximizing element in Y^k given p^{k*}. It follows that no component of p^{k*} can be negative. Also, from condition (iv), not all components can be zero. Therefore at least one component of p^{k*} is positive. Maximizing $p^{k*} \cdot y$ with respect to y in Y^k, we obtain

$$p_0^{k*}(c) - \psi_0^k \cdot c = 0 \qquad c \in C^k \tag{17.16a}$$

$$p_1^{k*}(c, \theta_1) - \lambda(\theta_1)\psi_1^k \cdot c = 0 \qquad c \in C^k, \theta_1 \in \Theta \tag{17.16b}$$

$$p_2^{k*}(c, \theta_1, \theta_2) - \lambda(\theta_1)\lambda(\theta_2)\psi_2^k \cdot c = 0 \qquad c \in C^k, \theta_1, \theta_2 \in \Theta \tag{17.16c}$$

where ψ_t^k, $t = 0, 1, 2$, are nonnegative l-dimensional vectors of Lagrange multipliers. By virtue of the existence of a maximum and the existence of at least one positive price, one of these Lagrange multipliers is positive. Thus

$$p^{k*} \cdot \xi^k = \psi_0^k \cdot e_0 + \psi_1^k \cdot e_1 + \psi_2^k \cdot e_2 > 0$$

since $e_t > 0$, $t = 0, 1, 2$. However, the measure which puts weight unity on the zero element of the underlying commodity space for all possible parameter draws has valuation zero under p^{k*}. Thus $p^{k*} \cdot \xi^k > \min p^{k*} \cdot X^k$ and the second part of the condition (i) cannot hold.

Now x_i^{k*} denotes the maximizing element for the agent type i in a competitive equilibrium of the kth restricted economy. For any i, $\{x_i^{k*}\}_{k=0}^{\infty}$ is a sequence in the space of $(1 + n + n^2)$-dimensional vectors of probability measures on the underlying consumption set C. This metric space is compact, and so a convergent sub-sequence exists. Since there are a finite number of agent types, it is possible to construct a sub-sequence of the sequence allocation $\{(x_i^{k*})\}$ which converges to some allocation (x_i^{∞}). This limit (x_i^{∞}) will constitute part of an equilibrium specification for the unrestricted economy.

For every restricted economy k, the price system is (17.16). Moreover, the price system can be normalized by dividing through by the sum of all the Lagrange multipliers so that in fact each Lagrange multiplier can be taken to be between zero and unity. Thus, we can again find a further sub-sequence of the sequence of vectors $\{\psi_t^k\}$ which converges to some number $\{\psi_t^{\infty}\}$ with components between zero and unity. Moreover, the Lagrange multipliers in $\{\psi_t^\infty\}$ must sum to unity. In what follows, then, we restrict attention to the subsequence of economies, indexed by h, such that, for every i, $x_i^{h*w} \to x_i^\infty$ and, for every t, $\psi_t^h \to \psi_t^\infty$.

For each economy h, the equilibrium price system is a linear functional v^h defined by

$$\begin{aligned} v^h(x) &= \sum_{c \in C^k} p_0^{h*}(c)x_0(c) + \sum_{\theta_1} \sum_{c \in C^k} p_1^{h*}(c, \theta_1)x_1(c, \theta_1) \\ &\quad + \sum_{\theta_1} \sum_{\theta_2} \sum_{c \in C^k} p_2^{h*}(c, \theta_1, \theta_2)x_2(c, \theta_1, \theta_2) \\ &= \sum_{c \in C^k} \psi_0^h \cdot cx_0(c) + \sum_{\theta_1} \lambda(\theta_1) \sum_{c \in C^k} \psi_1^h \cdot cx_1(c, \theta_1) \\ &\quad + \sum_{\theta_1} \lambda(\theta_1) \sum_{\theta_2} \lambda(\theta_2) \sum_{c \in C^k} \psi_2^h \cdot cx_2(c, \theta_1, \theta_2) \end{aligned} \tag{17.17}$$

Taking the limit as $k \to \infty$, we see that an equilibrium price system v^∞ for the unrestricted economy will be

$$\begin{aligned} v^\infty(x) &= \psi_0^\infty \cdot \int cx_0(dc) + \sum_{\theta_1} \lambda(\theta_1)\psi_1^\infty \cdot \int cx_1(dc, \theta_1) \\ &\quad + \sum_{\theta_1} \lambda(\theta_1) \sum_{\theta_2} \lambda(\theta_2)\psi_2^\infty \cdot \int cx_2(dc, \theta_1, \theta_2) \end{aligned} \tag{17.18}$$

Note that, since the sum of the Lagrange multipliers is unity, which is a strictly positive number, $v^\infty(\xi) > 0$. Finally,

$$y^\infty = \sum_i \lambda(i)x_i^\infty - \xi \tag{17.19}$$

is an equilibrium output for the firm.

The feasibility of the limiting allocation $\{(x_i^\infty)_{i \in \Theta}, y^\infty\}$ follows because both constraints X and Y are closed in the weak topology. Given that $v^h(x_i^{h*}) \leqslant v^h(\xi)$, taking the limit as h goes to infinity yields $v^\infty(x_i^\infty) \leqslant v^\infty(\xi)$. All that remains is to show that (a) there is no $\hat{x}_i \in X$ which satisfies the budget constraint and for which $W(\hat{x}_i, i) > W(x_i^\infty, i)$ and (b) there is no $\hat{y} \in Y$ for which $v^\infty(\hat{y}) > v^\infty(y^\infty)$.

The proof of (a) is by contradiction. If there is such an $\hat{x}_i$, then it is possible to select some h and $\hat{x}_i^h \in X^h$ such that $W(\hat{x}_i^h, i) > W(x_i^{h*}, i)$ and $v^h(\hat{x}_i^h) < v^h(\xi^h)$. This contradicts x_i^{h*} as maximizing in the hth restricted economy. To prove (b), the nonnegativity of the ψ^∞ implies that all points belonging to Y, that is, satisfying constraints (17.11)–(17.13), have a nonnegative value with respect to the price system v^{∞}. Since budget constraints are binding, that is $v^{\infty}(x_i^{\infty}) - v^{\infty}(\xi) = 0$, from (17.19) profits at y^{∞} are zero. Hence, y^{∞} is profit maximizing. This completes the proof of the existence of a competitive equilibrium.

It is readily verified that for a one-period economy (with period 0 only) there need be no randomness in a competitive equilibrium. Agents are risk averse, and the incentive compatibility conditions need not be imposed explicitly. In this sense, the work developed here reduces the standard competitive analysis when the information structure is private but not sequential.

5 The welfare theorems

We now turn to the two fundamental theorems of contemporary welfare economics and ask whether any competitive equilibrium allocation is optimal and whether any optimum can be supported by a competitive equilibrium. The first question has an affirmative answer.

Theorem 17.2
If the allocation $\{(x_i^*), y^*\}$, together with the price system v^*, is a competitive equilibrium and if no x_i^* is a local saturation point, then $\{(x_i^*), y^*\}$ is a Pareto optimum.

Proof. Suppose that a feasible Pareto superior allocation $\{(x_i), y\}$ existed. Then $v^*(x_i) \geqslant v^*(x_i^*)$ with strict inequality for some i. Multiplying by population fractions, summing over i, and using the linearity of v^* yields $v^*(x) > v^*(x^*)$. Profit maximization implies $v^*(y^*) \geqslant v^*(y)$. Thus, $v^*(\xi) = v^*(x - y) > v^*(x^* - y^*) = v^*(\xi)$, which is the contradiction.

Debreu (1954) establishes that the following five assumptions are sufficient to ensure that an optimum can be supported by a quasi-competitive equilibrium.

1 X is convex.
2 For $x', x'' \in X$ and $i \in \Theta$, $W(x', i) < W(x'', i)$ implies $W(x', i) < W(x^{\alpha}, i)$ where $x^{\alpha} = (1 - \alpha)x' + \alpha x'', 0 < \alpha < 1$.
3 For $x, x', x'' \in X$ and $i \in \Theta$, the set $\{\alpha \in [0, 1]: W(x^{\alpha}, i) \leqslant W(x, i)\}$ is closed where $x^{\alpha} = (1 - \alpha)x' + \alpha x''$.
4 Y is convex.
5 Y has an interior point.

For property 1, note that a linear combination of two probability measures is again a probability measure and that constraints (17.4) and (17.5) hold under convex combinations. Properties 2 and 3 follow immediately from the linearity of the objective function. Property 4 follows from the fact that constraints (17.11)–(17.13) hold under convex combinations. For property 5, pick a degenerate element of L such that (17.11)–(17.13) hold as strict inequalities.

However, with private information these conditions, together with Debreu's argument (Debreu, 1954, theorem 2), do not ensure that every Pareto optimum can be supported by a quasi-competitive equilibrium with an appropriate initial distribution of wealth. It is true that a separating hyperplane exists such that y^* maximizes value subject to the technology constraint. It does not follow, however, that x_i^* necessarily minimizes value over the set of points that yield utility to type i greater than or equal to $W(x_i^*, i)$. Rather, x_i^* minimizes value over the set $\{x \in X: W(x,i) \geqslant W(x_i^*, i) \text{ and } W(x,j) \leqslant W(x_j^*, j) j \neq i\}$. (For details, see Prescott and Townsend (1979).)

6 An example

In this section we present a simple example economy which we hope clarifies by illustration the definitions and concepts that we have developed throughout the chapter. For this economy, the equilibria are characterized by insurance contracts with options, the exercise of which is dependent on private information. In addition, the equilibrium contracts incorporate contrived randomness even though agents have convex preferences. For this example, all agents are alike *ex ante* but not *ex post*. This greatly simplifies the analysis, for by theorem 17.2, the optima are the competitive equilibrium allocations.

Following Becker and Lancaster, we give agents a household production function mapping a time endowment, a market-produced consumption good $c \in R_+$, and a private shock $\theta \in \Theta = \{\theta_1, \theta_2\}$ into an idiosyncratic nontradeable household consumption vector. The resulting indirect utility function is $U: R_+ \times \Theta \rightarrow R$. The function $U(c, \theta)$ is increasing, concave, and continuously differentiable in c. Further, $U'(\infty, \theta_1) = 0$, and $U(c, \theta_2) = \theta_2 c$ where $\theta_2 > 0$. Thus households of type θ_1 are *ex post* risk averse and households of type θ_2 are *ex post* risk neutral. This somewhat extreme assumption simplifies the analysis, but is not crucial. What is needed is that there are differences in curvatures *ex post*.

Households know that a fraction $\lambda(\theta)$ of the population will experience shock θ. This is the only information that they have for forecasting. We assume that agents' subjective probability beliefs are that the likelihood of being of type θ is $\lambda(\theta)$ (see note 5). Finally, all agents receive an endowment e of the consumption good with certainty and $U'(e, \theta_1) < \theta_2$.

Our first task is to determine a Pareto optimal allocation for this economy. This could be done formally as in section 3 by consideration of a linear programming problem in the space of lotteries, maximizing the expected utility of the representative household subject to the incentive compatibility and resource constraints. Here we find a solution to a simplified problem that takes into account the resource constraints only. We then modify that incentive incompatible solution to obtain an allocation which is both incentive compatible and resource feasible and which yields the same expected utility as the solution to the simplified problem.

If θ were public, an optimal allocation would be for type θ_1 to consume c_1^* and type θ_2 to consume c_2^*, where c_1^* and c_2^* are such that marginal utilities are equated across states and the endowment is exhausted. Essentially, this is full insurance. However, this allocation is not achievable if θ is private information. Type θ_1 prefers the larger consumption c_2^* to its allocation c_1^* (see figure 17.1). An equally good incentive-compatible allocation does exist, but it requires contrived randomness in the allocation. If, rather than receiving c_2^* with certainty, type θ_2 receives c_3^* with probability $\alpha^* = c_2^*/c_3^*$ and consumption 0 with probability $1-\alpha^*$, the expected utility of type θ_2

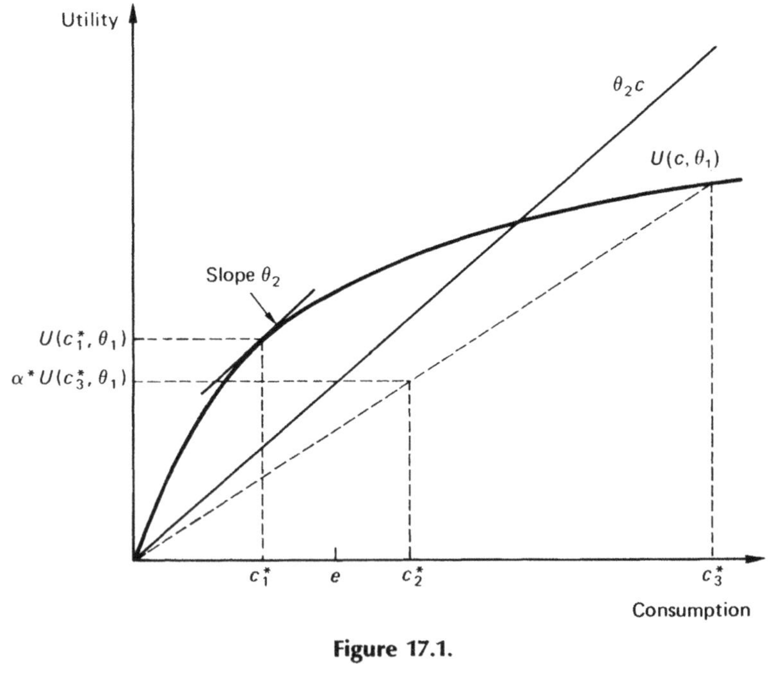

Figure 17.1.

continues to be $\theta_2 c_3^*$ as type θ_2 is risk neutral. Thus both allocations yield the same expected utility as well as having the same per capita consumption. Variable c_3^* can be selected sufficiently large to insure that the expected utility of this lottery for type θ_1 is less than the utility of the certainty consumption c_1^* (as in figure 17.1). To summarize, the allocation for which type θ_1 individuals receive c_1^* with certainty and type θ_2 receive a lottery that provides c_3^* with probability α^* and zero otherwise is an optimum. Further, no allocation without lotteries is optimal.

We will now argue that this optimum can be achieved in a decentralized competitive market for insurance contracts with individually effected and private information dependent options. Imagine, in particular, that households in the economy can buy and sell contracts (make commitments) in some planning period market. Clearly, with one consumption good, unconditional promises or commitments cannot be mutually beneficial. However, households want commitments to be conditional on their own individual circumstances, that is, on their own shocks θ. Of course, these shocks are privately observed. Still, assume that an insurance contract has options effected entirely by the household, once its θ value is known. Then some insurance may be possible. Of course, the household will choose the option which is best given its individual circumstances, and thus we can assume without loss of generality that options are such that the household announces its individual shocks truthfully. Finally, we allow options to affect random allocations of the consumption good.

More formally, then, a household is imagined to buy in the planning period market (say from a Walrasian auctioneer) an insurance contract $\{x(c, \theta)\}$, $c \in C, \theta \in \Theta$. (Here for simplicity we assume that set C is finite, though the more general analysis of this chapter allows C to contain a continuum of values.) Under this contract, the household is assumed to announce its actual shock θ in the consumption period and receive c with probability $x(c, \theta)$ (of course, $0 \leqslant x(c, \theta) \leqslant 1$ and $\Sigma_c x(c, \theta) = 1$). The household can choose, in principle, apart from budget considerations, any incentive compatible contract it wants, with the receipts varying over c in C and the probabilities varying between zero and unity inclusive. A price system $\{p(c, \theta)\}, c \in C, \theta \in \Theta$, determines the cost of a contract. As for revenue, note that the household is effectively endowed with probability measures $\xi(c, \theta), \theta \in \Theta$, each putting weight unity on the endowment point e. These endowments are sold in the planning period market. (Alternatively, we can view $x(c, \theta) - \xi(c, \theta)$ as excess demand.) In summary, the household can choose a contract $x(c, \theta)$ to maximize

$$\sum_{\theta} \lambda(\theta) \sum_{c} x(c, \theta) U(c, \theta) \tag{17.20}$$

subject to the budget constraint

$$\sum_{\theta}\sum_{c} p(c,\theta)x(c,\theta) \leqslant \sum_{\theta}\sum_{c} p(c,\theta)\xi(c,\theta) \tag{17.21}$$

and to incentive compatibility restrictions.

On the other side of the market, we assume that there are firms or intermediaries that make commitments to buy and sell the consumption good. A production–intermediation choice $y(c,\theta)$, $c \in C$, specifies the number of units of the bundle with c units of the consumption good which the firm–intermediary plans to deliver or sell to the market for use by consumers announcing that they are of type θ. Thus, if $y(c,\theta)$ is negative, there is a plan to take in or buy resources. The production–intermediation set Y of each firm–intermediary is defined by

$$Y = \left\{ y(c,\theta), c \in C, \theta \in \Theta : \sum_{\theta} \lambda(\theta) \sum_{c} c y(c,\theta) \leqslant 0 \right\} \tag{17.22}$$

In effect, (17.22) requires that in the consumption period each firm–intermediary does not deliver more of the single consumption good than it takes in. Note that each firm–intermediary takes the coefficients in Y, the weights on different bundles, as given and beyond its control. Note also that Y displays constant returns to scale, and so we act as if there were only one firm–intermediary.

The firm–intermediary obtains credit or debits for its commitments in terms of the price system $p(c,\theta)$. It takes the price system as given and maximizes profits

$$\sum_{\theta}\sum_{c} p(c,\theta)y(c,\theta) \tag{17.23}$$

It is thus clear that the specification of constant returns to scale of the production set (17.22) delivers prices up to some arbitrary normalization. In fact, if prices are expressed in terms of the consumption good, the equilibrium price system $p^*(c,\theta)$ must satisfy

$$p^*(c,\theta) = \lambda(\theta)c$$

This corresponds to actuarially fair insurance.

The Pareto optimal allocation to be supported in this competitive insurance market is

$$x^*(c_1^*,\theta_1) = 1, x^*(c_3^*,\theta_2) = \alpha^*, x^*(0,\theta_2) = 1-\alpha^*,$$
$$\text{and } x(c,\theta) = 0 \text{ otherwise} \tag{17.24}$$

Clearly, for an equilibrium we must have $y^* = x^* - \xi$. It can easily be verified under the price system p^* that x^* solves the household's problem and y^* solves the firm–intermediary's problem.

In this analysis, we used lotteries as an allocation device. This may seem unusual, but we argue that it is not. Indeed, the effects of a lottery can be mimicked exactly by indexing on the basis of a naturally occurring random variable that is unrelated to preferences and technology, provided that the random variable has a continuous density. (This was pointed out to us by Kenneth Arrow.) Such an arrangement would seem consistent with the existence of the usual Arrow–Debreu securities or contingent commodities.[9]

We might argue further that devices which generate lotteries or contrived risk may themselves be familiar. For, returning to our competitive market setup, assume that a group of households has entered into the contracts $\{x(c, \theta)\}$ with a broker, who acts as a firm intermediary, with terms of trade as specified in the $p^*(c, \theta)$.[10] This contract can be effected as follows.

Agents are required to surrender their endowment e to the broker and then, subsequent to the revelation of the shocks, they have a choice between two distribution centers. If they choose the first, they are guaranteed c_1^* units of the good. If they choose the second, they receive c_3^* units if it is available. Households choosing the second center are imagined to arrive in a random fashion and to receive c_3^* on a first-come first-served basis.[11] All households know that the likelihood of receiving c_3^* if they choose the second center is α^*. Agents are not permitted to recontract contingent upon whether or not they are served.[12]

Upon observing the number of unserved customers in the second center, a casual observer might find the scheme described above somewhat unsatisfactory. Since some go away empty-handed, the "price" must be too low; that is, the potential allotment of c_3^* is too high. In fact, if the receipt were lowered to c_2^*, all could be served.[13] But, of course, the allocation achieved by the resource-allocation scheme mentioned above is private-information optimal. The point is that the queue (rationing) is a device which induces the requisite artificial risk.

7 Concluding remarks

The essential difference between our private-information competitive analysis and the contingent claim approach of Arrow and Debreu is that options are needed and these options are exercised contingent upon private information. If we are to use competitive analysis to explain the existence of contractual arrangements with options, the exercise of which cannot be perfectly predicted given publicly available information, such a theory is needed. Given the wide use of such arrangements, we are optimistic that this formulation will prove useful in substantive economic analyses.

Notes

1 The reasons why we did not introduce names were that it would be notationally cumbersome and analytically difficult and would have no econometric implications. With randomness in the allocation *ex ante*, there can be different outcomes for *ex ante* identical agents, identical, that is, from the point of view of the econometrician.

2 The work of Harris and Townsend (1978, this volume, ch. 6; 1981, this volume, ch. 7) and Myerson (1979) provides the justification for these additional constraints.

3 The use of signed measures in general competitive analysis is not new. Mas-Colell (1975), and subsequently others, has exploited them in the study of economies with a continuum of differentiated products.

4 Despite the apparent generality, the analysis is limited in two ways. First, we do not allow for random privately observed shocks to endowments, though we suspect that our analysis can be extended in that direction. Second, we do not allow for statistical dependence in the preference shocks, so that agents would have private information on the probability distribution of future shocks at the time of initial trading. Current efforts (Prescott and Townsend, 1984, this volume, ch. 16) indicate that extensions of standard competitive analysis to such environments are not straightforward.

5 In assuming that the agents know only what the distribution of the parameters in the population will be, we avoid measurability problems. There are problems in going in the other direction, from independently and identically distributed random variables on the continuum to measurable sample spaces, which necessitate a redefinition of the integral (see Bewley and Radner, 1980).

6 In (17.6)–(17.8) the integration is coordinate-wise and the weak inequality holds for each of the l coordinates.

7 Mas-Colell (1975) also assumes that the underlying commodity space is compact.

8 We are assuming that each $\lambda(i)$ is rational. An extension to arbitrary real $\lambda(i)$ would entail a limiting argument.

9 Cass and Shell (1983) give an example of an economy with an equilibrium characterized by allocations being indexed by an exogenous random variable that is unrelated to either preferences or technologies.

10 In a literal sense, we would not expect to see the highly centralized Walrasian arrangement with an auctioneer who calls out prices until all markets are clear. We believe, though, that such an arrangement might well predict the outcome of arrangements in which the market-assignment process and the price determination process are explicit.

11 Obviously, for the analysis of some queues, we want to take starting times as choice variables. For our purposes here, we abstract away from such considerations.

12 We thank John Bryant for pointing out this implicit restriction.

13 Of course, this is not the only model of apparent underpricing. In a provocative paper, Cheung (1977) argues that apparent underpricing of better seats in theaters, so that they fill up early on, is a way of reducing the costs of monitoring seat assignments. But the theory developed here has something in common with that of Cheung – the use of apparent underpricing to discriminate among potential buyers with unobserved characteristics. Such discrimination also underlies the model of credit rationing given by Stiglitz and Weiss (1980), though they proceed in a different way and draw somewhat different conclusions than we do in this chapter (see also Akerlof, 1970; Stiglitz, 1976; Weiss, 1976; Wilson, 1980).

References

Akerlof, G.A. (1970) The market for "lemons": quality uncertainty and the market mechanism. *Quarterly Journal of Economics* 84, 488–500.

Arrow, K.J. (1953) Le rôle des valeurs boursières pour la répartition la meilleure des risques. *Econometrie*, pp. 41–8. Paris: Centre Nationale de la Recherche Scientifique.

Bewley, T.F. (1972) Existence of equilibria in economies with infinitely many commodities. *Journal of Economic Theory* 4, 514–40.

—— and Radner, R. (1980) Stationary monetary equilibrium with a continuum of independently fluctuating consumers. Working Paper, Northwestern University, Evanston, IL.

Cass, D. and Shell, K. (1983) Do sunspots matter? *Journal of Political Economy* 91, 193–227.

Cheung, S.N.H. (1977) Why are better seats "underpriced"? *Economic Inquiry* 15, 513–22.

Debreu, G. (1954) Valuation equilibrium and Pareto optimum. *Proceedings of the National Academy of Science* 40, 588–92.

—— (1959) *Theory of Value: An Axiomatic Analysis of Economic Equilibrium.* New Haven, CT: Yale University Press.

—— (1962) New concepts and techniques for equilibrium analysis. *International Economic Review* 3, 257–73.

Dunford, N. and Schwartz, J. (1957) *Linear Operators, Part I: General Theory.* New York: Interscience.

Gale, D. (1980) Money, information and equilibrium in large economies. *Journal of Economic Theory* 23, 28–65.

Harris, M. and Townsend, R.M. (1978) Allocation mechanisms of asymmetrically informed agents. Working Paper 35-76-77, Carnegie–Mellon University, Pittsburgh, PA. Reprinted in this volume as chapter 6.

—— and —— (1981) Resource allocation under asymmetric information. *Econometrica* 49(1), 33–64. Reprinted in this volume as chapter 7.

Hurwicz, L. (1971) On informationally decentralized systems. In *Decision and Organization*, eds R. Radner and B. McGuire. Amsterdam: North-Holland.

Lucas, R.E., Jr (1980) Equilibrium in a pure currency economy. In *Models of Monetary Economies*, eds J. Kareken and N. Wallace. Minneapolis, MN: Federal Reserve Bank of Minneapolis.

Mas-Colell, A. (1975) A model of equilibrium with differentiated commodities. *Journal of Mathematical Economics* 2, 263–95.

McKenzie, L.W. (1959) On the existence of general equilibrium for a competitive market. *Econometrica* 27, 54–71.

Myerson, R.B. (1979) Incentive compatibility and the bargaining problem. *Econometrica* 47, 61–74.

Neumann, J. von and Morgenstern, O. (1947) *Theory of Games and Economic Behavior*. Princeton, NJ: Princeton University Press.

Parthasarthy, K.R. (1967) *Probability Measures on Metric Spaces*. New York: Academic Press.

Prescott, E.C. and Townsend, R.M. (1979) On competitive theory with private information. Working Paper, Carnegie–Mellon University, Pittsburgh, PA.

—— and —— (1984) Pareto optimal and competitive equilibria with adverse selection and moral hazard. *Econometrica* 52(1), 21–45. Reprinted in this volume as chapter 16.

Stiglitz, J.E. (1976) Prices and queues as screening devices in competitive markets. Technical Report 212, Institute of Mathematical Studies of Social Science, Stanford University.

—— and Weiss, A. (1980) Credit rationing in markets with imperfect information. Part II: Constraints as incentive devices. Research Memorandum 268, Princeton University.

Weiss, L. (1976) The desirability of cheating incentives and randomness in the optimal income tax. *Journal of Political Economy* 84, 1343–52.

Wilson, C. (1980) The nature of equilibrium in markets with adverse selection. *Bell Journal of Economics* 11, 108–30.

Index

Printed and bound by CPI Group (UK) Ltd, Croydon, CR0 4YY

15/09/2026

14962390-0002